The Psychology of Learning

THE LIPPINCOTT COLLEGE PSYCHOLOGY SERIES

Under the Editorship of

Dr. Carl P. Duncan, Northwestern University
and Dr. Julius Wishner, University of Pennsylvania

The Psychology of Learning

John F. Hall

The Pennsylvania State University

J. B. LIPPINCOTT COMPANY | *Philadelphia & New York*

5.6610.2

Preface

A BASIC TOPIC in psychology is learning, and my primary objective has been to write a text for the advanced undergraduate which includes much of the material traditionally encompassed in its study. My approach has been an empirical one, and I have organized most of the text around an examination of those variables and/or conditions which contribute to the learning process. In so doing, I have included a discussion of a variety of learning situations rather than limiting my presentation of the topic to one or two of the traditional categories.

Charles K. Allen, Elmer Davidson, Robert Leeper, David S. Palermo, William F. Prokasy, and Jerome E. Singer all have read the complete, or portions of the, manuscript; and I should like to express my sincere thanks to them for their helpful suggestions. I am particularly indebted to Carl P. Duncan and Julius Wishner, co-editors of the Lippincott College Psychology Series, for their penetrating comments which resulted in a number of important changes. Finally, special thanks are due to my wife, Jean, whose help, like that with an earlier publication, began with the transcribing of original notes and continued through the typing of the final draft.

I should like to express my thanks to the following organizations who very kindly gave me their permission to use figures or quotations obtained from their publications: Academic Press; *The American Journal of Psychology;* The American Association for the Advancement of Science; The American Psychological Association for its several journals; Annual Reviews, Inc.; Appleton-Century-Crofts, Inc.; Cambridge University Press; University of California Press; Columbia University Press; *Journal of the Experimental Analysis of Behavior;* The Journal Press, McGraw-Hill Book Company, David McKay Company, Inc.; The University of Nebraska Press; *Perceptual and Motor Skills;* The University of Texas Press; John Wiley and Sons, Inc.; and Williams and Wilkins Company.

John F. Hall

University Park, Penna.
June, 1965

Contents

1

Introduction

FEW TOPICS ARE AS IMPORTANT or as basic to the psychologist as that which we describe as learning. A fair portion of our lives is spent in educational institutions where the primary purpose is to learn basic as well as technical and professional skills. There is little doubt that our abilities to add or subtract, or to read or to write, are largely products of learning. Similarly, an individual's talent in adjusting a carburetor, designing a house, or removing an appendix, has come about as a result of learning. In all probability, most of our behavior patterns which make up the uniqueness of our personality are also learned. The temper tantrums which Johnny exhibits at three, his aggressiveness at seven, or his hostility at twelve would appear to represent the products of learning. The pervasiveness of learning, then, is one of the primary reasons why psychologists have been greatly interested in its analysis.

Although the learning process makes such a tremendous contribution to our daily lives, the reasons why we learn (or why we do not) are not always clear. This obscurity is the product of a number of reasons. A primary one is that when learning does take place, it does so under very poorly controlled conditions; and, as a result, it becomes exceedingly difficult to determine those variables which have made the primary contribution. When we are

1

interested in getting someone to learn, we usually do a variety of things which we believe will facilitate his learning. We may threaten or cajole, reward or punish our learner. We may perform the act ourselves and get the learner to imitate us, or we may have him engage in his own trial and error behavior. Our practice sessions may be long or short, or a mixture of the two. Determining the relative contributions to the learning process of the many variables which we have manipulated in our everyday living conditions becomes an impossibility. This does not mean that the layman knows nothing about those conditions which influence learning, for it is obvious that he does. The designation of these conditions, however, has been typically done at a "common sense" level. It becomes important for the psychologist to demonstrate experimentally the operation of these common sense variables as well as to investigate those variables or conditions which have escaped the layman in his analysis of the learning situation.

In the experimental analysis of learning, it frequently has been found necessary to utilize learning situations of a relatively simple type in order to understand better those basic principles which underlie the learning process. Such simplicity is sometimes achieved by using animals in which, it is assumed, the learning processes involved are similarly simple. In fact, a large percentage of the learning studies which have been done have been carried out with animals as experimental subjects. At other times, it is necessary to use very simple tasks on a human level. Such tasks, for example, often entail the learning of a list of single words or, perhaps, pairs of words, although all learning tasks which are used in the laboratory are not of a simple variety.

In general, then, it is felt that the simple tasks learned by man or animal provide the psychologist with the best means by which he may tease out those variables which are of greatest significance. But, it should be recognized that in adopting this position, the psychologist assumes that some value from this approach will accrue to him when he undertakes the study of more complex problems. Under some circumstances, he may actually find that learning principles which have been discovered with the simple task will generalize to more complex tasks; in other circumstances, he may note that his chief gain has been findings that have served as a fruitful source of hypotheses.

TOWARD A DEFINITION OF LEARNING

A recurring problem in psychology has been the formulation of acceptable definitions of varying concepts which are then used to delimit given areas of inquiry. Learning is no exception, but one problem which must be faced is that at least a dozen different definitions of the concept can be found by examining standard works in the area.

A primary consideration in developing any acceptable definition is acknowledgment of the position that learning refers to a hypothetical construct, its presence being inferred from changes in the organism's performance.[1] A change in performance or behavior, then, becomes an indispensable part of any definition of learning. But all changes in performance cannot be attributed to the learning process; a number of investigators have demonstrated that some behavior changes must be attributed to maturation. As an example, both Stone (1922) and Beach (1942) have shown that copulatory behavior in the male rat is not learned but, rather, can be accounted for by developmental processes taking place within the organism. In Beach's (1942) study, 55 male rats following weaning were divided into three groups: (1) an isolation group in which each animal was not permitted contact with any other animal until copulation tests were made at approximately 100 days of age; (2) a segregation group in which 16 males were separated from females but lived together in a single large cage; and (3) a cohabitation group in which, beginning at 40 days of age, these animals were raised with females and thus had the opportunity to copulate. When each animal reached 100 to 110 days of age, it was placed in a cage with a receptive female and the incidence and pattern of copulatory behavior observed. Six additional observations were conducted with three days intervening between each period. Results indicated that the percentages of copulators in the varying groups were as follows: Isolation 69%, Cohabitation 53%, and Segregation 25%. Although the Isolation group had no opportunity to learn the mating pattern, it had the largest number who engaged in this kind of behavior. Of equal importance was the fact that an

---

[1] The distinction between performance and learning is one which has attracted considerable interest, but this topic shall be considered in Chapter 3.

examination of the specific mating pattern of the copulators within each group disclosed no significant differences among them. Twelve of fifteen copulators in the isolated group copulated normally at the first contact with the female. Thus, the early observations of Stone (1922) were confirmed by Beach (1942) who stated that the ". . . inexperienced male is capable of normal copulatory reactions upon his first contact with the receptive female."

One could cite a number of other examples in which maturation rather than learning has been used to account for a particular behavior change. As a result, there has been the belief that a training or practice component must be included in any adequate definition of learning. McGeoch and Irion (1952), for example, have defined learning as "a change in performance which comes under condition of practice," and Thorpe (1956) has stated that learning is "that process which manifests itself by adaptive changes in individual behavior as a result of experience."

The practice component cannot, however, be used as the sole criterion for differentiating the learning process from all others which are capable of producing changes in behavior. For example, a typist begins the morning typing at 80 words per minute but at the close of day, is typing just 60. It is obvious that a change in behavior has been accompanied by practice. And yet, one could hardly attribute such a performance change to the operation of the learning process. Rather, common sense dictates that another process, perhaps that of fatigue or inhibition, might be used to "explain" the performance change.

Behavior changes attributed to fatigue or some inhibitory process have been differentiated from learning by some writers by examining the duration of the change. Kimble (1961) has handled this problem by considering learning to be "a relatively permanent change in behavior potentiality. . . ." Behavior changes attributed to fatigue, then, would be of a temporary nature. Presumably, our typist would be typing 80 words per minute the next morning or after an adequate rest, since the change in performance was only temporary. But as Woodworth and Schlosberg (1954) have commented in examining this problem, the term "relatively" spoils our definition for "some things, like telephone numbers, are learned well enough for immediate use but are soon forgotten." The recent interest in short-term retention also leads to the conclusion that making learning dependent upon so-called permanent behavior changes can lead to considerable difficulty.

Some writers have distinguished between those performance changes attributable to learning as contrasted to those which arise from fatigue by taking cognizance of performance proficiency. Brogden (1951), for example, has stated, "Acquisition is a progressive incremental change in the proficiency of performance by an organism . . . ," but Hovland (1951) has supported an earlier definition by Hunter (1934) in which learning refers to a trend of improvement in performance.

But an adequate definition of improvement or performance proficiency may not always be easy to achieve, particularly when one is working with autonomic nervous system responses. Can changes in the galvanic skin response or heart rate be conceptualized in terms of increased proficiency?

From time to time, it can also be noted that some writers have introduced motivational constructs in order to help define learning. For example, Kimble (1961) has written of learning as "a relatively permanent change in behavior potentiality which occurs as a result of *reinforced* practice." But, it must be noted here that many theorists would object to the position that reinforcement is necessary in order for learning to take place, while many others would disagree about a definition of reinforcement.

This survey of the varying attempts to provide an acceptable definition of learning has not been completely successful, and any adequate definition must await further developments, perhaps of a neurological nature. The inability of individuals working in this area to come to a completely satisfactory definition is not as great a handicap to its study as one might believe. For there is little concern on the part of most investigators with the examination of an already existing behavior pattern and with an attempt to decide whether or not it has come about as a result of learning, or as a result of another process, e.g., maturation or fatigue. Rather, they have concerned themselves with examination of the contribution of specific variables to the learning process, and their modus operandi has been designed to provide the organism with an experimental situation in which it is obvious that the behavior change must be learned. When a college student changes his behavior so that at the end of a practice period he is capable of calling out a list of specific adjectives, it can be assumed that a learning process is involved.

Essentially this same point was made by Hilgard (1951) who stated (p. 518), "A precise definition of learning is not necessary, so long as we agree that the inference to learning is made from changes in performance that are the result of training or experience, as distinguished from changes such as growth or fatigue and from changes attributable to the temporary state of the learner. The experiments themselves define the field ostensively." [2]

For the reader who feels most secure with a definition, one would define learning as follows, recognizing that this definition, too, has basic limitations: Learning is a process which takes place within the organism and is inferred from specified changes taking place in the organism's behavior. Such changes in behavior (1) are directed toward certain standards or criteria which have been established and (2) can be related to the necessity of practice or experience in order to achieve such standards.

THE ROLE OF STIMULUS AND RESPONSE

Psychologists most frequently describe behavior in terms of stimulus and response, a kind of analysis which stems from the work of the early Behaviorists. Since these concepts have been used in almost all areas of psychology and have found important application whenever the study of learning is undertaken, a detailed examination of their use would be in order.

The reader has been made aware of difficulties involved in defining the concept of "learning"; there are problems also in determining precisely what is meant by "stimulus" and "response." [3]

---

[2] A similar approach can be found in many areas of scientific inquiry. For some time there has been considerable controversy among physicists regarding the nature of light. Some physicists have defined light by reference to wave theory, and others have preferred to conceptualize light in terms of quantum theory. The failure to agree upon a definition, however, has not precluded research in the area.

[3] Miller (1959) has pointed out that stimulus-response psychologists have frequently tended to bypass the problem of providing adequate stimulus and response definitions. Rather, they have concentrated on experimental situations in which stimulus and response has been so simple and manageable that the lack of a precise definition has not been of immediate concern, and they have concentrated on determining the laws which govern the connections or responses to stimuli. Thus, he has written, "Stimulus-response psychologists may be said to know and care relatively little about either stimuli or responses; they are specialists on the hyphen between the S and R and could more aptly be called 'hyphen psychologists,' or to use Thorndike's term, 'connectionists.' "

What Is a Response?

Typically, responses have been defined as (a) muscular contractions or glandular secretions or (b) acts of the organism which are directed toward producing some change in the environment, either of which are occasioned by a stimulus. This definition acknowledges a distinction between two ends of the response continuum which have been labeled (1) molecular and (2) molar.

The molecular position describes responses in terms of specific qualitative or quantitative variations of muscular contraction or glandular secretion. In an early conditioning study by Wickens (1939), for example, extensor movements of the finger were differentiated from flexor movements even though both movements resulted in withdrawing the finger from the source of shock.

The molar approach, on the other hand, describes responses in terms of the changes that the organism produces in the immediate environment, with differences in the detailed movement or patterns of muscular activity being ignored. A lever press in the Skinner box is treated as a single-response class regardless of the specific muscular movements which are involved in making the lever move. One lever press in the Skinner box is treated as any other, although the rat may have used his right paw to depress the lever on one occasion and his left paw to depress it on another.

An example of a position somewhere between these extremes has been taken by Logan (1956, 1960) who in his micromolar theory of behavior has stated, "Responses that differ in any way whatsoever are different in the sense that they may be put into different response classes so that separate response tendencies can be calculated for them." Thus, different speeds of a rat's running a straight runway, rather than being treated as a reflection of varying strengths of the same response (molar approach), are considered as different responses. As Logan has indicated, such an approach parallels the traditional analysis of the stimulus. As different wave lengths or different intensities of a visual stimulus can be considered as different stimuli, so different movements or different amplitudes of the same movement should be categorized as different responses.

It has been the molar approach to response measurement which has been most frequently adopted, however, and as shall be noted in Chapter 3, most response measures used in experimental investigations, e.g., lever pressing in a Skinner box, etc. are of this variety.[4]

The Mediating Response

One response class which deserves mention in this section, although it is not related to the molar-molecular distinction which has been made, is the mediating response. This type of response is hypothesized to act as a bridge between an external stimulus situation and an overt, observable response. Mediating responses are postulated to have stimulus characteristics to which are attached other mediated or possibly overt responses. Thus, the point of view is taken that the response which an organism makes produces characteristic stimuli which can serve as cues or other stimuli for further responses. Within a stimulus-response analysis, one can provide the following diagram: S–r–s–R in which the S and R are observables, and the r is a mediated response which has stimulus characteristics.

Mediated responses play an obvious role in human behavior since they can be conceptualized as thoughts or ideas or as implicit verbal responses which are produced by certain stimulus events but which at the same time become stimuli for other responses. For example, assume that a subject is required to learn the pair of words DOG—NINE so that when DOG is presented as a stimulus, the subject should respond with NINE. It is quite likely that the subject may use the mediating response CAT, with the association running from DOG to CAT to NINE since some already pre-established associations prevail between DOG and CAT and between CAT and NINE.

But the mediated response hypothesis has been posited to take place with animals as well. It is premature to examine the specific role of mediators at this time, but it will be found that they have been hypothesized to play an important part in many learning situations.

What Is a Stimulus?

An examination of many of the problems involved in the definition and role of the stimulus would encompass most areas of psychology. Stimulus selection and perception, in addition to learning, are only a few of the major topics which depend upon a

---

[4] The reader interested in the problem of response definition should consult Logan (1960) who has provided an excellent discussion of this topic.

proper understanding of the nature of the stimulus. In fact, Stevens (1951) has stated that the definition of the stimulus can be equated with the problems of all psychology. He has written (pp. 31-32) :

> In a sense there is only one problem of psychophysics, namely, the definition of the stimulus. In this same sense there is only one problem in all of psychology—and it is the same problem. The definition of the stimulus is thus a bigger problem than it appears to be at first sight. The reason for equating psychology to the problem of defining stimuli can be stated thus: the complete definition of the stimulus to a given response involves the specification of all the transformations of the environment, both internal and external, that leave the response invariant. This specification of the conditions of invariance would entail, of course, a complete understanding of the factors that produce and that alter responses. It is easy enough, of course, to decide upon arbitrary definitions of "stimulus objects". . . but the question is: what properties of these objects do the stimulating? Viewed in this fashion, it is evident that for no response have we yet given a complete definition of the stimulus. At best we have only partially determined the conditions and limits of invariance.

It is obvious that any inquiry of the role of the stimulus in psychology would prove too extensive to be covered here; and as a result, only a brief discussion can be provided.

Although stimuli are most frequently defined as those energy changes in the physical environment which excite a sense organ and initiate a response, there is increasing recognition of the need to distinguish among a number of different usages of the term. Spence (1956) , for example, has pointed out that the concept of stimulus has at least three different classes of referents. The first—situational stimuli—are those physical objects or events in the environment that may be specified by the experimenter and which are under his direct control. A second class—intraorganic stimuli—are specified on the basis of known physiological laws or specific hypothesized internal relations, and the third class—effective stimuli—refer to those energy changes which actually excite a receptor and produce a response.

More recently, both Gibson (1960) and Underwood (1963) have proposed somewhat similar classifications based upon the situational vs. effective distinction. Gibson (1960) has suggested that stimuli which are *capable* of exciting receptor cells be classified as potential stimuli, while stimuli which *actually* do result in receptor activity, neural impulses, sense organ adjustment, overt responses, etc. be given the term effective stimuli. Underwood (1963), examining the problem within the context of verbal learning, has suggested that the stimulus situation which is presented to the subject be known as the nominal stimulus and the characteristics to which the subject actually responds or "uses" to cue a response be called the functional stimulus.

It is, of course, the "effective" or "functional" stimulus concept which is of most concern to psychologists, and the definition of this term, it can be noted, is circular. It is readily acknowledged that it is impossible to define the concept of an effective stimulus independent of the response it purportedly elicits.

One approach to the problem of circularity of both stimulus and response definitions has been proposed by Miller and Dollard (1941), who define a response as (p. 59) ". . . any activity by or within the individual which can become functionally connected with an antecedent event through learning; a stimulus is any event to which a response can be so connected . . . Thus, 'sitting up' in dogs is known to be a response because it can be functionally connected by reward with the antecedent command, 'Sit up!'; the command is thereby known to be a stimulus."

Miller (1959) has acknowledged that this first step in stimulus identification is circular, because a specific response can be connected to it by learning. The second step is predicting from the assumption that an event which is the stimulus for the learning of one kind of response can also serve as a stimulus for other responses. As Miller states, "This second step is not circular because the assumption could, in principle, be disproved. In fact, the second step is far from safe; the assumption may actually turn out to be wrong."

Can any answer be provided to the problem of adequately defining a stimulus? Certainly not in any final sense. The Miller and Dollard (1941) position provides a working approach, but it does not represent a completely satisfactory solution to the problem. Perhaps the most important gain from any discussion is that experimenters become increasingly aware that a disregard for, or inattention to, the problem of discriminating the effective stimulus from the situational stimulus can lead only to confusion and pseudo-controversies.

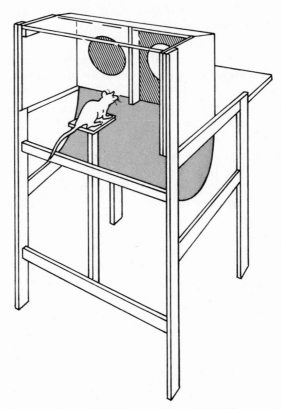

Fig. 1–1. Lashley jumping stand. The positive card falls over when the rat jumps against it, giving access to the food table. The negative card is locked and after jumping to it the animal falls into the net. *Adapted from Munn (1946)*

A good example of this is found in those learning situations which employ the Lashley jumping stand, an illustration of which is indicated in Figure 1–1. The general procedure is for the rat to learn to jump against one of the stimulus cards. If the card is the correct cue, it falls, permitting the animal to secure a reward on the platform behind the card. If the animal chooses the incorrect (and stationary) card, it bumps its nose and falls into the net below.

A number of investigators utilizing this kind of apparatus did not recognize that when the animal was placed in this type of situation, it oriented its head so that only the bottom portion of the card (effective stimulus) was seen just prior to jumping. Rather, they assumed that the animal observed the whole card (situational stimulus) .

Now it can be noted that it is possible to come to a different conclusion about the difficulty that an animal will have in solving a discrimination problem, depending upon whether the assumption is made that the animal fixates only the bottom of the card or sees the whole card. Ehrenfreund (1948) has experimentally demonstrated such to be the case. He was able to show that animals fixating the bottom of the card had great difficulty in discriminating between two visual stimuli. By raising the platform of their jumping stand, thus enabling the animal to "see" the upper portion of the card, such discrimination was made much easier.

2

The Learning Situation

ALTHOUGH SOME PSYCHOLOGISTS have indicated that there is no need for providing a precise definition of learning and that the experiments themselves define the field, it must be acknowledged that an examination of experimental studies in learning reveals a complex and bewildering array of different kinds of learning situations. As a result, a number of investigators have proposed different classifications or groupings of these situations in an effort to provide some order in the area. One of the more frequently employed taxonomies, the one which we should like to use in this chapter, categorizes learning situations into classical conditioning, instrumental conditioning, and verbal learning. However, this classification has certain inadequacies. For example, it does not represent completely separate and nonoverlapping classes. But, the primary concern in this section is to provide only a framework within which may be described some of the learning situations which are typically found in the laboratory. In so doing, the reader should gain a more adequate understanding of the learning process as well as an appreciation of some of the problems and complexities that are involved in the study of learning. In addition, attention can be directed to some of the varying types of apparatus and materials which are used, the organisms which are employed as experimental subjects, as well as general methodological considerations. Finally, this descriptive material will provide an opportunity to review some of the terms and operational procedures which are a basic part of the study of learning.

CLASSICAL CONDITIONING

It is appropriate to initiate a discussion of learning situations with the work of Pavlov, a familiar figure to most students of psychology. Pavlov, of course, was a famous Russian physiologist who was originally interested in examining the glandular secretions involved in digestion. While he was examining the gastric process, he became interested in the learning situation which has come to be known as classical conditioning. Pavlov's work provides reference experiments for the classical conditioned response, and the essential features of his procedure can be obtained from a description of a typical experiment in his laboratory.

Since he was interested in examining the salivary response of the dog, it was first necessary to devise a technique whereby such a response could be measured. By means of minor surgery, he was able to transplant the salivary duct through the surface of the dog's cheek so that saliva flowed to the outside of the animal's mouth. A small glass funnel was cemented over the opening to collect the saliva which could then be measured accurately.

The animal was trained to stand quietly in a loose harness on a table in a room which was sound-deadened to prevent distracting noises or vibrations. A small window permitted the animal to be observed by the experimenter. The general experimental procedure was as follows: a tuning fork was sounded and seven or eight seconds after its onset, a small quantity of powdered food was moved within reach of the dog's mouth. On the first trial, the tuning fork did not elicit salivation although the eating of the dry food did so. After a number of pairings of the tuning fork and the meat powder, the sound of the tuning fork was presented alone. Under such circumstances, the sound elicited salivation in the animal.

Pavlov's experimental procedure has resulted in a number of specific terms being used to describe the classical conditioning situation. In the experiment cited, the meat has been designated as an unconditioned stimulus (UCS); the response which was elicited by the meat powder is called the unconditioned response

(UCR). The sound arising from the tuning fork was referred to as the conditioned stimulus (CS), and the response of the animal to the conditioned stimulus was termed the conditioned response (CR).[1]

More general definitions of these terms, terms which are a part of the basic vocabulary of the psychologist, are as follows:

Unconditioned stimulus—any stimulus which will evoke a regular and measurable response in the organism for a long period of time. This capacity of the stimulus may be a product of an innate characteristic of the organism or of previous learning. The characteristics of the UCS usually determine whether or not the conditioning situation shall be termed appetitional or aversive. If the UCS is shock or some other stimulus which is noxious to the subject, the conditioning situation is usually classified as aversive; on the other hand, if the UCS is food or an object related to satisfying some need state of the organism, the situation is termed appetitive.

Unconditioned response—the response which is elicited by the unconditioned stimulus.

Conditioned stimulus—a neutral stimulus, or one which does not have the capacity at the beginning of the training session to elicit any aspect of the unconditioned response.

Conditioned response—that aspect or part of the unconditioned response which is elicited by the conditioned stimulus.

Further work by Pavlov indicated that once a conditioned response was established, the repeated presentation of the CS without it ever again being paired with the UCS resulted in the gradual cessation or diminution of the CR. This was termed experimental extinction—a topic which shall be considered in greater detail in a later chapter. This phenomenon is mentioned at this time because a number of investigators have used this measure from which to infer something about the strength of the conditioned response which was established during the training trials.

[1] Conditioned and unconditioned responses are the terms which are now used to describe the conditioning procedure. It is a matter of interest, however, that they were originally translated as conditional and unconditional reflexes. Some writers have pointed out that the term "conditional," rather than "conditioned," makes more sense since at the beginning of the experiment, the neutral stimulus is not a conditioned one but is conditional. Woodworth and Schlosberg (1954) state, "Consider the bell which will be experimentally associated with food; at the outset it is a to-be-conditioned stimulus but not yet a conditioned stimulus, though it is often so called."

Finally, Pavlov further discovered that if he waited for a time following the extinction of a response, the presentation of the CS would again elicit the CR. This phenomenon was termed spontaneous recovery since the recovery in strength of the CR appeared to be spontaneous.

The use of the classical conditioning procedure has not been limited to the salivary response in dogs. Rather, an examination of the experimental studies which have been conducted testifies to the fact that the classical conditioning situation has been used with a variety of responses in a number of different organisms. At the one end of the phylogenetic scale, there is some evidence to indicate that planaria can be conditioned; at the other end, man has been frequently used as a subject.[2] An unusual classical conditioning study is reported by Spelt (1948) who has found it possible to establish a CR (body movement) in the human fetus in utero during the last two months of gestation. Spelt found that a loud noise could serve as a UCS in eliciting movement of the fetus. Such movements were recorded by means of pairs of 55 mm. tambours taped to the abdomen. He then paired vibrotactile stimulation (buzzer placed on the abdomen) with this UCS and found that after a number of trials the vibrotactile stimulation was capable of eliciting movement. The response was recorded by the subject pushing a button whenever fetal movement was felt.

Involuntary as well as voluntary responses have been used. Mouth opening and swallowing, locomotion, finger withdrawal, and the eyeblink are examples of voluntary responses which have been conditioned, while changes in skin resistance (GSR), blocking of the electroencephalograph (EEG) alpha rhythm, and changes in heart rate illustrate involuntary responses which have been conditioned.

In general, classical conditioning studies most frequently found in current use involve changes in skin resistance (GSR) or the eyeblink. With the conditioning of the GSR, an electric shock

[2] In an early study, Thompson and McConnell (1955) reported the classical conditioning of planaria, wherein the UCS was a weak shock which elicited a longitudinal contraction of the animal's body. A change in illumination was used as the CS. Results indicated that the frequency of contractions increased significantly over control groups with the 150 training trials which were provided. Jacobson (1963) in his review of the literature has concluded that classical conditioning in planaria is a bona fide phenomenon. Warren (1965) has suggested, however, that experimenters adopt a measure of skepticism of these reported findings until more is learned of the nature of the UCR to frequently used stimuli such as light and electric shock.

usually serves as the UCS, with a tone or light serving as the CS. In conditioning the eyeblink, a puff of air is used as the UCS while a change in illumination or presentation of a tone serves as the CS.

Classical Conditioning Operations

A notable feature of the classical conditioning procedure is the fact that the experimenter generally has precise control over the onset and termination of both the CS and the UCS. With such control, it is possible to vary these stimuli in a number of ways, and these procedural variations have had different designations. Although many of them are only infrequently used, it is appropriate to indicate them.

DELAYED CONDITIONING. The most frequently used operation found in classical conditioning experiments is known as delayed conditioning. Such a procedure involves the presentation of the CS some time prior to the onset of the UCS and is indicated in Figure 2–1. The CS has been terminated with the onset of the

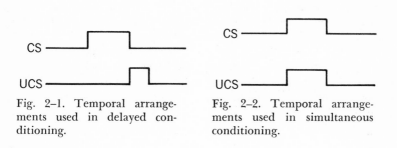

Fig. 2–1. Temporal arrangements used in delayed conditioning.

Fig. 2–2. Temporal arrangements used in simultaneous conditioning.

UCS, but other delayed conditioning procedures may be used. The CS may be terminated sometime during the presentation of the UCS, at the termination of the UCS, or even after the UCS has been terminated.

SIMULTANEOUS CONDITIONING. As Figure 2–2 reveals, simultaneous conditioning consists of presenting and terminating the CS and UCS at the same time.

TRACE CONDITIONING. With trace conditioning, the CS is presented and terminated prior to the onset of the UCS. Thus, there is an interval of time between the termination of the CS and the onset of the UCS. The term arises from the assumption that the neural trace left by the presentation of the CS acts as the CS, although, more objectively, time appears to act as the CS. If the interval of time is less than one minute, the procedure is frequently referred to as a short trace conditioning procedure, while if the interval is a minute or longer, it is known as a long trace. Figure 2–3 illustrates this operation.

TEMPORAL CONDITIONING. The temporal conditioning procedure is one in which the UCS is presented at regular intervals, e.g., once every two minutes, etc. With such a procedure, a conditioned response may appear at about the same time that the UCS is due to be presented. This kind of situation has been utilized very little by American investigators, but as the review by Dmitriev and Kochigina (1959) reveals, it has been employed frequently by Russian experimenters, beginning with Feokritova working in Pavlov's laboratory.

BACKWARD CONDITIONING. The last of these procedural operations is one in which the CS is presented after the termination of the UCS, and it is illustrated by Figure 2–4.

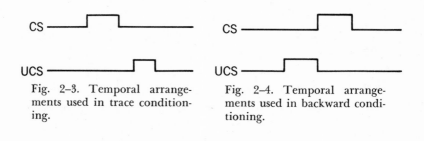

CS ⎯⎯⎯⎯⎯⎯⎯⎯⎯

UCS ⎯⎯⎯⎯⎯⎯⎯

Fig. 2–3. Temporal arrangements used in trace conditioning.

CS ⎯⎯⎯⎯⎯⎯⎯⎯⎯

UCS ⎯⎯⎯⎯⎯⎯⎯

Fig. 2–4. Temporal arrangements used in backward conditioning.

An Analysis of the Conditioned Response

Pavlov's analysis indicated that the CR was identical to the UCR, and this assumed identity led to the use of the expression—*substitution learning*—a term frequently employed to "explain" classical conditioning. During the course of the conditioning trials, it was assumed that the CS came to substitute for the UCS in eliciting the UCR.

This point of view, however, is contrary to fact. In those studies in which the CR does appear to be identical to the UCR the reason for such identity can be attributed to omissions or restrictions involved in the measurement of the response. It is now generally acknowledged that the CR may be viewed not as a replica of the UCR but rather as a response (1) which prepares the organism for the occurrence of the UCS or (2) one which is a component of the UCR.

In the Pavlovian study which was cited previously, the meat powder elicits in the hungry animal not only a salivary response but a chewing response which includes tongue smacking, licking, etc. On the other hand, the CS elicits only salivation. This salivary response seems to prepare the animal for the presence of the meat powder, but at the same time, it may be regarded as a fractional part of the total eating response. This point has been most aptly described by Zener (1937) who conditioned the salivary response to a bell and recorded with pictures the whole conditioning procedure. Zener states (p. 393) :

> Except for the component of salivary secretion the conditioned and unconditioned behavior is not identical. (a) During most of the time in which the bell is reinforced by the presence of food, chewing generally occurs with the head raised out of the food-pan but not directed either at the bell or into the food-pan, or at any definite environmental object. Yet this posture practically never, even chewing only occasionally, occurs to the conditioned stimulus alone. Despite Pavlov's assertions, the dog does not appear to be eating an imaginary food. (b) Nor is the behavior that does appear an arrested or partially unconditioned reaction consisting of those response elements not conflicting with other actions. It is a different reaction, anthropomorphically describable as a looking for, expecting, the fall of food with a readiness to perform the eating behavior which will occur when the food falls. The effector pattern is not identical with the unconditioned. (c) Movements frequently occur which do not appear as part of the unconditioned response to food: all the restless behavior of stamping, yawning, panting.

When a noxious stimulus is used as a UCS, a similar analysis can be made. If a dog is conditioned to raise one paw by pairing a tone (CS) with a shock (UCS), the response that is elicited by the shock is characterized by barking, tail and ear movements, and straining at the harness, all of which take place in addition to a lifting of a paw. On the other hand, the response elicited by the tone is substantially different, since the emotional behavior of the animal is virtually eliminated, and the response consists of only a simple raising of a paw.

Differentiating the CR from the UCR

As has just been noted, the CR cannot be viewed as a replica of the UCR; but in most conditioning studies the experimental procedure involves recording only a part of the organism's total response—a procedure which frequently obscures differences between the CR and UCR. In conditioning the GSR, for example, the shock which is used as the UCS elicits a complex response which includes skeletal as well as autonomic nervous system components. But the response which is measured is only the change in skin conductance. Now, if the experimental procedure is one in which the CS is consistently paired with the UCS, one may ask, "How do you know that the response which is elicited is one which arises from the presentation of the CS rather than the UCS?"

One way to make such a differentiation is to examine temporal relationships. For example, it may be noted that there is a two-tenths of a second delay between the onset of the UCS and the beginning of the UCR. Let us further assume that the CS is presented five-tenths of a second prior to the onset of the UCS. This would mean then, that on the average, the beginning of the UCR would follow the onset of the CS by seven-tenths of a second. Note, of course, that the response which occurred with this temporal interval would be classified as a UCR. After a number of trials, one might note that the interval between the onset of the CS and the beginning of the response would become progressively smaller. Obviously, if this interval was reduced to two-tenths of a second, it would have to be classified as a CR since (1) this time interval is the same as that which existed between the onset of the UCS and the beginning of the UCR, and (2) in this case, the onset of the response would take place prior to the onset of the UCS. In reality, all situations are not quite this simple, and the experimenter will invariably use some arbitrary time interval in order for the response to be classified as a CR. Some of the problems which are involved in differentiating the CR from the UCR can be found in the subsequent section on voluntary responding.

A second and simpler technique for differentiating the CR from the UCR is one in which the experimenter omits the presentation of the UCS. A typical procedure is to present the CS alone from time to time during the course of training. Such presentations become "test" trials (are actually extinction trials) which are used to assess the level of conditioning.

Some General Considerations

Two general problems are related to conditioned response learning. If the conditioned response is to be considered as a type of learned response, a basic and fundamental consideration is one which is related to the question of whether such a response has been acquired as a function of the presentation of the CS-UCS in some close temporal relationship over a series of trials.

If it can be demonstrated that the double stimulation procedure is not necessary, then one can seriously question whether or not the experimenter has succeeded in producing a response which can be truly designated as "conditioned." Secondly, if it is possible to acquire a conditioned response within a relatively few trials, such an acquisition may involve the subject's simply instructing himself to make an appropriate response whenever the conditioned stimulus is presented. Again, a number of investigators have questioned whether this type of situation should be designated as one of conditioned response learning.

Pseudoconditioning

If it is possible to obtain a "conditioned response" without using the double stimulation procedure (CS-UCS), one must raise the question as to whether or not such a response should be indicated as being "learned." The answer to this question must be found by comparing responses produced by regular conditioning procedures with responses which are obtained when there has been some change or deviation in the double stimulation procedure. In general, following the lead of Grether (1938), these deviant procedures have been classified as pseudoconditioning, and they consist of (1) presenting the CS singly and alone and/or (2) presenting both the CS and UCS singly but in random order. Following such training, extinction or test trials are introduced in order to determine if the response to the CS differs from that obtained when normal conditioning trials (double stimulation) have been utilized.

A number of studies examining a variety of responses in many different organisms have indicated that pseudoconditioning procedures are capable of eliciting responses similar to those found with normal conditioning operations. It has been noted in adult

TABLE 2–1

Performance During Extinction Trials

| CONDITION | PER CENT RESPONDING Extinction Trials | | | | | |
	1	2	3–4	5–6	7–8	9–10
Forward conditioning	90.0	70.0	60.0	35.0	30.0	35.0
Backward conditioning	84.6	46.1	30.7	23.0	26.8	23.0
Random conditioning	44.4	33.3	22.2	16.6	22.2	22.2
Pseudoconditioning	100.0	80.0	30.0	10.0	20.0	10.0

(Adapted from Harris, 1941).

humans by Grant and Hilgard (1940), Grant and Meyer (1941), Harris (1941), and Prokasy, Hall, and Fawcett (1962); in infants by Wickens and Wickens (1940); in monkeys by Grether (1938); in cats by Harlow and Toltzien (1940); in rats by Harris (1943), May (1948), and Wickens and Wickens (1942); and in goldfish by Harlow (1939).

In an early and extensive study in this area, Harris (1941) investigated pseudoconditioning of the finger withdrawal response. A loud tone served as the CS while a shock to the middle finger was used as the UCS. Forward and backward conditioning groups each received 80 presentations of tone and shock, while the pseudoconditioning group received only 80 shocks. A fourth group (random) of subjects was run in which the CS and UCS were presented 80 times.[3] Ten presentations of tone followed each training series. Results, as Table 2–1 indicates, reveal a larger percentage of responses for the pseudoconditioning group on the first extinction trial than for any other group, although it must be noted that the pseudoconditioning group also had the smallest percentage of responses for the last two trials.

Interpretations for pseudoconditioning have ranged from very specific explanations, based upon the nature of the response under investigation, to those explanations having greater generality. A discussion of these is beyond the scope of this text, although the interested reader can refer to the work of Grant and his associates [Grant (1943, 1943a, 1945); Grant and Norris (1947); Grant, Norris, and Boissard (1947)], Wickens and Wickens (1942), and May (1949) for appropriate discussion.

In conclusion, the basic significance of pseudoconditioning is

[3] Although Harris (1941) classified this group as a "random" group, the procedure utilized placed it within the pseudoconditioning group classification.

that the experimenter should be constantly on guard for the presence of pseudoconditioned responses arising from his experimental procedure. The failure to provide pseudoconditioned control groups may invalidate his experimental findings.

Voluntary Responding

It will be recalled that a second consideration was related to the subject at the beginning of the experiment simply instructing himself to respond whenever the conditioned stimulus was presented. Such responding has been given the label "voluntary." Since it has been frequently assumed that the establishment of a conditioned response is dependent upon the presentation of a series of CS-UCS trials, some question has been raised as to whether voluntary responses should be designated as being of the "conditioned" variety.[4]

Early investigators attempted to exercise some control over voluntary responders by providing what have been designated as neutral instructions just prior to the actual conditioning operations. Such instructions are illustrated in a study by Wickens (1943) who was interested in conditioning finger withdrawal. Part of the instructions provided to his subjects were as follows: "If you get conditioned, you will develop a tendency to respond to the tone before the shock goes on. I do not want you to fight against becoming conditioned, and at the same time you are not to respond voluntarily to the tone. If your finger wants to fly up just don't inhibit it."

The problem of eliminating voluntary responders (or responding) cannot always be solved by merely relying on the instructions provided the subject. In some instances, it is deemed desirable to use other criteria by which to differentiate the conditioned response from those responses which the experimenter believes are voluntary.

In an eyelid conditioning experiment, Spence and Taylor (1951) found that many of their subjects sought to "cooperate" and thus facilitate conditioning by voluntarily closing their eye

---

[4] Concern for this topic dates back to Bechterev (1932) (pp. 204–205) who wrote, "Is it possible to produce, by personal efforts, an imitation reflex through a 'volitional' movement of the foot or hand? This question, too, has been listed for solution in my laboratory, and there are data which lead us to suppose that the times at which a true association reflex and an imitation reflex are manifested give a clue by which to distinguish the one from the other."

to the conditioned light signal and keeping it closed until after the UCS had been presented. The authors indicate that these voluntary responses had extremely short latencies, and in order to eliminate this group from consideration, the latencies for all subjects were examined. The percentage of CR's less than three-tenths of a second in latency (as measured from the onset of the CS) was computed for each subject. Subjects who gave more than 50 per cent CR's with a latency of less than three-tenths of a second (with a one-half second CS-UCS interval) were discarded from this study.[5]

In a further examination of the form and latency of eyelid responses in conditioning, Spence and Ross (1959) provided 80 subjects with 100 conditioning trials with a relatively strong air puff as the UCS. A one-half second CS-UCS interval was employed. The criteria used in denoting a voluntary response were (a) a sharp, smooth complete closure and (b) a continuation of the closure until some time after the completion of the air puff. In contrast to voluntary responses, conditioned responses were characterized by a gradual, irregular closure. Results supported the earlier criteria used in the Spence and Taylor (1951) study in that a large number of responses judged to be voluntary in form were found to fall predominately in a two- to three-tenths of a second interval which followed the onset of the CS.

A comprehensive discussion of the problem of voluntary responders cannot be provided, but the complexity of the problem can be revealed as the studies of Hartman, Grant, and Ross (1960); Hartman and Ross (1961); and Gormezano and Moore (1962) have demonstrated. Hartman and Ross (1961) have pointed out that any criteria that are used to eliminate voluntary responders must take into consideration the general experimental

---

[5] In contrast to the "cooperative" subject who attempts to facilitate conditioning by a voluntary closing of the eye, McAllister and McAllister (1958) have pointed out that there has been some suggestion that the neutral instructions with which subjects are provided result in their adopting a negative set which protects them from appearing foolish by responding to the CS before the UCS is delivered. These authors hypothesized that if the subjects knew conditioning principles and the lawfulness of such behavior, the inhibitory set might be eliminated. In an experimental examination of this variable, two groups of subjects were run in which one group (knowledge) was given a brief explanation of what conditioning was while the other group (no knowledge) was not given such information. Although there was some indication that the "knowledge" group conditioned better than did the "no knowledge" group, the results were not significant, at least with regard to generally accepted levels of significance.

procedure that is employed. In their study, they did not employ a ready signal prior to the presentation of the CS.[6] As a result, these investigators found that the latency criterion proposed by Spence and Ross (1959) was inappropriate in their experimental situation, but they did find that a criterion which involved the slope of lid closure was a satisfactory substitute.

A second consideration in this area has been the "validating" of the voluntary responding criterion. In the Hartman, Grant, and Ross (1960) and Gormezano and Moore studies (1962), there has been an attempt to provide such validation by using a group of subjects who are told to blink in order to avoid the air puff. Responses obtained from this group are then compared to a "normal" conditioning group. Gormezano and Moore (1962) found that low UCS intensities resulted in those subjects who were provided with the voluntary blink instructions having responses of shorter latency and sharper lid closures than subjects who were provided with normal instructions. On the other hand, when the UCS intensity was increased, no difference between the groups was obtained. As the authors point out, these findings have important methodological implications for eyelid conditioning studies which have varied the UCS intensity and which have also employed a latency criterion to reject subjects as voluntary responders. Thus, "in the absence of cross validation of criteria, one is confronted with the possibility of erroneously classifying different numbers of subjects as voluntary responders."

Is there any answer to the problem of how most appropriately to deal with voluntary responders?[7] Probably not in any final sense. Extensive work in an area may provide the experimenter with cues or criteria which he may, at least in a specific situation, use to eliminate subjects who are voluntarily responding. But as

[6] In most studies performed in the Iowa laboratory, the conditioning procedure involves the presentation of a ready signal to which the subject is instructed to blink. A short time following the presentation of this signal, the CS is presented.

[7] One solution might be to use involuntary responses, e.g., GSR, but the problem here is that involuntary responses may be controlled by voluntary ones. For example, Razran (1935) found that conditioning of salivary responses in the human could be facilitated by having the subject think of eating pretzels. More recently, Shearn (1961) has shown that human subjects who were attending to their own pulse beat could learn to avoid electric shock by reducing their cardiac rate. Similarly, Razran (1961) reports that Lisina, a Russian investigator, has found that subjects watching their own plethysmograph records transformed digital vasoconstriction into vasodilation in order to avoid electric shock. In these cases, the subject's self-instructions initiated important defensive responses.

Hartman and Ross (1961) have demonstrated, such a procedure has its dangers. Perhaps the best solution in most situations would be to include all responders. Under such circumstances, subjects who voluntarily respond will be randomized over the varying experimental groups.[8] Such a position also has the advantage of placing these studies on the same continuum with the animal studies in which the problem of voluntary responding never arises.

INSTRUMENTAL CONDITIONING

About the time that Pavlov was investigating the conditioned response, Thorndike (1898) undertook a series of experiments in which cats and dogs learned to escape from a box in order to obtain food which was visible but which had been placed on the outside of the box. The box was so constructed that it was necessary for the animal to press a latch or pull a string which would open a door and permit access to the reward. Following the receipt of reward, the animal would be returned to the box.

An examination of the animal's behavior revealed that when it was placed in the box for the first time, it displayed a great deal of what has frequently been described as trial and error behavior. During the course of responding, the animal made a number of errors but eventually made a response which opened the door and thus enabled it to secure the reward. On subsequent trials, it was observed that the animal's activity was usually centered around that part of the box where the successful response took place. With continued trials, the irrelevant and erroneous responses dropped out so that the animal performed the correct response as soon as it was placed in the box.

Thorndike's work marked the beginning of an interest in trial and error learning situations which has continued to the present.

Maze learning has been a popular trial and error situation with one of the earliest studies in the area performed by Small (1899, 1900) who built a six- by eight-foot reproduction of the

[8] It should be recognized that there is the possibility that, at least with the operation of some independent variables, such a randomization procedure will not be effective. In examining the role of UCS intensity, for example, it may be that by increasing the strength of the UCS the number of subjects who become voluntary responders also increases, thus providing a bias to this condition.

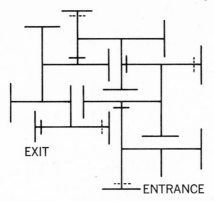

EXIT

ENTRANCE

Fig. 2–5. Floor plan of a multiple T-maze. The short solid lines indicate doors that are let down behind the rat to prevent retracing. The dashed lines represent dummy doors, causing the blind alley and the true path to have the same appearance to the animal from the choice point. *Adapted from Stone and Nyswander (1927)*

famous maze at Hampton Court in England. The maze was constructed of wire mesh placed on a wooden floor. Like Thorndike, Small found that the amount of time it took his subjects (rats) to go from the entrance to the middle of the maze where they found food decreased as a function of the number of trials they were given.

The complexity and general irregularity of this type of maze led other investigators to utilize different maze patterns which were believed to provide more reliable measures of learning. U-, Y-, and T-shaped mazes have all been used, with perhaps the latter type being the most frequently employed. The floor plan of one type of T-maze is illustrated in Figure 2–5. Construction may be in the form of an elevated pathway which permits the subject to use extra maze cues in learning, or the maze may be enclosed by walls and ceiling which limits the number of such cues that can be utilized.

In contrast to the spatial type of maze which has just been considered, a second type is of the temporal variety. Here there are no consistent spatial stimuli to provide differential cues for correct responses. The most frequently used of these was devised by Hunter (1920), an illustration of which is provided in Figure 2–6. It can be noted that there is just one choice point. When the animal reaches it, it must turn sometimes to the right and

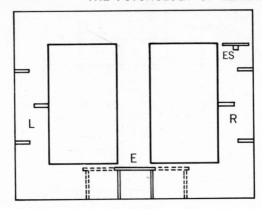

Fig. 2–6. Temporal maze. A stop, ES, may be placed in either alley, R or L, in order to prevent the animal from completing a tour on the wrong side. The animal is placed into the apparatus at E. The stop just below E may be shifted into the positions indicated by the dotted lines in order to force the animal into the central alley again after the completion of each tour. *Adapted from Hunter (1920)*

sometimes to the left in accordance with an arbitrary pattern provided by the experimenter. A relatively simple pattern would be alternation—R-L-R-L.

Although animals and most frequently rats have been favorite subjects for maze learning situations, it is interesting to note that human subjects have been used from time to time. Some of the early investigators [Hicks and Carr (1912), Perrin (1914)] devised outdoor mazes which were somewhat similar in floor plan to those which have been used with rats. Subjects were blindfolded and required to locomote through it with time and errors being used as performance measures. Construction and space problems involved with the use of such mazes resulted eventually in finger or stylus mazes being used whenever an experimenter desired to use human subjects. The typical finger maze consists of a small board with a maze pattern which is raised slightly above the surface so that the subject can follow it with one of his fingers. A path can be made with a variety of materials, although stiff wire is perhaps most frequently used. The stylus maze is similarly made except that the path is indented and the subject is given a stylus with which to trace the maze pattern.

A second type of learning situation, also involving trial and

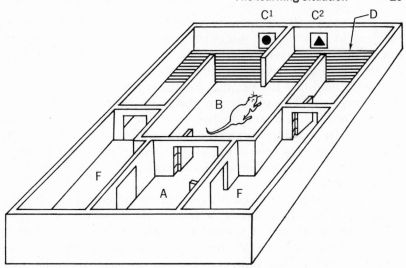

Fig. 2–7. The Yerkes-Watson discrimination apparatus. The animal is placed in Compartment A, and it moves to B where it chooses between C-1 and C-2. An incorrect choice will result in the animal's being shocked on the grid D. Food is found in Compartment F, from which point the animal moves into A for the next trial. *Adapted from Yerkes and Watson (1911)*

error behavior on the part of subject, is discrimination learning. Early discrimination problems were attacked using the Yerkes-Watson (1911) discrimination apparatus. Its essential features are shown in Figure 2–7. It can be noted that it consists of a reaction compartment from which the animal can look across an electric grid to two stimuli placed on either side of the partition. If the animal makes a correct response, it crosses the grid in front of the positive stimulus, turns, and pushes through a door to the compartment containing the goal object. If the animal makes an incorrect response, it gets shocked. In addition, the door of the food compartment is locked which forces the animal back to the reaction compartment where it can make another response.

As Harlow (1948) has written, this apparatus suffered from a number of limitations. For one, the stimuli were so arranged that the experimenter could not be assured that the animal was attending to and perceiving the stimuli when responding. A second problem was that the animal had to run away from the stimulus in order to secure the goal object. Finally, the fact that the goal object was temporally distant from the correct stimulus resulted in making the discrimination problem a very difficult one. These limitations were overcome by apparatus devised by Fields (1928) and Lashley (1930).

Fields modified the original Yerkes-Watson apparatus so that the subject could run under the forms to be discriminated and would continue in a straight line from the starting point to the goal box. In addition, the goal object was provided immediately after the correct response while an incorrect response was followed by detention in a chamber without the goal object. Electric shock was not used.

Lashley (1930) devised discrimination apparatus involving a jumping stand which has been previously illustrated in Figure 1–1. Here the animal is trained to jump directly at the stimuli which are used as cues for the location of an appropriate goal object. If the animal jumps to the correct card, the card falls, permitting access to a platform behind the card which contains the reward. If the animal jumps to the wrong card, it finds the window locked, and it falls into the net below.

Discrimination learning in monkeys has been studied most extensively by Harlow and his associates with the Wisconsin General Test Apparatus, illustrated in Figure 2–8. The animal responds by displacing one of two stimulus-objects covering the food wells in the tray before him. An opaque screen is interposed between the monkey and the stimulus situation between trials, and a one-way vision screen separates the monkey from the experimenter during trials. Simple discrimination tasks are those which require the monkey to choose one of two objects which differ in multiple characteristics (a green square vs. a red triangle) and which shift from left to right positions in a predetermined balanced order.

The discrimination problems which have been described involve the presentation of just two stimuli to the subject, but there is no reason that the learning situation must be so limited. One of the early pieces of apparatus employing multiple stimuli was the Yerkes (1916) multiple-choice apparatus illustrated in Figure 2–9. Here the subject could be presented with nine or more stimulus compartments. Subjects were required to respond consistently to such arrangements as "first on the left," "second on the right," etc.

Complex discrimination problems have also been employed

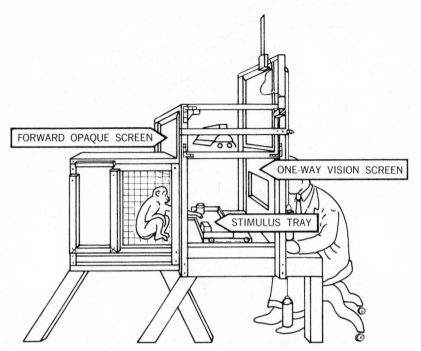

FORWARD OPAQUE SCREEN

ONE-WAY VISION SCREEN

STIMULUS TRAY

Fig. 2–8. Wisconsin General Test Apparatus. *Adapted from Harlow* (*1949*)

with the Wisconsin General Test Apparatus, with two such types being designated as either oddity or matching. With the oddity problem, two different pairs of identical stimulus objects are used. Three of the stimuli are presented together, with the odd stimulus being rewarded. Trials are so arranged that one member from each pair of stimuli is odd on half of the test trials. With the matching problem, the test tray is divided into a sample compartment having a single food well and a choice compartment having two food wells. All wells are covered by stimulus objects. The subject is first trained to displace the stimulus object found in the sample compartment, which is rewarded; then it is required to select the identical stimulus object found in the choice compartment.

Early investigators, being primarily interested in describing how learning took place, frequently used quite complex types of learning situations. Small's use of a replica of the Hampton Court

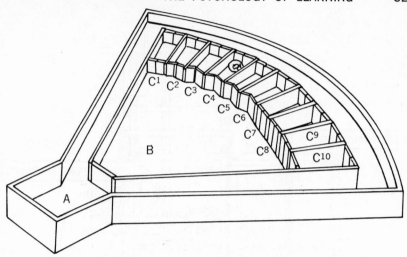

Fig. 2–9. The Yerkes multiple-choice apparatus. The animal responds to one of the test compartments from Compartment B. *Adapted from Yerkes (1916)*

maze is a good example. But as time passed, description was replaced with an interest in explanation—how specific responses came to be strengthened or weakened as a function of the manipulation of certain variables. Concomitant with this approach was the position that simple learning situations were the best means by which this interest could be pursued. As a result, classical conditioning situations, the two-choice discrimination problem, and the T-maze have had considerable contemporary popularity along with the straight runway and the Skinner box. With the straight runway, the animal has only to learn to run forward a few feet and enter a goal box which contains a goal object. The speed of the animal's running represents the response measure which is recorded. The Skinner box was developed by Skinner (1938). It consists of a simple box which contains only a single manipulandum—a lever or bar—the depression of which will provide the organism with a pellet of food.

This type of apparatus differs from the others discussed in that after the subject has made a response, he remains in essentially the same place ready to respond again. This kind of task has been designated as the free operant [Ferster (1953a)]. The methodological significance of the free operant is that most frequently the investigator does not use trials to measure learning; rather the subject is placed in the situation for a specified number of sessions, with each session consisting of a fixed interval of time, e.g., 30 minutes.[9]

Learning situations which have been categorized by a response-reward contingency have been described by Hilgard and Marquis (1940) as instrumental conditioning or learning—a classification which we have also used to describe learning situations in this section. As Hilgard and Marquis have written, "When the occurrence of the reinforcement [reward] is contingent upon the organism's behavior the procedure may be termed instrumental conditioning . . ."

The reader should be aware that some investigators have made a distinction between instrumental learning situations of the Skinner box or straight runway variety and those of the trial and error or discrimination type. Spence (1956), for example, has pointed out that the response measure used in the trial and error or discrimination learning experiment (selective learning) is a complex function of the operation of at least three concurrent processes: (1) the increasing strength of a correct stimulus-response relationship; (2) the successive weakening of incorrect stimulus-response tendencies; and (3) the spontaneous recovery of the incorrect stimulus-response tendencies between occurrences. In contrast, the Skinner box or straight runway learning situation (instrumental learning) is one in which the investigator hopes to limit the investigation to the study of the strengthening of only a single stimulus-response relationship.

This distinction may be more fictional than real. The rat when placed in a Skinner box (instrumental situation) does not immediately begin to press the bar. Rather, it engages in considerable trial and error behavior (e.g., exploring the box, sniffing, etc.) in much the same way as the animal which has been placed in the selective or trial and error situation. The basic difference between the two situations appears to be not in the behavior of the subject but in the behavior of the experimenter. In the instrumental learning task (i.e., Skinner box) the situation is so

---

[9] The reader should be aware of the fact that trials can be programmed in the free operant situation. One technique is to remove the manipulandum following each response. Thus, in Skinner box studies, a retractable lever may be used which is removed from the apparatus after each response. Each presentation of the lever constitutes a "trial."

arranged that errors cannot be readily identified; on the other hand, with the selective learning situation, errors become a basic datum.

The instrumental learning situations which have been described have typically used hungry or thirsty animals in which food or water has served as a reward. Accordingly, they can be classified as instrumental-reward situations. From time to time, some investigators have used noxious stimuli (i.e., shock) to motivate their subjects, and the use of such stimuli has given rise to other instrumental learning classifications—those of escape and avoidance learning.

Instrumental escape differs little from the instrumental reward situation which was previously described. A noxious stimulus is presented, and the organism must learn to make a response which terminates it. It can be noted that the presentation of such stimuli is not unlike the organism's being placed under some deprivation state, with the removal or termination of the aversive stimulus acting as reinforcement for an instrumental response in much the same manner that food serves as a reward for a hungry animal.

Instrumental avoidance situations differ from those of either instrumental reward or escape, and they may be classified into (a) active and (b) passive varieties. With active avoidance, a CS is presented which is followed by a UCS in the form of a noxious stimulus; the organism must learn to make an instrumental response during the presentation of the CS in order to avoid the UCS. If it does not respond during this period of time, noxious stimulation is received and the situation becomes one of instrumental escape.

With passive avoidance, the subject is first trained to make some response, following which it is provided with a noxious stimulus for continuing to respond in this fashion. An illustration of this situation can be found in a study by Kamin (1959). Here rats were first trained to avoid shock by running from one compartment to another. The CS was a buzzer, with shock being administered ten seconds following CS presentation. After the animals had learned this response, the animals were shocked upon reaching the second compartment; as a result, they had to learn to avoid this second shock by not responding to the CS (remaining in the first compartment). Shock was not presented in the first compartment during this second phase of training. The passive avoidance situation has been frequently subsumed under the topic of punishment.

One final type of learning situation which should be included in this section has been known as motor-skills learning. Following Fitts (1964) such situations may be described as involving highly organized receptor-effector-feedback processes, along with the use of what have been called graded responses. Some motor-skill behavior involves gross bodily activities such as walking, running, swimming, etc. Other forms involve only a part of the total response mechanism, e.g., reaching. Many such activities involve the manipulation of tools and objects or the control of machines, as in the case of typing, playing a musical instrument, driving a car, etc. Human subjects have been almost exclusively used with this type of learning situation. Early investigators concerned with examining motor-skill behavior typically used tasks which would be found in everyday experiences. Lashley (1915), for example, had subjects learn to shoot a bow and arrow using an outdoor range and standard equipment. An early study by Swift (1903) employed a ball-tossing or juggling task. (The subject had to toss two balls in the air with one hand.) Mirror tracing and card sorting were two other tasks which experimenters used to investigate motor-skills learning. The use of more complex tasks can be found in the early studies of Bryan and Harter (1897) and Book (1908), who investigated the acquisition of skill in sending and receiving telegraphic messages and learning to typewrite.

It was not until the beginning of World War II, however, that extensive programs on motor-skills learning commenced. One reason for considerable interest in the area was the fact that many investigators had acquired skill and familiarity with a number of different kinds of motor-skill apparatus—an outgrowth of a number of tests and a battery of hardware that psychologists had developed to select air crews for the United States Air Force. A second reason was that motor-skills learning was believed to be a particularly appropriate situation with which to examine some of the inhibition concepts which had been postulated by Hull (1943) in his *Principles of Behavior*.

An extended description of the varying motor-skill devices with which most systematic research is now being pursued would serve no useful purpose, although the interested reader can consult Bilodeau and Bilodeau (1961) who have recently provided a list. Perhaps the most frequently used apparatus is the rotary pursuit which consists of a turntable that turns at a fixed rate of speed. A small round target is set into the turntable and is flush with the turntable's surface. The task for the subject is to keep a stylus in contact with the target throughout a fixed practice period. The total time spent in such contact is typically used as the response measure.

An often used nonapparatus motor-skill task is upside-down alphabet printing. Here the subject is required to print the alphabet upside-down and backwards so that when the paper is turned through a 180-degree angle, the alphabet can be read from right to left in the usual manner. This task yields a sizable score in a relatively short period of time and is one in which young adults show rather rapid improvement.

VERBAL LEARNING

Although verbal learning situations have been frequently characterized as a type of instrumental learning, they are sufficiently different from the kinds of instrumental learning situations which have been described to merit separate discussion. Such differences are primarily related to the characteristics of the task and the type of material used. In addition, the use of human subjects usually results in experimenters' interest being directed toward the contribution of nonmotivational variables to the learning process.

Verbal Materials

An examination of verbal material used in the learning situation must begin with Ebbinghaus (1885) who introduced the nonsense syllable—two consonants separated by a vowel (e.g., siv)—in order to provide himself (he was his own subject) with verbal material which had the attributes of large numbers readily available, simplicity, and uniform difficulty—so presumed since there were no established associations between one nonsense syllable and another.[10]

The subsequent history of the experimental use of the non-

[10] It is interesting to note that the invention of the nonsense syllable prompted Titchener (1919) to write (pp. 380–381), "It is not too much to say that the recourse to nonsense syllables, as a means to the study of association, marks the most considerable advance, in this chapter of psychology, since the time of Aristotle."

sense syllable, or CVC trigram (consonant-vowel-consonant) as they are now categorized, reveals a continuing effort to calibrate and standardize their use. Varying rules have been proposed for the construction of nonsense syllable lists (i.e., a consonant should appear as the first letter of a syllable only once within a list; no vowel should occur more than once within any four consecutive syllables, etc.), and in contrast to Ebbinghaus' method of pronouncing the syllables, the practice of spelling them out has been recommended. Perhaps most important has been the recognition that nonsense syllables may differ in the number of associations they arouse within the subject. Since association value has been recognized as an important variable contributing to the learning process, calibration of nonsense syllables according to association value, as well as related constructs, e.g., pronunciability, has been undertaken by a number of experimenters.

Another type of nonsense material is the paralog or dissyllable which consists of a two-syllable nonsense combination of letters that are pronounceable but bear little resemblance to actual words. Except under very specific circumstances, in contrast to the nonsense syllable, they have found little favor with most experimenters.

Many investigators have considered the nonsense syllable as something less than the ideal verbal learning unit. When they are pronounced, they are capable of arousing associations in the same way that words or other meaningful units do. Thus they cannot be considered to have any unique verbal property. On the other hand, when they are spelled, there has been the increasing recognition that each nonsense syllable is not an integrated unit but, rather, only a collection of letters in which the probability of one letter following another will vary from syllable to syllable. The fact that such syllables are often difficult to learn frequently decreases subject motivation. As a result, the position has been taken that the nonsense syllable should be abandoned as an experimental verbal unit [i.e., Deese (1961)]; but surprisingly enough there has been little enthusiasm in adopting such a position.

Digits and words have also served as units of verbal material for the experimenter. The relationship that exists among words (e.g., synonyms, antonyms, etc.) has provided a semantic dimension which frequently cannot be utilized when using nonsense material. Recent experimental evidence has pointed to the necessity for words to be equated on the basis of word frequency in much the same way that nonsense syllables have been equated on the basis of association value.

Some investigators have been interested in using material similar to that which would be found in school or other everyday situations. As a result, they have employed connected discourse or material obtained from texts. Frequently, all of the material to be learned is presented to the subject in a "whole" fashion, with the subject given a fixed length of time to study it, following which some type of recall test is provided. As an example, in an early study by Gates (1917) subjects were presented with biographical material (e.g., John Clark, born in Indiana, June 4, 1867. Studied surgery and became a doctor in Philadelphia. Taught at Johns Hopkins, etc.) and given a fixed amount of time for study. Following this, they were asked to recall as much of the material as they could. A basic difficulty with such a procedure is that there is no assurance that the subject will spend equal amounts of time on the varying parts of the material.

TYPES OF VERBAL-LEARNING SITUATIONS

Serial Learning

In the serial-learning situation, the verbal material is presented in a fixed, serial order. Figure 2–10 illustrates such a list using common nonsense syllables as the material to be learned. Frequently, an anticipation method of learning is used. This consists of first instructing the subject to associate each item with the subsequent one, with an asterisk (or some other symbol) being used to cue the subject for the first item. When each item is exposed to the subject, it then serves as a stimulus to which the subject must respond with the next item on the list. Exposure time is typically fixed, usually two to four seconds per item.

Paired-Associate Learning

In learning serial tasks with the anticipation method, each item serves as a stimulus as well as a response. Investigators who wish to separate the stimulus and response characteristics of a verbal-learning task cannot use serial-learning situations, and as a result paired-associate learning tasks have been employed. This

```
*****
BEJ
DIW
GOK
JUQ
LUY
MEZ
QAM
SAJ·
VAK
ZUX
```

Fig. 2–10. A list of nonsense syllables. The **** serve as the stimulus for the subject to respond with the first syllable.

type of task consists of a series of pairs of items, with one item of the pair serving as the stimulus and the second item as the response. The anticipation method which has been frequently used with the paired-associate learning situation consists of the stimulus being presented for a short period during which time the subject must anticipate and call out the response which has been paired with that stimulus. The presentation of the stimulus is followed by the presentation of both the stimulus and response which provides the subject with the opportunity to learn the association. Presentation times have varied from one-half second to four seconds and sometimes longer, although two seconds has been the most frequently used time period. Thus a 2:2 presentation interval means that the stimulus is presented for two seconds followed by presentation of both the stimulus and response for two seconds.

As Battig (1964) has pointed out, the paired-associate anticipation procedure appears to incorporate the essential features of standard experimental procedures which have been used in the study of simple types of learning. That is, the material to be learned is separated into discrete stimulus and response categories, with the requirement that the subject make an appropriate response upon presentation of the stimulus. It also provides information to the subject as to whether a correct response has been made.

Although the anticipation method has been frequently employed with both serial- and paired-associate learning tasks, there is no requirement that it must be used and a whole variety of other verbal learning techniques have been utilized. In the serial-learning situation, for example, the material may be exposed, one item at a time, with the subject instructed to read each item and learn as many of them as he can. Following the presentation of the last item, he might be asked to write down or recall all that he can. Similarly, in the paired-associate situation, both stimulus and response items might be exposed, following which the stimulus items may be presented and the subject asked to attach the appropriate response to them.

Verbal-Discrimination Tasks

Verbal-discrimination tasks are similar to most discrimination learning situations except that verbal materials are used as the stimuli to be discriminated. The subject is presented with two, three, or possibly more verbal units for a fixed amount of time and is asked to choose the one which he believes the experimenter has arbitrarily designated as correct. Following his response, the correct item may be revealed or the experimenter may indicate whether or not the subject's choice was correct. As an example of this type of situation, McClelland (1942) presented pairs of words at approximately four-second intervals. Subjects were instructed to choose one word of each pair, and if their choice happened to be correct, a bell was rung. If it was incorrect, nothing happened. On the second trial, the subject's task was to recall which word of each pair had rung or would have rung the bell on the preceding trial.

A NOTE ON LEARNING CLASSIFICATIONS

The primary purpose of this chapter has been to provide the reader with a description of a number of different kinds of learning situations in order to acquaint him better with this topic. In doing so, a rather crude classification divided learning into: (1) classical conditioning and (2) instrumental and (3) verbal-learning situations. Having concluded a survey of learning tasks, it seems appropriate to consider two questions related to the classification itself: (1) Have other classifications been proposed? If so, what have they been? (2) Are different learning principles involved in these different learning situations?

Both of these questions are related to the general problem of how best to provide the psychologist with a taxonomy of learning. As Underwood (1964) has recently written, the most elegant approach to the problem would be in terms of some general theoretical structure in which the particular findings obtained in the varying experimental situations could be shown to be deductions from a master set of postulates.

A number of classifications have been made within the context of a particular theoretical point of view. For example, Thorndike (1932), Skinner (1938), Mowrer (1947), and Birch and Bitterman (1949) have all posited two major types of learning: (1) classical conditioning or the Pavlovian type of experimental situation based upon a stimulus-substitution or contiguity principle and (2) problem solving or trial and error learning situations based upon the law of effect or principle of reinforcement.

Spence (1956), although proposing a trichotomy consisting of (1) classical, (2) instrumental conditioning, and (3) selective learning, has been interested primarily in analyzing the classical and instrumental situations. His theoretical position, contrary to the point of view just expressed, is that classical conditioning is dependent upon a reinforcement principle and that instrumental conditioning is based upon contiguity.

In contrast to the "two-factor" theories, Tolman (1949) has proposed six different situations or learning relationships. He has suggested that classical conditioning, reinforcement, and expectancy principles are involved in the acquisition of some of these relationships, although for one situation, the learning of drive discriminations, he posited that no learning principles were available for their explanation. Unfortunately, none of these theoretical approaches has been successful in providing a taxonomy which has achieved general acceptability.

A learning taxonomy without specific theoretical orientation was proposed by Hilgard and Marquis (1940) in which (1) classical and (2) instrumental learning situations have also provided the major groupings. These authors pointed out that the temporal arrangement of stimuli was the distinctive feature in the classical conditioning situation, and with instrumental learning, the important consideration was the fact that reinforcement was presented only after the response had been made. In essence, as indicated earlier, the response was instrumental in bringing about reinforcement. Instrumental learning situations were further divided into four subcategories or training situations: (1) reward, (2) secondary reward, (3) escape, and (4) avoidance.[11]

Recently, both Bitterman (1962) and Grant (1964) have provided other nontheoretical taxonomies. Bitterman, limiting himself to animal learning tasks, has posited the following situations: (1) Thorndikian, (2) Pavlovian, and (3) avoidance.

The *Thorndikian* situation, so named because of Thorndike's pioneering role in its development, is one in which the experimenter sets out to change an organism's behavior by manipulating its consequences—by arranging a contingency between reinforcement and the behavior in question. The *Pavlovian* situation is, of course, illustrated by Pavlov's experimental work. As Bitterman states (pp. 87–88) :

> In a Pavlovian-experiment, reinforcement is scheduled without regard to response; the experimenter does not set out to mold behavior in some predetermined fashion, but only to study the way in which the functional properties of one stimulus are altered by virtue of its contiguity with another. Because their introduction is not contingent on the animal's behavior, Pavlovian reinforcements cannot be treated as rewards or punishments in any meaningful manner, nor can rewards and punishments be distinguished in a Pavlovian experiment.

Avoidance situations are given separate classification since Bitterman believes they cannot be classified unequivocally as Pavlovian or Thorndikian. He sees in them the Pavlovian and Thorndikian features closely intertwined, since a neutral stimulus paired with an aversive stimulus thereby acquires certain arousing properties, but the pairing is not independent of the animal's behavior—the aversive stimulus is introduced only if the CS fails to elicit some defined response.[12]

---

[11] Brogden (1951) has questioned the distinction that these authors have made among these four varieties of instrumental behavior. He has pointed out that reward and secondary reward training can be reduced to a single variety; avoidance and escape training can be similarly reduced if a CS is introduced into the escape training procedure. Brogden has concluded that the distinction of the four varieties of instrumental training is based primarily upon the lack of control exercised by the experimenter over the conditions under which acquisition takes place and the time at which responses occur.

[12] Bitterman has pointed out that the diversity of situations found in learning experiments cannot be encompassed by such a relatively small classification and has subsumed under these three major groupings three subdivisions: specifically, (1) unitary vs. choice, (2) generalized vs. discriminative, and (3) discrete vs. continuous.

Grant's (1964) classificatory scheme is too extensive for this discussion, but briefly, like Hilgard and Marquis (1940), he has posited the major categories of learning to be of a classical and instrumental variety. Classical conditioning situations, however, have been divided into four subclasses, and instrumental conditioning situations have been subdivided into six.

Are different learning principles involved in the different learning categories which have been posited? As already indicated, some writers have posited such to be the case, but others have not. The issue is open, but this presentation shall be one which regards classical and instrumental learning situations only as laboratory models from which one may observe the operations of certain variables which contribute to the learning process. Thus, no distinction shall be made between classical and instrumental conditioning based upon the application of different learning principles.

In short, following Underwood (1964) the continuity of the varying learning situations which are found in the laboratory shall be examined in terms of phenomena produced by comparable operations. For example, does increasing the amount of reward (UCS) influence the classical conditioning response in the same way that increasing amounts of reward change a response learned in the instrumental learning situation? In general then, this orientation asks whether a given variable influences learning in the same way regardless of the task involved.

As Underwood (1964) has further pointed out, this approach has the obvious limitation that some variables do not have relevance for some tasks. For example, it is impossible to manipulate a meaningfulness or isolation variable in a pursuit rotor task in the same way that these variables are manipulated in verbal learning.

Moreover, two dangers to this approach must be delineated. First, if different tasks are examined, there is considerable difficulty in specifying when certain operations are comparable. For example, the amount of reward for a rat in a Skinner box may be increased by providing the animal with four pellets instead of one. But, does increasing the amount of reward from 25 cents to a dollar for the college student in a verbal-learning situation provide a comparability of operation? Some investigators would take the position that if the tasks differ, the operations cannot be comparable; but the adoption of such a position would remove all hope of the empirical assessment of continuity of learning across tasks. But when this is attempted and different experimental findings are obtained, how can one assess the role of the factors which are involved? Divergent findings may arise because the operations are not comparable, but they also may arise because the measuring units are not coordinate or perhaps because the effects of the variable are different in the two situations.

But a second danger may arise when the experimental operations procedures produce similar findings. Although a frequent interpretation of such a finding is that the same processes are involved in producing the effect, this may not necessarily be true.[13]

In spite of the limitations and difficulties of this approach, it is believed to be the one which makes the most sense and gives the most hope for providing some integration of the many learning experiments which have been performed.

[13] Underwood (1964) has suggested that one way of evaluating the contribution of specific variables in different learning situations may be achieved by use of transition experiments. This procedure requires that the varying learning tasks be analyzed along descriptive dimensions, with the similarities and differences being catalogued. A continuum of tasks is then provided which reflects varying amounts of these dimensional attributes. The investigator may then proceed to examine the contribution of a given variable over these varying types of learning situations.

3

Measurement and Methodology

BEFORE PROCEEDING TO AN EXAMINATION of the role of relevant processes involved in learning, it would be helpful to consider problems involved in the measurement of learning, the distinction between learning and performance, and an analysis of learning curves.

PROBLEMS OF MEASUREMENT

From the examination in the previous chapter of a few of the many kinds of learning situations found in the laboratory it is apparent that it is possible to obtain a variety of response measures within the same experiment. In the classical conditioning of the salivary response, for example, one may measure the amount of time it takes the animal to salivate beginning from the time that the conditioned stimulus was presented (latency), or one may measure the amount of salivation elicited by the conditioned stimulus (amplitude). The number of trials it would take to experimentally extinguish the response can also be measured. In a trial and error learning situation, an example of which might be a rat learning to run to one side of a T-maze, one might measure the speed with which the animal leaves the starting box or traverses the total maze. Or one could measure the number of errors that the animal makes. As with the classical conditioning situation, one could also measure the animal's resistance to extinction. With a human, learning a paired-associate task, it would be possible to measure the speed with which an individual responds after having been presented with the stimulus word, or it would be possible to measure the correctness with which he responds. These examples, of course, represent only a sampling of the many different kinds of response measures that can be obtained from the subjects in the learning situation.

The selection of what is to be measured represents an arbitrary decision, and it is not surprising to find investigators using varying measures from which to infer learning. However, since it is necessary, frequently, to compare and contrast the experimental findings obtained from a number of experiments, it becomes important to answer some basic questions about these response measures.

One of these questions is related to an examination of the interrelationships that exist among the varying response measures which may be obtained from the same learning task. It might be assumed that if the varying measures obtained within a single task were measuring the same process, the resulting correlation among the various measures would be high. The results of a number of experimental studies, however, have not supported such an assumption. Table 3–1 presents some of the evidence on this question, and an examination of these data clearly reveals that it is difficult to predict one response measure from a knowledge of another.

The problem that most individuals working in the area have faced, however, has not been one of attempting to make predictions about one response measure from another but, rather, whether varying response measures reflect corresponding changes which occur as a result of the manipulation of what are considered to be basic learning variables. The question can be asked: If a certain reinforcement procedure (or other basic learning variable) decreased the latency of the response, would the amplitude of that response also show a corresponding change as a result of the manipulation of the reinforcement procedure? In answering this question, the correlational analysis among individual measures of response strength, such as presented in Table 3–1, is not completely appropriate since it introduces into the situation a

TABLE 3–1

Intercorrelations of Various Measures of Learning

| | | CORRELATION BETWEEN | | |
| | | FREQ. AND AMPL. | LAT. AND AMPL. | LAT. AND FREQ. |
INVESTIGATOR	TASK			
Kellogg and Walker (1938)	Conditioned flexion (dog)	.94	.22	−.18
Campbell and Hilgard (1936)	Conditioned eyelid (dog)	.63	−.15	−.54
Campbell (1938)	Conditioned knee jerk (man)	.63	−.27	−.27
Pennypacker (1964)	Conditioned eyelid (man)	.69	−.65	−.79
Brogden (1949)	Forelimb flexion (dog)	r between number of trials to reach acquisition criterion and extinction criterion = .19		
Hunter (1935)	Running response (rats)	Trials to learn and trials to extinguish = −.36		
Hall and Kobrick (1952)	Running response (rats)	Latency and running time = .45 Latency and extinction = .15 Extinction and running time = −.01		

number of sources of variance which reduce the value of any correlation that is obtained.

A hypothetical situation may make this a little clearer. Experimental procedure consists of giving four rats three reinforced trials along a straight runway. The animals are first placed in a starting box, the door is raised, and they are then free to run down the runway into the goal box. Response measures are: (1) latency, or the length of time it takes the animal to get out of the starting box, and (2) running speed, or the amount of time it takes the animal to run the length of the runway. In Figure 3–1 the latencies and running speeds have been plotted for the four subjects, A, B, C, and D. With animal A, the mean latency is four seconds, and the mean running speed is eight. The mean latency for subject B is seven seconds, and mean running speed is two seconds. Animal C's mean running speed and latency are identical —three seconds in each case. A similar situation prevails for animal D—mean latency and mean running speed measuring six seconds. The data is recorded in Table 3–2. Computation reveals that the rank-order correlation between the two response meas-

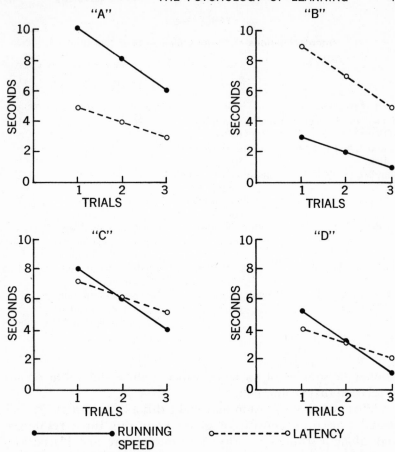

Fig. 3–1. Latency and running speed plotted for three learning trials and for four subjects, A, B, C, and D.

ures is only −.40. Increasing the number of subjects could further reduce it. On the other hand, both response measures decrease as a function of number of reinforced trials for all four subjects. It is this similarity of function which, at least at this stage of our science, is most important. In order to examine this kind of relationship, it is most appropriate to examine the similarity of function obtained with varying response measures. This can be done by visual inspection or by experimentally providing groups of subjects with varying amounts of the variable under consideration

TABLE 3–2

Computation of the Correlation between Running Speed and Latency

SUBJECTS	MEAN RUNNING SPEED	MEAN LATENCY	RANK R.S.	RANK LAT.	D	D^2
A	8	4	4	2	2	4
B	2	7	1	4	3	9
C	3	3	2	1	1	1
D	6	6	3	3	0	0
						$\Sigma 14$

$$\text{rho} = 1 - \frac{6 \cdot 14}{4\,(16-1)} = 1 - 1.4 = -.40$$

and then proceeding to make the appropriate correlational analysis.

The first method is illustrated by a study of Kessen (1953). In two experiments, rats learned to avoid shock by rotating a wheel in response to lights of varying intensities. The response measures used were: (1) latency or speed of responding as measured from the onset of the light (CS), (2) the probability of the response being made, (3) number of wheel turns made between trials, and (4) number of extinction responses. Figure 3–2 illustrates the results obtained from Kessen's Experiment II using three of these response measures. It can be noted that these three acquisition measures reflect similar functions as a function of the manipulation of the independent variable. Extinction data, on the other hand, were not related to the varying light intensities which were used.

Many other investigators, however, have not had the same success in finding that different response measures reflected similar changes as a function of the manipulation of some independent variable. In fact, it can be stated that very frequently, similar findings are not obtained when different response measures obtained from the same experiment are examined. Studies by Hillman, Hunter, and Kimble (1953); Levine, Staats, and Frommer (1959); Goodrich (1959); and Lachman (1961), to mention only a few, lend experimental support to this position.

Kobrick's (1956) study is one of the few designed to investigate this problem using the correlational method. In this experiment, rats were trained to run a 12-foot runway. Eight groups of

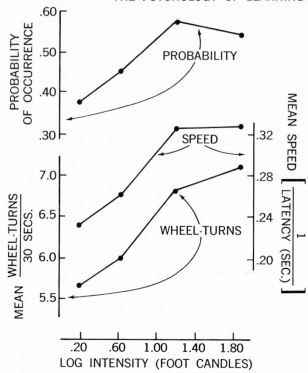

Fig. 3–2. Response strength during training as a function of log CS intensity, Exp. II. *Adapted from Kessen (1953)*

subjects were used with each group receiving either 4, 7, 10, 15, 20, 30, 40, or 50 reinforcements, followed by extinction trials. Individual's response measures were obtained by using the mean of each subject's last three acquisition trials. These individual means were, in turn, combined to provide group means. The response measures obtained were: (1) latency, or time required to leave the starting box, (2) speed of running, and (3) resistance to extinction. Intercorrelations among the measures were then obtained. It should be noted, of course, that rank-order correlations were used since the N in this instance was eight—the number of groups which received different numbers of reinforcements. Results indicated that latency and speed of running correlated quite highly (.86 for means, .74 for medians). On the other hand, there was little relationship between resistance to extinction and (a) latency (−.09 for means, .50 for medians) or (b) speed of running (−.28 for means, −.16 for medians). Kobrick's findings support the results of other investigators previously cited and reveal a fundamental difficulty when comparing one response measure with another.

Aware of the measurement problem, some investigators have attempted to solve it by concerning themselves with only a single response measure. Statistical learning theories as developed by Estes (1950) and others have placed major emphasis upon probability of response measures. Meyer (1953) and Pubols (1960), on the other hand, have made a distinction between measures which involve time (e.g., latency, running speed, rate of responding) and those which are time independent (e.g., errors or frequency of responding). These authors have hypothesized that time measures reflect performance changes, but time independent measures reflect learning—a distinction discussed in the next section.

Examination of the literature indicates the wisdom of differentiating among three types of response measurement. These are as follows:

1. Rate or Time Measures. These measures involve time as a basic parameter. Latency as obtained in classical conditioned response studies, or the amount of time required for an organism to leave a starting box or run a maze, would represent examples of this type of response measure. Moreover, the number of responses made within a given time interval, such as that frequently obtained in a Skinner box study, would be subsumed under this measure.

2. Amplitude or Magnitude Measures. These measures involve the amount or extent of a response and are only infrequently obtained, but they, nonetheless, constitute a measure which must be differentiated from others. In the examination of the classically conditioned salivary response, for example, some investigators have used the amount of salivation as a response measure. When conditioning the eyelid reflex or galvanic skin response, the amplitude of these responses is measured from time to time. Typically, such responses are graphically recorded with amplitude referring to the maximum distance the pen has deviated from the base line prior to the onset of the UCS. Although it might be pointed out that the amplitude of the response should reflect a time measure (it takes longer for the pen to make a large deflection than a small one) the time differential between small and large responses is so minute that at least for now, amplitude must be considered as a different measurement category.

Recently, Pennypacker (1964) has defined the magnitude of the conditioned eyelid reflex as the integral of the amplitude over the time course of the blink and has suggested that this measure provides a description of the physical properties of the response which is statistically superior to that provided by other measures. However, this measure shall be considered as merely one subcategory of amplitude and magnitude measures.

3. Probability Measures. This is undoubtedly the most frequently used measure, and it involves the measurement of the presence or absence of a response which is then often converted into a percentage value. The measurement of correct and incorrect responses also is subsumed under this category. For example, a common measurement operation for investigators examining classical conditioned responses is the noting of the percentage of such responses which are made over the course of a number of test trials. With the instrumental learning situation, the number of correct or incorrect responses that a subject makes in learning a T-maze or multiple T-maze becomes a basic performance measure.

Finally, the classification should be further divided into those measures which were obtained during acquisition trials as contrasted to those obtained during extinction.

This classification, unfortunately, does not solve all of the measurement problems. From time to time, some investigators have used response measures which involve two of the classifications presented. For example, an investigator who measures the number of correct (or incorrect) responses within a fixed period of time is obviously using a time or rate measure. But at the same time, it is a measure which is related to probability of responding as well. Probability of responding may also contribute to amplitude measures. For example, Humphreys (1943) and Hilgard (1951) have employed the term *magnitude* to refer to a response measure in which an amplitude measure is used and which includes all trials including those which resulted in no measurable response. The mean reflects the presence of zero values. On the other hand, the authors have used *amplitude* to denote a response which has been derived only from those trials on which a response occurred.

Of even greater difficulty is the fact that rate measures can be

TABLE 3–3

Speeds of Rats' Running Expressed in Two Ways

	FEET PER SECOND		SECONDS PER FOOT ($1/$FEET PER SECOND)	
	Rat A	Rat B	Rat A	Rat B
	2	4	.50	.25
	8	5	.125	.20
Total	10	9	.625	.45
Mean	5	4.5	.3125	.225

(Adapted from Edgington, 1960).

expressed in terms of amount performed per unit of time or amount of time per unit of performance and that, at least under certain circumstances, these two measures of performance can lead to contradictory conclusions. In an interesting demonstration of this, Edgington (1960) has presented the above table in which the speed of a rat's running a runway has been expressed in two ways. As shown in Table 3–3, the mean for rat A indicates it was faster than rat B when measured in terms of feet-per-second (A = 5, B = 4.5); but when measured by seconds-per-foot traveled, A was slower than B (A = .3125, B = .225). The non-linearity of the relationship between the two reciprocally related measures (Y = 1/x) reveals that there can be an inconsistency between them for any statistic that is derived from addition or subtraction of measurement values. The investigator points out that proposed solutions can be to either (1) use nonparametrics which employ only the rank-order of the original data or (2) use a logarithmic transformation of the measurement values.

Another difficulty, one which is also related to rate of response measures, is directed to *where* the rate measure is obtained. For example, the straight runway is frequently used in examining the influence of a number of learning variables. It is possible when using this type of apparatus to measure running speed (or rate of response) over different parts of the apparatus—latency, or speed of getting out of the start box; speed of running the middle portion of the runway; and speed of running the terminal portion of the runway which includes the animal's entering the goal box. There is no assurance that these varying response measures all reflect the contribution of a given independent variable. A good example is found in a study by Goodrich (1959) who examined running speed over three sections of a straight runway for rats given continuous and partial (50 per cent) reinforcement. Results are diagrammed in Figure 3–3. Here it can be noted that there is a crossover effect with the partial reinforcement group being superior to the continuous reinforcement group beginning midway through the learning trials, when performance is measured using starting speed or speed of running the middle section of the runway. Such an effect is not obtained, however, when running speed is measured over the terminal section of the runway.

A final problem which should be delineated is related to the one just discussed except that it concerns the use of probability of response measures. Bahrick, Fitts, and Briggs (1957) have pointed out that a basic difficulty arises when an experimenter uses a dichotomous score (error–no error, etc.) from which to infer the presence of the learning process which is assumed to be continuously distributed. The difficulty arises from the experimenter's selection of that point which differentiates errors from non-errors —thus, "the arbitrary choice of a cutoff point in the dichotomizing of continuous response distributions can impose significant constraints upon the shape of resulting learning curves, and . . . this can form the basis of misleading theoretical interpretations."

In a demonstration of their position, these investigators employed a continuous performance score (error magnitude expressed in the form of electrical voltage) and three different dichotomous time-on-target measures, all obtained from a tracking task which consisted of a ten cpm sinusoidal motion of a line on a cathode-ray-tube display. The three time-on-target measures were related to the subject keeping the cursor within one-tenth (small target), three-tenths (medium target), or six-tenths (large target) inches on either side of a target line. One group of male subjects and a second group of females were given 14 learning trials. Learning curves were plotted for both groups using each of the four response measures. Findings revealed different amounts of relative and absolute improvement during practice as a function of the response measure employed. For example, the curves for time-on-target scores all suggested that absolute as well as relative improvements during tracking were greater for male subjects than for the females, with this effect being particularly

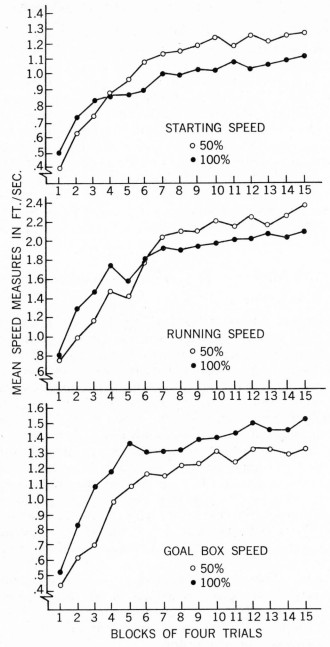

Fig. 3–3. Mean starting, running, and goal box speeds for the two groups by blocks of four trials. *Adapted from Goodrich (1959)*

apparent when performance on the smallest target was plotted. In contrast, when the continuous performance curve was plotted, greater improvement was noted for the females.

In selecting a response measure, an investigator will want to use one which promises to be of sufficient sensitivity that there is a high probability that it will reflect the manipulation of the independent variable. But other than this, since the selection of the response measure represents an arbitrary choice on the part of the experimenter, there are no correct answers to the problems which have been delineated in this section. However, experimenters should be increasingly aware of the problems involved in making comparisons among experimental studies which have utilized different response measures.

THE DISTINCTION BETWEEN LEARNING AND PERFORMANCE

In Chapter 1 learning was considered to be a process taking place in the nervous system and which was inferred from changes in the organism's behavior. Presumably, the manner in which an organism responds reflects the characteristics of the learning which has taken place. But it has also been recognized that this relationship between learning on the one hand and resultant behavior or performance on the other may not be perfect. Everyone knows of students who study diligently for an examination and presumably learn the material only to find the test-taking situation so traumatic that they are unable to respond appropriately. Since it is generally assumed that the student has not "forgotten" the material, his poor performance is readily distinguished from what he has learned. This contrast between how the organism *performs* and what it has *learned* has resulted in a number of investigators attempting to distinguish between these constructs.

Although Lashley (1929) had written earlier about differentiating between these two constructs, it was the experimental work of Tolman (1932) and his associates in their examination of latent learning which was most responsible for calling psychologists' attention to this distinction.

In an early study by Blodgett (1929), a Tolman associate, three groups of rats were given one trial a day on a six-unit

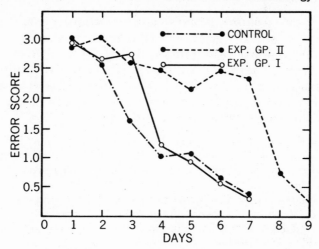

Fig. 3–4. The influence of reward on maze learning. The Control Group has been reinforced on every trial. Experimental Group I had reward introduced on Trial 3, while Experimental Group II had reward introduced on Trial 7. *Adapted from Blodgett (1929)*

multiple T-maze. The Control group (N = 36) was run for seven days, with each animal permitted to eat for three minutes in the goal box. Experimental Group I (N = 25) was also run for seven days. For the first two days, this group did not find food in the goal box but was retained there for two minutes. They were then placed in a cage and an hour later were given food. Reward was introduced on the third trial, and it continued to be present until the end of the study. Experimental Group II (N = 36) was treated similarly to Experimental Group I except that reward was omitted for the first six days and introduced on the seventh. These animals were then run two additional days. Results are illustrated in Figure 3–4. It can be noted that the discovery of food by Experimental Group I at the end of the third trial resulted in an error score on trial four not unlike that found by the Control group for trial four. This change in performance taking place as a function of finding reward on a single trial is even more dramatically revealed by the error scores made by Experimental Group II. As a result of finding food in the goal box on trial seven, performance for this group on trial eight is not significantly different from the performance on trial seven of the Control group.

Since the Control group's continuous rather than abrupt change in performance gives rise to the inference that the learning process does not take place rapidly, these findings have been used to make readily apparent the distinction between learning and performance. Learning in all groups was taking place at a uniform rate; reward was contributing only to the animal's performance. Or, as Tolman (1932) has written (p. 364) :

> The latent learning, which thus takes place without any strong differential effects, [introduction of food] does not, to be sure, manifest itself until after such effects have been introduced. But, once these latter have been provided, then the sizes of the immediate drops in the performance curves, which appear, indicate that the learning has been just as great as it would have been, if strong effects had been present throughout. Differential effects are, that is, necessary for *selective performance,* but they are not necessary, or at the most in only a very minor degree, for the mere learning *qua* learning which underlies such performance.

It has been pointed out that a primary reason for making a distinction between the two constructs is the need to isolate and identify those variables which contribute to learning as contrasted to those variables which contribute only to performance. It may be that in order for learning to occur, the organism must obtain some minimum amount of reward, but increases in this amount are not reflected in increasing the amount of learning. On the other hand, variations in the amount of reward that an organism receives may determine how it performs.

In order to separate learning from performance, it is necessary to find criteria by which one may be distinguished from the other. Two such criteria, stemming from certain assumptions that investigators have made about how learning takes place, have been related to (1) the presence (or absence) of reinforcement and (2) the opportunity for practice.

A number of investigators have held that the use of extinction trials represents a procedure from which inferences can be made about the contribution of a specific variable to learning or performance. A hypothetical example may illustrate this. Two groups of rats are placed on 20 hours of food deprivation and given 50 reinforced trials in learning to depress a bar in a Skinner box. Following these acquisition trials, an extinction series is instituted, with one group placed under 25 hours of deprivation while the other group has been placed under 15 hours. If the experimental findings reveal a difference in resistance to extinction between the groups—a difference which indicates the 25-hour deprived group to be superior—such a finding is assumed to reflect the contribution of hours of deprivation to performance, rather than learning. Such an inference is tenable, it is posited, inasmuch as the amount of learning taking place during the acquisition series was identical for both groups, and further learning could not take place during the nonreinforced extinction trials.

The reverse situation is one in which hours of deprivation would be manipulated during the acquisition series, i.e., one group placed under 15 hours of food deprivation and a second group under 25 but then held constant during extinction, i.e., both groups extinguished under 20. A significant difference between the groups (i.e., 25-hour group superior) would be used to support the position that the deprivation variable influenced learning, the logic being that since the deprivation variable was constant during extinction, any difference in extinction between the groups would be a reflection of a difference in the deprivation variable which was present during the acquisition series. Conversely, no extinction differences between the groups has been taken to mean that the deprivation variable has not contributed to the growth of the learning process.[1]

A second procedure which has been used to make a distinction between learning and performance rests upon the practice criterion and the level of learning. If a change in behavior takes place as a result of the manipulation of a given variable and if there has been no (or very little) opportunity for further learning to occur, the variable which has been introduced is assumed to influence performance. The lack of opportunity for further learning to take place has been manipulated by either (1) having the subjects learn until they reach some asymptote so that further practice trials produce only negligible amounts of performance increment or (2) not providing practice trials so that further learning cannot take place. This latter position is basically untenable since at least one trial must be given in order to determine if any effect has taken place. As a result, this position is typically modified to indicate that whatever effect is obtained could not have been produced by the learning process with only a single trial.

[1] More adequate experimental designs than these have been used to make this distinction and will be discussed in subsequent sections.

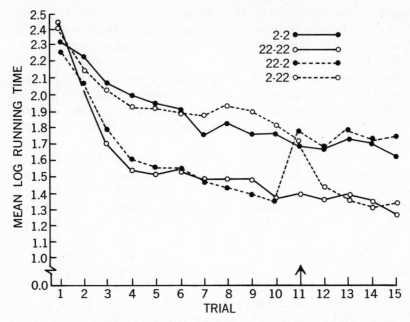

Fig. 3–5. Learning curves showing time scores for each experimental group as a function of trials. The arrow indicates the point at which the drive was changed for the two groups. *Adapted from Hillman, Hunter, and Kimble (1953)*

The Blodgett (1929) study previously referred to provides an excellent example of this latter position. It will be recalled that as a result of a single reinforced trial, the performance of his rats revealed a large increment in performance—significantly more than that found in the control group. Although one could not assume that learning was independent of reinforcement (since some learning could have taken place on the single trial in which reinforcement was provided), it is obvious that reinforcement makes a significant contribution to an organism's performance.

A more contemporary example is found in an experiment by Hillman, Hunter, and Kimble (1953) who placed rats under two or 22 hours of water deprivation and had them run a multiple T-maze for ten trials. On Trial 11, the group of animals on 22 hours of deprivation was subdivided, with half of them remaining on 22 hours of deprivation and the other half being switched to two hours of deprivation. Similarly, the original two-hour deprivation group was subdivided, with half continuing on two hours, whereas the other half was switched to 22. An examination of Figure 3–5 reveals that the two-hour group which was switched to 22 hours had a performance *increment* in a single trial which made it comparable with the 22-hour control group. Similarly, the 22–2 group had a performance *decrement* in a single trial which made it similar to the two-hour control group. The authors have concluded that since speed of maze running appears to depend almost entirely upon the amount of deprivation which is present during the particular trial on which it is measured, the deprivation variable must obviously influence performance. They have further contended that since the animals' performance on the first ten trials had essentially no influence on the subsequent trials, the amount of deprivation does not contribute to the amount learned. This latter position of the authors rests on the additional assumption that learning effects should be relatively permanent and they should carry over from one phase of training to the next, but performance effects should not.

A final distinction between learning and performance has been made from examination of the acquisition curve. Briefly, different rates of approach or growths to a performance asymptote presumably reflect learning, while different *asymptotes* reveal performance differences. Pubols (1960) states, "Many investigators have taken differences in rate of approach to asymptotic performance level as a function of incentive magnitude to reflect an effect on rate of learning, and different asymptotes to reflect a difference in performance." This criterion stems largely from Hull's (1951) theoretical system which posited that the asymptote (or motivational level) of an acquisition curve was determined by the amount of reinforcement provided the organism—a variable which Hull assumed to influence performance. Learning, or habit strength, he stated was influenced only by the number of reinforcements, each of which produced a given increment to the amount learned.

It is readily apparent that many of the assumptions which form the basis of the criteria which have been used to distinguish learning from performance are tenuous. One can seriously question the widespread use of extinction as a procedure for separating the two constructs, since we do not have any acceptable analysis of what takes place during the extinction operation. Moreover, empirical data have shown that in many situations extinction performance is unrelated to any of the response measures which have been obtained during the acquisition trials.

The distinction between learning and performance based upon rate of learning and asymptotic performance must also be questioned. To state that different asymptotic levels reflect performance rather than learning differences is dependent upon Hull's (1951) assumption that only the number of reinforcements can contribute to learning. If such an assumption is rejected, then there is a similar rejection of the distinction between the constructs based upon this criterion.

Perhaps the best criterion is related to the abruptness with which changes in performance take place. Abrupt changes of behavior are related presumably to performance variables, whereas continuous changes are related to learning variables. But a careful scrutiny of this criterion also reveals difficulties. Abrupt versus continuous is not a dichotomy but a continuum. To designate a certain class of behavior change as abrupt and another class as continuous undoubtedly does violence to the nature of the distribution. Moreover, what guarantee does one have that performance variables cannot reflect their influence in a continuous manner?

It would be only reasonable to say that the learning-performance dichotomy, although enthusiastically accepted by many investigators in the area, rests upon to-be-proven assumptions.[2] But in the last analysis the value of the distinction must rest upon pragmatic grounds. Does the making of such a distinction enable us to better understand behavior? An examination of the learning literature reveals that in a few areas investigators have been interested in the problem and have performed experiments

[2] With regard to a contemporary analysis of learning and performance, the writer would agree with a statement made by McGeoch (1942) who stated (pp. 598–599) that "the distinction between learning and performance is logically valid, but practically and operationally of little importance in a treatment of learning . . . The only way we can know that learning has occurred is by an observation of successive performances, since *learning is a relation between successive performances* . . . This does not mean that learning cannot occur without being measured, but only that we can never know that learning has occurred without measurement or observation of some kind. The statement that it can occur without being measured admits the validity of the logical distinction between learning and performance, while the statement that it cannot be known as a scientific datum without being observed or measured denies the operational validity of the distinction. Assertions that motive and effect influence performance but not learning become meaningless in the absence of quantitative demonstration, a demonstration which cannot be made without measurements of performance."

designed to evaluate the role of certain variables in learning and performance, at least as they have operationally distinguished between them. Wherever this has taken place, the relevant experimental findings shall be examined. It must be recognized, however, that most investigators have not been concerned with attempting to experimentally distinguish between the two concepts.

LEARNING CURVES

At times it is important for the experimenter to have some idea as to how learning progresses throughout the practice period, and one of the most appropriate techniques for supplying this information is use of a learning curve. Such curves are typically plotted by placing trials, or the independent variable, along the abscissa, while performance or the dependent variable is plotted on the ordinate. It is apparent that the particular type of performance measure utilized will determine whether the curve will rise or fall. Performance measures involving time (i.e., speed of running, latency of responding, etc.) or errors result in falling curves; whereas measures of positive performance (i.e., number or frequency of correct responses) produce rising ones.

When individual learning curves are constructed, a laborious procedure when many subjects are used, they will usually be quite irregular. As a result, the assumed orderliness of the learning process is obscured. For this reason, group curves are usually utilized.

The simplest way to construct a learning curve is to average the scores made by all the subjects on the first trial, then the second, etc. Then these values are plotted to reveal the course of learning. One difficulty with this technique is that when a criterion is used, the number of trials that each individual has taken to reach a criterion will vary.[3] One subject may reach criterion in 20 trials, another in 25, a third in 28, etc. Such being the case, it means that the varying points on a curve in which *trials* are used to define the abscissa will reflect differing numbers of subjects. It is possible, of course, to assume that once the individual has reached the criterion, his performance will con-

[3] The criterion, of course, represents an arbitrary standard of proficiency set by the experimenter.

tinue to reflect criterion performance thereafter. If the criterion is a very stringent one, such an assumption is reasonable. Frequently, however, the criterion is not severe, and individual subjects on post-criterion trials regress to a performance level lower than that obtained on the criterion trial.

One technique which has been used when the experimenter uses a criterion has been suggested by Vincent (1912). It is called a Vincent curve, although the original procedure as outlined by Vincent has been subjected to a number of modifications by later investigators. The basic procedure can be described as follows: Each individual's learning curve or trials to mastery is divided into equal fractions (i.e., tenths, twelfths, etc.) with performance at these varying fractional intervals being summated, averaged, and then plotted. On the abscissa, equal fractions of learning are used rather than trials. In her original article, Vincent (1912) suggested tenths of learning as the fractional interval to be used. In a number of instances, this meant that performance on fractional trials would have to be obtained; and in order to eliminate such fractional trials, it was suggested that the total trials be so divided that a whole number would be obtained, with the excess trials distributed over the beginning fractions. The performance value used at each fraction for an individual subject was obtained by summating scores over all the trials comprising the fraction and then getting the mean.

To illustrate the general procedure, if a subject required 22 trials to reach a criterion, each tenth of learning would be represented by two, rather than two and two-tenths, trials. Since there would be two additional trials, these would be distributed over the first two-tenths of learning. Thus, performance scores obtained on the first, second, and third trials would be summated and a mean obtained to represent that subject's performance on the first tenth of learning, while a similar procedure would be utilized with the fourth, fifth, and sixth trials in order to provide a value for the second tenth. All other fractional intervals would consist of obtaining mean performance values over two trials.

As Hilgard (1938) has stated, the arbitrary distribution of excess trials led later investigators to abandon Vincent's suggested procedure, and modifications by Hunter (1929), Kjerstad (1919), and others have been proposed. A number of investigators have followed Hunter's (1929) suggestion that trials be assumed to be continuous and that performance is uniformly

TABLE 3–4

Records for Three Subjects (A, B, and C) Learning a List of Eight Adjectives

| | TRIALS | | | | | | | | | |
	1	2	3	4	5	6	7	8	9	10
Subject A:										
No. Correct Responses	1	3	4	4	6	6	7	8		
Subject B:										
No. Correct Responses	2	4	3	4	5	5	6	6	6	8
Subject C:										
No. Correct Responses	1	4	5	7	8					

distributed within any trial, thus permitting fractional values to be used. In the previously cited illustration, the first tenth of learning would be represented by two and two-tenths trials, rather than by the first three as suggested by Vincent. A second modification proposed by Kjerstad (1919) has been to use the score or performance level which has been reached at the *end* of a given fractional interval, rather than to represent each interval with an average score.

Another method for obtaining a group-learning curve has been suggested by Melton (1936). This has been called a successive criteria technique, and it consists of computing the average number of trials to reach successive criteria. Here it can be noted that trials form the dependent variable, while successively more stringent criteria are plotted on the abscissa.

As an example of this technique, let us hypothesize that three individuals are asked to learn a serial list of eight adjectives to a criterion of one perfect trial. The following protocols are illustrated in Table 3–4.

The data employed to construct the successive criteria curve would be as noted in Table 3–5, and the curve itself can be observed in Figure 3–6.

Underwood (1957) has pointed out that the successive criteria curve represents the earliest point in learning in which the average subject reaches each criterion score; and if a picture of

TABLE 3–5

Data Used to Construct the Successive Criterion Curve

TRIAL ON WHICH EACH SUCCESSIVE CRITERION
WAS ACHIEVED

		1	2	3	4	5	6	7	8
	A	1	2	2	3	5	5	7	8
Subjects	B	1	1	2	2	5	7	10	10
	C	1	2	2	2	3	4	4	5
	Total	3	5	6	7	13	16	21	23
	X	1.0	1.7	2.0	2.3	4.3	5.3	7.0	7.7

learning is desired which combines maximum performance with the earliest achievement of the maximum, such a representation of group performance is adequate. On the other hand, if it is assumed that any learning situation actually involves fluctuations in performance, the successive criteria curve is a representation of performance which takes place only at performance peaks. In an effort to show cyclical fluctuations, Underwood (1957) has suggested obtaining performance data, which in addition to obtaining the average number of trials required to reach each successive criterion, includes the following: (a) lowest performance obtained after attaining each successive criterion, (b) number of correct responses on the trial just before the trial on which the subject attained each criterion, and (c) the number of correct responses on the trial just after the trial on which the subject attained each successive criterion. The plotting of these points will provide a graph which reveals systematic cycles in the performance curve.

The employment of group curves is an extremely useful technique for graphically depicting differences among the varying groups which have been used in the experiment. Sometimes investigators have attempted to use such curves in order to test certain hypotheses concerning basic learning processes or to make judgements about individual behavior. It has been recognized, however, that the group curve does not necessarily provide information which can be used to answer either of these questions. A number of individuals [Merrill (1931), Skinner (1938), Sidman (1952), Hayes (1953), Bakan (1954), Estes (1956), Spence (1956)] have raised serious questions concerning the valid-

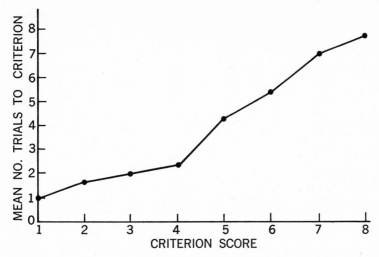

Fig. 3–6. Successive criteria curve derived from data in Table 3–5.

ity of any inference which has been made or obtained from group-learning curves. As Spence (1956) has written, the ". . . averaging of individual data often produces considerable distortion with the consequence that the group curve does not accurately reflect the individual curves."

A good example of this is noted in an experiment by Thompson and reported by Hayes (1953). Forty rats were trained in a brightness discrimination problem to a criterion of ten consecutive correct responses. The traditional learning curve for this experiment is revealed in Figure 3–7 where each point represents 400 choices—ten trials for each of 40 rats. The other lines in the figure are individual learning curves for the first, tenth, twentieth, thirtieth, and fortieth animals to reach criterion. As Hayes has pointed out, although due allowance may be made for the irregularity of the individual curves, the average curve grossly distorts individual data. In contrast to the typical, negatively accelerated curve, the individual curves suggest a period of little or no progress which is followed by uniformly sudden or insightful learning.

Stemming from the work of Skinner and his students, there has been in recent years an emphasis upon individual rather than group behavior. Consistent with this emphasis has been the presentation of individual learning curves rather than those

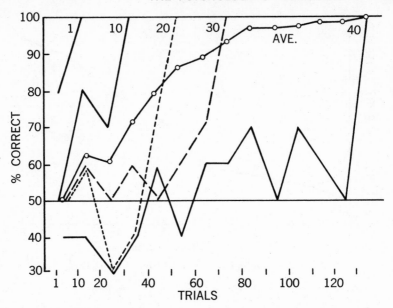

Fig. 3–7. Brightness discrimination learning in rats. The one line is the average learning curve (N = 40) ; other lines are individual curves for the first, tenth, twentieth, thirtieth, and fortieth rats to reach criterion. *Adapted from Hayes (1953)*

obtained from groups. Frequently this behavior has been depicted in terms of what has been called a cumulative curve, obtained by using a graph which shows the number of responses on the ordinate plotted against time on the abscissa. Figure 3–8 shows how a cumulative record is obtained. Each time the organism responds, the pen moves one step across the paper which is feeding through the apparatus. With this technique, it will be noted that if the organism does not respond at all, a horizonal line is drawn in the direction of the paper feed. The more frequently the organism responds, the steeper the line. Although the rate of responding is directly proportional to the slope of the curve, at slopes above 80 degrees, small differences in the angle represent very large differences in rate. With these kinds of curves, the *rate of responding* becomes the response variable which interests the investigator. Figure 3–9 shows cumulative curves which show a variety of rate changes.

In discussing this general approach, Skinner (1959) has written (p. 372) :

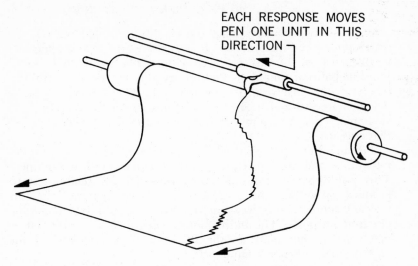

Fig. 3–8. Diagram of a cumulative recorder. *Adapted from Ferster and Skinner (1957)*

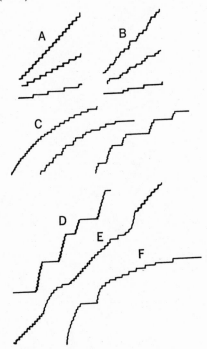

A   B

C

D

E

F

Fig. 3–9. Cumulative curves showing varieties of rate change. *Adapted from Ferster and Skinner (1957)*

In our study of anxiety, Estes and I published several curves, the reasonable smoothness of which was obtained by averaging the performance of 12 rats for each curve. The individual curves published at that time show that the mean curves do not faithfully represent the behavior of any one rat. They show a certain tendency toward a change in slope which supported the point we were making, and they may have appeared to justify averaging for that reason.

But an alternative method would have been to explore the individual case until an equally smooth curve could be obtained. This would have meant, not only rejecting the temptation to produce smoothness by averaging cases, but manipulating all relevant conditions as we later learned to manipulate them for practical purposes. The individual curves which we published at that time do not point to the need for larger groups but for improvement in experimental technique.

4

Motivation I:
The Role of Drive

MANY PSYCHOLOGISTS BELIEVE that motivation is the most important variable which contributes to the learning process. Consequently, it is not surprising that throughout the past three decades, the examination of motivational conditions in learning has occupied the attention of a number of investigators. It is important, however, that the reader be provided with a general understanding of what is meant by motivation prior to an examination of how it influences the learning process.

Two general approaches have been taken with regard to handling the concept of motivation within the learning area. One has been the examination of motivation from a functional point of view. Here, a motive is defined in terms of its functional characteristics. Following a whole host of writers [i.e., Richter (1922), Carr (1925), Dashiell (1928, 1937), Melton (1950)], a basic function of a motive has been assumed to be an energizing one. This refers to the fact that motives energize behavior, arouse activity, or provide the energy of movement. More specifically, it is assumed that they interact with learned or innate habits to produce overt behavior. Thus, most adults know how to write their names (a learned behavior tendency), but it is not until this habit is energized (motivated) that the overt behavior takes place.

The second approach has been a theoretical one. The energizing function has been accepted, but experimenters have hypothesized that such a function arises from, or is related to, a specified class of internal or external conditions. Typically, this is done within the context of a set of postulates which make up a particular learning theory. Miller [Miller and Dollard (1941), Dollard and Miller (1950)], for example, has defined a drive as any strong stimulus. Hull (1943), whose theory has been most widely accepted, has followed a number of earlier investigators in positing that primary or bodily-need states were the ultimate basis for motivation, with such needs arising from deficiencies within the body and their satisfaction necessary for the general health and well-being of the organism or the survival of the species. Needs were not directly incorporated into his system; rather, they were represented by the concept of drive. Need states were responsible for "driving" the organism about in its environment. "Because of this motivational characteristic of needs they are regarded as producing primary animal drives" [Hull (1943)]. A drive was thus conceptualized as an intervening variable which could be inferred from an examination of those antecedent and consequent conditions which were related to it. The hunger drive, for example, could be assessed by relating the number of hours of food deprivation on the one hand to the amount of activity expended by the organism on the other.

The reader should not make the assumption that drive is merely a synonym for a need. Under certain circumstances, there is an obvious relationship between the two, but under other conditions the two concepts can be clearly differentiated. For example, if a rat is deprived of food, its need for that substance increases progressively until the moment of death, but the strength of the hunger drive, as defined by the relationship between hours of deprivation and some behavioral consequent, i.e., amount of activity, will undoubtedly reveal a curvilinear function, first increasing with increasing hours of deprivation but then decreasing as the animal loses strength occasioned by the further lack of food.

The primary needs which Hull (1943) posited included the need for foods of various sorts (hunger), the need for water (thirst), the need for air, the need to avoid tissue injury (pain), the need to maintain an optimal temperature, the need to defecate, the need to micturate, the need for rest (after protracted exertion), the need for sleep (after protracted wakefulness), and the need for activity (after protracted inaction). The needs concerned with the maintenance of the species were those which lead to sexual intercourse and the needs represented by nest building and care of the young.

In brief, then, the origins of motivation were to be found in the biological needs of the organism, and the effect of such needs was to arouse activity. Such activity, of course, was hypothesized to be unlearned or "spontaneous"—presumed to arise from the metabolic processes in the organism.

How has such activity been measured? Perhaps the most frequently used technique has been the activity wheel. This consists of a circular drum which rotates freely around its axis, with the number of revolutions over a fixed period of time providing the experimenter with an index of the amount of activity exhibited by the organism. A second type is the stationary cage or stabilimeter. The stabilimetric cage is one in which the cage, frequently one used for normal animal occupancy, is placed upon tambours or microswitches. The animal's movements provide movement to the cage which in turn is measured. The stationary cage, on the other hand, is divided into halves or quarters by photoelectric cell units, and an interruption of the light beam produced by the organism's activity is transmitted to a recorder. Finally, the last type of activity measurement is one which uses a more unrestricted situation. Some type of open field apparatus is used in which the field is divided, usually into small squares, and movement of the animal from one square to another is recorded.

BIOLOGICAL NEEDS AND THE ENERGIZING FUNCTION

Early experimental work in this area was performed by Richter (1922) who found that the activity of the rat, as measured in a stabilimetric cage, increased up to two or three days of food deprivation.

Support for a deprivation-activity relationship has also come from experiments using an activity wheel, although recent investigators prefer to use weight loss as the independent variable rather than deprivation time.[1]

A whole host of experimenters [Hitchcock (1927) ; Wald and Jackson (1944) ; Finger (1951) ; Finger and Reid (1952) ; Hall (1956) ; Moskowitz (1959) ; Weasner, Finger, and Reid (1960) ; Treichler and Hall (1962) ; and Duda and Bolles (1963) to cite only a scattered sampling of them] have obtained results indicating level of activity to be a function of the amount of food and water deprivation as measured by either deprivation time or weight loss.

NEGATIVE EVIDENCE

During the last decade, there has been an ever-increasing amount of experimental evidence to indicate that deprivation states in rats, cats, monkeys, or adult humans do not produce increases in activity when such activity is measured by means other than the activity wheel. Such evidence is in conflict, of course, with the early Richter (1922) study as well as a later one by Siegel and Steinberg (1949). But Montgomery (1953), Strong (1957), DeVito and Smith (1959), Hall, Low, and Hanford (1960), Glickman and Jensen (1961), Bolles and DeLorge (1962), Bryan and Carlson (1962), Miles (1962), and Treichler and Hall (1962) among others, using activity measures other than the wheel, have been unable to demonstrate any relationship between level of deprivation and amount of activity. Strong (1957), for example, investigated activity as a function of food deprivation using two types of stabilimeters, with one type designed to be much more sensitive to movement than the other. The experiment consisted of dividing the subjects (rats) into varying groups matched on the basis of sex, age, and previous activity and then placing them under either 0, 24, 48, or 72 hours of food deprivation. Each group was given a series of 30-minute trials extending over a period of 30 to 45 days. Results revealed that when the less sensitive stabilimeter was employed, there was no significant difference between the activity of hungry and satiated animals. On the other hand, hungry rats were *less* active then satiated ones when activity was measured with the more sensitive instrument. Similar findings have been obtained by

[1] Here it is assumed that weight loss reflects an organism's need for water or food more adequately than deprivation time.

Treichler and Hall (1962) who examined the activity of rats when such activity was measured by a stabilimetric cage or the Dashiell checkerboard maze. These investigators found that activity did not change as a function of weight loss produced by continuous food, water, or combined food and water deprivation.

Bindra (1961) has pointed out that the activity as measured in the stabilimetric or stationary cage is itself composed of a variety of specific identifiable motor responses which include such categories as grooming, walking, sitting, stretching, etc. and that an examination of how these more specific responses are influenced by deprivation states merits attention. In one such study, Bolles (1963) examined the specific behaviors of rats maintained on a 23-hour deprivation—one-hour feeding cycle in contrast to animals which had food available at all times (fed ad lib). Each animal's behavior in its home cage was observed 24 times each hour, 24 hours per day, for a 12-day period. The behavior of the animals was categorized into eating; drinking; sleeping; resting; and activity which included the specific behaviors of locomotion, rearing-up, exploring and chewing on the cage. As the author points out, deprivation appeared to change primarily the pattern of waking activity rather than to increase the amount of it, although the activity response category for the deprived animals did show an increase over that noted for the ad lib animals during the last four days of the study.

As indicated earlier, strong support for a deprivation-activity relationship has come from activity wheel studies, and as noted, these findings are not in keeping with the results obtained with other types of activity measures. The Stevenson and Rixon (1957) study provides the possibility of reconciling the two sets of data. These investigators examined the relationship of deprivation and body temperature to activity wheel behavior. The running activity of rats placed on four days of continuous deprivation was examined under the following range of environmental temperatures: 5, 10, 15, 22, 27, 30, and 33 degrees Centigrade. Both skin and colonic temperature records were obtained from the animals. Results indicated that increases in activity wheel behavior under deprivation were an inverse function of environmental temperatures between 33 and 10 degrees Centigrade, with body temperature during this period being maintained. When the activity of the animals was severely restricted by placing them in a sling, body temperature declined as a function of deprivation. In discussing these findings, Stevenson and Rixon have pointed out that deprivation results in a deterioration in the insulation of the body and a concomitant reduction in body temperature. Muscular activity is one of several means by which body temperature can be increased. If the deprived animal is given the opportunity to exercise, body temperature can be maintained. One reasonable reconciliation of the activity wheel-stabilimetric cage data is that the activity wheel provides the animal with the opportunity to engage in vigorous muscular activity and thus maintain body temperature; whereas, the stabilimetric cage with its relatively restricted locomotor area does not. If this hypothesis is correct, activity does not arise from deprivation states per se; rather, the deprivation state contributes to activity only indirectly.

A second line of evidence that has been leveled against the postulation of a deprivation-activity relationship has come from the findings of studies which reveal that "spontaneous" activity is influenced by learning. For example, Finger, Reid, and Weasner (1957) and Hall (1958) have demonstrated that activity as measured in the activity wheel can be manipulated by the utilization of appropriate reinforcement schedules. In the Finger, Reid, and Weasner (1957) study, rats were placed on cycles of 23 hours of deprivation and one hour of feeding. Every other day, the animals were placed in activity wheels for one hour under 21 hours of deprivation. One group went immediately from the wheels to their home cages and were fed for one hour, while the second group was removed from the wheel and was placed in a neutral chamber for one hour prior to being fed in their home cage. As Figure 4–1 illustrates, the group which was fed immediately following running increased their activity over the group whose feedings had been delayed. Similarly, Sheffield and Campbell (1954) and Amsel and Work (1961) have demonstrated that activity as measured in the stabilimeter can also, at least in part, be attributed to a learning component.[2]

All of these findings, then, suggest that the behavior which is obtained in the activity wheel or stabilimeter does not spontane-

[2] The contribution of learning to activity wheel behavior should not be overemphasized since some investigators, i.e., Treichler and Hall (1962), have demonstrated increasing activity as a function of the amount of deprivation when the animals are placed in the activity wheel and never fed, thus precluding the learning of any wheel-running–reinforcement contingency.

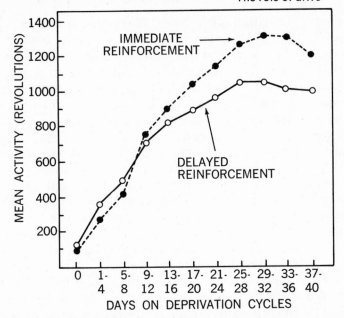

Fig. 4–1. Activity wheel records for the immediately reinforced group and for the delayed reinforced group. *Adapted from Finger, Reid, and Weasner (1957)*

ously arise as a result of the presence of some biological need but rather appears to be of an instrumental variety.

ACQUIRED DRIVES

Accounting for the initiation of large segments of human behavior on the basis of the operation of only biological needs has obvious difficulties; as a result, many experimenters found it necessary to look for other motivational sources.

In an early attempt to solve this problem, Dashiell (1937) hypothesized that when a neutral stimulus was associated with a primary need, such a stimulus could acquire motivational functions (i.e., energize behavior). A few years later, Anderson (1941, 1941a) attempted to validate experimentally such a position. He posited that if an internally aroused need was satisfied over a long period of time in a constant external stimulus situation, the need would become aroused by this external stimulus. Such an arousal, he termed "externalization of drive." He further assumed that the process of externalization spread from one stimulus constellation to another so that in time almost any stimulus object which was associated in any way with the drive would come to arouse that drive. Anderson's experimental findings utilizing hunger as the need state, although only partially supporting his position, nonetheless were used by many subsequent theorists as evidence that drives could be acquired.

Some years later, Hull (1951) incorporated into his *Principles* a corollary similar to Anderson's externalization of drive. Hull stated (p. 25): "When neutral stimuli are repeatedly and consistently associated with the evocation of a primary or secondary drive and this drive stimulus undergoes an abrupt diminution, the hitherto neutral stimuli acquire the capacity to bring about the drive stimuli (S_D) which thereby become the condition (C_D) of a secondary drive or motivation."

If contemporary experimental studies which have examined an acquired drive position are examined, it is found that they can be classified into those based upon (1) appetitional needs and (2) noxious stimuli.

When studies are examined in which appetitional needs have served as the foundation upon which to base an acquired need, both positive and negative findings have been reported. The findings of investigators who have reported positive results, however, frequently can be interpreted by recourse to the operation of other variables. Moreover, when these studies have been replicated, it has been difficult to confirm the original findings. As an example, Calvin, Bicknell, and Sperling (1953) placed two groups of rats in a black and white striped, triangular shaped box for 30 minutes a day for 24 days. One group received this daily experience under 22 hours of food deprivation while the other group was only one-hour deprived. Subjects were not fed during this 30-minute period. Following the 24-day training session, both groups were placed under 11.5 hours of deprivation and the amount of food consumed by both groups during four 15-minute eating periods was measured. Results, which revealed that the 22-hour deprived group consumed significantly more food than the one-hour group, presumably supported an acquired drive hypothesis.

A number of other interpretations of these findings are equally admissible. It is possible that the 22-hour deprived group, as a result of being fed only a short time each day, learned to eat rapidly, so that a short testing period reflected nothing more than faster eating on the part of these animals. Or it is possible that the one-hour deprived subjects had learned other responses during their daily experience in the striped box and that these responses interfered with the eating response when the animals were placed in the test situation. In any event, control groups were not employed to rule out these possibilities. Furthermore, Siegel and MacDonnell's (1954) replication of this study failed to confirm it.

Most experimental studies using appetitional needs have not supported an acquired drive position. Siegel's (1946a) replication of Anderson's early work yielded negative findings, and more recently, the experiments of Myers and Miller (1954), Greenberg (1954), Denny and Behan (1956), Andersson and Larsson (1956), Novin and Miller (1962), Howard and Young (1962), and Pieper and Marx (1963) have been representative of studies in which investigators have been unable to find experimental support for an acquired need based upon the primary needs of either food or water.

The experimental studies which have attempted to base acquired drives upon noxious or aversive states, in contrast to those just reviewed, have been quite successful. In one of the early studies, Miller (1948) trained rats to escape shock by running from the white to a black compartment. Following such training, when a door was placed between the compartments which blocked the escape route, it was found that some of the animals could learn to turn a wheel or press a bar which would raise the door thus permitting escape, even though shock was no longer used in the experimental situation. According to Miller's analysis, fear which accompanied pain produced by the shock was conditioned to the white box. The response of fear also had stimulus characteristics which functioned as a motive for the instrumental response of bar pressing or wheel turning. Accordingly, fear was conceptualized as a learned drive—learned since it was a response to a previous neutral cue (white box) and a drive since it was a stimulus which could energize performance in the same way as primary needs.[3]

In another early experimental demonstration of fear as acquired drive, Brown, Kalish, and Farber (1951) placed one group

[3] The use of fear in this context is an excellent example of a mediated response and its attendant stimuli being postulated to "explain" better a particular experimental finding.

of rats in a stabilimeter and provided seven paired presentations of a buzzer-light and shock on each of four successive days. It was assumed that this procedure would result in the subjects' learning to respond with fear to the presentation of the light-buzzer. Fear was inferred from a startle response which was produced by the shock. Interspersed among each day's conditioning trials were three test trials consisting of presenting the buzzer and light along with a loud, sharp sound produced by a toy pistol. A control group was given the same test trials, but the temporal spacing of the buzzer-light and shock was designed to minimize the learning of the fear response. These experimenters found that for the experimental subjects, the magnitude of the startle response, elicited by the sound of the toy pistol together with the presentation of the buzzer-light, increased as a function of conditioning trials. Control animals, on the other hand, revealed no tendency to improve their level of performance. The authors thus demonstrated that the startle reaction was a function of the strength of the conditioned fear state. Such findings provided additional support for the position that the paired presentation of a neutral and a noxious stimulus results in a neutral stimulus acquiring the capacity to elicit an emotional response of fear.

Since it has been acknowledged that fears are acquired, their acquisition should be a function of the same variables which have been found to make a contribution to other learned responses. Experimental work in this area, however, has not been extensive. Kalish (1954) and Desiderato (1964) have found that the strength of fear increases as a function of (1) the number of CS-UCS pairings and (2) weakens progressively with successive extinction trials.[4]

An interesting question arises: Why are learned drives based upon pain successful in contrast to those based upon need states? Miller (1951) has suggested that the gradualness of the onset of these need states might be a contributing factor—a condition which contrasts markedly with the use of shock. A recent experiment by Fromer (1962) has examined this hypothesis. His general procedure consisted of shocking animals in one compartment for a 51-second period, with all animals receiving two trials per day for ten days. Four experimental groups were used (as well

---

[4] Mathers (1957) has been unable to confirm this finding, and Goldstein (1960) has found that the number of CS-UCS pairings influenced performance only during the latter stages of the test period.

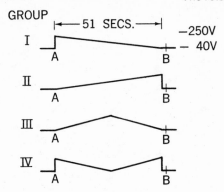

Fig. 4–2. Diagrammatic representation of the stimulus patterns. Base voltage was 40, while maximum voltage was 250. *Adapted from Fromer (1962)*

as a control), with two groups receiving sudden shock onset while two groups received gradual onset. Shock offset for each group was either gradual or sudden. These varying shock patterns are shown in Figure 4–2. Following the training trials, 50 test trials (two trials per day) were provided in which the animal was placed into the compartment where it had been previously shocked and a guillotine door was dropped which permitted the animal access into another compartment. Latency of running into the second compartment was recorded. Results are indicated in Figure 4–3, and it can be noted that the groups receiving sudden onset had shorter latencies than those receiving gradual onset, a finding in keeping with Miller's hypothesis.

Two points should be noted. First, since the two groups which received gradual shock onset did reveal significant amounts of learning, it must be acknowledged that the role of onset cannot completely account for the complete absence of learning which has been obtained in those acquired drive studies which have used food or water deprivation as the primary need source. Secondly, an unpublished study in which the need for water was abruptly produced also revealed negative findings. In this experiment [Greenberg (1954)], an almost immediate need for water was produced by injecting into rats a saline solution. A blinking light was then paired with the presence of this need state in order to determine if the light could acquire drive characteristics. Measures of the frequency and amount of the drinking response during

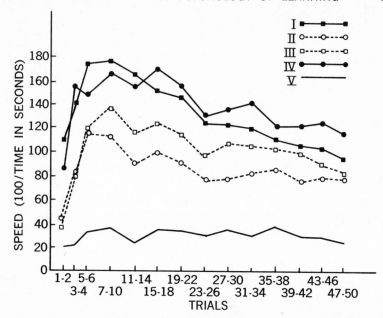

Fig. 4–3. Latency of responding during the testing phase. Groups I through IV are the experimental groups which received different patterns of shock during training. Group V is the control which received forty volts of constant stimulation. *Adapted from Fromer (1962)*

a test period in which the light was present revealed no increase in drinking over that noted when the saline injection was not utilized.

It may be that the critical factor in producing an acquired drive is the concomitant arousal of an emotional state, a condition which is not found when food or water deprivation states are manipulated.

OTHER POSTULATED DRIVE STATES

Beginning in the late nineteen-forties and early fifties, an increasing number of investigators began to express doubt that the biological needs should be viewed as the primary initiator of behavior. Harlow (1953), one of the advocates of a "new look" in motivation, wrote that there was no justification on phylogenetic, ontogenetic, or physiological grounds for assuming that motives aroused by one source were more basic or important than motives aroused by the other. Moreover, he pointed out (pp. 26–27) that the ". . . erroneous assumption that the homeostatic drives were the only unlearned, fundamental motivational mechanism has led to drastic overemphasis and over-interpretation of another psychological concept, the construct of secondary or derived drives." One result of this revolt was increasing emphasis placed upon external stimulation from which a variety of drives were posited to arise.

This experimental area, as a number of reviews have indicated, is an extensive one [Butler (1960), Fiske and Maddi (1961), Hall (1961), Cofer and Appley (1964)]. The reader should be provided with a general familiarity with the area, rather than an exhaustive survey of the work that has been done.

An examination of many of these studies reveals that two basic types of environmental manipulation have been employed. The first has enriched the organism's external environment, while the second has impoverished it.

Environmental Enrichment

NOVEL STIMULI—THE ROLE OF CURIOSITY AND EXPLORATION. Although both Dashiell (1925) and Nissen (1930) had written of curiosity drives, their experimental findings were not in keeping with the trend of the times, and interest in this area remained dormant until 1950 when Berlyne proposed that novel stimuli give rise to the motivational state of curiosity, with functioning based on two postulates. Briefly, Berlyne posited that: (1) when a novel stimulus impinged upon an organism's receptors there occurred drive stimulus producing responses which he termed curiosity; and (2) as the curiosity arousing stimulus continued to be present, curiosity diminished.

About the same time that Berlyne (1950) posited the existence of a curiosity drive, Montgomery (1951) published the first of a series of experimental studies supporting the presence of what he termed an exploratory drive. The exploratory drive, Montgomery proposed, was aroused by novel stimulation which elicited exploratory behavior. Such behavior decreased with the time that the organism was exposed to the stimulus but recovered during the period of nonexposure.

It can be noted, then, that the prominent features of this kind of behavior which are hypothesized to stem from the drive states of curiosity or exploration are (1) heightened interest in novel stimuli, (2) habituation of interest with continued exposure, and (3) recovery of responsiveness during unstimulated periods.[5]

Since Montgomery considered the exploratory drive to be a primary source of motivation, he was interested in pointing out its independence of physiological needs, as well as in demonstrating that exploratory behavior could not be considered as merely an expression of the general activity of the organism. Both Montgomery (1953) and Zimbardo and Montgomery (1957) obtained experimental findings which revealed that exploratory behavior was reduced (rather than heightened) by food and water deprivation and in another study Montgomery (1953a) found that moderate amounts of activity deprivation over an eight-day period did not influence the amount of exploratory behavior. Although other investigators [Hall, Low, and Hanford (1960), Glickman and Jensen (1961)] have been unable to confirm the finding that exploratory behavior is depressed by deprivation states, there has been the frequent finding of no significant relationship between deprivation and exploratory behavior. In any event, Montgomery's position of exploratory behavior being independent of deprivation is probably correct.[6]

Manipulative Stimuli

In an early study in this area, Harlow, Harlow, and Meyer (1950) provided one group of rhesus monkeys (Group A) with 12 days of experience in manipulating an *assembled* mechanical puzzle which had been placed in each animal's cage. A second group of monkeys (Group B) had *disassembled* puzzles placed in their cages during this same period of time. Neither group of

[5] This general behavior pattern, presumed to arise from the presentation of novel stimuli, is not completely invariant. Menzel, Davenport, and Rogers (1961) have found that if very young organisms are used, novel stimuli will produce a fear response which only after a time will elicit exploration. And Glickman and Hartz (1964), using the guinea pig, albino rat, chinchilla, gerbil, spine mouse, albino mouse, and hamster, have found that exploratory responses to a procedural variable (whether or not the subject had the opportunity to escape into a smaller darkened compartment) were found to differ as a function of the species employed.

[6] Fehrer (1956), in contrast to the reported experiments, did find that hungry rats entered a new environment more frequently than satiated ones, while Zimbardo and Miller (1958) found that food deprivation increased the speed of running to a novel stimulus after a delay in the start box. If there was no delay, the satiated animals had the faster running time. Richards and Leslie (1962) have found that hungry and thirsty rats, when given a choice between a novel and familiar tactile stimulus in a T-maze, chose the novel stimulus more often than satiated animals.

animals was placed on any deprivation schedule; rewards were not available to them for working the puzzle. On Days 13 and 14, assembled puzzles were placed in the cages of both groups of subjects, and the performance of the two groups was compared by examining the responses the monkeys made to the puzzle for five five-minute sessions. Each observation session was separated from another by one hour. Results indicated that Group A was significantly more efficient than Group B when measured by total number of solutions (disassembling the puzzle), solutions obtained in 60 seconds, and ratio of correct to incorrect responses.

In accounting for the behavior of these monkeys which had disassembled the puzzle, the experimenters have written (p. 233) :

> It is the opinion of the experimenters that a manipulation drive can best account for the behavior obtained in this investigation. The stimuli to the drive are external and, in conjunction with the animals' capacities, set the pattern of behavior. The manipulation is conceived of as having reinforcing properties that account for the precision and speed the subjects acquire in carrying out the solution, and the persistence they show in repeated performances.

Although some individuals have quarreled with this *explanation* for the behavior, a large number of subsequent investigations coming from Harlow's laboratory have testified to the reliability of the behavior obtained in this type of situation.

Environmental Impoverishment

SENSORY DEPRIVATION. In an early study, Butler (1953) placed a monkey in a wire cage, visually isolated it by covering the structure with an opaque material, and then presented a visual discrimination problem to the animal. The trial was begun by raising a screen and exposing the test stimuli to the animal. If the monkey pushed against one stimulus, identified by one color, the door would open and the animal would be permitted to view its surroundings for 30 seconds. If the incorrect stimulus was chosen, the door would not open, but rather an opaque screen would be immediately lowered. Two rhesus monkeys, following preliminary training, were given 20 trials a day for a total of 20 days. At the end of this period, an examination of the performance, as diagrammed in Figure 4–4, indicated that they had learned the problem. A subsequent study by Butler and Harlow (1954) has revealed that such behavior, reinforced only by visual explora-

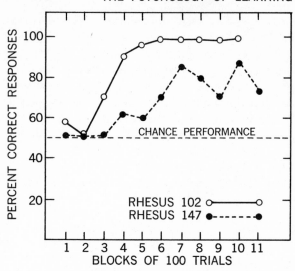

Fig. 4–4. Discrimination learning to visual-exploration incentives. *Adapted from Butler (1953)*

tion, extinguishes very slowly. One animal in this study, for example, worked for almost 20 hours before finally refusing to respond.

Butler has considered his work essentially a continuance of the earlier work coming from Harlow's laboratory which has emphasized the role of external stimulation. More specifically, he has hypothesized a visual exploratory motive in order to account for the behavior of his animals, postulating that such a motive represents another facet of externally elicited motivational states. An important consideration here is the fact that the animal's environment has been effectively impoverished by the experimental apparatus; thus, there is a kind of sensory deprivation which provides the appropriate environmental conditions for the eliciting of the instrumental behavior. That such behavior is related to deprivation effects is revealed in a subsequent study by Butler (1957) who kept his subjects in their experimental boxes for varying lengths of time (zero, two, four, or eight hours) prior to testing them. Reinforcement consisted of a 12-second view of the monkey colony outside the test cage. Results indicated that the number of responses to the visual incentive during a one-hour period of testing increased up until the four-hour deprivation period and then leveled off.

The work on sensory deprivation with humans appears to be a logical continuation of the work with primates, but actually there has been no such continuity. As Hebb (1961) has pointed out, this work began with the problem of brain washing, with the chief impetus being the dismay at the kind of confessions being produced at the communist trials. In an early experiment, Bexton, Heron, and Scott (1954) studied the effects of depriving male college students of visual, auditory, and many kinesthetic stimuli. The students were paid to lie 24 hours a day in a comfortable bed in a lighted, semi-soundproof cubicle which had an observatory window. Throughout the experiment, the subjects wore translucent goggles which admitted diffuse light but prevented pattern vision. Except when eating or at the toilet, cotton gloves and cardboard cuffs which extended from below the elbows to beyond the fingertips were worn, thus limiting tactual perception. A U-shaped foam rubber pillow, the walls of the cubicle, and the masking noise of the thermostatically regulated air conditioner as well as other equipment severely limited auditory perception. Subjective reports indicated that the subjects first spent some time in reviewing their work, making attempts to solve personal problems, and in general engaging in organized thought patterns. As time wore on this type of activity became harder because of the difficulty of concentrating, and the subjects preferred "just to let their minds drift." Finally, blank periods during which the subjects could think of nothing would frequently occur. During isolation, there were frequent reports of confusion, hallucinations, as well as an inability to concentrate.

Since the early Canadian studies in this area, a large number of investigators have been interested in this problem. As the Solomon, Kubzansky, *et al.,* volume (1961) reveals, research has been concerned chiefly with two major areas. The first has involved the relationship of parameters of sensory input to cognitive and behavioral efficiency; the second has dealt with sensory deprivation as a special technique for assessing dynamic patterns of individual adaptation to a novel situation.

One interesting experimental variation in this general area is a study by Jones, Wilkinson, and Braden (1961) who proposed that information deprivation functions as a motivational variable in much the same way as hunger, thirst, etc. Presumably, the information deprived subject will execute, with increasing frequency, instrumental responses which result in increasing the

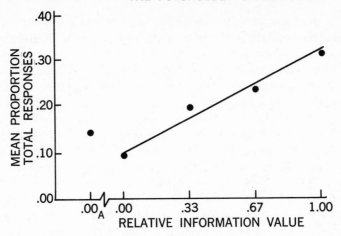

Fig. 4–5. Mean proportions of responses associated with the light series (Exp. II). The .00ₐ condition, not discussed in the text, was used to control for stimulus variability. *Adapted from Jones, Wilkinson, and Braden (1961)*

amount of information which is introduced into the environment. Two experiments were run, with the second providing the most conclusive findings. In this study, subjects were isolated for ten hours in a lightproof room in which noise was reduced to a minimum. The instrumental response available to the subject was a button press which resulted in a series of 24 light flashes, either red or green in color, appearing on a panel in the ceiling of the experimental room. Varying degrees of information in the light series were used; the relative information values being .00, .33, .67, and 1.00. Thus, information value of .00 provided no information, the 24 flashes being a single fixed color. Information value of 1.00 was represented by a random determination of color for each of the 24 flashes making up the series, while the intervening values of .33 and .67 were associated with one-third and two-thirds of the 24 flashes being determined randomly with regard to color. A "cafeteria" selection of the light series was made possible by a dial which could be manipulated by the subjects in the dark. Results are indicated in Figure 4–5, and one can note that the amount of responding is a function of the information value of the light series. An important conclusion drawn from this study is the proposal of the experimenters that the crucial aspect found in studies presumably investigating curiosity, exploration, and manipulation may be the reduction of uncertainty. Thus, this information theory concept may be of considerable help in achieving some unification of these diverse points of view.

Response Deprivation

In the studies which were just reviewed, emphasis has been placed upon stimulus deprivation, although it could be pointed out that there has been a concomitant restriction of the organism's activity. Some investigators have been interested in determining whether or not the restriction of such activity on the part of an organism would result in subsequent increases in activity and perhaps merit the postulation of an activity drive. Evidence for such a position would be the obtaining of a positive correlation between the amount of inactivity imposed upon an organism and the organism's subsequent activity level. Early studies in this area [Shirley (1928), Siegel (1946), and Siegel and Alexander (1948)] provided ambiguous findings, but Hill (1956) has demonstrated that the activity-wheel behavior of rats following 0, 5, 24, or 46.5 hours of confinement in a small cage did result in activity increases taking place as a function of the length of the confinement period. The positing of any simple relationship between these conditions is difficult, however, since when confinement periods ranging from 36 to 47 days were examined, activity as measured in a tilt cage immediately increased following release from the confined quarters but then decreased for several days thereafter. Activity when measured in the wheel, on the other hand, immediately decreased following such a confinement period [Hill (1958, 1958a)].

General Considerations

One problem with much of the research in this area has been the lack of concern of most investigators with the relating of the energizing function to their postulated constructs. The postulation of a biological need as a drive state was supported by the experimental evidence that such an event produced activity, thus giving rise to an inferred energizing function. But there have been few attempts to demonstrate that these other postulated drives (e.g., curiosity, manipulation) have such a function.

A second difficulty is that with some of the postulated drive states experimenters do nothing more than describe the behavior which they purport to explain. The positing of a manipulation drive, for example, does nothing more than describe the fact that animals engage in a type of behavior which has been labeled manipulation. There appears to be little difference between the positing of such drive states and the identification of instincts—a practice common in psychology some 40 years ago. The parallel has been noted by a number of writers and dissatisfaction with such a state of affairs has been frequently voiced. Estes (1958), for example, has stated (pp. 33–34):

> In a few well-studied experimental situations, involving for the most part food deprivation, water deprivation, or electric shock as antecedent conditions, all of the ingredients of the operational definitions are present and "drive" can at least be used without ambiguity as a descriptive, or summarizing, concept. Its usefulness in this role breaks down, of course, when enthusiastic proponents extend usage of the term to situations in which only one of the defining relations can be identified, thereby generating such ill-endowed mutants as "exploratory drive" and even "activity drive."

Frustration

This discussion of postulated drive states should not be terminated without calling attention to frustration. The Dollard, Doob, Miller, Mowrer, and Sears (1939) volume on frustration and aggression and the experimental work of Rohrer (1949) and Sheffield (1949, 1950) represent early contributions which treat frustration as a source of motivation, but Brown and Farber (1951) and Amsel (1951) have been primarily responsible for considering the concept of frustration as a source of drive within contemporary learning theory. Brown and Farber (1951) assumed that frustration, regarded as a hypothetical construct, was produced either by some inhibitory condition or by a competitive excitatory tendency aroused simultaneously with an already ongoing excitatory tendency. The strength of this inhibitory tendency varied as a function of (a) response blocking, (b) amount of work, or (c) nonreward. The primary consequence of frustration was that (1) it functioned as any other drive state in that it energized behavior and (2) it provided internal stimuli to which appropriate responses could be attached.

Amsel (1951, 1958, 1962) has taken a similar position, although he has been almost exclusively interested in the nonreward condition as the basic contributor to frustration. In brief, he has maintained (a) that under certain conditions nonreward is an active factor which may be termed frustrative nonreward; (b) that such frustrative events are antecedents to a primary, aversive motivational condition, frustration; and (c) that a secondary (learned) form of this primary aversive condition, termed fractional anticipatory frustration $(r_f—s_f)$, develops through classical conditioning. Thus, the $r_f—s_f$ construct is the fractional anticipatory response assumed to arise from a frustrating event, and it provides the mechanism for conceptualizing the active properties of nonreinforcement.[7]

In an early study which demonstrated the energizing properties of frustration, Amsel and Roussel (1952) deprived rats of food and trained them to traverse a runway into Goal Box 1. Following the eating of a pellet of food, the animals left the goal box and ran down a second runway into Goal Box 2. Eighty-four trials spaced over 28 days were provided, at the end of which time the animal's

[7] The $r_f—s_f$ mechanism is an excellent example of the kind of mediating response frequently employed by theoretical psychologists who have adopted a stimulus–response point of view. Amsel's postulation of the $r_f—s_f$ mechanism is part of a larger theoretical framework which makes use of varying types of fractional anticipatory responses, the most frequently posited one being the fractional anticipatory goal response (r_g). The basic position here is that as a result of making consummatory responses in the learning situation, the animal becomes conditioned to make anticipatory feeding responses to preceding stimulus events that have the appropriate temporal relation. It is assumed that (a) through stimulus generalization, stimuli farther removed in time and space acquire the capacity to elicit these fractional anticipatory goal responses and (b) these responses produce internal cues of their own (s_g) to which instrumental responses may be attached. Expressed in more concrete terms, this means that when a rat learns to run down an alley, the stimulus cues in the goal box and from that part of the runway which just precedes the goal box become conditioned to the goal-box response of eating (R_g). Through stimulus generalization, the stimulus cues still more distant from the goal box are also able to elicit R_g, or at least noncompetitional components that can occur without the actual presence of the goal object (i.e., salivating, chewing movements, etc.). These noncompetitional response components of R_g have been classified as fractional anticipatory goal responses and have been designated as r_g. Thus, r_g may be elicited by cues found in the start box. In addition, r_g produces an internal stimulus, s_g, which becomes a part of the total stimulus complex found in the learning situation, to which the instrumental response of running is attached. The $r_g—s_g$ mechanism has an associative property which contributes to the strength of the learned response; in addition, it is assumed that this mechanism also has motivational properties which vary with the magnitude or vigor of R_g and, in turn, r_g.

Spence (1956) in discussing the fractional anticipatory goal response has written, ". . . it is apparent that the subject in instrumental conditioning experiments not only learns to make a particular instrumental response but also acquires an expectation or an anticipatory response that prepares it for dealing with the impending event." As a number of writers [Behan (1953), Seward (1956), Kimble (1961)] have observed, the fractional anticipatory response appears to serve the same function as does the notion of expectancy.

running speed over the second runway had reached a stable value. Thirty-six test trials were then provided in which, on 18 trials, the reward in Goal Box One was absent while on the remaining 18 trials it was present. The omission of reward the investigators hypothesized to be frustrating, which should energize the running response on Runway Two and result in more rapid locomotion. A comparison between running speeds on this runway for the rewarded and nonrewarded (or frustration) trials supported the authors' position. This difference in vigor of performance following reward compared with nonreward has been termed by Amsel as the frustration effect (FE). Penney (1960), using a somewhat similar situation, has obtained such an effect with kindergarten children.[8]

McHose (1963), also using the double runway apparatus, has shown that continued nonreinforcement in Goal Box One will result in diminution of the frustration effect. In this study, Groups I and II (rats) were trained to find 100 per cent reinforcement in Goal Box One, but for a third group, reinforcement was never found in this goal box. Reinforcement was present, however, for all three groups in Goal Box Two. Seventy-two training trials were provided. Following such training, reinforcement in Goal Box One was changed. Group I found reinforcement in Goal Box One only 50 per cent of the time while for Group II, reinforcement was never found in Goal Box One. For the third group, reinforcement in Goal Box One continued to be absent. An examination of the speed of running in the second runway after the switch in reinforcement conditions revealed the usual frustration effect for Groups I and II. After 16 trials, however, Group II's running time increased, from which the experimenter inferred that the frustration effect had dissipated. In keeping with Amsel's position, McHose hypothesized that frustrative effects of nonreward are dependent on the expectancy of reward in Goal Box One. With continued nonreward, however, the frustration response extinguishes.

[8] There has been some debate as to whether frustration is truly a motivational state in that it has an energizing function or whether the experimental findings that have been obtained can be interpreted in terms of learning or associative factors—the animal learns to respond more vigorously in the presence of nonreward. One experiment by Marx (1956) has supported such an associative position, but findings from a study by Amsel and Penick (1962) have cast doubt upon such an interpretation.

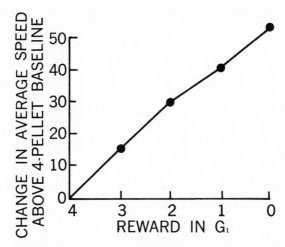

Fig. 4–6. Average change in speed of running the second runway following rewards of three, two, one, or zero pellets after training with four-pellet reward. *Adapted from Bower (1962)*

As might be anticipated, a number of investigators have been interested in examining how varying conditions contribute to the frustration effect. Bower (1962) was interested in examining whether this effect varied as a function of the amount of reward reduction. In one study, using the familiar two-runway apparatus, animals were given six training trials per day for 24 days in which four pellets of food were placed in Goal Box One and another four pellets in Goal Box Two. A test series was then provided in which the number of pellets found in Goal Box One was varied from the four obtained in the training series to either three, two, one, or zero. Goal Box Two continued to have four pellets. Results indicated (see Figure 4–6) that the frustration effect, as measured by running speed in Runway Two, was a function of the size of the reward obtained in Goal Box One.

A second area of interest for Bower was whether two frustrating events occurring close together in time would summate in their effects upon performance. In order to examine this effect, a third runway was added to the apparatus, with the subjects finding reward in three consecutive goal boxes.

The procedure involved the providing of various combinations of reduced rewards in Goal Box One and Goal Box Two and examining running speed in the third runway. Other than the change in the apparatus, training conditions were similar to those previously utilized. Thirty-three days of six trials per day represented the initial training with eight food pellets placed in Goal Box One, eight pellets in Goal Box Two, and one pellet in Goal Box Three. Following such training, the test series consisted of presenting different rewards in Goal Box One and Goal Box Two, with the reward in Goal Box Three remaining fixed at one pellet. During this test series, 15 combinations of reward were presented, corresponding to all possible pairs (except the regular 8–8 pair) formed by eight, four, one, and zero pellets in Goal Box One and Goal Box Two. Additional tests were given with the reward pairs of 6–8, 12–0, and 16–0. Each test pair of rewards occurred six times over the entire series, once in each of the six possible trial positions within the day's testing. In examining the results, it should be noted first that an inspection of running speed in the second runway was similar to that found in the previously cited study. That is, as the number of pellets in the first goal box became fewer than the customary eight, running became faster as a function of the size of the reduction. If the number of pellets was larger than the usual eight-pellet reward, running grew slower.

The principal results of the summation effect are illustrated in Figure 4–7 which plots the average summation effect, measured in terms of speed changes in the third runway, against reward in the second goal box, with the immediately prior reward in the first goal box serving as the parameter of each curve. In examining this figure, one can note that if zero pellets are found in the first goal box, and zero pellets in the second goal box, this results in the fastest running in the third runway; as more and more pellets are found in the second goal box, with zero pellets continuing to be present in Goal Box One, running time becomes slower.

The amount of time that the subject is confined in the frustrating situation (detention time) would appear to be another variable worthy of investigation, although in an early study, Amsel and Roussel (1952) were unsuccessful in finding differences in the amount of the frustration effect when detention times in Goal Box One were either 5, 10, or 30 seconds. In a second study by MacKinnon and Amsel (1964) detention times of 3, 15, or 90 seconds were investigated. In addition, a small as well as a large goal box was used at the end of the first runway in an effort

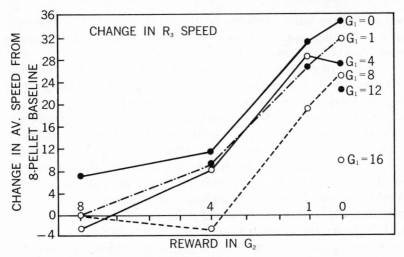

Fig. 4–7. Average change in running speed over the third runway following reduced test rewards in Goal Box Two. *Adapted from Bower (1962)*

to examine the contribution of this variable to the frustration effect. The general experimental procedure consisted of rats receiving 80 training trials in the familiar two-runway apparatus. On half of the trials, the first goal box was large (23″ x 3¼″ x 4″) while for the other half of the trials it was small (2″ x 2″ x 9″). Following such training, a 24-test trial period was employed with the subjects being randomly assigned to one of three detention conditions—detention in the first goal box being either 3, 15, or 90 seconds. Within the 24-test trials, 12 trials were run to the large goal box (at the end of the first runway) and 12 to the small; within each of these subgroups, 6 trials were rewarded, and 6 were nonrewarded. Starting, running, and goal box times were obtained for performance on the second runway. Results revealed that the size of the goal box was an important determiner of the performance of the animals on the second runway, although it influenced the findings in a complex manner. More specifically, *starting times* were shorter out of the small goal box than they were out of the larger goal box, but *running times* out of the small goal box were longer than out of the larger. With regard to detention times, results revealed that 90 seconds of detention attenuated the frustration effect. There was the suggestion that 15 seconds of detention maximized the frustration effect, although such a finding appeared to be confined to the running time measure when the small goal box was used.

Finally, in a counterpart to the acquired drive of fear findings, Wagner (1963) has demonstrated that it is possible to produce an acquired drive based upon frustration. In one part of his study, rats were run in a U-shaped apparatus. On half of the trials, the animals found food in the goal box following the running response. On the other half, a CS (flashing light and intermittent noise) was presented, which was followed by the absence of food in the goal box. It was presumed that the pairing of non-reinforcement (assumed to produce frustration) with the CS would result in the CS acquiring drive characteristics. Following such training, the animals were placed in a stabilimetric cage and the CS was presented along with a loud noise which produced startle. Twenty such test trials were provided. The amplitude of the startle response was measured on each trial. Findings indicated that the experimental subjects produced a more vigorous startle response than appropriate control animals which had never received the CS paired with nonreinforcement. The apparent energizing effect, inferred from the more vigorous startle response, was interpreted as supporting the investigator's position that stimuli associated with a frustrative nonreward situation could come to elicit a learned drive of conditioned frustration.

A Final Word

One last point must be noted. Most learning theorists have assumed that the performance of a given response must take place as a result of some habit tendency being energized or motivated, and, as noted, there has been a determined search for the operation of motivational variables whenever learned responses have been observed to take place. It seems possible, however, that at least for some types of behavior other approaches to the problem might be explored. For example, Earl (1957) trained two groups of mice to dig sand under 20 hours of food deprivation. Twelve sessions were provided during which each animal had to dig through nine pounds of sand in order to secure food. The mean number of pounds of sand dug during the first 15 minutes of each session was recorded. One group was then satiated, and the second group was placed under 16 hours of deprivation. Both groups were then permitted to resume digging. Fifteen

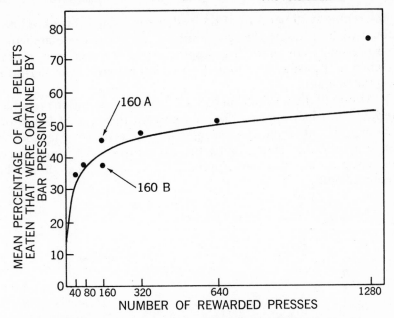

Fig. 4–8. Mean percentage of all pellets eaten during a 40-minute choice period where pellets were earned by bar pressing as a function of number of previous rewards. The A and B values plotted at 160 represent the performance of two groups given reinforcement under slightly different schedules. *Adapted from Jensen (1963)*

additional sessions were provided, and it was observed that the satiated animals were digging almost as rapidly as they had when they were deprived. No trend toward extinction was noted during this period. From the investigator's point of view, it appeared that the act of digging had developed "invitational character."

Or in a more recent study by Jensen (1963) rats were first trained to depress a bar in a Skinner box in order to receive pellets of food. Rewarded presses numbering 40, 80, 160, 320, 640, or 1,280 were provided, followed by giving the animals a choice between eating pellets from a dish attached to the floor of the box or pressing a bar to earn pellets. In Figure 4–8 the relationship between preference for bar pressing over eating pellets from a dish as a function of the number of rewarded bar presses prior to the choice period is apparent. Here it can be noted as the number of previously rewarded presses increases, the percentage of eaten pellets obtained by bar pressing increases so that with 1,280 presses almost 80 per cent of the pellets the animal eats have been obtained by pressing the bar. Jensen (1963) has postulated that bar pressing holds an intrinsic appeal for the rat—intrinsic appeal defined as a pleasant emotional state experienced while performing the operant.

Although the postulation of such terms as "invitational character" or "intrinsic appeal" does not explain this type of behavior, the experiments themselves suggest that for at least certain kinds of responses, the search for traditional motivational sources may be inappropriate and new approaches to the problem should be undertaken.

5

Motivation II:

The Role of Reinforcement
and Punishment

FROM THE FUNCTIONAL POINT OF VIEW, motives have been conceptualized as having a selective function in addition to the energizing function. More specifically, this refers to the fact that a motive operates to increase or decrease the probability of a response being made. This function has been usually attributed to the presence of reinforcement (or reward) and punishment. There has been some ambiguity in this matter, however, since a number of writers have considered reinforcement and punishment as distinct from motivation, although at the same time they have acknowledged the selective function to be a basic motivational property.

THE NATURE OF REINFORCEMENT

As with other constructs, it seems most appropriate to examine first how reinforcement is defined. Such an examination reveals empirical as well as theoretical definitions. A definition of the first sort takes the form of the empirical law of effect [McGeoch and Irion (1952)] which states that responses are fixated and eliminated as functions of their effects. Or as Spence (1956) has written, a reinforcing state of affairs belongs to the class of "environmental events exhibiting this property of increasing the probability of occurrence of responses they accompany. . . ."

Work done in the area of verbal reinforcement illustrates investigators utilizing the empirical law of effect. Thorndike (1932), for example, used the verbal responses of "right" and "wrong" to increase or decrease the probability of a variety of responses in the human being; and beginning with Greenspoon (1955), a number of experimenters have reported successful attempts to condition classes of verbal responses by using the verbal responses of "mmmm" or "huh-uh."

Theoretical definitions, in contrast to the empirical one, are concerned with the nature of the mechanisms which underlie the effect that is produced. Contemporary theoretical definitions undoubtedly begin with Hull's (1943) law of primary reinforcement, in which primary reinforcement has been defined as the reduction of a primary need. Some years later [Hull (1951)], this law was revised so that a reduction in the drive stimulus, rather than reduction of need, became critical in order for reinforcement to take place.

Miller [Miller and Dollard (1941), Dollard and Miller (1950)] has also assumed that drive reduction will act as reinforcement. As noted in Chapter 4, Miller has defined a drive as any strong stimulus, with the reduction of such stimulation serving as reinforcement for the organism.

Commencing in the early fifties, a number of investigators obtained findings which have cast considerable doubt on the position that reinforcement must be defined in terms of either need or drive reduction. Sheffield and Roby (1950) found that saccharin could serve as a reward for a rat's learning a position habit in a T-maze, and Hendry and Rasche (1961) have shown that the licking of a stream of cool air (air drinking) could serve as reinforcement for thirsty rats learning to run an alley-maze. Neither stimulus, of course, appears to provide need reduction for the animal. Sheffield, Wulff, and Backer (1951) have demonstrated that naïve male rats with no previous history of ejaculation would learn to run and climb hurdles, with the only reward being the opportunity to copulate with a receptive female. Need reduction in the form of ejaculation was not permitted.

A number of investigators have demonstrated that stimuli in the form of light, sound, or even the presence of another animal may take on reinforcing characteristics.

The studies of Marx, Henderson, and Roberts (1955); Kish (1955); Kling, Horowitz, and Delhagen (1956); Butler (1957); Hurwitz and De (1958); Roberts, Marx, and Collier (1958); Clayton (1958); Davis (1958); and Robinson (1961), to mention only a few, have shown that light increment or decrement has reinforcing properties. Studies by Butler (1957a), using monkeys, and Barnes and Kish (1961), using mice, have demonstrated that the onset of auditory stimulation also may act as a reward. Campbell and Pickleman (1961) have demonstrated that objects to which an organism has been imprinted may serve as a reinforcing stimulus in an instrumental learning situation. Angermeier (1960) has shown that simply the presence of an animal may serve as reward. Finally, a number of experimental findings have suggested the possibility that a unique environment may take on reinforcing characteristics if animals are raised in it from infancy and for relatively long periods of time [Hunt and Quay (1961), Warren and Pfaffman (1958)].

Reinforcement has also been demonstrated to take the form of an organism's response. Montgomery (1954) and Montgomery and Segall (1955) have shown that rats can learn T-maze problems if the correct response is followed by allowing the animal to explore a Dashiell checkerboard maze. Kagan and Berkun (1954) have found that rats can learn a bar-pressing response if this response is followed by permitting them to run in an activity wheel.

The studies cited, along with many similar ones, have raised serious question about the validity of both Hull and Miller's definitions of reinforcement.[1] As a result, a number of investigators have attempted to provide theoretical positions of their own. Such theoretical frameworks usually involve a consideration of one of the following: (1) the stimuli which are presented following the instrumental response, (2) the nature of the response that is made to the stimulus which follows the instrumental response, or (3) physiological or internal states which are related to the

[1] It is interesting to note that Miller (1957, 1959, 1963) on a number of occasions has written that in the future other investigators will probably refute his drive reduction hypothesis of reinforcement. He has also acknowledged that in situations in which there is no independent measure of drive, it is difficult to say whether or not drive reduction has occurred. As he has written (p. 76), "Unfortunately, many situations are of the latter kind, so that it is difficult to prove that the drive-reduction hypothesis is wrong, but at present one can make the more damning statement that it is irrelevant." [Miller (1963)]

action of either the stimulus which follows the instrumental response or the response itself.

The position most frequently taken regarding the contribution of the stimulus has been that environmental changes may act as reinforcement. As an example of such a point of view, Moon and Lodahl (1956) placed rhesus monkeys in a plywood box for 60 minutes during which time a lever-pulling response would result in either a decrease (60 watt lamp changed to 15 watts) or an increase (15 watt lamp increased to 60 watts) in the illumination of the box. Control groups were used in which the lever pull produced no illumination change. Results indicated that the experimental groups responded more frequently than the controls, and Moon and Lodahl have interpreted these findings to indicate that the effective reinforcing dimension was change per se rather than the direction of such a change. Forgays and Levin's (1958) experimental findings have also supported the position that a change in sensory stimulation may have reinforcing properties.

One problem with this position is that although it cannot be denied that a change in stimulation resulted in learning in the experiments which have been cited a number of other studies have been performed in which stimulation changes did not result in learning. Symmes and Leaton (1962) were unable to find any reinforcement effect occurring as a function of the presentation of a tone which followed a bar press, whereas Robinson (1959) found that light onset had a significant reinforcing effect on bar-pressing behavior but light termination did not.

A further difficulty lies in the fact that the reinforcing effects attributable to stimulation change are frequently temporary in nature and quite unstable. For example, Barnes and Kish (1961), using 1,000 mice as subjects, examined the influence of varying frequencies and intensities of tone in reinforcing a bar-pressing response. Although results revealed a weak positive reinforcing effect of tones at low frequencies and intensities, a subsequent study [Baron and Kish (1962)] was unable to replicate this finding.

In summary, although some experimenters have been interested in examining stimulus change parameters [Crowder and Crowder (1961), Barnes and Kish (1961)], most investigators have been content to merely demonstrate that some sort of stimulus change can act as reinforcement. Moreover, there has been a lack of a general theoretical position which would indicate when a stimulus change should or should not be reinforcing.

A second theoretical position which has attempted to explain the nature of reinforcement has been consideration of the consummatory response as being the basic mechanism. In the Sheffield and Roby (1950) study, previously referred to, the investigators pointed out (pp. 480–481) that the ". . . performance of a consummatory response appears to be more important to instrumental learning—in a primary, not acquired, way—than the drive satisfaction which the consummatory response normally achieves." The importance of the consummatory response has been further indicated in the Sheffield, Wulff, and Backer (1951) study, also previously cited, which demonstrated that the copulatory response but not ejaculation appeared to be a primary reinforcement mechanism. And in a subsequent study, Sheffield, Roby, and Campbell (1954) had rats learn to run a straight runway in which food reinforcement varied in sweetness as well as nourishment. Findings revealed that when speed of running was plotted as a function of rate of ingestion, a linear relationship was found between the two measures.[2]

One difficulty with this position is that recent experiments examining the relationship between an instrumental learning response and the consummatory response [Goodrich (1960) ; Snyder and Hulse (1961) ; Collier, Knarr, and Marx (1961)] have all yielded negative findings. In the Snyder and Hulse (1961) study, for example, three levels of water reinforcement (2.65, 1.50, and .75 cc.) and three numbers of total licks (295, 450, and 675) were investigated on the (1) running speed in an L-shaped runway and (2) varying aspects of the consummatory response. Thirty-four training trials were provided. Results did not reveal

[2] These investigators have pointed out that reinforcement may have an energizing or arousal function as well as a selective one. They have proposed (pp. 353–354) that ". . . the reward stimulus is at the outset of training an 'unconditioned' stimulus for the consummatory response in the sense that it will regularly elicit the response when presented. It would be expected that this terminal consummatory response would become conditioned to immediate neutral cues, especially those which just precede the onset of the reward stimulus. On successive experiences after the first these cues will arouse the consummatory response *ahead* of the reward. Moreover, this arousal of the incomplete consummatory response will work its way from the goal backward over the instrumental sequence since only the cues in this sequence invariably precede reward. Thus performing the correct responses —and only the correct ones—becomes a cue-producing situation that arouses the incomplete consummatory response."

any consistent relationship between running speed and either total volume consumed, total licks, volume per lick, or rate of licking. In the Collier, Knarr, and Marx (1961) study, rats were given 52 acquisition trials on a runway in which either a 4 or 32 per cent sucrose solution was used as reinforcement. Time permitted to drink was held constant at 20 seconds for the first twelve trials, 40 seconds for the next eight trials, and 60 seconds for the remaining trials. Results indicated that the rats receiving the 32 per cent solution had faster running speeds than the 4 per cent group. An analysis of the consummatory response in terms of total frequency of licks or total amount consumed revealed that after a large number of trials both measures differed significantly as a function of the intensity of the solution. It was found, however, that differences in starting time and running speed were in evidence long before differences in lick rate or amount consumed took place. As a result, the experimenters concluded that neither variations in the amount consumed nor the number of licks in one minute of reinforcement were necessary conditions for the production of differences in the instrumental response.

A last bit of evidence that has been used to attack the consummatory response position has been the studies of Hull, Livingston, Rouse, and Barker (1951) and Miller and Kessen (1952), as well as others, who have demonstrated it is possible for organisms to acquire an instrumental response by having food bypass the mouth and enter the stomach directly, thus eliminating the consummatory response.

In one such experiment, Miller and Kessen (1952) had small plastic fistulas sewn into rats' stomachs. These animals were then provided with two training trials per day on a T-maze; the first trial was one of free choice and the second trial was one which forced the animal to the side opposite to that chosen on trial one. A minimum of 25 days of training was provided. Three experimental groups were run: (1) stomach injection animals received an injection of 14 cc. of milk via the fistula when they went to the correct side and 14 cc. of isotonic saline when they went to the incorrect side; (2) no-delay animals received dishes containing 14 cc. of milk or saline in the correct or incorrect goal boxes respectively; and (3) delay animals received dishes of 14 cc. of milk for a correct choice or saline for an incorrect choice after a delay of 7 minutes and 35 seconds—the time normally taken to complete the injection which was received by the stomach injec-

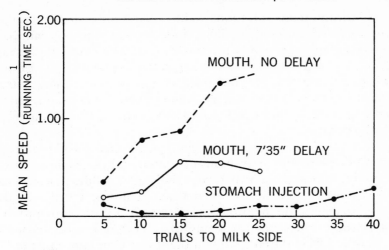

Fig. 5–1. Speed of running to the compartment in which milk was provided. *Adapted from Miller and Kessen (1952)*

tion animals. Figure 5–1 indicates the efficiency of receiving reinforcement via mouth (measured by rate or probability of responding), but it also reveals that learning is possible when milk is placed directly into the stomach.

Similar findings had been obtained by Kohn (1951) who deprived rats of food and then taught them to push a panel in order to secure milk. Following this, the animals underwent surgery in which a plastic fistula was sewn into their stomach. Following retraining, the animals were tested with three types of reinforcement: (1) 14 cc. of enriched milk via the mouth, (2) 14 cc. of enriched milk placed directly into the stomach, and (3) 14 cc. of saline placed directly in the stomach. Results, similar to the Miller and Kessen study, indicated that milk via the mouth was superior in obtaining a panel-pushing response than milk which was placed directly into the stomach. This latter condition, however, was superior to saline being placed in the stomach. Berkun, Kessen, and Miller (1952) replicated Kohn's experimental procedure but measured the consummatory response of drinking and obtained similar results.

A recent definition of reinforcement, also conceptualized in terms of an organism's response, has been proposed by Premack (1959) who has hypothesized (p. 219) that ". . . reinforcement results when an R [response] of a lower independent rate coincides, within temporal limits, with the stimuli governing the occurrence of an R of a higher independent rate." A familiar behavior pattern which illustrates this point of view is the rat pressing a bar for food. Since the typical experimental procedure utilizes a hungry rat, the independent rate of bar pressing is less than the independent rate of ingestion of pellets so that this latter response, in keeping with Premack's hypothesis, becomes a reinforcing event.

In an interesting test of his hypothesis, Premack had a pinball machine rewired for continuous operation and placed adjacent to a candy dispenser. Thirty-three first-grade children served as subjects, each child being tested twice. The first testing session served to determine the subject's relative rate of responding to the candy and to the pinball machine when both were unrestrictedly available. The children were told that there were two games to be played and they could play either or both of them as much as they cared to. Children who made more pinball machine responses than they ate pieces of candy were labeled "manipulators," and children who made more candy dispenser responses than pinball responses were labeled "eaters."

In the second session, which followed the first by three to four days, the "manipulator" group and the "eater" group were subdivided; one-half of each group was tested under an "eat-manipulate" contingency and the other half of each group was tested under a "manipulate-eat" contingency. More specifically, the arrangement was such that for the experimental group, the manipulators had to eat before they could manipulate while eaters had to manipulate before they could eat.[3] The higher rate response was made fully available to the control groups, and thus their behavior provided a measure of change in the lower rate response which might have occurred independently of the rate-differential contingency.

Results which supported the experimenter's hypothesis are indicated in Table 5–1 which presents the increase in responses made by the four groups during the second test session. Here it can be noted that for the manipulators there was a significant

---

[3] Because of time limited sessions, instructions were used to establish the first contingency. Thus, if three minutes elapsed without a response, the experimenter said, "Remember, there are two games." If this failed, the experimenter then said, "I wonder what would happen if you ate a piece of candy? Played the pinball machine?" according to which was appropriate.

TABLE 5–1

Increase in Lower Rate Response from First to Second Test

Manipulators

EATING CONTINGENT ON MANIPULATING (EXPERIMENTAL)	MANIPULATING CONTINGENT ON EATING (CONTROL)
Increment in number of pieces of candy eaten per subject	
16	0
16	4
19	19
22	0
14	5
14	10
28	0
19	0
26	7
81	child absent
Mean 25.5	Mean 5

Eaters

Increment in number of pinball machine responses per subject	
10	5
8	0
7	0
1	0
16	7
9	0
16	
Mean 9.4	Mean 2

(Adapted from Premack, 1959)

increase in the number of pieces of candy eaten providing such eating was followed by the opportunity to play the pinball machine. Similarly, with the eater groups, there was a significant increase in the number of times the pinball machine was played if such playing was followed by the opportunity to eat a piece of candy.

Support for this hypothesis has also come from a second study [Premack (1961)] in which a bar-pressing response and a licking response were used as the referent and contingent responses, respectively. Briefly, different lick rates were first obtained by permitting four groups of rats to lick either a 4 or 18 per cent sucrose solution from a drinking tube for either 30 seconds or eight minutes. The animals were then placed in a Skinner box where each bar press produced the previously licked sucrose solution. Results revealed that bar pressing was predictable from the lick rate order which was obtained during the first stage of training.

In an interesting demonstration of the effectiveness of this technique, Homme, DeBaca, Devine, Steinhorst, and Rickert (1963) have used Premack's principle to control behavior of nursery school children. High probability behavior patterns such as running around the room, pushing chairs, etc. were used to reinforce behavior which was desired by the teacher. For example, sitting quietly in a chair and looking at the blackboard would be intermittently followed by the sound of the bell, with the instruction: "Run and scream." At a later stage in the activity of the children, the children could earn tokens for low-probability behaviors which could later be used to purchase the opportunity for high-probability activities. With this kind of procedure, the experimenters reported that control was virtually perfect after a few days.

One interesting feature of Premack's hypothesis is that it indicates that reinforcement has relative rather than absolute properties. If the independent rates of several of an organism's responses are determined in advance and can be ranked in terms of rate, all possible contingencies between the ranked responses can be investigated. Thus, if A, B, and C represent three responses with independent rates of responding in the order stated, it would follow from Premack's position that A should reinforce both B and C, B should reinforce C but not A, and C should reinforce neither A nor B.

One problem, however, is the determination of the varying rates of responses which the organism may make; a second is related to the commensurability of behavior units. Thus, the criterion for determining what a behavior unit is and the relating of this to a rate measure is of primary importance. Although Premack (1959) has suggested some solutions, empirical research is needed before definitive answers can be provided.

Some of the studies surveyed in this section have been related not only to an examination of the role of the consummatory response, but they have also had something to say about some of the physiological mechanisms involved in reinforcement—the last of the theoretical interest areas. Some investigators interested in this area have assumed that the locus of the reinforcing effects of food would be found in the blood. Coppock and Chambers (1954) attempted to demonstrate this by depriving rats for three days, following which each animal was restrained in a snugly fitting cage. Under anesthesia, a hypodermic needle was inserted in the caudal vein at the base of the tail. The animal's head was placed between vertical beams of an infrared light so that horizontal flexion of the head to either side actuated the photo relay on that side. Following a ten-minute period in which the operant level of head turning was measured, there followed a 90-minute reinforcement period. During this period, experimental subjects received a 10 per cent glucose solution as long as they kept their heads in a given (right or left) position. Control animals were reinforced with saline. Results indicated that the 10 per cent glucose solution was more effective than saline in increasing the relative duration of, or preference for, a given right or left head position. Although Chambers (1956) was unable to obtain similar findings with dogs, confirming results were obtained in a second study when rabbits were used as the experimental subjects.

Another area of physiological interest in reinforcement has been the examination of electrical stimulation in the brain. The experimental work that has been done in this area has been so extensive, e.g., Sheer (1961), that only a few of the reference experiments in the area can be mentioned. The first study was reported by Olds and Milner (1954) who found that rats which had electrodes implanted in the septal region of their rhinencephalon, when placed in Skinner boxes in which brain stimulation followed the pressing of the bar, would continue to make the bar-pressing response again and again. (See Figure 5–2 for an illustration of implanted electrodes.) Such findings have been commonly interpreted in terms of the brain having a pleasure, reward, or reinforcing center.

About the same time as Olds and Milner (1954) reported their exciting findings, Delgado, Roberts, and Miller (1954) demonstrated that it was possible to motivate escape or avoidance behavior also by utilizing brain stimulation. In this study, cats were trained to turn a wheel in order to terminate peripheral shock. Electrical stimulation was then provided in the tectal area of the brain, and, after a number of trials, the animal learned to rotate the wheel in order to terminate and thus escape from such central stimulation. In a second study, the same procedure was used except that a tone was used as a CS and paired with central

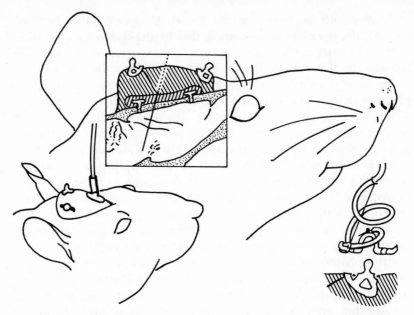

Fig. 5–2. Main features of a simple technique for using chronically implanted electrodes with rats. *Adapted from Miller, Coons, Lewis, and Jensen (1961)*

stimulation. If the wheel was turned within a short period of time, central stimulation could be avoided. Although the tone did not elicit any response at first, after a number of trials, the animals learned to avoid central stimulation. Cohen, Brown, and Brown (1957) have also demonstrated the feasibility of setting up a conditioned avoidance response via central stimulation.

Some investigators have demonstrated that both rewarding and punishing effects can be obtained from stimulation at the same location in the brain and at the same intensity. In one study by Roberts (1958), electrodes were placed at various locations in the posterior hypothalamus of the cat. The animals were then trained to press a bar in order to secure food. Extinction trials were then provided with the investigator administering a brief burst (one-half second) of stimulation after each bar press. When compared with normal extinction without stimulation, "rewarding" effects appeared as marked increases in the number of responses made during extinction. The subjects then received 30 avoidance training trials per day for three days.

The apparatus was a two-compartment box in which the animals were placed in one compartment. After five seconds, brain stimulation was provided and continued until the animal climbed through the hole in the barrier to the other side. Results revealed that an escape response was learned by observing the reduction of response times provided over the course of the 90 trials; avoidance responses (responses made prior to the onset of stimulation), however, were not learned.

In analyzing these findings, Roberts has pointed out that the fact that the cats would learn the escape response which was immediately followed by termination of the stimulation proved that the termination of such stimulation was reinforcing. The demonstration that the animals would learn to press the bar to obtain one-half second of the same level of stimulation could not be taken as conclusive evidence that stimulation onset was also rewarding, however, since the termination of the stimulation followed the bar-pressing response by only one-half second. Thus, there was the possibility that termination may have served as a reinforcing event for this response, too. In an attempt to determine whether the onset of stimulation possessed rewarding properties separate from termination, a second experiment was performed. In this second study, cats were trained to oscillate back and forth between two of the three arms in a symmetrical Y-maze. Entrance to one arm turned on stimulation, and entrance to another turned it off. Entries into the third arm were recorded as errors. At low voltages, the turning-on response was performed with few or no errors, but the turning-off response was performed at a chance level. At a higher voltage, however, the turning-off response improved markedly whereas the turning-on response deteriorated. Thus, increasing the voltage had opposite effects on the turning-off and turning-on responses. Roberts reasoned that since both responses would be expected to improve together if there was only one reinforcing event, this inverse relationship provided additional support for the position that onset of stimulation and its termination in the posterior hypothalamus can exert separate reinforcing effects which can be elicited by the same electrode at the same intensity.

Using rats as subjects, Bower and Miller (1958) have also found that stimulation of the same area in the brain would lead the animal to make a bar-pressing response in a Skinner box for stimulation onset and to respond to one side of a T-maze for termination of such stimulation. Like Roberts (1958), Bower and Miller were unable to obtain evidence that the animals could learn to respond appropriately in order to avoid such stimulation. Brown and Cohen (1959), however, have been able to get cats to learn to avoid a UCS consisting of three-tenths of a second of hypothalamic stimulation and also to get them to learn to run a straight runway in which the onset of the same intensity stimulation at the same hypothalamic location would serve as a reward.

SECONDARY REINFORCEMENT

In his *Principles of Behavior,* Hull (1943) postulated that primary reinforcement was effective for only a very short time in strengthening a stimulus-response relationship. There was thus an obvious difficulty in accounting for the learning of responses which were not followed immediately or almost so with reward. In an effort to extricate himself from this difficulty, Hull (1943) introduced the principle of secondary reinforcement. Briefly, this law stated that the power of reinforcement could be transmitted to any stimulus situation by consistent and repeated association of a stimulus with primary reinforcement.

Although Hull used an early experiment by Cowles (1937) to illustrate the operation of this law, a more contemporary example can be found in a study by Saltzman (1949). In this experiment, one group of rats was trained to run down a runway to a distinctively colored goal box which contained food. Following such training, the animals were placed in a U-maze in which the previously reinforced goal box was placed on one side and a neutral goal box on the other. Food was present in neither goal box. Fifteen maze trials were then given. Saltzman found that performance to the previously reinforced goal box was significantly better than would be expected by chance. His explanation for such behavior was that the goal box had acquired secondary reinforcing properties by its being previously associated with primary reinforcement.

It is interesting to note that although contemporary investigators have virtually abandoned further attempts to examine Hull's law of primary reinforcement, the concept of secondary reinforcement has continued to have a long experimental history. It is not possible to examine all of the experiments in this area, but the interested reader can refer to the reviews of Myers (1958) and

Kelleher and Gollub (1962). It is possible, however, to discuss some of the more important studies which have examined the operational parameters and theoretical significance of secondary reinforcement.

Before proceeding, attention should be directed to an examination of two frequently used procedures from which secondary reinforcing effects are inferred. In the first, the organism learns a new response during the test situation; the second examines the organism's resistance to extinction. The Saltzman (1949) study just described is an example of the first measure. The establishment of a secondary reinforcing stimulus took place as a result of the animal's traversing a runway and associating a distinctively colored goal box with food. This goal box then served as reinforcement for the animal in learning to make a new response. Somewhat similar procedures have been used with Skinner box studies. Animals first learn to approach a pellet dispenser, associating a click (secondary reinforcing stimulus) with the receipt of food. Following such training, a bar is inserted into the box and the animal learns to depress the bar, with the click serving as the sole reinforcing agent.

The second measure, resistance to extinction, is nicely illustrated by an experiment by Bugelski (1938). Rats placed in a Skinner box were trained to depress a bar in order to receive food. Associated with each pellet was the click of the food-release mechanism which, because of its association with food, was assumed to acquire secondary reinforcing characteristics. Following training, the bar-pressing response was extinguished; for one-half of the animals the response was followed by the customary click, but for the other half, it was not. Results revealed that the click-extinction group made significantly more bar presses than the nonclick group—a result which has been attributed to the reinforcing role played by the secondary reinforcing stimulus during the extinction trials.

PARAMETERS OF SECONDARY REINFORCEMENT

Amount of Primary Reinforcement

An examination of this variable has led some investigators to utilize what Lawson (1957) has termed the *differential* in contrast to the *absolute* experimental procedure. The differential method is one in which each subject serves as its own control;

thus, it learns to associate one amount of reinforcement with one stimulus and a different amount with another. A test situation is then presented in which the subject must make a choice between the two stimuli.

Using the differential technique D'Amato (1955) was able to demonstrate that the strength of the secondary reinforcing stimulus varied as a function of the amount of primary reinforcement with which it had been paired. Rats first learned to associate five pellets of food with a goal box of one color and just one pellet with a goal box of another color. The test situation consisted of utilizing a T-maze with the five-pellet box placed on one side and the one-pellet box on the other. The animals were given 15 test trials. Primary reinforcement, of course, was never provided in the test situation. Results indicated that the mean number of responses to the five-pellet box was significantly greater than chance; 18 of the 20 rats used in the study made eight or more responses to the goal box previously associated with five pellets of food. Lawson (1957) has confirmed D'Amato's findings.

The absolute method involves an experimental procedure which employs several groups of subjects, with each group having the opportunity to associate only one magnitude of reward with the secondary reinforcing stimulus. The experimental findings, in contrast to those obtained with the differential method, are somewhat controversial. The early studies of Lawson (1953) and Hopkins (1955) provided negative findings, but more recent experiments have provided positive results. In one of these [Butter and Thomas (1958)] rats received 48 trials in which the click of a reinforcement mechanism was associated with the animal's running to one end of a box and receiving either an 8 or 24 per cent sucrose solution. Following such training, a bar was introduced into the apparatus and all bar presses were reinforced by the click which served as secondary reinforcement. Experimental findings revealed that the 24 per cent solution group made a significantly greater number of bar presses than the 8 per cent group.

Frequency of Primary Reinforcement

A number of investigators [Hall (1951); Bersh (1951); Miles (1956)] have demonstrated that the strength of a secondary reinforcing stimulus is related to the frequency with which it has been paired with primary reinforcement. As an example of this general

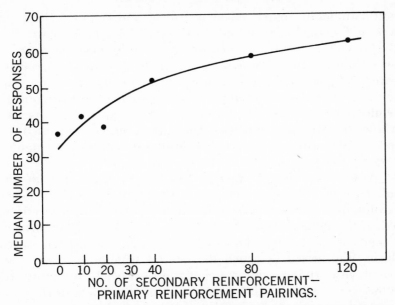

Fig. 5–3. Median number of bar-pressing responses made as a function of the number of secondary reinforcement–primary reinforcement pairings. *Adapted from Bersh (1951)*

finding, Bersh (1951) provided five groups of rats with 10, 20, 40, 80, or 120 reinforcements for bar pressing. Each response produced a three-second light, with reinforcement taking place after the light had been present for one second. A control group was given 120 reinforcements without the accompanying light. Following this, all groups were then extinguished, but the extinction situation did not include presentation of the light at any time. Presumably, this procedure reduced the bar-pressing response to the same level for all groups. Following this, a final testing session was provided in which each bar press resulted in the light being presented for one second. Results, presented in Figure 5–3, showed a positive relationship between the number of times that light was paired with food and the median number of bar-pressing responses for each of the groups.

The Role of Need States

One of the early questions that was asked was whether or not a secondary reinforcing stimulus could actually reduce a primary need. Studies by Simon, Wickens, Brown, and Pennock (1951) as well as Calvin, Bicknell, and Sperling (1953a) have shown that the presence of a secondary reinforcing stimulus does not reduce a primary need. In the Simon, *et al.*, study, the investigators compared the quantity of water consumed by thirsty rats whose bar-pressing responses had been previously accompanied by secondary reinforcement with water consumption of equally thirsty rats whose bar-pressing responses had not been accompanied by secondary reinforcement. No significant differences were obtained between the groups.

A second topic of interest has been concerned with the influence of need states on (1) the establishment of secondary reinforcing stimuli and (2) their subsequent operation. When the influence of the need state upon the establishment of secondary reinforcing stimuli is investigated, the need is varied during the period in which the neutral stimulus is being associated with primary reinforcement and then held constant during subsequent testing. In the second situation, the reverse is true; the need is held constant during the period in which the neutral stimulus is being associated with primary reinforcement but is then varied during the subsequent testing. The reference experiment in this area is a study by Brown (1956). In the first part of this study, a light and buzzer were paired with the presentation of food pellets in a Skinner box. The bar was not present. During this session, training trials were given to rats, half of which had been placed on a low-hunger drive and half on a high-hunger drive. In the second phase of the study, the bar was inserted into the box and each rat was permitted to make 20 bar presses. Each press was followed by the light and buzzer. During this session, each of the previous groups was subdivided so that half of the rats made their bar-pressing responses under high drive and half under low drive. Following this second phase, the last phase consisted of providing extinction trials in which neither food nor the secondary reinforcement of the light and buzzer was provided for bar pressing. This extinction session was immediately followed by a re-learning session during which the rats were given an hour of free responding in which each press was followed by the light and buzzer. Again, each group was further subdivided into high and low drive groups. Brown found that the strength of drive during the pairing session had no effect on subsequent responding—a finding in agreement with an earlier study made by Hall (1951a). On the other hand, Brown did find that the level of drive was an important variable in determining the strength of responding during the learning and re-learning situation. Again, this result is in keeping with the experimental findings of Miles (1956), who, following the establishment of a secondary reinforcing stimulus by pairing a light and click with food, extinguished the bar-pressing response with the animals being placed under either 0, 2.5, 5, 10, 20, or 40 hours of deprivation. It would appear that the level of an organism's need is not an important variable in the establishment of a secondary reinforcing stimulus, but its role is significant during its subsequent operation.

Temporal Relationships

Both Jenkins (1950) and Bersh (1951) have demonstrated the strength of a secondary reinforcer to be a function of the interval of time which separates the presentation of the neutral stimulus and the occurrence of primary reinforcement. Using a Skinner box with the bar removed, Bersh (1951) first paired light with the presentation of food but varied the interstimulus interval. Light and food were presented simultaneously to one group; for five other groups, either .5, 1.0, 2.0, 4.0, or 10.0 seconds intervened between the onset of light and the receipt of the reinforcement. Following training trials, the bar was introduced into the box, and conditions were so arranged that a bar press resulted in the presentation of light. The number of responses taking place during two 45-minute test sessions is shown in Figure 5–4.

Secondary Reinforcement Based upon Shock Termination

Reinforcement can be conceptualized as consisting of the termination of noxious stimuli as well as being related to the presentation of objects which satisfy appetitional needs. This consideration of secondary reinforcement has been limited almost exclusively to the consideration of stimuli associated with the presentation of food and water, and there has been no consideration as to whether or not secondary reinforcement can be established by associating neutral stimuli with the termination of noxious stimulation. Now it can be noted that a neutral stimulus and its association with noxious stimuli can be examined when the neutral stimulus is paired with the *onset* of the noxious stimulus and when the neutral stimulus is paired with the

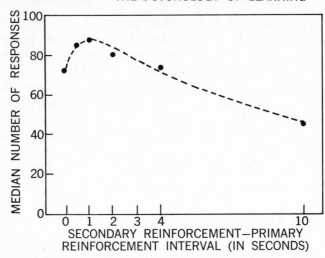

Fig. 5–4. Median number of bar-pressing responses made during two 45-minute test sessions combined. *Adapted from Bersh (1951)*

termination of the noxious stimulus. The first case is an example of an acquired drive of fear already discussed, but the second situation should lead to secondary reinforcement. Experimental proof that stimuli can acquire secondary reinforcing properties by being associated with the termination of a noxious stimulus however is controversial, with both positive and negative experimental findings being reported. A few of the studies which have yielded positive findings should be examined.

Smith and Buchanan (1954) trained one group of rats to cross a charged grid in order to obtain food in a black goal box and across a sponge runway to secure food in a white goal box. (The influence of color of the goal boxes was controlled by using a second group with the color of the boxes reversed.) In such a situation, the goal box which was associated with food as well as shock termination should take on greater secondary reinforcing strength than the goal box associated only with food. The test for the strength of the secondary reinforcing stimulus was conducted by having the animals learn a black-white discrimination problem on a Y-maze in which the black goal box contained food and the white goal box did not. [It should be noted that although this situation is similar to that used by Saltzman (1949) as well as others, it is different in the sense that the animals actually received food during the secondary reinforcing test trials.] Results revealed that the animals which had run to the black goal box during training and had thus received shock termination as well as food learned more rapidly than animals which had only received food during training. Presumably, the reduction of pain which was associated with the black box was responsible for the difference between groups. Positive findings have also been reported by Crowder (1958) in an unpublished study. The situation which he used consisted of a tail-shock apparatus in which the shock could be precisely controlled. The front of the apparatus contained a nose-key which the animal could press against and which could be used as the instrumental response. In one experiment, shock was gradually increased to a maximum intensity over a 25-second interval. The first response taking place after shock had reached its peak was followed by a one-half second presentation of light which was then followed by shock termination. In both extinction and reconditioning the presentation of this light as a reinforcer significantly increased response rate.

Although a number of investigators have reported negative findings [Littman and Wade (1955), Nefzger (1957)], contemporary writers [Kimble (1961), Mowrer (1960)] have considered the effect demonstrated, and Mowrer's presentation has included a careful consideration of why he believes many investigators have been unable to secure positive results. One basic difficulty is that during the testing situation, if the noxious stimulation is not used, the animal's motivation is frequently so reduced that it is difficult to get any relevant responding. Moreover, Mowrer points out that a stimulus which has been associated with shock termination in a given experimental situation will have little positive appeal to the subject in another neutral situation (where no shock has ever been experienced), for the reason that it will "remind" the subject of the original experimental situation and make him less rather than more comfortable. Or, perhaps more objectively, the neutral stimulus in the second situation results in the generalization of fear from one situation to the other. (Such an explanation means that Mowrer assumes the neutral stimulus which has been associated with shock reduction also acquires fear-producing properties.)

A recent analysis by Beck (1961) in which he has carefully examined the positive findings in this area has led him to point out (p. 34) that "In those instances where there has been a clear experimental effect the interpretation is generally confounded such that the concept of secondary reinforcement need not be invoked," and he has concluded his review by stating that there is almost no evidence to show that secondary reinforcement can be established by the association of a neutral stimulus with noxious-drive reduction.

A basic problem with some of the experiments revealing positive findings is the lack of distinction between what might be called a cue or eliciting function of a motive and its reinforcing or selective function. For example, in the Smith and Buchanan (1954) study, when the rat was at a choice point, it could see both the black and white goal boxes. As a result, it is very possible that the black box *elicited* the response of running toward it rather than strengthening it once it had been made. This situation is unlike the Saltzman (1949) study in which the animals had to first make a right or left response prior to their being in a position to see the color of the goal box.

Schedules of Reinforcement

A variable of considerable interest for a number of experimenters has been the schedule of primary and secondary reinforcement which is provided the organism during the training and the test situations. That is, during the establishment of a secondary reinforcing stimulus (training period), as well as during the test period, it is possible to provide the organism with a variety of schedules. Table 5–2 illustrates the varying combinations which may be used.

One methodological consideration should be called to the reader's attention. It is frequently possible to use a separate group design, or subjects may be used as their own control. With the separate group design, one group associates during training a secondary reinforcing stimulus with intermittently presented primary reinforcement, and a second group associates the secondary reinforcing stimulus with continuously presented primary reinforcement. A test situation which presents only the secondary reinforcing stimulus as a goal object provides the basis for a comparison between the groups. The second method is one in which subjects act as their own control. Here, subjects experience both continuous and partial reinforcement procedures during training, with each reinforcement contingency being associated with a different secondary reinforcing stimulus. A test situation is

TABLE 5–2

Types of Training Sessions Using Continuous and Intermittent
Primary and Secondary Reinforcing Schedules

		SECONDARY REINFORCEMENT SCHEDULE	
		Continuous	Intermittent
PRIMARY	Continuous	a	b
REINFORCEMENT			
SCHEDULE	Intermittent	c	d

then used which places the secondary reinforcing stimuli in
apposition.

In an early examination of the partial versus continuous
primary reinforcement training procedure and using subjects as
their own control, Mason (1957) trained rats to learn two discriminations. One consisted of black versus gray, with the black
positive, and the other discrimination consisted of white versus
gray, with the white positive. With one of the tasks, the positive
stimulus was primarily reinforced on only 50 per cent of the trials,
but on the other task, the positive stimulus was reinforced on 100
per cent of the trials. Following training, the black and white
stimuli were paired, thus forming a new discrimination task. The
animals were then given ten nonreinforced trials. Results indicated that 17 of the 20 animals made six or more choices to the
stimulus which had been associated with continuous reinforcement during the original training.

A study by D'Amato, Lachman, and Kivy (1958) utilizing a
slightly different training procedure has confirmed Mason's
findings. These investigators provided runway training in which
rats received partial reinforcement in a black (or white) goal
box and continuous reinforcement in white (or black). Following 88 training trials, 30 test trials (15 per day) with a T-maze
were provided. The black and white goal boxes used in the
runway procedure were placed at opposite ends of a T-maze but
primary reinforcement was not provided. As Figure 5–5 reveals,
entries into the goal box associated with continuous reinforcement were significantly greater than entries into the box associated with partial reinforcement. It can be noted, then, that
there is general agreement with the position that a continuous
primary reinforcement schedule is superior to a partial primary

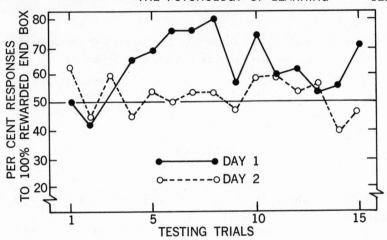

Fig. 5–5. Performance on unrewarded secondary-reinforcement test trials on the T-maze, with the continuously reinforced goal box on one side and the partially reinforced goal box on the other. *Adapted from D'Amato, Lachman, and Kivy (1958)*

reinforcement schedule in establishing the strength of a secondary reinforcing stimulus when subjects have experience with both types of secondary reinforcement.

As indicated earlier, a second experimental design employs separate groups. Using this type of design D'Amato, Lachman, and Kivy (1958) provided one group of rats with training on a runway in which reinforcement was obtained in a black goal box on every trial, whereas a second group was reinforced in the same black box on only 50 per cent of the trials. Following such training, both groups received 30 test trials (15 per day) on a T-maze which contained the previously reinforced goal box on one side of the T and a neutral goal box on the other side. Although no difference between groups in frequency of responding was found for the first 15 trials, an examination of the second 15 trials revealed that the partial reinforcement group was superior to the continuous group. Figure 5–6 presents this finding.

Confirmation of this general finding has been obtained by Klein (1959). In this study, six groups of rats were trained to run a straightaway for reinforcement. Each group of animals was given 120 training trials with one of the following primary reinforcement percentages: 20, 40. 60, 80, 90, or 100. The goal box served

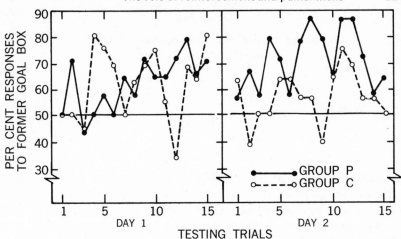

Fig. 5–6. Performance on unrewarded secondary reinforcement test trials on the T-maze, with the former goal box on one side and a "neutral" box on the other. *Adapted from D'Amato, Lachman, and Kivy (1958)*

as the secondary reinforcing stimulus. Twenty trials were given on a T-maze in which the previously reinforced goal box was placed on one side and a neutral goal box on the other. The median number of entries into the previously reinforced goal box for each of the varying groups can be noted in Table 5–3. Inspection of these data reveals that the strength of a secondary reinforcing stimulus increased as the percentage of the reinforced trials during acquisition trials decreased.

Armus and Garlich (1961) have obtained similar findings when the secondary reinforcing stimulus as well as primary reinforcement is presented intermittently. (See Table 5–2, a vs. c.) In this study, rats were first trained to press a bar in order to receive food. For the continuously reinforced group, each bar press was always accompanied by food as well as by secondary reinforcement (sound of the pellet dispenser and a two-second flash of light). The partially reinforced group was placed on a fixed ratio schedule in which primary reinforcement and the presentation of the secondary reinforcing stimulus were provided after every fifth response. The animals were then tested in a two-lever situation in which depression of one bar provided the secondary reinforcing stimuli but depression of the second bar

TABLE 5–3

Number of Entries into the Secondary Reinforcing
Goal Box during Testing

	REINFORCEMENT GROUPS					
	100	90	80	60	40	20
Median No. Responses	11.5	12.5	14.5	16.0	18.0	18.5

(Adapted from Klein, 1959)

did not. An examination of 150 test trials revealed that the fixed ratio group, as measured by percentage of correct responses, was superior to the continuously reinforced group.[4]

The findings of D'Amato, Lachman, and Kivy (1958), Klein (1959), and Armus and Garlich (1961) suggest then that when a separate group design is used to evaluate the contribution of partial reinforcement of the strength of a secondary reinforcing stimulus, the partial reinforcement regimen is superior to the continuous.

In the studies which have been examined, although partial reinforcing situations have been utilized during the training period, the secondary reinforcing stimulus has been continuously presented during the testing period. A logical question which follows is: What takes place when the secondary reinforcing stimulus is presented intermittently during the testing period? An early study by Zimmerman (1957) was directed toward answering this question. In this study, a Skinner box situation was used and a training period was utilized in which a two-second buzzer was followed by the operation of a water delivery dipper. Although early training utilized a continuous reinforcement schedule—the presence of the buzzer being followed always by the operation of the water dipper—as training continued, water reinforcements were omitted following the buzzer, at first on alternate presentations and then successively in longer runs. The ratio of the rewarded to nonrewarded presentations during training varied somewhat randomly, but the mean number of reinforcement omissions gradually increased, with a 1:10 ratio finally estab-

---

[4] Fixed ratio, fixed interval, variable ratio, and variable interval schedules of reinforcement are types of partial reinforcement programs used in the free operant situation. It is suggested that the reader scan the appropriate material in Chapter 8 in order to familiarize himself with these schedules inasmuch as they shall be referred to throughout this section.

lished. During this training, the vigor with which the animal went to the water delivery apparatus following the buzzer did not lessen although the frequency of rewarded presentations progressively decreased.

Following the training procedure, the buzzer was tested for its secondary reinforcing properties by presenting it as a consequence of the rat's pressing a small bar which was placed in the apparatus. Instead of having the buzzer always follow the bar pressing, the procedure again involved intermittent reinforcement. Here, the animal was required to make a large number of bar presses, with the buzzer following the response only a small percentage of the time. Zimmerman found that such a procedure was quite effective in maintaining the bar-pressing response at an exceptionally high level although primary reinforcement was never used.

A second study by Zimmerman (1959) verified the findings of the first, although he utilized a somewhat different experimental apparatus. In this situation, the animal was first trained to traverse a runway and secure food in the goal box. More specifically, the animal was first confined to a starting box for 30 seconds before each run. A ready signal—a buzzer—was then sounded, and two seconds later the starting box door was raised. After running down the alley, the animal went into the goal box and secured food. Following 33 continuous reinforced trials, a variable ratio scheduling procedure was used. Here, nonreinforced trials were interspersed among reinforced ones. Following 93 training trials, a bar was inserted into the starting box and when the animal pressed the bar, the buzzer, or ready signal, was presented which was then followed two seconds later by the lifting of the door. The animal was permitted to run to an empty goal box and was then removed to a waiting cage. After a number of trials in which each bar press resulted in the door's opening, a fixed ratio schedule was instituted in which the animals had to press the bar a number of times before the door would open. By the fifth test day, the fixed ratio schedule was increased to 1:20 and remained at this value thereafter.

Results showed that the number of bar presses made by the experimental animals was significantly greater than those provided by appropriate control groups. The findings further revealed that the experimental animals' performance lasted for ten to fourteen one and one-half hour daily sessions during which thousands of responses were made. In fact, the behavior was comparable to that generated by variable ratio and fixed ratio schedules in which primary reinforcement was used. Although the runway behavior became disrupted after several sessions, a fragment of it—jumping from the starting box onto the runway—persisted much longer and permitted the bar-pressing behavior to be maintained.[5]

Zimmerman's studies merit attention, not only for providing empirical information about a particular secondary reinforcing situation, but also because they hold promise of answering a very fundamental question which had arisen in the minds of many theorists who had posited that secondary reinforcing stimuli made an invaluable contribution to the better understanding of human rewards. That is, although a host of parametric studies investigating secondary reinforcement had provided overwhelming evidence that secondary reinforcing stimuli could increase the probability of a response being made, there had been persistent doubt in the minds of many as to whether or not secondary reinforcing stimuli were durable—capable of accounting for the protracted behavior sequences which were typical of human behavior. Until the Zimmerman studies, there had been no experimental demonstration that secondary reinforcement could sustain prolonged behavior sequences.

The experimental findings cited above have been of limited scope in their examination of the influence of reinforcement schedules on the strength of a secondary reinforcing stimulus. Studies by Myers (1960) and Fox and King (1961) have been much more extensive.

In Myers' study, children between the ages of three and six were presented with a clown game. When the nose of the clown was pressed, a token was delivered from the clown's mouth. The token was then inserted into the ear of the clown, and pressing of the nose provided a piece of candy. Twenty trials constituted the training session. Four major experimental groups were formed, utilizing either 50 or 100 per cent secondary reinforcement (tokens) and either 50 or 100 per cent primary reinforcement (candy). The varying groups were scheduled as follows:

[5] A series of studies by Wike and his associates [Wike and Platt (1962); Wike, Platt, and Knowles (1962); Wike, Platt, and Scott (1963)] has raised a number of questions about this experiment. An important finding that these investigators have obtained is that the opportunity for the animal to escape from the starting box, and not the buzzer, appears to serve as the basic source of reinforcement for the bar-pressing response.

GROUP I		GROUP II	
Primary 100%	Secondary 100%	Primary 100%	Secondary 50%
GROUP III		GROUP IV	
Primary 50%	Secondary 100%	Primary 50%	Secondary 50%

(Adapted from Myers, 1960)

Each major group was then divided following training so that for the 40 extinction trials which were provided one-half of the subjects received tokens and the other half did not.

Results are presented in Figure 5–7, and some general kinds of findings can be noted. First, the presentation of tokens during extinction trials prolongs experimental extinction—evidence which supports the secondary reinforcing characteristics of the tokens and confirms the findings of a number of previous investigators.

Secondly, examination of those groups which were presented the secondary reinforcing stimulus during extinction trials reveals that the intermittent presentation of both primary and secondary reinforcement resulted in the highest percentage of responding,

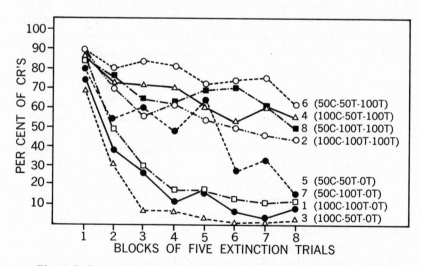

Fig. 5–7. Percentage of responses for successive five-trial blocks of extinction trials for the varying experimental groups. C = candy; T = tokens. *Adapted from Myers (1960)*

TABLE 5–4

Mean Number of Responses for Test Session I during Stage II

STAGE I CONDITION	STAGE II CONDITION		
	Partial	Continuous	Control
Partial	70.6	23.6	17.7
Continuous	21.0	31.5	11.5

(Adapted from Fox and King, 1961)

but the continuous presentation of primary and secondary reinforcing stimuli during training produced the lowest.

Fox and King's (1961) study differs from Myers' in that these investigators provided for the intermittent presentation of the secondary reinforcing stimulus during the testing situation as well as intermittent reinforcement during the training session. The experimental design which they used was as follows: During Stage I (i.e., the establishment of a secondary reinforcer), a continuous reinforcement group received 100 presentations of a buzzer which were always paired with the presentation of water. A partial reinforcement group received 200 presentations of the buzzer, but only 100 reinforcements of water presentation were provided. The ratio of buzzer to water presentations was not fixed but took place as follows over five training sessions: 50:50; 50:30; 50:15; 50:5. Thus, the final ratio of buzzer to water presentations was 10:1. Stage II consisted of a test for the strength of the secondary reinforcer. A bar was introduced into the apparatus, and its pressing could be followed by the sound of a buzzer. Subjects from both the continuous and the partial reinforcement groups were randomly assigned to one of three Stage II groups: (1) Those on a continuous schedule received the buzzer as a consequence of each bar depression, (2) those on a partial reinforcement schedule received the buzzer on a fixed interval (one-minute) schedule, and finally, (3) a control group never received the buzzer as a consequence of bar depression. Two one-hour experimental sessions comprised Stage II. The mean number of bar presses for the first hour for each of the varying groups is indicated in Table 5–4 and reveals the clear superiority of using a partial reinforcement schedule during both stages. Statistical analysis revealed that all experimental groups gave significantly more responses than their appropriate control groups; but more important, the partial-partial group responded significantly more frequently than any of the other experimental groups.

In summary, the findings which have been obtained offer strong support for the position that the intermittent presentation of the primary reinforcing stimulus during training and the intermittent presentation of the secondary reinforcing stimulus during the test situation lead to the most durable secondary reinforcing effects.

The Nature of Secondary Reinforcement

It is obvious from the studies which have been cited that neutral stimuli may acquire the capacity to serve as a reinforcing stimulus. Do such stimuli serve any other function? And what is the specific nature of the operations which must be employed in order for a neutral stimulus to acquire secondary reinforcing characteristics? A number of investigators have been interested in these problems.

The Discriminability of Secondary Reinforcing Stimuli

One question concerning the nature of secondary reinforcing stimuli is related to the discriminability of the secondary reinforcing stimulus. In an early study in the area by Schoenfeld, Antonitis, and Bersh (1950), two groups of hungry rats were provided food pellets for bar-pressing responses. For the experimental group, a light of one-second duration went on at the beginning of eating, rather than being paired with the bar-pressing response which is typically the case in secondary reinforcing studies. The light stimulus was not presented to the control group. Secondary reinforcement was measured by noting the number of bar presses during extinction when only the light was presented following the making of the response. No difference was obtained between groups, and the investigators concluded that the secondary reinforcing stimulus must precede the primary reinforcer if it is to achieve reinforcing strength. They further proposed that discrimination training was required in order to obtain secondary reinforcing effects. In essence, neutral stimuli, if they are to become secondary reinforcers, must be discriminative stimuli as well. (A discriminative stimulus is one whose presence serves as a cue for responding and whose absence is a cue for not responding.) In the experiment cited, the light was not a discriminative stimulus, hence it did not serve as a secondary reinforcer.

Since this early study, a number of other investigators [Webb and Nolan (1953), Dinsmoor (1950), McGuigan and Crockett (1958), and Myers and Myers (1963)] have supported the position that some type of discrimination training is necessary if a neutral stimulus is to acquire secondary reinforcing properties.[6]

Whether or not some type of discrimination training is a necessary condition for the establishment of a secondary reinforcing stimulus, however, is debatable. A study by Stein (1958) has important implications for this question. In this study, rats first received a series of six daily one-hour sessions in a two-lever Skinner box. Pressing one lever produced a one-second tone, whereas pressing the other had no effect. An examination of the number of responses made to each lever revealed a slight preference for the no-tone lever. The animals were then presented with the tone followed by five-tenths of a second of brain stimulation for 100 trials per day for a four-day period. These sessions took place in the apparatus with the levers removed. Following this training the levers were again placed in the box, and for the next three days daily one-hour test sessions were provided with a procedure which was similar to that used previously—i.e., one lever produced a tone but the second lever did not. Results are diagrammed in Figure 5–8. Here it can be noted that the pairing of the tone with brain stimulation resulted in a significant increase in the number of presses on the bar which produced the tone—a finding which supports the position that the tone had acquired secondary reinforcing characteristics. A control group of

[6] Wyckoff, Sidowski, and Chambliss (1958) have argued that investigators should make a distinction between the cue function and the reinforcing function of secondary reinforcing stimuli. That is, they have pointed out, if a response is learned as a function of the action of a secondary reinforcer, one should demonstrate that such an effect cannot be attributed to the cue function. The experiment which they have reported is one which attempted to differentiate the reinforcing function from the cue function and which consisted of training rats to approach and lick a water dipper in response to a buzzer. Such training was followed by a test period during which time the lever pressing produced a buzz but no water. Control subjects were given identical training; but during the test period each animal was "yoked" to an experimental subject so that whenever the experimental animal pressed the bar and received the buzz, the control animals also received the buzz. The experimenters argued that this type of control group was necessary in order to establish control for the cue action of the buzzer which would result in the subject's running to the water dipper. Such activity would bring the animal into the vicinity of the bar, and any resultant activity would increase the probability of a lever-pressing response. Experimental findings revealed no differences in bar pressing between groups. As a result, the secondary reinforcing data gathered in Skinner box studies have been deemed suspect by the investigators.

A series of studies by Crowder and his associates [Crowder, Morris, and McDaniel (1959) ; Crowder, Gill, Hodge, and Nash (1959) ; Crowder, Gay, Bright, and Lee (1959) ; and Crowder, Gay, Fleming, and Hurst (1959)] has not been able to verify the Wyckoff, et al., findings.

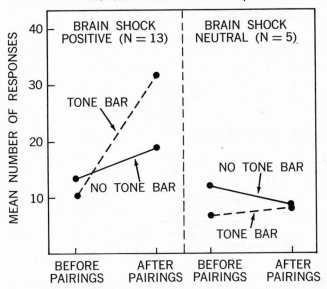

Fig. 5–8. Mean number of responses at the two bars for the experimental sessions before and after the pairings phase for both groups. *Adapted from Stein (1958)*

animals which were provided similar training and testing except that they received their stimulation in a neutral section of the brain did not reveal the same increase in lever presses. These results are also shown in Figure 5–8.

Secondary Reinforcement as Providing Information

Egger and Miller (1962, 1963) have conceptualized secondary reinforcing stimuli as providing the subject with information about the occurrence of primary reinforcement. The hypothesis examined in these studies has been that in a situation in which there is more than one stimulus predicting primary reinforcement the most informative stimulus will have the greatest secondary reinforcing strength. Moreover, these investigators have asserted that the necessary condition for establishing any stimulus as a secondary reinforcer is that the stimulus provide information about the occurrence of primary reinforcement.

In their second study [Egger and Miller (1963)], which incorporated the salient features of the first, a Skinner box situation was employed and the animals first were trained to press the bar

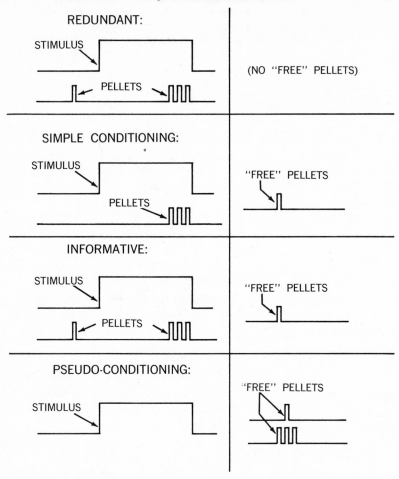

Fig. 5–9. Schematic representation of the training procedure of the four experimental groups. *Adapted from Egger and Miller (1963)*

for food. Then the bar was removed and the following training procedures were instituted. A *redundant* group received at variable intervals 15 occurrences per session of a two-second stimulus (either a flashing light or tone), the last one-half second of which overlapped the delivery of three food pellets. Each of these two-second stimulus–three food pellet pairings, however, was preceded by one-half second by the delivery of a single food pellet. The two-second stimulus in this case is redundant since the single pellet of food indicates to the organism that three pellets will be

TABLE 5–5

Total Number of Bar Presses for Three
Ten-Minute Testing Periods

Simple conditioning	218
Informative	212
Redundant	162
Pseudoconditioning	137

(Adapted from Egger and Miller, 1963)

forthcoming. An *informative* group received exactly the same food pellet–two-second stimulus–three more pellets sequence as did the redundant group, but 35 individual pellets were presented at random throughout each session. In this case, the two-second stimulus becomes informative since the presentation of a single pellet does not always signal three additional pellets. Two additional groups were run as controls: (1) a simple conditioning group which received 15 two-second stimulus-food pairings during each session, without the pellet preceding the stimulus, plus 35 pellets delivered at random during the session and (2) a pseudo-conditioning group which received 35 occurrences of a single pellet and 15 occurrences of triple-pellet deliveries unpaired with 15 occurrences of the two-second stimulus. Events for the pseudo-conditioning group were separated by at least seven and one-half seconds. Figure 5–9 diagrams the varying training procedures which were used.

Following nine 25-minute training sessions, the animals were given additional bar-pressing training where the subjects were permitted to press for 30 pellets with every third response being rewarded. The bar was then disconnected from the feeder, and subjects were extinguished for ten minutes. Extinction was followed by 21 minutes of pressing for one-second occurrences of the training stimulus; 48 hours later subjects were provided 25 minutes during which they were again allowed to press the bar for stimuli. The second session was followed 48 hours later by a third of 25 minutes duration. Presentation of the training stimulus was on a fixed ratio schedule of 3:1.

Results for each group in total presses during the first ten minutes summated for the three test periods revealed that the simple conditioning and informative groups were not significantly different, but these groups differed significantly from the redundant and pseudoconditioning groups. See Table 5–5 for a summary of the findings.

Knowledge of Results

In the human organism, in which language plays an important role in guiding behavior, the individual very frequently obtains information about his actions. Such information often has been termed knowledge of results (KR) or feedback. Since it has been shown that KR has the capacity to increase or decrease the probability of a response being made, it thus has a selective function and qualifies as a type of motivational variable.

One of the earliest experiments was performed by Judd (1905) who set up an experiment in which subjects attempted to determine the correct continuation of a line which formed an angle when only part of the line was exposed to view. Nine lines drawn at various angles (+60, +45, +30, +15, 0, −15, −30, −45, and −60 degrees) were presented 20 times per day for ten days with the subjects given no indication of the accuracy of their responses. Results revealed that the subjects performed as well during the early trials as they did during the later ones, indicating that learning had not taken place.

Although subsequent studies by Spencer (1923) and Smith (1933) indicated that improvement in performance could take place *without* KR, a large number of the experiments that were done in the late twenties and thirties supported the generalization that learning was a function of KR. One of the most frequently reported of these studies was performed by Thorndike (1932) who blindfolded subjects and requested them to draw lines three inches long. If the subject was not provided with KR, performance did not improve. On the other hand, if the experimenter provided KR by saying "right" when the line drawn was within one-eighth inch of the three-inch standard and "wrong" when the line deviated by more than this, rapid improvement took place. The extensive work that has been done in this area since these early studies has provided additional evidence that KR is an important motivational variable.

Interest in learning theory has resulted in many contemporary investigators considering KR as a kind of reward or reinforcement, undoubtedly of a secondary variety. There is an obvious similarity between the two since, as indicated earlier, the selective function is common to both. In fact, in many studies with humans, the constructs may be viewed as identical. The verbal response "right" which follows a response, for example, may be viewed not only as reinforcement for the subject; it also carries with it information that the response which has been made is correct. Furthermore an examination of those studies in which KR has been manipulated reveals that frequently the findings that are obtained are quite similar to those that are obtained when reinforcement has been varied. Typically, there is a progressive improvement as a function of trials followed by KR, and there is a deterioration of performance when KR is removed.

Bilodeau and Bilodeau (1958), however, have disagreed with experimenters who have considered KR and reward as equivalent, pointing to a number of differences between them. As they have written (p. 379):

> Reward is typically provided after one of a dichotomy of responses, KR more often varies with the *degree* of response error. . . . In the human skills context, the task is usually one of learning to make graded responses by means of a graded error signal, KR being a quantitative index of how and by how much subsequent behavior should be modified. In the KR study, verbal instructions to S generally define the general problem, limit the response types, and establish the range within which the correct response lies. Absence of KR does not usually signify anything at all. On the other hand, in studies of reward, gradations of response are commonly irrelevant, a common reward being administered for any one of many responses meeting a broadly defined criterion such as, "turning right."

In a subsequent article [Bilodeau and Bilodeau (1961)] they stated (p. 252) that in their examination of the similarities and differences between KR and reinforcement as exemplified by food they "have found sufficient reason to believe that, in almost every case, E's use of reward with his animals differs substantially from his use of KR with human Ss." Finally they point out, "This does not invalidate the work on either side of the fence, but it does mean that there is no special virtue in generalizing theoretical similarities *ad infinitum* in the absence of data obtained under comparable procedures."

As the Bilodeaus have indicated, there is no doubt that there are fundamental differences between the use of primary reinforcers, e.g., food with animals and KR with humans. But perhaps this is only one facet of a more basic difference between animal and human experiments—the contribution of language. If analysis were restricted to humans, however, it would appear that KR may be profitably viewed as a construct under the reinforcement rubric.

THE NATURE OF PUNISHMENT

In examining the varying functions of a motive, it will be recalled that one aspect of the selective function was that if certain stimuli follow the making of a response, the probability of that response being made again will decrease. This function has been frequently attributed to the action of punishment—a topic which now should be considered.[7]

A problem arises in this area because investigators have failed to agree upon a general definition of punishment. For example, some writers have defined punishment merely as the presentation or occurrence of a stimulus *they* consider to be noxious. Thus, the fact that a derogatory verbal statement or an electric shock has been used in an experiment becomes sufficient evidence that punishment is being applied. It is imporant, however, to obtain an independent criterion of the fact that punishment is being used. As a result, some investigators [Solomon (1964)] can be found defining punishment as a noxious stimulus which will support by its termination or omission the growth of new escape or avoidance responses, whereas others [Deese (1958)] have looked upon punishment as noxious stimulation, applied to moderately well or highly motivated behavior, which reduces the probability that such behavior will reoccur. The last two definitions place emphasis upon (1) the termination of the noxious stimulus, utilizing an increased probability of responding as the criterion for the effectiveness of the stimulation, or (2) the onset of stimulation, using as the criterion the decreased probability of responding of a previously occurring response.

This examination of punishment shall be primarily related to situations in which the presentation of a particular stimulus is presumed to weaken or decrease the probability of a response being made.

One of the earliest investigators to examine punishment from this point of view was Thorndike (1913). As contained in his early *Law of Effect,* Thorndike stated that responses which were

[7] The interested reader can refer to Church (1963) and Solomon (1964) for a much more extended presentation.

closely followed by discomfort to the organism will have their connection with the situation weakened so that when the situation recurs, such responses will be less likely to occur. Viewed within an S-R framework, the greater the discomfort, the greater the weakening of the bond. In this formulation, it should be noted, discomfort was defined as a state of affairs which the organism commonly avoids and eventually abandons.

Some 20 years later Thorndike (1932) revised his position. In *The Fundamentals of Learning* he stated, "In the early statements of the *Law of Effect* the influence of satisfying consequences of a connection in the way of strengthening it was paralleled by the influence of annoying consequences in the way of weakening it. . . . I now consider that there is no such complete and exact parallelism." This conclusion that punishment did not weaken an S-R connection was arrived at only after a large number of experiments had presumably indicated the inefficiency of punishment in weakening a stimulus-response relationship.[8]

The following experiment illustrates Thorndike's procedure as well as the reasoning which he used to support his general position. Subjects were presented with 200 rare English words. For each word they had to choose the correct meaning from five alternatives which were provided. The sample below provides an example of the material:

desition: crossing   situation   ending   craving   legal paper
dowlas: bowie   fabric   grief   Indian soldier   howls
edacious: daring   tractable   sober   devouring   polite
eidolon: laziness   benefice   gift   duck   phantom
ern: long ago   foretaste   zeal   merit   eagle

On each trial, the subject chose one of the alternatives and underlined it. If the chosen word was correct, the experimenter rewarded the subject by stating "right"; if the word was wrong, the experimenter "punished" the subject by stating "wrong." Twelve or more repetitions of the series were provided.

In the analysis of results, Thorndike considered cases in which

[8] In a chapter on the influence of rewards and punishments which deals with this topic, ten experiments were reported. In addition to the experiment cited below, other experiments involved a blindfolded subject drawing three-, four-, five-, or six-inch lines; the learning to estimate the area of paper surfaces; the learning to associate some motor response (turn head to the right, pull head back, etc.) with a card having a nonsense figure on it, etc. In all instances, the association of the correct response with the stimulus was followed by the announcement of "right" and the incorrect response was followed by the statement "wrong."

the response was right on the second trial but not on the first and cases where the response was wrong on the second trial but was not the same wrong response that had been given on trial one. The reason for not using cases where the same response had occurred on Trial 1 as on Trial 2 was that Thorndike wished to exclude from the experiment (a) all records with words whose meanings were known to the subject by reason of experiences prior to the experiment and (b) records of words that may have had some strong connection with a particular response, right or wrong. The third trial represented the test trial in which the influence of the announcement of "right" or "wrong" was measured. The results obtained were corrected for the number of right and wrong responses that could be expected on the basis of chance—that is, by subtracting 20 per cent from the obtained number of right responses and 80 per cent from the obtained wrong ones. If hearing "wrong" spoken by the experimenter acted as an immediate consequence to weaken the bond, the response it followed should be weakened as evidenced by a shift to some other response on the next trial. On the other hand, if hearing "right" had a fixative effect, the response it followed should be repeated on the next trial.

Thorndike's analysis revealed that although "right" strengthened the making of a response, "wrong" had little weakening influence. In fact, it was noted that a response gained more in strength from simply occurring than it lost from being followed by the word "wrong." As a result, Thorndike reasoned that an annoying aftereffect had no uniform weakening influence; if there was any effect, its method of action was indirect. That is, the subject was led by the annoying aftereffect to vary his response which then increased the probability of the occurrence of the correct one.

Following these experiments with humans, Thorndike (1932a) carried out a series of discrimination learning experiments with chicks, 13 to 50 days of age, in which incorrect responses were "punished" by confinement to a small nonrewarded goal box. The results from these studies, confirming his earlier finding, resulted in his writing: "The results of all comparisons by all methods tell the same story. Rewarding a connection always strengthened it substantially; punishing it weakened it little or not at all."

A different approach to the problem of punishment has been taken by Skinner (1938), Estes (1944), Dinsmoor (1954, 1955),

Mowrer (1960), and others who have looked upon the punishment situation as a type of avoidance learning and who have postulated that the noxious or punishing stimulus is a negative reinforcer which produces emotionality on the part of the subject.[9]

In an early study illustrating this approach, Skinner (1938) examined the effect of punishment or negative reinforcement upon extinction. Such negative reinforcement was produced by a sharp slap to the foot of a rat when it pressed a lever in a Skinner box.

In one experiment, two groups of four rats were periodically conditioned to press a bar in the Skinner box. The response was then extinguished in both groups for two hours on each of two successive days. In the experimental group, all responses were followed by a slap during the first ten minutes of the first day. An examination of the extinction curves revealed that although the response rate of the experimental group was depressed during the period when the slap was being administered, after the punishment period the response rate rose more rapidly than the response rate of the control animals. By the end of the extinction period, there was no difference between the two groups of animals with regard to the total number of responses made during the two days of extinction. Skinner pointed out that although the punishment resulted in the temporary suppression of a response, all responses that were in the animal's "reserve" eventually emerged without further positive reinforcement. The behavior of the animal, Skinner postulated, was in accord with the assumption that the slap or punishment established an emotional state of such a sort that any behavior associated with feeding was temporarily suppressed and that eventually the lever itself and incipient movements of pressing the lever become conditioned stimuli capable of eliciting the emotional state.

Six years later, Estes (1944) made a much more extensive examination of the influence of punishment. His experimental procedure was similar to Skinner's. Rats were trained first to depress a lever in the Skinner box in which such responses were

[9] It is interesting to note that the Hullian system, undoubtedly the most influential in psychology, did not treat the concept of punishment. Rather, pain or tissue injury was considered as only another primary drive state, the termination of which resulted in reinforcing those responses which immediately preceded it.

reinforced every four minutes. Two or three hours of such periodic reinforcement, sufficiently long to produce a stable rate of responding, were provided followed by extinction trials in which the influence of punishment was examined. Estes, in contrast to Skinner's use of a slap, used shock as his noxious stimulus. Typically, responses were punished during the first extinction period, but during subsequent periods all shock was omitted.

Results from his first study supported the earlier findings of Skinner. The effect of a short period of mild shock produced a temporary depression in rate of responding which was followed later by a compensatory increase in rate, so that the total number of responses to reach the extinction criterion was equal to those which would have been required if no punishment had been administered. In a second study, Estes examined the influence of more severe punishment. Here the immediate effect of punishment was a rapid decrease in the rate of responding until at the end of the first ten minutes of extinction the animal stopped responding. For the next three extinction days, there was some responding on the part of the previously punished animals, but the rate was still markedly depressed. On the fourth extinction day and for the remaining three extinction days, however, responding by the experimental subjects did not differ from that of the controls.

Estes stated that his investigation, although procedurally different from Thorndike's, provided findings which tended to confirm the Thorndikian formulation that punishment does not directly weaken a stimulus-response relationship. Rather, and like Skinner, Estes assumed that any influence that punishment had upon the punished response could be attributed to competing responses aroused by the noxious stimulus. More specifically, he posited that the noxious stimulus produced an emotional state within the organism and that any stimulus which was presented simultaneously with the noxious stimulus became a conditioned stimulus capable of arousing this state on subsequent occasions. (Such conditioned stimuli could be incipient movements of making the to-be-punished response as well as stimuli which were present when the punishment was administered.) Estes (1944) concluded (p. 36), "From the results of the present investigation, we may conclude that a great part of the initial effect of punishment is due to this sort of emotional conditioning."

A further point which Estes has made is that the punished response is not eliminated from the organism's repertoire of responses. It continues to exist at a state of considerable latent strength. Thus, when punishment is discontinued, the withdrawing response that the organism learned to make in the presence of the noxious stimulus is weakened and the original response recovers in strength. While the punished response is being suppressed, it not only is protected from extinction but may also become a source of conflict.[10]

Mowrer (1960) has expressed the position that punishment emerges as a subprinciple of an application of fear conditioning, and he has proposed that punishment be termed passive avoidance learning. (A passive avoidance-learning situation is one in which, in order to avoid a noxious stimulus, the organism learns *not* to make a given response.) The mechanism involved is similar to that indicated by Estes. The response which is followed by punishment produces certain stimuli of both an internal and external variety which, by virtue of their contiguity with punishment, take on the capacity to arouse fear. When the organism starts to repeat such an action, the resulting fear produces a conflict with the motivation underlying the original response. If the fear is sufficiently strong, the original response, as a consequence, will be inhibited or at least in some fashion modified.[11]

[10] It must be noted that the early studies of Masserman (1943), Klee (1944), and Lichtenstein (1950), in contrast to Estes' position, have demonstrated that a response can be continuously inhibited by severe punishment. In Masserman's (1943) study, for example, cats which were feeding in an experimental situation and then subjected either to a blast of air or shock at the moment of feeding inhibited their feeding response for long periods of time despite severe hunger. Similarly, Lichtenstein (1950) observed that dogs which were shocked at the forepaw while eating refused to eat and that this inhibitory state lasted for weeks and sometimes months without further presentation of shock. More recent studies of Storms, Boroczi, and Broen (1962); Appel (1963); and Walters and Rogers (1963), using the free operant situation, have confirmed these findings. Both rats and monkeys have inhibited their bar-pressing responses for food for weeks or months when severe shock has been associated with the bar-pressing response.

[11] In a very interesting series of papers, Dinsmoor (1954, 1955), in what was essentially a reply to the Skinner and Estes position, has rejected the necessity for the postulation of fear in order to better understand punishment. He has pointed out that the effects of punishment can be examined within an avoidance response position and that such effects can be deduced from those principles involved in secondary aversive stimulation and avoidance training. His hypothesis is one which states that the punished response is one member of a series of responses which are linked together by a series of discriminative as well as secondary reinforcing stimuli. Stimuli which come immediately before the punished response are paired by the response itself with the punishment. By virtue of this pairing, such stimuli

In brief, two learning situations (or two processes) are involved. First, there is fear conditioning, and, secondly, the subject learns to make an instrumental response which eliminates or controls the fear.[12]

The primary concern in this section has been to consider punishment only as a type of motivational antecedent, and discussion of the effect of punishment on behavior has been delayed until a subsequent chapter. It should be acknowledged, however, as Solomon's (1964) recent review indicates, that this is a complex topic, with the influence of punishment on behavior being related to a wide variety of conditions.

Although not conceived in the passive avoidance tradition, an examination of the role of punishment in learning would not be complete without calling attention to the work of Muenzinger and his associates who have conducted a long series of studies and who have interpreted their findings as indicating that the pairing of punishment (electric shock) with the correct response does not disrupt but rather facilitates performance. Muenzinger has hypothesized that there is a general sensitizing factor in punishment which serves to slow down the organism and make it more sensitive to those cues which are to be discriminated at the choice point of a maze. It has been suggested that only relatively mild shock may provide such facilitation. It should also be pointed out

---

"gain an aversive property in their own right." Basically, then, his position is that the inhibitory or suppressive reaction of punishment is due to the conditioning of avoidance responses which conflict with the original behavior being punished. Punishing an organism for making a given response results in cues or discriminative stimuli for this response which correspond to warning signals that are typically used in avoidance training studies.

Mowrer (1960) in commenting upon Dinsmoor's position agrees that for some purposes it makes little difference whether one assumes that a danger signal elicits an emotional state which then acts to motivate, and through its reduction rewards behavior, or whether one assumes that the danger signal itself becomes aversive so that its presence is directly motivating and its removal rewarding. On the other hand, he believes that the postulation of the emotional state provides greater flexibility in accounting for more complex situations. Moreover, Mowrer questions the fact that stimuli gain aversive properties in their own right, pointing out that aversiveness is a property of the affected organism and not of the stimulus itself.

[12] Mowrer's general position is that both active and passive avoidance-learning situations can be explained by a common set of principles. The important distinction is related to the characteristics of the stimuli to which the fear gets connected. With passive avoidance (or punishment situations), the stimuli are produced by the behavior for which the subject is being punished. With active avoidance, the fear arousing stimuli are not response-produced; they arise from external sources usually provided by the experimenter.

that the facilitation effect is obtained when the group given shock for making a correct response (shock-right group) is compared with a second group which is not given shock for making an incorrect response (no-shock group). If the shock-right group is compared with a group given shock for making a wrong response (shock-wrong group), the performance of this latter group is almost always superior. Recent work of Muenzinger and his associates has been to examine shock-right group performance as related to whether a correction or noncorrection procedure is utilized, as well as to further examine the sensitizing function of shock. In one study, Muenzinger and Powloski (1951) have found that providing shock for making a right response results in superior performance when the animal is permitted to correct his errors but not when a noncorrection situation is used.

In a second study, Muenzinger, Brown, Crow, and Powloski (1952) hypothesized that shock, although making the animal more sensitive to the cues to be discriminated, also produced a tendency in the animal to avoid the alley in which it had been shocked. As a result, they posited that if it should be possible to train an animal to adapt itself to this avoidance effect, it might then exhibit the sensitizing effect more clearly. In an effort to test this hypothesis, three groups— (1) no-shock, (2) shock-wrong, (3) shock-right—were used with three different training procedures. The first was no pre-training, the second was pre-training with shock, and the third was pre-training without shock. Following training in which rats were given 120 trials on a runway and where appropriate received shock on 55 of these, the animals were subsequently trained by the noncorrective method to learn a black-white discrimination. Although significant differences between the shock-wrong and shock-right groups were present in the no-pre-training and pre-training without shock, there were no differences between these groups when pre-training was given with shock. Thus, the investigators pointed out that if the tendency to avoid shock is overcome prior to training in the discrimination situation the accelerating function will manifest itself unequivocally.[13]

---

[13] Muenzinger's conclusions have not been universally accepted. For one thing, conclusions based upon "no difference findings" are tenuous. Moreover, the non-correction procedure that Muenzinger has typically used varies from that used by most other investigators. His procedure is one in which if the animal makes an incorrect choice it continues to the goal box where it is detained, but it is then per-

THE ROLE OF INCENTIVES

This examination of the varying motivational determinants, at least as they have been related to a motive's functions, has been concerned primarily with the energizing and selective functions. But some writers have posited that motivational constructs may also have an incentive function.

Two definitions of an incentive can be delineated. First, stimuli which increase or decrease the probability of a response being made have been classified as incentives, positive or negative depending upon the direction of the change in probability. This definition equates an incentive with reward or punishment and incorporates the selective function. Second, incentives have been also defined as goal objects, which when perceived or anticipated direct behavior toward or away from them. This position that behavior is directed by the anticipation of goal objects corresponds probably to what many individuals regard as a motive's basic function.

This latter function has been only recently gaining acceptance.[14] It was not included in the Hullian system, since Hull (1943) considered an incentive as only "that substance or commodity in the environment which satisfied a need, i.e., which reduced the drive."

Not all psychologists, however, have adopted the Hullian

---

mitted to enter the starting box from which it again moves to the choice point. The subject may make any number of incorrect responses, with each incorrect response being followed by the animal's moving into the starting box and proceeding to the choice point; each trial continues until the subject makes a correct response and receives reinforcement. It is only at this time that the appropriate discriminative stimulus may be changed. The result is that the typical trials to criterion measure cannot be used with Muenzinger's results; rather, the dependent variable may be the number of reinforcements required to reach the criterion or incorrect responses made prior to reaching the criterion.

Muenzinger's findings have also been questioned by the different results obtained by Wischner (1947) and Wischner, Fowler, and Kushnick (1963).

[14] Hilgard (1956) in discussing this point of view has written (p. 428), ". . . this rather primitive nature of goal-experiences was largely lost sight of in the theorizing of the last decade or two. To be sure, it could not be ignored entirely, but striving and goal-seeking had to be derived from more primitive principles before the familiar facts could be recognized as valid. The circumstances that led away from attributing positive qualities to incentives probably arose historically through the turn toward objectivity and away from conceptions that appeared tainted with animism or teleology."

position. McClelland (1951) has defined a motive as "a strong affective association, characterized by an anticipatory goal reaction and based on past association of certain cues with pleasure or pain," and both Tolman (1955) and Woodworth (1958) have also acknowledged the role of anticipation of rewards or punishment as basic features of a motive. Similarly, Mowrer (1960), in his revised two-factor theory, has placed emphasis upon the role of the attractiveness or unattractiveness of goal objects. The constructs of hope and fear—emotional states based upon anticipated events—are fundamental in his theorizing.

Spence (1956), working within the Hullian system, has conceptualized the role of incentives somewhat differently. The contribution of an incentive variable, designated as K, is posited to act as a drive in much the same way that deprivation states have drive characteristics. The mechanism which Spence has speculated to underlie K is the fractional anticipatory goal response. When a hungry rat learns a T-maze, for example, Spence assumes that stimulus cues in the goal box and from the alley just outside the goal box become conditioned to the goal response, Rg (eating). Through stimulus generalization, the stimulus cues at earlier points in the runway are also assumed to acquire the capacity to elicit Rg or at least noncompetitional components of Rg that can occur without the actual presence of food (e.g., salivation, etc.). These fractional conditioned responses have been designated as r_g, and it is hypothesized that they move forward to the beginning of the instrumental response sequence. Since the fractional anticipatory goal responses produce interoceptive stimuli (s_g), they also become a part of the stimulus complex in the alley and thus become conditioned to the instrumental locomotor responses.

The motivational aspect of the r_g-s_g mechanism has been related not to the posited directive function but, rather, to an energizing function. Spence has suggested that conflict might take place when the tendency for the r_g to occur at an early point in the response sequence is opposed by tendencies to make other responses and that this conflict generates tension which increases the existing level of drive and thus adds to the energizing function.

Since the basic mechanism which underlies K is the classical conditioned Rg, a number of assumptions can be made which are related to the variables that determine K's strength. For example, Rg should vary with the number of conditioning trials provided in the goal box; in fact, any property of a goal object which produces unconditioned consummatory responses of different intensities or vigor will presumably determine the value of K.[15]

Apart from the different theoretical conceptualizations of how incentives contribute to behavior, a number of additional experimental studies in this area have been reported.

In an early study, Tinklepaugh (1928) placed food under one of two stimulus objects while his subjects (monkeys) were looking but were prevented from immediate access to the objects and food. In one part of this delayed response experiment, after the monkey had observed a piece of banana being hidden, the experimenter, unbeknown to the subject, substituted for it a lettuce leaf—a less preferable foodstuff. The monkey, after displacing the object, did not accept the lettuce but engaged in searching behavior, presumably looking for the banana. Similarly, studies by Nissen and Elder (1935) and Cowles and Nissen (1937) revealed that a chimpanzee's performance in a delayed response situation was strongly influenced by the size of the goal object which had been received on preceding trials. The previously experienced consequence (reception and ingestion) of seeing small and large incentives placed in the delayed response container was demonstrated to be an important variable in determining the accuracy of the response. Such a factor was acknowledged to be "the expectancy value of the incentive" [Cowles and Nissen (1937)].

A few years later, Crespi (1942) had rats run to a goal box which contained either 16, 64, or 256 pellets of food. He noted that the 64- and 256-pellet groups were considerably more excited than the 16-pellet group when brought to the starting box and, as a result, posited that with varying incentive amounts there arises among groups of animals varying amounts of anticipatory tension, excitement, or eagerness at the prospect of their acquisition. It is this variable, he posited, which accounted for the differences he found among groups in their runway performance.

More recent experimental support for an incentive function can be found in some of the studies of Marx and his associates

[15] Several fundamental differences between the point of view expressed by Spence (1956) and McClelland, Tolman, etc. can be noted. Spence prefers to deal with behavioral mediators, i.e., fractional anticipatory goal responses, rather than cognitive ones, i.e., anticipations or expectancies. Second, Spence has hypothesized that the role of the incentive makes its contribution to behavior via the energizing function rather than a directive one.

[Marx (1958), Marx (1960), Marx and Murphy (1961)]. In the Marx and Murphy (1961) study, rats were trained to make an instrumental response (poking their head into a small compartment) in order to secure food. A discriminative cue (buzzer) was paired with the presentation of food pellets for the experimental animals. Control subjects also received buzzer and food but not temporally contiguous. Ninety trials were given over a three-day period in which the experimental subjects were required to make the learned response to the buzzer (poking head into compartment) on at least 20 of the final 30 trials. The animals were then trained to run down a runway and obtain food in the goal box. Following 20 training trials, the subjects were given massed extinction trials in which the buzzer or discriminative stimulus was introduced on the sixteenth trial and presented on every fifth trial thereafter. The buzzer was sounded just after the subject was placed in the start box. When the start door was raised, the buzzer stopped. Results revealed that the experimental group took significantly longer to extinguish than the controls (118.25 trials vs. 95.75), although latencies and running speeds for the first 15 extinction trials were similar. The effect of the buzzer was examined by comparing the first seven buzzer presentation trials with the seven trials immediately preceding these and on which, of course, the buzzer was not presented. Figure 5–10 provides the appropriate comparisons. These findings clearly indicate the facilitating effect of the buzzer as an initiating or eliciting stimulus although its training role was that of a secondary reinforcer. As Marx and Murphy have written, the extent to which secondary reinforcers generally can be shown to operate through such motivational properties—and thus perhaps should more properly be called secondary motivators—is an interesting and important development.

A somewhat similar outcome has been reported by Longstreth (1962) working with children. Pre-school children were given preliminary training in which candy was associated with the presentation of a red light and no candy followed the presentation of a blue light. Following such an incentive experience, the subjects were given test trials. When a light was activated, they were instructed to run down a 12-foot runway in order to push a response button. Results revealed faster running to the red light (the stimulus which was associated with reward during the incentive experience phase of training), but there was a decre-

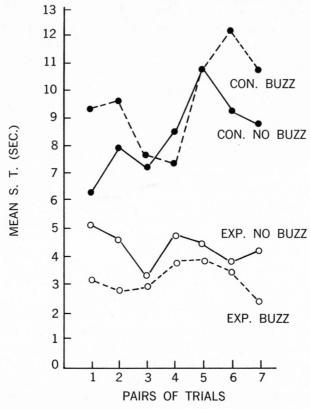

Fig. 5–10. Mean starting times for buzzer and no-buzzer conditions on seven critical pairs of trials in extinction. *Adapted from Marx and Murphy (1961)*

ment in response speed to the blue. These findings clearly indicated that the stimulus associated with the incentive, and independent of the instrumental response, produced reliably faster speeds during test trials.

6

The Contribution of Motivational
Variables to Learning I:

The Role of Need States

ALTHOUGH, AS NOTED in the two previous chapters, different points of view have been expressed regarding the definition, function, and operation of motivational constructs, there has been a general acceptance of the position that needs and rewards play important roles in the learning process. In this chapter the contribution that need states make to learning will be examined, and in Chapter 7, the contribution of rewards will be considered.

The need states most often examined have been those which involve food or water deprivation. The presentation of noxious stimuli in the experimental situation has been also subsumed under need states—the need to avoid tissue injury. There are, however, some fundamental differences in the operations of those need states involving food or water deprivation and the need to avoid tissue injury.

First, the amount of reinforcement that is provided on any single learning trial rarely reduces substantially the need for food or water, but when a noxious stimulus is used to motivate the organism, an appropriate response typically brings complete and immediate pain reduction. Secondly, the food or water deprivation state which is assumed to energize the organism can be differentiated from the reinforcement which is related to the selective function. Thus, as in the case of experimental extinction, it is possible to manipulate one (deprivation) without influencing the other. On the other hand, the energizing function which is related to the onset of the noxious stimulus is intimately tied to the selective function which is occasioned by the cessation of such stimulation. Unlike food or water deprivation states, the energizing function cannot be manipulated without also influencing the selective function.[1]

THE RELATIONSHIP BETWEEN NEED INTENSITY AND RESPONSE ACQUISITION

What is the relationship between the intensity of an organism's need and the acquisition of a learned response? A frequent approach to this problem has been the experimental manipulation of the level of the need state, followed by an examination of the organism's performance in the learning task.

Classical Conditioning

In many classical conditioning studies, the need state has been the avoidance of tissue injury and its manipulation has been through the use of a UCS taking the form of electric shock or an air puff to the cornea of the eye. The experimental findings reported by Passey (1948); Spence and Taylor (1951); Runquist, Spence, and Stubbs (1958); Prokasy, Grant, and Myers (1958); Ross and Spence (1960); Gormezano and Moore (1962); and Beck (1963) have revealed that when the intensity of the UCS is increased the frequency of responding also increases.[2] In the early

---

[1] This is true for most learning situations employing noxious stimuli, although it may be possible to use special procedures to separate the two functions. For example, in a study by Spence, Haggard, and Ross (1958) a classical conditioning situation was employed, with the intensity of the UCS being manipulated as the independent variable. One group of subjects received a strong puff of air as the UCS, but a second group received a weak puff. Interspersed among the conditioning trials was an equal number of trials with the UCS alone. The group conditioned with the strong puff of air received solitary trials with a weak puff whereas the group conditioned with the weak puff received solitary trials with a strong puff. It was assumed that this procedure equated (on the average) the drive level, or energizing function arising from noxious UCS, although the amount of reinforcement or drive reduction arising from the termination of the puff and available to strengthen the CS-CR relationship was not fixed.

[2] The experiments using noxious stimuli are considered to reflect the operation of varying a need or drive state, although, as pointed out earlier, the amount of reinforcement arising from their cessation also varies.

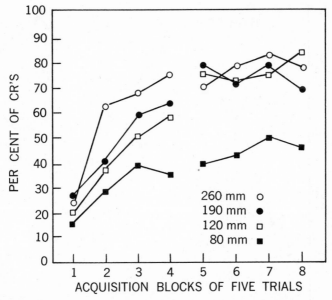

Fig. 6–1. Percentage frequency of CR's during acquisition with UCS intensity as the parameter. *Adapted from Prokasy, Grant, and Myers (1958)*

Passey study (1948), four experimental groups consisting of ten subjects per group were conditioned to blink to a tone in which the UCS was a puff of air to the cornea. Air puffs of 7.5, 18, 44, and 88 pounds per square inch were used. When the mean numbers of conditioned responses were plotted, results revealed a negatively accelerated function between the number of such responses and the intensity of the UCS. In general, weak puffs of air produced fewer CR's than did strong puffs, although an examination of Passey's data revealed an inversion between the groups given the 44- and 88-pound puffs. The 44-pound group was clearly superior to all others throughout the entire course of conditioning. Prokasy, Grant, and Myers (1958), also examining the conditioned eyeblink response, manipulated UCS intensity by regulating the amount of fall of a column of mercury—50, 120, 190, or 260 mm. —which in turn controlled the intensity of an air puff. A light served as the CS. Twenty acquisition trials were provided on Day 1, followed on Day 2 by 20 more acquisition trials and then 20 extinction trials. As Figure 6–1 reveals, the percentage of condi-

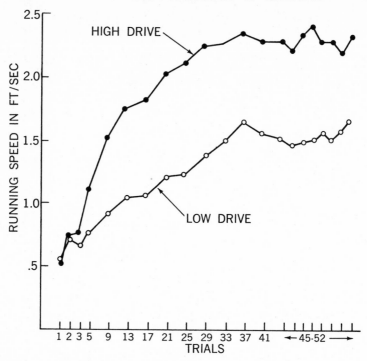

Fig. 6–2. Comparison of acquisition trials under different drive strengths. *Adapted from Barry (1958)*

tioned responses was a function of the intensity of the UCS on Day 1, although differences among the three strongest groups on Day 2 were small.

Instrumental Conditioning

In the simple instrumental reward learning situation using rate of response as the dependent variable, the experimental evidence is essentially unequivocal and follows that found with classical conditioning. Almost all of the studies which have been done support the position that performance, as measured by rate of responding, improves as a function of the intensity or amount of the need state. Table 6–1 provides a summary of many of these experiments. An example of the general findings in this area is an experiment by Barry (1958) who examined the running speed of rats which had been placed under 2.5 hours (low need) or 26.5 hours (high need) of food deprivation. Figure 6–2 reveals the

TABLE 6–1

The Role of Intensity of Motivation on Rate of Responding during Acquisition Trials

SOURCE OF MOTIVATION	INTENSITY	TASK	RESPONSE MEASURE	ORGANISM	INFLUENCE OF INTENSITY ON RESPONSE MEASURE	INVESTIGATOR
Food depriv.	12, 24, 48 hours	multiple T-maze	running time	rat	positive	MacDuff (1946)
Water depriv.	12, 35, 36 hours	runway	running time	rat	positive	O'Kelley and Heyer (1948)
Food depriv.	16, 20 hours	runway	running time	rat	positive	Campbell and Kraeling (1954)
Water temp.	15, 30 deg.	multiple T-maze	swimming time	rat	positive	Braun, Wedekind, and Smudski (1957)
Food depriv.	run 24 hours after fed 3 grams or 12 grams	type of Skinner Box	latency of door raising	rat	negative	Reynolds (1949)
Food depriv.	0, 1, 2, 8, 15, 24 hours	guillotine feeding apparatus	latency of pushing door	rat	positive	Kimble (1951)
Food depriv.	0, .5, 1, 2, 23 hours	guillotine feeding apparatus	latency of pushing door	rat	positive	Horenstein (1951)
Food depriv.	0, 6, 16, 22 hours	runway	running time	rat	positive	Cotton (1953)
Food depriv.	15, 22, 25, 37 hours	runway	running time	rat	time is a function of deprivation up to 25 hours, then decreases with deprivation increases	Birch, Burnstein, and Clark (1958)
Food depriv.	2.5, 26.5 hours	runway	running time	rat	positive	Barry (1958)
Air depriv.	0, 3, 6, 9, 12, 18 seconds	Y-maze	swimming time	rat	negative	Denenberg and Karas (1960)
Food depriv.	1, 5, 22 hours	T-maze	running time	rat	positive	Jensen (1960)
Food depriv.	3, 22, 44 hours	runway	running time	rat	positive	Reynolds and Pavlik (1960)
Food depriv.	2, 22 hours	runway	running time	rat	positive	Lewis and Cotton (1960)
Food depriv.	1, 22 hours	type of Skinner Box	rate of bar pressing	rat	positive	Batten and Shoemaker (1961)
Water depriv.	4, 44 hours	Y-maze delayed alternation	running time	rat	positive	Lachman (1961)
Food depriv.	2, 26, 50 hours		latency	monkey	negative	Gross (1963)
Food depriv.	2, 26, 50 hours	delayed response	latency	monkey	positive	Gross (1963)

animals' running speed as a function of their need for food. When a more complex task is used, similar findings have been obtained. Hillman, Hunter, and Kimble (1953) placed rats under two or 22 hours of water deprivation and measured their speed of running a ten-unit multiple T-maze. They found that the 22-hour deprived group traversed the maze significantly more rapidly than the two-hour deprived group.

When instrumental escape learning situations in which shock is used as the source of motivation are examined, rate of response measures continue to reveal a positive relationship between intensity and performance. Amsel (1950), Campbell and Kraeling (1953), and Trapold and Fowler (1960) have all demonstrated that speed of running is related to the intensity of the shock. Amsel (1950) found that speed of locomotion in a runway was a function of shock intensity—rats given a high intensity shock ran significantly more rapidly than those given low intensity. In the Trapold and Fowler (1960) study, five groups of rats were trained to escape shocks of either 120, 160, 240, 320, or 400 volts by running to an uncharged goal box. Twenty massed trials were provided to all subjects. The results, revealed in Figure 6–3, indicate that running speed was a negatively accelerated function of the intensity of the shock which was used; starting speed, on the other hand, first increased and then decreased with increasing shock intensity.[3]

Finally, the positive findings obtained in the instrumental escape runway situation have been extended to the free operant. Boren, Sidman, and Herrnstein (1959) have shown that the latency of a bar-pressing response which must be made to terminate shock in a Skinner box is related to the intensity of the shock which is given.

In an interesting study which examined the mechanism underlying the differential response rate taking place as a result of differing levels of need, Cotton (1953) measured the rat's actual

---

[3] These findings do not confirm those of Campbell and Kraeling (1953). In this study, groups of animals were trained to run from a starting box to a goal box in order to escape shock which varied in intensity (200, 300, or 400 volts). Although large and significant differences appeared early in the acquisition series, after 10 to 12 trials such differences became smaller and nonsignificant, with all groups reaching the same asymptote. As Trapold and Fowler (1960) have pointed out, Campbell and Kraeling included both starting and running speed within the same running speed measure, which might have contributed to the lack of differences obtained at the end of training.

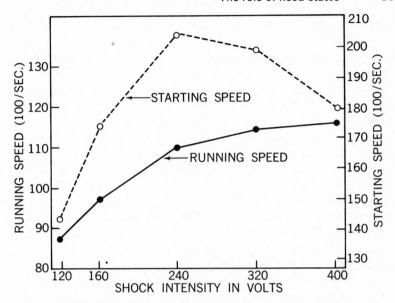

Fig. 6–3. Mean performance over the last eight trials as a function of shock intensity. *Adapted from Trapold and Fowler (1960)*

running as well as competing responses which were made on a straight runway. He found that animals under low deprivation states made many responses extraneous to running which competed with the basic running response. If the time required to make these competing responses was subtracted from over-all running time, findings revealed that the influence of the intensity of the need state on running time was virtually nonexistent. On the other hand, Cicala's (1961) results have not been in keeping with Cotton's early findings. Cicala found that even when competing response trials are removed from the data running speed varies as a function of the deprivation state. Support for Cicala's findings has come most recently from Kintsch (1962) who observed the lack of competing responses in rats running an alley-maze and yet found differences in running time taking place as a function of varying deprivation states.

It will be recalled that avoidance learning can be divided into passive and active avoidance learning situations. The findings of most investigators using the passive avoidance situation are in accord with results obtained in the instrumental reward and escape situations. In a study by Annau and Kamin (1961) rats were given ten hours of bar-press training under a two and one-half-minute variable interval (VI) food reinforcement schedule. Following such training, ten daily two-hour bar-pressing sessions were provided with the same VI schedule maintained. Four CS-UCS pairings were introduced into each session. The CS was white noise presented for three minutes followed by a five-tenths second delivery of one of five intensities of shock (.28, .49, .85, 1.55, 2.91 ma.) which served as the UCS. The decrement in the rate of the bar-pressing response for food during the ten daily sessions was found to be a function of the intensity of the shock which was used.[4,5] A subsequent study by Appel (1963), also using a bar-pressing response for food and providing varying intensities of shock (.1, .2, .3, .4, .5, .6, .7, or .8 ma.) to suppress this response, has confirmed Annau and Kamin's findings—the degree of suppression was a function of the intensity of shock.

There is some question, however, as to whether these findings can be unequivocally generalized to the active avoidance learning situation. In a study by Kimble (1955), rats were trained to turn a wheel within a five-second interval in order to avoid shock. A buzzer served as the CS, and one of four intensities of shock (.2, .5, 1.0, or 2.0 ma.) was used as the UCS. Latency was the response measure used. Results, as Figure 6–4 indicates, produced a curvilinear relationship in which latency decreased as a function of shock intensity.[6]

Boren, Sidman, and Herrnstein (1959) using the free operant situation have also reported positive findings between the rate of avoidance responding and the intensity of shock used.

In contrast to these findings, Brush (1957) has been unable to

----

[4] The response measure in experimental situations such as these is frequently termed *conditioned suppression*. In this situation, the bar-pressing decrement was measured by using a suppression ratio, defined as the ratio between the number of responses made during the presentation of the CS of three minutes duration and the number of responses made during the three minutes immediately preceding presentation of the CS.

[5] Responses obtained in the free operant situation are related to both rate and probability measures. They are arbitrarily considered to be a rate of responding measure.

[6] A careful examination of this figure reveals that the relationship is primarily a function of the performance of the .2 ma. group—little difference is evident among the groups shocked with the other three intensities. The mean response latency for the .2 ma. group is approximately nine seconds; since this is longer than the five-second CS-UCS interval which was used, it means that many of the responses which were made for this group were of the escape rather than avoidance variety.

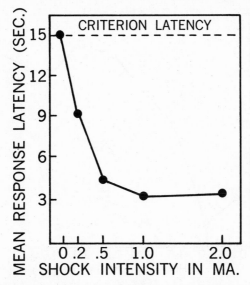

Fig. 6–4. Response latency as a function of shock intensity. *Adapted from Kimble (1955)*

obtain an intensity effect on the acquisition of an avoidance response in dogs, also as measured by latency of responding. Dogs were trained to jump a hurdle in a modified Mowrer-Miller shuttle box in which the UCS was one of five intensities of shock (.70, 2.06, 3.20, 4.82, or 5.59 ma.). The CS was a raising of the gate between the boxes and the extinguishing of a light. Brush reported that variations in shock intensity had no influence on the latency of the response.

Finally, Moyer and Korn (1964), also using the shuttle-box situation, gave rats 30 trials a day for four days. Varying groups of subjects received either .5, 1.0, 1.5, 2.5, 3.0, 3.5, or 4.5 ma. of shock during training. The termination of a light as well as the onset of a tone served as the CS. Results, contrary to the findings of both Kimble (1955) and Brush (1957), indicated that increasing the intensity of the shock interfered with the acquisition of the avoidance response. The mean latencies of avoidance responses for all groups as a function of the shock level employed are presented in Figure 6–5.

The differences in the experimental findings which have been reviewed cannot be reconciled easily. It would appear that the

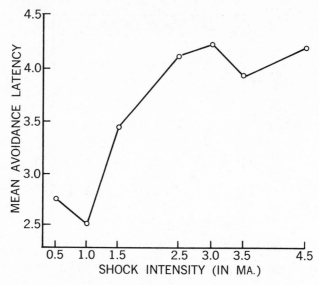

Fig. 6–5. Mean latency times for the varying groups as a function of shock level. *Adapted from Moyer and Korn (1964)*

contribution of the kind of response which is used and the CS-UCS interval, as well as other procedural variables, must be investigated before any definite conclusions can be drawn regarding the role of the intensity of the noxious stimulus in the active avoidance learning situation.

When probability of response measures are used, as indicated by the number of errors, or frequency of correct response, it is difficult to provide any general statement regarding the relationship between level of need and performance in the instrumental reward situation. (See Table 6–2.)

An early study by Dodson (1917) revealed that rats which were deprived of food for 41 hours learned a visual discrimination habit more rapidly than animals deprived for 24, 31, or 48 hours. Studies by Tolman and Honzik (1930) and MacDuff (1946) using multiple T-mazes also demonstrated that performance as measured by probability of response was related to the intensity of need. In the MacDuff study, for example, rats were placed on 12, 24, or 48 hours of food deprivation and given one trial per week on a 16-unit multiple T-maze (Experiment I). She found that the 12-hour group took the largest number of trials (and made the most errors) to reach a criterion of one errorless trial;

TABLE 6–2

The Role of Intensity of Motivation on Probability of Responding during Acquisition Trials

SOURCE OF MOTIVATION	INTENSITY	TASK	RESPONSE MEASURE	ORGANISM	INFLUENCE OF INTENSITY ON RESPONSE MEASURE	INVESTIGATOR
Food depriv.	2, 6, 12, 24, 36, 48 hours	problem solving	correct solution	chimp.	intermediate depriv. condition best	Birch (1945)
Food depriv.	12, 24, 48 hours	multiple T-maze	errors	rats	positive	MacDuff (1946)
Food depriv.	12, 24, 48 hours	multiple T-maze	errors	rats	negative	MacDuff (1946)
Food depriv.	1, 23, 47 hours	discrimination reversal	errors	monkeys	negative	Meyer (1951)
Food depriv.	1, 7, 15, 22 hours	T-maze	errors	rats	negative	Teel (1952)
Water depriv.	2, 22 hours	multiple T-maze	errors	rats	negative	Hillman, Hunter, and Kimble (1953)
Water depriv.	1.5, 20.5 hours	T-maze	correct responses	rats	positive	Buchwald and Yamaguchi (1955)
Food depriv.	4, 22, 46 hours	discrimination	errors	rats	positive	Eisman, Asimow, and Maltzman (1956)
Food depriv.	1, 23 hours	discrimination	errors	monkeys	negative	Warren and Hall (1956)
Food depriv.	3.5, 21.5 hours	T-maze	errors	rats	negative	Armus (1958)
Food depriv.	1, 5, 20 hours	discrimination	correct responses	monkeys	negative	Miles (1959)
Food depriv.	1, 5, 22 hours	T-maze	correct responses	rats	1 hour group best; 5 hour group poorest	Jensen (1960)
Water depriv.	4, 44 hours	Y-maze	correct responses	rats	negative	Lachman (1961)
Food depriv.	0, 2, 4, 6 hours	delayed response	correct responses	gibbons	positive or negative depending upon type of food	Berkson (1962)
Food depriv.	0, 26, 50 hours	delayed resp. and delayed alternation	correct responses	monkeys	positive	Gross (1963)

the 48-hour group required the smallest number of trials. More recently, Buchwald and Yamaguchi (1955) had rats learn a position habit in a T-maze in which the animals were under either 1.5 or 20.5 hours of water deprivation. Results revealed that the high deprivation animals learned significantly more rapidly than animals placed under low deprivation. Similar findings have been obtained by Eisman, Asimow, and Maltzman (1956) who had rats learn a black-white discrimination problem under either 4, 22, or 46 (actually 45.5) hours of food deprivation. The rats were given six trials per day to a criterion of learning set at 14 correct responses in 16 trials. Findings indicated that the 46-hour group made least errors. The difference between the 4- and 22-hour deprivation groups was not significant.

In contrast to these positive findings, the studies of MacDuff (1946); Hillman, Hunter, and Kimble (1953); and Lachman (1961), using rats as experimental subjects, have provided negative results. MacDuff (1946) placed rats on 12, 24, or 48 hours of food deprivation and had them learn a 16-unit multiple T-maze (Experiment II). No performance differences among these groups were found when a learning criterion of one errorless trial was used. Similarly, Hillman, Hunter, and Kimble (1953) placed rats on two or 22 hours of water deprivation and had them learn a ten-unit multiple T-maze. Although they obtained differences between groups in running speed, they were unable to obtain differences between groups when the number of errors was used as a measure of performance. As the investigators stated, "There is, in short, no evidence that the number of errors is related to strength of motivation at *any* point in learning."

A more recent experiment by Lachman (1961) has supported this conclusion. After examining the learning of a brightness discrimination situation for groups of rats placed on either high or low drive states (water deprivation), Lachman concluded that "drive level produced a highly significant effect upon locomotion while at the same time producing no observable influence upon choice behavior."

Studies by Meyer (1951), Warren and Hall (1956), and Miles (1959) in which monkeys were used as subjects have also been unable to demonstrate any relationship between the amount of need as measured by hours of deprivation and the learning of discrimination problems. In Miles' (1959) study, naïve monkeys were placed under either 1, 5, or 20 hours of food deprivation and

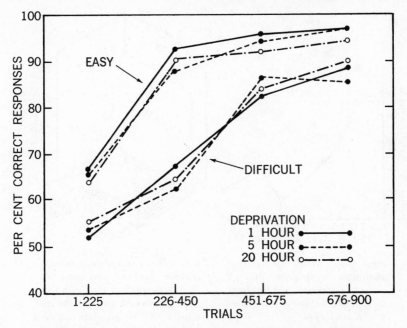

Fig. 6–6. Mean percentage of correct responses as a function of trials and deprivation conditions. *Adapted from Miles (1959)*

given easy or difficult discrimination problems. As Figure 6–6 indicates, there are no differences in performance as a function of hours of deprivation, although there are performance differences between the easy and difficult task.

The more recent studies of Berkson (1962) and Gross (1963) have indicated, however, that deprivation states can influence primate learning. Berkson (1962) using gibbons as his experimental subjects, in two separate experiments, found that food deprivation of zero, two, four, or six hours did not result in increasing the number of correct responses in a delayed response experiment. In a third experiment, however, Berkson did demonstrate that varying deprivation times were not effective conditions when preferred foods were used as rewards but were effective when nonpreferred foods (celery) were used. Gross (1963) employing monkeys which were deprived of food for either 2, 26, or 50 hours as subjects also has demonstrated the influence of deprivation states on both delayed response and delayed alternation problems when the percentage of correct responses was used

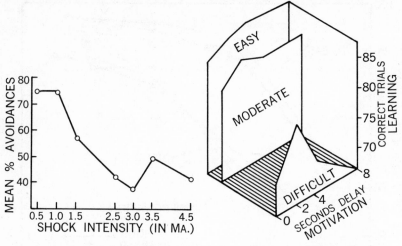

Fig. 6–7. Mean percentage avoidance responses for all groups as a function of intensity of shock. *Adapted from Moyer and Korn (1964)*

Fig. 6–8. A three-dimensional surface showing the relationship between learning in a discrimination task and (a) the intensity of the air deprivation and (b) the level of difficulty of the task. *Adapted from Broadhurst (1957)*

as the performance measure. These findings suggest that the length of the deprivation period as well as the characteristics of the reward must be taken into consideration in attempting to derive generalizations about the role of the deprivation state.

Finally, the study by Moyer and Korn (1964) which was mentioned previously is puzzling since these investigators have shown that the probability of responding in an active avoidance learning situation is inversely related to the intensity of the shock which is used. Moyer and Korn have found that the greatest probability of avoidance responding takes place when a relatively light shock (.5 or 1.0 ma.) is used. As shock intensity is increased, the mean percentage of avoidance responses declines. (See Figure 6–7.)

Need Intensity and Task Difficulty

In the experimental studies just examined, different tasks have been used; some of these have been quite simple, e.g., traversing

TABLE 6–3

Breakdown of Learning Scores

DIFFICULTY OF DISCRIMINATION

MOTIVATION LEVEL (AIR DEPRIVATION)	EASY MEAN	MODERATE MEAN	DIFFICULT MEAN
0 sec.	84.8	81.3	71.1
2 sec.	86.4	84.7	79.5
4 sec.	87.7	83.0	71.6
8 sec.	86.8	83.2	66.1
All	86.4	83.1	72.1

(Adapted from Broadhurst, 1957)

a runway, but others have been more complex. Some investigators have examined the relationship between the intensity of a need and the difficulty of the task. The reference experiment is one by Yerkes and Dodson (1908) who used mice as experimental subjects and employed a visual discrimination task involving three degrees of difficulty. Three different intensities of shock served as the motivation. Results revealed that with the easy discrimination problem correct responses increased as a function of the strength of the shock. With the medium and difficult discrimination tasks, however, increases in the intensity of the shock resulted in first increasing but then decreasing the number of correct responses. These findings, which provided the basis for what has been known as the Yerkes-Dodson Law, indicated an optimum intensity of shock for a specific degree of task difficulty. The more recent studies of Hammes (1956) and Broadhurst (1957) have provided confirmation of the earlier findings. In the Broadhurst study, need intensity was manipulated by delaying the rat for either zero, two, four, or eight seconds underwater, with three levels of difficulty of an underwater brightness discrimination task being used. As Figure 6–8 reveals, increases in the intensity of air deprivation resulted in increasing performance on the easy task; on the other hand, slight increases in air deprivation resulted in an increase in performance for the difficult task, but as the deprivation period was further increased, inferior performance was obtained. Table 6–3 provides a breakdown of these learning scores.

Spence has used Hullian theory to predict the relationship between need intensity and task difficulty. Briefly, he has hypothesized that in learning situations in which the organism has but a single response tendency, or where correct response tendencies predominate over incorrect ones (an easy task), an increase in the organism's need will result in the facilitation of performance. On the other hand, if incorrect response tendencies predominate over correct ones, thus providing a difficult task, an increase in an organism's need state will result in a performance decrement. This general hypothesis was derived from a basic Hullian assumption that the need or drive state multiplies the strengths of all response tendencies, correct as well as incorrect. Thus, increasing an organism's need results in increasing the amount by which the excitatory strength of one response tendency exceeds the strength of the other.

Spence's early formulation suggested that (1) easy tasks should be learned as a function of the intensity of the need or drive state and (2) difficult tasks should be learned most rapidly by subjects under a low drive. In later discussions, Spence (1958) pointed out that with difficult tasks low drive groups should be superior to those under high drive during only the early stages of training, following which performance of the high drive group should eventually reach and then overtake the performance of the low drive group. Such a postulation means that the performance curves for the two groups should be expected to cross sometime during the acquisition series.

An examination of the research that has been done in this area over the last decade reveals that a number of techniques have been utilized in order to manipulate motivational strength and a variety of tasks have been employed. The manifest anxiety scale (MAS) has been used most frequently as a technique for examining emotional responsiveness from which motivational level has been inferred. This measure has been derived from a subject's responses as expressed on a scale of items obtained from the Minnesota Multiphasic Personality Inventory. Classical conditioning situations frequently have served as the easy tasks, and trial and error or problem solving situations have been utilized as the difficult.

Spence (1958) recently has indicated that the type of situation most appropriate to investigate the relationship between need intensity and type of task is the paired-associate learning situation.

Since this task consists of forming a number of more or less iso-lated stimulus-response relationships, it is possible to manipulate these units so that competition among them can either be mini-mized or maximized. Little competition among units typically produces an easy task, but greater competition among units re-sults in a more difficult learning situation.

Table 6–4 summarizes a number of the experimental studies which have been based upon Spence's theoretical analysis, and it will be noted that most of the findings agree with his hypothesis. There is a sufficient number of divergent findings, however, to raise some question about the nature of the variables which contribute to these results. Spence (1964), in a recent evaluation of findings which have been obtained using the classical con-ditioned eyelid response, has pointed out that the studies which have supported his hypothesis have used relatively large numbers of subjects whereas those which have not supported his position have used fewer subjects. Moreover, he has indicated that the ex-perimental conditions of the nonsupporting studies did not appear to be as emotion-arousing as those found in the studies which have yielded positive findings. In addition, some experi-menters failed to remove voluntary responders.

In summary, Spence has called attention to a number of conditions which experimenters must employ if positive findings in this area are to be obtained. Whether or not he is correct can be answered only by experimentation.

THE ROLE OF IRRELEVANT NEEDS

The basic question considered in this section is: Do needs which are irrelevant play any role in learning? Interest in this area has stemmed primarily from the Hullian position that irrelevant needs which are present in the organism combine with those which are relevant to increase the subject's motivational level. The distinction between relevant and irrelevant needs is related to the nature of the reward secured by the organism in the experimental situation. A need which is not satisfied by the goal object found in the learning situation would be classified as irrelevant.

In order to understand more fully the experimental findings obtained in this area, these studies will be divided into those

TABLE 6-4

A Summary of a Number of Studies Examining the Relationship between Drive Level and Learning

TYPE OF MOTIVATION	TYPE OF TASK	RESULTS	INVESTIGATOR
Taylor Manifest Anxiety Scale	Eyelid conditioning	High anxious group conditioned more rapidly than low anxious group	Taylor (1951)
Taylor Manifest Anxiety Scale	Eyelid conditioning	High anxious group conditioned more rapidly than low anxious group	Spence and Farber (1953)
Taylor Manifest Anxiety Scale	Differential eyelid conditioning	High anxious group exhibited more CR's to positive stimulus than low anxious group	Spence and Farber (1954)
Taylor Manifest Anxiety Scale	Differential eyelid conditioning	High anxious group exhibited more CR's to positive stimulus than low anxious group	Spence and Beecroft (1954)
Shock, threat of shock, or no shock; also Taylor Manifest Anxiety Scale	Eyelid conditioning	Shock-involved groups exhibited better conditioning than no shock group; shock-involved high anxious group exhibited more CR's than nonanxious, shock-involved group	Spence, Farber, and Taylor (1954)
Emotional responsiveness as measured by pulse rate changes and conductance	Eyelid conditioning	More emotionally responsive group gave more CR's than nonemotional group	Runquist and Ross (1959)
Emotional responsiveness as measured by muscle action potential (MAP)	Eyelid conditioning	Mean number CR's was found to be an increasing function of MAP response ($r = .52$)	Runquist and Ross (1959)
Emotional responsiveness as measured by pulse rate increase and skin conductance increase	Eyelid conditioning	More emotionally responsive group showed higher performance than nonemotional group	Runquist and Ross (1959)
Taylor Manifest Anxiety Scale	Eyelid conditioning	r of .40 between total number of CR's and level of anxiety	Baron and Connor (1960)
Taylor Manifest Anxiety Scale, with .25 and 2.0 pounds per sq. inch UCS	Eyelid conditioning (no warning signal)	High anxious groups superior to low anxious groups, regardless of whether .25 or 2.0 UCS used	Spence and Weyant (1960)

Threat of strong UCS, or no threat	Eyelid conditioning	Threat group produced higher percentage of CR's than control subjects	Spence and Goldstein (1961)
Anxiety as measured by psychometric indices as well as by performance to stress situation	Galvanic Skin Response	High anxious group conditioned more rapidly than low anxious group	Bitterman and Holtzman (1952)
Anxiety scale	Eyelid conditioning	No relationship between amount of anxiety and ease of conditioning	Hilgard, Jones, and Kaplan (1951)
24 hours deprivation of food, water, and tobacco	Eyelid conditioning	No difference in conditioning between experimental and control group	Franks (1957)
(Exp. I) Taylor Manifest Anxiety Scale (Exp. II) Welsh Anxiety Scale, and Taylor Manifest Anxiety Scale	Eyelid conditioning	Both experiments revealed no difference between high and low anxious groups	King, Kimble, Gorman, and King (1961)
Taylor Manifest Anxiety Scale	Eyelid conditioning	No difference in conditioning between experimental and control group	Prokasy and Truax (1959)
Taylor Manifest Anxiety Scale	Eyelid conditioning	High anxious group superior for first 40 trials; no difference between groups on subsequent trials	Caldwell and Cromwell (1959)
Taylor Manifest Anxiety Scale	Eyelid conditioning	When ready signal was used, high anxious group conditioned more rapidly; when no ready signal was used, no difference between high and low anxious groups	Prokasy and Whaley (1962)
Taylor Manifest Anxiety Scale	Serial learning of words (difficult task)	Low anxiety group superior	Taylor and Spence (1952)
Taylor Manifest Anxiety Scale	Paired-associate task (easy & difficult S-R combinations)	Low anxious group superior on difficult S-R combinations; no difference between groups on easy S-R combinations	Ramond (1953)
Taylor Manifest Anxiety Scale	Three lists of words, i.e. difficult, medium, and easy	High anxious group learned easy list most rapidly; low anxious group learned difficult list most rapidly	Montague (1953)

A Summary of a Number of Studies Examining the Relationship between Drive Level and Learning (*Continued*)

TYPE OF MOTIVATION	TYPE OF TASK	RESULTS	INVESTIGATOR
Taylor Manifest Anxiety Scale	Paired-associate task: easy and difficult lists	High anxious group learned easy list most rapidly; low anxious group learned difficult list most rapidly	Spence, Farber, and McFann (1956)
Taylor Manifest Anxiety Scale	Serial list of easy words	High anxious group superior to low anxious group	Taylor and Chapman (1955)
Taylor Manifest Anxiety Scale	Paired-associate task: easy and difficult lists	High anxious group superior on easy list; low anxious group superior on difficult list	Spence, Taylor, and Ketchel (1956)
High tension (pressing of dynanometer during learning trials)	Paired-associate task: easy and difficult S-R combinations	High tension group superior for easy S-R combinations; low tension group superior for difficult S-R combinations	Lovaas (1960)
No tension group			
Varying combinations of Taylor Manifest Anxiety Scale and shock	Transfer paired-associate task in which S-R combinations were easy or difficult	For no shock groups: high anxious group was superior on easy S-R combinations; low anxious group was superior on difficult task; for shock groups: high anxious group was superior on both easy and difficult S-R combinations	Lee (1961)
Stress as inferred by indicating that task was (1) part of entrance examination (high anxious) (2) test of interest only (low anxious)	Easy and difficult list of nonsense syllables	High anxious group superior on easy task; no difference between groups on difficult task	Willett and Eysenck (1962)
Stress as inferred from paced or nonpaced instructions	Discrimination task consisting of easy and difficult parts	High stress group superior on easy part; low stress group superior on difficult part	Castaneda (1956)

Stress as inferred from type of instruction provided to subjects	Discrimination task consisting of easy and difficult parts	Low stress group superior on difficult part of task; no difference between groups on easy part of task	Castaneda and Palermo (1956)
Stress as inferred from paced or nonpaced instructions	Discrimination task consisting of easy and difficult parts	High stress group superior on easy part; low stress group superior on difficult part	Palermo (1957)
Taylor Manifest Anxiety Scale	Simple addition task (Exp. I) Simple discrimination task (Exp. II)	High anxious group superior on both tasks	Reynolds, Blau, and Hurlbut (1961)
Heineman forced choice anxiety scale, and threat of mild or strong shock	Digit letter substitution	No difference between high and low stress groups	Katz and Greenbaum (1963)
Taylor Manifest Anxiety Scale	Stylus maze learning	Maze performance of anxious subjects significantly poorer than nonanxious subjects, with more difficult choice points providing greatest difference between groups	Farber and Spence (1953)
Taylor Manifest Anxiety Scale	Stylus maze learning (replicated Farber and Spence study)	No difference between anxious groups	Axelrod, Cowen, and Heilizer (1956)

which have measured the influence of an irrelevant need on (1) acquisition and (2) extinction.

In a very early study, Kendler (1945) compared the learning of one group of rats, motivated by 22 hours of food deprivation, with the learning of a second group, which was motivated by 22 hours of food deprivation and 22 hours of water deprivation. Since the animals were reinforced with food only, water deprivation was an irrelevant need. Results indicated that the addition of an irrelevant need *retarded* the learning of a spatial discrimination habit in the T-maze.

It has been generally acknowledged, as indicated by a study of Verplanck and Hayes (1953), that an animal which has been deprived of water will not eat as much as it would normally; similarly, the animal which has been deprived of food will decrease its consumption of water. Thus, if one deprivation state is manipulated, the other cannot be considered as irrelevant. As a result, investigators have used other combinations of need states, combinations which presumably are unrelated one to the other, in order to examine the role of irrelevant needs in the learning process. Studies by Amsel (1950); Braun, Wedekind, and Smudski (1957); and Levine, Staats, and Frommer (1959) have all shown that the addition of an irrelevant need increases learning as measured by rate of response, although there is some question as to whether it influences probability measures. In the Braun, Wedekind, and Smudski (1957) study, rats learned to traverse a multiple T-maze in order to escape from the water which filled the apparatus. Two levels of need were produced by using water temperatures of either 15 degrees or 35 degrees Centigrade. Results reveal that an irrelevant need of 22 hours of food deprivation resulted in significant decreases in swimming time and number of errors when compared with animals not deprived of food. Levine, Staats, and Frommer's (1959) study was similar in that they also used the need to escape from water, but the irrelevant need was produced by shocking the animals just prior to the first trial of each day's learning session. It was hypothesized that the emotionality arising from the shock would serve as an irrelevant need. Although the experimenters were not able to find differences in number of errors between the experimental group and a group not given shock, swimming speed for the shocked group was significantly more rapid than for the non-shocked group.

A number of investigators have studied the effect of manipulating the irrelevant need during extinction. In some experiments the relevant need has been satiated; in other cases, the relevant need continues to be present. Early studies in the area by Siegel (1946a), Webb (1949), and Brandauer (1953) provided mixed findings, but this is not surprising since in all instances food and water acted as the relevant and irrelevant needs. The problems produced by these sources of motivation have been considered previously.

Ellis (1957), Miles (1958), and Webb and Goodman (1958) have performed experiments when the irrelevant need apparently is not related to the relevant one. Both the Ellis (1957) and Miles (1958) studies failed to find performance differences (rate of response measure) during extinction as a result of an irrelevant need being present. Webb and Goodman (1958) provided positive findings, but the procedure utilized by these investigators differs substantially from that used by Ellis (1957) and Miles (1958). In the Webb and Goodman (1958) study, hungry rats were trained to push one of two bars in order to obtain food. Following training, they were satiated and returned to the box for a five-minute test session in which the number of times they pushed the correct bar was recorded. Following this, the floor of the apparatus was flooded and the subjects were given a second five-minute test session. The animals' performance under conditions of satiation without flooding acted as a control for their bar-pressing performance with flooding. Results revealed that the irrelevant need to escape from the water significantly increased the number of correct bar-pressing responses.

Clearly, the Hullian hypothesis regarding the role of irrelevant needs in performance is oversimplified and a new hypothesis is needed. It could be proposed that the contribution of an irrelevant need to behavior is not dependent upon any energizing function but only upon its cue function. To the extent that an irrelevant need elicits responses which are incompatible with the response demanded by the experimenter, the presence of an irrelevant need will result in poorer acquisition or more rapid extinction. On the other hand, if the irrelevant need elicits a response which is compatible with the response demanded by the experimenter, better performance during acquisition should take place. In any event, workers in this area should not only examine carefully any relationship which might exist between the relevant and irrelevant need, as was noted in the case of food and water deprivation, but they should also be aware of the nature of the response (or responses) which have been attached to those cues arising from the irrelevant need.

THE ROLE OF NEEDS IN PERFORMANCE AND LEARNING

In Chapter 3, it was pointed out that some investigators have been interested in distinguishing between performance and learning. This has been particularly true of those experimenters who have adhered to Hullian theory, for Hull (1943) was careful to distinguish between variables which contributed to habit strength (learning), as contrasted with those which contributed to reaction potential (performance). In the studies which have been reviewed, it has been held that the examination of behavior during acquisition trials does not enable the investigator to determine whether or not the intensity of a need is making its contribution to learning or performance. Spence (1953), for example, has pointed out that since performance or response strength is a function of both habit strength and drive strength it is possible that the increments of habit strength do not vary with the intensity of the deprivation state but that only drive strength does. Or, it may be possible that the differences in the intensity of the deprivation state might result in differences in both habit strength and drive strength.

The procedure used most frequently to distinguish between learning and performance has been the extinction operation since, as indicated in Chapter 3, it has been assumed that learning does not take place during extinction. Thus, if it is desired to examine the influence of the intensity of a need state on performance, all subjects are placed under the same amount of need and given an equal number of reinforcements in the learning of a particular task, e.g., bar pressing. Following such training, the subjects are then divided into varying groups, with each group being placed under a different deprivation state and the response extinguished. Differences among the groups, as measured by their resistance to extinction, presumably reflect the contribution of need level to performance with learning or habit held constant, since it has been assumed that performance and not learning can be influenced by the operation of the varying intensities of need which were present when the response was extinguished.

The reverse situation has been used to examine the influence of need intensity on learning (habit strength). Subjects are placed under varying deprivation levels and then given a constant number of reinforcements. Following such training, the intensity of the need is equated for all groups and resistance to extinction is measured. With this type of experimental design, it is assumed that performance differences among groups during extinction trials should reflect the contribution of varying levels of need, each of which presumably contributed to the formation of habit strength (or learning) which took place during the acquisition trials.

The experimental findings which have used this type of design to investigate the contribution of deprivation level in performance provide some confirmation of the results which have been obtained when performance during acquisition trials is measured. The experimental findings of Perin (1942), Koch and Daniel (1945), Saltzman and Koch (1948), and Yamaguchi (1951) all support the position that the rate of response, as measured by lever pressing in the Skinner box during extinction trials, is a function of the intensity of the organism's need state.[7] In the Perin study (1942), for example, 40 rats were placed under 23 hours of food deprivation and then given 16 reinforcements in the Skinner box. The animals were then divided into four groups, with each group given extinction trials under either 1, 3, 16, or 23 hours of food deprivation. The findings indicated that the mean number of responses to extinction increased as a function of hours of deprivation. If the experimental findings of the investigators which have been cited are pooled, performance as measured by resistance to extinction as a function of hours of deprivation is revealed by Figure 6–9.

The functional relationship between hours of deprivation and performance as indicated in Figure 6–9 is sufficiently complex that it would be most unusual to find its replication by other investigators using different learning situations or different need states. On the other hand, a reasonable prediction would be that a negatively accelerated function would express the relationship between the intensity of a need and performance. Studies by both

[7] It should be noted that when extinction findings are examined the rate of response almost invariably is used as the response measure.

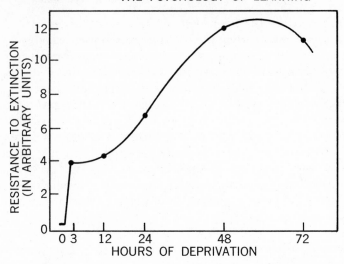

Fig. 6–9. Proposed representation of the relationship of resistance to extinction (in arbitrary units) to hours of food deprivation. *Adapted from Hall (1961)*

Kimble (1951) and Cautela (1956) have supported such a prediction. In the Kimble (1951) study, rats were first taught a panel-pushing response under 24 hours of deprivation. Response latencies for five trials were then obtained under deprivation periods of 10, 30, 50, and 60 minutes as well as 2, 8, 15, and 24 hours. The relationship between latency of response and deprivation time could be best expressed by a negatively accelerated curve.

Cautela's (1956) study differs from the other investigators' in that a discrimination task was utilized. A black-white discrimination habit was acquired by rats placed under 23 hours of food deprivation. The animals were then extinguished under 0, 6, 12, 23, 47, or 71 hours of deprivation. Extinction was defined by an animal's refusing to run for three minutes. Results revealed that both mean and median number of responses to extinction increased up to 23 hours and then gradually declined to the 71-hour group. Differences between the 23-, 47-, and 71-hour groups, however, were not significant.

It will be recalled that the second part of this general investigation has been the examination of the role of need states in learning, with performance variables presumably held constant. The reference experiment here is a study by Strassburger (1950) who had rats learn a bar-pressing response. In Experiment I the animals were deprived of food for either 4, 11, 23, or 47 hours, with each group receiving 30 reinforcements. The animals in Experiment II were deprived for either .5, 1, 4, or 23 hours and permitted to receive 10 reinforcements, and in Experiment III they were deprived for either 1, 11, 13, or 47 hours and provided only a single reinforced trial. All animals in the three experiments were extinguished under 23 hours of deprivation. Results revealed that although the number of reinforcements contributed to resistance to extinction this response measure was not related to the amount of deprivation provided during the original training situation. A subsequent study by Carper (1953) has confirmed the Strassburger findings that varying the deprivation level during extinction trials does not influence resistance to extinction.[8]

The experimental studies which have been reviewed and in which an attempt has been made to distinguish between learning and performance have all suffered from the inability of the experimenter to control stimulus generalization effects which occur when the organism is changed from one deprivation state during the training period to another deprivation state during extinction. In the Strassburger (1950) study just cited, it can be noted that animals (Experiment I) were placed first under either 4, 11, 23, or 47 hours of food deprivation during training and then extinguished under 23 hours of deprivation. A basic difficulty is that no allowance has been made for the fact that the 23-hour group did not have its deprivation schedule changed whereas all other experimental groups underwent a change. Furthermore, it has been demonstrated [Yamaguchi (1952), Barry (1958)] that a change in deprivation from acquisition to extinction has an effect of its own in addition to the influence provided by the specific amount of the deprivation state. A number of investigators have attempted to solve this problem by using a factorial design in

[8] It must be noted that these findings are at variance with an early study by Finan (1940) who deprived rats of food for 1, 12, 24, and 48 hours and then provided each group 30 reinforcements in learning to press a bar in order to obtain food. All animals were then extinguished under 24 hours of deprivation. Results revealed that learning (as inferred from resistance to extinction) increased from a relatively low level produced by training under one hour of deprivation to a maximum of 12 hours of deprivation and then declined at a negatively accelerated rate through the 24 and 48 hours of deprivation.

TABLE 6–5

Factorial Designed Study to Examine the Influence of Drive on Learning and Performance

		ACQUISITION		
HOURS OF DEPRIVATION		10	20	MEANS
	10	a	b	$\overline{X}$ab
EXTINCTION	20	c	d	$\overline{X}$cd
	MEANS	$\overline{X}$ac	$\overline{X}$bd	

which the effects of deprivation on both learning, or habit strength, and performance are examined simultaneously.

In this experimental design the deprivation level is manipulated during extinction as well as during acquisition. In Table 6–5, the acquisition series is conducted with subjects placed under either 10 or 20 hours of deprivation. Each group is then divided into subgroups and extinction is carried out under either 10 or 20 hours of deprivation.

An examination of means Xab and Xcd, in which acquisition has been carried out under both 10 *and* 20 hours of deprivation but extinction has been examined under *either* 10 or 20 hours of deprivation, provides information about the role of deprivation in performance. An examination of means Xac and Xbd reveals something about the role of deprivation in learning or habit strength.

It is disconcerting to find that the reasonably consistent findings relating level of need to habit strength and performance obtained in nonfactorial designed studies have produced equivocality when the findings of factorial studies are considered. Teel (1952), using a probability of response measure, and Campbell and Kraeling (1954), using rate of response, have reported findings which indicate that deprivation level affects neither habit strength nor performance in any systematic way. Hillman, Hunter, and Kimble (1953), on the other hand, have found some support for the position that the intensity of a need influences performance but not habit—a finding in keeping with some of the nonfactorial studies. Lewis and Cotton (1957) and Barry (1958) have found that the amount of deprivation not only effects performance but has some influence on habit as well.

7

The Contribution of Motivational
Variables to Learning II:
The Role of Rewards

As INDICATED PREVIOUSLY, in this chapter the contribution of rewards or reinforcement to learning will be examined. Current psychological thought concerned with this area reveals a fundamental indebtedness to Hull (1943) who, in his *Principles of Behavior,* proposed that three reward or reinforcement conditions were of prime importance in influencing behavior: (1) the number of reinforcements, (2) the quantity and quality of the reinforcing agent, and (3) the delay of reinforcement. Almost all of the experimental studies examining the role of reinforcement have taken their point of departure from one of these conditions. It is most interesting to note that the distinction between learning and performance, which has occupied the attention of many experimenters when examining the role of needs, has been almost totally ignored when reinforcement variables are considered.

NUMBER OF REINFORCEMENTS

An examination of most learning experiments in which the organism is presented with a series of continuously reinforced trials reveals that performance during these trials, as measured by either rate, amplitude, or probability of response, is a function of the number of reinforcements which have been provided. An example of such a finding is an experiment by Felsinger, Gladstone, Yamaguchi, and Hull (1947) who trained rats to press a bar in a Skinner box. The acquisition trials consisted of permitting the animal to make a single reinforced response until its latency of responding had reached a stable minimum. A decreasing negatively accelerated function was obtained between the latency of response and the number of reinforcements provided.

This type of experimental evidence frequently has been interpreted as supporting the position that learning takes place in incremental steps, each reinforcement adding one increment to the total habit strength (or learning) of the organism.[1]

When resistance to extinction is used as the response measure, the evidence is somewhat controversial. The early studies of Williams (1938) and Perin (1942) and, more recently, by Harris and Nygaard (1961) and Dyal and Holland (1963) all support a decreasing negatively accelerated relationship between the number of reinforcements and resistance to extinction. In Perin's study, rats were placed on 23 hours of food deprivation and trained to depress a bar in order to obtain food pellets. Following the presentation of either 5, 8, 30, or 70 reinforced trials, the animals were placed on three hours of deprivation and extinguished. In the Williams study, a similar experimental procedure was utilized. The animals were given 5, 10, 30, or 90 reinforced trials and then extinguished under 22 hours of deprivation. The experimental findings obtained in both studies revealed that resistance to extinction increases as a negatively accelerated function of the number of reinforced trials. The Harris and Nygaard

[1] Other positions, however, have been taken. Early objections were made by Krechevsky (1932) and Lashley (1938) who have supported what has become known as a noncontinuity position. In their examination of discrimination learning, they took the position that learning does not take place in incremental steps; rather, the organism adopts varying hypotheses about what represents the correct solution to the problem. The actual connection between a hypothesis and a response takes place very rapidly. A second point of view which has much in common with the noncontinuity position is one-trial learning. This position, espoused by Estes (1960) and others, also supports a nonincremental point of view. More specifically, it has been posited that the connection between the stimulus and response takes place in a single trial or on an all-or-none basis. The many experiments with their diverse experimental techniques which have been performed to throw light on this controversy cannot be discussed in detail here. The interested reader, however, can refer to Postman (1963) for an excellent summary of much of the work that has been done in this area.

(1961) study was similar in design to Williams' except that water deprivation was used and the animals were provided 45, 90, or 360 reinforcements prior to extinction. Although the group receiving 360 reinforced trials made more bar presses than the group which received only 90, the difference was not significant, indicating that with this type of task 90 reinforcements result in near asymptotic performance.

It is interesting to note that these findings cannot be generalized to the simple runway situation when speed of running over a fixed number of extinction trials is used as the response measure. North and Stimmel (1960) found that rats which were given either 90 or 135 reinforcements in running a straight runway had slower running speeds during extinction than animals given 45 reinforcements. Siegel and Wagner (1963) have corroborated these findings.

Ison (1962) examining extinction as a function of a greater variety of acquisition trials has also obtained findings which indicate that at least with a minimum number of reinforcements extinction performance is inversely related to the number of acquisition trials. In his study, rats were trained to traverse a runway and given either 10, 20, 40, 60, 80, or 100 rewarded acquisition trials. Following the acquisition series, extinction was carried to a minimum of 80 trials, with five trials being provided each day. Running speed over three days of running (15 extinction trials) is indicated in Figure 7–1. Here it can be noted that animals which had been given the largest number of reinforcements ran slowest and the subjects which were given the smallest number of reinforcements ran most rapidly.[2]

AMOUNT OF REWARD

Before examining the empirical findings amassed in this area, it is appropriate to call attention to one methodological problem. When the amount of reward is manipulated by varying either the

---

[2] The findings of Hill and Spear (1963a) using running speeds as their response measure have not confirmed the findings of either North and Stimmel (1960), Ison (1962), or Siegel and Wagner (1963).

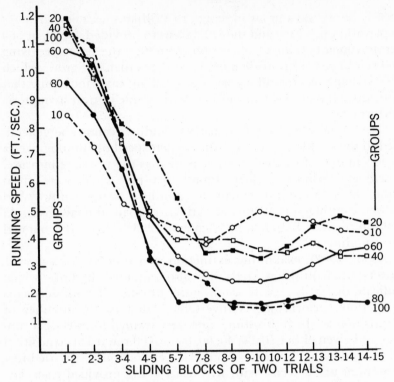

Fig. 7–1. Mean running speed in sliding blocks of two trials over the first three days of extinction. The first trial of each day is omitted. *Adapted from Ison (1962)*

actual weight of the food or the number of units, it is obvious that conditions other than the actual amount of reward will also vary.

As Guttman (1953) has pointed out, the stimulation which is derived from the goal object prior to the consummatory behavior will vary, the number of calories or amount of nutrition will vary, as will the amount of consummatory activity and the amount of time spent in the goal box. The relationship of these variables to the amount of reward has not been systematically explored, although the work of Wolfe and Kaplon (1941), Kling (1956), Spence (1956), Wike and Barrientos (1957), and Logan (1960) has indicated that these variables can make a contribution to the organism's performance. For example, Wolfe and Kaplon (1941) found that a grain of rice cut into four quarters will produce faster running times than when the same amount is presented in a single piece. Similarly, Wike and Barrientos (1957) found that five ml. of water which was obtained by rats drinking through a narrow tube resulted in superior performance on a T-maze than if the water was obtained through a wider tube.

Spence (1956) has reported an experiment by Czeh in which three groups of rats were trained to run a straightaway and two of these groups were rewarded with a large pellet of food. The third group was rewarded with a small pellet. One of the large-pellet groups was permitted to consume the whole pellet in the goal box, which required about four minutes of eating time. The other two groups were permitted to eat in the goal box for 30 seconds—a period of time sufficient for the group provided with the small pellet to finish eating. The 30-second large-pellet group was removed from the goal box and permitted to finish eating in its feeding cage. Results revealed that latency of responding was related to the time spent in the goal box and not to the size of the pellet.

As a result, many investigators following the lead of Guttman (1953) have manipulated the amount of reward by varying the concentration of a sucrose solution that is provided the organism. By so doing, it is possible to control the amount of time the animal spends in the goal box as well as the amount of the animal's consummatory activity.

When performance during acquisition trials is measured by either rate, amplitude, or probability of response, the majority of studies using animals reveal that performance during acquisition trials is related to the amount of reinforcement that is provided. This generalization appears to hold whether the amount of reward is manipulated by varying the number or weight of the units or by varying the percentage of a sucrose solution. Tables 7–1 and 7–2 provide a summary of many of these studies with typical findings revealing a negatively accelerated curve expressing the functional relationship between performance and the amount of reward provided.

An interesting variation in manipulating the amount of reward variable has been to provide the animal with a choice between varying magnitudes. The general procedure has been to place subjects in a discrimination task in which one cue leads to one amount and a second cue leads to another. In a study by

TABLE 7-1

The Role of Amount of Reinforcement on Rate of Responding during Acquisition Trials

TYPE OF REINFORCEMENT	AMOUNT	TASK	RESPONSE MEASURE	ORGANISM	INFLUENCE OF AMOUNT OF REINFORCEMENT ON THE RESPONSE MEASURE	INVESTIGATOR
Food	0, 1, 2, 4 and 6 grains units	runway	running time	chicken	positive	Grindley (1929)
Food	1, 4, 16, 64, 256	runway	running time	rat	positive	Crespi (1942)
Food	2, 5 seconds of eating	Skinner Box	rate of pecking	pigeon	positive	Jenkins and Clayton (1949)
Food	.05, .20, .40, .60, .80, 1.60, 2.40 gm.	runway	latency	rat	positive	Zeaman (1949)
Food	60, 120, 160 mg.	Skinner Box	time for 25 bar presses	rat	negative	Reynolds (1950)
Sucrose	4, 8, 16, 32 per cent	Skinner Box	time for 500 bar presses	rat	positive	Guttman (1953)
Food	1, 5 pellets	multiple T-maze	running time	rat	positive	Maher and Wickens (1954)
Food	1, 5 pellets	runway	running time	rat	positive	D'Amato (1955)
Sucrose	2, 6, 18, 54 per cent	Skinner Box	rate of lever pressing	monkey	positive	Conrad and Sidman (1956)
Sucrose	8, 24 per cent	Skinner Box	speed of approaching bar	rat	positive	Butter and Thomas (1958)
Food	45, 450 mg.	runway	starting and running times	rats	positive	Armus (1959)
Food	1, 3, 6, 12 pellets	runway	starting and running times	rats	negative	Weiss (1960)
Food	.1, 1.0, 2.0 gm.	runway	running time	rats	positive	Reynolds and Pavlik (1960)
Sucrose	3, 12, 24, 48 per cent	runway	running time	rats	positive	Goodrich (1960)

TABLE 7-2

The Role of Amount of Reinforcement on Probability of Responding during Acquisition Trials

TYPE OF REINFORCEMENT	AMOUNT	TASK	RESPONSE MEASURE	ORGANISM	INFLUENCE OF AMOUNT OF REINFORCEMENT ON THE RESPONSE MEASURE	INVESTIGATOR
Food	small, large piece	discrimination	correct response	chimpanzee	positive	Cowles and Nissen (1937)
Food	30, 160 mg.	discrimination	trials to criterion	rat	negative	Reynolds (1949)
Food	85, 271 mg.	discrimination	errors	rat	positive	Greene (1953)
Food	20, 75, 250, 2500 mg.	multiple T-maze	errors	rat	negative	Furchtott and Rubin (1953)
Food	1, 5 pellets	multiple T-maze	errors	rat	negative	Maher and Wickens (1954)
Food	.1, .7 gm.	multiple T-maze	correct response	rat	positive	Denny and King (1955)
Food	1, 2, 4 pellets	discrimination	correct response	monkey	positive	Schrier and Harlow (1956)
Food	10, 150 seconds eating time	E-maze	correct response	rats	positive	Powell and Perkins (1957)
Food	.5, 2 peanuts	discrimination	errors	monkey	positive	Leary (1958)
Water	10, 40 seconds drinking time	U-maze	errors	rats	negative	Fehrer (1956a)

Hill and Spear (1963) all groups of rats received four pellets of food on one side of a T-maze, but one of these groups received two, a second group one, and a third group zero pellets on the incorrect side. Learning, as measured by correct responses, was inversely related to amount of reward on the incorrect side. Davenport (1963) has used a somewhat similar procedure except that the amount of reinforcement variable was investigated by manipulating the percentage of reinforced trials to the incorrect side. His findings were in keeping with those obtained by Hill and Spear (1963).

The results with human subjects, in contrast to those obtained with animals, provide controversial findings. Siegel and Andrews (1962), using children four to five years of age, examined the influence of amount of reward in the classical two-choice uncertain outcome experiment. This situation was one in which two identical containers were placed before the subject with the container in one of the positions, e.g., left, holding the reward 75 per cent of the time whereas the other container would hold it just 25 per cent of the time. In the low reinforcement condition, the reward was a button, selected to have minimum interest for the child, along with a knowledge of the results of each trial as to which container held the object. In the high reward condition, the object was a small prize which the child could keep if he responded correctly. One hundred trials were first given to the subject under one of the reward conditions. If the low reward condition was first presented, it was followed by 100 additional trials of the high reward condition. On the other hand, if the high reward condition was first presented, only 12 additional trials of the low reward condition were given since the child was usually reluctant to continue without receiving reward for an activity for which he had previously received a prize. Findings revealed that children exhibited a greater tendency to maximize the probability of the correct response when the high reward was used.

Miller and Estes (1961) and Estes, Miller, and Curtin (1962), on the other hand, have been unable to find performance differences as a function of the amount of reward provided. In the Miller and Estes (1961) study, nine-year-old boys were required to discriminate between drawings of faces which differed only in the height and spacing of the eyebrows. Pictures were presented tachistoscopically for two-second intervals with subjects receiving either 50 cents, 1 cent, or knowledge of results after each correct choice. A subsequent study by Estes, Miller, and Curtin (1962), using the same experimental procedure, was performed with college students as subjects; a reward of 25 cents, 1 cent, or knowledge of results was provided for a correct response. In neither experiment did differences in performance accompany differences in the amount of reward received.

It is likely that a resolution of this conflict is dependent upon an adequate understanding of what constitutes a reward to the human subject. It is quite possible that for the typical college student the amount of monetary reward that can be provided in an experiment means far less than certain intangible rewards. The satisfaction in pleasing the experimenter or the interest in making a good score may far outweigh any small monetary reward obtained. Since these intangibles would appear to assume increasing importance with increasing age, it may mean that the experimenter must be first aware of their contribution before attempting to assess the amount of reward variable with human subjects.

It will be recalled from the discussion of the role of need intensity in performance that some experimenters were interested in examining the learning task as related to competing and noncompeting responses. A similar approach has been taken when examining the amount of reward variable. Pereboom and Crawford (1958) found that only relatively slight increases in running speed (although statistically significant) were obtained with rats when the amount of reward was varied from 10 mg. to 50 mg. and only forward progress in the runway was measured. A basic problem with this study was that the investigators included all of the forward running, which included retracing, done by their animals. Marx and Brownstein's (1963) recent experiment was an attempt to examine the amount of reward variable without such a confounding measure. Rats were given one trial daily on a 14-foot runway for a total of 73 acquisition and 72 extinction trials. Four groups were used, each receiving a different incentive—8, 16, 32, or 64 per cent sucrose solution. Starting time and total running time was recorded. In addition, forward progress time was obtained by measuring only when the animal was locomoting in a forward direction; retracing time, either forward or backward, was not included. They found a significant effect for amount of concentration when forward progress time was measured, although, as Figure 7–2 reveals, the effect was due primarily to the slower running of the 8 per cent group.

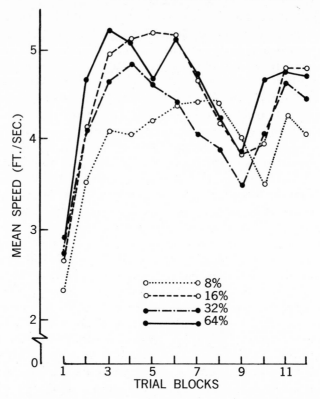

Fig. 7–2. Mean forward-progress speeds by sucrose concentrations for twelve blocks of six trials in acquisition. *Adapted from Marx and Brownstein (1963)*

Of considerable interest in this study was the fact that once the animals had reached an asymptote there was a decline in running speed, with the approaching of a somewhat lower asymptote. That this phenomenon was genuine is suggested by the fact that the decline took place in each of the concentration groups. Moreover, it came at progressively later points for the various concentrations, occurring first for the 64 per cent subjects, next for the 32 per cent subjects, etc. Although only 20 seconds of daily licking was provided, which involved a total daily liquid volume of less than one ml., even this relatively small amount of sucrose appeared to be sufficient to produce a kind of satiation effect which appeared to be related to loss of incentive value rather than being mediated by physiological factors.

When performance is measured during extinction trials, an examination of Table 7–3 reveals that most investigators have found that extinction rate is a function of the amount of reward obtained during the acquisition trials. It is likely, however, that the extinction findings reflect nothing more than the fact that large reward groups were responding at a higher level at the end of the acquisition period than the small reward groups and that extinction superiority was merely a reflection of this terminal acquisition response disparity. Such a position has support from Metzger, Cotton, and Lewis (1957) who equated performance levels for varying reward groups at the beginning of extinction trials by using analysis of covariance. No differences were obtained between groups, suggesting that the amount of reward variable affects extinction performance through differential levels of performance found at the end of acquisition rather than producing its effect on extinction directly.[3,4]

Intra-subject Reward Variability

One interesting amount of reward variable is the experience that the organism has had with reward in the experimental situation. As Meyer (1951a) and, more recently, Bower (1961) have pointed out, the amount of reward variable should not be considered a static parameter; its influence depends upon the context in which a given amount of reward occurs. In an excellent

[3] The problem of comparing extinction performances when a correction for systematic differences at the end of the acquisition trials is necessary has been discussed at some length by Anderson (1963).

[4] Some investigators have obtained findings at variance with those typically obtained. Armus (1959) trained two groups of rats to traverse a runway, with one group receiving only one 45-mg. food pellet and the second group receiving ten such pellets. Following 75 acquisition trials, 150 extinction trials were provided. The results revealed that the ten-pellet group, which showed superior running times at the end of the acquisition trials, extinguished more rapidly than the one-pellet group. A recent study by Lewis and Duncan (1961) using college students as subjects and a lever pulling task failed to find differences in resistance to extinction between subjects provided a fifty-cent reward and subjects given a one-cent reward for lever pulls during acquisition trials. There was, however, no measure of terminal acquisition performance for the varying groups. Finally, a study by Hulse (1958) has revealed additional complexities in this area. In this experiment, rats were provided with either a 1.0 gm. or an .08 gm. pellet for running a straightaway. Partial reinforcement (46 per cent) as well as continuous reinforcement groups were used. Twenty-four acquisition trials were provided followed by 19 extinction trials. Extinction trial performance revealed that if continuous reinforcement was used animals receiving the smaller pellet of food took longer to extinguish, but if partial reinforcement was utilized the larger-pellet group took longer to extinguish.

TABLE 7–3

The Role of Amount of Reinforcement on Resistance to Extinction

TYPE OF REIN-FORCEMENT	AMOUNT	TASK	ORGANISM	INFLUENCE OF AMT. OF REINF. ON RESISTANCE TO EXTINCTION	INVESTIGATOR
Food	5, 10, 30, 90 pellets	lever pressing	rat	positive	Williams (1938)
Food	.05, .20, .40, .80, 1.60, 2.40 gm. cheese	runway	rat	positive	Zeaman (1949)
Food	60, 120, 160 mg.	lever pressing	rat	negative	Reynolds (1950)
Food	3, 12, 50 mg. (combined with different tastes)	lever pressing	rat	positive	Hutt (1954)
Sucrose	4, 8, 12, 32 per cent	lever pressing	rat	positive	Guttman (1953)
Sucrose	2, 6, 18, 54 per cent	runway	rat	18% group best, 6% group poorest	Young and Shuford (1955)
Food	2, 5, 8 pellets	runway	rat	when perf. level at beginning of extinction is equated, no diff. among groups	Metzger, Lewis, and Cotton (1957)
Food	.08, 1.0 gm.	runway	rat	positive if partial reinforcement was used; negative if continuous reinforcement was used	Hulse (1958)
Food	10, 45 mg.	runway	rat	negative	Armus (1959)

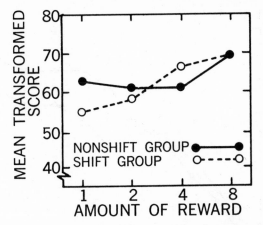

Fig. 7–3. Mean arcsin-transformed percentage of correct responses as a function of the number of pellets provided as reward. Each point on the curve for the nonshift group represents a different subgroup, whereas each point on the curve for the shift group represents the same subjects. *Adapted from Schrier (1958)*

demonstration of this effect [Schrier (1958)], one group of monkeys received a one-pellet reward for each correct response made throughout a series of discrimination problems. A second group received two pellets and a third and fourth group received four and eight pellets, respectively. All the groups were designated as nonshift groups since the amount of reward remained constant throughout the entire experiment. A fifth group of subjects (shift group) experienced each of these reward amounts. That is, one amount would be used for correct responses on one problem, a different amount would be used for correct responses on a second problem, etc. Figure 7–3 reveals the performance of the varying groups as a function of the amount of reward received. It can be noted that for the nonshift groups rewards of one pellet, two pellets, or four pellets produced similar performances. It required eight pellets to facilitate the organisms' learning. On the other hand, each variation in the amount produced an increasing percentage of correct responses for the shift group.

Studies by Bevan and his associates [Bevan and Adamson (1960); Black, Adamson, and Bevan (1961)] have obtained somewhat similar findings when shock (and shock reduction) are used. In the Black, Adamson, and Bevan (1961) study, three

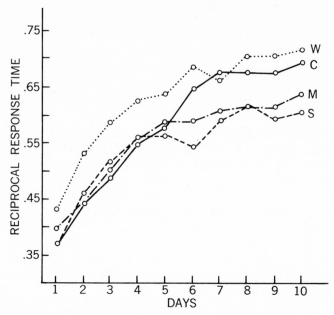

Fig. 7–4. Mean reciprocal daily response times for the escape response in the straightaway with a shock of the same physical, but of different relative, intensity. *Adapted from Black, Adamson, and Bevan (1961)*

groups of rats received ten trials per day in a shuttle box in which either (1) strong, (2) medium, or (3) weak shock was used to motivate the animals to run to the other side where shock reduction was obtained. Following each days' shuttle-box trials, ten additional test trials were provided in a straight runway with medium shock being used to motivate all three groups to run. A control group received only the test trials on the straightaway. As Figure 7–4 indicates, a comparison of the performance curves for those groups which received pre-test shuttle-box experience reveals that the most rapid running times were associated with the group that received the weak shock in the shuttle-box, whereas slowest running times were obtained from the group receiving the strong shock. The investigators have used Helson's (1959) adaptation level theory found in psychophysics as an explanation for their findings. More specifically, Black, Adamson, and Bevan have proposed that the magnitude of reinforcement is defined by the difference between the intensity of a present stimulus process and an internal norm which is derived from a pooling of previous relevant information.

The use of differing rewards within the same experimental problem calls attention to an interesting phenomenon first reported by Crespi (1944). He reported that if a rat was shifted from one or four pellets of food to sixteen its performance in running a straight runway rose above the level of performance characteristic of a 16-pellet group which had reached its asymptote in running speed. On the other hand, if the amount of reward was reduced from 256 or 164 pellets to 16, running speed was slower than that found with a constant 16-pellet group at its limit of practice. Increased performance as a result of going from a small to a large reward was termed positive contrast or an "elation" effect, whereas the poorer performance associated with going from a large to a smaller amount of reward was termed negative contrast or "depression" effect.

The replicability of Crespi's findings has been controversial. Although Zeaman (1949) has confirmed Crespi's findings, a number of other investigators have been unable to obtain such effects. Spence (1956), citing unpublished work from his laboratory, has suggested that the positive contrast effect obtained by Crespi was a function of the original high-reward group subjects' not having reached their asymptote and that the shift group responded at the higher level because of the additional training trials. He did report, however, that negative contrast effects were obtained.

In a recent experiment, Bower (1961) was also unable to find positive contrast effects, although he, too, obtained negative contrast effects. The experimental design that he utilized was somewhat different from that employed by other investigators in that for his experimental group he associated different cues with differing amounts of reward. More specifically, rats in the contrast or experimental group received a large reward (eight pellets) when run in a black (or white) alley and a small reward (one pellet) when run in a white (or black) alley. Trials employing the different alleys were randomly presented. Performance for this group was then compared to two control groups in which one group received a large reward and one received a small reward on every trial. One hundred and twenty eight trials were provided, and results revealed that asymptotic performance of the experimental group when running to the small reward was inferior to that of the small reward control group. On the other hand, performance for the experimental group when running to the large reward was slightly, but not significantly, inferior to that of the large reward control group.

Throughout the experimental history of the contrast effect, many investigators have hypothesized that the organism learns something about the reward which is found in the learning situation. Subjects are thus presumed to be able to perceive as well as respond to discrepancies between prevailing and previously encountered reward states. Therefore, one could assume that it would be possible for an experimenter to manipulate the presentation of rewards so that the contrast effect would disappear. In one study of this variety, Gonzalez, Gleitman, and Bitterman (1962) trained three groups of rats to run a straightaway in which one group received a reward of two pellets, the second group received eight pellets, and the third group 32 pellets. Following 27 trials, the two-pellet group continued to run to two pellets, but the eight-pellet group was shifted abruptly to two pellets. One-third of the 32-pellet group continued to run to 32 pellets, one-third was shifted abruptly to two pellets, and one-third was shifted gradually so that at the end of a 15-day period it was also receiving two pellets. Results revealed that the magnitude of the depression effect increased with the magnitude of the reward decrement; no depression effect appeared when a gradual decrement in reward took place.[5]

Homzie and Ross (1962) examined the effects of reducing reward by varying the concentration of a sucrose solution. In this experiment, rats were trained to traverse a runway, with starting speed, running speed, and goal box speed being the response measures obtained. One group of subjects was given a 20 per cent sucrose solution as reward, whereas a control group was given a 1 per cent solution. Following 84 training trials, the 20 per cent group was subdivided into three groups. One group was switched to a 1 per cent solution, a second group was given distilled water, and the third group was given no reward. The 1 per cent control group continued to receive the 1 per cent solution. Results revealed that during the acquisition trials the 20 per cent group, as might be anticipated, went to a higher asymptote of performance than the

---

[5] One difficulty with this study was the fact that the investigators were unable to find differences in running speeds among the varying reinforcement groups during the 27-trial training period.

control group. This difference was reflected in all response measures. A reduction in the concentration of the solution from 20 per cent to 1 per cent led to the expected decline in performance but this decline was not abrupt, requiring more than 20 trials to reach this level. Moreover, the depression effect was absent since the switched group did not show significantly poorer performance than the control group.[6]

A somewhat different approach to the problem of manipulating reward is found in an extensive series of studies by Logan (1960). In these investigations, he trained rats to run a straightaway and varied the amount of reward the animal received from one trial to another. He concluded that if the amount of reward is varied between two equally likely values, as contrasted with the average of these amounts constantly being provided, differences in speed of running between the two conditions are dependent upon whether the average amount is small or large. If the average amount is small, moderate degrees of variable amounts provide superior performance, as contrasted with the constant amount. On the other hand, if the average amount is large, variable amounts provide inferior performance, as contrasted with the constant amount. For example, 20 pellets is a large reward to a rat, and a constant 20-pellet amount provides better performance than a variation of 19 and 21 which, in turn, is superior to a variation of 18 and 22. On the other hand, a constant four-pellet reinforcement results in poorer performance than does variation of three and five.[7] One surprising aspect of these studies is the apparent ability of the animals to discriminate among the varying numbers of pellets. It would appear to be quite difficult for a rat to

[6] When an investigator uses pellets of food as his reward and during the course of an experiment his animals are required to go from one amount to another, a number of other stimulus conditions also change (visual aspects of the reward, number of consummatory responses, and length of stay in the goal box). When there is a change in sucrose solution, only the percentage of sugar is changed; and since all of these other variables remain the same as before, it would appear that the animal has greater difficulty in discriminating between the two reward values. As a result, it may be that this increased difficulty in discriminating between the two different rewards can account for the lack of positive findings.

[7] Yamaguchi (1961) has been unable to confirm this generalization. In this study, one group received a constant five units of reinforcement for 40 acquisition trials, and a second group received eight units on a random half of the trials and two units on the other half. A third group received a nine-one varied magnitude reinforcement schedule. A fourth group received a ten-zero reinforcement schedule. Results revealed no significant differences among groups over 40 acquisition trials.

discriminate between 19 and 21 pellets which, in turn, is necessary if differential performance for this group, as contrasted to an average 20-pellet group, is to be obtained.

INTERACTIONS BETWEEN NEED AND AMOUNT OF REWARD

In the studies reported in Chapter 6, the experimenters have examined the influence of need states on performance. In this chapter, interest has been directed toward examining the role of rewards. During the past decade, a number of investigators have manipulated simultaneously both of these variables in order to ascertain whether or not there is any interaction between them. Rate of responding has been the response measure utilized.

In a study by Kintsch (1962), rats were trained under three levels of water deprivation and received three different magnitudes of reward for running down a straight runway. Water deprivation for the high drive group was 23 hours; the medium drive group was also deprived for 23 hours but was permitted to drink three cc. of water just prior to each experimental session. The low drive group was also placed under 23 hours of deprivation but permitted to drink six cc. prior to the experimental session. High reward subjects received 3.5 cc. of water; medium reward subjects received 1.75 cc.; but the low reward subjects received only .25 cc. Latency of responding as well as running speed were the response measures obtained. The results revealed that both latency and running speed increased as a function of drive strength and magnitude of reward. The findings, portrayed in Figure 7–5, indicate an interaction between drive and reward which is multiplicative—that is, differences in performance among the three drive conditions depend upon the amount of reward that is received, i.e., the larger the reward, the greater the difference in performance arising from different drive conditions. Thus, the low reward figure reveals small differences among performance measures as a function of the strength of drive. One can also make the same conclusion on the basis of the low drive figure. On the other hand, an examination of the high reward figure reveals that differences in performance arising from the varying drive states are large, and a similar finding is noted from an examination of the high drive figure.

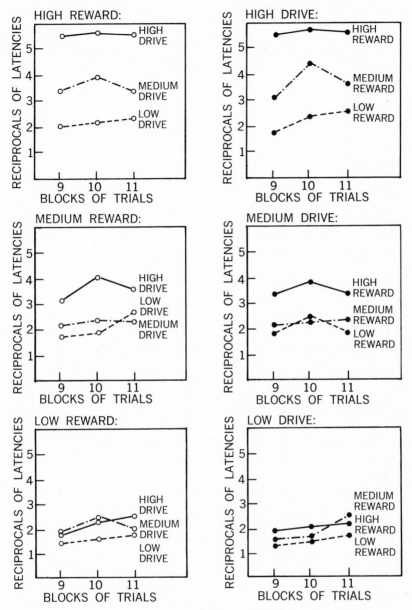

Fig. 7–5. Asymptotic starting speeds for all drive and reward conditions. *Adapted from Kintsch (1962)*

A number of experiments performed prior to the Kintsch (1962) study have also revealed a significant interaction between need and reward [Seward, Shea, and Elkind (1958) ; Seward and Procter (1960) ; Seward, Shea, and Davenport (1960) ; Ehrenfreund and Badia (1962) ; Stabler (1962)].[8]

DELAY OF REINFORCEMENT

A third reinforcement variable described by Hull (1943) as having primary importance in learning is the delay of reinforcement. But it must be recognized that this parameter refers to a number of different operations, depending upon the learning situation which is examined. With classical conditioning situations, it frequently has reference to the CS-UCS interval. This is also true for the instrumental avoidance type learning situation.[9] On the other hand, delay of reinforcement with instrumental reward or escape learning situations involves the examination of the time interval occurring between the making of a response and the securing of reward or termination of the noxious stimulation.

Classical Conditioning: the CS-UCS Interval

As indicated above, the delay of reinforcement in classical conditioning situations will be considered as referring to the amount of time elapsing between the onset of the CS and the onset of the UCS. Frequently, this has been referred to as the interstimulus interval (ISI). A primary concern of investigators working in this area during the past 30 years has been the determination of that time interval which is optimal for condi-

[8] The studies of Reynolds and Pavlik (1960), Weiss (1960), Hulicka (1960), Snyder (1962), and Pavlik and Reynolds (1963) have found no significant interaction between these two variables. For example, Reynolds and Pavlik (1960) provided 90 rats with 72 reinforced trials on a straight runway. Three amounts of reinforcement (one-tenth, one, or two grams of wet mash) were utilized along with three levels of food deprivation (3, 22, or 44 hours). Although performance increased as the level of both reward and drive increased, the investigators were unable to find any significant interaction. A second study by Pavlik and Reynolds (1963) using 6 and 30 hours of deprivation combined with two levels of reward magnitude supported their earlier findings that these variables do not interact in their effect on performance.

[9] It is recognized that in many of the classical conditioning studies, and of course in all of the instrumental avoidance ones, the reinforcement that is present arises from the termination, not the onset, of the UCS. Strictly speaking, delay of reward should not be equated with the CS-UCS interval in such situations.

tioning. Table 7–4 summarizes the results of many of these studies (classified by response) which have employed humans as subjects. From these findings, it appears that the most effective interstimulus interval is five-tenths of a second plus or minus one-quarter.

Differential conditioning studies have supported these simple conditioning findings only in part. Hartman and Grant (1962) examining the conditioned eyelid response employed CS-UCS intervals of .4, .6, .8, or 1.0 second. The positive and negative stimulus was each presented 44 times, with each stimulus assigned randomly but balanced within each block of eight trials. Results are indicated in Figure 7–6. Here it can be noted that the .6 and .8 second CS-UCS intervals provided the greatest percentage of responses to the positive stimulus, a result in keeping with the findings of many of the simple conditioning studies which have been examined. However, Kimmel and Pennypacker (1963) were unable to obtain similar findings. These investigators examined the differential conditioning of the GSR and used CS-UCS intervals of .25, .50, 1.0, and 2.0 seconds. Their results indicated that no optimal CS-UCS interval could be found.

The complexity of the area is further indicated by the results of a number of investigations which suggest that the optimal CS-UCS interval is two seconds when animals are used as subjects. Table 7–5 presents summaries of a number of these experiments.

The fact that in the simple conditioning situation both voluntary (skeletal) responses and involuntary (autonomic) responses in humans have approximately the same optimal interval has been incorporated into different theoretical positions on classical conditioning. A view posited by some investigators, e.g., White and Schlosberg (1952), is that classical conditioned response learning is primarily of a stimulus-stimulus variety, with the important variable being the time interval between the onset of the CS and the onset of the UCS. Thus, the characteristic of the response (whether it be skeletal or autonomic) is of no particular concern.

The second explanation, provided by Moeller (1954) and Smith (1954), is that classical conditioning is dependent upon reinforcement principles and that the conditioning of involuntary responses such as the GSR is in reality a conditioning of some unspecified skeletal response which in turn is dependent upon reinforcement. As Smith (1954) has argued, ". . . every 'conditioned visceral response' is in reality an artifact, an innate

TABLE 7–4

A Summary of Studies Using Human Subjects Examining the Interstimulus Interval and Classified by Response Conditioned

Response: Galvanic Skin Response

INVESTIGATOR	CS	UCS	CS-UCS INTERVALS EXAMINED	RESULTS
White and Schlosberg (1952)	Light	Shock	0, .25, .50, 1.0, 2.0, 4.0 seconds	.5 second superior as measured by amplitude for 5 extinction trials
Moeller (1954)	Noise	Shock	.25, .45, 1.0, 2.5 seconds	.45 seconds superior as measured by amplitude during 4 test trials interspersed among conditioning trials
Prokasy, Fawcett, and Hall (1962)	Tone	Shock	0, .5, 1, 3, 5 seconds	Neither CR latency nor amplitude varied as a function of the interval employed; magnitude of CR revealed .5 second interval superior; all measures based upon the first extincton trial

Response: Pupillary Dilation

Gerall and Woodward (1958)	Cessation of noise	Light offset, shock	.125, .50, 1.50, 2.50 seconds	1.5 second interval superior; no conditioning found with 2.50 second interval

Response: Finger Withdrawal

Wolfle (1930)	Tone	Shock	−.50, −.25, 0, .25, .50, .75, 1.00, 1.25, 1.50 seconds	Sixty test trials interspersed among 280 CS-UCS presentations revealed .50 second interval group superior as measured by per cent responding
Wolfle (1932)	Tone	Shock	−2.00, −1.00, −.6, −.2, 0, .2, .3, .4, .6, 1.00, 2.00, 3.00 seconds	Varying numbers of trials provided although all Ss had a minimum of 600 CS-UCS pairings; results indicated .2 and .3 second interval groups superior as measured by per cent responding
Spooner and Kellogg (1947)	Tone	Shock	.5, 1.0, 1.5 seconds	Twenty test trials interspersed among 80 CS-UCS pairings; .5 second interval group superior as measured by per cent responding

Study	CS	UCS	Interval	Results
Fitzwater and Reisman (1952)	Tone	Shock	−.5, 0, .5 seconds	Twenty test trials interspersed among 80 CS-UCS pairings; .5 second interval group superior as measured by per cent responding
Fitzwater and Thrush (1956)	Tone	Shock	0, .1, .2, .3, .4, .6 seconds	Twenty test trials interspersed among 80 CS-UCS pairings; .4 second interval group superior as measured by per cent responding
Response: Eyeblink				
Bernstein (1934)	Click	Shock	−.90, −.50, .10, .20, .25, .30, .50, 1.0, 1.48 seconds	When CS precedes UCS by a range of .30 to 1.48 seconds, there is no variation in the amount of conditioning
Reynolds (1945)	Click	Airpuff	.25, .45, 1.15, 2.25 seconds	Acquisition curves for 90 reinforced trials reveal that .45 second interval was superior as measured by per cent responding
Kimble (1947)	Light	Airpuff	.1, .2, .225, .250, .3, .4 seconds	For six test trials obtained within 60 reinforced acquisition trials, .4 second interval was superior as measured by per cent responding
Kimble, Mann, and Dufort (1955)	Light	Airpuff	.5, .8, 1.5 seconds	Sixty acquisition trials: analysis of trials 51–60 reveal .5 group superior as measured by per cent responding
McAllister (1953)	Tone	Airpuff	.1, .25, .45, .70, 2.0 seconds	Twenty test trials interspersed among 80 reinforced trials indicated .25 group superior, although difference between .25 and .45 second intervals not significant, as measured by per cent responding
Ebel and Prokasy (1963)	Light	Airpuff	.2, .5, .8 seconds	.5 second group superior although not significantly so when frequency of responding over 400 acquisition trials was examined

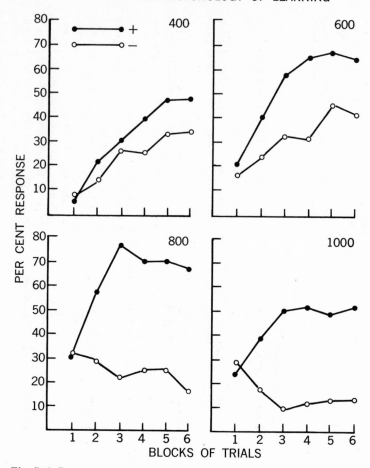

Fig. 7–6. Percentage frequency of anticipatory responses to the positive and negative stimuli during successive blocks of acquisition trials for the four CS-UCS intervals. The first block was four trials; subsequent blocks were eight trials each. *Adapted from Hartman and Grant (1962)*

accompaniment of the skeletal responses inculcated by the conditioning process." Being more specific, Smith has pointed out that in the conditioning of the GSR the subject soon comes to regard the CS as a signal for the "bracing" against the noxious stimulus to come. This bracing is a muscular response and a matter of reinforcemental learning. At the same time, the skeletal activity is accompanied by the GSR as a matter of innate neural connec-

TABLE 7–5

A Summary of Studies Using Infrahuman Subjects Examining the Interstimulus Interval

INVESTIGATOR	EXPERIMENTAL SUBJECTS	CS	UCS	CONDITIONED RESPONSE	CS-UCS INTERVALS EXAMINED	RESULTS
Noble, Gruender, and Meyer (1959)	Mollienisia (Fish)	Increase in illumination	Shock	Vigorous forward and backward movement; also cessation of movement	.5, 1.0, 1.5, 2.0, 3.0, 4.0 seconds	Per cent frequency of CR was maximum at 2.0 seconds
Noble and Adams (1963)	Mollienisia (Fish)	Increase in illumination	Shock	As above	.5, 2.0, 4.0 seconds	Per cent frequency of CR was maximum at 2.0
Noble and Adams (1963a) Exp. I	Pigs	Increase in illumination	Shock to rear leg	Leg flexion, head movements; bracing	.5, 1.0, 1.5, 2.0 seconds	2.0 provided reliably better conditioning than any other interval
Exp. II	Pigs	Increase in illumination	Shock to rear leg	As above	1, 2, 4, 8 seconds	During early conditioning trials (1–15) conditioning was best for 1- and 2- second intervals; later trials (16–35) conditioning was best with 4- and 8- second intervals
Noble and Harding (1963)	Rhesus monkey	Increase in illumination	Shock to waist	General bodily response	.5, 1, 2, 4 seconds	Only 2-second interval provided significantly more CR's than control
Klinman and Bitterman (1963) Exp. I	Mollienisia (Fish)	Increase in illumination	Shock	General activity	.5, 2, 4 seconds	Probability and magnitude of CR declined from maximum at .5 seconds (1.5 min. between trials)
Exp. II	Mollienisia (Fish)	Increase in illumination	Shock	General activity	.5, 2, 4 seconds	Influence of CS-UCS interval not significant (4.0 minutes between trials)
Exp. III	Goldfish	Increase in illumination	Shock	General activity	.5, 2, 4 seconds	Influence of CS-UCS interval not significant

tions. "The occurrence of the conditioned GSR is thus hardly surprising, and it can be explained without recourse to a principle of autonomic learning."

A number of recent developments seem to hold promise for a better understanding of this area. One of these is the proposal by Boneau (1958) and Prokasy and his associates that the CR behaves as an instrumental response in that its characteristics can be altered or changed by the reinforcing contingencies that are found in the experimental situation. These investigators have examined this position by shifting the interstimulus interval within blocks of acquisition trials that are provided the subject.

In a study by Boneau (1958), a group of subjects received 50 conditioning trials (eyelid response) with an interstimulus interval of five-tenths of a second. The group was then subdivided into (a) one which was shifted to a 1.0-second interstimulus interval for 100 additional trials and (b) a second group which was shifted to a 1.5-second interstimulus interval for 100 additional trials. Two control groups were given 150 trials with either a 1.0- or 1.5-second interstimulus interval. If a conditioned response is defined as a response appropriate to a short CS-UCS interval, i.e., lying in the latency range of .31 to .50 seconds, the results are similar to those obtained in an earlier study by McAllister (1953a) in that there was a decline in the percentage of conditioned responses for both the 1.0 and 1.5 shift groups. However, it must be kept in mind that a conditioned response defined as a response found in the latency range of .31 to .50 seconds is not appropriate for either the 1.0 or 1.5 interstimulus interval groups since the making of a response at this latency (.31 to .50 sec.) would undoubtedly result in the individual's opening his eye just prior to the onset of the UCS. On the other hand, if the conditioned response is defined by a latency of .66 to 1.0 second for the 1.0-second interstimulus interval group and 1.01 to 1.50 seconds for the 1.5-second interstimulus interval group, an increasing percentage of conditioned responses is noted as a function of trials with this new interstimulus interval.

Ebel and Prokasy (1963), also using the conditioned eye blink, examined the shifting of the ISI over 1,200 training trials. They have confirmed Boneau's findings that the latency of the response is related to changes in the interstimulus interval. Nine treatment groups were used, and three interstimulus interval conditions were employed in the study, i.e., .2, .5, and .8 second. Of the nine

TABLE 7–6

Latency Means and SD's (Msec.) over Three Blocks of
Four Sessions

GROUP	BLOCK 1		BLOCK 2		BLOCK 3	
	MEAN	SD	MEAN	SD	MEAN	SD
222	268	67	245	65	231	57
252	342	137	425	163	302	97
282	306	135	465	199	286	129
555	527	128	413	82	305	69
525	499	153	314	131	469	153
585	393	87	575	158	420	107
888	760	193	773	145	693	171
828	623	213	308	116	515	224
858	647	172	508	106	558	181

(Adapted from Ebel and Prokasy, 1963)

treatment conditions, three involved only a single interstimulus interval value provided throughout training but the remaining six involved shifts from one interstimulus interval to another. Following 400 trials with a .2-second interstimulus interval, one group was shifted to a .5-second interstimulus interval, and a second group was shifted to an .8-second interstimulus interval for 400 trials. Following these trials, they were then shifted back to the original .2-second interstimulus interval. Two other groups following 400 training trials with a .5-second interstimulus interval were shifted to either .2-second interstimulus interval or .8-interstimulus interval for 400 trials and then returned to .5. Finally, two other groups following 400 training trials on a .8-interstimulus interval were shifted to either .2- or .5-interstimulus interval and then returned to a .8-interstimulus interval.

In general, Ebel and Prokasy found that increases or decreases in the interstimulus interval resulted in correlated changes in latency means and standard deviations. Table 7–6 provides this information. The .2, .5, .2 group's mean latency of responding, for example, was .342 for the first 400 trials (.2 ISI), increased to .425 for the second 400 trials (.5 ISI), and then returned to a mean latency of .302 (.2 ISI).

The experimenters, in complete agreement with Boneau, have supported the position that reinforcement in classical conditioning is contingent at least in part upon the amount of time which separates the CR and UCS events, with the temporally appropriate location of the CR with respect to UCS onset strongly suggesting a kind of instrumental shaping. Ebel and Prokasy further point out that the interstimulus interval function should reflect the efficiency with which the subject is able to maximize the CR-UCS reinforcement contingency. Thus, the optimal value of an interstimulus interval would be one in which it is possible for the subject to make a response just prior to UCS onset. Since subjects apparently are unable to make an eyelid response with a latency of much under .18 second, interstimulus intervals of less than this will result in reducing the effectiveness of the CR. As the interstimulus intervals increase beyond .5 second, the appearance of a CR (defined as a response with a latency of .31 to .50 second) will reduce the effectiveness of reinforcement since, presumably, the individual will be opening his eye when the UCS is presented. This, therefore, should result in a delayed latency of responding which will be related to the length of the interstimulus interval, with the result that the eyeblink should just precede the presentation of the UCS regardless of the length of the interval.

A finding by Prokasy, Ebel, and Thompson (1963) using the conditioned eyelid response is also in keeping with the general position that the classical conditioned response can be shaped by appropriate training procedures. In this study, one group of subjects was given trials in which the subjects began their training with an interstimulus interval of .63 second, but then the interval was gradually shifted to one of 2.497 in six steps over a 360-trial period. More specifically, 40 trials were given with an interstimulus interval of .63 second, 40 trials with .791, 50 trials with .996, 50 trials with 1.246, 60 trials with 1.570, 60 trials with 1.977, and 60 trials with 2.497. A second group received 300 trials with an interstimulus interval of .63 and then was shifted for the last 60 trials to 2.497. Finally, a third group received all 360 trials with an interstimulus interval of 2.497. Results revealed that for the last 60 trials the frequency of response was considerably greater for the gradually shifted group (approximately 60 per cent) than for the other two groups (approximately 30 per cent) which had identical interstimulus intervals but were either switched rapidly or started training at this interval.

In summary, the studies of Boneau (1958) and Prokasy and his associates are noteworthy in that they place the classical conditioning situation, at least for eyelid conditioning, within an instrumental learning context, with the CR-UCS interval being of basic importance.

A second development is a theory proposed by Jones (1962) in which classical conditioning is presumed to involve the operation of both contiguity and reinforcement principles. She has pointed out that when the CS-UCS interval is varied two temporal relationships which are of basic importance are affected: (1) the CS-UCR interval and (2) the CR-UCS interval. One optimum condition for the establishment of a conditioned response is that the CS and the UCR be contiguous in time (the greater the degree of temporal separation of these events, the weaker the resulting connection), since a contiguity principle is assumed to operate with this relationship. The second optimum condition is that the temporal relationship between the CR and the UCS also be contiguous. A reinforcement principle is assumed to operate here (the UCS serves as the reinforcing agent), and the primary reinforcement gradient indicates that the longer the interval between these two events, the less effective the reinforcing agent. Jones has hypothesized that early in the conditioning trials the efficiency of performance is determined by the contiguity of the CS and the UCR, whereas late in the conditioning trials the contiguity between the CR and UCS assumes primary importance in strengthening the CR.

The basic problem is that no single CS-UCS interval can be chosen which maximizes the operating efficiency of both contiguity and reinforcement. For example, in any given experimental situation, the response which is being measured always has some latency. Thus, the CS-UCS interval which maximizes the operation of a contiguity principle presumed to operate with the CS-UCR relationship is backward conditioning. But this relationship minimizes the efficiency of the CR-UCS relationship since the presentation of reinforcement (UCS) takes place prior to the appearance of the CR. As Jones has written, "If the interstimulus interval is such as to favor the effect of either the gradient of contiguity or of reinforcement, it necessarily follows that the other is operating at less than maximum efficiency." In predicting the optimum CS-UCS interval, the combination of the overlapping contiguity and reinforcement gradients must be considered. Jones has proposed that these combine in an additive fashion to influence the strength of the conditioned response.

Two of the varying performance functions which Jones has deduced from her theoretical position seem particularly important. First, when groups are trained with a short CS-UCS interval, they should perform relatively well initially but then show a decrement in performance. On the other hand, groups trained with longer CS-UCS intervals should show less rapid initial learning but should perform better in later training. Second, when responses which differ in latency are conditioned, the interstimulus interval function for the longer latency response would be less sharply peaked and a wider range of CS-UCS intervals should be effective. In an experimental examination of these hypotheses [Jones (1961)], in which CS (tone) -UCS (shock) intervals of 20, 235, 440, 660, 860, 1,045, and 1,245 milliseconds were used, a response with a short latency (finger movement) as well as long latency (GSR) was conditioned. The experimental findings were in keeping with her position.

In summary, it may be the ease of manipulating the CS-UCS interval which has blinded experimenters to the fact that the temporal relationship between the CR-UCS and CS-UCR is of critical importance in conditioned response learning. The work of Boneau, Prokasy, etc. suggests that the interstimulus interval problem be approached from this vantage point.[10]

Backward Conditioning

A topic which in essence involves the CS-UCS interval and yet which deserves special mention is backward conditioning. The arrangement is to provide the UCS prior to the presentation of the CS. A problem of considerable interest has been to determine whether or not conditioning can take place with such an arrangement. Pavlov (1927) wrote, "It is . . . necessary that the conditioned stimulus should begin . . . before the unconditioned stimulus. . . . If this order is reversed . . . , the conditioned reflex cannot be established at all."

Although experiments by Cason (1935) and Porter (1938) tentatively supported the Pavlovian position, the findings of Switzer (1930), Wolfle (1932), Bernstein (1934), Grether

---

[10] A third development in this area should be noted, although it is one which continues to view the CS-UCS relationship in terms of an optimal interval. Wickens and his associates have been interested in the CS-UCS interval as it is related to the presentation of a compound conditioned stimulus in which the onset of different elements of this stimulus bear different temporal relationships to the onset of the UCS. Their general problem has been one of attempting to predict responses to these elements based upon the principle that the optimal CS-UCS interval is five-tenths of a second. Their findings have been quite complex and not easy to summarize. [See Wickens (1959); Wickens, Gehman, and Sullivan (1959); and Wickens, Born, and Wickens (1963).]

(1938), and Harlow (1939) all appeared to indicate that backward conditioning could take place in such a situation. However, the more recent studies of Spooner and Kellogg (1947); Fitzwater and Reisman (1952); Champion (1962); Kamin (1963); and Trapold, Homzie, and Rutledge (1964), examining a variety of responses, again have questioned the position that backward conditioning is a bona fide phenomenon.

In the Spooner and Kellogg (1947) study, a classical conditioned finger withdrawal experiment was set up in which a tone served as the CS and shock to the finger served as the UCS. Six groups of subjects were used in which three of the groups had the tone precede the shock by 1.5, 1.0, and .5 second, respectively. Simultaneous conditioning was employed for the fourth group and for two backward conditioning groups, the UCS preceded the CS by .50 and .25 second, respectively. One hundred trials were provided which included 20 nonshock or test trials, making up the principal source of the data reported. An analysis of the findings revealed that the backward and simultaneous conditioning procedures produced a decremental or extinction effect which is the reverse of that present in forward conditioning. Thus, the so-called CR which occurs in the simultaneous and backward situation generally appears in the early stages of training and disappears as training continues. For example, approximately 20 per cent conditioned responses were found for the backward and simultaneous groups during the first 20 trials. For Trials 41 to 60, this percentage decreased to approximately 10 per cent, and by Trials 81 to 100, it was less than 5 per cent. Spooner and Kellogg also point out that there are marked differences in the latency of the backward CR as contrasted to the forward CR, with the latency of the forward CR tending to increase with practice whereas the latency of the backward CR reveals no such progression. The investigators concluded that although backward conditioned responses may be obtained under the proper experimental circumstances they differ in so many ways from the typical forward conditioned response that there is a real question as to whether they should be considered as conditioned responses at all.

One major difficulty with Spooner and Kellogg's (1947) conclusions was that their study lacked a pseudoconditioned control group. In the Fitzwater and Reisman (1952) study, in which this deficiency was remedied, the classical finger withdrawal response was examined utilizing a procedure similar to that employed by Spooner and Kellogg (1947). In addition to the normal forward conditioning group which utilized a five-tenths of a second interstimulus interval, simultaneous, backward, and pseudoconditioning control groups were used. For the simultaneous group both CS and UCS were presented simultaneously, but for the backward conditioning group, the UCS onset preceded the CS onset by five-tenths of a second. Finally, a pseudoconditioning group was used in which shock was presented alone for 80 trials; these were interspersed with 20 test trials in which the tone was presented alone. Results revealed no significant differences among the backward, simultaneous, and pseudo modes of presentation, although each differed significantly from the findings obtained with the forward group. As a result, it appears that backward conditioning cannot be recognized as a phenomenon distinct from pseudoconditioning.[11]

THE ROLE OF THE CS-UCS INTERVAL IN INSTRUMENTAL AVOIDANCE LEARNING

It will be recalled that instrumental avoidance learning situations can be categorized into (1) active and (2) passive avoidance.

---

[11] Two investigators who believe that backward conditioning is a genuine conditioned response phenomenon are Razran (1956) and Jones (1962). Reviewing the data from a number of Russian and American experiments, Razran concluded that "A sum total of the reviewed experimental studies leaves no doubt that backward conditioning is a genuine CR-associative phenomenon that is obtainable and maintainable under special conditions." Razran has indicated that the conditions favorable for the formation of backward CR's are a UCS that is not too strong and a CS that is not too weak. If shock is used as a UCS, backward conditioning appears to be possible only when the CS is applied after the shock has ceased and not when it is applied during the presentation of shock. With food used as the CS, backward conditioning is more readily obtained when the UCS-CS interval is 15 seconds than when it is five seconds and more readily when five than when two seconds.

Jones (1962) on the basis of her two-process theory of classical conditioning has hypothesized that backward conditioning emerges as a special case of the CS-UCS interval effect rather than differing qualitatively from forward conditioning. Such an effect, she avers, is dependent primarily upon the operation of a contiguity principle which leads to an initial increase in performance during the early conditioning trials, followed by a decrease. Trapold, Homzie, and Rutledge (1964), however, were unable to find any evidence of backward conditioning in either the GSR, finger withdrawal, or eyeblink as a function of the number of UCS-CS pairings.

TABLE 7–7

Number of Trials Required to Reach the Last
Shock Trial as a Function of CS-UCS Interval

TRIALS	CS-UCS INTERVAL					
	5″	10″	20″	40″-a	40″-b	40″
Mean	9.4	16.0	25.8	55.5+	10.0	28.2+
Median	6.0	8.5	28.5	57.5+	7.0	18.5

Note: Kamin pointed out that early in training, six of the ten dogs making up the 40″ group developed a tendency to respond spontaneously, with the response not appearing to be elicited by the CS. The data for these six subjects are indicated under the heading 40″ b and the remaining four subjects in the 40″ group are presented under 40″ a. Data under 40″ includes all ten subjects.

(Adapted from Kamin, 1954)

Active Avoidance

In the active avoidance learning situation, the CS-UCS interval refers to the time interval measured from the onset of the CS to the onset of the UCS. In an examination of the effects of this interval, Kamin (1954), using dogs as subjects, employed a shuttle box situation in which the animal had to jump a barrier in order to get from one side to the other. The CS was the sounding of a buzzer for two seconds in the compartment in which the animal was placed. Following an interval of either 5, 10, 20, or 40 seconds, measured from the onset of the CS, the UCS was presented. The short duration of the CS, it should be noted, resulted in a trace conditioning procedure. An acquisition criterion of five consecutive avoidance trials was employed. Once the criterion was reached, extinction trials were begun and continued until an extinction criterion of five consecutive failures to respond to the CS was observed. If extinction had not taken place within ten days (100 trials), extinction trials were discontinued. Results revealed that the briefer CS-UCS intervals led to more rapid acquisition of the avoidance response as well as to greater resistance to extinction. Table 7–7 reveals the mean number of trials required to reach the last shock trial as a function of the CS-UCS interval (acquisition). Figure 7–7 reveals resistance to extinction as a function of the CS-UCS interval.

A subsequent study by Davitz, Mason, Mowrer, and Viek (1957), using rats as subjects, has provided similar findings. Training consisted of 20 trials in which the CS, a two-second

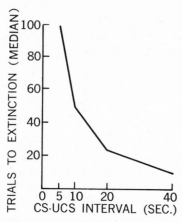

Fig. 7–7. Resistance to extinction as a function of the CS-UCS interval. *Adapted from Kamin (1954)*

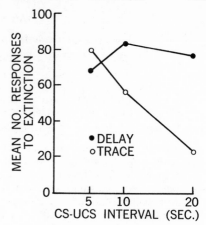

Fig. 7–8. Mean number of responses to extinction as a function of the CS-UCS interval in a delayed and trace conditioning procedure. *Adapted from Church, Brush, and Solomon (1956)*

blinking light, was paired with a three-second electric shock serving as the UCS. The CS was presented at intervals of 0, 2, 5, 10, 30, 120, and 600 seconds before the onset of shock.[12] Each subject received four training trials a day for five days. Following such acquisition, a testing procedure designed to determine whether or not the CS at each of the varying CS-UCS intervals had acquired the capacity to evoke an emotional response was begun. The behavioral index of this response was the tendency on the part of the animals to "freeze" or inhibit activity which was produced by the presentation of only the CS. A gradient similar to the extinction gradient obtained by Kamin (1954) was obtained.

A study by Brush, Brush, and Solomon (1955) examined the effects of the CS-UCS interval with a delayed conditioning procedure, in contrast to a trace conditioning procedure used by Kamin (1954). With the delayed conditioning procedure, the CS is

[12] It should be noted that this procedure involves trace conditioning for the 5-, 10-, 30-, 120-, and 600-second CS-UCS intervals. The zero interval is a simultaneous conditioning situation, and the two-second interval represents a delayed conditioning procedure.

TABLE 7–8

Indices of Avoidance Learning as a Function of CS-UCS Interval in
Trace (Kamin) and Delay (Church, Brush, and Solomon) Procedures

	TRACE CS-UCS INTERVAL			DELAY CS-UCS INTERVAL		
	5″	10″	20″	5″	10″	20″
Mean no. of shocks						
Mean..................	6.5	11.0	18.7	11.7	12.0	8.7
Median...............	4.0	6.5	18.5	11.0	11.0	7.0
Mean trial of 1st avoidance						
Mean..................	4.5	5.1	6.9	7.1	5.4	6.3
Median...............	4.5	4.5	6.5	7.0	4.0	5.0
Mean trial of 5th avoidance						
Mean..................	10.8	13.5	15.4	15.4	16.4	12.4
Median...............	9.5	11.5	15.5	16.0	15.0	12.0

(Adapted from Church, Brush, and Solomon, 1956)

presented until the onset of the UCS. In the avoidance learning situation, this requires that the CS be presented during the entire CS-UCS interval. In this study, the experimenters had considerable difficulty comparing their findings to those of Kamin (1954) since there were a number of procedural differences which precluded a bona fide comparison. As a result, a second study was undertaken by Church, Brush, and Solomon (1956) in which Kamin's methodology was duplicated, with the delayed conditioning technique being the only procedural difference. Results from the two studies for comparable groups are presented in Table 7–8, which reveals acquisition findings, and Figure 7–8, which presents the extinction findings. It can be noted that in the trace conditioning procedure poorer learning results as a function of lengthening the CS-UCS interval; however, this is not true when a delayed conditioning technique is used. Rather, learning appears to be independent of the CS-UCS interval. Similarly, resistance to extinction appears to be independent of the CS-UCS interval.

The theoretical explanation that Church, Brush, and Solomon (1956) have proposed for their own as well as Kamin's (1954) findings is based upon a two-process theory of avoidance learning, first proposed by Mowrer (1947) and later elaborated upon by Solomon and Wynne (1954) and Turner and Solomon (1962). The first process is the establishment of a conditioned emotional response which takes place as a result of the contiguous presentation of the CS and UCS. In learning these emotional responses, the interval between the onset of the CS and the onset of the UCS becomes the important temporal variable. The second process is the reinforcement of the instrumental escape response which takes place by means of drive reduction, i.e., elimination of the shock. During the course of learning, the escape response is replaced by an avoidance response; drive reduction continues to take place, although it is of a secondary variety, i.e., fear or anxiety reduction. The important time interval in the reinforcement process is the interval between the occurrence of the instrumental response and the CS or UCS termination.

The operation of the reinforcement process is inferred from measuring the escape or avoidance response which is dependent upon either CS (avoidance) or UCS (escape) termination. Church, Brush, and Solomon (1956) point out that in trace conditioning, where the CS always is terminated after two seconds of presentation, only those responses with latencies as short as two seconds could maximally benefit from secondary drive reduction resulting from the termination of the CS. Thus, the shorter CS-UCS interval groups would benefit from this effect more than the longer interval groups. Since the differential effect between CS-UCS groups is not possible in the delay procedure (the termination of the CS always follows the response regardless of the CS-UCS interval), the CS-UCS interval gradient should be more pronounced in the trace procedure than in the delay procedure, a prediction in keeping with the experimental findings. As a result, the experimenters concluded that the rate of avoidance learning is not strictly a function of the onset of the CS-UCS interval; rather, it is related to response termination of the CS.

Furthermore, it can be inferred from the two-process theory that resistance to extinction should be greater with delayed conditioning than that found with trace conditioning because the delay groups have the advantage of response termination of the CS and the secondary drive reduction resulting from such termination. Only with the short CS-UCS interval group in the trace procedure could this effect possibly be operating. Such a position means that resistance to extinction should be an inverse function of the CS-UCS interval in the trace procedure and either independent of or minimally related to the CS-UCS interval in the delay procedure. The experimental data from the two studies cited support these predictions.[13]

Passive Avoidance

In the passive avoidance situation, the organism first learns a response and is then presented with a noxious stimulus following the response. Although Warden and Dymond (1931) and Bevan and Dukes (1955) also examined this problem, Kamin's (1959) study is the most extensive. In this investigation, consisting of two separate studies, rats were first trained to avoid shock by running from one compartment of a shuttle box to another. The CS was a buzzer (Experiment I) or a buzzer plus lifting of a gate separating the two compartments (Experiment II). The UCS was a shock administered through a grid floor, with the CS-UCS interval being ten seconds. After the animals had reached a criterion of 11 consecutive avoidances, punishment trials were instituted in which the animals received shock either 0, 10, 20, 30, or 40 seconds after making the avoidance response. Thus, punishment might occur immediately or as much as 40 seconds after the response. A control group which did not receive punishment for responding was also used. The results of both studies, indicated in Figure 7–9, show similar delay of punishment gradients. As it will be noted, there is considerable similarity between this kind of gradient and the primary reinforcement gradient found in instrumental reward studies.

INSTRUMENTAL REWARD AND ESCAPE LEARNING SITUATIONS

Both Hull (1952) and Spence (1956) have indicated the importance of differentiating between what they have called (1)

---

[13] Low and Low (1962), using rats learning a barrier-jumping response under a delayed conditioned procedure with the CS-UCS intervals of 2, 4, 6, 8, and 10 seconds, were unable to confirm the experimental findings of Church, Brush, and Solomon (1956). The Lows found that the number of avoidance responses or the mean number of trials to reach a criterion of four consecutive avoidance responses *was* a function of the CS-UCS interval. A negatively decelerated curve best described this relationship, with the two-second CS-UCS interval group requiring the largest number of trials to reach the criterion and the ten-second CS-UCS group the smallest. No differences among groups were obtained during extinction when either latency of responding or number of responses was used as the extinction measure.

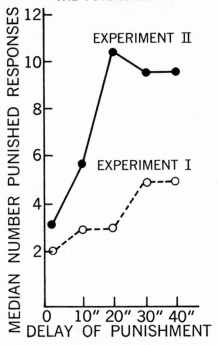

Fig. 7–9. Median number of extinction responses as a function of delay of punishment. *Adapted from Kamin (1959)*

response delay and (2) temporal delay in instrumental reward learning situations. The response delay situation is one in which the instrumental response chain, or the length of the behavior sequence, varies. Thus, there are different distances between the first part of the sequence, or initial portion of the chain, and the reinforcement received at the end of the behavior sequence. Temporal delay, on the other hand, involves the introduction of a period of time between the organism's making an instrumental response and the securing of the reinforcement. It must be recognized that this latter classification represents only a convenient way of describing a set of operations in which the experimenter does not require the organism to make any additional responses between the making of one required response and the securing of reward, since it is obvious that responses of one type or another fill this delay interval just as they fill the interval which is utilized in the response delay situation.

Response Delay

In 1932, Hull formulated the goal gradient hypothesis which stated (pp. 25–26) that "there exists an excitatory gradient extending with positive acceleration approximately according to the logarithmic law in an upward direction from the beginning of the maze to the goal box," and "the goal reaction gets conditioned the most strongly to the stimuli preceding it, and the other reactions of the behavior sequence get conditioned to their stimuli progressively weaker as they are more remote in time or space from the goal reaction."

A survey of almost all of the response delay studies reveals that they have been used to examine the adequacy of the goal gradient hypothesis. These studies can be divided into (1) the order of elimination of blind alleys in a complex maze, (2) the preference for the shorter of the two paths to a goal, and (3) the speed of locomotion gradient.

THE ORDER OF ELIMINATION OF BLIND ALLEYS IN THE MAZE. Although a number of early investigators were interested in how errors were distributed throughout a complex maze [Watson (1907), Vincent (1915), Hubbert (1915), Carr (1917), Hubbert and Lashley (1917), Warden (1923), Warden and Cummings (1929)], it was Hull (1932) who deduced from his goal gradient hypothesis that errors found in the maze situation should be eliminated in a backward direction—the first correct response to be learned should be closest to the goal box, etc.

A number of investigators, however, have been unable to obtain findings which support Hull's position. Spence's (1932) careful examination of many of these findings led him to conclude, "There is considerable evidence of some backward order principle of learning operating in the maze situation. In general, the blinds are more difficult the farther they are from the goal." At the same time, he also pointed out that other learning principles are involved in the order of blind alley elimination. For example, the animal will tend to make anticipatory errors; that is, blind alleys which point in the direction of the goal will tend to be entered more often than those pointing away and will thus become harder to eliminate.[14]

[14] Hull (1952), in a later attempt to examine the mechanisms underlying the order of elimination of maze errors, added the role of fractional anticipatory goal responses to the goal gradient hypothesis. Such responses are important in de-

LEARNING TO TAKE THE SHORTER PATH TO A GOAL. A second deduction stemming from the goal gradient hypothesis was related to the learning of a discrimination between pathways involving different distances to a goal object. According to the goal gradient hypothesis, the differential strength between the two paths will develop as a function of the different delays of reinforcement that each path involves. Each path should be taken equally often at the beginning of training, but a differential effect of reinforcement should develop in favor of the shorter path because this response receives a greater increment of habit strength per trial than does the long path. Eventually, this differential habit strength reaches a sufficient magnitude to offset all other factors which are operating and results in the organism's consistently taking the shorter path to the goal.

Such a deduction was confirmed in a study by Grice (1942). Five groups of white rats were run in a maze situation in which they were required to select the shorter of the two paths to a goal. The lengths of the two maze paths used for Group I were 6 and 12 feet; for Group II, 12 and 18 feet; for Group III, 18 and 24 feet; for Group IV, 24 and 30 feet; and for Group V, 30 and 36 feet. Four trials were given each day. For the first two trials the animals were forced to go once each way, but on the last two trials they were permitted free choice. Training continued until the rats took the shorter path to the goal box on both of the free trials for three consecutive days. Results revealed that all groups learned to take the shorter path to the goal box thus confirming, at least in part, the goal gradient hypothesis.

The ratios of the long path to the short (long/short) for the varying groups were as follows: Group I, 2.00; Group II, 1.50; Group III, 1.33; Group IV, 1.25; and Group V, 1.20. As Figure 7–10 reveals, when the number of errors for the varying groups are plotted as a function of these ratios, a negatively accelerated gradient is obtained.

Grice altered not only the ratio of the long path to the short but also the absolute lengths of the alternative paths. Thompson (1944) was interested in ascertaining whether the difficulty of learning to discriminate between paths of different lengths would be constant for different absolute lengths if their ratios remained constant. In one experiment, five groups of rats were utilized and

---

terminining the ease or difficulty of learning correct responses at places in the maze other than the last choice point.

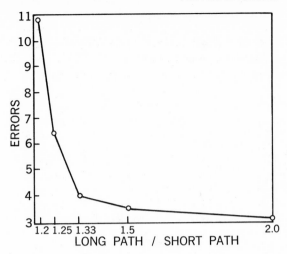

Fig. 7–10. Errors made by the five groups. *Adapted from Grice (1942)*

with each group, the ratio of the long to the short path remained constant at 2.0, although the absolute length of the paths differed. The second experiment involved a constant ratio of 1.3. Here, six groups of animals were used. The general procedure which Thompson employed was to provide four daily trials; on the first two trials, the animal was permitted a free choice, but the next two trials were forced—the object being that for each four daily trials, two were made to the long path and two to the short. The learning criterion was choosing the shorter path on the two free choice trials for three consecutive days. If the subjects had not satisfied this criterion after 20 days of training, they were dropped from the experiment. Table 7–9 provides the varying conditions of the two studies as well as the appropriate findings. Grice's general conclusions should be modified since an examination of the mean number of errors reveals that the relative difficulty of learning the short path is dependent upon the absolute lengths of the paths as well as the ratio of the long to the short path. It is not clear, however, precisely what form the modification should take since Thompson's findings are sufficiently complex that no simple relationship is evident.

SPEED OF LOCOMOTION GRADIENT. If, as the goal gradient hypothesis indicates, responses closer to the goal are conditioned

TABLE 7–9

The Percentage of Animals in Each Group that Reached a Learning Criterion of Six Successive Free Runs to the Short Path along with the Mean Number of Errors Made in 20 Days for 40 Free Trials

RATIO 2.0

GROUP	N	SHORT PATH	LONG PATH	PERCENTAGE OF RATS REACHING CRITERION	MEAN NUMBER OF ERRORS
I	20	6 feet	12 feet	100	4.45
II	20	12 feet	24 feet	100	6.85
III	20	15 feet	30 feet	100	6.75
IV	17	18 feet	36 feet	100	4.64
V	13	29 feet	58 feet	100	6.61

RATIO 1.3

I	10	6 feet	7.8 feet	70.0	13.00
II	10	11 feet	14.3 feet	80.0	10.60
III	14	15 feet	19.5 feet	92.8	6.64
IV	9	20 feet	26.0 feet	88.8	9.22
V	9	32 feet	41.6 feet	22.2	18.44
VI	7	45 feet	58.5 feet	71.4	13.14

(Adapted from Thompson, 1944)

more strongly than remote responses, an animal's speed of running should also be a function of its nearness to the goal object—the closer it gets, the more rapidly it runs. Hull's (1934) investigation of the rat's speed of locomotion in the straight runway was an examination of the adequacy of the goal gradient hypothesis in this kind of learning situation. A 40-foot runway was utilized, with the runway being divided into eight five-foot sections. Five trials per day were given, and an examination of performance revealed that running speed was a function of the runway section on Days 1 and 2. In general, the gradient which was obtained approached the form that the goal gradient hypothesis would predict, although there was a slight retardation in running speed just as the goal was about to be reached. On the other hand, a relatively flat gradient, with little differences in running speeds among any of the sections, was obtained after Days 6 and 7. Although Hull believed that his results substantiated his deduction from the goal gradient hypothesis, they had at the same time revealed "a rich complexity of phenomena not demanded by the hypothesis." One of these was a tendency toward slowing down as the goal was approached, and the second was a kind of inertia characteristic of starting.

Subsequent experimental work by Bruce (1937), Morgan and Fields (1938), and Drew (1939) has failed to obtain clear evidence to support the speed of locomotion gradient. As is frequently the case, the attempt to explain the learning of even a simple response based upon only a single principle was not successful.

TEMPORAL DELAY

Although Watson (1917), Hamilton (1929), and Wolfe (1934) provided experimental findings relevant to this area, their experimental procedures produced uncontrolled secondary reinforcement effects; as a result, contemporary studies of temporal delay of reinforcement typically begin with Perin (1943). In this study, Perin found that if a delay of 30 seconds or more was introduced between the rat's making a bar-pressing response and its receiving food the animal was unable to learn. Subsequent studies by Perkins (1947), Grice (1948), and Smith (1951) have indicated that this time interval should be further reduced. In Grice's (1948) study, groups of rats were required to learn a black-white discrimination problem. Delays of 0, .5, 1.2, 2, 5, and 10 seconds were introduced between the animal's making the correct response and its securing food. (It should be noted that the delay periods used in Grice's study were not all of the temporal variety. In some cases, a response delay was used.) The criterion of learning was 18 correct responses out of 20 trials. Learning curves for the varying groups revealed that the 0 delay group learned most rapidly, followed by the .5, 1.2, and 2.0 groups. When a delay of five seconds was introduced, the animals experienced great difficulty in learning; with as many as 700 trials, the animals' responses were only 80 per cent correct. The group provided a delay of ten seconds did not learn the discrimination task although in some cases the animals were given as many as 1,400 trials. Figure 7–11 presents these findings.

Fowler and Trapold (1962) have shown that the speed of rats' running down a charged runway is significantly slower when reinforcement, defined by shock reduction, is delayed following

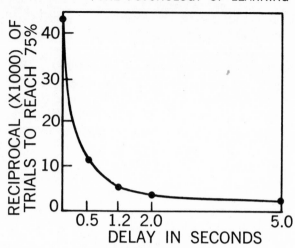

Fig. 7–11. Rate of learning as a function of delay of reward. The experimental values are represented by black dots, and the smooth curve is fitted to these data. *Adapted from Grice (1948)*

the behavior which is instrumental in securing it. The delays used by these investigators were 0, 1, 2, 4, 8, or 16 seconds. These findings, Fowler and Trapold have observed, are analogous to those of Grice (1948) and others and suggest that similar laws underlie both types of experimental situations.

Finally, Keesey (1964) has reported similar findings using a discriminative bar-pressing response and intracranial self-stimulation. In this study, groups of rats who had electrodes implanted in their posterior hypothalamus were first trained to depress a single bar for stimulation which was provided either 0.0, 0.5, 1.0, 2.0, 3.0, or 5.0 seconds after the bar press. Following such training, the subjects were placed in a two-bar discrimination situation in which they were to choose between two bars, over one of which a light had been placed. A response on the lighted bar, whose position was randomly varied, resulted in the delivery of intracranial stimulation after the same temporal interval which animals had experienced in their first training session. A response to the nonlighted bar provided no stimulation. Following a response on either bar, the discriminative and house lights were extinguished for ten seconds. The reciprocal of the mean number of errors made by each group over 500 trials as a function of the delay interval is revealed in Figure 7–12. The similarity between

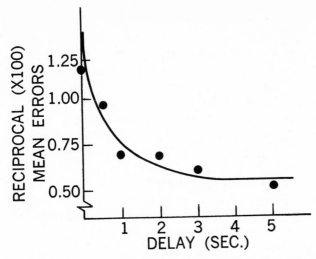

Fig. 7–12. Rate of learning as a function of the delay of reward. The curve has been visually fitted to the data points. *Adapted from Keesey (1964)*

this function and that obtained by Grice (1948) can be readily noted.[15]

The interaction of delay of reinforcement with other reinforcement variables has been investigated, although not extensively. Studies of instrumental learning situations in which the rate of response has been the response measure have indicated that drive level and delay combine additively [Ramond (1954), Renner (1963)]; Logan (1960) also has reported that delay combines additively with amount of reward.

In an examination of the mechanisms involved in the delay of reinforcement, Spence (1947) originally suggested that ". . . it would not seem unreasonable to hypothesize that there is no primary gradient of reinforcement but that all learning involving

[15] A recent study by Brackbill (1964) has not been in keeping with these general findings. In her first experiment, third grade children were required to learn a series of discrimination problems with either zero or ten seconds interpolated between the making of a choice and the securing of reward. During the ten-second delay condition, the children were required to copy pairs of random numbers. After the subject made the correct response, a lamp flashed on, a loud buzzer sounded, and a marble which could later be exchanged for a toy dropped into a receptacle. Brackbill found that the delayed reinforcement group required significantly fewer trials to reach the learning criterion than the group provided immediate reinforcement.

delay of primary reward results from the action of *immediate* secondary reinforcement which develops in the situation." Spence further proposed that although it might be possible to eliminate secondary reinforcement from the external environment it could arise from proprioceptive stimulation resulting from the organism's making differential responses.

More recently, in distinguishing between response and temporal delays of reinforcement, Spence (1956) has theorized that in temporal delay there is the reduction of K, an incentive motivation variable, which in turn involves the classically conditioned consummatory response. He has proposed that the consummatory response is weakened as a function of the length of the delay. Since this response and its related fractional anticipatory response are related to the strength of K, any reduction in K is reflected in poorer learning. A second and presumably more potent factor in producing poorer performance with temporally delayed reinforcement concerns the interfering responses which take place during the delay period. When a delay is introduced, the organism makes a variety of extraneous responses during the time interval, and because these responses are made to the same stimulus components as is the to-be-learned instrumental response, they likewise become conditioned to them. Since such responses take place during training trials, poorer learning is reflected in the increased time taken to run off the appropriate response sequence or in the competition they provide to the to-be-learned response.

An analysis of the responses which are made during the delay period would indicate that if the organism can maintain an orientation toward the response manipulandum (e.g., a bar in a Skinner box) or is so trained that specific responses serve as secondary reinforcing stimuli it is possible to reduce or perhaps eliminate any response decrement which might take place. A number of studies utilizing a variety of learning situations have provided support for such a position.

Spence (1956) has reported a series of studies by Carlton, Harker, and Shilling which have shown that the delay in reinforcement is related to the opportunity for competing responses to occur during the delay period. In one of these studies (Carlton), two groups of rats were trained to leave a starting box and run down a short runway, at the end of which was a response bar which had to be pressed in order to secure a pellet of food which dropped into a small food cup. Following each bar press, one group of animals received immediate reinforcement, whereas a second group was delayed for ten seconds. Each group was divided into subgroups (making four groups in all); one immediate reinforcement subgroup and one ten-second delay subgroup had to run over an enclosed runway which was just two inches wide and three inches high. It was presumed that these confining conditions would discourage the animal from turning away from the food cup during any delay which was imposed and thus increase the likelihood that the animal would maintain an orientation toward it. The other two subgroups had to run over a runway which was much larger—the runway in this case was 17 inches wide and 11.5 inches high. Here it was assumed that the large area would encourage the occurrence of responses incompatible with the maintenance of an orientation to the food cup.

Results supported Spence's position. For the two groups which were given immediate reinforcement, no difference in bar-pressing performance was obtained as a function of the size of the runway. On the other hand, the size of the runway did make a differential contribution to learning for those groups which were given the ten-second delay; the group running over the confined runway indicated superior performance.

Studies by Ferster (1953) and Dews (1960) illustrate the use of a pigeon's responses bridging the temporal interval to aid in the learning situation. In Ferster's study, a stable pecking response was first established with no delay of reinforcement. He then introduced a 60-second delay period which resulted in the animal's rate of pecking declining to an operant level. Short reinforcement delays were then introduced in which the length of the delay gradually increased as the pecking response became stable under each specific delay condition. Ferster found that by using this graded delay technique it was possible to obtain a normal response rate with a 60-second delay period—a delay magnitude which had previously resulted in only operant level responding.

Lawrence and Hommel (1961) have confirmed this finding using rats learning a black-white discrimination task. After their subjects had learned the discrimination, in which no delay of reinforcement was provided, fifty training trials were given with delay intervals of 20, 30, and 60 seconds. The experimenters reported that the animals continued to respond correctly in spite of the delay which was imposed.

It has been demonstrated, then, that delay of reinforcement, like amount of reinforcement, is not a static parameter but that the effect of delay depends upon the way in which the organism is permitted to acquire responses during the delay period which can be used to bridge the temporal interval.

In a recent study, Champion and McBride (1962) examined how the characteristics of the activity which fills the delay interval operate with human subjects. A paired-associate task was provided, and college students were required to read a list of words between the response which was made by the subject and the exposure of the word which would indicate whether or not a correct response had been made. For example, the word "needle" was used as the stimulus word to which the individual had to respond with the word "thread." Between the subject's response and the exposure of the response word in the apparatus, the subject had to read a list of words which would be expected to interfere with the response word, i.e., sharp, pin, sew, steel, eye, point, thimble, sewing. Two- and five-second delay periods were used, with half of the subjects in each delay period required to read lists of words during the delay whereas the remaining subjects were instructed to fixate on the word appearing in the memory drum. Response latencies for the varying groups are revealed in Figure 7–13 and in essence confirm Spence's position that performance is related to the characteristics of the competing responses which fill the delay period.

Variable Temporal Delays of Reinforcement

In examining the amount of reward variable, it was noted that some investigators varied the amount of reward required by the organism within the learning situation. A similar technique has been utilized by investigators studying the delay of reward variable. In one of the early studies, Crum, Brown, and Bitterman (1951) provided one group of rats with a 30-second delay of reward on one-half of the training trials and immediate reinforcement on the other half. The second group received immediate reinforcement on all trials. One hundred acquisition trials were provided. The results revealed that the running speed for the variable delay group was as fast as for the immediate reinforcement group.

Somewhat similar findings have been reported by Logan, Beier, and Ellis (1955). In this study, groups of subjects received

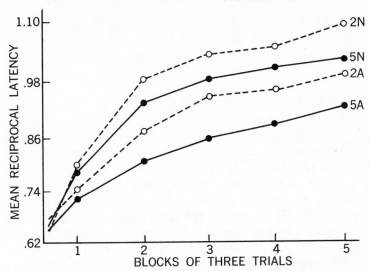

Fig. 7–13. Performance curves for groups learning with two- and five-second delay of reinforcement and with activity (A) or inactivity (N) during the delay period. *Adapted from Champion and McBride (1962)*

either (1) a constant one-second delay, (2) a constant five-second delay, or (3) a one-second delay on one-half of the trials and a nine-second delay on the other half. The task consisted of having the animals traverse a runway for 48 trials. The experimenters reported that there was no difference in running speed between the constant one-second delay group and the variable one–nine-second group. Both groups, however, were superior to the constant five-second delay group.

Pubols (1962), who examined the role of delay employing a Y-maze and using a probability of response measure, has confirmed the findings of other investigators that variable delay of reinforcement results in performance which is superior to that found with constant delay.

Finally, Logan's (1960) extensive experimental work in this area has resulted in his general conclusion that when the delay of reward is varied between two equally likely values, then among conditions having the same average delay, performance is better the wider the range of variation. Thus, a constant 20-second delay produces a rate of response which is inferior to variations of 18

THE PSYCHOLOGY OF LEARNING

and 22 which, in turn, result in poorer performance than do variations of 16 and 24. The limiting case and thus the best condition would be when zero delay is provided on one-half of the trials.[16]

The Role of Reward Delay in Extinction

Almost all of the early investigators examining the role of delay of reward confined their attention to acquisition measures; more recent studies have examined such effects on resistance to extinction. One of the first studies, and one which was discussed in the previous section, was performed by Crum, Brown, and Bitterman (1951) who trained rats to run down an alley. One group of animals was given reward immediately on every trial (zero delay) whereas a second group was rewarded immediately on one-half of the trials and after a delay of 30 seconds on the remaining half. Following 100 acquisition trials, 50 extinction trials were provided. Results showed that the variable delay group extinguished less rapidly than the group which had been provided immediate reinforcement during the acquisition period. A subsequent study by Scott and Wike (1956) replicating the Crum, et al., study has confirmed these findings.

A number of other investigators also have shown that variable delays of reinforcement which are provided during the acquisition trials produce resistance to extinction which is superior to that of groups given immediate reinforcement. For example, Peterson (1956) provided two groups of rats with 96 acquisition trials in running a straightaway. One group was given delays of reinforcement which consisted of 0, 10, 20, or 30 seconds presented in a random order, whereas a second group was given a constant zero delay (immediate reinforcement). Extinction trials were then provided in which a criterion of two successive trials with running time greater than one minute was used. The experimenter found

---

[16] Studies by Peterson (1956) and Wike and Kintsch (1959) have not confirmed this conclusion, although the experimenters have utilized more complex delay programs. In Peterson's study, two groups of rats were given 96 trials in running a straightaway. One group was given varied delayed reward trials—the delay consisting of either 0, 10, 20, or 30 seconds provided in a random order—and a second group was given zero delay. Peterson found that the zero delay group had significantly superior running times. In the Wike and Kintsch experiment, five groups of rats were used; and 20-second delay periods were provided on either 2, 21, 50, 80, or 100 per cent of the acquisition trials. On all of the other trials, a zero delay period was used. Findings indicated that runway speed was a function of the number of the trials on which zero delay was provided.

that the variable delay groups were significantly more resistant to extinction than the immediate reward group.

One limitation to these findings has been proposed by Logan, Beier, and Kincaid (1956) who found that variable delays of reinforcement increase resistance to extinction only if the difference in the delay periods making up the variable condition is rather large. In one experiment, the investigators had rats run down a runway in order to secure food. In addition to a group which received immediate reinforcement on all trials, a second group received a 0- and a 9-second delay; a third group received a 0- and 30-second delay. In the case of the varied delays, on one-half of the trials (randomly selected) one delay period was used and on the remaining trials the other delay period was used. Following 50 training trials, 20 extinction trials were provided. Findings indicated that although the 0- and 30-second delay group was significantly more resistant to extinction (as measured by running time) than either the immediate or the 0- and 9-second varied delay group there was no difference between the two latter groups.[17]

In summary, Renner's (1964) careful survey of the experimental findings obtained in this area has led him to conclude ". . . that at least under conditions where the delay interval is relatively long (e.g., 30 seconds) and is present on both acquisition and extinction, partial or variable delay of reinforcement increases resistance to extinction. . . ."

The mechanism which is responsible for producing superior resistance to extinction for delayed reinforcement is not apparent. As Renner (1964) has pointed out, it may be the delay per se or it may be the variability that is present—the fact that delay is present on only part of the trials. The few studies in which this problem has been examined have yielded controversial findings. Fehrer (1956a) and Pubols (1958) have found that a constant delay of reinforcement does lead to increased resistance to extinction.[18] On the other hand, Logan, Beier, and Kincaid (1956) and Logan (1960) have been unable to confirm this finding, and a recent study by Renner (1963) has yielded inconclusive results.

[17] The reader should be aware that all investigators have not been able to confirm the findings that variable delay results in superior resistance to extinction. See studies by Wike and Remple (1959) and Wike and Kintsch (1959).

[18] Pubols actually used a reversal learning situation, but it has been generally agreed that resistance to extinction and difficulty of reversal learning correlate highly.

Delay of Knowledge of Results

The last topic considers the role of delay as related to knowledge of results (KR). One of the early studies in this area was performed by Lorge and Thorndike (1935) who had subjects throw a ball at a target 40 times. Delays of zero, one, two, four, and six seconds were interpolated between the subjects' making the response and their KR. Results, generally, were negative in that a delay of zero seconds did not provide performance superior to that found when a six-second delay was utilized.

Results from some of the more recent studies, with KR being frequently subsumed under a reinforcement rubric, have been controversial. Saltzman (1951), Greenspoon and Foreman (1956), and Bourne (1957) have all obtained positive findings. In the Greenspoon and Foreman (1956) study, for example, subjects were required to draw a three-inch line while blindfolded. Fifty lines were drawn, with 30 seconds between each trial. For Group I, the information of "long," "short," or "right" was given immediately upon completion of the drawing of the line. Subjects in Groups II, III, and IV were also provided this information but delayed either 10, 20, or 30 seconds following their response. A control group received no information concerning the correctness of their performance. As Figure 7–14 reveals, results demonstrate the efficiency of immediate KR.

In Bourne's (1957) study, the subjects' task was to classify geometric patterns into four categories with zero, five-tenths, one, two, four, or eight seconds delay of KR. The investigator also added varying amounts of irrelevant information which produced tasks of varying difficulty. Findings indicated that the number of errors that subjects made was a function of the delay of KR regardless of the difficulty of the task. An interaction of delay with difficulty, however, was not obtained.

However, one can contrast the results of these studies with those of Saltzman, Kanfer, and Greenspoon (1955); Noble and Alcock (1958); and Bilodeau and Bilodeau (1958a), all of whom were unable to secure positive findings.

Bilodeau and Bilodeau (1958a) have been responsible for calling attention to two methodological considerations which frequently have been ignored and thus contribute to the difficulty of securing stable findings. The first, which was already discussed in other delay of reinforcement studies, concerns how the delay

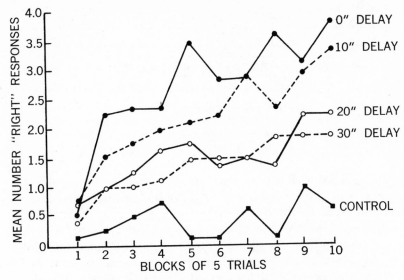

Fig. 7–14. Mean number of "right" responses of the control and experimental groups for successive blocks of five trials. *Adapted from Greenspoon and Foreman (1956)*

interval is filled. Most investigators have not been concerned with this variable, but the Bilodeaus have pointed out that whether or not the delay of KR contributes to learning may depend upon whether or not the delay interval is relatively free of interpolated activity. Their hypothesis has been that if a simple task is used, and no formal interpolated activity before or after KR is required, little or no differential effect of delay of KR should be expected. A systematic variation of the activity performed in the delay interval, however, has not yet been undertaken.

A second consideration is that a KR study involves the relationship among three temporal intervals—the time between the response and KR, the post-KR interval, and the intertrial interval—rather than only one. Figure 7–15 diagrams the sequence of events and nomenclature of the temporal intervals in a typical KR study.

Bilodeau and Bilodeau (1958a) performed five related studies, all of which were designed primarily to examine the influence of these varying temporal intervals on performance. The responses involved in the varying learning tasks were fairly simple, and there was no formal activity interpolated before or after the

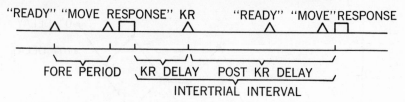

Fig. 7–15. A schematic representation of the sequence of events and the nomenclature of a typical knowledge of results study. *Adapted from Bilodeau and Bilodeau (1958a)*

subject received KR. In their first study, for example, the subjects' task was to learn to twist a knob eight 360 degree turns, with KR given either 5, 15, or 20 seconds following the making of a response. The two shorter delay groups had a reminder of KR five seconds before the signal indicating the commencement of a new trial. Since the intertrial interval was held constant at 28 seconds, the post-KR delay period decreased as the KR delay period increased. Following ten trials, the response was changed from eight to four turns and five additional trials were provided. Results revealed that the two shorter KR groups failed to differ significantly from the 20-second KR group.

These findings, along with the results of four other experiments, led the Bilodeaus to conclude that the delay of KR did not contribute to performance decrement, a finding in keeping with their hypothesis. They did find, however, that a critical variable was the intertrial interval since they observed that performance varied inversely with its duration.

8

The Role of Nonreinforced
Responses in the Learning Situation

THE PREVIOUS CHAPTER WAS DEVOTED to an examination of the contribution of reinforcement to learning, and in the situations which were examined the organism received continuous reinforcement; that is, a reward was obtained whenever a correct response was made. A number of experimenters, however, have examined the contribution of nonreinforcement to the learning process. In pursuing this interest, three operational procedures typically have been employed: (1) partial reinforcement, (2) nonreinforced trials in discrimination learning, and (3) experimental extinction. The breadth of this last topic demands that it be considered in the next chapter.

PARTIAL REINFORCEMENT

Partial reinforcement, as Jenkins and Stanley (1950) have written, ". . . refers to the reinforcement given at least once but omitted on one or more of the trials or after one or more of the responses in a series." Skinner (1938) was one of the early investigators to become interested in this procedure, but it was Humphreys' (1939) conditioned eyelid response study which was primarily responsible for producing widespread interest in the

231

area. In this study, three groups of college students were provided with the following types of training: (1) 96 trials with 100 per cent reinforcement, (2) 96 trials with 50 per cent reinforcement, and (3) 48 trials with 100 per cent reinforcement. Although no significant differences in responding were noted among the three groups during the acquisition series, there were striking differences among the groups during extinction, with the partially reinforced group extinguishing much more slowly than the groups given continuous reinforcement.

An examination of the work on partial reinforcement which has been done since the Humphreys study reveals that it can be divided into two general interest areas. First, some investigators have been interested in what can be described as empirical findings or parameters. That is, interest has centered around an examination of the contribution of varying partial reinforcement procedures on performance, as measured by both acquisition and extinction, without great concern for theoretical explanations. The second area of interest has been an attempt to account for partial reinforcement effects via a given theoretical position. As Lewis (1960) has acknowledged, it has been this second area which has piqued the interest of most investigators. Some of the basic material in both of these areas will be examined. First, however, some of the methods which have been used to manipulate the partial reinforcement procedure will be presented.

Techniques of Presentation

If the investigator uses a task in which it is possible to provide the organism with discrete trials, the partial reinforcement situation takes the form of providing reinforcement on some trials but not on others. For example, if an experimenter is examining the influence of partial reinforcement on a rat's running a straightaway, it is a simple matter to determine on what trials the animal shall (as well as shall not) receive reinforcement.

When such situations demand that the partial reinforcement group be contrasted with a continuously reinforced group, it is customary to equate groups on the basis of trials and to permit the number of reinforcements to vary. Any superiority of the partial reinforcement group takes place in spite of the greater number of reinforcements presented to the continuous group.

In a number of learning situations, e.g., Skinner box, the experimental procedure may be such that discrete trials cannot be provided and the situation becomes one of free responding. In these instances, the relevant partial reinforcement dimension cannot be trials. Rather, it is the number of responses made by the organism or the amount of time that elapses between reinforcement presentations. It has been acknowledged that these response or time contingencies may be fixed or variable. The permutations of these conditions provide the following four types of partial reinforcement schedules for the free responding situation.

1. *Fixed interval.* Here, reinforcement follows the first response which the organism makes after some fixed period of time as measured from the last reinforcement. With a 30-second fixed interval schedule, for example, reinforcement is provided for the first response which occurs 30 seconds or more following receipt of previous reinforcement.

2. *Variable interval.* With this schedule, reinforcement is provided after a variable, rather than a fixed, period of time which separates one reinforcement from the next. Thus, a 30-second variable interval schedule consists of a schedule of reinforcement administered for the first response which follows randomly selected time intervals which average 30 seconds.

3. *Fixed ratio.* Here, reinforcement is provided after every nth response. For example, a 20:1 fixed ratio schedule means that every twentieth response is followed by reinforcement.

4. *Variable ratio.* With this schedule, the number of responses which must be made in order to secure reinforcement varies, but the varying numbers of responses are averaged to provide a descriptive statement of the kind of schedule employed. Thus, a 10:1 variable ratio schedule would be produced by the following: 4 responses (reinforcement); 14 responses (reinforcement); 10 responses (reinforcement); 6 responses (reinforcement); and 16 responses (reinforcement).

Empirical Findings

How do varying percentages of reinforcement influence performance during acquisition trials? In an early classical conditioning experiment, Grant and Schipper (1952) investigated the strength of the eyelid CR in which the following percentages of reinforcement (presentation of the UCS) were used: 0, 25, 50, 75, or 100 per cent. A light served as the CS and an air puff as the UCS. Sixty training trials were given on Day 1 and 32 training trials on Day 2. Response probability was an increasing function

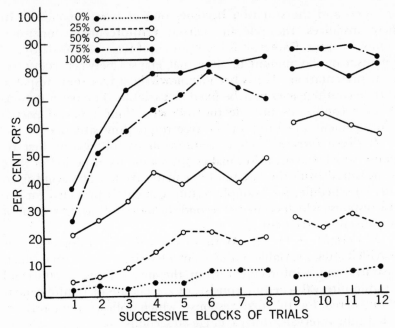

Fig. 8–1. The course of acquisition and extinction of the eyelid CR with varying percentages of reinforced trials during training. Per cent frequency of CR's is plotted against successive blocks of trials. The size of the block during training is eight trials except for Block 8 which is four trials. *Adapted from Grant and Schipper (1952)*

of the percentage of UCS presentations, although there was an inversion of the 100 and 75 per cent reinforcement conditions on Day 2. Figure 8–1 presents these findings.

In a verbal conditioning situation, Grant, Hake, and Hornseth (1951) obtained findings similar to those just presented. In this study, one light was presented and subjects were instructed to guess whether or not a second light would go on. The presentation of the second light was considered to be a "reinforced" trial. Subjects were given 60 training trials followed by 30 extinction trials. Five different training procedures were used in which each procedure varied only with regard to the percentage of "reinforced" trials presented. These percentages were the same as those utilized in the Grant and Schipper (1952) study, i.e., 0, 25, 50, 75, or 100 per cent. The number of positive responses which were made during the acquisition series was found to be a function of the percentage of "reinforced" trials provided during the training series.

The Grant and Schipper (1952) and Grant, Hake, and Hornseth (1952) studies confirmed the findings of a number of earlier experiments [Finger (1942, 1942a); Denny (1946)] which had led Jenkins and Stanley (1950) in their review of the partial reinforcement literature to write: "All other things equal, performance under a partial reinforcement schedule tends to be somewhat lower than that under a continuous reinforcement one as measured in terms of single responses."

Recent studies have indicated that this generalization does not hold for some instrumental learning situations when late acquisition trials of a prolonged learning series are examined. Weinstock (1958) provided six groups of rats with either 16.7, 33.3, 50.0, 66.7, 83.3, or 100 per cent reinforcement for traversing an enclosed runway. Subjects were placed under 22 hours of water deprivation and given one trial per day. All animals received continuous reinforcement for the first 12 days; for the next 96, they were reinforced according to the group to which they had been assigned. Thus, within every 12 trial block, one group received two reinforced trials, a second group four reinforced trials, etc. Water was available for 30 seconds on all reinforced trials. On the nonreinforced trials, the subject was left in the goal box for the same period of time. Following the 108 acquisition trials, all animals were given 60 (one per day) extinction trials. Response measures included both latency and speed of running; but since these measures yielded the same findings, Weinstock has presented only latency measures. Acquisition curves for the varying reinforcement groups are indicated in Figure 8–2. Although it can be noted that the continuously reinforced group had latencies similar to the partial reinforced groups at the end of 30–35 trials, by the fortieth trial the continuously reinforced group had the longest latencies, an effect maintained until the end of acquisition.

The complexity of the problem is revealed in the more recent studies of Goodrich (1959) and Wagner (1961) who have found that Weinstock's results are related to the response measure which is used. In Goodrich's (1959) study (Exp. I), two groups of rats were given 60 acquisition trials; one group received 50 per cent reinforcement and the other group 100 per cent. All animals were placed under 23 hours of food deprivation. The apparatus was a

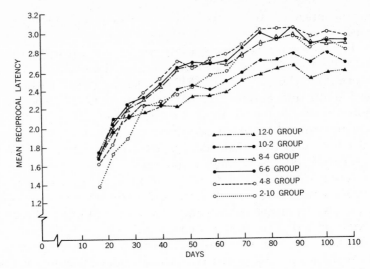

Fig. 8–2. Mean reciprocal latency as a function of trials by blocks of six for the acquisition series. *Adapted from Weinstock (1958)*

straight alley consisting of an eight-inch start box, a 13-inch runway, and a 12-inch goal box. Starting, running, and goal box response measures were provided by three timing circuits activated by the interruption of infrared photo cell beams located 6, 12, and 24 inches beyond the starting doors which separated the eight-inch start box from the alley. It can be noted that the last beam was one inch from the end of the goal box and went across the top of the food cup. The findings obtained in Goodrich's first experiment are shown in Figure 8–3 and demonstrate that, for both starting and running speed measures, the partial reinforcement group was slower than the continuous reinforcement group during early trials but was faster at performance asymptote. In contrast to these findings, goal box speed was consistently slower for the partial reinforcement group.[1]

A more recent study by Wagner (1961) who utilized a five-foot runway and obtained starting, running, and goal box speed measures has confirmed the Goodrich (1959) findings.

[1] A second experiment [Goodrich (1959)] employing an identical procedure but utilizing a slightly different apparatus has confirmed the starting and running speed findings. Analysis of goal box speed revealed no difference between the continuous and partial reinforcement groups.

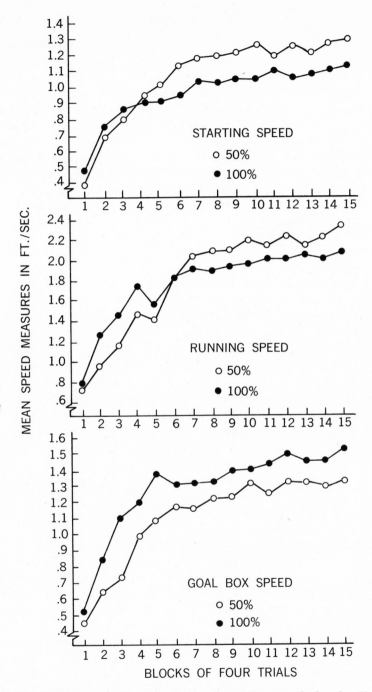

Fig. 8–3. Mean starting, running, and goal box speeds for the 50 per cent and 100 per cent reinforcement groups, by blocks of four trials. *Adapted from Goodrich (1959), Exp. I*

One final area regarding the influence of partial reinforcement on acquisition trials should be mentioned. The paired-associate learning situation has been considered by some investigators to be analogous to classical conditioning. The stimulus member of the paired-associate corresponds to the CS, and the response member as presented to the subject and the subject's response parallels the UCS-UCR relationship. The elicitation of the subject's response by the stimulus is assumed to be comparable to the formation of a CS-CR association. Goss, Morgan, and Golin (1959) and Schulz and Runquist (1960) have conceptualized the paired-associate verbal learning situation in these terms and have investigated learning as a function of the percentage occurrence of presentation of the response member (ORM) of the paired-associate. In the Schulz and Runquist study, a paired-associate list was constructed with either 20, 40, 60, 80, or 100 per cent occurrence of the response member of the pair. Thus, with the 20 per cent ORM, a response was paired with its stimulus member on only one of each block of five trials. Subjects learning the ORM list were warned that the response members of the pairs would be omitted a certain proportion of the time and that they should do their best in spite of this handicap. The criterion for learning was one perfect recitation. Twenty-four hours later, the subjects were instructed to relearn the material, with this relearning session taking place with 100 per cent ORM.

The findings, similar to those of Goss, *et al.* (1959), were that the number of correct responses as well as the mean number of trials required to reach criterion decreased as the percentage of ORM increased. The mean number of correct responses on the first trial of the relearning session (recall trial), however, was unaffected by variations in percentage of ORM during acquisition.

Although acquisition measures have been of some concern, it has been the resistance to extinction measure which has interested most investigators. Before examining some of the experimental findings, the reader should be aware that at times extinction trial data produce a basic problem with which too few investigators have been concerned.

At the end of the acquisition series in which varying percentages of reinforcement have been used, it is not uncommon to note that the varying experimental groups have different terminal levels of performance. Performance during extinction trials obviously will be influenced by the terminal level of acquisition, in addition to whatever role other variables may play. Many investigators have ignored terminal performance differences in their examination of extinction measures—a procedure which obviously confounds the experimental findings. As Anderson (1963) has recently written, equating resistance to extinction measures when a correction for differences in initial extinction response level is required is a difficult problem for which no single solution is appropriate.

Jenkins and Stanley (1950) in examining the contribution of partial reinforcement to resistance to extinction have concluded, "All other things equal, resistance to extinction after partial reinforcement is greater than that after continuous reinforcement when behavior strength is measured in terms of single responses." Furthermore, of 17 studies which these investigators examined, only three failed entirely or in part to find extinction differences significant at the 5 per cent level of confidence favoring those groups which were provided partial reinforcement during training as contrasted to continuously reinforced groups.[2]

A number of investigators have not been content to examine extinction measures as related only to the continuous versus partial continuum. Rather, they have been interested in examining extinction as influenced by different partial reinforcement regimens. More specifically, the percentage of reinforced trials, as well as the reinforcement patterning, has been investigated.

Extinction findings from the Grant and Schipper (1952) classical conditioning eyelid study, which was mentioned previously, indicated that the 50 per cent and 75 per cent reinforce-

[2] A series of studies by Bitterman and his associates [Wodinsky and Bitterman (1959, 1960); Longo and Bitterman (1960)] gave promise of demonstrating that this finding could not be generalized to experiments in which fish were subjects. When the number of trials was equated and frequency of reinforcement was left to vary, continuous reinforcement schedules, in contrast to partial, provided superior resistance to extinction whether practice was massed or distributed, whether few or many training trials were provided, and whether the prevailing level of motivation was high or low.

More recently, Gonzalez, Eskin, and Bitterman (1962, 1963) have demonstrated that when the number of reinforcements is equated and the number of training trials is left to vary a partial reinforcement schedule does produce superior resistance to extinction. As they (1963) have written (p. 374), "The earliest experiments—with equated trials—seemed to show fish and rat to be differently affected by partial reinforcement, but in the light of subsequent work with equated reinforcements the first results were seen to be a function only of differential sensitivity to frequency of reinforcement."

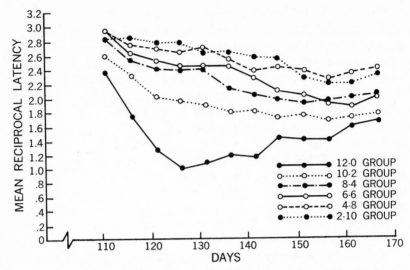

Fig. 8–4. Mean reciprocal latency as a function of trials by blocks of five for the extinction phase. *Adapted from Weinstock (1958)*

ment groups provided greatest resistance to extinction, followed by the 25 per cent and then the 100 per cent reinforcement group. Since the 0 per cent group revealed little or no conditioning, for this group there was no resistance to extinction.

Instrumental learning situations have not always provided similar findings. It will be recalled that in Weinstock's study (1958) groups of rats were provided with either 16.7, 33.3, 50, 66.7, 83.3, or 100 per cent reinforcement for running down an enclosed alley. Following 108 acquisition trials, 60 extinction trials were provided. The results, indicated in Figure 8–4, show that animals receiving the smallest percentages of reinforcement exhibited the greatest resistance to extinction whereas animals receiving the largest percentage of reinforcement exhibited the least resistance to extinction.

In contrast to Weinstock's instrumental learning situation in which a number of trials were needed in order for the organism to learn the task, Lewis (1952) and Lewis and Duncan (1956, 1957, 1958) have undertaken a series of studies in which the role of learning has been minimized. Human subjects were studied in a type of "gambling" situation. In the Lewis study (1952), the subjects were young children between 6.5 and 7.5 years of age.

The task was one in which each child was first given 20 toys and was then asked to push one of four buttons. If the pressing of one of these buttons was followed by the presentation of a red light, the child won an additional toy. If the pressing of a button was followed by a blue light, the child lost a toy. A ten-trial acquisition series (one button press equals one trial) was given in which reinforcement was provided on either 0, 50, 60, or 100 per cent of the trials. Extinction trials followed the acquisition series, with no discernable "break" between the two conditions. The children were permitted to play until they wanted to quit or until they ran out of toys. Lewis found that the 50 per cent and 60 per cent groups were most resistant to extinction, followed by the 0 per cent group and then the 100 per cent group.

In the Lewis and Duncan (1956, 1957, 1958) studies, the task for the subject was to pull the handle of a slot machine. College students were used as subjects. In the first study [Lewis and Duncan (1956)], the acquisition series consisted of eight plays (trials) in which the following percentages of reward were provided: 100, 75, 50, 37.5, 25, 12.5, and 0. Reinforcement consisted of the subject's receiving a disc which could be exchanged for five cents. Extinction trials immediately followed the acquisition series, in which the subjects were permitted to play as long as they desired. An examination of the number of pulls by each group indicated that resistance to extinction was an inverse function of the reinforcement percentage obtained during the acquisition trials. Figure 8–5 presents these findings.

Both the 1957 and 1958 studies in which the same apparatus and procedure were used have, in general, confirmed these findings. In the 1957 [Lewis and Duncan (1957)] study, nine acquisition trials were provided with the following percentages of reinforcement: 0, 11, 33, 67, and 100. In addition to obtaining the number of plays to extinction, the subjects' expectation of winning or losing on the next trial was obtained. The investigators found that the smaller the percentage of reward, the more plays made during extinction with one exception: the 0 per cent group played slightly fewer times than the 11 per cent group. Loss of expectancy of winning during extinction was a function of the percentage of reward, with greatest expectancy loss taking place with the highest percentage of reward. In the 1958 study [Lewis and Duncan (1958)], three percentages of reinforcement (33, 67, and 100) were combined with four numbers of acquisition trials

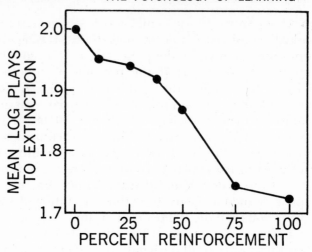

Fig. 8–5. Mean log trials to extinction as a function of the percentage of trials reinforced during acquisition. *Adapted from Lewis and Duncan (1956)*

(3, 6, 12 and 21). Again, the general trend was for smaller percentages of reinforcement to produce a larger number of plays to extinction.

Can any general conclusions be drawn regarding the role of percentage of reinforced trials and resistance to extinction? Lewis' (1960) review of the literature has led him to conclude that an inverted U-shaped function is found most frequently, with high and low percentages of reinforced trials resulting in poorest resistance to extinction. Thus, the studies of Grant and Schipper (1952), Lewis (1952), and Lewis and Duncan (1957), which have been reviewed, as well as one by Grant, Hake, and Hornseth (1951) have supported this position. However, as has been noted also, the experimental findings of Weinstock (1958) and Lewis and Duncan (1956, 1958) have produced a different function— resistance to extinction is an inverse function of the percentage of reinforcement which is provided during the acquisition trials.

It seems reasonable to assume that until the extinction process is more thoroughly understood the apparently opposing findings cannot be reconciled.

The patterning of reinforcement–nonreinforcement presentations has been also of contemporary interest. The experimental findings from classical as well as instrumental conditioning studies generally have agreed that a patterned effect, as indicated by a single alternation (reinforced–nonreinforced–reinforced–nonreinforced) procedure, results in poorer resistance to extinction than does a procedure which is provided by a random schedule. For example, Longenecker, Krauskopf, and Bitterman (1952) conditioned the galvanic skin response using either a random or single alternation reinforcement procedure. The random procedure group was found to be significantly more resistant to extinction than was the single alternation group.[3]

Tyler, Wortz, and Bitterman (1953) who examined an instrumental learning situation with rats as subjects also found a single alternation group less resistant to extinction than a random reinforcement group.

Grosslight and his associates have examined patterned effects as related to a series or block of trials. In the design which has been used, a partial reinforcement procedure with nonreinforcement termination (RU) has been contrasted with partial reinforcement with reinforcement termination (UR). As an example of these procedures, Grosslight, Hall, and Murnin (1953) used a Humphreys light expectancy procedure with the patterning of training trials as indicated by Table 8–1. (It will be recalled that the subject has to indicate whether or not a second light will go on after a first light has been presented. The presentation of the second light is considered to constitute a reinforced trial.) Following the fifth series of trials, an extinction session of ten trials was provided and the number of positive responses was determined for the three groups. Mean number of extinction responses for the UR group was significantly larger than for either the RU or for the continuously reinforced (RR) groups. Similar findings have been reported by Ishihara (1954).

Subsequent studies by Grosslight and Radlow (1956, 1957)

---

[3] One exception is an eyelid conditioning study by Grant, Riopelle, and Hake (1950) who ran four different reinforcement groups: (1) a 100 per cent reinforcement group, (2) a single alternation group in which a nonreinforced trial always followed a reinforced trial, (3) a double alternation group in which two nonreinforced trials always followed two reinforced trials, and (4) a random reinforcement group in which reinforced trials were provided randomly throughout the acquisition series. Surprisingly enough, the random group extinguished most rapidly.

TABLE 8–1

Patterning of Training Trials

GROUP			GROUP		
RR	RU	UR	RR	RU	UR
	Series 1			Series 4	
R	R	R	R	R	R
R	R	U	R	R	R
R	U	U	R	R	R
R	U	R	R	R	R
	Series 2		R	R	R
R	R	R	R	R	R
R	R	R	R	R	U
R	R	R	R	U	U
R	R.	R	R	U	U
R	R	U	R	U	R
R	U	U		Series 5	
R	U	U	R	R	R
R	U	R	R	R	U
	Series 3		R	U	U
R	R	R	R	U	R
R	R	R			
R	R	U			
R	U	U			
R	U	R			

(Adapted from Grosslight, Hall, and Murnin, 1953)

using rats have supported the position that a patterned effect, in which a reinforced trial follows a nonreinforced trial, can significantly prolong resistance to extinction.

Theoretical Explanations

As indicated in the introduction, a great deal of interest has been directed toward attempting to provide a theoretical explanation for the many experimental findings which have been obtained using the partial reinforcement procedure. A number of hypotheses have been proposed, and some of these will be outlined briefly. This presentation is abbreviated, and the reader should consult the reviews of Jenkins and Stanley (1950) and Lewis (1960) for a more extensive discussion.

Perhaps the earliest explanation for the partial reinforcement effect was based upon expectancy, most widely associated with Humphreys' early studies. Responses during acquisition were made to conditioned stimuli because these stimuli led the subject to "expect" the unconditioned stimulus. In extinction after continuous reinforcement, the response dies out quickly because there has been a rapid and easy shift from a regular expectancy of 100 per cent to one of 0 per cent. Partial reinforcement, on the other hand, produces an irregular expectation of reinforcement, and it becomes difficult for the subject to change from an irregular expectation produced in the acquisition trials to the regular one needed in the extinction series.

This interpretation has been criticized for its anthropomorphic, vague, and *ad hoc* nature. As Sheffield (1949) has stated, subjects after experiencing continuous reinforcement during an acquisition series could find it harder to believe that more reinforcement was not forthcoming during the extinction series. Lewis (1960) has pointed out that the expectancy hypothesis has been so discredited during the past 20 years that it appears to have no remaining articulate supporter.

A second explanation has been proposed by Sheffield (1949) on the basis of what frequently has been termed an aftereffect or stimulus generalization hypothesis. Sheffield has written: "The basic hypothesis is that extinction necessarily involves different cues from those used during training. Omission of reinforcement alters the context and makes extinction a case of 'transfer of training' in which a certain amount of generalization decrement is expected because of the change in cues." Sheffield has posited that reinforcement on trials of a *continuously reinforced series* results in specific stimulus aftereffects which become part of the stimulus pattern on every trial after the first. That is, the chewing movements and food in the mouth—stimulus effects which were present during eating in the goal box—become part of the stimulus situation for the animal when placed in the starting box for the next trial. The running response becomes attached to these cues. When extinction trials are provided, such stimulus aftereffects are no longer present in the starting box, and, as a result, the running response loses strength. On the other hand, with *partial reinforcement* the animal encounters cues on the non-reinforced acquisition trials which are also present during extinction. Since the running response has been conditioned during these training trials to cues which are characteristic of extinction trials, there is less loss in response strength through a change in the conditioned stimulus pattern when reinforcement is not provided during extinction.

Sheffield (1949) reasoned that the aftereffects of reinforcement (or nonreinforcement) dissipate with time and that if distributed acquisition trials were used the contribution of such aftereffects on extinction would be negligible. As a result, she compared the resistance to extinction of groups given distributed training with those receiving massed trials. Animals receiving massed acquisition trials were given 15 seconds between trials whereas groups receiving distributed training received 15-minute intertrial intervals. Partial (50 per cent) and continuous reinforcement (100 per cent) groups were run within each of these basic conditions. Results revealed that resistance to extinction following massed training was significantly greater in the partial reinforcement group than in the continuously reinforced group. On the other hand, following distributed training, resistance to extinction was not significantly different between the two groups. Such findings, of course, supported an aftereffect hypothesis.

Unfortunately, a number of subsequent experiments have been performed in which the investigators, also manipulating the length of the intertrial interval, have been unable to confirm Sheffield's findings [Wilson, Weiss, and Amsel (1955); Lewis (1956); Grant, Schipper, and Ross (1952); and Weinstock (1958)].

Weinstock's study is most damaging to Sheffield's theoretical interpretation of partial reinforcement. His general procedure was presented in a previous section. Briefly, it will be recalled that he used six groups of rats and provided them with varying percentages of reinforcement ranging from 16.7 per cent to 100 per cent for running down an alley. One hundred and eight acquisition trials were followed by 60 extinction trials, with 24 hours intervening between each trial. Because of the long delay between trials, there was little opportunity for the aftereffects of reinforced trials to be associated with those which were nonreinforced, and yet the animals receiving the smallest percentage of reinforcement exhibited the greatest resistance to extinction.

Capaldi and his associates [Capaldi, Hart, and Stanley (1963); Capaldi and Spivey (1963)] have taken a new look at the aftereffects hypothesis. Capaldi has theorized that aftereffects do not undergo diminution as a function of time; rather, a given aftereffect remains a functional unit until replaced by another aftereffect. According to this position, and in contrast to the one assumed by Sheffield and other investigators, the length of the intertrial interval is irrelevant and the primary concern is the nature of activities which take place during the intertrial interval.

In a study by Capaldi, Hart, and Stanley (1963) examining this position, two groups of rats were given 30 acquisition trials in running an alley under identical patterns of partial (50 per cent) reinforcement. A third group received continuous reinforcement. Following such training, 20 extinction trials were provided. The salient feature of this experiment was the provision of seven intertrial reinforcements to the two partial reinforcement groups. The intertrial reinforcement procedure was as follows: the intertrial interval which subjects normally spend in a neutral waiting box was divided into two equal intervals. The subject spent the first interval in the waiting box; then it was placed directly in the goal box where it was fed. For one partial reinforcement group (PN), intertrial reinforcements were given following those nonreinforced runway trials which preceded reinforced trials; for the second partial reinforcement group (PR), intertrial reinforcements were given following reinforced trials. The investigators reasoned that for the PN group the intertrial reinforcement procedure prevented the stimulus characteristics of response during nonreinforced runway trials from becoming conditioned to the instrumental response. This, of course, was not true for the PR group, which, although given an equal number of intertrial reinforcements, did not receive these reinforcements following nonreinforced trials. The results supported the researchers' hypothesis: Group PN was not more resistant to extinction than the consistently reinforced group, and Group PR was significantly more resistant to extinction than either Group PN or the continuously reinforced group.

If it is assumed that the events which fill the intertrial interval are of primary importance, a basic consideration concerns the nature of the goal box in which intertrial reinforcement is provided. The more dissimilar it is to the goal box which is used in training trials, the greater the probability that a portion of the nonreinforced aftereffects will survive the intertrial reinforcement experience and be available for conditioning on a subsequent reinforced trial. In an examination of this position, using rats in a straight runway, Capaldi and Spivey (1963) found that as similarity between the goal box used in the acquisition series and the intertrial interval goal box decreased, resistance to extinction increased.

A third explanation for partial reinforcement was proposed by Denny (1946) who attempted to account for such effects on the basis of secondary reinforcement. Denny hypothesized that if secondary reinforcing stimuli were present on the nonrewarded trials of the partial reinforcement situation response strength during acquisition should be similar to that obtained with continuous reinforcement. On the other hand, if secondary reinforcement was absent on the nonrewarded trials, acquisition performance should be inferior. Denny used a T-maze in which frequency of correct responding was used as the response measure; the findings supported his hypothesis. He obtained a significant difference in acquisition between partial (50 per cent) and continuous (100 per cent) reinforcement when the experimental conditions minimized the influence of secondary reinforcing stimuli, but when there was no attempt to minimize secondary reinforcement, no difference between the partial and continuous reinforcement groups was obtained.[4]

Denny (1946) suggested that resistance to extinction is increased by the presence of secondary reinforcing stimuli and hypothesized that their removal during the extinction series should result in poorer extinction performance. However, Denny's findings were not in keeping with his hypothesis since he found no difference between partial and continuous reinforcement groups with secondary reinforcement either maximized or minimized.[5]

One explanation for partial reinforcement which appears to have promise is the discrimination hypothesis. This hypothesis had its origins in a study by Mowrer and Jones (1945) in which four groups of rats were trained in a Skinner box to make either one, two, three, or four bar depressions before receiving food. A fifth group received a food pellet after either one, two, three, or

[4] Rubin (1953) examined the acquisition of a panel-pushing response acquired under conditions of continuous reinforcement and under conditions of partial reinforcement with secondary reinforcing stimuli minimized during the nonreinforced trials. Using a rate of response measure, Rubin found no differences between his groups in speed of responding—a finding in contrast to those obtained by Denny. Similarly, Hulse and Stanley (1956) were unable to confirm Denny's findings. Using a rate of response measure, no differences were obtained among three reinforcement conditions: (a) continuous reinforcement, (b) partial reinforcement with secondary reinforcement minimized, and (c) partial reinforcement with secondary reinforcement maximized.

[5] This result is unusual and contrary to the findings of most investigators who have reported the superiority of partial reinforcement groups during extinction. Perhaps the fact that Denny used only 12 extinction trials and employed a probability of response measure accounts for his results.

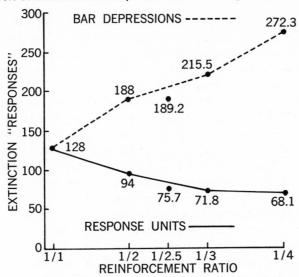

Fig. 8–6. The upper curve shows the average number of bar depressions and the lower curve plots response units, both as a function of the reinforcement ratio. *Adapted from Mowrer and Jones (1945)*

four presses; the presentation was random but on the average after 2.5 bar presses. Following extensive training, extinction sessions were provided on three successive days. Results are shown in Figure 8–6. Resistance to extinction, as indicated by total number of bar presses, was a function of the number of bar presses or reinforcement ratio which was required to obtain food during acquisition. Thus, the group which was required to press the bar four times in order to obtain a single food pellet took longest to extinguish, whereas the group which was required to press only once extinguished most rapidly. Mowrer and Jones proposed as one explanation for their findings that when the change from acquisition to extinction was difficult to discriminate there should be greater resistance to extinction than when such a discrimination was easy.[6]

[6] As a second explanation for their findings, the investigators proposed that a response could be defined as a set of nonreinforced responses which are strengthened by terminal reinforcement. Thus, for the first group, a response unit would be defined as one press followed by reinforcement, whereas for the second, third, and fourth groups, a response would be defined as two, three, or four presses followed by reinforcement. When a response was measured this way, the number of responses during extinction was a function of the ratio of presses to reinforcement. (See lower curve in Figure 8–6.)

Applied to typical partial reinforcement findings, it would be hypothesized that acquisition trials during which a partial reinforcement procedure is employed are more difficult for the organism to discriminate from extinction trials than if continuous reinforcement is provided during acquisition.

One test of this position would be to provide a random versus fixed pattern of partial reinforcement, keeping the percentage of reinforced trials the same in each group. Studies, previously cited, by Longenecker, Krauskopf, and Bitterman (1952) and Tyler, Wortz, and Bitterman (1953) demonstrated that a simple alternation pattern of reinforcement and nonreinforcement resulted in more rapid extinction than a random pattern—a finding which supports the discrimination hypothesis.

Since the extinction situation is one in which zero per cent reinforcement is provided, it would be expected that an acquisition series containing a small percentage of reinforced trials should produce greater resistance to extinction than an acquisition series in which a larger percentage of reinforced trials was given. Much of the evidence in this area has already been examined, noting that an inverted U-shaped function frequently has been obtained between the percentage of reinforcement provided during acquisition and resistance to extinction. However, there is some question as to whether a zero per cent reinforcement condition can be properly called partial reinforcement since no reinforced trials are given. A second consideration is that with many learning situations, e.g., classical conditioned response learning, a minimum percentage of reinforced trials is necessary in order for learning to take place. In the studies which reveal small percentages of reinforcement during acquisition resulting in little resistance to extinction, an examination of terminal acquisition performance also reveals that little learning has taken place.

A recent test of the discrimination hypothesis has been made by Theios (1962), who varied the number of continuously reinforced trials interpolated between a partial reinforcement series and an extinction series. Theios proposed that the longer the block of continuously reinforced trials provided after partial reinforcement, the greater the similarity between acquisition trials and extinction. As a result, resistance to extinction would be expected to decrease as a function of the number of continuously reinforced trials interpolated between the partial reinforcement regimen and extinction.

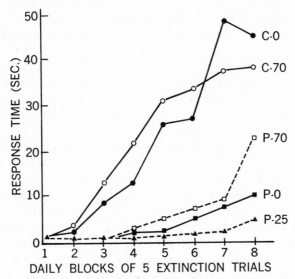

Fig. 8–7. Response times during extinction. *Adapted from Theios* (*1962*)

His experiment consisted of running three groups of rats on a runway, each group receiving 70 trials of random 40 per cent reinforcement. Following this training, either 0, 25, or 70 continuously reinforced trials were provided. Thus, three experimental groups—partial-0, partial-25, and partial-70—were used. Two control groups received continuous reinforcement during the 70-trial training period and either 0 or 70 additional training trials. All groups were then given a minimum of 40 extinction trials. Extinction findings are presented in Figure 8–7. Theios found no significant difference between the two control groups, but the partial-70 group was significantly superior to both. There was no significant difference in resistance to extinction between the partial-0 and partial-25 groups, but both of these were significantly superior to the partial-70 group. Theios has pointed out that the partial reinforcement effect of increasing resistance to extinction is relatively unaffected by continuous reinforcement following partial reinforcement since the partial-70 group revealed more resistance to extinction than did the continuous reinforcement groups. He has suggested further that any adequate theory of partial reinforcement must have constructs representing relatively permanent effects of nonreinforcement which can be sustained through blocks of continuous reinforcement. Presumably, the discrimination hypothesis could not account for these findings.

Not all investigators would agree with the experimenter's interpretations since the partial-70 group did reveal significantly less resistance to extinction than the partial-0 and partial-25 groups, indicating that the 70 continuous reinforced trials did have some influence on extinction.[7]

Spence, Homzie, and Rutledge (1964), studying the classically conditioned eyelid response, have provided a somewhat different version of the discrimination hypothesis. They have hypothesized that the discrimination of the change from conditioning to extinction trials leads the subject to adopt an inhibitory set not to blink. Extinction is extremely rapid since the set interferes with the appearance of the conditioned response. Partial reinforcement precludes or delays this discrimination so that the decrement in the frequency of the conditioned response under such conditions is more gradual and reflects the cumulative development of inhibition of nonreinforcement, not the presence of an inhibitory set. The experimenters have pointed out that their version of the discrimination hypothesis has been "put forward primarily to deal with the extremely rapid extinction (one or two nonreinforced trials) that occurs only in humans on the initial extinction of a CR."

The last explanation of partial reinforcement effects which will be discussed has been made in terms of the presence or absence of mediating responses. In some cases, the mediating response has been considered an emotional one (frustration) whereas in other cases investigators have not specified its nature.

Wilson, Weiss, and Amsel (1955) have argued for the role of a frustration response. It has been assumed that during the partial reinforcement situation frustration develops when the animal runs into the goal box and does not find reward. Through stimulus generalization, this emotional response "works backward" and is eventually elicited by the stimuli found in the

---

[7] Theios' findings are puzzling in that the partial reinforcement groups were not superior to the continuously reinforced groups in running speed during late stages of acquisition trials, a finding reported by a number of recent investigators. The fact that there was no difference in resistance to extinction between the 100 and 170 continuous reinforcement groups is also at variance with the findings of other investigators.

starting box. However, in addition to emotionality being a response, it also has stimulus properties with such stimuli becoming conditioned to the instrumental response of running. When extinction trials are provided with the empty goal box resulting in frustration, the partially reinforced subjects have already been trained to respond by running in the presence of frustration stimuli, whereas the consistently reinforced subjects have not. As a result, this response for the continuously reinforced group is considerably weaker and extinguishes more rapidly.

Kendler, Pliskoff, D'Amato, and Katz (1957) have provided an almost identical explanation except that they have not identified the mediating response (or responses) other than to call them distinctive, nonconsummatory end box responses.

What can be concluded from this survey of the varying explanations for partial reinforcement effects? One obvious conclusion is that there is no single theory which can successfully account for all of the experimental findings—a conclusion also voiced by Lewis (1960) in his exhaustive survey of the literature. The major difficulty appears to be that most theorists have assumed that any explanation (1) must be able to handle partial reinforcement effects as measured by a variety of response measures obtained in a number of different learning situations, without regard to species, and (2) must be related to the operation of a single variable or condition, e.g., aftereffects, secondary reinforcement, expectancy, etc.[8] In this regard, Gonzalez, Eskin, and Bitterman (1962) have written that resistance to extinction in any species is undoubtedly determined by a variety of interrelated factors whose relative values undoubtedly vary

---

[8] Two exceptions to this point of view should be noted. Grant and Schipper (1952) have posited that partial reinforcement effects found in classical conditioned eyeblink responses should be interpreted in terms of two processes. The first is a minimal amount of reinforcement necessary to produce a learned response, whereas the second is related to the difficulty of the discrimination of the shift from the training to extinction procedure. Spence, Homzie, and Rutledge (1964) have hypothesized that the extinction of the classically conditioned eyeblink response is based upon the adoption of an inhibitory set by the subject and that the partial reinforcement situation, in contrast to the continuous, precludes the adoption of such a set. These investigators also have pointed out that this explanation cannot be applied to eyelid conditioning studies employing nonhumans, in which such higher order inhibitory sets would not be present. The specificity of this explanation is a reflection of Spence's (1960) more general position that the mechanisms involved in the extinction of responses based upon appetitional needs and rewards are probably very different from those operating in the extinction of responses learned under aversive motivation.

from species to species and that whether the same factors operate in all species and to the same degree remains to be established.

THE ROLE OF NONREINFORCEMENT IN DISCRIMINATION LEARNING

As indicated in the introduction, a nonreinforcement procedure may be used in discrimination learning situations. The experimental question has been one of examining the role of nonreinforced trials in the learning that takes place.

The basic approach to this problem has been one in which the acquisition series contains differing numbers or percentages of nonreinforced trials. In an early study, Denny and Dunham (1951) had groups of rats learn a simple black-white discrimination task. One group of animals received two reinforced and one nonreinforced trial each day. A second group received two reinforced trials and four nonreinforced trials each day, thus running six trials per day, in contrast to the three trials per day which the first group received. Nine days of training were provided, with free as well as forced choices being used to provide each group with the appropriate number of correct and incorrect responses. Results as measured by the first two free-choice trials indicated that Group II performed significantly better as measured by the percentage of correct responses than did Group I.

A few years later, Cantor and Spiker (1954) performed a somewhat similar study with children three to five years of age. A simple discrimination task was used in which two differently colored cars served as the discriminanda. One group of subjects received eight blocks of forced trials in which each block consisted of two reinforced and two nonreinforced trials. A second group received the same number of blocks of trials; each block consisted of two reinforced trials but only one nonreinforced trial. Reinforced and nonreinforced trials were provided by presenting only one car at a time, followed by reinforcement or nonreinforcement depending upon which car was presented. Each block of trials was followed by a free-choice trial in which both cars were presented and the child had to choose one of them. The findings, agreeing with Denny and Dunham (1951), showed that the group which received two nonreinforced trials made significantly more correct responses on the eight free choice trials than the group which had received only one.

Both the Denny and Dunham (1951) and Cantor and Spiker

TABLE 8–2

Discrimination Performance on the Test Trials

	ONE TRAINING TRIAL Per Cent Correct			TWO TRAINING TRIALS Per Cent Correct		
	Test Trial 1	Test Trial 2	Test Trial 3	Test Trial 1	Test Trial 2	Test Trial 3
Test Stimulus Rewarded	74	95	96	79	93	96
Test Stimulus Nonrewarded	93	92	95	97	98	99

(Adapted from Moss and Harlow, 1947)

(1954) studies support the position that the nonreinforcement of an incorrect response, at least in the simple discrimination learning situation, is an important factor in learning about the correct response. In both studies, it should be noted that the varying experimental groups had unequal numbers of learning trials. Although it can be concluded that the presentation of a nonreinforced trial is better than providing no trial at all, a basic condition to be investigated would be to keep the number of trials constant and to vary the ratio of reinforced to nonreinforced trials.

In an early study involving this procedure, Moss and Harlow (1947) trained eight monkeys on 90 discrimination problems under three conditions of reward. The Wisconsin General Test Apparatus was used, and the training consisted of providing either one or two trials in which only a single stimulus was presented. With Condition 1, the stimulus was always rewarded, but with Condition 2 the single stimulus was never rewarded.

Following such training, two stimulus objects were presented in order to provide a typical discrimination problem to the subject. These stimuli consisted of a neutral stimulus and the stimulus object which was rewarded in the first condition and never rewarded in the second condition. Table 8–2 provides the percentage of correct responses on test trials 1, 2, and 3 as a function of whether or not the animals received a reward for the single stimulus presentation and also as a function of whether one or two training trials were provided. As Table 8–2 reveals,

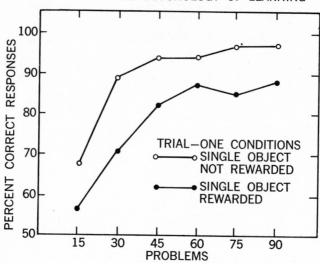

Fig. 8–8. Discrimination learning set curves based on Trial 2 responses following rewarded and unrewarded Trial 1 responses. *Adapted from Harlow and Hicks (1957)*

performance on the first test trial was clearly superior when the subject did not obtain reward during the training trials. Thus, the nonreward training condition resulted in the monkeys' rapidly shifting to the other stimulus object during the test trials.

Perhaps an even clearer demonstration of the influence of non-reward is revealed in a subsequent study by Harlow and Hicks (1957). The same procedure as previously described was used; on Trial 1, only a single stimulus object was presented to the monkey. In one condition the stimulus object was never rewarded, whereas in the second condition it was always rewarded. On Trials 2 through 6, the subject was given a discrimination problem in which the object which had been presented on the first trial was used as one of the discriminanda. If this object had been rewarded on Trial 1, it continued to be reinforced on the following trials; if it had not been rewarded on Trial 1, it continued not to be rewarded. Figure 8–8 presents the percentage of correct responses on Trial 2 over 90 problems which were provided the animals.[9] It can be noted readily that nonrewarding

[9] With two-choice object discrimination problems, the second trial becomes a most useful one in the examination of the learning of the problem. The first trial should reflect chance responding but the information acquired on this trial can be used by the organism to provide a correct response on Trial 2.

the stimulus during the first trial, in contrast to rewarding it, resulted in superior learning.

Fitzwater's (1952) work has been similar except that rats have been used as the experimental subjects. Training consisted of providing varying groups of subjects with 40 trials in a single-alley, nonchoice apparatus. Groups I, II, and III received 5, 10, or 20 reinforced trials to a subsequently reinforced cue (vertical striped card) and 35, 30, or 20 nonreinforced trials to the subsequently nonreinforced cue (horizontal striped card). Groups IV, V, and VI were controls for each of the above experimental groups, with the number of reinforced trials provided to the subsequently reinforced cue (vertical striped card) equal to those of the experimental groups. The control groups differed, however, in that 35, 30, or 20 nonreinforced training trials were not to the subsequently nonreinforced cue but to a neutral stimulus (black card). A seventh group received all 40 reinforced trials to the subsequently reinforced cue.

Following the last training trial, animals were placed in a two-choice discrimination learning situation. The cue cards previously associated with reward and nonreward for the experimental groups comprised the stimuli to be discriminated. All groups were given 16 trials per day for six days. The number of correct responses made on Day 1 is presented in Figure 8–9. It can be noted that 40 reinforced training trials produced poorer learning than those training conditions in which the number of reinforced trials was reduced to either 20, 10, or even 5.

The studies of both Birch (1955) and Lachman (1961), although using a slightly different procedure, have confirmed these general findings in indicating the importance of nonreinforced trials in the learning situation. Reinforced and nonreinforced trials were manipulated within the actual learning experiment. Lachman (1961) had rats learn a simple brightness discrimination in a Y-maze. Three experimental groups were given different ratios of correct to incorrect responses—either 3:1, 1:1, or 1:3. This was accomplished by programming blocks of four trials, with one free and three forced. Twenty trials were given on Day 1 and 40 trials each on Days 2 through 5. Day 5 consisted of only free choice trials. Although an examination of the percentage of correct responses on the free choice trials for Days 1 through 4 revealed little differences among the three groups, the free choice trials on day 5 produced rather divergent curves. As Figure 8–10 shows, during the last ten trials of Day 5,

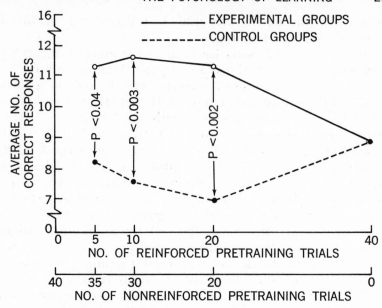

Fig. 8–9. Empirical curves showing the effects upon choice performance of differential amounts of single-alley reinforcements with
and without nonreinforced practice. *Adapted from Fitzwater (1952)*

the group receiving only one correct response to every three
incorrect was responding close to 90 per cent correct whereas the
three correct and one incorrect response group was performing at
the 70 per cent level.

Although the studies which have been examined clearly
indicate the importance of providing nonreinforced trials to the
subject in the two-choice discrimination learning situation, very
little about the specific ratio of nonreinforced to reinforced
responses which provides optimal learning can be said. Fitzwater's
study demonstrated little difference among the following nonreinforcement–reinforcement ratios: 7:1, 3:1, and 1:1. In contrast,
Lachman's experiment indicated that a 3:1 ratio was superior to
that of a 1:1 which, in turn, was superior to that of a 1:3. Birch
(1955) found that a 1:1 ratio was superior to either a 1:3 or a 3:1,
but, as he states, it is to be expected that such factors as conditions
of reward, extent of pretraining, etc. will, in the last analysis,
determine what the optimal ratio will be.

A general conclusion would be that a continuously reinforced

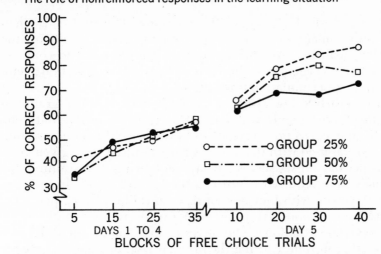

Fig. 8–10. The percentage of correct responses on free choice trials for forced choice response schedule groups. *Adapted from Lachman (1961)*

series of trials does not contribute to the learning process as much as do nonreinforced trials combined with reinforced ones. Presumably, the organism must learn what responses are incorrect as well as those which are correct. Such a conclusion, however, must be limited to the two-choice discrimination learning situation. When more than two choices are presented, the role of nonreinforcement remains to be investigated.[10]

Correction Versus Noncorrection Procedures

In examining the role of nonreinforcement in the discrimination learning task, the learning situations were so structured that when the animal made an incorrect response it was confined to a goal box which did not contain reinforcement. This is known as a noncorrection procedure and can be contrasted with the correction method—a procedure in which, although the animal may make an incorrect response, the incorrect goal box

[10] It would appear that some of Thorndike's work which was reviewed in the discussion of punishment is relevant to this section. It will be recalled that he found that a nonreinforced response (experimenter's saying "wrong") had little influence on learning when a five-choice discrimination task was used.

door is locked which necessitates retracing. The trial ends when the animal makes a correct response and secures reward in the positive goal box. An interesting problem has been to compare the relative efficiency of the correction and noncorrection methods in the discrimination learning situation.

In an early study, Hull and Spence (1938) had two groups of rats first learn to go to the right (or left) in a T-maze. With one group the correction procedure was used; the noncorrection method was used with the second group. Subjects were given eight trials per day on six successive days. Following such training, the animals were required to turn to the left (or right) in order to secure reward, with four days of reversal training being provided. Correction or noncorrection procedures were also employed in the reversal situation. The investigators found no difference between groups in learning the original task, but they believed it was performance in the reversal training situation which provided the basis for comparison between the two procedures. An examination of these findings indicated that on Day 1 the correction group made significantly fewer errors than the noncorrection group. Performance differences between the groups grew progressively smaller on Days 2, 3, and 4 so that the advantage of the correction method was lost after the second day. A second experiment confirmed the findings of the first.[11]

The experimental findings of Seward (1943) and Besch, Morris, and Levine (1963) have not been in keeping with the Hull-Spence conclusions. Seward was interested in examining the role of the length of the correct versus incorrect path in the T-maze. At the same time, he was interested in examining the efficiency of the correction versus noncorrection procedures. Three length-of-path conditions were run. The first was one in which both the correct and incorrect paths were three feet long; the second condition was one in which the correct path was 12 feet long and the incorrect path was three feet long; in the third condition both the correct and incorrect paths were 12 feet long. Correction and noncorrection groups were run to a criterion of nine correct out of ten trials. As Table 8–3 indicates, regardless of

---

[11] It is interesting to note that Hull and Spence have restricted the generality of their finding as follows (p. 130) : "Since success in competing excitatory tendencies requires merely that one excitatory tendency shall obtain a certain margin of strength over the other, it follows that success in a trial-and-error situation may be attained equally well [by either method] when *both* reaction tendencies are at a relatively high, or when they are at a relatively low, excitatory strength."

TABLE 8–3

Maze Performance for Correction and Noncorrection Groups

			ERRORS		TRIALS TO CRITERION	
CONDITION		N	Corr.	Non-corr.	Corr.	Non-corr.
Correct-3 ft.	Incorrect-3 ft.	12	9.0	4.7	15.1	9.1
Correct-12 ft.	Incorrect-3 ft.	10	10.8	5.1	24.5	11.6
Correct-12 ft.	Incorrect-12 ft.	12	13.5	6.2	30.1	12.4

(Adapted from Seward, 1943)

the length of task condition, the noncorrection method provided statistically superior learning.[12]

Besch, Morris, and Levine (1963) examined the influence of a correction versus a noncorrection procedure in a drive-discrimination experiment. The task consisted of training rats to turn right when they were hungry and left when they wanted social reinforcement—the presence of another rat in the correct goal box. Sixty days of training were provided which, with the exception of Day 1, consisted of six trials per day. Correction as well as noncorrection procedures were used. Using the percentage of correct choices as the response measure, the experimenters found that the subjects in the noncorrection group responded significantly above chance during the last half of the learning period, whereas animals in the correction group did not achieve this level of performance.

Can any general conclusion be reached on this topic? Unfortunately, it does not seem likely at this time. The findings of Seward (1943) and Besch, Morris, and Levine (1963) seem most compatible with the earlier findings which have been presented which indicate that the presence of a nonreinforced response in the two-choice discrimination learning situation can aid learning materially. However, these conclusions probably are limited to the kind of situations which these investigators studied. To date, there has been no systematic analysis relating specific learning variables to the method used. Until this is done, little can be said about the superiority of one method over the other.

[12] Kalish (1946), using a much different type of learning situation, also has obtained findings which indicate the superiority of the noncorrection procedure, and some writers [Munn (1950), Woodworth and Schlosberg (1954)] have cited his study in their discussion of this topic. Kalish, however, has written that he did not believe that his findings have applicability to the correction versus noncorrection procedure comparison.

9

Experimental Extinction

EXPERIMENTAL EXTINCTION WAS DESCRIBED in Chapter 2, at which time it was indicated that many investigators have used it as a measure from which to infer something about the strength of the learning process. In Chapter 3, its relationship to other learning measures was considered. Since these early chapters, it has been noted also that it has played an important role not only as a measure of learning but also as an operation which has been used to distinguish between learning and performance.

The behavior which is found in the extinction situation has interested investigators also as a basic behavioral phenomenon. There has been considerable interest in an empirical examination of some of the variables which influence it as well as in positing and testing the theories which presumably "explain" it.

The variables related to experimental extinction can be classified into four categories: (1) motivational variables, (2) work or effort variables, (3) temporal variables, and (4) stimulus variables.

MOTIVATIONAL VARIABLES

Since experimental extinction has been used as a behavioral outcome from which learning and/or performance has been inferred, the studies which are relevant to this section have been examined in Chapters 6, 7, and 8. In brief, increasing the intensity of a need typically results in greater resistance to extinction if such increased intensity is provided during the extinction trials.

With regard to the motivational variable of reinforcement, it will be recalled that four parameters frequently have been investigated: (1) number of reinforcements, (2) amount of reinforcement, (3) delay between the making of the response and the securing of reinforcement, (4) continuous versus intermittent presentation of reinforcement.

Although a number of experimenters have supported the position that resistance to extinction is a function of the number of reinforced trials, others have not been able to replicate these findings and, at least in some instances, resistance to extinction has been found to be inversely related to the number of reinforcements. The issue remains unresolved.

Most investigators have found that resistance to extinction is an increasing function of the amount of reward obtained during the acquisition trials; such superiority is undoubtedly a reflection of the differences which were present at the end of the acquisition trials. Providing reinforcement delay during acquisition appears to increase resistance to extinction. Perhaps the most consistent reinforcement finding is that partial reinforcement, in contrast to continuous, will result in increasing resistance to extinction.

WORK OR EFFORT VARIABLES

Mowrer and Jones (1943) were two of the early investigators who called attention to the growing body of evidence which indicated that extinction was a mode of adjustment in which fatigue played an important role; thus, extinction of an effortful habit should take place more rapidly than would the extinction of a relatively effortless but otherwise comparable habit. The experimenters hypothesized that the extinction situation involves a conflict in which the fatigue generated by the original response elicits a resting response which is incompatible with, and thus tends to inhibit, the original response.

In an experimental test of their position, rats were given training in a Skinner box. Twenty bar presses per day for a food reward were provided, with the bar weighted differently on

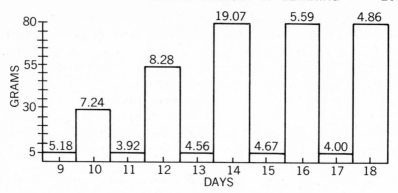

Fig. 9–1. Diagrammatic representation of procedure used to teach subjects to press bars requiring varying amounts of effort. The values given at the top of each column represent the average times (in minutes) required by all subjects to make twenty responses constituting each day's training performance. *Adapted from Mowrer and Jones (1943)*

different days to provide reinforcement at varying effort levels. Figure 9–1 portrays the amount of effort required to receive reinforcement on the last ten days of training (Day 9 through Day 18). It will be observed that on the last six days' training alternated between a five-gram and 80-gram weight. It may also be noted that at the end of the training period (Days 17 and 18), the amount of time it took the animals to make 20 responses with the 80-gram weight was not much longer than the time required to make the same number of responses with the five-gram weight. Following training, the animals were randomly divided into three groups, and extinction took place with bar weights of either 5, 42.5, or 80 grams. Three 20-minute extinction sessions were used for each group. The results, shown in Figure 9–2, reveal that the average number of responses made by the five-gram group was significantly greater than that made by either the 42.5- or 80-gram group—a finding supporting the experimenters' hypothesis that extinction was related to the amount of effort required to perform the task.

Five years later, Solomon (1948) confirmed the findings obtained by Mowrer and Jones (1943) using a different type of learning situation. Two groups of rats were trained to jump different distances in a Lashley jumping stand in order to reach a landing platform and food reinforcement. The acquisition condi-

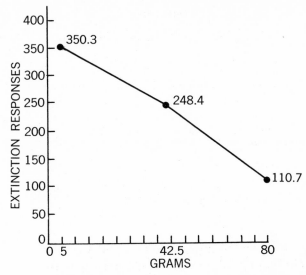

Fig. 9–2. Curve showing the average number of responses made during three standard extinction periods as a function of the effortfulness of the task. *Adapted from Mowrer and Jones (1943)*

tions are indicated in Table 9–1. Following 20 acquisition trials, the extinction series was begun immediately. As in the acquisition trials, each rat was permitted 30 seconds in the reward box and then was returned to the starting box. The criterion for extinction was refusal to jump within two minutes. Five successive extinction sessions were conducted at 24-hour intervals, with the last four sessions differing from the first in that ten relearning trials preceded each extinction session. The results are indicated in Figure 9–3 and reveal that the group required to jump 16 inches extinguished more rapidly than the group required to jump eight inches.

Both studies have been criticized on the grounds that the groups whose tasks required more effort had smaller amounts of learning. For example, in the Mowrer and Jones study, 180 trials were given with the five-gram weight, 20 trials each with 30-gram and 55-gram weights, and 60 trials with the 80-gram weight. Similarly, an examination of Solomon's (1948) training conditions revealed considerably fewer reinforcements for the 16-inch jump group than for the 8-inch jump group. However, even when this variable is controlled, most investigators [Applezweig

TABLE 9–1

Acquisition Conditions for Both Groups

GROUP A		GROUP B	
TRIAL	DISTANCE	TRIAL	DISTANCE
#1	0″	#1	0″
#2 to 5	4″	#2 to 4	4″
#6 to 12	6″	#5 to 8	6″
#13 to 20	8″	#9 to 12	8″
		#13 to 14	12″
		#15 to 16	14″
		#17 to 20	16″

(Adapted from Solomon, 1948)

(1951) ; Stanley and Aamodt (1954) ; and Capehart, Viney, and Hulicka (1958)] report a positive relationship between effort and resistance to extinction.

In the Capehart, *et al.*, (1958) study, rats received 15 reinforced responses per day for six days in depressing a bar for food in a Skinner box. Three bar loadings were used: 5, 40, and 70 grams; each subject received 30 reinforced trials at each weight. The 27 subjects were then divided into three groups equated for latency of responding. Group I was extinguished on 5 grams, Group II on 40 grams, and Group III on 70 grams. Extinction was measured in two ways: (1) the number of responses made during a 30-minute extinction session on each of two successive days and (2) the number of responses to a five-minute no-response criterion on each of two consecutive days. Since the experimenters noted that there was no statistical difference between the two measures, only the number of responses to the five-minute no-response criterion were presented, and the findings, as Figure 9–4 reveals, provide confirmation of the earlier studies which have been cited.[1]

TEMPORAL VARIABLES

The amount of time that is interpolated between extinction trials has commonly been referred to as the intertrial interval. One of the earliest investigators of temporal variables was Pavlov

[1] The Maatsch, Adelman, and Denny (1954) study, using bar loading weights of 5, 40, and 80 grams, is one of the few failing to confirm this general finding.

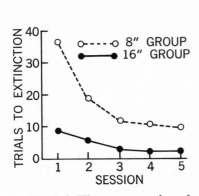

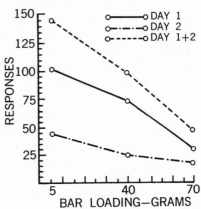

Fig. 9–3. The mean number of responses required for extinction to take place under two conditions of effort. *Adapted from Solomon (1948)*

Fig. 9–4. Number of responses to the five-minute no-response criterion. *Adapted from Capehart, Viney, and Hulicka (1958)*

(1927), who wrote (p. 52), "Yet another important factor in determining the rate of experimental extinction is the length of pause between successive repetitions of the stimulus without reinforcement. The shorter the pause the more quickly will extinction of the reflex be obtained, and in most cases a smaller number of repetitions will be required." An illustration of this phenomenon was provided by extinguishing a dog's salivary response. The intertrial interval was either 2, 4, 8, or 16 minutes. Pavlov reported that with an interval of two minutes extinction was obtained in 15 minutes; with an interval of four minutes, extinction was obtained in 20 minutes; with an interval of eight minutes, extinction was obtained in 54 minutes; with an interval of 16 minutes, extinction was incomplete after two hours.

A few years later, Hilgard and Marquis (1935) also reported that spaced extinction trials (10 every other day), in contrast to massed (60 trials every other day), resulted in greater resistance to extinction.

There has been some question, however, concerning the validity of these findings. As Guthrie (1935) has pointed out, Pavlov's data are concerned with time rather than with the number of responses made by the animal. If these data are reanalyzed by dividing the intertrial interval into the total time required for extinction, one can note that there is little difference among the total number of extinction responses made at each intertrial interval. Hilgard and Marquis' conclusions must be viewed with some caution also since only one subject was used and the investigators cautioned their readers that this experiment was exploratory.

The more recent classical conditioning studies of Porter (1939), Grant, Schipper, and Ross (1952), and Howat and Grant (1958) who investigated the role of the intertrial interval during extinction have not yielded consistent findings. Porter (1939) and Grant, Schipper, and Ross (1952), conditioning the eyelid response, were unable to find that the distribution of extinction trials was a significant variable in determining resistance to extinction. The Grant, Schipper, and Ross (1952) study is interesting in that the experimenters found an interaction between the distribution of acquisition trials and the distribution of trials during extinction. They found that extinction following massed acquisition trials was most rapid if the extinction trials were spaced, whereas extinction following spaced acquisition trials was most rapid when extinction trials were massed. As the experimenters state, "Changing the distribution of trials when the transition is made from training to extinction results in a more rapid extinction of the CR's."

In contrast to these findings, Howat and Grant (1958), also examining the conditioning and extinction of the eyelid response, provided training trials in which the intertrial interval was random but averaged 35 seconds. Extinction trials were carried out with a massed group which was provided random intertrial intervals averaging seven and one-half seconds and a distributed group provided random intertrial intervals averaging 35 seconds. In this study, spaced extinction trials resulted in more rapid extinction.

Instrumental reward studies also have failed to provide consistent findings. The studies of Gagne (1941), Rohrer (1947, 1949), and Teichner (1952) have supported the position that the distribution of extinction trials increased resistance to extinction, but the evidence has not been strong. In Gagne's (1941) study, for example, varying groups of rats learned to run an elevated pathway with intertrial intervals of either .5, 1, 2, 3, 5, or 10 minutes. Animals were then given extinction trials. The intertrial intervals were the same as those which had been previously employed during acquisition. Although Gagne found that extinction was most rapid for the groups provided the two shortest intertrial intervals, he also found that there were substantial differences among groups at the end of training, with resistance to extinction for the varying groups being perfectly correlated with the level of performance at the end of the acquisition trials.

In Rohrer's (1947) first study, rats were trained to raise a horizontal bar by an upward movement of the head in order to obtain food reward. The apparatus was a fairly complex one in which the animal's head was placed in a stock and a wire cage fitted over the body to permit the subject to remain in a natural sitting position. Following a long pre-training period, regular training trials were provided. All animals were placed on approximately 23 hours of food deprivation; one group was given nine reinforcements; a second group was given 59 reinforced trials. During the acquisition series, the intertrial interval varied between 40 and 75 seconds, with a mean of 49.5 seconds. Following the ninth or fifty-ninth trial, the animals were permitted to eat until they were satiated. When the subjects were returned to the experimental situation six or 30 hours later, they were given one additional reinforced trial, making ten or 60 reinforced trials in all, and then extinguished. Extinction trials were given with an intertrial interval of either ten or 90 seconds.

Resistance to extinction, as measured by failure to respond in ten seconds for two successive trials, was greatest with the 90-second interval when 60 reinforcements had been provided. Such an effect was present whether or not the animals had been extinguished under six or 30 hours of food deprivation. However, extinction data resulting from the six- and 30-hour deprivation groups which were given ten reinforcements, provided no conclusive evidence that massing or distributing the extinction trials influenced extinction.

Teichner's (1952) study indicates that although the influence of massing or distributing extinction trials may have some effect on resistance to extinction a much more important consideration appears to be the relationship between the intertrial interval used during acquisition and that provided during extinction—a finding which was also obtained in the Grant, Schipper, and Ross (1952) conditioned eyeblink study. In Teichner's study, rats were trained to depress a small bar-like food chute in order to receive a pellet of food. A guillotine door slid up and down in front of the

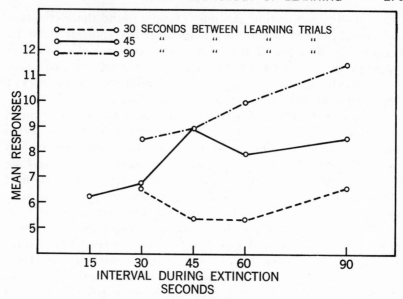

Fig. 9–5. Extinction as a function of the intertrial interval during extinction for three learning conditions. *Adapted from Teichner (1952)*

chute preventing free access to the chute and enabling the experimenter to provide discrete trials to the subjects. In his first experiment, subjects were given 15 training trials with 45 seconds between trials. Subgroups were then extinguished with either 15, 30, 45, 60, or 90 seconds between trials. In a second study, one-half of the subjects were provided 15 training trials with 30 seconds between trials, whereas the other half had a 90-second intertrial interval. Immediately following such training, subjects were given extinction trials in which 30, 45, 60, or 90 seconds were provided between trials. The response measure was the latency of responding obtained between the raising of the guillotine door, permitting access to the food chute, and its depression. The extinction criterion was three consecutive failures to respond, with a ten-second period available for the making of the response.

The extinction findings obtained from the two experiments are presented in Figure 9–5. The middle curve shows how response strength, as measured in terms of the mean number of responses occurring in the extinction period for the first experiment, varied with the intertrial interval. The curve rises with an increase in the intertrial interval used during extinction, indicating that extinction tends to speed up with the massing of trials. A complicating factor, however, is the relation between the interval employed during extinction and that used during the acquisition trials. Thus, the "bump" in the curve at the 45-second intertrial interval suggests that resistance to extinction is, other things being equal, greater when the intertrial interval used in extinction is the same as that under which the original learning took place.

The upper and lower curves of Figure 9–5 present the mean number of responses made during the first 20 trials of the extinction period by the two learning groups in Experiment II. As in Experiment I, the findings suggest that the intertrial interval used during the learning trials was an important factor in determining the influence of the intertrial interval used during extinction.

A number of experimenters have examined the role of massed versus distributed extinction trials within the context of a theoretical position posited by Sheffield (1950). She has stated that in instrumental reward situations, particularly those in which a runway is used (p. 312),

> . . . frustration generated by the omission of reinforcement during extinction has a motivational effect, which shows up as an increased vigor in performing whatever response the subject has a tendency to perform. With massed extinction trials, the increased motivation produced by absence of reinforcement on one trial would still be present when the animal was put into the apparatus for his next trial and would maintain the vigor of the running response, causing the animal to continue to go down to the end of the alley trial after trial and thus slowing extinction. With spaced extinction trials, on the other hand, the frustration and its accompanying increase in motivation would have dissipated, in greater or less degree depending on the interval used, by the start of the following trial, resulting in a relatively weaker response and faster extinction.

In an experiment designed to test this hypothesis, Sheffield (1950) trained 72 rats to run a straightaway for food with one-half of the animals being trained with a 15-second intertrial interval and the other half with a 15-minute intertrial interval. Each group was subdivided for extinction trials, with one-half being extin-

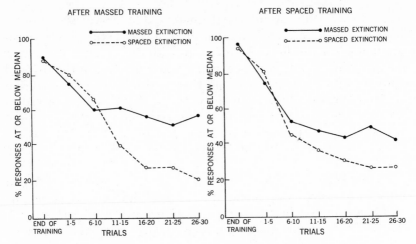

Fig. 9–6. Comparison of massed and spaced extinction following massed training and following spaced training, showing percentage of responses which equalled or were below 16.3 seconds (the overall median response time). The reference points at the beginning are the values for the last five training trials. *Adapted from Sheffield (1950)*

guished with a 15-second intertrial interval and one-half with a 15-minute intertrial interval. During the extinction trials, whenever either starting or running time exceeded two minutes, the animal was removed from the apparatus; all animals, however, were given 30 extinction trials. When extinction performance was examined, regardless of how the animals were trained, Sheffield found that extinction took place more rapidly when extinction trials were spaced than when they were massed. A closer examination of the findings indicated that for the group trained with massed trials spaced extinction was significantly more rapid than with massed extinction trials. For the group trained with spaced trials, spaced extinction trials also produced more rapid extinction than massed, but the difference was not significant. (See Figure 9–6.)

A number of subsequent instrumental reward experiments [Stanley (1952); Wilson, Weiss, and Amsel (1955); Cotton and Lewis (1957)] have confirmed Sheffield's findings, although at least one investigator [Lewis (1956)] has been unable to do so. Wilson, Weiss, and Amsel (1955) replicated Sheffield's procedure. In their first experiment, they found that the performance of a group given 15 seconds between extinction trials resulted in greater resistance to extinction than a group provided a 15-minute intertrial interval when massed acquisition trials were given. No difference was obtained between the two groups, however, after spaced acquisition trials. In a second experiment, in which water instead of wet mash was used as reinforcement, the investigators found that groups provided massed extinction trials were more resistant to extinction than groups given spaced extinction trials, regardless of whether massed or spaced training trials were used.

Stanley's (1952) study (Part 1) is interesting in that he used a T-maze and obtained two response measures—running time and number correct—during extinction. Findings indicated that the running-time measure supported Sheffield's position, but when the probability of response measure was used massed extinction trials produced least resistance to extinction.

In some situations, it may be that frustration will elicit responses which are incompatible with the previously learned response; this, in turn, should result in poorer resistance to extinction. In a study by Rohrer (1949) two groups of rats, after being trained to press a bar in a modified Skinner box, were given extinction trials; one group received the nonrewarded trials at ten-second intervals, the other group at 90-second intervals. The distributed group showed significantly greater resistance to extinction. Rohrer, like Sheffield, assumed that the massed non-rewarded trials produced frustration. Unlike Sheffield, he posited that the responses which were elicited as a result of this drive state were incompatible with the previously learned response (bar pressing). Thus, resistance to extinction was decreased as a result of interfering responses.

The role of massed versus distributed extinction trials in instrumental escape and avoidance learning situations has been examined by both Edmonson and Amsel (1954) and Hall (1955a), with conflicting findings. In the Edmonson and Amsel study, rats were given one trial a day in learning to escape a shocked runway by running into a goal box. After each subject had reached a criterion of a stable running time (seven out of eight consecutive trials with five-thousandths of a minute variation or less), it was assigned to one of three experimental groups and given extinction trials. The first group received one, the second five, and the third group 15 extinction trials per day for a total of 60 trials. The findings showed that the massed trial groups (five and 15 trials per day) were much less resistant to extinction than the group given only one trial a day. The difficulty with this study is that the one trial per day group was also the group which did not have its intertrial interval changed in going from acquisition trials to extinction.

Hall (1955a), controlling for this variable by using the factorial design and employing an avoidance learning situation, was unable to find extinction differences as a function of the intertrial interval used during extinction trials. In this study, rats, placed in a black-white shuttlebox, learned to avoid shock by running from one side to the other within two seconds from the time a door separating the compartments was raised. A massed group was given ten seconds between trials, and a distributed group was provided 90. Following the reaching of a learning criterion of three consecutive trials in which the subject learned to avoid shock, one-half of each group was given extinction trials with ten seconds between trials whereas the other half was given 90 seconds. Thus, four experimental groups, massed–massed, massed–distributed, distributed–massed, distributed–distributed, were used. The extinction criterion was the failure of the animal to leave the first chamber within 15 seconds on three consecutive trials. No difference in responding during extinction trials was obtained among the four groups.

In summary, what generalizations can be made about temporal variables? Unlike the conclusions which can be reached concerning the influence of effort, and in spite of the large number of studies which have been carried out, it is difficult to arrive at stable conclusions. In instrumental reward situations, particularly those in which the runway is employed, the massing of extinction trials appears to increase resistance to extinction, perhaps via a frustration effect. However, when more complex responses are examined, there is some indication that distributed extinction trials prolong extinction. In some situations, the relationship between the intertrial interval used during the acquisition trials and that used during extinction also appears to be of some importance, although the specific contribution of this variable to the experimental findings has not been determined.

ALTERED STIMULUS CONDITIONS

It should be recognized that a partial or continuous reinforcement regimen which is given over a series of acquisition trials provides a particular stimulus pattern which makes up part of the total stimulus complex to which the organism learns to attach a response. During extinction there is a change or alteration of the total stimulus complex because reinforcement is no longer present. A similar analysis can be made with the other variables which have been discussed in this section. Thus, if an organism is required to expend a given amount of effort in making an instrumental response or if it is provided with a specific intertrial interval, it would be expected that these conditions would become a part of the total stimulus complex to which the organism has learned to respond. If the experimenter decides to change these conditions at the start of the extinction series, the total stimulus complex undergoes some change. It follows, then, that altering the stimulus to which an organism has learned to respond will produce a response decrement.

Many of the studies which have been reviewed in this section can be conceptualized as reflecting altered stimulus conditions, and the findings of a large number of them indicate the fruitfulness of considering extinction as a procedure which involves altered stimulus conditions. It will be recalled, for example, that Grant, Schipper, and Ross (1952) pointed out that "changing the distribution of trials when the transition is made from training to extinction results in a more rapid extinction of the CR's."

Although an altered stimulus condition variable appears to be of some importance in accounting for differential performance levels in extinction, there are a sufficient number of exceptions to reject the position that all extinction findings can be attributed to the operation of this single variable. Moreover, Marx (1958) and Brown and Bass (1958) have demonstrated that the prediction of extinction effects based only upon the operation of an altered stimulus variable is not always correct.

Marx (1958) trained rats in a simple runway situation to find food in a glass cup. Following 36 training trials distributed over six days, animals were randomly placed into an experimental or control group and given massed extinction trials. Control subjects always found the empty glass cup in the goal box on these trials. For the experimental subjects, 50 per cent of their trials were run to the empty glass cup, but on the other 50 per cent of the trials, the cup was not present. The extinction criterion was failure to complete a run within 180 seconds on two consecutive trials, but all subjects were given a minimum of 36 trials. Marx found that the experimental subjects had greater resistance to extinction.

He has pointed out that the stimulus conditions were altered the least for the control animals (food cup always present in both acquisition and extinction) and yet this group extinguished most rapidly.

In the Brown and Bass (1958) study, two groups of rats were trained to traverse a 3.5-foot alley for food. For one group, the same environmental cues were present on all acquisition trials, but for the second group training trials were administered under varying stimulus conditions. The different stimulus conditions were provided by using three different runways. For example one runway was 5.5 inches wide, painted flat black, and had a smooth floor. Vertical aluminum baffle plates in the middle section forced the animal to either the right or left as it ran toward the goal box. The second alley was 3.75 inches wide, painted gray, and had a hardware cloth floor. Three aluminum baffle plates were so positioned in the middle section that the animal was required to step over the first, duck under the second, and step over the third in order to get into the goal box. The third alley was only 2.5 inches wide, painted a glossy white, and had a floor covered by a thin layer of sand. Following 24 acquisition trials, one-half of each group was extinguished under a constant or variable stimulus condition. Extinction trials consisted of 12 massed trials with six per day on the two days immediately following acquisition. Performance measures included starting as well as running times. Figure 9–7 indicates the latter performance measure for the varying groups.

As one can observe, behavior during extinction is more profoundly affected by the characteristics of the extinction situation than by the circumstances under which behavior was originally learned. When external stimuli are held constant from trial to trial during extinction, both starting and running times deteriorate rapidly, but when extinction stimuli are varied, extinction is retarded. It may be, of course, that the varied stimulus conditions present during extinction elicited curiosity in the subjects which contributed to the findings.

THEORETICAL EXPLANATIONS

One of the early explanations for extinction was posited by Guthrie (1935) and Wendt (1936) who assumed that the presen-

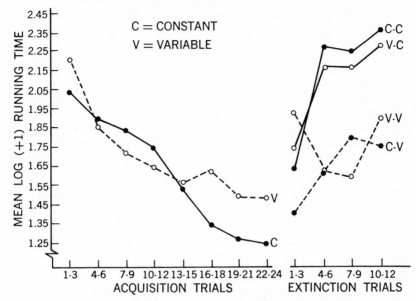

Fig. 9–7. Mean log (+1) running times for subjects trained and extinguished under constant and variable stimulus conditions. *Adapted from Brown and Bass (1958)*

tation of the conditioned stimulus without the unconditioned stimulus resulted in the organism's making responses in the experimental situation which interfered with the making of the conditioned response. The strength or frequency of these interfering responses eventually precluded the appearance of the conditioned response and, as a result, extinction was said to have taken place.

In contrast to the interference theory was the position taken earlier by Pavlov (1927). He stated that extinction represented one manifestation of a central inhibitory state which built up with the presentation of the conditioned stimulus (without UCS pairing) and which, although dissipating rapidly, nonetheless accumulated sufficient strength to prevent the conditioned response from being made.[2]

Early investigators found merit in both theoretical positions.

[2] Pavlov's conceptualization of an inhibitory process was anchored in the physiological foundations provided by Sherrington (1906) who had discovered the phenomenon of reciprocal inhibition.

The interference theory had the obvious advantage of parsimony since it was not necessary to posit a second process (inhibition) in order to account for extinction phenomenon. In addition, the observation of subjects in the extinction situation frequently revealed that the organism actually was engaging in some other type of response. For example, Wendt (1936) had observed that monkeys, trained to open a drawer to a stimulus in order to obtain food, revealed an increase of other activities such as pulling the drawer, biting, and vocalizing during extinction trials.

On the other hand, many arguments were directed against an interference theory interpretation. Three of these, as indicated by Hilgard and Marquis (1940), were (1) the role of spontaneous recovery, (2) the effect of rate of elicitation, and (3) the effect of drugs. First, spontaneous recovery, interpreted within an interference framework, could take place only to the extent that the interfering response (which competed with the conditioned response) was weakened during the interval coming between experimental extinction and the test for spontaneous recovery. The experimental facts, however, indicated that spontaneous recovery could be obtained with very short intervals of time, with these time periods generally acknowledged to be too short for the response to be forgotten. Moreover, if a conditioned response was "extinguished" by counter-conditioning—a procedure which clearly denotes the characteristic of the interfering response— there was virtually no spontaneous recovery.

The second point was derived from an examination of the effect of rate of elicitation of training and extinction trials. The massing of training trials generally retards learning, but such massing of extinction trials, at least based upon the evidence obtained by Pavlov (1927) and Hilgard and Marquis (1935), tends to hasten extinction. As Hilgard and Marquis (1940) wrote: "If the extinction process were essentially similar to the conditioning process, one would expect a positive correlation between rates of acquisition and extinction, that is, rapid conditioning corresponds to rapid extinction, slow conditioning corresponding to slow extinction." However, the numerous correlations which these investigators cited, some of which were cited in Chapter 3, are predominantly negative and, thus, do not support the interference position.[3]

[3] There is considerable question as to whether this evidence has contemporary validity. As indicated earlier, the experimental work of Pavlov (1927) and Hilgard

Finally, there was evidence to indicate that certain drugs could produce differential effects on conditioning and extinction. For example, caffeine and benzedrine were found to increase the rate of learning a conditioned response but to decrease the rate of extinction. To these specific difficulties could be added a general one—the lack of a description of the characteristics and growth of the interfering response as well as its source of motivation.

In contrast, the fact that the inhibitory process was tied to a physiological foundation appealed to many. Moreover, the findings from a number of experimental studies were in keeping with the operation of an inhibitory process. Thus, the phenomenon of spontaneous recovery could be accounted for easily since inhibition was presumed to dissipate with time, permitting the reappearance of the conditioned response. In addition, the early studies of Pavlov (1927) and Hilgard and Marquis (1935) which revealed that distributed extinction trials produced superior resistance to extinction were also compatible with the postulation of an inhibitory process which dissipated with time.

It was Hull (1943), however, who utilized both points of view by positing a two-factor theory of inhibition. Basing his approach upon the work of Pavlov (1927), as well as Miller and Dollard (1941) and Mowrer and Jones (1943), Hull postulated that inhibition was made up of (1) reactive inhibition and (2) conditioned inhibition.

Reactive inhibition was defined as follows: "Whenever any reaction is evoked in an organism there is left a condition or state which acts as a primary negative motivation in that it has an innate capacity to produce a cessation of the activity which produced the state." A basic corollary was that such an inhibitory state diminished progressively with the passage of time according to a simple decay or negative growth function.

The second inhibitory process—conditioned inhibition—was considered to be something similar to "conditioned resting." During continuous work, reactive inhibition accumulates, thus providing a negative drive state. When rest actually does occur, this drive is reduced by the reactive inhibition being dissipated. If a signal (CS) precedes the rest, it is possible for the resting re-

---

and Marquis (1935) showing experimental extinction to be hastened by the massing of trials is questionable, and some question also should be raised concerning the interpretation given the correlation coefficients which have been cited. (See Chapter 3.)

sponse to become conditioned to the signal and, thus, be reinforced by the reduction of the drive for rest. It was posited that reactive inhibition summated with conditioned inhibition in order to produce a total inhibitory potential which was subtracted from the organism's reaction potential.

The reactive and conditioned inhibition constructs could readily account for experimental extinction and spontaneous recovery.[4] It was assumed that extinction trials produced an accumulation of both reactive and conditioned inhibition sufficient to prevent the appearance of the learned response. Since reactive inhibition dissipated with time, the subsequent presentation of the conditioned stimulus resulted in a spontaneous recovering of the conditioned response. The lowered level of responding in this situation, however, presumably reflected a response decrement produced by conditioned inhibition which was hypothesized not to dissipate with time.

Hull's treatment of inhibition has not gone unchallenged, and a number of investigators have pointed to empirical and conceptual difficulties as well as paradoxical derivations from the theory.[5]

These difficulties are too extensive to be discussed in detail. However, two extinction areas which frequently have been cited as being difficult to incorporate within Hullian inhibition theory should be examined: (1) silent or subzero extinction and (2) latent or nonresponse extinction. Both are concerned with the fact that extinction can be hastened by a procedure which does not demand that the organism respond.

Silent Extinction

Pavlov (1927) demonstrated that when a conditioned response had been extinguished so that further responses could not be elicited by the presentation of the conditioned stimulus, further nonreinforced presentations of the conditioned stimulus would nonetheless serve to strengthen the extinction effect as measured by a decrement in spontaneous recovery. More contemporary experimental evidence for this effect is found in an experiment by Brogden, Lipman, and Culler (1938). In this

[4] Hull's theory of inhibition has been applied to a broad spectrum of behavioral phenomena, i.e., inhibition of reinforcement, alternation behavior, reminiscence, etc. However, only extinction will be discussed.

[5] See Koch (1954), Gleitman, Nachmias, and Neisser (1954), and Cotton (1955). See also Jensen (1961) who has reviewed attempts by other investigators to reformulate Hull's treatment of inhibition.

study, four dogs were conditioned to flex their right forelimb when a 1,000 cycle tone (CS) was presented. Shock served as the UCS. Following acquisition training, extinction trials were provided until the conditioned response could not be elicited by the CS. Two dogs were then reconditioned, but 400 extra extinction trials were provided the other two prior to their being reconditioned. Reconditioning was much more readily obtained with the two animals which did not receive the additional 400 extinction trials. Both groups of animals, however, were then given a sufficient number of training trials to be brought to the same acquisition criterion and then again extinguished. The two animals which had previously received the 400 extra extinction trials were reconditioned immediately following their reaching the extinction criterion, whereas the other two were provided with 400 extra extinction trials. Results indicated that these latter two animals took longer to extinguish than the two other animals.[6] Here, then, was evidence which indicated that differential extinction effects are not necessarily dependent upon different amounts of responding—a finding which appears to question Hull's reactive inhibition postulate.

Latent Extinction

A related area but one of greater contemporary interest than silent extinction has been latent extinction or what some writers have termed nonresponse extinction.

In an early study demonstrating the phenomenon, Seward and Levy (1949) provided 33 rats with ten training trials in learning to run a narrow elevated path from one platform to another; reward was found on the second platform. Following such training, the animals were divided into two groups, with one group being placed directly on the second platform with the food cup empty and allowed to remain for two minutes. Control animals spent a similar amount of time on a neutral platform. Five such sessions, referred to as nonresponse or pre-extinction trials, were used. Regular or response extinction trials were then provided in which the experimental animals first spent two minutes on the second platform before being run and then were confined to the same platform two minutes after reaching it during a regular ex-

[6] The experimenters have pointed out that this effect took place only for the first two conditioning and extinction cycles; subsequent cycles did not reveal any differential effect as a function of additional extinction trials.

tinction trial. Control animals were confined to the neutral platform for two minutes prior to each extinction trial. After reaching
the second platform during the extinction trials, they were confined
there for 20 seconds and for the last 100 seconds they were
confined to the neutral platform. The investigators found that the
experimental group's running time on the first extinction trial
was significantly slower than on its last training trial, but the
corresponding difference for the control group between running
time on the last training trial and the first extinction trial was not
significant. Moreover, the experimental group achieved the extinction criterion in a mean of 3.12 trials whereas the control group
reached it in 8.25.

Deese (1951) obtained a similar finding using a discrimination task. Following 24 acquisition trials in which all animals
learned to go to one side of a U-maze, subjects in the experimental
group were placed directly in the goal box from which food had
been removed. Four such "trials" were provided with a one-
minute intertrial interval. All animals were then given eight
extinction trials. Deese's findings confirmed those of Seward and
Levy (1949). The mean percentage of correct responses for the
experimental group was significantly lower than that found for
the controls.

Almost all of the studies which have been done since the
Seward and Levy (1949) and Deese (1951) experiments have
supported the position that latent extinction is a bona fide
phenomenon.[7] Contemporary investigators have directed their

---

[7] Two notable exceptions are the studies of Bugelski, Coyer, and Rogers (1952)
and Scharlock (1954). As Bugelski, Coyer, and Rogers have pointed out, the experimental designs of both the Seward and Levy (1949) and Deese (1951) studies are
weak. In the Deese study, control subjects were not given any "controlled" pre-
extinction training, i.e., pre-extinction training in a neutral goal box. In the Seward
and Levy study the control animals were treated differently during the extinction
trials in that they spent only 20 seconds on the reward platform and the remaining
100 seconds on the neutral platform. (It must be pointed out, however, that
first-trial findings of Seward and Levy in which different extinction procedures were
not involved continue to support a latent extinction effect.) The first experiment
in the Bugelski, Coyer, and Rogers study was a replication of that of Seward and
Levy, except that an additional control group was used. This group was permitted
to spend the total 120-second period on the second platform. No significant
differences were obtained between groups. Scharlock's (1954) study examined the influence of pre-extinction training on the extinction of both place and response learning in a T-maze. In this study, one group of subjects was trained to make a particular turn (right or left), whereas a second group of subjects was trained to go
to a constant location. Following seven days of training, pre-extinction trials were
given in which the experimental subjects were confined on a reward platform with

interest toward providing appropriate theoretical explanations for the effect.

Since Hull postulated that both reactive and conditioned inhibition could develop only in the course of responding, it is obvious that there is difficulty in accounting for latent extinction effects within inhibition theory. Aware of the problem, Moltz (1957) has suggested that the operation of another Hullian construct, the r_g–s_g mechanism, may be used to provide an explanation.[8] He has posited that the pre-extinction trials result in the animal's making fractional anticipatory goal responses (r_g) to cues found in the goal box. Continuing, he has theorized (p. 233),

> . . . successive nonreinforced emissions of r_g will produce a sharp reduction in its response strength with respect to cues in the goal location. If these cues are similar to those at the choice point, and if delay of reward during training was at a minimum, the extinction effects of r_g will generalize readily to antedating segments of the behavior sequence, so that at the start of the test trials, r_g either will not be elicited at the choice point or will be elicited with greatly reduced excitatory potential. If latent extinction is effective in reducing the strength of r_g . . . then s_g, of course, will also not be available, and the associative connection established during training between s_g and the instrumental response will no longer contribute to the habit strength of that response.

In addition, any decrease in the strength of r_g will reduce the value of the incentive motivational variable K, which, in turn, will also contribute to extinction effects.

Two predictions have arisen from this hypothesis. The first is that increasing the animal's drive level during the pre-extinction trials should increase the amount of latent extinction; second, increasing the number of pre-extinction trials (or placements) or increasing the length of each trial should also increase the amount of latent extinction. The reasoning has been that each condition should increase the probability of fractional anticipatory responses being made by the subject during the pre-extinction

---

an empty food cup; control animals were given training with a "neutral" platform placed outside the experimental apparatus. Following such training, 25 extinction trials were provided. A variety of response measures was taken (number of errors, time at choice point, starting time, running time, and number of times the animal looked into the food cup). Results, regardless of the measure used, failed to support a latent extinction effect.

[8] See Chapter 4 for a discussion of the r_g–s_g mechanism.

training. Since these responses are nonreinforced, their strength is reduced which, in turn, is reflected in the decreased strength of the instrumental response. The studies of Moltz and Maddi (1956), Thomas (1958), Young, Mangum, and Capaldi (1960), and Dyal (1962) all have relevance to these predictions.

Moltz and Maddi (1956) provided 40 runway trials to rats which were deprived of food for 22 hours. Seven of each day's ten trials were to a goal box of one color in which the animals received reinforcement (positive); for the other three trials, the animals ran to a goal box of a different color in which reward was not present (negative). Following the last training trial, experimental and control groups were each divided into three subgroups, with each subgroup being placed under 0, 22, or 44 hours of deprivation. Latent, or pre-extinction, trials which were provided to the experimental subjects consisted of placing the animals in the previously positive goal box for four one-minute periods without food. Control animals were not given this experience. Regular extinction trials were provided in the form of 15 T-maze trials with all animals being placed under 22 hours of deprivation. One arm of the maze contained the previously positive goal box, and the other arm contained the previously negative goal box. It should be noted that this procedure, in contrast to that used by Seward and Levy (1949) and Deese (1951), examined the influence of latent extinction on the capacity of secondary reinforcing stimuli to mediate the learning of a new response.

The mean number of correct choices for all control subjects was 9.67—significantly in excess of chance—and a result which demonstrated the efficiency of the secondary reinforcing stimulus in mediating the learning of a new response. Responses from all of the experimental animals did not differ from chance expectancy. When performance for the varying experimental groups was examined, results indicated that the 44-hour deprived group had the smallest number of responses to the previously correct goal box (6.30), followed by the 22-hour group (7.10), which was then followed by the 0-hour deprived group (9.30). In brief, the experimental findings supported the position that increasing deprivation during the pre-extinction trials significantly retarded the reinforcing strength of the positive goal box during the new learning situation.

The studies of Thomas (1958), Young, Mangum, and Capaldi

(1960), and Dyal (1962) have all demonstrated that the number as well as the duration of the pre-extinction trials also contribute to latent extinction effects. In Dyal's (1962) study, rats were given five trials per day on a Y-maze until they reached a multiple criterion of learning: (1) all subjects have a minimum of 25 training trials; (2) nine out of the last ten trials correct; (3) the error, if any, must not have been made on the first trial of the last day of training. Following such training, experimental subjects were given pre-extinction training which consisted of either one, five, or ten placements in the previously reinforced goal box in which the duration of each trial was either 30, 60, or 300 seconds. Control animals were given similar pre-extinction training in a neutral goal box. Ten regular extinction trials followed, with the number of errors as well as goal box time being recorded. The latter response measure was obtained by measuring the time taken to run the last 2.5 inches of the runway and the first 8.5 inches of the goal box. On the first extinction trial, both response measures indicated the presence of a strong latent extinction effect as a function of both the number of placements and the duration of the placement; this effect grew progressively weaker, however, as extinction trials were continued. Young, Mangum, and Capaldi (1960) have also shown that running time during extinction trials increased as a function of increases in pre-extinction confinement time.[9]

As noted earlier, an important aspect of Moltz's (1957) fractional anticipatory goal response hypothesis is that the extinction effects of r_g should generalize from the goal box to other segments of the apparatus. Accordingly, a third prediction would be that by using a goal box similar to the alley of the maze greater amounts of generalization would take place which, in turn, would produce greater amounts of latent extinction. The studies of Hughes, Davis, and Grice (1960) and Koppman and Grice (1963), however, have been unable to support this prediction.

In summary, the fractional anticipatory goal response hypothesis as posited by Moltz (1957) has had considerable, although not complete, success in predicting latent extinction effects. A some-

---

[9] Thomas (1958) also found that increasing the length of time the animals were confined in the goal box during pre-extinction trials (single placements of 1, 5, or 15 minutes) significantly reduced the number of correct runs on a T-maze during the regular extinction series. Unlike Young, Mangum, and Capaldi (1960) and Dyal (1962), however, Thomas' running-time measure failed to reveal any latent extinction effect.

what different analysis of latent extinction effects, although not incompatible with the position of Moltz (1957), is found in the studies of Coate (1956), Ratner (1956), Rozeboom (1957), and Denny and Ratner (1959).

This approach considers complex behavior patterns as being composed of a number of separate stimulus and response units or chains and the question which has been raised is: If one part of the chain is extinguished or weakened, what effect does this have on the total behavior pattern? Within a latent extinction context, it would be assumed that the pre-extinction trials result in the extinction of certain goal box behavior which leads to a more rapid extinction of the total behavior pattern. Both Coate (1956) and Ratner (1956) using Skinner box situations obtained evidence that the extinction of one part of the chain resulted in decreasing resistance to extinction of the total behavioral unit.

CONTEMPORARY POINTS OF VIEW

Difficulties with Hull's theory of inhibition, some of which have been reviewed, have resulted in renewed interest in an interference theory, with many investigators attempting to determine the motivational source of the competing response. One such source has been posited to be frustration. Following the lead of Amsel and his associates, it has been posited that frustration arising from the removal of the reward from the learning situation may elicit a competing response which eventually interferes with the previously learned one.

An important consideration in the frustration hypothesis is whether or not the competing response, which is elicited by frustration, is compatible with the previously learned one. Adelman and Maatsch (1955) made the prediction that if a compatible response was elicited by frustration, extinction would be significantly slower than if frustration was to elicit an incompatible response. Their experiment consisted of first training rats to run down a path, with food serving as reinforcement. Following such training, the animals were divided into three groups, differentiated by the type of response which was permitted to be made during the extinction trials. For the "jump" group, the plate glass cover of the goal box was removed and the animals were allowed to jump to the top of the goal box where they remained for 20

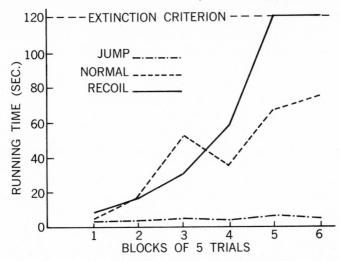

Fig. 9–8. Group medians of the median running times of each subject for successive blocks of five trials during extinction. *Adapted from Adelman and Maatsch (1955)*

seconds prior to being returned to their individual cages. Animals which did not jump within a five-minute period were aided by the experimenter in climbing to the top of the goal box. It can be noted that the jumping response was temporally compatible with that of running. The second group (recoil) was permitted to come out of the goal box following nonreward. Upon re-entering the runway, the goal box door was closed. Twenty seconds later the animal was returned to its cage. It was assumed that this group was learning a response incompatible with running and should extinguish most rapidly. Finally, the third group was given typical extinction trials. All groups received three days of ten spaced extinction trials per day. As can be noted from Figure 9–8, the experimenters' predictions were in keeping with the experimental findings, with the "jump" group showing relatively little extinction and the "recoil" group revealing the most. The experimenters concluded that these findings demonstrate that resistance to extinction is a function of how the response which is elicited by frustration interacts with the original habit.

A basic problem in this study is how so-called incompatible responses which are elicited in the goal box are able to interfere with a response which takes place somewhere else in the learning situation. The interfering responses must take place in the starting box and the runway in order to prevent the animal from reaching the goal box within a specified period of time—the extinction criterion. In the study cited, the incompatible response takes place following the running response. Thus, there is some problem in seeing how a response learned *following* the running response can interfere with it. Perhaps the explanation is related to the role of stimulus generalization, with parts of the apparatus other than the goal box eliciting the incompatible response which interferes with the running response.

Recently, Marx has conceptualized that extinction is primarily a function of the loss of the specific motivating properties of the stimulus complex. Specifically, his position is that resistance to extinction is a function of the degree to which motivation to make the response is maintained. Stated somewhat differently, a decrease in a subject's motivation is the primary factor responsible for the response decrement which takes place during the extinction trials. Marx's first study in this series was described previously. In this experiment, Marx (1958) trained rats to run a straightaway at the end of which they found food in a glass cup. Following 36 training trials, they were divided into an experimental and a control group. Experimental subjects were extinguished with an empty food cup present in the goal box on one-half of the trials, whereas control subjects were extinguished with the food cup continuously present as during training. Resistance to extinction was greatest for the experimental group.

Marx has interpreted these findings by positing that intermittent presentation delays the extinction of a motivational cue—in this case, the glass food cup.

Verification of this general finding was provided in another study [Marx (1960)] in which rats ran to three distinctive goal boxes (white, black, and striped), although food was found in only one of these. Seventy-two trials (24 to each box) comprised the training series. Following this, massed extinction trials were provided. One group of animals was given trials only to the formerly positive goal box, a second given trials to one of the formerly negative goal boxes, a third group given trials to both negative goal boxes, and a fourth group was run using both negative goal boxes as well as the positive one. The fourth group showed superior resistance to extinction. Marx hypothesized that the formerly positive goal box acted as a strong motivator when interpolated among formerly negative goal boxes.

In a third study, Marx and Murphy (1961) provided three days of discrimination learning to groups of rats. In this training, all subjects were required to make an instrumental response (head probe) to obtain food pellets. For the experimental subjects, a discriminative cue (buzzer) was paired with the presentation of food, whereas for the control animals, the buzzer was presented separately from food presentation. Following such training, all animals were trained to run down an alley where they secured food. After ten training trials, massed extinction trials were provided. On Trial 16 and every fifth trial thereafter, the discriminative stimulus was introduced. The buzzer was sounded just after the subject was placed in the start box, and when the door was raised it stopped. Findings showed that the number of trials to the extinction criterion was significantly greater for the experimental animals than for the controls. However, on the first 15 extinction trials, before the introduction of the buzzer, the two groups exhibited similar behavior. A more direct test of the effect of the buzzer was made by comparing the first seven buzzer presentation trials with the seven trials immediately preceding buzzer presentation. Figure 9–9 presents the mean starting times for these seven pairs of buzzer and no-buzzer trials. The difference is statistically significant. It can be noted that the differential action of the buzzer is especially evident for the first two buzzer presentations when its effect would be expected to be greatest if adaptation to it took place in later trials. The results of the study lend further support to the position that extinction should be considered primarily as a loss of motivation of activating factors. Thus, a cue previously associated with reinforcement serves to increase resistance to extinction when introduced differentially during extinction trials. The present study differs from secondary reinforcement experiments in that the cue was introduced prior to, rather than following, the making of the instrumental response.

Finally, a further test of Marx's position has been provided in an experiment by Marx, Tombaugh, Cole, and Dougherty (1963). It was assumed that an animal which was offered progressively more desirable incentives during acquisition trials would be more strongly motivated to respond during extinction trials

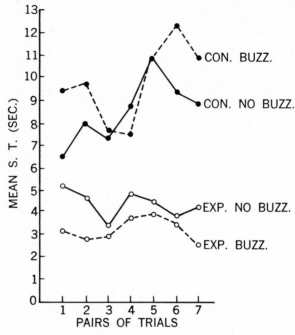

Fig. 9–9. Mean starting times for buzzer and no-buzzer conditions on seven critical pairs of trials in extinction. *Adapted from Marx and Murphy (1961)*

than an animal offered progressively less desirable incentives. Following a training period in which rats learned to depress a bar for water, two groups of subjects were formed—an increasing incentive group and a decreasing incentive group. The general test series consisted of providing each animal with four 30-second trials each day for a 12-day period during which time they could depress the bar. One group of animals received increasing concentrations of a sucrose solution (4, 8, 32, and 64 per cent) following bar-pressing responses and a second group received decreasing concentrations (64, 32, 8, and 4 per cent). Thus, for the first 30-second period, an animal would receive, following each bar press, a 4 per cent (or 64 per cent) solution; during the second 30-second period it would receive an 8 per cent (or 32 per cent) solution, etc. Following each four daily training trials, four 30-second nonreinforced trials were provided. Bar pressing during each 30-second period was recorded.

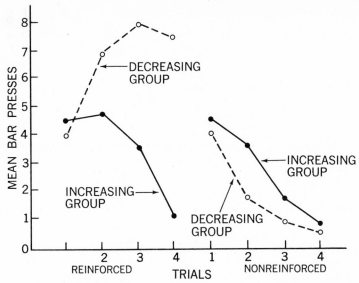

Fig. 9–10. Mean bar presses on reinforced trials and nonreinforced trials. *Adapted from Marx, Tombaugh, Cole, and Dougherty (1963)*

Results are presented in Figure 9–10. The mean number of bar presses during reinforced trials grows progressively larger for the decreasing concentration group, whereas bar pressing decreases for the increasing concentration group. This latter effect is not unexpected since saturated concentrations of sucrose appear to result in a rapid satiation effect on the part of the animals—a finding also obtained by Collier and Willis (1961). An examination of the number of bar presses taking place during the non-reinforced trials supports Marx's general position that extinction should be explained in terms of a reduction in performance due to a motivational decrement.

It must be pointed out, of course, that these findings can also be explained on the basis of frustration theory which assumes that (1) it is more frustrating to shift from a high, desirable incentive to a weak incentive than from a weak incentive to no incentive and (2) there is a positive correlation between amount of frustration and the vigor of the response. In a previous chapter, a study by Bower (1962) which supports such a position was mentioned.

10

The Role of Task Variables I

IN THE PRECEDING CHAPTERS, the primary concern has been one of investigating the role of motivational variables in learning. A number of experimenters, however, have not been so concerned; rather, their interest has been one of examining the variables related to the task itself. In the next two chapters, the task-related variables which have been regarded by most investigators as being of primary importance in terms of their contribution to learning will be examined. It is of interest to note that task-related variables have played a prominent role in the verbal learning situation, perhaps because motivational variables in the human are so difficult to manipulate.

MEANINGFULNESS AND THE RELATED CONCEPTS OF ASSOCIATION VALUE, FREQUENCY, FAMILIARITY, AND PRONUNCIABILITY

All things considered, perhaps the most important variable found in the verbal learning task is the meaningfulness of the material that is used. However, prior to examining how learning is influenced by meaningfulness, it is appropriate to examine the construct itself. Most individuals who work in the area acknowl-

edge that verbal material may vary with regard to its meaningfulness, but a definition of this construct, or the identification of
those particular characteristics which define meaningfulness, has
been a problem for many investigators.

Approaches to the problem have involved measuring (1) the
frequency, latency, or number of associations elicited by a verbal
item, (2) the frequency with which the item is experienced, (3)
the familiarity, or (4) the pronunciability of the verbal item, as
indicated by rating scales designed to measure these attributes.

Association Value

Most of the early work examining the association value of
verbal material utilized nonsense syllables, the first systematic
work being done by Glaze (1928). In this study, 15 subjects were
presented with more than 2,000 syllables; each syllable was
presented one at a time for two or three seconds. Subjects were
instructed to indicate in one or two words what the syllable meant
to them. If the stimulus meant nothing, nothing was to be said.
The association value of each syllable was obtained by computing
the percentage of subjects who indicated that a given syllable
provided some association.

The early studies of Hull (1933) and Krueger (1934) employing nonsense syllables, and Witmer (1935) employing consonant
syllables (3 consonants), also examined the association values for
such material. Krueger (1934) had his subjects first write the
syllable and then note any ideas which the syllable aroused. The
time allotted for each response was thus considerably longer than
Glaze permitted. Witmer (1935) exposed each syllable for four
seconds on a memory drum, with the subject instructed to spell
out the syllable and then indicate what it meant. In contrast to
these techniques, Hull (1933) had his subjects learn lists of
nonsense syllables but at the same time report what the syllable
made them think of. The subject was not to attempt to think of
associations, but if they did occur he was to report them. Each list
was presented three times, with 20 subjects being used. The
association index was the number of associations which were
reported for each syllable from the 60 presentations of the
material.

Although the operations just described measure some aspect of
association, a common practice has been to consider these association measures as measures also of meaningfulness. For example,

McGeoch and Irion (1952) state ". . . the meaningfulness of nonsense syllables has been measured by Glaze in terms of the percentage of subjects having associations aroused by each syllable."

Noble has defined meaningfulness (m) also in terms of association value, but his measurement operation has been different from those which have been reviewed. Beginning by defining meaning as a relation between stimulus and response, and coordinated by Hull's theoretical construct of habit, Noble (1952) has postulated that meanings increase as a simple linear function of the number of S-multiple R connections acquired in a particular organism's history. When this is translated into behavior, an appropriate index of meaningfulness is provided by the average number of continued written associations made by a sample of subjects during a standard time interval—frequently 60 seconds. In his original study [Noble (1952)], 96 items were obtained by using two-syllable nouns taken from the Thorndike-Lorge (1944) frequency count and supplemented by 18 artificial words. Subjects (N = 119) were presented with one item at a time and given 60 seconds to write down as many words as they could think of which were associated with the stimulus word. Subjects were instructed to respond only to the stimulus word, but not to use any of the responses as stimuli to which to respond. Thus, if the word "lemur" was presented and the subject responded with "hope" and continued with "faith" and "charity," it would seem reasonable to assume that "faith" and "charity" were responses to "hope," rather than to "lemur," and were unacceptable. Table 10–1 provides the m values for the varying items which Noble used.

A few years later, Mandler (1955) using Noble's operations obtained the meaningfulness of a list of 100 selected nonsense syllables.

Recently, both Archer (1960) and Noble (1961) using still different association measurement operations have provided meaningfulness values for virtually all consonant-vowel-consonant (CVC) combinations. Noble's (1961) technique consisted of providing 200 subjects with 2,100 CVC combinations and having them rate the number of things or ideas that each syllable provided. Five rating categories were used: (1) none, (2) below average, (3) average, (4) above average, and (5) very many. Two scores were then obtained for each combination. The first, designated as a, was similar to the measure used by Glaze (1928) and was obtained by

TABLE 10–1

List of Dissyllable Words (Nouns) in Rank Order of Increasing Meaningfulness (m) as Defined by Mean Frequency of Continued Associations in 60 Sec. (N = 119)

RANK	m-VALUE	WORD	RANK	m-VALUE	WORD
1	0.99	GOJEY	49	2.69	OVUM
2	1.04	NEGLAN	50	2.73	ROSTRUM
3	1.05	MEARDON	51	2.76	VERTEX
4	1.13	BYSSUS	52	2.80	BODICE
5	1.22	BALAP	53	2.89	TANKARD
6	1.22	VOLVAP	54	3.06	PALLOR
7	1.24	TAROP	55	3.21	SEQUENCE
8	1.24	XYLEM	56	3.34	ARGON
9	1.26	LATUK	57	3.36	RAMPART
10	1.26	QUIPSON	58	3.51	JITNEY
11	1.27	GOKEM	59	3.55	ENTRANT
12	1.28	NARES	60	3.62	PALLET
13	1.28	ZUMAP	61	3.64	NAPHTHA
14	1.30	POLEF	62	3.77	PIGMENT
15	1.33	SAGROLE	63	3.91	ORDEAL
16	1.34	NOSTAW	64	4.44	ZENITH
17	1.39	BODKIN	65	4.60	YEOMAN
18	1.50	ULNA	66	4.68	QUOTA
19	1.53	WELKIN	67	5.10	QUARRY
20	1.54	ICON	68	5.13	EFFORT
21	1.55	KUPOD	69	5.32	UNIT
22	1.60	DELPIN	70	5.33	FATIGUE
23	1.71	ATTAR	71	5.47	KEEPER
24	1.73	MATRIX	72	5.52	KENNEL
25	1.74	DAVIT	73	5.61	MALLET
26	1.78	WIDGEON	74	5.94	LEADER
27	1.79	BRUGEN	75	5.98	QUARTER
28	1.82	KAYSEN	76	5.98	REGION
29	1.84	MAELSTROM	77	6.02	HUNGER
30	1.84	TUMBRIL	78	6.15	ZERO
31	1.86	RENNET	79	6.24	INCOME
32	1.90	ROMPIN	80	6.57	UNCLE
33	1.95	GAMIN	81	6.75	YOUNGSTER
34	2.09	FEMUR	82	6.83	TYPHOON
35	2.09	LOZENGE	83	6.88	CAPTAIN
36	2.13	FERRULE	84	7.12	ZEBRA
37	2.14	STOMA	85	7.17	GARMENT
38	2.15	GRAPNEL	86	7.28	VILLAGE
39	2.19	FLOTSAM	87	7.39	INSECT
40	2.26	CAROM	88	7.58	JEWEL
41	2.26	NIMBUS	89	7.70	JELLY
42	2.28	LEMUR	90	7.91	HEAVEN
43	2.41	CAPSTAN	91	7.95	OFFICE
44	2.43	PERCEPT	92	8.12	WAGON
45	2.48	LICHENS	93	8.33	DINNER
46	2.54	JETSAM	94	8.98	MONEY
47	2.59	ENDIVE	95	9.43	ARMY
48	2.63	TARTAN	96	9.61	KITCHEN

(Adapted from Noble, 1952)

noting the relative frequencies of responses which exceeded the "none" category. The second measure, a', was the mean rating of associative frequency obtained by assigning the ordinal weights of 1, 2, 3, 4, or 5 to the five categories.[1,2]

Archer (1960) utilizing a somewhat larger CVC population (so enlarged because he permitted Y to serve as either a consonant or a vowel) employed 216 subjects who viewed each trigram for four seconds on film strip. They were instructed to pronounce each trigram to themselves and ask themselves the following questions: Is it a word? Does it sound like a word? Does it remind me of a word? Can I use it in a sentence? Subjects indicated their judgements on a two-choice IBM answer sheet, responding "yes" if they could answer at least one of the four questions in the affirmative or "no" if answers to all four were negative. The percentage of subjects who made "yes" responses to each trigram defined the association value, or meaningfulness, of the varying trigrams which were used.

Objections have been raised to the measurement operations of both Noble and Archer. Archer (1961) has pointed out that Noble's multiple presentation of trigrams undoubtedly resulted in his subjects' making comparisons among the items. Moreover, such multiple item presentation does not prevent subjects from spending more time on less meaningful trigrams and less time on more meaningful ones. Saltz and Ager (1962) as well as Archer (1961) have also objected to Noble's assigning of weights to the varying scale values since this assumes that there is an equality of the psychological distances between each value—a questionable point.

Noble (1961) has written that ". . . the novelty of Archer's four questions raises doubt concerning the psychological status of this index of wordness."[3]

---

[1] Noble (1963) has reported that this rating technique provides a measure which closely approximates his measure of meaningfulness as obtained by his previous (production) method ($r = .91$).

[2] Battig and Spera (1962) and Cochran and Wickens (1963) have used a similar rating scale to provide association values for numbers ranging from 0 to 100.

[3] Noble (1961) has stated that Archer's association values can be identified most closely with his a value and has reported a correlation of .955 between 120 of Archer's association values and Noble's corresponding a' values. Archer (1961) has reported a similar value (.949) when the entire range of values is sampled but has pointed out that a more adequate test of communality would be one which restricts the range of values. Archer has shown that when the range is restricted to 20 per cent intervals on his scale correlations between his values and Noble's are considerably lower, ranging from .32 to .68.

Frequency

A second variable which has been considered as a dimension of meaningfulness is frequency, conceptualized as the number of times that a subject has experienced a given item of verbal material. It often has been assumed that such experience is related to the frequency with which such material appears in print, and frequency values for common English words can be found in the Thorndike-Lorge (1944) frequency count. This count was obtained by examining a wide range of printed materials and tabulating the frequency with which the various words occurred. Although Thorndike and Lorge have provided different word counts depending upon the source examined, the most frequently used one is the general word count (G), which reflects all of the sources of materials which the researchers perused and which categorizes words on the basis of occurrences per million words examined. Words found more than 100 times per million are given a ranking of AA, and words found from 50 to 100 times per million words are listed as A. Frequency counts less than 50 are indicated by their actual number, i.e., 48, 36, 2, etc. A basic question which must be asked when using this measure for learning experiments is whether or not this measure faithfully reflects total frequency of occurrence including material written, spoken, and listened to, rather than only the written.

Since this list was published in the early forties, a second question is whether or not the frequency values obtained at that time continue to reflect accurately contemporary word frequencies.

Frequency counts of single letters and two-letter (bigram) and three-letter (trigram) combinations have also been provided by a variety of sources. The interested reader can refer to Underwood and Schulz (1960) for a compilation of many of these frequency counts.

Familiarity

More than thirty years ago, Robinson (1932) suggested that the concept of acquaintance was an important learning variable; a number of later investigators have pointed out that this concept is similar to familiarity [Waters (1939) ; Hovland and Kurtz (1952) ; Epstein, Rock, and Zuckerman (1960)]. The operations for producing acquaintance or familiarity can be typically reduced to those involving (a) learning or (b) frequency. Waters (1939), for example, had his subjects "familiarize" themselves with the material to be learned by reading it aloud, and Hovland and Kurtz (1952) had subjects become "familiar" with nonsense syllables by studying them in a constantly changing order until they knew the syllables well enough to recognize them and to supply missing letters when parts of the syllables were presented individually.

Noble, on the other hand, has defined familiarity as the frequency with which a subject has contact with a word, and in one study (1953) using the 96 verbal units which had been used in his previous study (see Table 10–1) asked 200 subjects to rate each one for familiarity. It was possible for the subject to give one of five possible ratings (never, rarely, sometimes, often, and very often) to each item. When Noble correlated his index of meaningfulness (m) with the median scale value defining familiarity, the r value was .92.

More recently, Lindley (1960) provided an index of familiarity for nonsense syllables by recording the number of times that the various syllables occur as the first three letters in words found in the Thorndike-Lorge frequency count.

Pronunciability

Underwood and Schulz (1960) have presented evidence that one dimension of meaningfulness, at least for trigrams, may be pronunciability. In one experiment, which they have reported, subjects were given instructions to rate on a nine-point scale the relative ease or difficulty of pronouncing 178 different combinations of three letters, among which were 100 nonsense syllables which Noble, Stockwell, and Pryer (1957) had scaled for meaningfulness. The other 78 units consisted of common three-letter words as well as consonant syllables. For the 100 common items, there was an r of .78 between the scale values obtained by Noble and the mean ratings for pronunciability.

Interrelationships among Measures of Meaningfulness

Table 10–2 provides a concise picture of the measurement operations which have been used to investigate the varying attributes of meaningfulness. Serious reflection about these dimensions would lead most investigators to conclude that they have much in common. Moreover, an examination of the correlations among these measures, some of which have been reported, supports

TABLE 10–2

Varying Measures of Meaningfulness

MEASURE	FREQUENTLY USED SYMBOL	BASIC MEASUREMENT OPERATION
1. Association	a	Percentage of population indicating that a given verbal item elicits an association, where each item is presented individually
		May also be obtained by using a rating scale (see 2), and calculating relative frequencies of responses exceeding the No Association category
2. Association	a′	Mean ratings of association frequency where: no association = 1; below average = 2; average = 3; above average = 4; very many = 5
3. Association		Percentage of population indicating that a verbal item elicits a "yes" response to one of four questions all related to whether or not the item seems like a word (See text for questions)
4. Association	m	Number of associations provided by a subject to a verbal unit in a specified amount of time, frequently 60 seconds
5. Association	m′	Similar to 2 except rating frequencies are transformed into deviates of the normal curve by Thurstone-Attneave method of successive intervals
6. Familiarity	f	Frequency with which subject has come in contact with specified verbal items as measured by five-point rating scale: never, rarely, sometimes, often, very often; rated frequencies transformed into deviates of normal curve as in 5
7. Frequency	F	Frequency of verbal items (words) as found in Thorndike-Lorge word count
8. Frequency		Frequency of trigrams as measured by contiguous three-letter combinations obtained from words randomly selected from the Thorndike-Lorge word count
9. Pronunciability	P	Ease or difficulty in pronouncing a verbal item as measured by a nine-point rating scale

this conclusion. In fact, most of the correlations which have been reported do not go substantially below .80.

One question which can be asked is whether or not these varying dimensions of meaningfulness, at least insofar as they will predict the rate of learning, can be best understood in terms of the operation of only a single variable. Underwood and Schulz (1960) have examined the position that meaningfulness should be defined in terms of the number of associations (Noble's m) a given verbal unit will elicit. As they point out (p. 45), its potential seems great. Thus,

> In a paired-associate task the subject must learn to associate two items; he must learn to say B when A is presented. The basic postulate of the theory could state that the greater the M of these items—the greater the number of associates which they elicit—the greater the probability that associates from the two items will link up in some manner so that B is connected to A via already existent associations. The link might be made directly (at one extreme) in that an associate of A *is* B. At the other extreme the link may come via one or more mediated associations.

They have, however, rejected such a position for a number of reasons. For one, such an approach leaves no room for "raw" learning. That is, there must exist within the individual the opportunity to learn material which does not already exist in his repertoire. A second difficulty is related to what has been called the interference paradox—a finding obtained with transfer studies. There has been some experimental work which indicates that the greater the number of responses attached to the stimulus, the greater the negative transfer. The application of the association hypothesis, on the other hand, would assert that the greater the number of associates, the greater is the likelihood that an associative connection (positive transfer) would be made.

The findings from a number of early studies led Underwood and Schulz (1960) to consider seriously the dimension underlying meaningfulness as being frequency. But subsequent experiments utilizing trigrams differing widely in frequency revealed only insignificant differences in learning as a function of the material used. On the other hand, a high correlation obtained between pronunciability and learning resulted in the experimenters' concluding that pronunciability was the major variable in learning rate and that frequency derived its causal status by being correlated highly with pronunciability.

MEANINGFULNESS AND LEARNING

Learning as a Function of Association Value and Frequency

Since meaningfulness has been defined in a variety of ways, the examination of the relationship between meaningfulness and learning is dependent upon how meaningfulness is measured. As might be anticipated, a large number of studies have been done in this area; only a sampling of the findings can be discussed here. For a more extended presentation, the reader can refer to Underwood and Schulz (1960).

One of the early studies investigating learning as a function of meaningfulness, defined by Glaze's association values, was done by McGeoch (1930). Lists of nonsense syllables with varying association values (0, 20, 46, 53, 73, and 100 per cent) were constructed. All of the syllables were presented to the subject at one time with two minutes given for study. A two-minute recall session was then provided.[4] A second experiment was conducted in which similar procedures were followed except that only one minute was provided for list presentation. Results from both studies revealed that the learning of the varying syllables was a function of their association value.

When the rote serial learning task is comprised of materials which differ in meaningfulness, as measured by Noble's m, similar findings are obtained. Noble (1952a) constructed three 12-item serial lists using his scaled material. The items on the first list had a mean m value of 1.28 (low m), the second list had a mean value of 4.42, and the third list had a mean value of 7.85 (high m). Learning was carried out to one perfect trial.

---

[4] As indicated in Chapter 2, verbal learning situations are sometimes used in which material is presented to the subject for a period of time, e.g., two minutes, following which he is asked to "recall" as much of the material as he can. Investigators have frequently termed this situation free recall. Inasmuch as recall has been generally regarded as a measure of retention, it may seem unusual to consider these studies within a learning framework. Following Melton (1963) it is believed that the area of retention should primarily reflect an investigator's interest in that interval of time (or the events which fill this interval) between a given learning trial (N) and a subsequent one (trial $N + 1$). Inasmuch as the interval of time between the presentation of the material and its "recall" typically is of no concern to experimenters using the free recall situation, these experiments will be considered as learning rather than retention studies, even though the term *recall* is used to describe the findings.

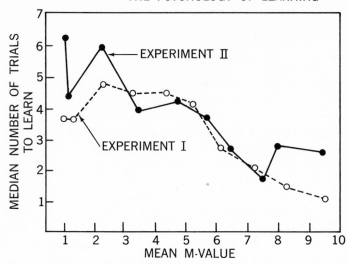

Fig. 10–1. Median number of trials to learn each pair of terms in Experiments I and II. The abscissa values are mean *m* value of each pair. *Adapted from Kimble and Dufort (1955)*

Significant differences among groups were obtained as a function of the meaningfulness of the material used. The more recent studies of Dowling and Braun (1957), Braun and Heymann (1958), and Sarason (1958) have confirmed these findings.

When a paired-associate learning situation is used, results are similar to those obtained with the rote serial presentation. Mandler and Huttenlocher (1956) used the nonsense syllables which Mandler (1955) had scaled for meaningfulness. The range of meaningfulness values was divided into eight equal intervals with one pair of syllables chosen from each interval. The findings, which were later confirmed by Noble, Stockwell, and Pryer (1957), showed learning to be a function of the meaningfulness of the material.

Kimble and Dufort (1955) have also obtained similar findings when the paired-associates list consisted of pairs of words which varied in meaningfulness, also defined by Noble's *m*. In their first study, which was replicated by a second, ten pairs of associates made up the list with each pair consisting of a different *m* value. Thus, NEGLAN–MEARDON represented the least meaningful pair, and ARMY–KITCHEN represented the most meaningful. Using the anticipation method, 20 subjects in each experiment

TABLE 10–3

Varying Meaningfulness
Combinations Utilized

STIMULUS	RESPONSE
High	High
High	Medium
High	Low
Medium	High
Medium	Medium
Medium	Low
Low	High
Low	Medium
Low	Low

(Adapted from Cieutat, Stockwell, and Noble, 1958)

were run to a criterion of one perfect trial. Figure 10–1 presents the findings.

One extension of the experimental work investigating mean-ingfulness and the learning of paired-associates has been to examine the role of meaningfulness on the stimulus and response items individually. In the studies examined, the meaningfulness of the stimulus and response items making up the pair was considered together. Cieutat, Stockwell, and Noble (1958) em-ployed nonsense syllables and three levels of meaningfulness (high, medium, and low) of stimuli and responses (Experiment II). Thus, nine different combinations of the meaningfulness of stimulus and response syllables were employed and are indicated in Table 10–3. Subjects received 20 trials on an appropriate experimental list. Table 10–4 represents the average performance of each group for each list and it seems clear that the average difference among groups due to the meaningfulness of the re-sponse is greater than that due to the stimulus.

L'Abate (1959) using nonsense syllables calibrated by Glaze in order to form four conditions of stimulus and response meaningfulness (high-high, high-low, low-high, and low-low) confirmed Cieutat, Stockwell, and Noble's (1958) findings. The learning of nine paired-associate nonsense syllables as a function of the meaningfuless of the stimulus and/or response is shown in Figure 10–2.

When the verbal material which Noble scaled for meaningful-ness is used, similar findings are obtained. Cieutat, Stockwell, and

TABLE 10–4

Mean Total Correct Responses During Trials 1–20

MEANINGFULNESS OF STIMULUS	MEANINGFULNESS OF RESPONSE			ROW MEANS	STIMULUS DIFFERENCE (HIGH − LOW)
	Low	Medium	High		
Low	6.0	16.7	30.5	17.7	
Medium	17.4	31.4	77.5	42.1	23.3
High	21.0	47.2	54.8	41.0	
Column Means	14.8	31.8	54.3		
Response Difference (High − Low)		39.5			

(Adapted from Cieutat, Stockwell, and Noble, 1958)

Noble (1958) (Experiment I) utilized the same four combinations of meaningfulness of stimulus and response units which were reported for L'Abate (1959). Eighty subjects were given 12 trials, and the results, in terms of percentage of correct response as a function of trials, are indicated in Figure 10–3. The similarity between this figure and that provided by L'Abate (1959) can be noted. Recently, Kothurkar (1963) also using material obtained from Noble's (1952) list and employing a paired-associate task in which the varying combinations of stimulus and response were manipulated (LL, HL, LH, and HH) has obtained findings confirming the results of Cieutat, Stockwell, and Noble (1958).[5]

When frequency of verbal material, as measured by the Thorndike-Lorge (1944) word count, is manipulated, the learning of such material is also a function of this variable. Although Peters (1936) was unable to find any relationship between frequency of word count and learning, the restricted range of words which he used can undoubtedly account for his negative findings. Hall (1954), on the other hand, using a wider range of material was able to find a positive relationship. In his study, four lists of 20 words per list were constructed. The words selected were seven letters long and were chosen at random from the Thorndike-Lorge word count. One list consisted of words occurring one per million; a second, 10 per million; a third, 30 per

[5] One notable exception to the findings presented has been provided by Mandler and Campbell (1957) who were unable to find ease of learning as a function of associative frequency. Underwood and Schulz (1960), however, have provided some cogent criticisms of this study.

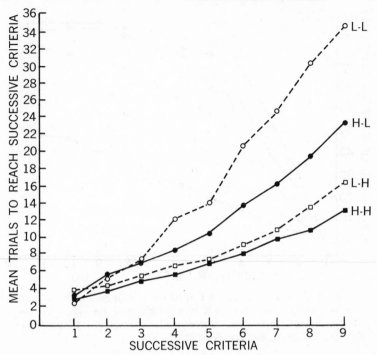

Fig. 10–2. Mean trials to reach successive criteria as a function of different associative values. *Adapted from L'Abate (1959)*

million; and a fourth, 50 to 100 per million. Each list was presented five times at a rate of five seconds per word. Following the last presentation, the subjects were given five minutes to write all the words they could recall. The results, as presented in Table 10–5, show a direct relationship between frequency and mean number of words recalled. Subsequent studies by Jacobs (1955), Bousfield and Cohen (1955), and Bousfield, Cohen, and Whitmarsh (1958) have confirmed the frequency-learning relationship.[6]

[6] Deese (1960) has presented evidence which supports the position that differences among free-recall scores taking place as a function of the frequency of the words presented are largely the result of differences between frequencies of interword associations. In Deese's experiment, lists of 12, 25, 50, and 100 words were used; all lists were homogeneous with regard to frequency of usage. Within each list length, the following word frequencies were used: (1) more frequently than 100 times per million (AA); (2) words occurring between 50 and 100 times per million (A); (3) words between 49 and 21 per million; (4) words between 20

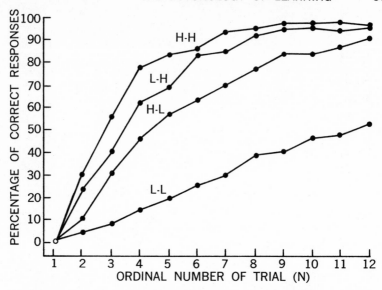

Fig. 10–3. Learning curves for lists of ten paired-associates as a function of practice. The four S-R combinations of low (L) and high (H) meaningfulness (*m*) represent the parameter. *Adapted from Cieutat, Stockwell, and Noble (1958)*

The Underwood and Schulz (1960) monograph represents an impressive array of experiments, many of which were designed to investigate the role of frequency in learning. In their early studies, frequency was manipulated by having each subject recite different nonsense syllables varying numbers of times. When these items were placed in a paired-associate learning situation, it was observed that learning was a function of the frequency with which the subject had experienced such material. Confirming the findings from other studies which have been reported, the investigators noted that frequency made its greatest contribution to learning when the items which appeared frequently were used as responses rather than stimuli.

and 9 per million; (5) words between 8 and 3 per million; and (6) words occurring 1 or 2 times per million. The general procedure was to present each word at a 1.5-second rate. At the end of such presentation, the subjects were asked to write down as many words of each list as they could recall. In order to calculate the inter-word association index for each of the lists, free association norms were obtained for all 600 words which were used. Findings indicated that as inter-word association decreased the frequency of recall also decreased, thus supporting Deese's hypothesis.

TABLE 10–5

Learning as a Function of Thorndike-
Lorge Word Frequency

T-L FREQUENCY COUNT	MEAN RECALL
1 per million	12.04
10 per million	13.31
30 per million	15.02
50–100 per million	15.04

(Adapted from Hall, 1954)

In a subsequent series of experiments, however, Underwood and Schulz found that the learning of a list of trigrams was not related to measured trigram frequency, but a significant relationship between trigram pronunciability and rate of learning was obtained. As a result, they concluded, as indicated earlier, that pronunciability (at least of trigrams) was the major variable in learning rate and that frequency derived its causal status by being correlated highly with pronunciability.[7]

A number of writers [Johnson (1962), Terwilliger (1962)] have taken issue with the Underwood and Schulz (1960) position that frequency is not a key variable, basing their argument on the experimenters' method of measuring trigram frequency. The method which Underwood and Schulz used involved counting all successive or contiguous three-letter combinations which were found in a word. Thus, the word "learning" contains the following trigrams: lea, ear, arn, rni, nin, ing. Johnson (1962) has proposed that frequency should be defined in terms of the occurrence of trigrams as discrete or relatively discrete sound units in spoken English. Measuring trigram frequency in this manner, he has found that frequency was significantly related to the rate of verbal learning but pronunciability was not.

The experimental results obtained by both Lindley (1963) and Gibson, Bishop, Schiff, and Smith (1964) are also in keeping with Johnson's findings. Lindley constructed four lists of trigrams which were used in a serial learning situation. The lists were so

---

[7] The investigators, leaving the door open for a frequency interpretation, pointed out that if one defines trigram frequency as the frequency with which the three-letter combination occurs as a sound in the English language frequency may serve as an adequate predictor of the rate of verbal learning.

TABLE 10–6

Characteristics of the Lists Used

LIST	ASSOCIATION VALUE	PRONUNCI- ABILITY	FAMILIARITY
1	Low	Hard	Unfamiliar
2	Low	Easy	Unfamiliar
3	High	Easy	Familiar
4	High	Easy	Unfamiliar

List 1 vs. 2 examines pronunciability
List 3 vs. 4 examines familiarity
List 2 vs. 4 examines association value

(Adapted from Lindley, 1963)

constructed that by comparing two specific lists it was possible to assess separately the contribution of one of three variables—pronunciability, association value, or familiarity—to learning. Table 10–6 provides an analysis of the lists which were used as well as the comparisons which were made. All lists were learned to a criterion of one perfect recitation or 25 trials, whichever took longer, although subjects were not tested for longer than 60 trials. Lindley found that variations in pronunciability, when familiarity and association values were held constant, did not contribute to ease of learning. The only significant variable was association value.

The Gibson, Bishop, Schiff, and Smith (1964) study is interesting in that the same letters were used to examine both pronunciability and meaningfulness of trigrams. This was done by using a meaningful trigram such as IBM, FBI, or TVA and rearranging the letters to make an easily pronounceable unit, i.e., BIM, BIF, or TAV. Control trigrams were generated by rearranging the letters still differently, i.e., MBI, IFB, or AVT. Twelve such trigrams comprised the material. Perceptual thresholds were obtained for all trigrams, following which the trigrams were presented via film strip for three trials. At the end of each trial, subjects were given instructions to recall all of the items that they could. The recall curves are provided in Figure 10–4. It can be noted that although trigrams which can be pronounced are recalled better than those making up the control list, the meaningful trigrams were recalled best.

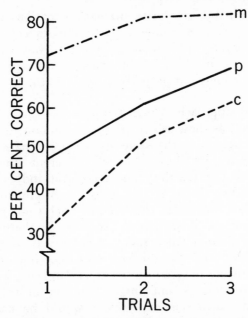

Fig. 10–4. Recall curves for three types of trigrams (meaningful, pronounceable, and control). *Adapted from Gibson, Bishop, Schiff, and Smith* (*1964*)

Similarity of Stimulus and Response

The similarity of the stimuli or responses which make up the learning task represents a second dimension or task variable which has interested experimenters. But, as observed with meaningfulness, a problem arises as to how it should be defined. Wallach (1958) has suggested a number of definitions, two of which appear to be particularly relevant. The first, derived from Hume (1939), defines similarity in terms of communality or *common environmental properties.* Stimulus objects which have a large number of common and usually formal environmental properties are judged to be more similar than objects which have few such properties. This way of defining similarity has been used frequently in verbal learning studies; thus, the nonsense syllable "qed" is more similar to "qew" than it is to "fiz." One obvious advantage, of course, is that this definition enables the experimenter to define similarity independently of his experiment; but, on the other hand, similarity in many situations cannot be so manipulated. At least under some circumstances, it would be more likely for an individual to perceive "vase" and "urn" as more similar than "vase" and "base," although in terms of common environmental properties (letters), the latter two words are more similar.

A second approach which Wallach has taken is to define similar stimuli as those which produce common responses. If an individual responds in the same way to two situations, although these situations may be objectively different, they would be classified as similar. On the other hand, if an individual responds differently to two situations despite the environmental properties that the situations have in common, no such similarity would be inferred. The problem here, of course, is that this type of definition is circular since there is no way to judge similarity independently of the response which the experimenter is trying to predict. Following the lead of Meehl (1950), who wrote of trans-situational reinforcers, one might conceive of trans-situational similarity in which one experiment would be used to define similarity whereas another would then be run to examine its influence on the dependent variable.

Similarity and Learning

In classical conditioning studies, the manipulation of similarity has been confined primarily to the CS, and these studies have been generally subsumed under the topic of stimulus generalization—an area which will be discussed in Chapter 12. However, it can be pointed out that the most usual finding in this area has been that the strength of the tendency to elicit a CR is related to the similarity of the test stimulus to the CS.

When instrumental conditioning studies are examined, particularly those involving discrimination, a common finding has been that the ease of learning is related to task difficulty. An examination of the characteristics of the task which make for ease or difficulty in learning indicates that a frequently observed feature is the similarity of the stimuli that must be discriminated. In general, it has been shown that as such stimuli become more similar the discrimination task becomes more difficult. The early studies of Yerkes and Dodson (1908), Cole (1911), and Dodson (1915) as well as more recent ones by Hammes (1956) and Broadhurst (1957) have supported such a position. In the Broadhurst study, which was referred to

TABLE 10–7

Analysis of Learning Scores

MOTIVA-TION LEVEL (AIR DEP-RIVATION)	DIFFICULTY OF DISCRIMINATION							
	EASY		MODERATE		DIFFICULT		ALL	
	MEAN	SD	MEAN	SD	MEAN	SD	MEAN	SD
0 sec.	84.8	6.6	81.3	6.3	71.1	9.0	79.1	9.4
2 sec.	86.4	4.7	84.7	5.9	79.5	4.8	83.5	6.0
4 sec.	87.7	3.9	83.0	7.1	71.6	6.2	80.8	9.0
8 sec.	86.8	3.9	83.2	5.9	66.1	6.5	78.7	10.6
All	86.4	5.0	83.1	6.5	72.1	8.3	80.5	9.1

(Adapted from Broadhurst, 1957)

earlier, the animals had to learn to discriminate between two levels of illumination. A large difference between levels of intensity constituted the easy task, whereas the difficult task was defined by a small difference. It was found that regardless of the level of motivation utilized the greater the similarity between the stimuli the longer the time required for learning to take place. Table 10–7 presents the learning scores for the varying tasks as a function of the level of motivation.

Spiker (1956) obtained similar findings for children. His study consisted of having four- to six-year-old children learn a discrimination task. The similarity of the discriminative stimuli used in the task was manipulated by using lights of various colors to which the child responded. The lights used for the highly-similar task consisted of one yellow-green and one green; the stimuli used in the medium-similar task consisted of a yellow-green and a blue-green light. The least-similar task consisted of one light which was yellow-green and another which was deep blue. The task consisted of presenting the two lights simultaneously and having the subject push one of two buttons; the correct response was indicated by one of the lights going out. All subjects received at least 30 stimulus presentations (or trials). Subjects who failed to reach the criterion of nine correct choices in ten consecutive trials by Trial 30 were given additional trials until this criterion was reached or until a total of 96 trials had

TABLE 10–8

Trials to Learn and Errors per Trial during Learning

| | TRIALS | | ERRORS | |
LIST	Mean	σm	Mean	σm
High Association				
High similarity	25.86	1.18	1.47	.07
Low similarity	19.27	.92	1.47	.07
Low Association				
High similarity	42.57	1.72	1.61	.07
Low similarity	29.18	1.54	1.32	.06

(Adapted from Underwood and Richardson, 1956)

been given. Spiker found that the number of errors made was a function of the amount of similarity between the lights that were used. The task which utilized highly-similar lights resulted in 28.92 errors; the use of medium-similar lights produced a mean of 24.59 errors; the task utilizing the least-similar lights resulted in only 9.72 errors.

Studies in human verbal learning have provided findings similar to those just cited. In the rote serial learning of nonsense syllables, Underwood and Richardson (1956) and Underwood and Schulz (1959) have found that high intra-list similarity resulted in slower learning than did low intra-list similarity. In these studies, similarity was defined by the use of nonsense syllables which had common letters. In the Underwood and Richardson (1956) study, four lists of syllables were constructed. Two lists were made up of syllables with association values of 93.3 to 100 per cent; the other two lists utilized syllables with association values of 0 to 20 per cent. One of the two lists at each level of association value had high intra-list similarity, whereas the other had low intra-list similarity. Four hundred subjects, 100 per list, learned this material to a criterion of one perfect trial. The results, as shown in Table 10–8, indicated that learning was a function of amount of intra-list similarity, although the difference was much greater for lists containing low-association syllables. These general findings were confirmed and extended in a study by Underwood and Schulz (1959) who constructed four lists of low-association nonsense syllables, with intra-list similarity increasing from List 1 through List 4. Table 10–9 illustrates the material used in each list. An added variable had to do with whether or not

TABLE 10–9

Lists of Nonsense Syllables Used

LIST 1	LIST 2	LIST 3	LIST 4
CEF	SIW	GOK	XAZ
DAX	QAS	GUW	ZAX
GAH	QUW	GYK	XEY
MEQ	KOJ	KIG	YOZ
SIJ	BEJ	KEZ	ZUY
TOV	YAB	WUG	YUZ
NUB	YOV	WEZ	XIY
YIL	XEZ	ZIK	ZEY
ZOK	ZIK	ZYW	YIX
WUP	VUX	ZOW	ZOY

(Adapted from Underwood and Schulz, 1959)

massed (two-second intertrial interval) or distributed practice (17-second intertrial interval) was used. Forty learning trials per list were presented, with 60 subjects learning each list. Figure 10–5 reveals learning to be a function of intra-list similarity, with the massed practice condition providing somewhat stronger support for this generalization than the distributed practice condition.

Similar findings have been obtained by Underwood and Goad (1951) when the rote serial list consisted of adjectives, with similarity being defined by synonymity. A list of adjectives consisting of elated, gleeful, carefree, jolly, laughing, pleasant, festive, sunny, blissful, genial, smiling, cheerful, and hearty was much more difficult to learn than a list consisting of the following: fiery, worldly, blotchy, hostile, fiscal, swarthy, agog, crumbly, flashy, sallow, puny, irksome, vulgar, and bearded.

In contrast to rote serial learning situations in which each member of the list serves as both a stimulus and a response, paired-associate learning situations have provided the opportunity to investigate independently the influence of similarity of stimuli and responses. In one of the early studies in this area, in which stimulus similarity was manipulated, Gibson (1942) compared the ease of learning different lists which consisted of figures paired with nonsense syllables. A low similarity list was comprised of 12 different stimulus figures, and three lists were composed of stimuli in which a good deal of similarity existed among the figures. Findings indicated that the lists having highly similar stimulus figures were significantly more difficult to learn than the lists

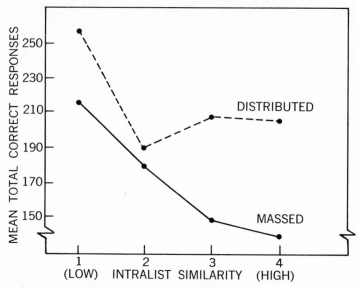

Fig. 10–5. Total correct responses over forty trials as a function of intra-list similarity and intertrial interval. *Adapted from Underwood and Schulz (1959)*

which utilized low similarity stimulus figures—a finding which supported Gibson's hypothesis that generalization frequently occurs between items of the list, which results in making the list more difficult to learn.

A number of studies by Underwood (1951, 1953, 1953a) and Newman and Buckout (1962) are also relevant to this area. Although Underwood (1951) found that lists containing many similar nonsense syllables took significantly more trials to learn than did low similarity lists, he did not attempt to examine the specific contribution of either stimulus or response similarity. In his second study, Underwood (1953) ran five experiments, with stimulus and response similarity for each experiment as indicated in Table 10–10.

Each list consisted of ten pairs of nonsense syllables; a learning criterion of one perfect trial was used. Although the precise operations which were used to define either low, medium, or high similarity cannot be discussed in detail, over-all, 20 different consonants were used to make up the ten items comprising the low similarity stimulus (or response) list; ten different consonants

TABLE 10–10

Experiments Used in Examining Variations in
Stimulus and Response Similarity

EXPERI-MENT	STIMULUS SIMILARITY	RESPONSE SIMILARITY
1	low	low
2	medium	low
3	high	low
4	low	medium
5	low	high

(Adapted from Underwood, 1953)

were used to make up medium similarity items; only six consonants were employed for the high similarity items. Similarity
between each stimulus and response pair was kept as low as
possible, with the basic principle being followed that no letter
used to start a syllable on the stimulus side could be used to start
the syllable on the response side. The results indicated that the
difficulty in learning increased as *stimulus* similarity among the
lists increased—a finding in keeping with other studies which
have been cited. Learning was not related to differences in
response similarity.

In a second study, Underwood (1953a) utilized paired adjectives in order to examine the same problem area. Ten pairs of
words comprised a given list. Within each list, considering
stimulus and response words independently, similarity was defined
by manipulating the degree of synonymity among the three
groups of words which made up the list. A high similarity
stimulus list, for example, consisted of one group comprised of
four very similar stimulus words and two other groups, each of
which had three similar stimulus words. A low similarity list also
was comprised of three groups of words, but the similarity
relationship among the words within each group was low. As an
example, the following list was defined as having high similarity:
(angry, enraged, pained, wrathful) (royal, regal, kingly) (double,
dual, twofold) . A low similarity list consisted of the following:
(fickle, heedless, fitful, giddy) (sickly, bedfast, feeble) (complete,
perfect, utter) . Lists were learned to a criterion of one perfect
trial. Six experiments were run with stimulus and response
similarity for each experiment as indicated in Table 10–11.

TABLE 10–11

Experiments Used in Examining Variations
in Stimulus and Response Similarity

EXPERI- MENT	STIMULUS SIMILARITY	RESPONSE SIMILARITY
1	low	zero
2	medium	zero
3	high	zero
4	zero	low
5	zero	medium
6	zero	high

(Adapted from Underwood, 1953a)

The results, in keeping with the findings of the earlier study obtained with nonsense syllables, showed that increasing the similarity of the responses had no influence on the rate of learning. Variation in stimulus similarity did not, however, support the findings of the previous study. In this study, both high and low stimulus similarity lists were learned at about the same rate; the medium stimulus similarity list, however, was learned significantly slower.

In a more recent study, Newman and Buckout (1962), using nonsense syllables and a paired-associate learning situation, examined four similarity conditions: low similarity among stimuli and low similarity among responses (LL), low similarity among stimuli and high similarity among responses (LH), high similarity among stimuli and low similarity among responses (HL), high similarity among stimuli and high similarity among responses (HH). High stimulus similarity syllables were made up by utilizing a pool of only four consonants (fvxy) throughout the list; similarly, a pool of only four consonants (hjqz) was used to make up the response syllables. On the other hand, eight consonants (fvxydmnt) were used to make up the low similarity stimulus syllables and eight other consonants (hjqzcgls) were used to make up the low similarity response syllables. Thirty-nine trials were provided, with a three-second rate for presentation of the stimulus and three seconds for stimulus and response. Results revealed that the group learning the LL list learned significantly more rapidly than any of the other three groups, but differences among these latter groups were not significant.

In summary, the bulk of the evidence supports the generalization that increasing the similarity of material within the serial learning situation results in increasing the difficulty of learning. With the paired-associate learning situation, increasing both stimulus and response similarity increases the difficulty of learning. When stimuli and responses are manipulated separately, the similarity among the responses which make up the list appears to play no role in learning, but learning does seem to be a function of stimulus similarity. Thus, high similarity among the stimulus members appears to retard learning whereas low similarity seems to facilitate it.

It must be acknowledged, however, that if the learning situation is one in which it is not necessary for the subject to learn the material in any given order, in contrast to the serial learning situation, the studies of Aborn and Rubenstein (1952), Rubenstein and Aborn (1954), Horowitz (1961), and Ekstrand and Underwood (1963) have shown that learning is facilitated by the similarity of the material to be learned. The Horowitz (1961) study is exceptionally interesting in this regard. His material consisted of 12-item lists of trigrams of either high or low similarity. The trigrams in the high-similarity list contained only four different letters whereas those in the low-similarity list contained 12. Each list was presented to two groups of secondary-school students with one group required to learn the items by the method of free-recall; the other group was required to learn the order of the items but not the items themselves. This latter procedure was accomplished by giving the subjects, following each presentation, a packet of slips of paper, each of which had a single trigram printed on it. Subjects were instructed to arrange these slips so that the order corresponded to the order in which the original material had been presented. The free-recall procedure was one in which the subjects were instructed to record on answer sheets, in any order, as many of the items as they could remember. Ten presentations of the material were provided; a free-recall session followed each presentation. High intra-list similarity facilitated free-recall early in learning, although this superiority was lost on later trials. Low intra-list similarity, on the other hand, facilitated the learning of the trigrams' order over all presentations.

A more recent study by Ekstrand and Underwood (1963) has confirmed Horowitz's findings that free-recall is facilitated with similar material. Ekstrand and Underwood's (1963) low-similarity list consisted of 12 unrelated words whereas their high-similarity list consisted of the names of 12 countries. The material was presented using a memory drum. Free-recall periods were provided between trials, which consisted of permitting the subject to write down all of the words that he could remember. The high similarity list was recalled better than the low.

Finally, a different facet of similarity is related to its influence on sequence of presentation. If the experimenter uses a paired-associate list of items comprised of different groups of similar stimuli and different responses (i.e., VKIH-star, VKIF-road, VKIW-yard, LDAQ-tree, LDAX-coat, etc.), the experimental findings of Gagne (1950) and Rotberg and Woolman (1963) indicate that a sequence of presentation in which similar items are grouped results in learning superior to that which results from a sequence in which the items are presented with maximum separation of the similar items.

Stimulus and Response Identity

A question which is related to the examination of the role of similarity in learning is: How does an *identical* item which serves as a stimulus for one paired-associate and as a response for another paired-associate influence learning?

Umemoto and Hilgard (1961) and Young (1961) have found that lists containing identical items which serve as both stimulus and response are more difficult to learn than lists in which unrelated items are used. Young's study revealed that such an identity effect was present regardless of whether high or low meaningful units were employed; whereas, Umemoto and Hilgard (1961) have examined learning as a function of the number of identical units comprising the list. Their experimental materials consisted of three lists of paired-associates, with each list consisting of eight pairs of nonsense syllables. On List 1, each syllable which was used as a stimulus was also used as a response, resulting in only eight different syllables being employed in making up the list. Thus, if baf-joc represented one of the paired-associates used, joc would serve as a stimulus for a second pair and baf would serve as a response for a third pair. On List 2, only one-half of the eight pairs used had common stimulus and response units, resulting in 12 different syllables making up the list as contrasted with eight in List 1. On List 3, none of the syllables making up the eight pairs

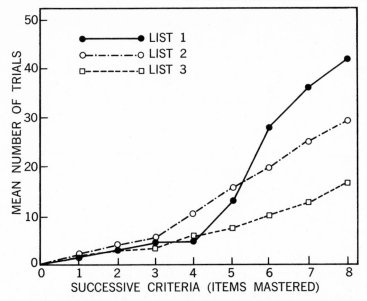

Fig. 10–6. Learning as a function of the number of items which are common to both the stimulus and response. List 1 has all items common to both S and R, List 2 has half of the items in common, while List 3 has none in common. *Adapted from Umemoto and Hilgard (1961)*

was repeated so that 16 different syllables were employed. Learning was to a criterion of one errorless trial. The findings revealed that List 3 was the easiest list to learn, and List 1 was the most difficult. As Figure 10–6 indicates, the learning of List 1 was somehow interrupted when about one-half of the list was learned.

The investigators have interpreted their findings as being related to the inhibiting effects of backward associations. When baf appears, the subject has to learn to respond with joc but Umemoto and Hilgard have hypothesized that a backward association is set up also between joc and baf. When joc appears as a stimulus for another pair of items, there is a tendency for it to elicit baf which interferes with the learning of the correct response. In the experiment reported, as the number of responses which also serve as stimuli decreases, interfering backward associations also decrease.

The investigators also posited that the use of some identical items combined with other items which are similar may result in

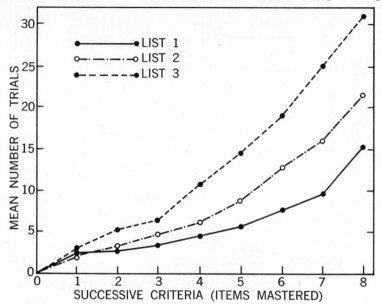

Fig. 10–7. Mean number of trials to successive criteria. In List 1 both members of similar adjective pairs are associated with the same nonsense syllable, in List 2 half the pairs have both members associated with the same nonsense syllable, in List 3 no similar adjective pair has its members associated with the same syllable. *Adapted from Umemoto and Hilgard (1961)*

facilitation rather than inhibition. Such a result takes place because the backward association which is produced facilitates new learning because of a synonymity or association effect. This kind of situation is illustrated by a subject learning the following paired-associates: faultless-yav; yav-perfect. The yav-faultless backward association aids the subject in learning the yav-perfect pair. In a second experiment, the investigators tested this hypothesis by constructing three lists which varied with regard to the number of identical-similar stimulus and response pairs. All lists contained eight pairs of items, with nonsense syllables and adjectives serving as both stimulus and response. For all lists, the same nonsense syllables and adjectives were utilized. On List 1, adjectives and synonyms were used to provide the facilitating relationship which has just been described; i.e., yav-perfect; faultless-yav; noonday-gid; gid-midday; etc. The adjectives used in List 3 were not so paired; i.e., yav-perfect; faultless-zot; gid-vacant; empty-keb. One-half of the pairs found in List 1 and one-half in List 3 were used to make up List 2. As Figure 10–7 indicates, the findings revealed that List 1 was easiest to learn and List 3 most difficult—a result in keeping with the investigators' hypothesis.

Isolation Effects

It has been noted over a wide range of conditions that as the similarity is decreased among the varying items that comprise the experimental material, such material becomes much more easy to learn. A logical extension of this position would be that if some part of the stimulus material was considerably different from the rest, learning for this part would become easier.

In an early study investigating such a possibility, Van Buskirk (1932) demonstrated that a nonsense syllable printed in red and placed on a green background, when learned as a member of a list of more conventional nonsense syllables, was recalled better than a corresponding member of a homogenous list. A year later, von Restorff (1933) found that a two-digit number was learned more easily if it was placed in a list of nonsense syllables than if placed in a list of other two-digit numbers. Although Van Buskirk believed that his findings were a function of the "vividness" of the material, von Restorff attributed her results to the "isolation" of the stimuli. Briefly, she posited that materials which are different or isolated can be conceived of as a figure whereas homogenous material in which the isolated item has been embedded is thought of as the ground. Most later investigators have referred to the general findings in this area as illustrating an "isolation" principle or von Restorff effect.[8]

Since these early studies, a number of investigators have examined various aspects of the isolation phenomenon. For

[8] Green (1956) has hypothesized that the von Restorff effect can be explained by the surprise or attention produced by an unexpected change. Although this effect might be defined and measured in terms of physiological responses, e.g., GSR, Green has suggested that it could be related to the forseeability of an event. In keeping with such a position, he hypothesized that a verbal item preceded by a long series of numerical items has more surprise value than the same item preceded by a shorter series. Moreover, the first item in new material has more surprise value than later, equally isolated items. From this hypothesis, Green predicted that in a list containing two equally isolated items, the first will be recalled significantly more often than the second even after serial position effects and other relevant variables have been balanced out. Experimental findings have supported this prediction. To the extent that attention, surprise, or forseeability can provide better predictions than isolation, they deserve serious consideration as explanations for this effect.

example, how does the more rapid learning of the isolated material affect the learning of the rest of the material? Or, what is the influence of the isolated material on the familiar bell-shaped curve which usually is found in serial learning situations?

In an early study using the serial learning situation, Jones and Jones (1942) made up two lists of ten nonsense syllables in which all of the syllables in one list were written in black. In the other list the seventh syllable was written in red; all the others were in black. Subjects were asked to learn the material to one errorless trial, and, a week later, they were requested to relearn the material to the original criterion. Results indicated that although the red syllable was more readily learned and better retained than its counterpart a comparison of the learning and retention of the two lists revealed no difference between them.

A few years later, Smith (1949) and Smith and Stearns (1949) obtained similar findings using adjectives. In this latter study two lists were made up which consisted of 13 two-syllable adjectives. In the experimental list, one adjective was printed in red and all others in black. Results indicated that although the learning of the isolated item took place very rapidly there was no difference in the learning of the total lists since the increased recall of the isolated item was accompanied by a decreased recall of the rest of the list. This finding has been confirmed by almost all of the investigators who have been interested in this effect.

Recently, Erickson (1963) has demonstrated that the isolation effect does not need to be related to the structural or absolute qualities of the material used but can operate with relationships as well. In this study, a nine-item paired-associate list was constructed in which four pairs consisted of three-digit numbers as stimuli associated with consonant syllables as responses (217-SWJ). Four other pairs were constructed in which consonant syllables were used as stimuli and associated with three-digit numbers as responses (CIG-472). The ninth and isolated pair consisted only of consonant syllables (KSC-ZNH). Thus, the stimulus syllable for the isolated item could not be viewed as isolated since four other stimulus items were also consonant syllables. Similarly, the critical response syllable could not be considered to be isolated since four other response items were consonant syllables. The isolated pair was better learned, however, than its nonisolated counterpart.

An extension of these experimental findings has been to manipulate the amount of isolation. That is, as the isolated unit becomes more and more similar to the material in which it is embedded, it should grow progressively more difficult to learn. In an examination of this hypothesis, Kimble and Dufort (1955) had four groups of subjects learn serial lists of 13 words which were identical except for the middle word. Twelve words on the list were obtained from Noble's (1952) 14 most meaningful words; the thirteenth word which occupied the middle position of the serial list varied in terms of its meaningfulness and ranged from the nonsense word "gojey" through "rampart," "kennel," and "office." The word "office" was in the same meaningfulness category as the 12 words which comprised the remainder of the list. Analysis of variance revealed that the relative difficulty of learning the critical word differed significantly from group to group; "gojey" was easiest to learn whereas "office" was most difficult.

Similar to this result is a finding by Erickson (1963) whose experiment was reported previously. This investigator has found that if the critical item in the list is made even more isolated by printing it in red, in contrast to the usual black, the addition of color increased the size of the isolation effect.

Kimble and Dufort (1955) have assumed that the isolation phenomenon was primarily perceptual and have hypothesized that the isolation effect should manifest itself when the isolated unit was placed on the stimulus side but not on the response side of the task. The findings obtained from an experiment using paired-associates as the experimental material confirmed their hypothesis.

However, Nachmias, Gleitman, and McKenna (1961) in a much more extensive examination of the effect of stimulus versus response isolation have been unable to support the general conclusions of Kimble and Dufort (1955). In their study, three types of material were employed: two-digit numbers, nonsense syllables, and common five-letter adjectives. Twelve different paired-associate lists were constructed. Each list consisted of nine paired-associates, seven pairs of a single type material and two pairs representing the isolated material. Six lists were used to examine the influence of stimulus-isolation, and six lists were used to examine the role of response-isolation. The make-up of the lists

TABLE 10–12

Schematic Representation of the Composition of the
Twelve Lists (A = Adjectives; N = Numbers;
S = Nonsense Syllables)

CONDITION	LIST	TYPE OF STIMULUS MAKING UP LIST		TYPE OF RESPONSE MAKING UP LIST	
		ISOLATED	OTHER	ISOLATED	OTHER
	1	A	S		N
	2	A	N		S
Stimulus-Isolation	3	S	A		N
	4	S	N		A
	5	N	A		S
	6	N	S		A
	7		N	A	S
	8		S	A	N
Response-Isolation	9		N	S	A
	10		A	S	N
	11		S	N	A
	12		A	N	S

(Adapted from Nachmias, Gleitman, and McKenna, 1961)

used is indicated in Table 10–12. The experimenters found that the isolation variable was effective on both the side of the stimulus and of the response to about the same extent. (See Table 10–13.)

Verbal Context

In the verbal learning task of either a serial or paired-associate variety, ten to fifteen items or S-R pairs usually comprise the material to be learned. Usually, the experimenter so arranges this material that one item or pair bears no relationship to the other— in a sense, the units may be conceptualized as being functionally isolated. Such material is in contrast to what Deese (1961) has called "connected discourse," or English prose, in which each item has some dependence upon the others which comprise the passage. A continuum going from the isolated unit to prose, with the varying points along this continuum being indicated in terms of what Miller and Selfridge (1950) have called approximations to English, can be noted. A basic question is: How is learning related to these varying approximations? Before proceeding to this

TABLE 10–13

Mean Number of Errors in Isolated and
Nonisolated Pairs

| | ALL ERRORS | |
| | Isolated | Nonisolated |
CONDITION	Pairs	Pairs
Stimulus-isolation	21.3	28.8
Response-isolation	23.6	33.3

(Adapted from Nachmias, Gleitman, and McKenna, 1961)

question, the concept of approximations to English will be discussed.

Miller and Selfridge (1950) have proposed that for any given number of words in a passage there are varying approximations to English. With a ten-word passage, for example, zero order approximation would be obtained by drawing the ten words at random from a dictionary. First order approximation would be obtained by selecting words according to their relative frequencies in English usage. A second order approximation would reflect the relative frequencies of occurrence of pairs of words, and higher orders would reflect trios, quartets, etc. with tenth order approximation being obtained from actual written English (prose).

The technique which the investigators used to obtain a specific approximation was to provide a subject with a given sequence or number of words and then have him use these in a sentence. Thus, for second order approximation, a common word such as "he" would be presented to a subject who would be instructed to use the word in a sentence. The word used directly after "he" would be noted and then presented to another subject for a second sentence. The word used directly after the one given this second subject would be noted and given to still another subject. This procedure would be repeated until the total sequence of words would be of the desired length.

Having obtained varying approximations to English for 10-, 20-, 30-, and 50-word passages, the investigators then proceeded to examine the learning of such material. Lists were read aloud and the subjects were instructed to write the words they remembered as nearly in their correct order as possible, although order was not used as a criterion for scoring. The results are presented in Figure

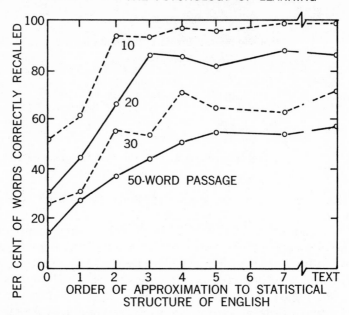

Fig. 10–8. Percentage of words correctly recalled as a function of the order of approximation to the statistical structure of English. *Adapted from Miller and Selfridge (1950)*

10–8. Surprisingly enough, these results reveal that there seems to be little improvement in learning, as measured by recall, above fifth order approximations.

The investigators' interpretation has been that learning of multiple-unit material is dependent upon the presence of familiar, short-range associations between words, with the varying higher approximations reflecting these short-range associations equally well. Sharp (1958), Richardson and Voss (1960), and Postman and Adams (1960) using the same material as that used by Miller and Selfridge (1950) were able to replicate their findings, although Epstein, Rock, and Zuckerman (1960) have not been able to do so.

It must be noted that Marks and Jack (1952) and more recently Coleman (1963) have called attention to the fact that the methodology and materials employed in the Miller and Selfridge study limit the generality of the conclusions. In the Marks and Jack (1952) study, the investigators have pointed out that, first, the scoring method which Miller and Selfridge (1950) used was

TABLE 10–14

Number of Words in Longest Segment Correctly Recalled as a Function of Order of Approximation to Statistical English

ORDER OF APPROX.	N	MEAN	SD
Second	20	7.7	1.5
Third	20	8.4	2.3
Fifth	20	10.0	2.6
Text	20	15.1	3.2

(Adapted from Marks and Jack, 1952)

concerned with only the number of words recalled, regardless of whether the consecutive order of the presented material was followed. Such a procedure permits the subject to form his own associations; thus, the results may not be attributable to the "short-range associations" inherent in the material. Secondly, the textual material used by Miller and Selfridge is somewhat misnamed in that parts of more than a single sentence appear in the longer lists. In the Marks and Jack study, second, third, and fifth orders of approximation were used in addition to textual material. The material used by Miller and Selfridge was lengthened to contain 261 words. These 261 word sequences were then broken down into consecutive segments of 6, 7, 8, 9 . . . 23 word units. For the textual material, complete sentences of similar lengths were chosen from novels and biographies. In individual testing sessions, subjects were presented segments of increasing length until two consecutive segment failures were obtained. A failure was defined as any omission, inversion, or addition of a word or words. The subject's score was the number of words in the longest segment he was able to recall correctly. The results, revealed in Table 10–14, clearly indicate that the order of approximation significantly affects recall, but, unlike Miller and Selfridge's findings, textual material was recalled significantly better than fifth order approximation. As the investigators state, "When a different measure of retention is used, as in the present study, recall seems to be very much a function of the a priori relative meaningfulness of the materials."

Coleman (1963) has called attention to additional difficulties. In one part of his investigation, he had expert linguists rank the varying approximations, which Miller and Selfridge (1950) had used, as to their grammaticalness. It was found that the linguists rated those approximations beyond fifth order as deviant from English grammatical rules as was the fifth order approximation. As Coleman states, "As order of approximation becomes higher apparently the grammatical constructions gradually become more awkward and implausible; that is, the subjects do not agree so well with their verbs, nor the verbs with their direct objects, nor the modifiers with the words they modify, etc."

Furthermore, Coleman (1963a) has pointed out that the complexity of the words used in the varying Miller and Selfridge approximations were not the same. Complexity, in this instance, was defined by (1) the number of uncommon words (all those occurring less than 100 per million) found in the approximation, (2) the number of syllables obtained for each 100 words in the approximation, and (3) the number of morphemes obtained for each 100 words in the approximation. The findings were in agreement with the linguistic ratings in that eighth order approximation and prose material were more complex than approximations below this level.

Finally, Coleman replicated the Miller and Selfridge procedure, but he used material in which the prose and all approximations were matched in syllabic length and in word frequency. Moreover, recall was scored in correct two-word, correct three-word, and up to correct 17-word sequences. The results, supporting the Marks and Jack (1952) findings, revealed that prose was recalled significantly better than the higher order approximations. Moreover, as recall was scored in longer sequences, the advantages for the higher order approximations became greater.

In conclusion, although the Miller and Selfridge (1950) findings have been accepted as basic whenever the role of context of learning is examined, it appears that their findings have little generality beyond the specific material used and the scoring techniques they have employed.

In a series of studies, Epstein (1961, 1962) has investigated the influence of syntactical structure on the learning of multiple-unit material, with syntax being defined as the generalized pattern or schema which determines the sequence of words available to the subject. Epstein hypothesized that since verbal messages in ordinary usage are encoded according to a set of grammatical rules, the learning of this material may be very different from the learning

TABLE 10–15

Examples of Verbal Material Used

A haky deebs reciled the dison tofently um flutest pav.
Deebs haky the um flutest reciled pav a tofently dison.

Wavy books worked singing clouds to empty slow lamps.
Worked clouds slow empty to wavy singing books lamps.

(Adapted from Epstein, 1962)

of a series of independent items. This position has been confirmed in a series of experiments, one of which will be described [Epstein (1962)].

Two general classes of material (nonsense syllables or meaningful words) were placed in either a grammatically structured sequence or in a sequentially meaningless sequence. Table 10–15 illustrates the two arrangements. The procedure consisted of providing the subjects with a seven-second presentation of one of the arrangements with instructions to learn the material in the order in which it was arranged. The subjects were then given thirty seconds for recall. Additional trials and recall periods were provided until the subject was able to reproduce the series perfectly. It was found that syntactically structured material was more rapidly acquired than matched, unstructured material, with such a finding being true regardless of whether the material was meaningful or not.

11

The Role of Task Variables II

MANY TASK VARIABLES can contribute to learning. In this chapter an examination of their influence will be continued, examining the role of instructions, stimulus intensity, stimulus position, the additivity of cues, and, finally, the distribution of practice.

THE ROLE OF INSTRUCTIONS

In most experiments it is necessary to provide instructions to the subjects which indicate something about the nature of the task. It generally has been assumed that one set of instructions is as effective as another. As a result, relatively few investigators have examined the influence of this variable on learning. One exception to this has been in the area of classical conditioning where a number of experimenters have been concerned with determining how the role of instructions can control the acquisition and extinction of a CR.

In one of the early studies, Miller (1939) provided different instructions to two experimental groups and one control group prior to their receiving a training session of 50 trials during which there was an attempt to condition the eyelid response. A light served as the CS and an air puff as the UCS. All groups received

TABLE 11–1

The Influence of Supplementary Instructions on Frequency of Conditioned Responses

GROUP	INSTRUCTIONS	PERCENTAGE OF TRIALS ON WHICH CR APPEARED
1. (Inhibitory)	"Please refrain from winking when the light comes on. Be sure that you do not wink or start to wink before you have felt the puff. Keep your eyelids motionless if you possibly can, and above all, do not let them move from the time you look up at the glass until after the puff."	26
2. (Control)	(No supplementary instructions provided)	38
3. (Facilitatory)	"Please do not try to prevent this wink or do anything about it. And in case you feel your eyes closing or starting to close as soon as the light comes on, do nothing to prevent it. Just be sure you are willing to let your eyes and eyelids react automatically. Do not control them."	71

(Adapted from Miller, 1939)

the following preliminary instructions which were necessary for photographic recording: "Before each trial during the experiment, I will give you a ready signal by saying 'ready.' When you hear me say 'ready,' look at the cross. Between trials you may keep your eyes open or closed as you prefer." In addition, supplementary instructions were provided to the two experimental groups; one group received instructions designed to facilitate conditioning, whereas the other experimental group received instructions designed to inhibit conditioning. The control group received no additional instructions. The nature of these supplementary instructions and the experimental findings are indicated in Table 11–1.

It can be observed that the level of conditioning parallels the instruction continuum in which, at one end, instructions are of an inhibitory nature whereas at the other end they are facilitatory. Statistical examination of the findings, however, did not reveal significant differences between the group receiving instructions which were of an inhibitory nature and the control group.

Norris and Grant (1948) believed that in the Miller study the sensitization of the beta response, a secondary response of the eyelid to light, was not controlled adequately and that the instructions may have been forgotten quickly once the experiment began. As a result, they did not accept completely Miller's conclusions that negative or inhibitory instructions had only negligible effects upon conditioning. This became the focus of their experimental interest.

To this end, two major groups of subjects were provided with eyelid conditioning trials; one group received passive or neutral instructions ("Do not attempt to control your natural reactions to these stimuli."); a second group received inhibitory instructions ("Be sure you do not wink before you feel a puff."). Each of these two major groups was then subdivided into thirds. One-third of each group was given the additional instructions that if they winked or started to wink before the puff was felt an unpleasant shock would be delivered to the right wrist. This group was classified as the "shock explanation" group. The second third of each major group was also shocked for anticipatory blinks but was not provided any explanation for the shock. The last third was given no shock. Forty conditioning trials were provided on Day 1 and 30 additional trials on Day 2. Figure 11–1 presents the findings. It can be noted that in terms of frequency of responding the passive group clearly surpassed the inhibitory groups in all instances—a result not in keeping with Miller's findings. An interesting outcome was the fact that in spite of the group's being instructed not to respond prior to their feeling the puff, and that they would be shocked whenever this occurred, a substantial amount of conditioning took place.

Nicholls and Kimble (1964) have recently confirmed the findings of Norris and Grant (1948) in demonstrating that inhibitory instructions ("Concentrate on not blinking until you feel the puff of air. That is, try not to blink after the light comes on until you feel the air puff.") resulted in significantly poorer conditioning than did giving facilitative instructions ("Let your reactions take care of themselves. If you feel your eye closing or about to close do nothing to stop it.") Like Norris and Grant (1948) these investigators also obtained a significant amount of conditioning with their inhibitory group. (See Figure 11–2.)

The fact that instructions to the subject play an important

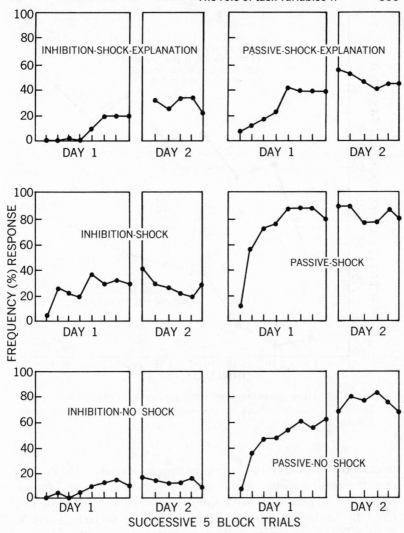

Fig. 11–1. Average percentage frequency of conditioned eyelid responses. Data are grouped into successive five-trial blocks. *Adapted from Norris and Grant (1948)*

role in conditioning responses which are under the voluntary control of the subject suggests that involuntary responses, e.g., GSR, can be used in order to eliminate this variable. The problem, however, is that involuntary responses may be con-

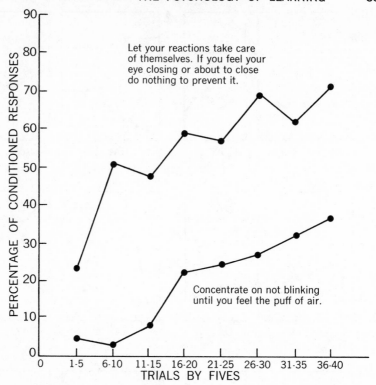

Fig. 11–2. Mean percentage of CR's for subjects conditioned with facilitative and inhibitory instructions. *Adapted from Nicholls and Kimble (1964)*

trolled by voluntary ones. For example, Razran (1935) found that the conditioning of the salivary response in the human, a response which is usually considered involuntary, could be facilitated by having the subject think of eating pretzels. Cook and Harris (1937) experimentally demonstrated that a "conditioned" GSR could be obtained merely by instructing the subject that electric shock (UCS) would follow a green light (CS). Thus, their experimental findings revealed that, following such instructions, the presentation of 15 or 30 conditioning trials did not increase the strength of the CR beyond that which was obtained when only a single conditioning trial plus instructions was used. The resistance to extinction measure (four consecutive responses of zero magnitude) showed that the mean number of responses for the single-trial group was 26.4, 30.0 for the 15-trial group, and 18.0 for the 30-trial group.

In another part of this study, the investigators found that instructing the subject that shock would no longer follow the light produced an elimination or marked weakening of the CR, a result confirmed by Wickens, Allen, and Hill (1963) and Grings and Lockhart (1963).[1]

The finding that immediate or rapid extinction can take place as a function of verbal instructions to the subject has been verified by Notterman, Schoenfeld, and Bersh (1952) and Chatterjee and Eriksen (1962) with another type of involuntary response—heart rate. Lindley and Moyer (1961) have also obtained similar extinction findings with the conditioned finger withdrawal.

THE ROLE OF STIMULUS INTENSITY

Another variable which has interested a number of investigators has been the intensity of the conditioned stimulus. After reviewing a large number of Russian conditioning studies, most of which have been unavailable to American psychologists, Razran (1957) stated that a cursory examination of these protocols reveals that a variation in the intensity of the CS is a significant determiner of conditioning efficiency as measured by either the speed of the CR formation or the magnitudes and latencies of resulting CR's.

[1] There have been a number of very specific findings in this area which undoubtedly need further investigation to demonstrate their generality. For example, Wickens, Allen, and Hill (1963) using the conditioned GSR found that instruction indicating that there would be no more shock produced relatively rapid extinction over the five extinction trials which were given; however, no difference was found between the instructed and a noninstructed group on the first extinction trial. Silverman (1960) also examining the conditioned GSR found that a group conditioned under a six-second CS-UCS interval and given instructions that there would be no more shock did not reveal any larger decrement in the magnitude of the GSR during extinction than a similarly conditioned but noninstructed group. (He was able, however, to obtain the usual finding when a five-tenths of a second CS-UCS interval was used.) Silverman postulated that in the long delay conditioning situation an anxiety response develops which is not affected by instructions and which functions to maintain GSR responding during extinction. In contrast, the Wickens, Allen, and Hill (1963) and Silverman (1960) findings have not been confirmed by Grings and Lockhart (1963). In the latter study, the GSR was conditioned using a five-second CS-UCS interval. An instructed group ("There will be no more shock.") revealed a large and significant response decrement on the first extinction trial—a finding not obtained with the noninstructed group.

What have American investigators found? Although Carter (1941) was unable to find differences in response strength as related to CS intensity, some of the more recent studies have yielded positive findings. Both Barnes (1956) and Walker (1960) have found that the rate of acquisition of a CR is a function of the intensity of the CS.

Barnes (1956) employed a classical conditioning procedure in which a 1.7 ma. shock (UCS) was applied to the right hind leg of a dog and paired with either a 60 or 80 db, 800 cps tone (CS). A second variable which interested this investigator was related to the temporal relationship existing between the CS and UCS. More specifically, the duration of the CS was either 1, 6, 16, or 31 seconds, with the UCS being presented nine-tenths of a second after the onset of the CS and continuing for one-tenth of a second. This procedure provided for CS-UCS overlaps of 0, 5, 15, or 30 seconds. Four trials per day were given each subject for the first seven days, followed by three trials per day for the next six days. Results indicated that the mean number of CR's as well as mean reciprocal latency varied directly with the intensity of the CS. Figure 11–3 reveals the number of CR's plotted for both CS intensities as a function of the varying lengths of CS-UCS overlap.

Walker (1960) has used human subjects in examining the influence of CS intensity. In brief, she believed that some of the negative findings which had been obtained in this area [Carter (1941), Grant and Schneider (1948, 1949)] might be related to the level of the UCS which was employed in these studies. She hypothesized an interaction between the CS and UCS in which the intensity of the CS would have a greater effect on performance under strong UCS intensity than under weak UCS intensity. The experimental procedure consisted of conditioning the eyelid with four different stimulus conditions: weak CS–weak UCS, strong CS–weak UCS, weak CS–strong UCS, strong CS–strong UCS. The CS was a tone of 1,000 cps, either 30 or 80 db above average threshold, and the UCS was an air puff of either five-tenths of a pound or five pounds per square inch. Eighty acquisition trials were provided to each subject in a single session.

The mean percentage of anticipatory responses for the acquisition trials can be noted in Figure 11–4. It can be seen that the intensity of the CS was an important determinant of the rate of acquisition. The CS-UCS interaction, which according to her hypothesis should have been significant, was not significant. However, the fact that the difference between weak and strong CS

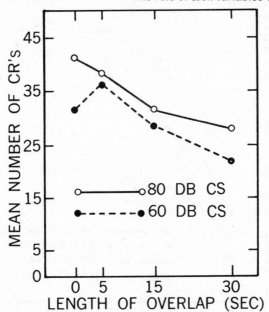

Fig. 11–3. Mean total number of CR's made by each CS intensity group as a function of duration of CS-UCS overlap. *Adapted from Barnes (1956)*

intensity was significant under the strong UCS, but was not reliable under the weak UCS, was consistent with her position.

Although the Barnes (1956) and Walker (1960) studies have yielded positive findings, it should be pointed out that the contribution of CS intensity to acquisition performance has been rather small. Recently, Beck (1963) has also examined the influence of two CS intensities on the conditioning of the eyeblink. Instead of using separate groups to investigate this variable, she administered the two intensities of the 1,000 cps tone (30 db and 80 db) to all subjects in an irregular order throughout 100 conditioning trials. Findings indicated a large and significant effect of the intensity variable.

Grice and Hunter (1964) have confirmed Beck's finding that the use of an experimental design in which each subject experiences the varying intensities of the CS produces a large CS intensity difference, in contrast to the separate groups design in which each subject experiences only a single CS intensity. In their study, the eyeblink response was conditioned using a 50 and/or 100 db tone as the CS. One group of subjects was conditioned for

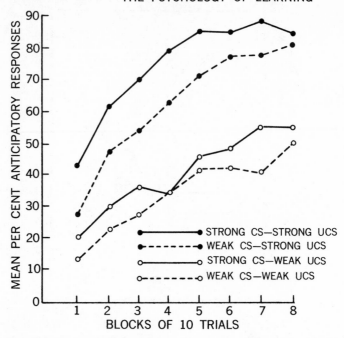

Fig. 11–4. Mean percentage of anticipatory responses during acquisition per block of ten trials for the four stimulus conditions. *Adapted from Walker (1960)*

100 trials with only the loud tone; a second group was conditioned with only the soft tone. A third group received 50 trials with the soft tone and 50 trials with the loud in which the tones were presented in a random order. The results for the last 60 trials to the loud and soft tones under the one- and two-stimulus conditions are presented in Figure 11–5. It can be noted that exposing each of the subjects to two values of a CS intensity during conditioning substantially increased the effect of the intensity variable as contrasted with the use of a single value with separate groups.[2]

[2] GSR studies by Kimmel and his associates (1959, 1962) have not supported the general findings that the CR is a function of CS intensity. In Kimmel's first study (1959), a GSR was conditioned to a 1,000 cps tone of three intensities: 35, 75, or 115 db. Twenty acquisition trials were provided, with the amount of conditioning measured in terms of the amount of GSR produced by the CS over and above the amounts of GSR produced by the CS on preliminary trials. A pseudoconditioning control group which received unpaired presentations of tone and shock was also run.

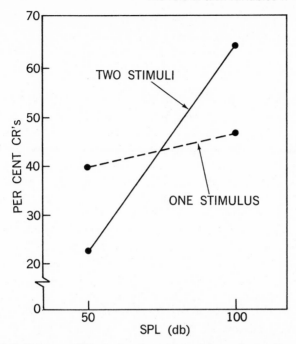

Fig. 11–5. Per cent CR's during last sixty trials to the loud and soft tones under the one- and two-stimulus conditions. *Adapted from Grice and Hunter (1964)*

Positive intensity effects have been also reported for acquisition trials in instrumental learning situations. The results of Brown's (1942) early study as well as those of Hull (1949), Perkins (1953), and Kessen (1953) have been consistent with the findings of the classical conditioning studies which have been reported. Hull (1949) has reported an unpublished study in

The results revealed that conditioning occurred only in the experimental group which received the 35 db CS; groups which received the more intense CS failed to become conditioned.

In the second study also using the GSR [Kimmel, Hill, and Morrow (1962)], CS (1,000 cps) intensities below and just above 35 db were examined. More specifically, intensities of 12, 17, 22, 27, 32, 35, and 42 db were used. The investigators found that GSR differences (mean amplitude) among the seven CS intensity values were not statistically significant, although the highest response value was associated with the weakest intensity used. It should be pointed out that Kimmel's inability to find conditioning with tones above the 35 db intensity level is in sharp contrast with the findings of a number of investigators who have commonly obtained GSR conditioning with CS intensities considerably above this value.

which 20 rats were reinforced for jumping against a black card and 20 others were trained to jump against a white card. Latencies for the animals jumping to white (the greater intensity stimulus card) averaged 1.70 seconds whereas those jumping to black averaged 7.54.[3]

In a much more extensive examination of the role of the CS intensity, Kessen (1953) trained ten albino rats to avoid electric shock by turning a wheel. Six lights of different intensities provided by frosted light bulbs of 6, 15, 40, 75, 150, or 300 watts served as the CS. The intensity values were converted to a logarithmic scale in order to provide more nearly even intensity increments; specifically, .16, .63, 1.19, 1.50, 1.90 and 2.26 log foot candles. The subjects received 11 trials with each light for a total of 66 training trials. The general procedure was to present the light and approximately 5.8 seconds later to charge the grid. The animal could learn to avoid shock by responding within the 5.8-second period that the light was presented without shock. In a second factorial study, 32 rats were used with four intensities of light—6, 15, 40, or 150 watts—serving as the CS. Subjects in this experiment received 42 trials. In both experiments three measures of response strength were obtained: (1) number of avoidance responses (transformed into a probability of response measure), (2) latency of the response as measured from the onset of the CS, and (3) number of wheel turns made between trials. Figure 11–6 reveals the response measures for the acquisition trials for the two experiments, with the data supporting the position that learning is a function of the intensity of the CS.

As previously noted, within the Hullian analysis of behavior, an examination of acquisition trials does not indicate whether or not the independent variable (in this instance, CS intensity) is contributing to learning or performance. As a result, a number of investigators have utilized the factorial design in an effort to provide a solution to this problem. Unfortunately, the results from factorial designed studies provide the same kind of equivocal findings as those obtained with drive level.

In one of the early factorial studies, Grant and Schneider (1948) examined the conditioning of the eyelid response utilizing four CS intensities. A light was used as the CS and the intensity

---

[3] This finding is contrary to the findings of many investigators who have found that rats will respond more rapidly to black stimulus objects than to white.

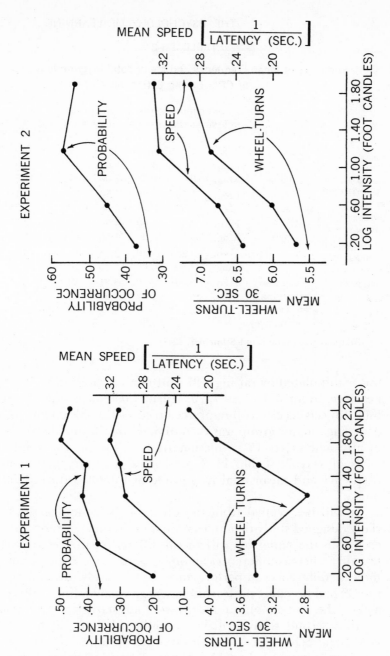

Fig. 11–6. Response strength during training as a function of log CS intensity. *Adapted from Kessen (1953)*

TABLE 11–2

Summary of Mean Frequency and Mean Total Magnitude (mm.)
of CR's During Extinction

STIMULI		CONDITIONED STIMULUS INTENSITY DURING EXTINCTION (MILLILAMBERTS)				ROW MARGINALS (LEARNING)
		7	70	320	1050	
1050	Freq.	0	3.25	5.00	5.25	3.38
	Mag.	0	31.75	55.00	60.75	42.50
320	Freq.	1.25	3.75	3.50	4.25	3.19
	Mag.	29.50	111.00	42.75	61.75	61.25
70	Freq.	4.25	1.00	4.50	1.25	2.75
	Mag.	38.25	2.00	71.50	14.00	31.44
7	Freq.	5.25	2.00	2.25	1.75	2.81
	Mag.	77.50	36.00	55.50	26.50	48.88
Column marginals (Performance)	Freq.	2.69	2.50	3.81	3.12	3.03
	Mag.	36.31	45.19	61.81	40.75	46.02

CONDITIONED STIMULUS INTENSITY DURING REINFORCEMENT (MILLILAMBERTS)

(Adapted from Grant and Schneider, 1948)

was manipulated by raising a 27 millilambert pre-stimulus brightness level by an additional 7, 70, 320, or 1,050 millilamberts. Sixty-four subjects received 50 reinforced trials—25 trials on each of two days. Each major group was then divided into four subgroups (16 in all) and given 15 extinction trials following the reinforced trials of Day 2. Table 11–2 presents a summary of the mean frequency and mean total magnitude of the CR's during extinction.

It will be recalled from the previous discussion of the factorially designed study that an examination of the differences among groups in the same row will reveal differences in the strength of learning whereas differences among groups down the column will indicate differences in performance. In this study, the intensity of the CS had no effect on learning or performance since differences among the row or column means were not statistically significant.

In a second study utilizing a similar design and procedure, Grant and Schneider (1949) examined the intensity variable in the conditioning of the GSR. A 200 cps tone of either 76, 86, 96, or 106 db intensity served as the CS, and a brief electric shock served as the UCS. Again, nonsignificant findings with regard to both learning and performance measures were obtained.[4]

An analysis of the extinction findings for the Kessen (1953) and Walker (1960) studies—experiments for which the acquisition findings have been reported—confirm the Grant and Schneider (1948, 1949) results. In Kessen's second experiment, which was described previously, four groups of rats learned to turn a wheel in order to avoid shock; one of four different intensities of light (6, 15, 40, or 150 watts) served as the CS. Following 42 avoidance training trials, each group was divided into four subgroups and given 30 extinction trials in which each subgroup was extinguished under a different CS intensity. An examination of the extinction findings arranged by row and column revealed no reliable differences among the means. Neither learning nor performance as inferred from extinction data was related to the intensity of the conditioned stimulus. In attempting to account for the failure of the intensity variable which was manipulated during extinction (as contrasted with acquisition findings) to influence behavior, Kessen (1953) posited that the elimination of the UCS during extinction reduced the organism's drive level and thus permitted the strengthening of responses antagonistic to the wheel-turning response.

Walker's (1960) conditioned eyeblink study is interesting since she utilized a technique which permitted the presentation of the UCS during extinction which presumably provided a test of Kessen's position. This procedure, utilized previously by McAllister (1953a), consisted of presenting the UCS 2,500 milliseconds after the CS. McAllister's work had revealed that such an interval results in the experimental extinction of the CR although it presumably permits the drive level of the subject to remain constant during extinction. Since Walker's (1960) findings revealed that the intensity of the CS did not influence extinction findings even though the UCS continued to be present, she rejected Kessen's hypothesis.

In summary, the bulk of the experimental evidence supports the position that by increasing the intensity of the stimulus

[4] In both studies there was an implicit assumption that the conditioned stimuli were discriminably different in the experimental situation. There is some question as to whether or not such an assumption can be made. [See Slivinske and Hall (1960)].

learning, regardless of how measured during acquisition trials, increases. As was noted from the Grice and Hunter (1964) study, this effect is substantially increased if the varying intensities are exposed to the same subject. Extinction measures, however, do not reflect this relationship.

In accounting for such increased learning, an explanation would be that increasing the intensity of the CS increases the probability that the CS will become the effective stimulus to which a response can be attached. Since the CS represents the only stimulus which is consistently associated with the UCS, the probability that learning will take place is increased. Opposed to this conclusion is Razran's (1957) statement that an examination of Russian studies in which CS intensity has been manipulated reveals that in the upper portion of the CS intensity continua an inverse relationship between CS intensity and performance prevails. That is, beyond a certain point, the more intense the stimulus, the slower the formation of the CR. Razran has rejected the possibility that such poor conditioning might be attributed to the fact that the CS at high intensity values becomes painful by pointing out that mildly painful stimuli (none of the sensory conditioned stimuli could be more than mildly painful) are readily conditionable. Moreover, he has stated that the reversal in conditionability begins at a point below that judged by human subjects to be painful. He has concluded that the reverse conditionability must be attributed to CS intensity per se irrespective of possible accompanying pain as a general antagonist.

Champion (1962a) has written recently that no precisely articulated theory of stimulus-intensity effects has been established firmly, although Hull (1951, 1952), Perkins (1953), Logan (1954), and Grice and Hunter (1964) have proposed hypotheses to deal with this effect. Hull (1951) assumed that there was a relationship between the strength of a response and the intensity of the stimulus to which it was attached, describing such an effect as "stimulus-intensity dynamism."

In his *Behavior System,* Hull (1952) limited the stimulus dynamism process only to the onset of the stimulus and to short latency responses such as the eyeblink. However, the Grice and Hunter (1964) findings are clearly at variance with this position since this study demonstrates that the dynamogenic property of a given stimulus, at least to a large extent, depends upon what other stimuli are presented.

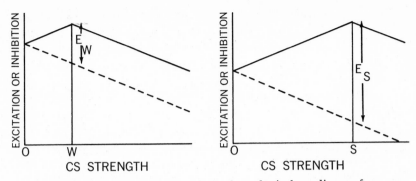

Fig. 11–7. Schematic diagram of the hypothetical gradients of excitation (continuous line) and inhibition (broken line) after reinforcement of responses to the onset of a weak CS (W) and a strong CS with nonreinforcement of responses to the intertrial stimulus of "silence" (O). (Net excitation is greater for the strong CS—E_s—than for the weak CS—E_w.) *Adapted from Champion (1962a)*

The second theory of stimulus intensity effects has been proposed by Perkins (1953) and Logan (1954). This theory has been expressed in terms of a differential conditioning situation in which a reinforced response gains excitatory strength which generalizes to similar stimuli, whereas the occurrence of the same response to other stimuli which are not reinforced provides inhibitory properties which also generalize. This situation is indicated in Figure 11–7. If a tone, for example, is used as a CS, the response attached to it is presumed to acquire the same degree of gross excitatory strength, regardless of the intensity of the CS. Such excitatory strength generalizes along the stimulus intensity dimension as indicated. When a response is given to the intertrial stimulus of "silence" during the training period, it is not reinforced. This response acquires inhibitory strength which also generalizes as revealed in Figure 11–7. The further assumption that inhibition is subtracted from excitation to provide net excitation permits this theory to predict greater net excitation for a response conditioned to a strong CS than a response conditioned to a weak CS. The various experimental tests of this hypothesis cannot be discussed in detail, but confirmation has been provided by a number of investigators [Perkins (1953), Bragiel and Perkins (1954), Johnsgard (1957), Nygaard (1958), and Champion (1962a)].

The Grice and Hunter (1964) finding which indicated that the response strength to the loud tone was significantly increased by the presence of the soft tone does not support the differential conditioning theory, which predicts that the addition of a weak stimulus to the conditioning situation should result in weaker, rather than stronger, absolute response strength to the stronger CS. This follows since the inhibitory gradient arising from the weak intensity CS should start at a higher level than the inhibitory gradient derived from the intertrial stimulus of "silence."

Finally, Grice and Hunter (1964) have suggested that the intensity effect may be interpreted in terms of a dynamogenic effect, but, unlike Hull, they have pointed out that some form of contrast effect is an important element in this phenomenon. They have proposed that Helson's (1959) adaptation level (AL) concept appears to be particularly fruitful in this regard. As Grice and Hunter have written (p. 252) :

> One could make the simple assumption that the dynamogenic potency of a stimulus depends upon its departure from adaptation level (AL) rather than upon absolute intensity. In the case of the single stimulus situation, then, the AL should be near the stimulus value. This would lead to the prediction of minimal intensity effects, since, irrespective of absolute intensity, departure from AL would be small. In the two-stimulus situation, however, the AL might be expected to lie between the two values. With the weak stimulus below AL and the strong above, an exaggerated intensity effect would be expected.

STIMULUS POSITION

The learning of many complex tasks, e.g., the driving of an automobile, the recitation of a poem, etc., usually can be divided into separate parts in which one part follows another in a fixed or sequential relationship. These tasks have been described as serial learning, and in the laboratory, multiple T-mazes or lists of verbal material frequently have been utilized as examples of this kind of learning situation. In this section, position as a basic variable in the learning of complex tasks will be considered. However, the process by which serial learning takes place will not be discussed.

Serial Lists

From the discussion of learning situations in Chapter 2, it will be recalled that one technique for presenting verbal material was in a serial order, with the subject having to anticipate each word prior to its being exposed in the memory drum. Thus, with the serial anticipation method, each word serves as a response for the preceding word and as a stimulus for the word that follows.

When verbal material is learned in such a fashion, although the material has been previously equated for difficulty, the number of errors that are made in learning are not equally distributed over the items making up the list. Rather, a type of bow-shaped curve is obtained. In general, items just past the middle are most difficult to learn, and the items placed first and last in the list are easiest to learn.

In a very early study, Smith (1896) made up a list of ten nonsense syllables and presented them to eight subjects. He noted that when the subjects were asked to recall them, the items which were at the end of the list were recalled best whereas the middle syllables were most difficult to recall. Since this early study, many investigators have supported and extended these early findings. The studies of both Ward (1937) and Hovland (1938) illustrate this phenomenon. In Ward's study, 24 subjects serially learned a list of 12 nonsense syllables. Figure 11–8 portrays his findings. This figure reveals the effect of serial position at varying stages of practice from Trial 1 on which only three nonsense syllables were learned through those trials on which five, seven, nine, and eleven items were correct. Until the trial on which the subjects correctly anticipated 11 of the 12 syllables on the list, the familiar bow-shaped curve, with some irregularities, of course, was obtained.

A number of investigators have been interested in determining how certain variables affect the bow-shaped curve. Hovland (1938) has shown that the serial position effect is steeper under massed than under distributed practice, a finding illustrated by Figure 11–9. Moreover, he [Hovland (1940a)] has found that this steepness increases as the length of the list increases from eight to 14 items.

McCrary and Hunter (1953) and Braun and Heymann (1958) have also demonstrated that the serial position curve is much less bowed when meaningful material is used in contrast to less

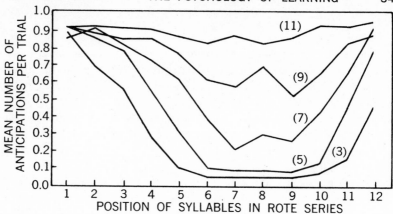

Fig. 11–8. Mean number of correct anticipations at each point in the rote series for five levels of mastery. The individual curves are each marked with the level of mastery represented. Curves are given for levels of mastery of 3, 5, 7, 9, and 11 correct anticipations, respectively, in a single learning trial. *Adapted from Ward (1937)*

meaningful. In the McCrary and Hunter (1953) study, for example, subjects serially learned a list of 14 nonsense syllables and a list of 14 names which were familiar to the subjects. In order to balance out any unevenness in the difficulty of the specific items, each subject started the list at a different point. Items were presented at a two-second rate with an eight-second intertrial interval. Learning, completed in a single session, was to a criterion of one correct anticipation. When mean errors are plotted for the syllables and names as a function of their serial position, the curves illustrated in Figure 11–10 result. It can be noted that the curve for the names is much flatter than that found for the nonsense syllables. This finding was confirmed by Braun and Heymann (1958) who used high and low meaningful material as defined by Noble's *m* scale.

McCrary and Hunter (1953) have found that when the serial position curve was plotted, not in terms of the mean number of errors made at each position, but in terms of the percentage of total errors that occur at each position, the meaningfulness variable had no effect on the curve's steepness. Thus, Figure 11–11 plots the data obtained from Figure 11–10 in terms of the percentage of total errors at each position, and it can be noted

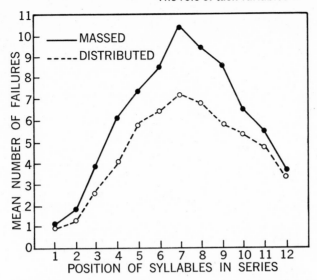

Fig. 11–9. Serial position curves showing mean number of errors at various syllable positions as a function of massed and distributed practice. *Adapted from Hovland (1938)*

that the curves become remarkably similar. A subsequent study by Braun and Heymann (1958) has confirmed these findings.[5]

This examination of serial position effects has been confined primarily to the studies which have used the method of serial anticipation. What findings have been obtained when other learning procedures are utilized? In one experiment, Deese and

[5] These findings have given rise to two general observations. On the one hand, Murdock (1960) has concluded that since the shape of the serial curve is not a function of the meaningfulness of the material—a variable which frequently has been demonstrated to have an effect on learning—position is not a learning variable. Rather, he has suggested that the shape of the curve results from the unequal distinctiveness of the items which make up the list.

On the other hand, Jensen (1962) has proposed that serial rote learning data may be analyzed into three components: (1) difficulty of the task—as measured by the number of trials to reach a given criterion, (2) efficiency of learning—as measured by the percentage of errors or correct responses, and (3) relative difficulty of learning the items at the various positions. It is only the latter measure, he avers, from which a true serial position curve should be obtained, although he notes that the serial position curve as most frequently found in the literature confounds at least two of the above mentioned components. He has suggested a new measure—the Index of Relative Difficulty—as the only satisfactory method of representing the serial position effect. Space does not permit a discussion of this measure, but the interested reader may consult the Jensen (1962) article for specific details.

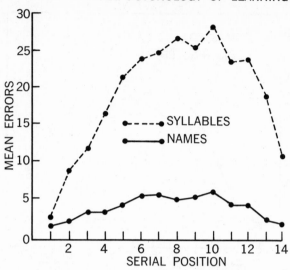

Fig. 11–10. Serial position curves as a function of the characteristics of the material used. *Adapted from McCrary and Hunter (1953)*

Kaufman (1957) examined the characteristics of free recall (actually free learning) for serially unstructured material as well as for connected prose. In this study, groups of subjects were presented with lists of words drawn randomly from the Thorn-dike-Lorge word list. One group learned and recalled lists of words which were ten items in length, and a second group recalled lists of words 32 items in length. A third group was presented with passages of connected discourse made by altering selections obtained from the 1953 *World Almanac*. These passages were approximately 100 words in length and consisted of ten simple statements organized into sentences and clauses. The statements were such that by minor rewording they could be presented in different orders. All material was presented orally; the subjects were instructed to try to remember what they had heard. A test for recall was obtained immediately after each list or passage had been read. The results for the 10-item and 32-item lists are indicated in Figure 11–12, and the findings obtained with the textual passages are presented in Figure 11–13. It can be noted that there was superior recall for the last items found in the 10- and 32-item lists—a finding in contrast to that obtained with serial anticipation learning where the first items are recalled best.

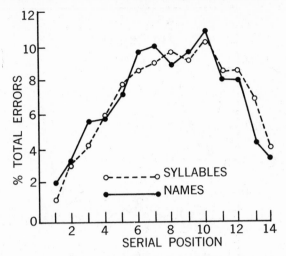

Fig. 11–11. Serial position curves as a function of the characteristics of the material used. Note that the ordinate expresses performance in terms of percentage of total errors. *Adapted from McCrary and Hunter (1953)*

The serial position curve for the learning of statements from the passages of connected discourse, however, indicates that statements located at the beginning of the passage were recalled best. The curve is much like the classical curve obtained using serial anticipation. The similarity of the serial anticipation curve and the recall of connected discourse curve has suggested to Deese and Kaufman that the association process involved in these situations may be similar.

In a second experiment, the investigators attempted to examine further the learning of connected discourse by utilizing varying approximations to prose as measured by Miller and Selfridge (1950). Fifty-item lists of words varying in order of approximation, in addition to a textual passage, were presented to all the subjects. The material was read at a rate of one word per second with recall requested immediately following the reading of the list. An examination of recall as a function of approximation to prose supported the findings of the first experiment. With zero order approximation, the last items which were presented were recalled best whereas items in the middle of the list were recalled poorest. This was also true for first order approximations to prose.

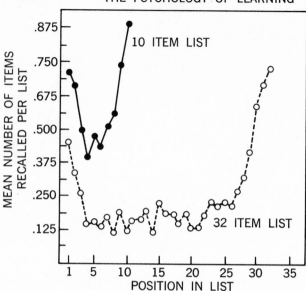

Fig. 11–12. Mean frequency of recall per list as a function of position of items in the list. *Adapted from Deese and Kaufman (1957)*

However, as order increased, the shape of the curve began to change. By the seventh order, material which was presented first was recalled best, and the shape of the curve approximated that found with serial anticipation learning.

Murdock's (1962) more recent examination of the serial position effects of unrelated words in the free-recall situation has confirmed the findings of Deese and Kaufman (1957). In this study, lists were constructed by randomly selecting common English words. Lists of 10, 15, 20, 30, or 40 words in length were used. Following the presentation of a list, the subjects were instructed to write down as many words as they could remember in any order that they wished. Serial position curves were plotted, with probability of recall being examined as a function of serial position. In keeping with the Deese and Kaufman study, a bow-shaped effect was obtained, with the material at the end of the list being recalled better than that presented at the beginning of the list.[6]

[6] Bousfield, Whitmarsh, and Esterson (1958) and Jahnke (1963) have obtained findings in the immediate free-recall situation which are not in complete agreement with Deese and Kaufman's (1957) and Murdock's (1962). Bousfield, Whitmarsh, and

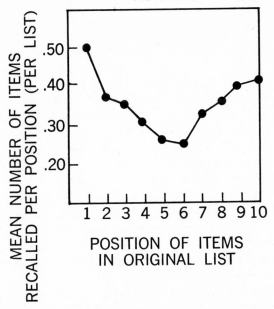

Fig. 11–13. Mean frequency of recall for statements in textual passages as a function of the position of the statements. *Adapted from
Deese and Kaufman (1957)*

Maze Learning

The learning of a fixed sequence of responses may also be
examined by employing some type of maze situation. A stylus or
finger maze frequently has been used with human subjects, and
alley-mazes of one variety or another commonly have been used
with animals.

Esterson examined serial position effects of meaningful words using the length of list
as the basic independent variable. Lists of 5, 10, 20, and 40 words were used, with
these words selected so as to be as similar as possible in frequency as measured by
the Thorndike-Lorge word count. Words were presented at a two and one-half-
second rate with recall immediately following such presentation. Jahnke's study was
basically similar except that his stimulus materials were consonants and either five,
six, seven, eight, or nine of these were presented following which subjects were
asked to recall them in the order given. Both studies revealed that although serial
effects were not obtained for the short series of material the bowing effect became
more pronounced as the length of the list increased. Unlike other findings, both
studies also indicated that recall of the first items in the list was greater than recall
of the final items. It is possible, however, that the findings of both investigations
might be attributed to the character of the instructions which were provided the
subjects since such instructions emphasized that the subjects were to recall the
material in the order in which it was given.

Obviously, there is a certain similarity between learning a list of words in serial fashion and learning a sequence of motor responses required to traverse a maze. There are a number of differences, however, which must be considered. The temporal factors in the verbal learning situation are usually fixed. Thus, it is the experimenter who determines at what rate the presentation of stimuli shall be made, and the response of the subject must then be tied to such presentation of stimuli. This is not true in the maze situation. The individual may spend varying amounts of time at each choice point. Furthermore, the opportunity for the subject to vary his response differs. In the maze situation, the kind of response that the subject can make is limited to a number of specific choices. A subject in a multiple T-maze, when confronted with a choice point, can turn only to the left or to the right, but in a verbal learning situation, the number of responses available to the subject are usually more than two and typically are dependent upon other variables.

Finally, the locomotor activity which takes place in the maze results in a number of error tendencies which typically are not found in the verbal serial learning situation. Rats frequently are found to have right or left turning preferences as well as other dispositions referred to as forward-going tendencies [Dashiell and Bayroff (1931)] or centrifugal swing [Schneirla (1933)].[7] The result is that the typical multiple T-maze situation rarely provides the bow-shaped performance curve when errors are plotted as a function of the sequence or position of individual choice points.

THE ROLE OF ADDITIVITY OF CUES AND CONTEXT

In examining task variables, a frequently adopted approach is one in which the investigator defines the stimulus arbitrarily and then proceeds to manipulate one of its attributes or dimensions in order to examine its influence on the dependent variable. Usually, the experimenter has taken care to provide the organism with a relatively simple task characterized by a dominant stimulus element. The success of many experiments testifies to the fact that the effective stimulus was isomorphic to the stimulus designated by the experimenter.

In many learning tasks, however, the stimulus situation is

[7] Centrifugal swing is the tendency, when momentum carries the animal to the outside wall of an alley, to follow that wall and to make a turn continuous with it.

quite complex, comprised of a number of elements or cues. With these situations in mind, one question which arises is: How is learning related to the number of cues which are present and available to the organism?

In classical conditioning situations, the experimental procedure designed to answer this question has taken one of two forms. The first has been to condition separately the same response to a number of different stimuli. The learning which takes place in this situation is then compared to the learning which takes place when the stimuli are presented together. The experimental evidence supports the position that the compound stimulus situation results in better learning than a single stimulus presentation. In an early study by Pavlov (1927), for example, the odor of oil of camphor (CS) when presented alone elicited 60 drops of salivation, whereas the presentation of mild shock (CS) produced 30 drops. When these stimuli were combined to provide a compound conditioned stimulus, they elicited 90 drops.

Although more recent studies have verified the general conclusion that stimuli which are presented together will elicit a stronger response than either presented singly, the simple additive effect which was obtained in Pavlov's study has not been verified. For example, Hull (1940) conditioned eight subjects to a weak light, with the UCS being an electric shock and the response being the GSR. Then a weak vibratory stimulus was paired with the shock and also conditioned to the GSR. When presented alone, the light elicited a reaction of 3.5 mm, and the vibrator evoked a reaction of 3.6 mm; when light and vibrator were presented simultaneously, the response was 4.4 mm.

Miller (1939a) demonstrated the same phenomenon with the conditioned eyelid response, utilizing separate groups. Group I received a visual stimulus as the CS (movement of a black pointer on a white background); Group II received an auditory stimulus (change in pitch); and Group III was simultaneously presented with both auditory and visual stimulation. The analysis of 50 acquisition trials revealed that the mean percentage of CR's for the visual stimulus group (Group I) was 22.2; for the auditory stimulus group (Group II), it was 45.4; for the compound or combined stimulus, it was 81.0. Not only did the compound conditioned stimulus provide significantly more CR's than either of the other conditions, but the response variability within this group was consistently smaller.

In the studies which have been examined, a tendency for

separately conditioned stimuli to summate has been noted, thus producing a CR of greater response strength than that produced when either CS is presented alone. Grings and O'Donnell (1956) examined the operation of the summation principle when non-reinforced as well as "nonpresented" stimuli became part of the stimulus compound. Their procedure involved presenting lights of various colors singly as the CS and shock as a UCS to elicit the GSR. Their acquisition series involved the presentation of three colored lights, with each light being presented singly as a CS. Two of the singly presented lights were always paired with the UCS: the third light was not. In essence, then, two of the lights were always accompanied by reinforcement whereas one was not. Test trials consisted of presenting two lights together in the following combinations: (1) two previously reinforced lights, (2) one reinforced and one nonreinforced light, (3) one reinforced light and one light not previously presented. The investigators found that the response to the stimulus compound comprised of the two reinforced lights was significantly greater than the response to any other compound. The magnitude of the response to the stimulus compound which combined the reinforced and nonpresented stimulus was greater than that to the combination of the rein-forced and nonreinforced stimulus. These findings support the position that a response to a compound stimulus reflects not only the presence of excitatory tendencies, developed as a result of reinforcing specific stimulus elements, but also inhibitory tenden-cies produced by the association of a stimulus element without reinforcement.

Eninger (1952), examining the instrumental learning situa-tion, has also found a tendency for stimuli to summate. In his experiment, one group of rats was required to choose the right arm of a T-maze after passing through a black stem pathway and the left arm after going through a white stem pathway (visual group). A second group of subjects was required to choose the right arm when a tone was sounded and the left arm when no tone was presented (auditory group). A third group had these cues combined (auditory-visual group). The findings showed that performance for the auditory-visual group was markedly superior to that of the other two experimental groups.

In the experiments cited above, the compound stimulus situation was made up of specific stimulus elements, i.e., a tone and light, separate lights, etc. Does the additive principle apply when varying dimensions or attributes of a single stimulus element are considered? More specifically, can a green circle be discriminated more easily from (1) a red circle or (2) a red square? Note that in the first comparison the stimuli differ along only a single dimension, i.e., color (red versus green), but in the second comparison, there are two dimensions along which the stimuli differ, i.e., color (red versus green) and form (circle versus square).

Lashley and Wade (1946) have supported what has become known as a perceptual dominance hypothesis. This position suggests that in situations of the type which have been outlined the organism responds only to the dominant cue and all other cues become irrelevant to the organism. Thus, Lashley and Wade (1946) state, "If a monkey is trained to choose a *large* red circle and avoid a *small* green one, he will usually choose any red object and avoid any green but will make chance scores when like colored large and small circles are presented." In such a situation, then, color is the dominant cue and size is irrelevant.

Warren's work [Warren (1953, 1954); Hara and Warren (1961)] with monkeys and cats is particularly relevant to this discussion. In an early study, Warren (1953) used 210 pairs of geometrical figures cut from colored paper. Each pair of figures which formed a discrimination problem varied in either color, form, or size or in combinations of these taken two or three at a time (i.e., color and form, color and size, form and size, or color, form, and size). Seven ten-trial discrimination problems, one taken from each of the cue categories, were used each day for 30 days which resulted in each subject (monkeys, N = 7) being presented with a total of 210 problems. An analysis of the findings, as indicated in Table 11–3, reveals significant differences among stimulus cue categories. Tukey's gap test reveals that the color, color-form, color-size, and color-form-size categories constitute a homogeneous group of categories and that performance on these categories is significantly superior to the performance on the form, size, and form-size categories.

The results of this study provide some evidence for the additivity of cue hypothesis since the presentation of size alone resulted in more errors than did the presentation of both form and size; the smallest number of errors occurred when color, form, and size were presented to the organism. Similarly, increasingly better learning is found when (1) form, (2) form and size,

TABLE 11–3

An Analysis of the Role of Various Cues in
Discrimination Learning

STIMULUS CATE-GORY	PERCENTAGE OF ERRORS
Color, form, size	6.6
Color, form	7.6
Color, size	8.5
Color	8.9
Form, size	20.7
Form	22.7
Size	25.5

(Adapted from Warren, 1953)

and (3) form, size, and color are used as cues. On the other hand, the data support Lashley in demonstrating that color is a dominant cue. Performance is not improved significantly when the cues of form and size are added to color.

The fact that certain cues in a given situation may be quite dominant and thus obscure any additive effect could be related to the discriminability of the cues themselves. For example, the difference between two colors in a discrimination study may be quite large whereas the difference in size and form between the stimuli may be considerably smaller. In almost all of the early studies in this area, the stimulus values were chosen arbitrarily with the implicit assumption that the difference between any two colors, i.e., red and green, was about the same as the difference between any two other dimensions, i.e., size or color.

The Hara and Warren (1961) study is noteworthy since these investigators examined stimulus additivity in the discrimination performance of cats when the differential limens (thresholds) for visual form, size, and brightness discrimination were known. The experimental situation consisted of first determining these limens by the method of constant stimuli. Psychophysical functions were thus obtained for individual cats on each of the three dimensions. For each cat it was possible to specify which stimulus values were just above and below the threshold, i.e., which could be discriminated with approximately 80 per cent and 70 per cent success, respectively. Fifty-five training trials were then presented each day for a period of 14 days. The first 15 trials on each day consisted of

TABLE 11–4

Percentage of Correct Responses to
the Varying Stimulus Compounds

CUES	PERCENTAGE CORRECT
None	53.5
c	71.8
C	82.2
cc	81.7
Cc	88.3
CC	90.0
ccc	87.5
Ccc	94.8
CCc	94.0
CCC	99.0

c = subthreshold stimulus difference
C = suprathreshold stimulus difference

(Adapted from Hara and Warren, 1961)

providing the animal with three five-trial sets in which easily discriminated stimulus pairs within each of the three dimensions (form, size, brightness) were employed. This was done in order to maintain the basic discrimination habits. These trials were then followed by four sets of ten trials in which all 27 possible combinations of two and three subliminal (70 per cent success) and supraliminal (80 per cent success) cues together with a control condition of no stimulus difference were employed.

As Table 11–4 reveals, cats discriminate stimuli differing along three dimensions better than they do stimuli differing on two dimensions, and two dimensional stimuli result in performance which is superior to that produced by stimuli differing on only a single dimension. The generality of the additivity principle has been extended to monkeys learning a conditional discrimination [Warren (1964)] and to humans solving discrimination problems [Restle (1955), Trabasso (1960)].

The Role of Stimulus Context

In many learning situations, the experimental operations are so arranged that one part of the stimulus seems to stand out from other or background stimuli which make up the total situational stimulus. For example, a light presented as a CS in a conditioning experiment is received by the subject along with other visual stimuli which are present in the experimental setting. These other stimuli provide a background for the presentation of the light. Similarly, a word presented on a memory drum tape has the tape background against which it has been placed. Again, the characteristics of the tape, that is, its color, texture, etc., could be considered as background stimuli. Background stimuli frequently have been termed contextual stimuli, and a number of investigators have examined the contribution of such contextual cues to learning as well as to retention.

One can acknowledge that this area of interest bears a marked similarity to the area which has just been examined. That is, the question can be asked: Do contextual cues summate with those which shall be designated as figure in order to produce better learning?

In one of the early studies in this area, Weiss and Margolius (1954), using nonsense syllables, examined both the learning and retention of paired-associates when the context variable was manipulated. In the learning phase of this study, the part which is relevant to this section, lists of nine paired-associates were learned to a criterion of one errorless trial. For one group, each pair of syllables was placed on a solid color background with a different color used for each pair. A second group learned the same list, but, in this case, the material to be learned was placed on a homogeneous gray background. The investigators found that the different contextual cues, i.e., the varying colored backgrounds associated with each pair of items, aided learning. Thus, the first group required fewer trials to reach the criterion than the second.[8]

A basic explanation for the summation effect stems from Hull's (1943) position that the reinforcement procedure results in associative strength developing between a specific response and all the stimuli which the subject receives. More specifically, and as Weiss and Margolius have suggested in interpreting their findings, the experimental group developed associative strength between the response to be learned and (1) the nonsense syllables which served as stimuli as well as (2) the colors which provided the context. In contrast, the control group did not have the benefit of the added associative strength occurring from the contextual cues.

Although Hill and Wickens (1962), using a verbal learning

<hr/>

[8] Sundland and Wickens (1962) were unable to replicate the Weiss and Margolius (1954) findings.

situation similar to that employed by Weiss and Margolius, obtained findings which indicated that contextual cues aided learning, their results also revealed that the influence of such multiple stimulus presentation did not take place early in learning. As a result, they have suggested that the superior performance of the multiple stimulus group was due to the fact that the subjects had the opportunity to select as the effective or functional stimulus that dimension of the entire stimulus pattern which was either most compatible with the response or which reduced interference with other stimulus-response relationships which made up the list. In essence, then, the investigators have rejected the summation hypothesis and have proposed a position which bears a marked similarity to Lashley's perceptual dominance position.

A recent study by Underwood, Ham, and Ekstrand (1962) is interesting in that the investigators used a transfer situation to assess the role of context. At the same time, their experiment demonstrates the complexity of the problem area. Their general experimental design was as follows: a compound stimulus consisting of a word or a trigram on a colored background was paired with response terms consisting of single-digit numbers, two through eight. Learning was continued until the subjects achieved one perfect recitation of the list. Following such learning, transfer tests were provided in an effort to determine what stimulus the subject had used. In one such test, only the background colors were used as stimuli, whereas a second test situation consisted of presenting only the verbal stimuli, with a homogeneous background. In addition, control groups were utilized in which the transfer task consisted of continued presentation of both verbal and contextual stimuli.

Figure 11–14 presents the acquisition curves on the transfer trials for both trigrams and words. An examination of that part of the study which utilized words reveals that words as well as colors were used by some individuals as stimuli to which to attach responses. The fact that transfer was greater when words were used as the sole stimulus condition than when colors were used supports the position that the subjects used words as stimuli for most associations.

It is the findings with the trigrams, however, which provide most interest. When colors were presented alone, there resulted virtually complete transfer, the performance of the color group

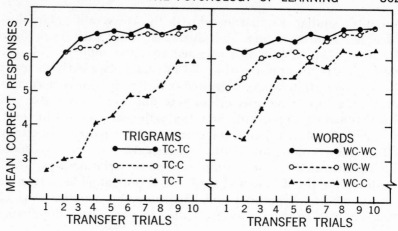

Fig. 11–14. Acquisition curves on the ten transfer trials. *Adapted from Underwood, Ham, and Ekstrand (1962)*

being only slightly below the control group, which was provided both the trigram and color on the transfer tests. Some transfer, however, can be noted for the group which was provided the trigrams but not color. Trigrams, at least in certain instances, served as effective stimuli. It may be that some trigrams, quite independently of the color component, become associated directly with the response term; or, it may be that some associative connection developed between the color and trigram components of the stimulus compound. During the transfer tests when the trigram was presented, the correct response was mediated by associations running from the trigram to the color to the response term. Data from this experiment, however, does not permit a choice between these two alternatives.

In summary, it can be noted that the bulk of the experimental evidence has supported the position that a compound stimulus will result in learning which is superior to that which results if only a single stimulus element is provided. Such a generalization appears to hold whether classical conditioning, instrumental conditioning, or verbal learning situations are used. The mechanism by which this effect takes place, however, is not clear.

This examination of the variables which are related to the stimulus and response parameters which make up the task is now complete. There is, however, one final variable, although it cannot be considered as being directly related to the task, which does deserve consideration. This variable is concerned with how the learning trials are distributed throughout the practice period.

MASSED VERSUS DISTRIBUTED PRACTICE

If an experimenter wants a rat to learn a simple T-maze and decides to provide the animal with five trials per day, it is necessary to decide whether the trials should be continuous or whether the animal should be permitted to rest between trials. If the decision is to provide rest, it must be decided specifically how much.

This example acknowledges the fact that learning, at least in the laboratory, takes place over a series of trials and that experimenters must decide how to distribute these trials over the training period. If trials are given continuously, the practice is designated as massed; if a rest interval is interpolated between trials, it is classified as distributed. In reality, the distinction between massed and distributed practice is relative and specific to the experimental situation. Thus, if one investigator compares a six-second intertrial interval with one of twelve, the latter rest period is described as distributed; on the other hand, if a second investigator compares a twelve-second intertrial interval with one of twenty-four seconds, the twelve-second rest period is described as massed.

Experimental investigations of the efficiency of massed versus spaced practice began with Ebbinghaus (1885). Many of the early experimenters examined this variable in order to determine the most efficient method for a given learning situation; many of the later studies have been designed primarily to test Hull's theory of inhibition—a topic which was discussed in Chapter 9. This theory predicts that the distribution of trials will permit the dissipation of reactive inhibition which has accumulated as a result of the organism's making a response and thus lead to superior performance.

The classical conditioning studies of Humphreys (1940), Calvin [as reported by Hull (1943)], Spence and Norris (1950), and Prokasy, Grant, and Myers (1958) have supported the Hullian position that superior conditioning should be obtained when the training trials are distributed rather than massed. In the

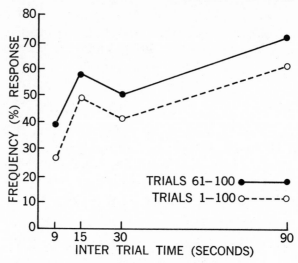

Fig. 11–15. Curves showing the relationship between the amount of conditioning and the intertrial interval. The upper curve shows the per cent frequency of CR's for trials 61–100, the lower curve the per cent frequency for all trials (1–100). *Adapted from Spence and Norris (1950)*

Spence and Norris (1950) study, four intertrial intervals (9, 15, 30, and 90 seconds) were used in the conditioning of the eyeblink. Four groups of 15 subjects per group were run, with 100 presentations of the CS and UCS. The results, presented in Figure 11–15, show that the frequency of responding is a function of the length of the intertrial interval.

Prokasy, Grant, and Myers (1958) have confirmed these findings. Three intertrial intervals (15, 45, and 135 seconds) were utilized in establishing the conditioned eyelid response. Twenty training trials were provided on Day 1 and 20 additional trials on Day 2. Figure 11–16 summarizes the findings.[9]

A recent study by Prokasy and Whaley (1961) is interesting since these investigators did not use the typical independent group

[9] Some contradictory evidence has been presented. Baron (1952) and Vandermeer and Amsel (1952) who examined the conditioned eyeblink have been unable to find any relationship between the learning of a CR and the length of the intertrial interval. In the Vandermeer and Amsel (1952) study, the CS was presented either three or nine times per minute. Baron (1952) examined intertrial intervals of 120 and 270 seconds. It is reasonable to assume, of course, that beyond a given length of intertrial interval increasing the length of the rest period should not make any contribution to performance.

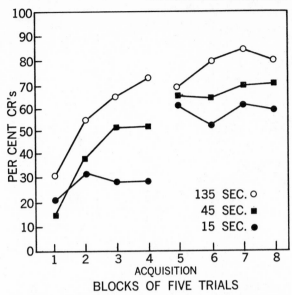

Fig. 11–16. Percentage frequency of CR's during acquisition trials with intertrial interval during acquisition as the parameter. *Adapted from Prokasy, Grant, and Myers (1958)*

design. Moreover, they varied the intertrial interval after the subjects had reached performance asymptote. Six intertrial intervals of 5, 10, 15, 20, 25, and 30 seconds were used; each subject was given 97 reinforced trials in each of the seven conditioning sessions. The first session was designated as a pre-training session designed to bring the subject to asymptote, and the remaining six were test sessions in which the last 78 trials in each test session were utilized in the analysis. (The first 19 trials were eliminated to minimize recovery or regression effects arising from the test situation.) The trials were ordered in such a way that each intertrial interval appeared 13 times during each session. Response data following each interval of time were pooled. The results indicated that response probability was not differentially affected by the immediately preceding intertrial interval. Figure 11–17 provides the response frequencies as a function of the intertrial intervals which were used for the 12 subjects in the study.

In summary, the findings from classical conditioning studies have generally supported the Hullian prediction that superior conditioning should be obtained when the training trials are

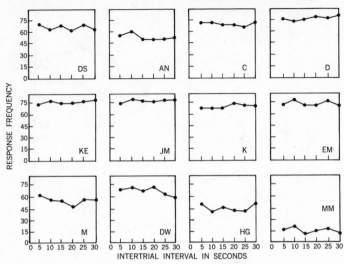

Fig. 11–17. Response frequency as a function of intertrial interval for each subject. *Adapted from Prokasy and Whaley (1961)*

distributed rather than massed. The Prokasy and Whaley study suggests, however, that once performance asymptote is reached the distribution of trials does not make any contribution to enhancing or depressing performance.

Motor skills learning situations have been also utilized to examine the massed–distributed practice variable. One of the most extensive studies in this area was performed by Kientzle (1946) who had subjects print the alphabet upside down so that when the paper was turned through a 180-degree angle the alphabet could be read from right to left in the usual manner. In this study, one-minute trials were provided, separated by the following rest periods: 0, 3, 5, 10, 15, 30, 45, 60, and 90 seconds, and seven days. All the subjects received 20 trials except the 90-second and seven-day groups which received 15 and 12 trials, respectively. Figure 11–18 shows learning to be a function of the varying rest periods, although it can be observed that rest intervals which are longer than 30 seconds do not appreciably increase performance.

Ammons (1950) examined the role of varying lengths of intertrial intervals in rotary pursuit performance. In one part of his study, intertrial rest periods of 0 seconds, 20 seconds, 50 seconds, 2 minutes. 5 minutes, 12 minutes, or approximately 24

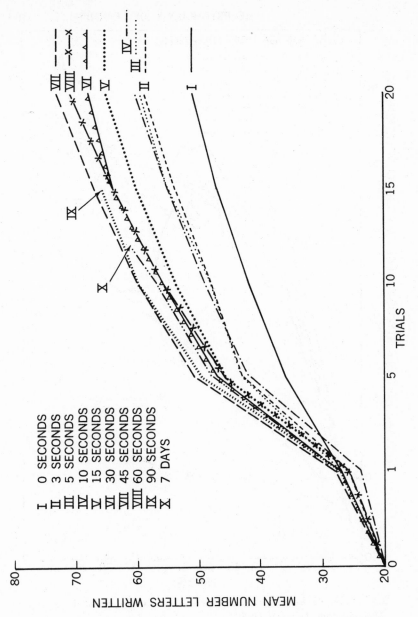

Fig. 11–18. Alphabet printing as a function of the length of the intertrial interval. *Adapted from data from Kientzle (1946)*

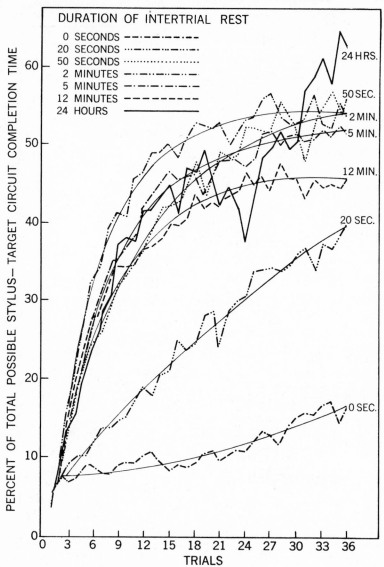

Fig. 11–19. Performance as a function of the intertrial interval.
Adapted from Ammons (1950)

hours were placed between 22-second trials. Thirty-six such trial
periods were employed in which performance was measured
during the last 20 seconds of each trial. (The two-second preliminary period was introduced at the start of every trial in an attempt

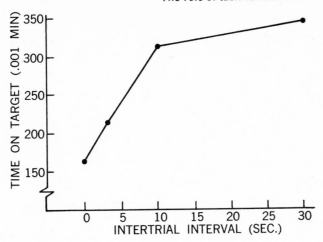

Fig. 11–20. Final performance level as a function of the intertrial interval. *Adapted from Adams (1954)*

to equate the preparedness to practice of the various groups.) Time on target was the performance measure.

Results for the various groups are indicated in Figure 11–19, with smoothed curves revealing the course of performance.[10] By the end of the trials, best performance appeared with the 50-second and two-minute rest period groups. These findings confirm those of an earlier study by Spence, Buxton, and Melton (1950) who found that subjects performed progressively better on a pursuit rotor task as intertrial intervals were increased from 0 to 20 seconds.

Later studies by Adams (1954) and Denny, Frisbey, and Weaver (1955), also employing the pursuit rotor task, have similarly indicated that performance is an increasing function of the length of the intertrial interval. In Adams' (1954) study, 150 thirty-second trials were given on the pursuit rotor with either 0-, 3-, 10-, 20-, or 30-second rest periods. Time on target for the final five trials, as a function of the intertrial interval, is indicated in Figure 11–20.

In summary, many of the experimental findings which have been obtained with motor-skill-tasks are in agreement with the

[10] Ammons has not provided a smoothed performance curve for the 24-hour intertrial interval group. He has pointed out that performance for this group was atypical in that initial scores were so low that they could not be matched with those of the other groups. Moreover, an examination of this group's performance indicated much greater variability than that found with the other groups.

classical conditioning studies and show that some type of distributed practice is superior to massed—a finding in keeping with the Hullian prediction of the efficacy of distributed practice.

As in a few other areas of inquiry, some investigators have made a learning versus performance distinction, hoping to find from their experimental studies some indication of whether or not the distribution of practice variables influences learning or performance. Most frequently, the position taken has been that the gain in performance arising from distributed practice can be considered a performance rather than a learning increment.

As an example, in a study by Adams and Reynolds (1954) groups of subjects were given 40 15-second trials on a rotary pursuit task. Experimental groups had either 5, 10, 15, or 20 massed trials, with a five-second intertrial interval, followed by a ten-minute rest period. The balance of the 40 trials was given under distributed practice (45-second intertrial interval). A control group had 40 uninterrupted practice sessions under the distributed practice condition. Performance of the varying experimental groups for the post-rest trials did not stabilize at a level below that of the distributed practice control group but rather converged upon it. The fact that all of the experimental groups readily shifted to the level of the control group suggested to the experimenters that the massing of practice leads to a decrement in performance but not in learning. Thus, the same performance level for all groups over the final post-rest trials suggested that the same habits had been acquired but that the massing of trials produced some inhibitory effect which dissipated with rest. Figure 11–21 presents these findings.

Somewhat similar findings have been reported by Archer (1954) and Starkweather and Duncan (1954), as well as a number of other investigators. In brief, it has been shown that providing subjects with an interpolated rest period following massed practice results in performance during post-rest trials which converges upon performance curves which have been established by groups which were given their training under distributed practice without an interpolated rest period.

One should be sure that the performance increment does not arise from additional learning taking place during the post-rest trials rather than from the dissipation of inhibition through rest. The fact that such increments are sufficiently large to bring performance near asymptote within a very few trials adds strength

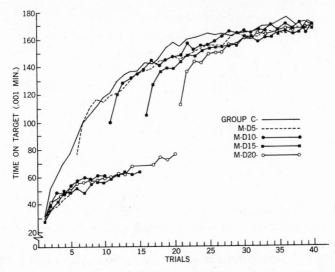

Fig. 11–21. Performance curves for the control group (C), which had distributed practice throughout training, and the four experimental groups, which had massed practice in the pre-rest trials and distributed practice in the post-rest trials. *Adapted from Adams and Reynolds (1954)*

to the position that the temporal interval interpolated between trials contributes to performance rather than learning.

In the motor-skill studies which have been examined, it is to be noted that the length of the work period has been held constant but the length of the rest period has been systematically varied. A final area of interest with this type of learning situation has been to investigate the distribution of work. That is, how the length of the work period influences performance when the rest period is held constant. Kimble and Bilodeau (1949) were two of the early investigators who studied this problem. In fact, they went one step further and compared the distribution of work periods with the distribution of rest periods, attempting to determine whether work or rest variables were more important in determining performance. The task utilized was the Minnesota Rate of Manipulation test, which consists of a large board with four rows of 15 holes. A cylindrical block of wood was fitted into each hole, and it was the subject's task to overturn the board and replace as many of the blocks of wood as possible in a given period of time.

TABLE 11–5

Experimental Design Illustrating the Work and
Rest Period Conditions

CONDI-TION	WORK PERIOD	REST PERIOD	REFERENCE NOTATION
1	10 sec.	10 sec.	10–10
2	10 sec.	30 sec.	10–30
3	30 sec.	10 sec.	30–10
4	30 sec.	30 sec.	30–30

(Adapted from Kimble and Bilodeau, 1949)

Four conditions were used, and these are indicated in Table 11–5. Subjects in the two 30-second work periods were given ten trials with either 10- or 30-second rest periods, and those in the two 10-second work conditions were given 30 trials in which 10- or 30-second rest periods were also utilized. Total work time was thus 300 seconds for all groups.

The results are indicated in Figure 11–22 and reveal that the 10-second work period groups, regardless of whether 10- or 30-second rest periods were used, performed better than the 30-second work groups. That is, if the length of the work period is held constant, performance may be significantly increased by lengthening the rest interval. However, when the length of rest period is held constant, increasing the length of the work period significantly decreases work output. The investigators, on the basis of these experimental findings, concluded that the amount of work which makes up a trial appears to be more important than the amount of rest in determining performance.

The specificity of these findings to the particular task is indicated by Kimble (1949a) who examined two conditions from the earlier Kientzle (1946) study and two conditions from a study of his own [Kimble (1949)]. Both investigators used the upside-down alphabet printing task, and the varying work and rest conditions are indicated in Table 11–6. These findings are indicated in Figure 11–23, and it can be noted that they do not confirm those obtained by Kimble and Bilodeau (1949). It appears that it is the length of the rest period that is of primary importance. Unfortunately, few investigators have made subsequent inquiries into this area, although it appears to be a challenging as well as an interesting one.

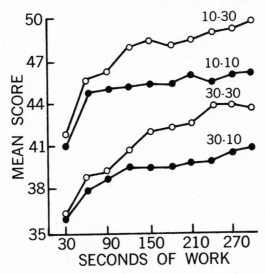

Fig. 11–22. Learning curves showing the performance of each of the four groups as a function of the number of seconds of practice. *Adapted from Kimble and Bilodeau (1949)*

Instrumental reward learning studies which have utilized animals have been somewhat controversial, although the bulk of the evidence indicates that the massed–distributed variable does not contribute to learning. Gagne (1941) had varying groups of animals learn to run an elevated pathway with intertrial intervals of either one-half, one, two, three, five, or ten minutes. The level of performance at the end of the acquisition trials was perfectly correlated with the length of the intertrial interval—the ten-minute group running most rapidly, followed by the five-minute group, etc.

However, the subsequent runway studies by Sheffield (1949), Wilson, Weiss, and Amsel (1955), Scott and Wike (1956), Lewis (1956), and Cotton and Lewis (1957) provide no evidence that running speed during acquisition trials depends upon the length of the intertrial interval. In Sheffield's study, for example, two groups of rats were trained to run a path under massed (15 seconds between trials) and under distributed practice (15 minutes between trials). Each group was divided, with one subgroup receiving partial reinforcement and the other subgroup receiving continuous reinforcement. Findings indicated no signifi-

TABLE 11–6

Experimental Design Illustrating the Work and
Rest Period Conditions

CONDI-TION	WORK PERIOD	REST PERIOD	REFERENCE NOTATION	INVESTIGATOR
1	60 sec.	5 sec.	60–5	Kientzle (1946)
2	60 sec.	30 sec.	60–30	Kientzle (1946)
3	30 sec.	5 sec.	30–5	Kimble (1949)
4	30 sec.	30 sec.	30–30	Kimble (1949)

(Adapted from Kimble, 1949)

cant differences among the four groups when running speed was used as the response measure.

In contrast to the negative findings using instrumental tasks in which appetitive states have served as the source of motivation, the intertrial interval generally has been shown to have an influence when shock and an avoidance response are examined. Its effect, however, appears to be dependent upon the particular nature of the task. Murphy and Miller (1956), in an early study in this area, conditioned three groups of rats to jump a barrier in a shuttle box when a CS (buzzer) was presented. The UCS (shock) was delivered five seconds after the CS presentation if the subject failed to make the jumping response. Group I was conditioned with an intertrial interval of 20 seconds, and Group II was conditioned with an intertrial interval of 40 seconds. Group III began conditioning sessions with an intertrial interval of 60 seconds which was progressively reduced to 50, and then 40, 30, and finally 20 as training continued, for an average intertrial interval of 40 seconds. Ten trials per day were provided, with the acquisition training taking place over 15 days. The findings, presented in Figure 11–24, indicate that the smallest intertrial interval group (Group I) had the poorest performance, whereas the variable interval group (Group III) had the best performance, although this was not significantly different from that of Group II.[11]

The Murphy and Miller (1956) study is interesting since, like the classical conditioning eyeblink study of Prokasy and Whaley (1961), it introduced a changing intertrial interval into the

[11] Hall (1955a) also using a shuttle box situation was unable to find avoidance learning to be a function of the length of the intertrial interval.

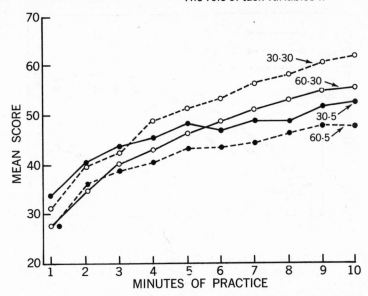

Fig. 11–23. Learning curves showing mean numbers of letters printed during successive minutes of practice. The notations on the curves refer to number of seconds of practice and number of seconds of rest in that order. Points for the thirty-second practice groups were obtained by adding scores for two trials. *Adapted from Kimble (1949a)*

experimental procedure. Levine and England (1960) made a further attempt to investigate the role of a changing intertrial interval in the avoidance learning situation. Again, a shuttle box was used in which a buzzer (CS) was presented for three seconds at which time the UCS (shock) was presented and continued until the subject made the appropriate running response. A Spaced-Fixed group was given 60 seconds between CS presentations, and a Spaced-Variable group was given intertrial intervals which varied from 40 to 80 seconds but, like their Spaced-Fixed counterpart, averaged 60 seconds. A Massed-Fixed group was given 20 seconds between trials, and the intertrial interval for the Massed-Variable group also averaged 20 seconds but varied from 10 to 30. Each subject was given 30 trials per day for five days. The results are indicated in Figure 11–25. Unlike Murphy and Miller's results, the fixed interval groups were superior to their variable counterparts, although the fact that massed training produced

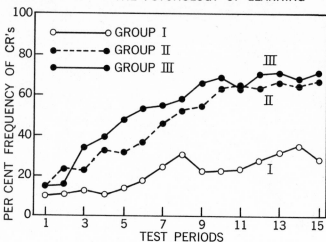

Fig. 11–24. The percentage frequency of CR's during the conditioning phase for all subjects. *Adapted from Murphy and Miller (1956)*

poorer performance than spaced confirms this part of the Murphy and Miller findings.[12]

Finally, Pearl (1963) has shown that with a different type of avoidance conditioning task short intertrial intervals produce superior performance. His experimental procedure utilized an avoidance task in which the rat had to press a lever in a Skinner box in order to avoid receiving a shock. The CS was the illumination of a small light above the lever in a Skinner box. It was presented for 20 seconds followed by seven seconds of shock (UCS). A lever press either terminated the CS and prevented delivery of the shock or simultaneously terminated the CS and UCS. For the short intertrial interval group (SIG), the CS was presented every 40 seconds, whereas the intermediate intertrial interval group (IIG) received the presentation of the light every 80 seconds. Finally, a long intertrial interval group (LIG) received the CS every 180 seconds. Two hundred training trials were provided on each of four consecutive days. The median number of lever presses was found to be an inverse function of the length

[12] It must be acknowledged that the Levine and England variable experimental procedure differs from that employed by Murphy and Miller since the latter investigators employed a progressively decreasing intertrial interval, in contrast to a randomized procedure employed by Levine and England.

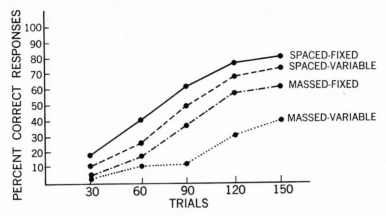

Fig. 11–25. Percentages of avoidance responses per session during acquisition. *Adapted from Levine and England (1960)*

of the intertrial interval. (See Figure 11–26.) In accounting for these findings, and in contrast to those obtained in the shuttle box, Pearl has hypothesized that shocking the animal in this type of situation leads to the perseveration of the lever-pressing response so that short intertrial intervals increase the probability that the perseverative response will be made during the presentation of the CS. In contrast, the shuttle box situation virtually prohibits perseveration because the animal must re-enter the compartment in which it has just been punished.

Verbal Learning

A large amount of work in the massed–distributed area has been done with verbal material. Although an early investigation by Lyon (1914) and one by Patten (1938) had indicated that distributed practice was the more effective method by which to learn a serial list of nonsense syllables, a series of studies by Hovland (1938, 1939, 1940, 1949) and by Underwood and his associates represents the most extensive investigations with this type of presentation.

The findings from Hovland's experiments are in keeping with the Hullian prediction that lengthening the intertrial interval tends to dissipate inhibition which, in turn, results in more rapid learning. In his first study [Hovland (1938)], 32 subjects learned 16 lists of nonsense syllables under massed (six seconds between

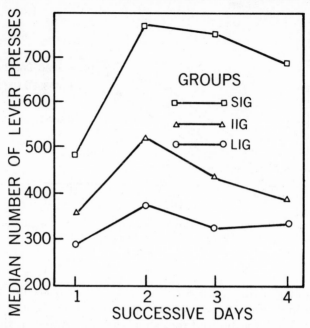

Fig. 11–26. Lever pressing as a function of the length of the inter-trial interval. *Adapted from Pearl (1963)*

trials) and distributed (two minutes and six seconds between trials) practice. The distributed practice condition produced a significant increase in ease of learning as measured by the number of trials necessary to reach a criterion of seven out of twelve correct. In a second study [Hovland (1940)], the massed–distributed practice condition was examined as a function of the length of the list. Lists consisting of either 8, 11, or 14 nonsense syllables were used, and again findings indicated that the distributed practice condition was superior for all lengths of list. Moreover, the superiority of the distributed practice condition grew progressively greater the longer the list. Finally, Hovland (1949) found that when the presentation of each nonsense syllable was reduced from the normal two-second rate to just one second the superiority of the distributed practice condition increased.

Underwood's series of studies has been primarily functional in character, in which he has attempted to examine the varying conditions under which distributed practice yields superior learning. As previously noted, the similarity variable has been significant in verbal learning, and in the first study of the series, Underwood and Goad (1951) were interested in the interaction of the distribution of practice and intra-list similarity in the serial learning situation. In this study, 14-item lists of adjectives were constructed in which there was either high or low similarity of material. An intertrial interval of either 2, 15, or 30 seconds was employed. The 15- and 30-second groups were superior when the high similarity list was being learned, although there was no difference among the varying intertrial interval groups in learning the low similarity list.

The finding of an interaction between similarity and the conditions of practice has not been confirmed, however, in later studies. Thus, Underwood (1953) ran five experiments in which the similarity of the adjectives comprising the list ranged from very low to very high, with 2-, 30-, or 60-second intertrial intervals being used.[13] The 30- and 60-second groups were superior in learning all lists, with no interaction being obtained between similarity and the intertrial interval. Similar findings have been obtained when nonsense syllables have been used [Underwood (1952), Underwood and Schulz (1959)]. In the Underwood (1952) study, three lists of nonsense syllables ranging from low to high intra-list similarity were used with 2-, 30-, or 60-second intertrial intervals. The Underwood and Schulz (1959) study employed four lists of nonsense syllables ranging from low to high similarity with either two- or 17-second intertrial intervals. Both studies indicated that the distributed practice condition was superior for all lists. Again, no interaction between similarity and intertrial interval was found.

The role of massed versus distributed practice has been investigated in interlist (as well as intra-list) similarity. In a study by Underwood and Richardson (1955) seven lists, each consisting of six consonant syllables, were so constructed that intra-list similarity was minimized but interlist similarity was maximized. The first list was learned using a two- or 30-second intertrial interval. The next five lists were learned with a two-second

[13] The reader should be aware that the technique for manipulating intra-list similarity for this experiment was different from that used by Underwood and Goad (1951). The 14 items which were used in each list were formed into four sets of three words and one set of two words. In varying similarity, synonymity of items within sets was varied; thus, for low similarity the items within sets making up the lists had low synonymity whereas for the high similarity the items within sets had high synonymity ratings.

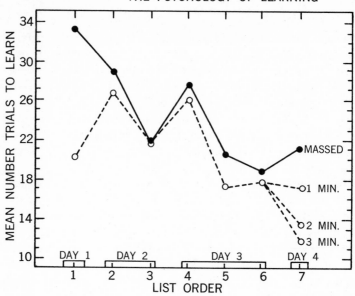

Fig. 11–27. Mean number of trials to attain one perfect recitation on each of the seven lists. *Adapted from Underwood and Richardson (1955)*

intertrial interval. Finally, the seventh list was learned with either a two-second, one-, two-, or three-minute intertrial interval. The results are presented in Figure 11–27. It can be observed that the 30-second group was superior to the two-second group in learning the first list, whereas the longest distributed practice group (three minutes) was superior to all other groups in learning the seventh list.

The last serial learning variable to be considered is the stage of learning. That is, does the distribution of practice interact with the learning of successive lists when one group learns all of the lists with distributed practice and another group learns all of the lists under massed practice? In an early study by Underwood (1951a) four serial lists of 14 adjectives per list were learned by either massed (two seconds between trials) or by distributed practice (30 seconds between trials). Only one list was learned per session. The findings showed that learning by distributed practice was consistently more rapid than was learning by massed practice, with the difference between the two conditions being

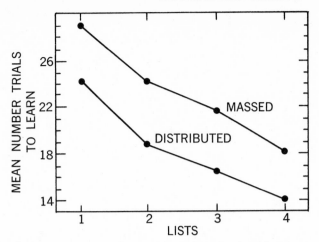

Fig. 11–28. The effect of stage of practice on learning by massed and by distributed practice. *Adapted from Underwood (1951a)*

essentially constant for the four sessions. Figure 11–28 presents these findings.

In summary, the bulk of the experimental evidence supports the position that distributed practice results in superior learning in the serial learning situation.

In contrast, the role of distributed practice in paired-associate learning has been somewhat controversial. In an early study, Hovland (1939), using nonsense syllables, found that learning did not take place more rapidly under distributed practice than under massed practice. However, in a subsequent study [Hovland (1949)] he was able to find such an effect.

Underwood has also found it difficult to obtain consistent findings. In one of his early studies [Underwood (1951)], lists of ten paired adjectives were used, with the lists having either high or low intra-list similarity. Four-, 30-, or 120-second intertrial intervals were employed. The results indicated no difference in learning as a function of the length of the intertrial interval.

Similar findings were obtained in two subsequent studies [Underwood (1953, 1953a)] in which stimulus and response similarity was manipulated separately. In one study [Underwood (1953a)], six experiments were performed in which adjectives served as the experimental material. Table 11–7 provides the similarity relationships between stimulus and response. The

TABLE 11–7

Experiments Used in Examining
Variations in Stimulus and
Response Similarity

EXPERI-MENT	STIMULUS SIMILARITY	RESPONSE SIMILARITY
1	Low	Zero
2	Medium	Zero
3	High	Zero
4	Zero	Low
5	Zero	Medium
6	Zero	High

(Adapted from Underwood, 1953a)

intertrial intervals employed were 4, 30, or 60 seconds. In another study [Underwood (1953)], stimulus response relationships were also manipulated in five experiments in which the same intertrial intervals were used. Nonsense syllables served as the material to be learned. Neither study revealed differences in learning as a function of the length of the intertrial interval.

In a more recent study [Underwood and Schulz (1961)], eight paired-associate lists were constructed using adjectives and non-sense syllables. Four lists were made up in which adjectives served as stimuli and nonsense syllables served as responses (A-S). Four other lists were constructed with nonsense syllables serving as stimuli and adjectives as responses (S-A). The nonsense syllables were so arranged that there was considerable interlist similarity but this was not true for the adjectives. Each subject learned four lists [(A-S) or (S-A)], with the first and fourth lists being learned under massed or distributed practice and the second and third lists under massed practice. Massed practice consisted of a four-second intertrial interval; distributed practice consisted of a 60-second intertrial interval. The findings, presented in Figure 11–29, indicate that for the learning of the S-A lists there was no difference between massed and distributed practice for the first list. However, for the fourth list, distributed practice provided poorest performance. As interference increases among the stimuli across lists, distributed practice produces poorer learning.

An examination of the adjective–nonsense syllable (A-S) pairings, however, reveals that distributed practice had little

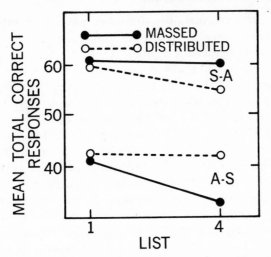

Fig. 11–29. Learning as a function of massed and distributed practice for syllable-adjective (S-A) lists and adjective-syllable (A-S) lists. *Adapted from Underwood and Schulz (1961)*

influence on the learning of the first list but did facilitate the learning of the fourth list. Thus, as interlist interference builds up among responses, the probability that distributed practice will facilitate acquisition increases.

In a second study by Underwood and Schulz (1961a), similar findings were obtained when the response interference introduced into the experimental situation resulted from language habits which the subject brought to the laboratory rather than being produced experimentally as was done in the previous study.

The role of massed versus distributed practice has been examined also in other types of verbal learning situations. One was the verbal discrimination learning experiment in which the subject is presented with a pair of words. His task is to indicate which word of the pair he believes is correct. In an early study by Underwood and Viterna (1951), two experiments were run in which similarity between members of each pair was high whereas in two other experiments similarity among pairs was low. Three intertrial intervals were employed within each experiment: 4, 15, or 60 seconds. In a study by Underwood and Archer (1955), intertrial intervals of 4, 30, or 60 seconds were used. Two experiments in the study employed high interlist similarity, but in the third experiment, intra-list similarity was low. Findings from all experiments revealed that the influence of the intertrial interval on learning was not significant.

The controversial findings with paired-associate learning situations have been reconciled, at least in part, by Underwood's (1961) two-stage learning hypothesis and a consideration of the variables which contribute to the learning which takes place in the two stages. Briefly, he hypothesized that the first stage of learning the paired-associate task consists of response learning in which the subject must acquire the verbal material as part of his response repertoire. In the second stage, identified as the associative or hook-up stage, the response must be attached or hooked-up to a specific stimulus. Underwood (1961) has observed that not only do these stages seem to be logically necessary but the behavior of subjects in learning paired-associates appears to correspond closely to the two stages.

The two-stage hypothesis is important in understanding the effects of distributed practice because when distributed practice facilitates learning it is a result of interference present during the response learning stage. Such interference is derived either from the formal similarity of materials produced by duplicating letters among the materials used on the response side of the list or from habits which have been learned either in the laboratory or during the lifetime of the subject.

It is assumed that when response interference is high the massing of trials results in the interfering response tendencies being only suppressed; thus, they arise from time to time during the course of learning to preclude the rapid acquisition of the complete list. The distribution of trials, on the other hand, permits the error tendencies, arising from interfering responses, to recover in strength; but with the subsequent occurrences of the correct response, these error tendencies are extinguished. The extinction procedure is hypothesized to represent a more effective elimination of the deleterious effects of the interfering responses than their suppression. However, as Underwood (1961) has pointed out, the length of the intertrial interval is critical. If it is too long, it will result in the weak associative strengths of the correct responses being forgotten, with the recovery of the incorrect responses persistently blocking or replacing the correct response. If the intertrial interval is too short, it may not permit sufficient time for the incorrect response tendencies to recover in strength, with the result that they are only suppressed.

All of the evidence that Underwood (1961) has used to support his position cannot be presented. Part of it is based upon the findings of studies which have demonstrated that when response competition has been virtually absent, as in the case of the verbal discrimination learning studies [Underwood and Viterna (1951), Underwood and Archer (1955)], or where responses are common words, thus, readily available to the subject, distributed practice has not facilitated learning. On the other hand, in a number of studies in which response competition was maximized by having the subjects learn a number of lists [Underwood and Schulz (1961, 1961a)] distributed practice did result in superior learning.[14]

[14] It is interesting to note that Underwood (1961) has not given serious consideration to the role of distributed practice in serial learning because the serial learning situation is "not a task providing sufficient isolation between stimulus and response functions to produce critical theoretical decisions." Thus, if an investigator cannot specify the locus of interference among stimulus or among response terms, the value of the task is considerably reduced for the study of distributed practice.

12

Stimulus and Response Generalization

IN DISCUSSING LEARNING up to this point, the basic emphasis has been placed upon empirical variables. Thus, the primary concern has been the examination of such constructs as reinforcement, stimulus intensity, distribution of practice, etc. The analysis of learning processes which develop as a function of the operation of these variables, i.e., excitation, inhibition, etc., although not ignored, has been of secondary importance. In this chapter, a different organization will be used to examine two processes which have been hypothesized to be of primary importance in learning: (1) stimulus generalization and (2) response generalization.

STIMULUS GENERALIZATION

Pavlov's early experimental work provided a foundation upon which the process of stimulus generalization rests. In writing about these early experiments, Pavlov (1927) stated, ". . . if a tone of 1000 d.v. is established as a conditioned stimulus, many other tones spontaneously acquire similar properties, such properties diminishing proportionally to the intervals of these tones from the one of 1000 d.v." Although a second Russian investiga-

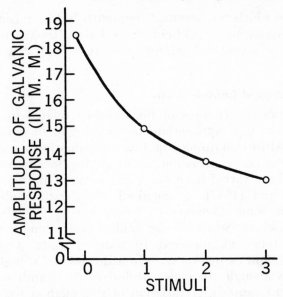

Fig. 12–1. Composite curve of generalization of conditioned excitatory tendencies. Galvanic skin response to conditioned frequency of tone (0) and to other tones 25, 50, and 75 j.n.d.'s removed in frequency (1, 2, and 3 respectively). *Adapted from Hovland (1937)*

tor, Bechterev (1928), also called attention to the topic, it was Pavlov's research which provided the impetus for a number of American investigators to become interested in the area.

Hovland's (1937, 1937a, 1937b, 1937c) studies have long been regarded as classic examples of the demonstration of the generalization process. In his first study [Hovland (1937)], a psychophysical method was used to obtain four tones which were separated in pitch by 25 jnd's. The frequencies which were obtained using this scaling procedure were 153, 468, 1,000, and 1,967 cps. A conditioning experiment was then undertaken in which either the highest tone (1,967 cps) or the lowest tone (153 cps) served as the CS and shock was used as a UCS to elicit a GSR. Following sixteen conditioning trials, extinction trials were given in which each subject was presented with each of the four tones four times in a random order. The extinction data were combined for both groups, and a single curve representing the generalization of tones separated by 25, 50, or 75 jnd's was plotted. As revealed in Figure 12–1, a concave gradient was obtained. The stimulus generalization curve which was obtained frequently has been conceptualized as representing a gradient of excitatory tendencies which have arisen as a result of reinforcing only a single S-R relationship.

Methodological Considerations

Before examining some of the variables related to stimulus generalization, it is appropriate to consider methodology. The basic method in examining stimulus generalization has been the use of an extinction situation, although the specific extinction operations have varied from one experiment to another. As just noted, Hovland (1937) presented all of the test stimuli to each subject, but some investigators have used only a single test stimulus. Wickens, Schroder, and Snide (1954), conditioning the GSR to a tone, administered 16 training trials. These were followed by eight extinction trials in which the test stimulus was a tone of only a single frequency. Different test stimuli were used with different subjects. A variation of this method has been to provide only a single extinction trial following the conditioning trials, a method utilized by Grant and Schiller (1953) and Hall and Prokasy (1961).

In recent years, a large number of stimulus generalization studies have been done with instrumental conditioning situations, many of which have been of a free operant variety [Ferster (1953a)].[1] An example of this procedure was demonstrated by Guttman and Kalish (1956) who trained pigeons to peck at an illuminated key in order to receive food. Different groups of subjects were trained under a variable reinforcement schedule to respond to different hues, i.e., 530, 550, 580, and 600 mμ. Sixty-second-stimulus-on intervals were alternated with ten-second-stimulus-off intervals, with 30 stimulus presentations during each daily session. The stimulus-off (blackout) condition was used to enable the experimenter to change the color of the key for the subsequent stimulus generalization tests. Following training, generalization tests were carried out using extinction trials. Eleven different hues were randomized within a test series, and twelve different series were presented to each subject. As with training trials, stimulus presentation consisted of 30 seconds

[1] It will be recalled that the free operant refers to any apparatus that generates a response which takes a short time to occur and leaves the animal in the same place ready to respond again.

followed by a ten-second-stimulus-off interval, although reinforcement was not provided. An examination of the number of extinction responses which were made to each stimulus presentation provided the basic data from which the generalization gradient was plotted. Although a number of variations of this general technique have been utilized, the basic data obtained with the free operant situation is the frequency of response during the generalization test.

Stimulus Generalization Gradients

As can be observed in Figure 12–1, Hovland's (1937) experimental data indicated a concave stimulus generalization gradient. The shape or form of the gradient has been regarded by many investigators as being of considerable importance in psychological theory. For some time following Hovland's study, it was generally assumed that the shape of the generalization gradient was invariant across dimensions and, more specifically, it was considered to be concave.[2] A second development regarding the shape of the generalization curve was the position taken by Hull (1943) that the diminishing response strength extended *symmetrically* in both directions along the stimulus dimension. Such a position, of course, was an extrapolation from the original Hovland data, since it will be recalled that although Hovland used stimuli at both ends of the stimulus dimension as his CS, his data were pooled so that the curve extended in only one direction.

In recent years, most investigators have recognized that no single form can describe all generalization gradients. What are some of the underlying reasons for their taking such a position? A primary one is related to measurement. Since different response measures or different measurement operations may not be measuring the same thing, there is little reason to assume that generalization gradients obtained with different testing methods should be similar. It will be recalled that Hovland (1937), presenting all of the test stimuli to his subjects, obtained a concave gradient. On the other hand, Wickens, Schroder, and Snide (1954), also examining the conditioned GSR but utilizing a generalization test series consisting of the presentation of only a single stimulus, obtained a bell-shaped curve. Studies by Gutt-

---

[2] It is interesting to note that the general acceptance of a single form for the stimulus generalization curve is reminiscent of the search for a single form of the learning curve.

man and Kalish (1956) and Kalish and Haber (1963) employing
an instrumental conditioning situation have also demonstrated
different gradients as a function of whether single or multiple
stimuli are used in the test series.

In one part of the Kalish and Haber (1963) study, pigeons
were trained to peck at a monochromatic stimulus of 550 mμ. Following the reaching of a learning criterion, each subject in a given
group was provided 132 extinction sessions in which only one of
the following monochromatic stimuli was presented as the test
stimulus: 550, 540, 530, 520, 510, or 490 mμ. Both training and extinction sessions consisted of 30-second presentation periods alternated with ten-second blackout periods. The number of responses
made by the varying groups during the first three, or first twelve,
extinction sessions was plotted to provide a stimulus generalization
gradient. Thus, this gradient was derived from an experimental
procedure in which subjects were exposed to only a single
stimulus during extinction. In the Guttman and Kalish (1956)
study, subjects were trained to peck at a 550 mμ stimulus, but
during extinction sessions each animal was tested with a range of
stimulus values extending from 490 to 610 mμ. The gradient
which was generated from these data has been labeled "multiple
stimuli" since the same subject is represented at each point on the
curve. An examination of Figure 12-2 presents a comparison of
the stimulus generalization gradients obtained with the different
testing procedures. As noted with the Hovland (1937) and
Wickens, Schroder, and Snide (1954) studies, it is obvious that
different testing procedures can produce different generalization
gradients.[3]

A second consideration in the examination of the generalization gradient is related to the stimulus units which are placed on
the abscissa. Hovland's (1937) technique of using jnd's to scale
the stimuli which he used has been followed by many other
investigators, but the assumption that this is the appropriate unit
for measuring similarity (or discriminability) can be questioned.
There is no doubt that psychophysical scales can be established,
but it must be pointed out that such scales invariably are the
product of extensive training of experienced observers. Although

---

[3] Some investigators [Hiss and Thomas (1963)] have not been able to obtain
differences in the shape of the gradient as a function of whether a single or multiple
stimulus testing procedure is utilized. The bulk of the experimental evidence, however, does support the position that the form of the gradient is dependent upon the
type of training as well as the testing procedure.

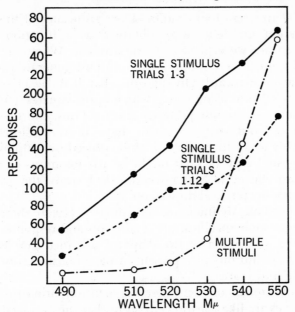

Fig. 12–2. Stimulus generalization gradients obtained as a function of single or multiple stimulus test sessions. *Adapted from Kalish and Haber (1963)*

they may approximate the limits of sensory functions, there is nothing in the resultant scale which indicates anything about the discriminability of stimuli or attributes of the external world which are initially selected and perceived by the subject *in the conditioning situation.* The problem of what the effective stimulus is in such situations is an important one.

Moreover, there is some question as to whether or not a continuum as would be indicated by the use of jnd's actually exists. Razran (1949), for example, has suggested that in the conditioning study there is only a crude qualitative categorizing of stimulus dimensions, one which consists of just a few steps. The difficulty of securing psychophysical scales with animals has led experimenters using infrahuman subjects to plot their stimulus units along some physical dimension, but this, of course, represents an arbitrary procedure.

In a recent study Vandament and Price (1964) examined stimulus generalization using the conditioned eyeblink response. Subjects were trained to respond to a light of 3.20 apparent foot candles and then tested to lights of less intensity, i.e., 1.364, .4267, and .07459 apparent foot candles. The significance of this study is that different gradients were obtained as a function of what stimulus values were placed on the abscissa. When the physical values of the CS were plotted, the resultant generalization curve was concave downward. On the other hand, if the physical scale was converted into a log scale (which approximates a jnd scale) the gradient was almost perfectly linear. Thus, the investigators have pointed out that ". . . the shape of the gradient varies considerably according to the scaling procedure employed" and have suggested that ". . . it might be parsimonious to disregard scaling procedures in generalization and study the parameters relating to some physical dimension."

In any event, Mednick and Freedman's (1960) dictum ". . . that without some specification of stimulus and response measurement scales, discussion of the shape of obtained gradients must proceed very cautiously" represents a basic consideration for any work done in this area.

One additional comment deserves mention. Stimulus generalization curves are like learning curves in that the averaged gradient is not necessarily representative of the generalization phenomenon for a single subject. As Guttman and Kalish (1956) have reported in their study in which they examined the response performance for both individual subjects and the group, ". . . for some Ss the curves are bilaterally convex, for some, concave, and for others, concave on one side and convex on the other. Certain Ss . . . exhibit linearity over a major portion of the gradient." These curves were in contrast to the group curve which was a bilaterally concave gradient.

AN EXAMINATION OF THE STIMULI USED IN STIMULUS GENERALIZATION

Many experiments have indicated that stimulus generalization can be observed using a variety of different stimuli. The presentation of a sampling of these will illustrate the experimental findings which have been obtained.

Auditory Stimuli

Hovland (1937) was one of the first American investigators to use human subjects to obtain generalization gradients when auditory stimuli varying in pitch and loudness were manipulated. Many subsequent experimenters have used these same frequency and intensity values in obtaining generalization gradients. Miller and Greene (1954) and Jenkins and Harrison (1960) have also used auditory stimuli with rats and pigeons in obtaining stimulus generalization gradients.

One interesting effect obtained when pitch is used as the stimulus dimension is known as the octave effect. In an early study, Humphreys (1939a), using college students, conditioned the GSR to a tone of 1,967 cps and then tested for generalization. The response to a test tone of 984 cps—one octave below the reinforced tone—was significantly greater than the response to a test tone of 1,000 cps, although in terms of frequency only, the 1,000 cps tone is more similar to the 1,967 cps tone than is the 984 cps tone.

Blackwell and Schlosberg (1943) obtained a similar finding with rats. In this study, a group of rats was trained to run to food when any one of a number of tones was presented. The tones used were 3,000, 5,000, 7,000, 8,000, and 10,000 cps. When the running response to these frequencies was of a uniform latency, the rats were extinguished to all frequencies except the 10,000 cps tone which continued to be reinforced. The extinction procedure was, in effect, counter conditioning, which took place by charging the grid which the animals had to cross in order to get into the food box. Generalization gradients obtained over six daily sessions were plotted from the response measures of latency and frequency of responding. [Each extinction session consisted of presenting the positive (reinforced) tone 24 times and each negative (nonreinforced) tone six times.] Both response measures revealed that an octave effect was clearly present at the 5,000 cps tone presentation on the first session, although by the last testing session it was not very pronounced.

Visual Stimuli

In a number of studies, the investigator has been interested in examining stimulus generalization effects as they are related to visual stimuli. One visual stimulus dimension has been size, and, in an early study, Grice and Saltz (1950) trained rats to run a two-foot runway in order to secure food. At the end of the runway was a white disc which had a small square door in its center. Attached to the back of the disc, and just below the door, was a food dish. It was thus possible for the animal to obtain food by

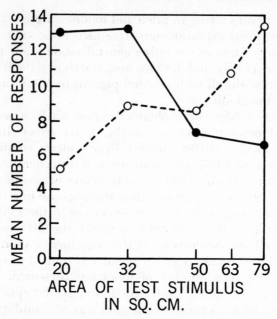

Fig. 12–3. Generalization functions showing mean number of extinction responses for each test group. The solid line indicates the group trained on the twenty centimeter disc; the dotted line indicates the group trained on the seventy-nine centimeter disc. *Adapted from Grice and Saltz (1950)*

pushing its nose through the door. One group of animals was first trained to respond to a disc which was 20 square cm., and a second group was trained to respond to a 79 square cm. disc. The training series consisted of providing each animal with 20 reinforced trials per day for three days. Five additional reinforced trials were presented just prior to the beginning of the generalization test which consisted of 25 trials. For the test series, the 79 square cm. disc group was divided into five subgroups; the subgroups were extinguished on discs of either 79, 63, 50, 32, or 20 square cm. The group which was trained on the 20 square cm. disc was divided into four subgroups, with these subgroups being extinguished on discs of 20, 32, 50, or 79 square cm. The number of responses which were made during the extinction test series was recorded; if an animal did not respond within 60 seconds it was scored as a failure of response. The mean number of responses made by the

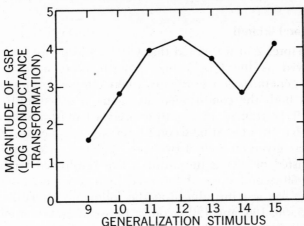

Fig. 12–4. Averaged GSR magnitudes in log conductance units to different generalization stimuli on the first extinction test trial. All Ss had been trained with the twelve-inch CS. *Adapted from Grant and Schiller (1953)*

varying groups to the varying test stimuli can be noted in Figure 12–3. Although both gradients show a decreasing amount of generalization as a function of the difference in size from the training stimuli, the curve forms are significantly different.

Grant and Schiller (1953) conditioned the GSR to a CS consisting of a rectangle of light 12 inches high and one inch wide. One hundred and five subjects were given 25 reinforced trials, followed by 15 extinction trials in which one of seven generalized stimuli, i.e., a rectangle one inch wide by 9, 10, 11, 12, 13, 14, or 15 inches high, was presented. The experimenters believed that the first test trial was of primary importance in obtaining a generalization gradient in which the discrimination process was minimized. Responses on the first test trial, indicated in Figure 12–4, reveal a very complex gradient.

Beginning with the Guttman and Kalish (1956) study, a number of investigators have used the free operant situation to examine stimulus generalization gradients when visual stimuli are varied along the frequency dimension. Since two of these studies were described previously [Guttman and Kalish (1956) and Kalish and Haber (1963)], the reader can refer to these for the procedures which were used and the findings which were obtained.

Temporal Stimuli

In Chapter 2, it was noted that CR's could be set up in which time served as the CS. A few experimenters have examined stimulus generalization gradients when temporal intervals have served as both the conditioned and generalized stimuli. Rosenbaum (1951) trained 16 rats to depress a bar in a Skinner box, with the bar inserted at 60-second intervals. Forty-eight reinforcements were given on each of two days. The test series on the third day consisted of giving the animals five reinforced trials at the standard 60-second interval followed by a series of test trials in which the bar was introduced at the following intervals: 15, 30, 45, 60, 75, 90, 105, and 120 seconds. Between each two test trials, five presentations of the bar at the standard interval were provided so that the disruption of the established temporal rhythm by the interpolation of irregular test intervals was minimized. The order of presentation of the test intervals was varied systematically to preclude any serial position effect. During the test series, one-half of the animals were placed under 22 hours of food deprivation (the same as during the training series) and the remaining animals were placed under a somewhat lower drive condition. This was produced by feeding the animals four grams of food just prior to their being placed in the experimental situation.

The findings are illustrated in Figure 12–5. As can be noted, when the bar was presented at intervals shorter than the one to which the subjects had been trained, they took progressively longer to respond. When the bar was inserted at increasingly greater temporal intervals, response latency also tended to increase but the difference between any of the longer intervals and the 60-second interval was not statistically significant.

Verbal Stimuli

One interesting dimension along which stimulus generalization has been shown to operate is related to language. As Osgood (1953) has pointed out, semantic generalization studies can be grouped into three categories: (1) sign to sign, (2) object to sign, and (3) sign to object. The sign-to-sign category refers to an experimental situation in which a response is conditioned to one word, with the generalization test taking the form of presenting another word—one which bears some relationship to the first, i.e., synonym, antonym, etc. The object-to-sign situation is one in

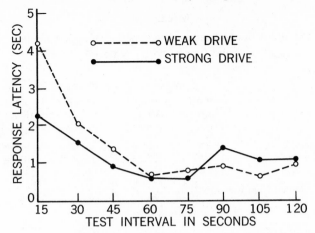

Fig. 12–5. Generalization gradients as measured by latency of responding for the two drive conditions. *Adapted from Rosenbaum* (*1951*)

which an object serves as a stimulus to which a response has been conditioned, and the generalization test consists of presenting a word which represents or is related to the object. Finally, the sign-to-object category is just the reverse of this.

Almost all studies have been of the sign-to-sign variety. In one such early experiment, Razran (1939) utilized synonyms and homophones as his test material. A salivary CR was established by using words such as "style" and "urn" as conditioned stimuli, and pretzels, small sandwiches, or candy served as unconditioned stimuli to elicit a salivary response. (This response was measured by placing a roll of dental cotton under the tongue of the subject and removing it after a specified length of time—usually one minute. The amount of salivation was measured by comparing the weight of the cotton before and after being placed in the subject's mouth.) After the CR had been established, test stimuli consisting of presenting synonyms such as "fashion" and "vase" as well as homophones, i.e., "earn." The results indicated that it was possible to obtain a CR to both synonyms and homophones, with the synonyms providing the greater amount of generalization.

Other semantic generalization studies have been reported by Diven (1936), Lacey and Smith (1954), and Lacey, Smith, and Green (1955). In a very interesting study in this area, Riess (1946) demonstrated that semantic generalization was a function of the age of the subject. Four groups of subjects differing in

TABLE 12–1

Stimulus Generalization as a Function of Age of Subject
and Type of Verbal Material

	MEAN PERCENTAGE OF GAIN			
	Group I (7 yrs., 9 mos.)	Group II (10 yrs., 8 mos.)	Group III (14 yrs.)	Group IV (18 yrs., 6 mos.)
Homophones	158.57	65.18	59.92	52.16
Antonyms	139.10	97.23	76.96	103.08
Synonyms	129.43	59.86	109.76	148.50

(Adapted from Riess, 1964)

chronological age were used. Group I had a mean age of seven years, nine months; Group II had a mean age of ten years, eight months; Group III had a mean age of fourteen years; Group IV had a mean age of eighteen years, six months. Varying verbal stimuli served as the CS, and a loud buzzer was used as the UCS to provide a GSR. Following the establishment of the CR to varying conditioned stimulus words, test words consisting of either homophones, antonyms, or synonyms were presented. The findings, as can be noted in Table 12–1, indicated that either homophones, antonyms, or synonyms provided the greatest generalization effects, depending upon the age of the subject.

Lang, Geer, and Hnatiow (1963) have examined stimulus generalization as it is related to the aggressiveness or hostility of the verbal stimuli which are employed. In this study, words which had been previously scaled for hostility by Buss (1961) were used as the verbal stimuli.[4] The training period consisted of presenting 12 highly hostile words, e.g., annihilation, along with ten neutral ones, e.g., abstract, with each hostile word being followed by shock which elicited a GSR. Following the training period, the generalization test was provided. This consisted of singly presenting 16 words, organized in blocks of four; each block included one member of each of the four word classes, i.e., high hostile (HH), medium hostile (MH), low hostile (LH), and neutral (N). The gradient of GSR responses which was obtained is indicated in Figure 12–6.

[4] Buss and his associates [Buss (1961), Geer and Buss (1962)] were among the first to examine the generalization of verbal stimuli which vary along the hostility dimension.

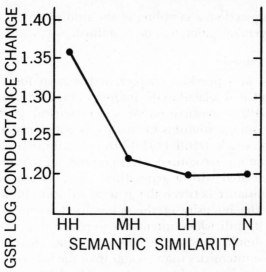

Fig. 12–6. Mean GSR scores of the experimental group for the four categories of hostile word stimuli. *Adapted from Lang, Geer, and Hnatiow (1963)*

Finally, Abbott and Price (1964) have demonstrated stimulus generalization of the conditioned eyelid response when nonsense syllables which varied in formal similarity from the CS were used as the test stimuli. Ninety acquisition trials were provided in which the syllable XUH served as the CS, followed by a puff of air (UCS). Ten generalization test trials were provided in which either the original syllable or other syllables which had two, one, or no letters in common with XUH were used. Using the percentage of responding for the first test trial or for all ten test trials the investigators obtained a negatively decelerated curve which so frequently has been found in stimulus generalization studies.

VARIABLES INFLUENCING THE GENERALIZATION PROCESS

The ready acceptance of stimulus generalization as a basic process involved in learning has resulted in a number of investigators attempting to examine how certain variables influence it. In the following section, a sampling of the studies which are related to stimulus generalization will be examined.

Stimulus Intensity

As noted in a previous chapter, it has been found that the strength of a CR is related to the intensity of the CS which is used. In Hull's (1943) postulation of a symmetrical generalization gradient the role of stimulus intensity was not considered, but in a subsequent article [Hull (1949)] the contribution of an intensity dimension was recognized. Hull pointed out that the response strength associated with a generalized stimulus was related not only to the distance between the generalized stimulus and the CS but also to the intensity of the generalized stimulus. In brief, generalized stimuli whose intensities were less than the intensity of the CS should produce *weaker* responses than generalized stimuli whose intensities were *greater* than the intensity of the CS. Since the intensity variable could provide differential contributions to response strength, it would follow that the stimulus generalization gradient would not always be symmetrical. Hull stated: "When a response is conditioned to a weak stimulus and generalizes toward a fairly strong extreme of the stimulus-intensity continuum, the resulting effective gradient is convex upward." But "when a response is conditioned to the strong extreme of the above stimulus-intensity continuum and generalizes toward the weak extreme, the resulting effective gradient is concave upward." Figure 12–7 provides an illustration of a stimulus generalization gradient in which the gradient has been influenced by the intensity variable.

A number of studies have demonstrated an asymmetrical form of the generalization curve when the stimulus dimension is intensity. If the assumption is made that larger objects result in more intensive stimulation (there is some evidence to support the position that large stimuli appear brighter than small stimuli), the studies of Grice and Saltz (1950) and Grant and Schiller (1953), which were cited previously, reveal an upward gradient when generalized stimuli are larger than the CS.

Razran (1949) has presented data obtained from 54 different experiments in Pavlov's laboratory, all examining the role of stimulus intensity and generalization effects of salivary conditioning in dogs. As Table 12–2 indicates, there is clearly an increase in

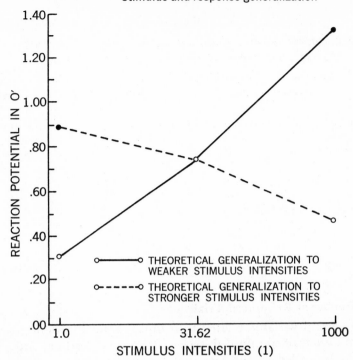

Fig. 12–7. Graphic representation of theoretical stimulus-intensity generalization as modified by stimulus intensity when extending from weak toward strong stimulus intensities and from strong toward weak intensities. The solid circles represent the origin of the respective gradients. *Adapted from Hull (1949)*

response strength as higher intensity generalized stimuli are used.

Hall and Prokasy's (1961) generalization study also has demonstrated the operation of an intensity variable. Groups of subjects were given 16 GSR conditioning trials in which a 30 or 80 db 1,000 cps tone served as the CS. Eight extinction trials followed with either a 30, 54, or 80 db 1,000 cps tone being presented. The analysis of generalization effects was confined to GSR responses made on the first test trial. The findings showed that when the 30 db tone served as the CS a generalized performance increment was noted to both the 54 and 80 db tones. When the 80 db tone was used as the CS, there was a generalized performance decrement to

TABLE 12-2

Stimulus Intensity Generalization of Salivary Conditioning in Dogs.
Data from 54 Different Experiments in Pavlov's Laboratory

Each entry is a mean percentage of conditioned salivation to the nonconditioned generalization stimuli. Figures in parentheses are numbers of determinations.

CONDI- TIONED STIMULI	LOWER INTENSITY STEPS			HIGHER INTENSITY STEPS		
	I	II	III	I	II	III
Lights	79(14)	69(11)	58(8)	118(14)	128(9)	149(8)
Whistles	68(12)	58(11)	49(9)	137(13)	149(8)	165(8)
Bells	72(11)	64(9)	56(7)	124(10)	138(8)	149(6)

(Adapted from Razran, 1949)

presentation of the 54 and 30 db tones. Figure 12-8 presents these findings.

Number of Reinforced Trials

A second variable related to stimulus generalization effects is the number of reinforced trials. Before proceeding, attention should be called to the fact that the learned response becomes stronger as the number of reinforcements increases. As a result, groups given a large number of reinforcements, in contrast to groups provided a smaller number, will have learned more at the end of the training period. This will be reflected in shorter latencies, faster running times, etc. The differences among groups should be corrected for in order to obtain a meaningful generalization curve by using either a statistical technique (analysis of covariance) or expressing the amount of generalization as a percentage of the generalized response strength to the strength of the response which was made to the CS during the latter stage of training. This problem is similar to the problem of comparing extinction measures following different acquisition trial performance which was discussed in an earlier chapter.

In one of the early GSR conditioning studies by Hovland (1937c) different groups of subjects were provided with either 8, 16, 24, or 48 CS-UCS presentations. For one-half of each group the CS was a 40 db tone, and for the other half it was an 86 db tone. Eight test trials were then presented, consisting of the presentation of the 40 and 86 db tones in a counterbalanced order. Figure

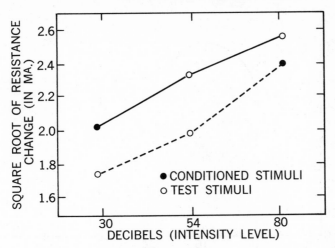

Fig. 12–8. Generalization gradients obtained as a function of the intensity of the CS. *Adapted from Hall and Prokasy (1961)*

12–9 reveals the percentage of generalization as a function of the number of reinforcements which were provided. Except for the group given 16 reinforcements, there was little difference among the groups. One interpretation would be that the 16-trial group's performance was a product of sampling error and that, basically, the number of reinforcements does not contribute to differences in relative amounts of generalization.

A more complete examination of stimulus generalization as a function of the number of reinforced trials should provide a group of curves—with each curve representing a generalization gradient arising from a specific number of reinforced trials. Margolius (1955) has provided data relative to this point. In his study, four groups of rats were trained to run down a two-foot runway and open a door placed in the center of a white circle 79 square cm. in area. These groups received either 4, 16, 64, or 104 reinforced trials to the training stimulus. Following training, each group was divided into five subgroups of seven subjects, each of which received 30 nonreinforced trials to either the 79 cm. training circle or to a circle of 63, 50, 32, or 20 square cm. Test performance was evaluated in terms of (1) the latency of responding over the first three test trials, (2) the total number of responses made, and (3) the number of responses made within a 60-second period. (The latter measure was obtained by adding

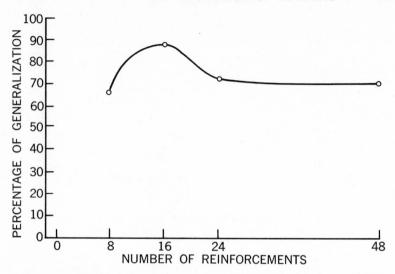

Fig. 12–9. Degree of generalization after varying numbers of reinforcements. *Adapted from Hovland (1937c)*

the latency of each succeeding response until a total of 60 seconds
was reached.) Figure 12–10 depicts a group of curves which was
obtained when the median latency for the first three test trials was
used as the response measure. Unfortunately, absolute response
values have been used, and, since differences in responding at the
end of the training trials were not corrected for, the curve values
undoubtedly reflect these differences. Figure 12–11 reveals the
relative generalization gradients for the varying criteria which
were used as a function of the number of training trials.[5] In
contrast to Hovland's findings, relative generalization for all of
the response measures increased as a function of the number of
training trials which were provided.

In a more recent study, Jensen and Cotton (1961) trained
four groups of rats to traverse a four-foot runway and open a door
placed in the center of a white square 50 square cm. in area.
Running speed was used as the response measure. These groups
received either 10, 30, 70, or 190 reinforced trials; following
training, each group was divided into nine subgroups which

[5] In order to obtain relative generalization values, response measures for the
varying generalization test points were combined and a mean value computed for
each training level.

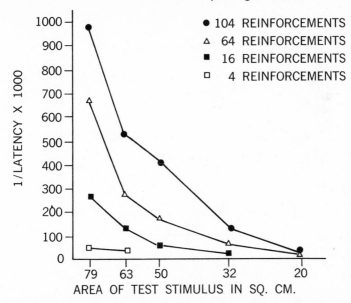

Fig. 12–10. Generalization gradients based upon the median latency of the first three test trials as a function of stimulus area and training trials. *Adapted from Margolius (1955)*

received 20 nonreinforced trials to either the 50 square cm. training square or to squares of 10, 20, 30, 40, 60, 70, 80, or 90 square cm. Differences in terminal acquisition performance, corrected for by analysis of covariance, revealed no differences among any of the groups—a finding in contrast to that obtained by Margolius (1955).

In summary, the bulk of the evidence supports the position that when relative measures of stimulus generalization are used the number of reinforced trials which are provided during training results in no differential responding during the test situation.

Number of Test Trials

As noted, it is customary for experimenters working in this area to provide the subject with a number of test trials, the intent often being to obtain a relatively stable response measure. A question which arises when this procedure is used is whether or not the stimulus generalization gradient varies as a function of the number of test trials which are provided. The studies of Wickens,

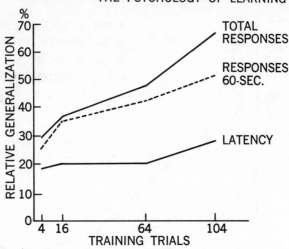

Fig. 12–11. Mean relative generalization of all test stimuli as a function of training trials and criterion. *Adapted from Margolius (1955)*

Schroder, and Snide (1954), using the conditioned GSR with humans, and Guttman and Kalish (1956), using pigeons with the free operant situation, have demonstrated that the generalization function appears to become steeper with continued testing.

Both of these studies were mentioned earlier in the chapter. In brief, Wickens, Schroder, and Snide (1954) administered 16 conditioning trials to three groups of subjects, in which a tone (either 153 or 1,000 cps) was followed by shock which produced a GSR. Following such training, eight test trials were provided. One group was given these trials with the CS serving as the test stimulus, and the two other groups were tested with a tone either 25 or 50 jnd's distant from the CS. The results are revealed in Figure 12–12; it is apparent that the generalization gradient becomes progressively steeper as a function of the number of test trials which are administered.

Guttman and Kalish (1956) have reported similar findings. In their study, pigeons were placed in a Skinner box and trained to peck at a disc illuminated by a light of a particular wavelength. Following a variable interval reinforcement schedule, twelve generalization test sessions were provided, with each test session consisting of the presentation of ten different wavelengths in addition to the original CS, for a total of 132 stimulus presenta-

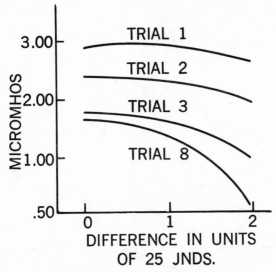

Fig. 12–12. Gradients of generalization after different numbers of extinction trials. *Adapted from Wickens, Schroder, and Snide (1954)*

tions. Reinforcement was never provided during these test trials. Figure 12–13 provides the generalization gradients for successive fourths of the total test series, and although the gradient is not the same shape as that obtained by Wickens, Schroder, and Snide (1954) a progressive steepening of the curve can be observed.

Time of Testing

There is some evidence to support the position that delaying the test for generalization results in a flatter generalization gradient than does providing such a test immediately after training. In an early study by Perkins and Weyant (1958), four groups of rats were trained to run a black (or white) three-foot runway in order to secure food. Eighty-six trials spaced over a 12-day training session were provided, with intermittent reinforcement being given during the latter stages of training. Following such training, all subjects received a total of 18 test trials on two successive days. For two groups of subjects, eight such trials were provided 60 seconds immediately following the last training trial; ten additional trials were given 24 hours later. One of these groups was tested on the colored runway over which the animals had been given training trials whereas the other group was given

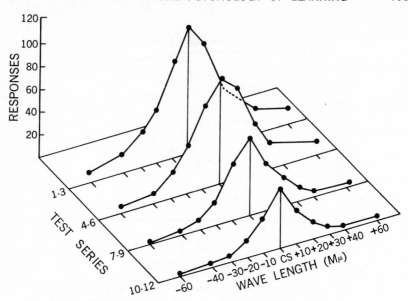

Fig. 12–13. Mean generalization gradients for successive fourths of the test series. *Adapted from Guttman and Kalish (1956)*

test trials on a runway over which it had not been given training. For the remaining two groups, eight test trials were provided seven days following the end of training, with ten additional trials being provided 24 hours later. As with the immediate testing situation, one group of subjects was tested on the colored runway over which it had been given training trials, and a second group was given test trials on a runway over which it had not been given training. In brief, then, four experimental groups of subjects were utilized: same runway–immediate testing, different runway–immediate testing, same runway–delayed testing, different runway–delayed testing. Using running speed for the first eight test trials as the response measure, results are as indicated in Figure 12–14. A much flatter gradient can be noted for the delayed testing groups than for the groups provided immediate testing.

Thomas and Lopez (1962), using pigeons in a free operant learning situation, have obtained findings supporting those of Perkins and Weyant (1958). In the Thomas and Lopez study, three groups of pigeons were trained to peck a key illuminated by a 550 mμ hue. After ten days of variable interval reinforcement

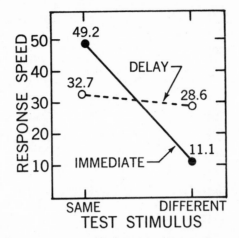

Fig. 12–14. Median response speed (100/response time in seconds) on the first eight test trials for each condition. *Adapted from Perkins and Weyant (1958)*

training, the subjects were divided into three groups matched for rate of responding. Group I was tested for generalization one minute after the completion of training; Group II was tested one day later; Group III was tested one week later. Generalization testing consisted of presenting 11 different stimuli—500 mμ to 600 mμ in 10 mμ steps—randomized within a series, with eight different series presented to each subject. (The 550 mμ CS was not presented.) A second generalization test was administered to each subject 24 hours after the first test, with no training intervening between the test periods. The findings showed that a much flatter gradient was obtained for the groups tested either one day or one week following training, in contrast to a relatively steep gradient obtained for the group given the test immediately following training. Since there was no difference between the gradients obtained by the one-day and one-week groups, Thomas and Lopez concluded that the process contributing to the flattening of the gradient appeared to be complete within 24 hours.

Finally, McAllister and McAllister (1963) obtained somewhat similar findings using an avoidance learning situation. In this study, a two-compartment apparatus was used in which a CS (increase in illumination) was presented for four seconds following which shock (UCS) was presented for two seconds; both the CS and UCS were terminated simultaneously. Rats learned to

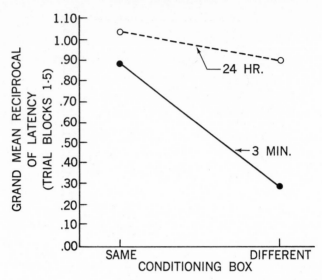

Fig. 12–15. Stimulus generalization gradients obtained with post-conditioning delays of three minutes and twenty-four hours. *Adapted from McAllister and McAllister (1963)*

jump a hurdle on the presentation of the CS in order to avoid shock. Following training, the test situation consisted of placing animals in the same or in a different conditioning box either three minutes or 24 hours following training. Using latency of responding as their response measure, the investigators obtained the results presented in Figure 12–15. They are unusual, and different from the Perkins and Weyant (1958) study, in that the delayed testing group, in contrast to the immediate testing group, revealed superior retention when the same conditioning box was used. They are similar to the Perkins and Weyant (1958) and Thomas and Lopez (1962) findings, however, in revealing a flatter generalization gradient for the group given the delayed test.

One interpretation for the obtaining of a flatter generalization gradient would be that the original and generalized stimuli would be discriminable immediately following the training session but would not be discriminable after a delay. As a result, the latter condition should produce less differential responding which, in turn, should result in a flatter gradient. As McAllister and McAllister (1963) have pointed out, however, this explanation is circular in the absence of independent evidence of this postulated difference in discriminability.[6]

Differential Training and the Problem of Discriminability

A basic problem which Hull (1943) considered in his examination of stimulus generalization was the problem of stimulus discriminability. He wrote (p. 188) that

> . . . it is clear that there can be no primary stimulus generalization unless there is some parallel physical variability in the stimulus energy to serve as its basis; for example, there could be no generalization in the stimulus dimension of frequency or amplitude of soundwaves if soundwaves did not present such dimensions of variability. Secondly, generalization cannot take place on a given stimulus dimension if the relevant receptor does not respond differentially to variability in that dimension; for example, organisms which are colorblind, i.e., those whose light receptors do not yield differential responses to variations in wave length of light, can hardly be expected to show a generalization gradient along this stimulus dimension.

Hull then postulated the presence of an "afferent generalization continuum" which he defined as being "the differential afferent response (s) corresponding in varying degrees to variation in a given stimulus continuum." This continuum is contrasted to the stimulus dimension which respresents a continuum of different physical energies. Furthermore, Hull pointed out that although there was a relationship between these two continua, the relationship was not perfect, citing the octave effect found when auditory stimuli were used. He did believe, however, that the afferent gen-

[6] Using a discriminated operant learning situation, Thomas, Ost, and Thomas (1960) were unable to obtain results consistent with those which have been presented. In this study, three groups of pigeons were trained to peck at a 550 mμ hue and not to respond to one of 570 mμ. Positive and negative stimuli were provided in a random order with discrimination training being provided until the subject reached a criterion of five successive periods in which no responses were made to the nonreinforced stimulus although the subject continued to respond when the reinforced stimulus was presented. Group I was tested for stimulus generalization the day following training, and Group II was tested seven days later. A third group was tested 21 days later. The test situation consisted of presenting 11 stimuli (stimuli used in the training were not used) ranging from 490 to 610 mμ in 10 mμ steps. The investigators found no difference in the shape of the generalization gradient as a function of when the generalization test was presented. Two procedural differences between this study and the others should be noted. One is that Thomas, Ost, and, Thomas had their subjects learn a discrimination task; the second difference is that they used no immediate testing group—the earliest test was 24 hours following training.

eralization continuum was best expressed by the discrimination threshold or jnd's.

From Hull's analysis of the role of stimulus discriminability and stimulus generalization gradients, one should expect to find a relationship between the discriminability of varying stimuli which make up a stimulus dimension and the characteristics of the stimulus generalization gradient.

In an early study, Guttman and Kalish (1956) attempted to examine this relationship. They noted that for both the pigeon and human the ease of discriminating two colors which are separated by a constant frequency is not constant over the spectrum. By an appropriate selection of conditioned stimulus values, the investigators reasoned that it should be possible to produce a set of curves whose slopes should reflect the ease (or difficulty) of the discrimination demanded of the subject. If two stimuli are difficult to discriminate, the generalization gradient should be relatively flat; but if two other stimuli are easy to discriminate, the gradient should be steep. The free operant situation with pigeons pecking at an illuminated disc was used. Subjects were divided into four groups, and each group was trained on a different CS (530, 550, 580, or 600 mμ). Following training, test trials were provided in which the wavelengths presented to each group were variable but in general ranged from 470 mμ to 640 mμ.

An examination of the four generalization gradients obtained with varying conditioned stimuli is presented in Figure 12–16, along with the discriminability function of the stimuli as measured in both humans and pigeons. There is little similarity between the two functions; thus, the results do not support the hypothesized relationship between the characteristics of the gradient and the discriminability function. For example, when a CS of 530 mμ was used it would be expected that a 510 mμ stimulus should elicit almost as many responses as the original CS since the pigeons' discriminability function reveals that the pigeons had considerable difficulty in discriminating between these stimuli. An examination of the number of responses made, however, reveals a sharp decrement. On the other hand, the discriminability function indicates that a difference between a 620 and a 630 mμ stimulus is quite marked, but an examination of the number of responses made to these stimuli indicates little difference between them.

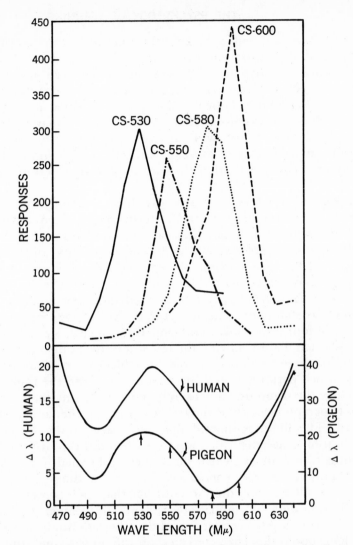

Fig. 12–16. The upper curve illustrates the mean generalization gradients obtained for the four experimental groups, each trained to respond to a different CS. The lower curve presents hue discrimination as a function of wavelength for pigeons, as adapted from data provided by Hamilton and Coleman (1933) and for humans, as adapted from data provided by Boring, Langfeld, and Weld (1948). *Adapted from Guttman and Kalish (1956)*

The failure to find a relationship between the discriminability and generalization function is puzzling. It may be, however, that the hypothesized relationship between discriminability and generalization is incorrect. Or, it may mean that the difference thresholds obtained in the pigeon are not accurately depicted. Or, as an extension of this latter point, it may be that discriminability of stimuli will vary as a function of the testing conditions and one cannot assume that because two stimuli are discriminable in one situation they are necessarily discriminable in another.

Kalish (1958) a few years later was able, however, to support the predicted relationship. In this experiment, a procedure similar to that which had been used in the Guttman and Kalish (1956) study was employed, although college students rather than pigeons served as subjects. The procedure consisted of presenting one stimulus as a standard, and the subject was instructed to view it and to try to remember it.[7] Hues of 500, 530, 560, and 580 mμ were used as standards. The test stimuli which were presented consisted of four hues above and below the standard, separated by intervals of ten mμ. In general, the test stimulus was presented for a period of three seconds, followed by a blackout of five to ten seconds which permitted the experimenter to record the response and change the stimulus. Subjects responded by lifting their hand from a telegraph key only if the test stimulus was the same as the standard. The findings showed that the shape of the stimulus generalization gradients which were obtained did conform to the discriminability curves which have been obtained for other human subjects. Kalish concluded that the findings provided "striking evidence for the supposition that the processes of generalization and discrimination, as generally defined, bear an inverse relationship to each other and that they are fundamentally dependent upon the characteristics of the underlying continuum."

Thomas and Mitchell (1962) have essentially replicated and confirmed Kalish's (1958) findings; Ganz (1962) using monkeys as subjects has also obtained a stimulus generalization gradient which was related to the monkeys' discriminability function.

[7] It should be noted that the procedure employed by Kalish (1958) using human subjects differed from the procedure used with pigeons in that the tendency to respond to the standard stimulus was created by instructions rather than by reinforced trials.

Generalization of Inhibition

This examination of stimulus generalization has been limited primarily to studies in which a stimulus has been reinforced during training, with the test situation examining the strength of the organism's response to other stimuli. One can conceive of these experiments as reflecting the generalization of excitatory tendencies built up by the reinforced trials.

A number of investigators also have demonstrated that generalization gradients can be obtained when the basic operation is one of nonreinforcement. In such instances, it has been assumed that there is the generalization of inhibition. An early study demonstrating such an effect was performed by Hovland (1937). In this study, subjects received a number of CS-UCS pairings in which different auditory stimuli served as the CS (153, 468, 1,000, 1,967 cps) and shock served as the UCS to elicit a GSR. In effect, GSR's were conditioned to each tone. An extinction series was then provided by presenting either the highest or lowest tone 16 times without reinforcement. Following the extinction series, a generalization test was made which consisted of presenting the four tones in a counterbalanced order. When the response strength to each tone was examined, decreased responding as a function of the locus of the test stimuli was noted. Figure 12–17 illustrates the gradient obtained in this study.

Studies of this general variety have not been as numerous as generalization of excitation studies, although Ellson (1938), Youtz (1939), Kling (1952), Grice and Goldman (1955), Honig (1961), and Kalish and Haber (1963) have all demonstrated such effects.

Kling (1952) utilized an instrumental response situation similar to that previously employed by Grice and Saltz (1950). In Kling's study, rats were trained to obtain food pellets by opening a small door placed in the center of a circle at the end of a runway. Each subject was given training on two circles of varying areas. Eight groups were employed, and each group was trained on one of the following area combinations: 79–20, 79–32, 79–50, 79–79, 20–79, 20–50, 20–32, or 20–20 cm. Each animal was provided 45 reinforced trials to one circle and 45 reinforced trials to the other. The response to the first circle of the training pair was then extinguished; the extinction criterion was no response on four out of five consecutive trials for two consecutive days. Following the

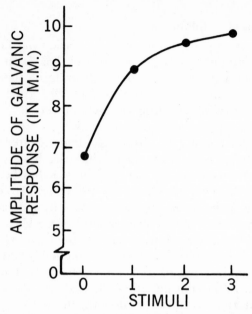

Fig. 12–17. Generalization of inhibition. All stimuli were provided reinforced trials, but only Stimulus 0 was given sixteen extinction trials. The test for generalization of inhibition consisted of presenting the four tones in a counterbalanced order. *Adapted from Hovland (1937)*

attainment of this criterion, generalization of extinction was examined by presenting the second circle of the training pair. Generalization gradients plotted in terms of the median latencies of the first response are indicated in Figure 12–18.

The Role of Discrimination Training

Many investigators have examined how discrimination training in general, and varieties thereof in particular, influence the nature of the generalization gradient. In one of the early studies, Hanson (1959) provided four groups of pigeons with discrimination training in which a 550 mμ hue served as the positive stimulus, with the negative stimulus being either 555, 560, 570, or 590 mμ. Such discrimination training was not provided to a control group, which was trained to respond only to the presentation of a 550 mμ hue. All groups were trained under a variable interval reinforcement schedule. Following the training sessions,

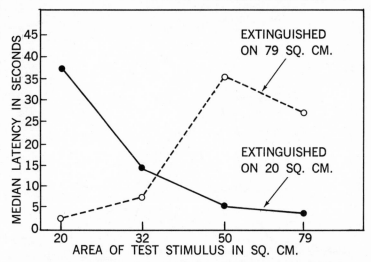

Fig. 12–18. Generalization functions, showing median latency to the first response for each group on the test trials. *Adapted from Kling (1952)*

the subjects were given tests for generalization in which the test stimuli used for all subjects were 13 hues: 480, 500, 510, 520, 530, 540, 550, 560, 570, 580, 590, 600, and 620 mμ.

A basic finding was that the amount of training required to reach the discrimination criterion (no responding to five consecutive presentations of the negative stimulus, but continued responding to the positive) was a function of the amount of the difference between the positive and negative stimulus. As might be anticipated, as the difference between the two stimuli grew smaller, the amount of training needed to reach the criterion grew larger. The generalization gradients for the varying groups are indicated in Figure 12–19, and it can be noted that the control group, which did not have the benefit of discrimination training, produced a different type of gradient than that obtained with other groups. In general, the gradient increased in steepness as the value for the negative stimulus approached the value of the positive stimulus.

Hanson's (1959) results have been supported by Thomas (1962) who has also found that discrimination training produces a general steepening of the stimulus generalization gradient. Thomas also examined the role of drive level, but differences in

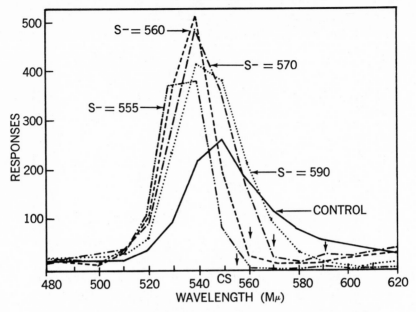

Fig. 12–19. Mean generalization gradients for the control and four discrimination groups, identified by the values of the negative stimulus. Arrows indicate the positions of the negative stimuli. *Adapted from Hanson (1959)*

responding among three groups of pigeons which had been maintained at either 60, 70, or 80 per cent of their normal weight could not be demonstrated at a statistically acceptable level of confidence.

The discrimination training which Hanson (1959) and other investigators utilized involved reinforcing one stimulus and not reinforcing a second. Hanson (1961) and Thomas and Williams (1963) have extended this area of inquiry by using a three-stimulus discrimination training situation. In Hanson's (1961) study, one group of pigeons was given discrimination training in which a 550 mμ light served as the rewarded stimulus but the presentations of 540 and 560 mμ lights were not reinforced. Discrimination training continued until subjects met a criterion of complete suppression of response to both the nonreinforced stimuli for three successive presentations of each negative stimulus. A control group was trained to respond only to the 550 mμ light. Following training, twelve generalization test sessions were

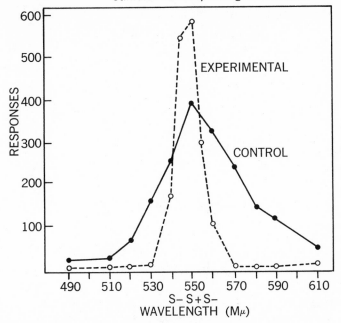

Fig. 12–20. Mean generalization gradients for a control group not given discrimination training and an experimental group trained on a discrimination with the 550 mμ stimulus reinforced and the 540 and 560 mμ stimuli not reinforced. *Adapted from Hanson (1961)*

provided which consisted of the random presentation of 11 or 13 stimuli ranging from 490 mμ to 610 mμ. The stimuli used for the control group were 490, 510, 520, 530, 540, 550, 560, 570, 580, 590, and 610 mμ. The same stimuli as well as two others, 545 and 555 mμ, were used for the experimental group. The results showed, as Figure 12–20 indicates, a relatively symmetrical gradient for both groups of subjects, although responding by the experimental group was essentially restricted to those stimuli bounded by the two nonreinforced stimuli.[8]

In contrast to Hanson's discrimination procedure, which employed a single positive stimulus and two negative stimuli,

[8] An interesting phenomenon which this study reveals is that the response to the CS (550 mμ) was significantly greater for the experimental group than it was for the control. Such increased responding during the generalization test appears to be a product of the discrimination training which is provided the experimental group and has been called a contrast effect. See Reynolds (1961, 1961a).

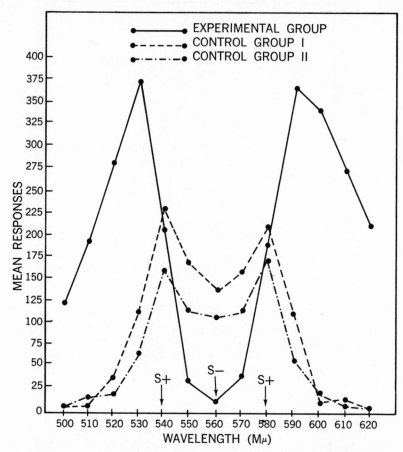

Fig. 12–21. The mean generalization gradients of the experimental and control groups. The control groups were not given discrimination training. The experimental group was trained on a discrimination with the 540 and 580 mμ stimulus being reinforced and the 560 mμ stimulus not reinforced. *Adapted from Thomas and Williams (1963)*

Thomas and Williams (1963) employed a single negative stimulus surrounded by two positive stimuli. Their general procedure closely paralleled Hanson's. Pigeons were trained to respond to a 540 and 580 mμ light and to withhold responding to a 560 mμ hue. The two control groups were trained to respond only to the positive stimuli. The only difference between these groups was that one was given a total of ten training sessions whereas the

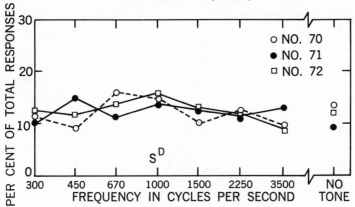

Fig. 12–22. Generalization gradients following nondifferential training with a 1,000 cps tone as the reinforced stimulus. *Adapted from Jenkins and Harrison (1960)*

other was given 22. Following training, the generalization test consisted of the presentation of 13 stimuli ranging from 500 mμ through 620 mμ in 10 mμ steps. Eight test series were provided. The generalization gradients for the experimental group and the control groups are presented in Figure 12–21.

Jenkins and Harrison (1960) have examined the influence of discrimination training on generalization gradients when auditory stimuli are employed. In their first experiment, control subjects (pigeons) learned to peck a key on a variable interval reinforcement schedule to the continuous presentation of a 1,000 cps tone. Experimental subjects received discrimination training consisting of periods in which the 1,000 cps tone was presented and reinforced on a variable interval reinforcement schedule and other training periods during which no tone was presented and responses which were made were not reinforced. Reinforced and nonreinforced periods for the experimental group were presented in a random order; daily training sessions continued until the average rate of response during the reinforced sessions was at least four times greater than that obtained during nonreinforced periods. In testing for generalization, eight test stimuli were presented which consisted of seven tones approximately equally spaced along a logarithmic scale of frequency (300, 450, 670, 1,000, 1,500, 2,250, 3,500 cps) and a no-tone presentation. The percentage of responses made to each test stimulus for the control

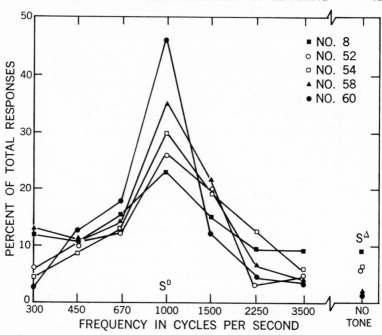

Fig. 12–23. Generalization gradients following discrimination training in which a 1,000 cps tone served as the reinforced stimulus and no tone was nonreinforced. *Adapted from Jenkins and Harrison (1960)*

subjects is indicated in Figure 12–22, and the generalization gradients for five subjects who were given discrimination training are indicated in Figure 12–23.

The flat gradient produced by the control subjects is in contrast to the reasonably well defined gradients obtained by a nondiscrimination training procedure when visual stimuli are used —see the performance of the control group in Figure 12–17. In attempting to account for the different findings, Jenkins and Harrison have written, "Since the training procedures appear to be the same in all important respects it may be concluded that the difference lies in the use of visual—as compared with an auditory stimulus. It does not appear that a lack of physiological capacity to detect or to make discriminations among auditory stimuli can account for the contrast in the results obtained with visual and with auditory stimuli."

A second experiment was designed to examine further generalization gradients using auditory stimuli. In this study, a three-stimulus discrimination training procedure was utilized in which the experimental group was reinforced when tones of either of two frequencies (450 or 2,500 cps) were presented but responses during a no-tone presentation were not reinforced. Control subjects were not given discrimination training. With this group, tones of 450 and 2,500 cps were presented and always reinforced. Following training, generalization tests were made with the following tones: 250, 450, 670, 1,000, 1,500, 2,500, 4,000 cps, and of course, no tone. The results showed that (1) the gradient which was obtained by the control group was similar to that obtained in the first experiment and (2) the discrimination training resulted in producing a bi-winged gradient with responses being maximal to the tones which were reinforced during training. In this regard, the findings are similar to those obtained by Thomas and Williams (1963) who used visual stimulation.

The Role of Experience

The final variable to be considered is the role of experience. One might ask how the role of experience contributes to the form of the generalization gradient. Peterson (1962) and Ganz and Riesen (1962) have attempted to answer this question from the results of their studies.

In the Peterson (1962) study, four ducklings were raised in white-walled cages which were illuminated by a monochromatic light of 589 mμ. As a result, these animals were exposed to only a narrow range of colors. Two other ducklings were raised in a regular laboratory environment in which typical tungsten filament lamps were used to illuminate the cages. All ducklings were deprived of water for 22 hours and trained to peck at a key which was illuminated by a light of 589 mμ frequency. Following 15 conditioning sessions in which a variable interval schedule was utilized, a test for stimulus generalization was conducted in which eight different wavelengths ranging from 490 mμ to 650 mμ were used to illuminate the pecking key. Results for the test sessions are indicated in Figure 12–24 and show that for the four ducklings raised in monochromatic light a flat gradient best describes the findings. On the other hand, the frequently found decremental gradient was obtained for the two subjects raised in the normal environment.

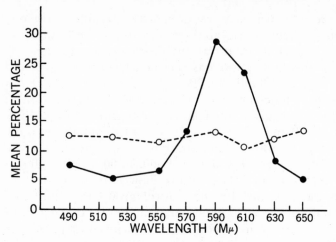

Fig. 12–24. Stimulus generalization gradients obtained for the birds raised in a monochromatic environment (broken line) and for the birds raised in an environment whose chromaticity was not controlled (solid line). *Adapted from Peterson (1962)*

In the Ganz and Riesen (1962) study, one group of infant monkeys was reared in total darkness and a second group was raised in a normally illuminated and visually patterned environment. At ten weeks of age, the experienced subjects joined the naïve group in the darkroom environment. Both groups were then trained to make a key-press response during the presentation of one monochromatic stimulus which was reinforced by a sucrose solution and not to respond during a 15-second blackout interval. During training, the left eye of each subject was covered by a black occluder so that the stimulus exposure was always monocular. This training period took a relatively long time, requiring an average of more than three months for the naïve group and approximately two months for the experienced group.[9]

Following training, generalization tests were administered over seven days, with each test period consisting of the presentation of seven monochromatic hues, one of which was the previously reinforced stimulus. The number of key presses made to the CS and generalized stimuli over the seven-day test period is indicated in Figure 12–25. The group reared in darkness provides

---

[9] It is possible, of course, that the long training period during which the experienced group was confined to the darkroom did much to provide this group with a visual experience similar to that provided the naïve group.

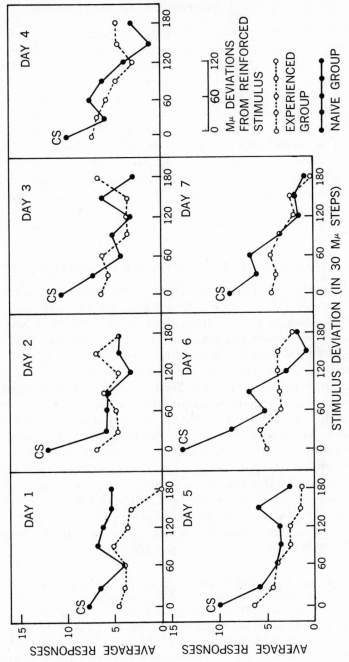

Fig. 12–25. Generalization gradients on seven testing days. *Adapted from Ganz and Riesen (1962)*

a somewhat flatter gradient than the experienced group for the first day of testing—a finding in keeping with that obtained by Peterson (1962). One might be tempted to assume that because the animals lacked visual experience they did not learn to make discriminations among visual stimuli which, in turn, resulted in a flat generalization gradient. But contrary to such a position are the findings obtained for the six experimental days following the first. It can be noted that the naïve group's responses produce the typical decremental gradient—a gradient which is steeper than that obtained by the experienced group. Thus, the role that experience plays in determining the shape of the generalization gradient seems to be quite complex.

INTERPRETATIONS OF STIMULUS GENERALIZATION

A number of points of view can be taken in interpreting stimulus generalization. The first is one which considers stimulus generalization as a term which describes an empirical phenomenon. Brown, Bilodeau, and Baron (1951), for example, have considered the construct within this framework and have written, "The empirical phenomenon of stimulus generalization is simply this: an organism that has been trained (or instructed) to respond to a designated stimulus will also respond, under certain specifiable conditions, to formerly neutral stimuli on which no training has been given (or to stimuli to which responses have been prohibited by instructions)...." This is undoubtedly the least controversial position, since it conceptualizes stimulus generalization as a kind of transfer of training situation.

A second position, posited by Lashley and Wade (1946), has become known as "a failure of discrimination" hypothesis. A somewhat similar proposal has been presented by Prokasy and Hall (1963). Lashley and Wade pointed out (p. 81) that

"stimulus generalization" is generalization only in the sense of failure to note distinguishing characteristics of the stimulus or to associate them with the conditioned reaction. A definite attribute of the stimulus is "abstracted" and forms the basis of reaction; other attributes are either not sensed at all or are disregarded. So long as the effective attribute is present, the reaction is elicited as an all or none function of that attribute. Other characteristics of the stimulus may be radically changed without affecting the reaction.

A further point that these investigators have made is that the gradient of stimulus generalization is a product of the test period and develops as a result of the subject's attention being directed to the relevant stimulus dimension. Thus, no decremental generalization gradient will be noted unless the CS is contrasted with a generalized stimulus so that the relevant stimulus dimension is made manifest to the subject. Lashley and Wade have specifically suggested that the method of single stimulus training, followed by a single test with the generalized stimulus, represents a crucial test of their position.

Most investigators, however, have adopted the position of Hull (1943) who posited that stimulus generalization was a basic organismic process arising from the reinforcement procedure. The generalization process was given particular prominence in resolving what Hull called the "stimulus-learning" and "stimulus-evocation" paradoxes.

A basic assumption made in the Hullian system was that a bond was established between a very specific stimulus and a response. Hull indicated, however, that the "flux of the world to which organisms must adapt has infinite variety, and therefore stimuli, especially conditioned stimuli, are never exactly repeated. . . . Since the stimuli are not exactly repeated, how can more than one reinforcement occur?" This, then, was the stimulus-learning paradox. It might be assumed, of course, that it was possible for a single reinforcement to produce a bond of maximum strength, but even if such a possibility did exist, a second question could be raised, How could such a stimulus ever again evoke a response since the exact stimulus to which the response had been conditioned would never again be encountered? This was the stimulus-evocation paradox.

By using the stimulus generalization process Hull was able to answer both questions. A response which was involved in the original learning situation became attached to a considerable zone of stimuli other than, but adjacent to, the stimulus present in the original learning. Thus, learning or habit strength was built up between these generalized stimuli and the organism's response. Moreover, such habit strength summated in order to

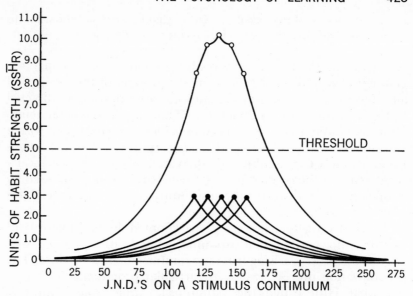

Fig. 12–26. Graph showing how the subthreshold primary stimulus generalization gradients from five distinct points on a stimulus continuum theoretically may summate to superthreshold values not only at the points of reinforcement but at neighboring points which have not been reinforced at all. Solid circles represent the results of single reinforcements; hollow circles represent the results of summation. The reaction threshold is arbitrarily taken at five. *Adapted from Hull (1943)*

produce a response of greater than threshold value. Figure 12–26 reveals how Hull (1943) conceptualized the summation of sub-threshold primary stimulus generalization gradients from five points in order to produce an overt response.[10]

A second point of interest in the Hullian system was the distinction between primary and secondary stimulus generalization. In primary generalization, it was assumed that the similarity dimension of the stimulus was, a product of the innate characteristics of the organism; in secondary generalization, it was assumed that the similarity dimension had been acquired through previous learning.

In contrast to Lashley and Wade (1946), supporters of the Hullian position have denied that subjects are unable to discrimi-

[10] Tests of Hull's summation hypothesis have confirmed it only in part. See Bilodeau, Brown, and Merryman (1956), and Kalish and Guttman (1957).

nate among the stimuli which are used in the test situation. The studies conducted by Hovland in which auditory stimuli used in the generalization test were 25 to 50 jnd's apart have been used to support this point of view. Moreover, a number of other experiments have been cited in which the confusion of stimuli, at least on common sense grounds, appears unlikely. Kimble (1961), for example, has called attention to the studies of Bass and Hull (1934) and Brown, Bilodeau, and Baron (1951) to support the position that generalization does not arise from the subject's failure to discriminate among stimuli. Bass and Hull (1934) obtained a stimulus generalization gradient when a GSR, originally conditioned to a tactual stimulus presented on the shoulder, was obtained when the stimulus was presented on the calf of the leg. Brown, Bilodeau, and Baron (1951) instructed individuals to lift their finger to one light and then found that responses were made when a light several inches away from the original one was presented.

Razran (1949) has taken a third position by proposing a two-factor theory of stimulus generalization which indicates that there is (1) pseudo-generalization and (2) true generalization. The first is accounted for by the organism's failure to discriminate among the varying stimuli which are presented during the test situation and correlates negatively with organismic capacity. True generalization, on the other hand, is a positive capacity of the organism and consists of an ability to generalize absolute characteristics of stimuli.[11]

Recently, Mednick and Freedman (1960) have proposed a "unit hypothesis" in which it is suggested that the extent of a subject's response to a given test stimulus is proportional to the number of stimulus units that separate the training stimulus from the generalized stimuli (GS). The number of stimulus units is defined in terms of the population of stimuli the subject has experienced within the immediate experimental situation. Thus, they have written (p. 195), "Let us say that in an experiment on pitch generalization, Stimulus 0 is 1000 cps and one S receives a 1400 cps GS and another S receives an 1800 cps GS on the first test trial. For each S in terms of his experience in the experimental situation, his GS will be only one unit removed from Stimulus 0." The prediction made from the hypothesis would be that

[11] Razran (1963) has modified this point of view, but his position was presented so recently that it could not be included in this discussion.

response strength to the 1,400 and 1,800 cps stimuli should be equivalent. With continued testing, the subject's GS unit hierarchy should change as he experiences the full range of GS used in the experiment.

Mednick and Freedman have pointed out that the unit hypothesis predictions tend to break down at the extremes of the stimulus continuum being tested. A subject trained to respond to 50 cps and tested at 20,000 cps will not behave the same as a subject trained at 50 cps and tested at 100 cps, despite the fact that the test stimulus is one unit of separation away in both cases.[12]

It does not appear that any of the theoretical explanations for stimulus generalization can satisfactorily account for all of the experimental findings which have been reported. As noted with the problem of reinforcement, it seems appropriate to conceive of stimulus generalization as an empirical phenomenon, with future research being directed toward examining basic parameters within a specific type of learning situation and with a standard methodological procedure for testing.

However, two fundamental considerations should be mentioned in examining this concept. First, it does appear that the stimulus generalization gradient is related to the discriminability of the stimuli which are used in the generalization test. But it should be recognized that because two stimuli have been judged to be discriminable in one situation does not necessarily mean they are discriminable in another. For example, Hovland (1937, 1937a, 1937b, 1937c) used a psychophysical scaling procedure to determine the discriminability of tones which varied in loudness and pitch. He then used these tones in his generalization studies, assuming that tones which were discriminable in a psychophysical experiment were equally discriminable in the conditioning study. But Slivinske and Hall (1960) have obtained experimental evidence to indicate that the tones which Hovland had selected for loudness were not absolutely discriminable in a situation which paralleled the conditioning experiment.

In the Brown, Bilodeau, and Baron (1951) study, subjects were instructed to lift their finger to the lighting of the center one of seven spatially arranged lamps but not to respond to the lighting of any of the others. Following a series of training trials in

[12] Gewirtz, Jones, and Waerneryd (1956) and Thomas and Hiss (1963) have been unable to obtain findings which support the unit hypothesis.

responding to the center lamp, the other lamps were lighted in a random order and the number of responses made to these lamps was recorded. The response frequencies plotted against the spatial position of the stimulus revealed a relatively smooth, symmetrical generalization gradient.

There is no doubt that the subjects were capable of discriminating among the various locations of the lamps but the point to be stressed is that the instructions which were given emphasized that the subject should respond as rapidly as possible and ignore false responses. Thus, the discriminability of the stimuli was a function of the situation. Had the instructions emphasized accuracy, as well as unlimited time to respond, it is highly probable that no "gradient" would have been obtained. In fact, the investigators have acknowledged such a position by stating, "If the subjects had been instructed to take plenty of time in responding . . . it is relatively certain that no false responses would have been observed."

All this leads to the general position that although stimuli can be discriminated under one set of circumstances it does not mean that they can be discriminated under another set.

The second consideration concerns the nature of the effective stimulus. It will be recalled that in Chapter 1 attention was called to the problem of defining the effective stimulus in an experiment. Most investigators who are interested in conditioning have assumed that the effective stimulus in the learning of a CR is the CS. If the experimenter presents a 1,000 cps 70 db tone to a subject, it is believed that the effective stimulus is isomorphic to the tone's physical characteristics. There is, however, no reason to assume that the experimenter's delineation of a physical event is the same as a subject's perception of it. What represents an important dimension of the physical event to the experimenter may not exist as a part of the effective stimulus to the subject. It is possible, also, that a subject may perceive aspects of the stimulus situation which have been ignored by or are unknown to the experimenter.

In keeping with the problems involved in specifying the effective stimulus, Prokasy and Hall (1963) have called attention to the fact that in many of the generalization studies, and particularly in those which employ the GSR, a change in the environmental situation which is produced by presentation of the CS provides a stimulus attribute or dimension to which the organism may be responding. As indicated in Chapter 2, frequently there is great difficulty in differentiating responses obtained using pseudoconditioning procedures from responses obtained by regular conditioning methods.

RESPONSE GENERALIZATION

A logical continuation of the examination of stimulus generalization is the examination of its counterpart, response generalization. An early example of response generalization is found in the work of Bechterev (1932) who wrote ". . . that if a dog is prevented from realizing an association reflex in that extremity in which it has been inculcated, it is replaced in the extremity of the other side."

Hull (1943) did not consider the topic of response generalization in his *Principles of Behavior,* but an extended presentation of the Hullian position is found in a study by Arnold (1945) who used one of Hull's unpublished manuscripts. Hull assumed that ". . . each reinforcement sets up connections between each point of the stimulus zone and all the points of an analogous zone of *contraction intensities* and, possible, of contraction speeds of each muscle concerned in the reaction of the reinforcement process." Contraction intensity and rate were considered as response dimensions analogous to the stimulus dimension of intensity and frequency used in stimulus generalization studies.[13]

A distinction was also made between primary and secondary response generalization. As noted previously, intensity and speed of contraction represented dimensions found with primary response generalization; secondary response generalization, it was assumed, was mediated by the habit family hierarchy. This construct was viewed as the potentiality of a number of alternative behavior patterns which lead from a given stimulus situation to a given reinforcement. Although these varying behavior patterns differ in habit strength, they are equivalent in the sense that they are interchangeable in the attainment of reinforcement.

Arnold's (1945) experiment investigating primary response generalization consisted of examining the downward intensity of a lever-pressing response in rats when a minimum push of 30 or 60

[13] The reader should note the similarity between this position and that taken by Logan (1960) presented in Chapter 1.

grams was required for each reinforcement. A tabulation of the pressures exerted by an animal in making these responses indicated that a distribution was obtained around a mean pressure which was somewhat greater than that required to actuate the mechanism. Presumably the varying response pressures reflected a response generalization gradient.

An example of secondary response generalization is found in the studies of Wickens (1938, 1939, 1943). In Wickens' first study, finger withdrawal, which utilized an extensor movement, was conditioned to a buzzer with shock serving as the UCS. Following such training, the hand was turned over so that a flexor movement, rather than extensor, had to be made in order to withdraw the finger from the electrode. With the hand in this new position, the CS was presented. Ten out of 18 subjects responded by making the appropriate movement (flexor) in this new situation, and the remaining subjects made such a movement after only a very few reinforced trials. In a second part of this study, following the establishment of the conditioned extensor response, the hand was turned over and the flexor response was extinguished. Then the hand was turned to its original position and the CS presented. It was found that extinguishing the flexor response served either to inhibit or depress the extensor response.

In a second study [Wickens (1939)], an extensor movement of the finger of the right hand was conditioned to a buzzer with shock serving as the UCS. Following the subject's learning to respond to the buzzer, the process of differentiation was begun in which the presentation of a bell was not followed by shock but the buzzer was presented with shock. After a number of trials, differentiation had become sufficiently stable that the subject was consistently failing to respond to the bell and was equally consistent in responding to the buzzer. Following this, the subject's hand was turned over so that a flexor rather than an extensor movement had to be made to remove the finger from the electrode. The test for transference was then made in which the buzzer and bell were each presented ten times in a random order but were never accompanied by shock. Seven subjects participated, for a total of 70 presentations of the buzzer and 70 presentations of the bell. Results indicated that only two responses out of 70 were made to the bell but 45 were made to the buzzer.

Most contemporary investigators who have examined response

generalization have adopted an empirical definition of the concept: If Response B is associated with Stimulus A, other responses similar to B have a greater than chance probability of being elicited by A. The influence of response generalization has been inferred from performance changes which accompany the manipulation of material along a response similarity dimension.

Underwood frequently has used the response generalization concept in order to account for certain classes of responses found in the verbal learning situation. For example, in one study [Underwood (1948a)] subjects learned two lists of paired-associates in which the material was two-syllable adjectives. The lists were so constructed that two responses had to be learned to the same stimulus. Either one minute, 5, 24, or 48 hours after learning these lists, the subject was asked to respond to the stimulus words with one of the responses which he had learned. If no response was given within ten seconds, the subject was asked, "What response does this stimulus make you think of?" If no response was elicited in 20 seconds, the subject was instructed to give any word which occurred to him. Although one of the two responses which appeared on the previously learned lists occurred most frequently, in a number of cases responses were given which were similar to one of the responses which had been learned. Examples of this would be the subject's saying, "inane" instead of "witless," "gaiety" instead of "festive," or "misty" instead of "filmy." The most reasonable interpretation of these findings, Underwood concluded, was the positing of a response generalization process.

In a second study by Underwood and Hughes (1950), subjects learned a list of ten dissimilar adjectives as responses to ten dissimilar nonsense syllables. One week after learning, the ten stimuli were presented and the subject was asked to give a response to each. Judges scaled the errors which were made during the learning and recall sessions along several dimensions of similarity to the correct responses. Errors which had the highest degree of scaled similarity to the correct responses occurred most frequently, thus providing a gradient of response generalization.

Morgan and Underwood (1950) have hypothesized that the reinforcement of a specific response during the learning of a task results in the strengthening of similar responses—a process which they have referred to as parasitic reinforcement. Their finding of increasing facilitation in the learning of a second list of verbal materials following the learning of a first list, with increasing response synonymity between the two lists, has been used as evidence to support this position.[14]

Duncan (1953, 1955) has employed a perceptual-motor task to examine the operation of response generalization. The task was one in which the subject responded to a colored light by moving a lever, grasped by the right hand, into a slot. The apparatus contained six slots, 60 degrees apart, arranged as radii of a circle and six differently colored lights presented on a ground glass screen. The subject had to learn to associate a given colored light with a particular slot. In one study, Duncan (1953) gave subjects either 10, 40, 80, or 180 trials with one combination of light–slot pairings. Following these trials, he had them learn a second task in which different pairings of lights and slots were provided. For one condition (low similarity), all six lights and slots were paired in new combinations. For a second condition (medium similarity), four lights were paired with different slots, and two light–slot combinations remained the same. For the third condition (high similarity), only two lights were paired with different slots, and four light–slot combinations remained the same. Duncan found that the learning of the second task increased as a function of the amount of learning provided on the first task and the amount of similarity between the first and second tasks. He has argued that response generalization was at least partially responsible for the positive transfer which was obtained. In a second study [Duncan (1955)], the frequency of errors made by subjects in the original learning of this perceptual-motor task was demonstrated to be a function of the spatial similarity of the correct to the incorrect response.[15] Again the response generalization process was posited in order to account for the findings.

[14] Duncan (1955) has suggested, as an alternative to the hypothesis that generalized responses are strengthened by parasitic reinforcement, the possibility that the extinction or relative weakening is greater for generalized responses which are less similar to the correct response. As he has written, ". . . instead of assuming that more similar generalized responses are more strengthened by parasitic reinforcement, we could assume that less similar generalized responses are more rapidly extinguished."

[15] It should be noted that this finding was evident during only the last ten trials of a 60-trial training period.

13

Theory and Controversy in Some Selected Learning Situations

THE APPROACH TAKEN IN DISCUSSING learning situations has been primarily a functional one in that the contribution of empirical variables to the learning process has been emphasized. Although theoretical issues have been considered from time to time, they have not played an important part in the discussion. It would not be correct, however, to leave the reader with the impression that theory has played a minor role in the psychology of learning. On the contrary, it would be possible, as some writers have done, e.g., Hilgard (1956), to examine learning almost exclusively from this point of view. In this chapter some of the theoretical issues and controversies which have arisen in the course of analyzing certain kinds of learning situations will be discussed.

MAZE LEARNING

The Problem of Sensory Control

With the introduction of the rat as a laboratory animal, many early investigators became interested in examining which sense organ the animal used to learn the maze. One of the earliest studies was performed by Small (1901) who reported that blind rats were as efficient in learning a maze (a modified Hampton Court maze) as normal rats. As a result, he concluded that when a rat learned a maze it was not learned with visual cues but, rather, on the basis of tactual-motor or kinesthetic processes. The actual learning consisted of the association of the motor image of turning in one direction with success and the motor image of turning in another direction with failure.

Watson's (1907) early monograph also was devoted to an examination of the sense organs used by the rat in maze learning. His general procedure was to exclude one sense organ at a time and then determine whether rats which had been so deprived could learn the maze as quickly as normal animals. Visual sensitivity was eliminated either by removing the animal's eyeballs—an operation from which the animal recovers quite rapidly —or by darkening the room. Hearing was eliminated by removing the eardrum and ossicles and filling the middle ear with wax, and the olfactory bulbs were removed to eliminate the sense of smell. The elimination of some tactual stimulation was accomplished by anesthetizing the soles of the animal's feet and cutting off the vibrissae.

Watson's findings indicated that blind or anosmic rats could learn a maze as rapidly as normal animals; that animals which were deaf learned as rapidly as animals with normal hearing; that rats which had the soles of their feet anesthetized or vibrissae removed learned as readily as animals without such sensory deficits. As Small (1901) had concluded some years earlier, Watson (1907) wrote, "The white rat makes the correct turns in the maze on the basis of intra-organic sensations—the kinesthetic sensations coupled with the organic probably, and possibly with the static." The learning of the maze was conceptualized to be a chain of kinesthetically released movements, with one movement automatically leading to the next until the food box was reached.

Certainly by contemporary standards, Watson's study suffered from many limitations. Only a single response measure—running time—was used, and relatively few animals comprised each group. Only a single animal, for example, had more than a single sense organ eliminated. Although this blind, anosmic, and vibrissaeless rat had difficulty in learning the maze, Watson attributed such difficulty to poor motivation rather than to a sensory deficit. But Watson recognized limitations in his study. One was the difficulty in accounting for an obvious increase in the number of errors made by his subjects when the maze was rotated. If kinesthetic stimuli were the only cues involved in the animal's learning the maze, rotation of the maze should not result in making the learning more difficult. Watson also was aware that other learning situations might emphasize external cues which, of course, would provide a different pattern of findings.

In the large number of experiments which followed Watson's, many of which were specifically designed to test his hypothesis, these limitations were forgotten. Studies by Vincent (1915), Walton (1930), Robinson and Wever (1930), and Snygg (1935) all revealed that the rat could learn on the basis of only visual cues, and experiments by Lashley and Ball (1929) and Ingebritsen (1932) indicated that if the kinesthetic sense was eliminated by an operative technique the animals were still capable of learning. This operation consisted of transecting the afferent path going from the muscle of the trunk and legs up the dorsal column of the spinal cord. The effect was to produce a dragging of legs and sprawling gait in the animal which provided evidence of poor kinesthetic sensitivity. Ingebritsen's (1932) experiment revealed that rats which underwent this operation before training learned the maze as rapidly as normal animals, whereas Lashley and Ball's (1929) study indicated that animals which had learned a maze prior to such an operation were capable of running it almost perfectly after surgery.

Hunter (1930) pointed out that Watson's conclusions did not necessarily follow from his data. Thus, Hunter wrote (p. 460):

> Let us now suppose that Watson had eliminated proprioception from otherwise normal animals. This was logically his next step. It is possible, I think probable, from the above results and others that these rats would have mastered the maze. Watson's line of argument would then have compelled him to conclude that the maze habit is not controlled by any sensory process, since each in turn can be dispensed with.

Honzik's (1936) extensive experimentation provides the most comprehensive finding in this area. His monograph reports the findings of some 20 experiments in which the maze learning of normal, blind, anosmic, deaf, and vibrissaeless rats, as well as combinations of these sensory deficits, was examined. His general findings were as follows: (1) In normal rats vision assumes the dominant role, olfaction plays a relatively minor role, and tactual and auditory stimuli do not seem to be directly involved. (2) When

rats are deprived of vision, olfaction assumes a larger role in learning and audition plays a role second only to that of olfaction.
(3) Learning by use of kinesthetic cues alone is not possible.
(4) Abolishing a sense by operative techniques retards learning
to a greater extent than does constantly changing the stimuli which
are received. Honzik concluded that the ". . . motor responses
that constitute the maze habit are made, not to specific, individual
stimuli, but to complexes or patterns of stimuli," echoing an earlier position of Hunter (1930) who had posited that maze learning
was under multiple stimulus control.

Thus, from the original statement posited by Small (1901) and
Watson (1907) that only one sense modality was involved in maze
learning, later investigators concluded that almost all senses were
involved and that any particular sense organ could be brought
into play if some other sense organ or combination thereof was
eliminated.

Place versus Response Learning

In the 1940's Tolman undertook a series of studies designed to
examine some of the important implications derived from his theoretical position. In the second study of this series, Tolman,
Ritchie, and Kalish (1946) investigated the role of what they
termed place learning versus response learning. Their experimental procedure was as follows: two groups of rats were trained
on a single-unit T-maze in which the starting path on one-half of
the trials led into the choice point from one direction and on the
other half of the trials from the opposite direction. Figure 13–1
shows the type of maze with the two starting points. One group of
animals (response group) learned to turn always to the right, but
the second group (place group) learned to go always to the same
arm of the maze. This meant that on one-half of the trials the place
group had to turn to the right, but on the other half it had to turn
left. The investigators found, as Figure 13–2 indicates, that the
place group was clearly superior in learning the maze, and they
concluded that the disposition to orient toward a place was simpler
and more primitive than the disposition to make a specific response.

Close examination of the Tolman, Ritchie, and Kalish (1946)
study reveals a marked similarity to the problem of sensory
control. In effect, the question that these investigators posed
involved the nature of the stimuli which the animal used in

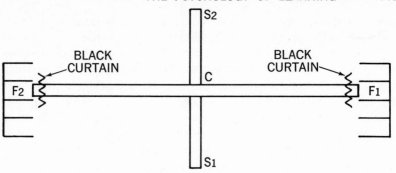

Fig. 13–1. Type of maze used. A block is placed at the center point (C) to force the animal to make a right or left choice. *Adapted from Tolman, Ritchie, and Kalish (1946)*

learning a maze, and the conclusion of the investigators could be rephrased to read that visual stimuli were more important (or more primitive) than kinesthetic.

The large number of experiments which were conducted in order to verify or refute the Tolman, Ritchie, and Kalish (1946) position resulted in a controversy similar to that which Watson had precipitated. For example, studies by Blodgett and McCutchan (1947), Tolman, Ritchie, and Kalish (1947), Blodgett, McCutchan, and Mathews (1949), Tolman and Gleitman (1949), Galanter and Shaw (1954), and Waddel, Gans, Kempner, and Williams (1955) revealed that place learning was more rapid than response learning; however, Glanzer (1953) and Scharlock (1955) found that response learning was faster. Thompson and Thompson (1949) found that either place learning or response learning could be more rapid depending upon the intertrial interval which was used.

The Hunter (1930) and Honzik (1936) conclusion concerning sensory control of maze learning was echoed by Restle (1957) who, in his analysis of the place versus response controversy, wrote that the theory was ill-formulated and that there was nothing in the nature of the rat which made it a "place" or "response" learner. Rather, he pointed out that the most important factor determining the outcome was the amount of extramaze visual stimulation which differentiated the region around and behind the one goal box from the region around and behind the second goal box. Such visual cues were obviously relevant in place

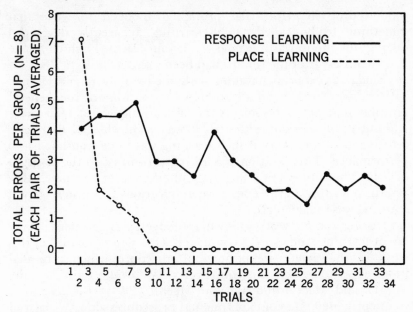

Fig. 13–2. Errors as a function of trials. *Adapted from Tolman, Ritchie, and Kalish (1946)*

learning but irrelevant in response learning. The rat in a maze will use all of the relevant cues, and the importance of any class of cues depends upon the amount of relevant stimulation provided, as well as upon the sensory capacities of the organism.

Latent Learning

A third controversy spawned by the maze learning situation was the problem of latent learning. In Chapter 3, in distinguishing between learning and performance, an early study by Blodgett (1929) who gave three groups of rats one trial a day on a six-unit multiple T-maze was described. One group was run for seven days, and each animal was permitted to eat after every trial. A second group was also run for seven days, but for the first two days this group did not find food in the goal box. Reward was provided on the third trial and continued to be present thereafter. For the third group, reward was omitted for the first six days and introduced on the seventh. This group was then run two additional days. Abrupt decreases in errors were found following each experimental group's finding food in the goal box. It was this sudden drop in errors that prompted Blodgett to write that something to be called latent learning apparently developed during the nonreward period—a latent learning which made itself manifest after the reward had been presented.

Blodgett's experiment, along with one by Tolman and Honzik (1930), was used by Tolman (1932) to support the general position that at least some types of learning could take place without reinforcement, although it was acknowledged that reinforcement was necessary if such learning was to be translated into performance. This position was in sharp contrast to the position held by Thorndike, Hull, Spence, and others who postulated that certain rewarding "after-effects" or reinforcement was necessary if learning was to take place.[1]

During the 25 years following Blodgett's experiment, many latent learning studies were conducted. One salient feature of this work was the variety of experimental procedures which were used in an effort to resolve this controversy. Following Thistlethwaite (1951) and MacCorquodale and Meehl (1954), the five most frequently used types of experimental procedures along with brief summaries of the findings which have been obtained will be presented.

Type I: Nonrewarded trials followed by rewarded trials.

The Blodgett (1929) experiment which was cited previously is an excellent example of this type of latent learning situation. In brief, the animals are deprived of food or water and given a series of trials in a complex maze without receiving food or water in the goal box. Reward is then introduced, and the abrupt decline in errors following the first reinforced trial is used to support the position that learning was taking place during the nonrewarded trials. Positive findings using this type of design have been reported by Simmons (1924), Elliott (1929), Williams (1929), Tolman and Honzik (1930), Herb (1940), Wallace, Blackwell, and Jenkins (1941), Meehl and MacCorquodale (1953), and Muenzinger and Conrad (1953), in addition to Blodgett (1929).

[1] As Thistlethwaite (1951) has pointed out, there has also been some controversy as to whether the latent learning studies are crucial in evaluating the reinforcement vs. nonreinforcement issue. Tolman (1938), Leeper (1935), and Seward (1949), for example, considered latent learning data as bearing directly on the issue. Other investigators, i.e., Meehl (1950), Postman (1947), do not believe this to be the case. As Meehl (1950) has written (p. 70), "Even the Strong Law of Effect is . . . compatible with the latent learning experiments."

Negative results have been reported by Reynolds (1945a) and Meehl and MacCorquodale (1951).

Type II: Exploration followed by rewarded trials.

This situation is similar to Type I except that the experimental animals are first permitted to explore the maze freely, usually under some deprivation state. They are then rewarded in the goal box, followed by one or more learning trials. The criterion of latent learning is met if this group makes fewer errors than would be expected on the basis of chance or when compared with a control group not given the opportunity to explore that particular maze.

A study by Buxton (1940) illustrates this general procedure. Varying groups of experimental subjects lived in a 12-unit T-maze for varying numbers of nights. Their place of entry and departure in the maze was varied from one night to the next so that fixed entrance and exit associations could not be formed. Following such free exploration, a test trial was provided. The investigator found that from 48 to 63 per cent of the subjects achieved a score of three errors or less. This score was in contrast to a score of six errors which would be predicted by chance and to a score of 5.8 errors which was actually achieved by a control group which had first lived 48 hours in a runway, was placed directly in a goal box and permitted to eat, and finally given a trial in the maze.

In addition to Buxton's findings, positive results have also been reported by Lashley (1918), Haney (1931), Daub (1933), and Karn and Porter (1946).

Type III: Trials provided with incentive present, but the drive state is weak and irrelevant; test trials are provided with subjects being motivated for the incentive.

In a third type of latent learning situation, the animals are satiated for food and water and given a series of trials in a T-maze in which food and/or water is present in the goal boxes. The animals are then deprived of food or water and provided test trials in order to determine if they have learned the location of the goal objects during the trials in which they were satiated. Responding to the correct goal box significantly better than chance or being superior to a control group which was given training with empty goal boxes provides a positive indication of latent learning.

A study by Spence, Bergmann, and Lippitt (1950) illustrates

this situation. Rats were given four trials per day for seven days in a T-maze in which one path led to water and the other to food. The animals were satiated, and, in order to get them to run during these trials, a cage mate was placed in the goal box. Test trials were given on the day following the training trials. For the first test series, one-half of the animals were placed under water deprivation and the other half under food deprivation. For the second test series provided on the following day, the motivational conditions for each subject were reversed. Results for the first test series revealed a significant shift from the pre-test choice of the subjects to the alley containing the goal object for which they were motivated. Results for the second test, on the other hand, were entirely negative, revealing little or no shift in the direction of the appropriate alley.

Positive findings have been reported by Szymanski (1918), Spence and Lippitt (1940), Meehl and MacCorquodale (1948), Seward, Levy, and Handlon (1950), MacCorquodale and Meehl (1951), Thistlethwaite (1951a), and Kendler and Levine (1953), in addition to Spence, Bergmann, and Lippitt (1950). Kendler (1947) and Maltzman (1950) have been unable to find this effect.

Type IV: Trials provided with incentive present, but the drive state is strong and irrelevant; test trials are provided with subjects being motivated for the incentive.

This situation is similar to Type III except that the animals have been placed under food or water deprivation and the incentive which is present in the goal box is irrelevant to this need. Following a number of training trials, the animal is appropriately deprived and test trials are provided. The criterion for latent learning is similar to that used with Type III.

An example of this experimental situation is found in a study by Spence and Lippitt (1946). Two groups of rats, deprived of water but satiated for food, were given five trials a day for 12 days in a simple Y-maze, in which for the control group the right alley led to water and the left alley to an empty goal box. For the experimental group of subjects, the right alley led to water and the left to food. Following training, all the animals were motivated for food and satiated for water. Food was found in the goal box located in the left alley. Five test trials were provided each day until a criterion of nine out of ten successive choices of the food alley was reached. The investigators found that on the first trial under hunger motivation all subjects continued to go down the alley which had previously led to water. A comparison between the two groups of subjects in reaching the criterion revealed no difference between them.

Positive results, using this type of design, have been reported by Diesenroth and Spence (1941), Walker, Knotter, and DeValois (1950), Strange (1950), Walker (1951), Bendig (1952), Christie (1952), Johnson (1952), and Thistlethwaite (1952). On the other hand, negative findings, in addition to Spence and Lippitt's (1946) study, have been reported by Walker (1948), Gleitman (1950), Kendler and Kanner (1950), Littman (1950), Shaw and Waters (1950), Christie (1951), and Fehrer (1951).

Type V: Exploratory trials followed by reinforcement in a discriminable goal box; test trials provided to examine the animal's choice of goal boxes.

The last latent learning situation to be described consists of first permitting deprived animals to explore a T-maze containing discriminably different but empty goal boxes. Following such training, the animals are placed in one of these goal boxes and fed. A test trial is then provided by placing the animal at the choice point and noting the animal's tendency to choose the side which leads to the goal box in which he had been fed.

Seward's (1949) study illustrates this type of design. In this experiment, goal boxes that differed in color, i.e., white or black, or in tactual sensitivity, i.e., hardware cloth floor or sponge rubber floor, were used in a T-maze. Three 10- to 15-minute periods of free exploration were followed by three additional sessions in which the animals were permitted to run once to each of the two goal boxes. Following such training, the animals were fed directly in one of the goal boxes and then placed at the choice point and given a free trial. The results, supporting a latent learning position, indicated that of 32 subjects, 28 went directly from the choice point to the goal box in which they had been fed.

Using this type of experimental procedure, positive findings have been reported by Seward (1949), Tolman and Gleitman

(1949), Iwahara and Marx (1950), Gilchrist (1952), and Strain (1953); but negative results have been obtained by Denny and Davis (1951) and Seward, Datel, and Levy (1952).

General Conclusions and the Present Status of Latent Learning

By 1955 most experimenters, guided by the experimental findings obtained in many of the studies which have been cited, had taken the position that latent learning was a demonstrable phenomenon. However, the investigators were unable to provide an unequivocal sorting of the experimental situations which would provide "positive" findings in contrast to those which would provide "negative."

The preponderance of positive findings, however, was obtained (1) when a complex learning situation was utilized and (2) when weak irrelevant motivation was employed. The use of strong irrelevant motivation with the simple type of learning situation, on the other hand, provided equivocal findings with negative results reported as frequently as positive. The identification of the necessary and sufficient conditions for latent learning to take place under strong irrelevant motivation was undertaken by Thistlethwaite (1951) who examined a number of variables which he believed were of basic significance in better understanding the phenomenon: (1) weak irrelevant motivation, (2) hunger rather than thirst as the irrelevant drive, (3) weak position preferences, (4) symmetry of reward during training, (5) free rather than forced trials, (6) discriminating contact with the undesired goal object, (7) previous exploratory or "need" differentiation training, and (8) large amounts of training under conditions which do not produce strong asymmetrical preferences.

Since 1955, interest in latent learning has declined, and it now seems unlikely that this controversy will ever again occupy a position of importance in learning theory. The reasons are diverse but two appear to be particularly important.

The first is that there has been a revision and elaboration of the Hullian position which has resulted in these theorists' being better able to explain at least some of the positive findings which have been obtained. One example is the introduction of K, an incentive variable. This construct is related to the quantity and quality of the reinforcing agent provided the subject and has been posited to contribute to performance rather than to learning. As Seward (1950) has pointed out, the introduction of reinforcement into the maze situation is posited, via K, to have an immediate effect which is reflected in the animal's increased performance on the next trial, a finding similar to that obtained by Blodgett (1929) in his early study.

Another example is the use of the fractional anticipatory goal response. In latent learning experiments where one incentive is present in one goal box, and a second in the other goal box, and the animal is satiated, it has been proposed that when the animal goes into the goal box the sight of the incentive elicits conditioned fractional eating or drinking responses, depending upon the nature of the incentive. Through stimulus generalization, these responses become conditioned to the cues arising from the particular alley which leads to that incentive. The reinforcement for such learning is assumed to arise from secondary sources, i.e., sight of food or water, lifting the animal out of the box, etc. When the animal is placed under a drive state and test trials are provided, the anticipatory act related to the goal for which the subject is motivated will, because of the greater strength of the particular drive stimulus, be much stronger than the other and will produce stronger proprioceptive cues. Thus, if the subject is made thirsty, the proprioceptive cues arising from the anticipatory drinking responses will be stronger than those arising from anticipatory eating. Inasmuch as these cues have been conditioned to the response of entering the alley leading to water, they will tend to elicit this response.

A second reason is that the reinforcement–nonreinforcement issue, which, of course, incorporates the latent learning controversy, no longer occupies a position of importance in learning theory for many investigators. The Hullian position of motivation, based upon biological need states and primary reinforcement and used as a point of departure for many of the latent learning studies, has gradually eroded under the rising tide of experimental evidence which has pointed to the existence of a number of other drive states as well as a variety of reinforcing events. One outcome has been that interest in the area of motivation, as applied to learning theory, frequently has been confined to problems of relatively limited scope, with the general recognition that the larger and more grandiose problems cannot be solved by "crucial" experiments.

DISCRIMINATION LEARNING

The Theoretical Positions of Hull and Spence

How does the rat learn to discriminate a black stimulus from a white one? a vertical striped card from a horizontal one? a rough textured floor from a smooth one? The problem of how the organism discriminates has been of interest to a number of learning theorists.

Both Spence (1936, 1937, 1937a) and Hull (1939, 1943, 1950, 1952) proposed theories of discrimination learning based upon the following postulates: (1) every reinforced trial leads to an increment in excitatory strength for a given stimulus and its reinforced response, (2) every nonreinforced trial results in an inhibitory increment to a given stimulus and its nonreinforced response, (3) both excitatory and inhibitory tendencies generalize to stimuli along a stimulus continuum, (4) there is the algebraic summation of excitatory and inhibitory increments which results in (5) a discriminatory response based upon these algebraic summations. As Hull (1943) has written, the phenomenon of simple discrimination learning is generated as a secondary principle based upon the interaction of the stimulus generalization gradients of excitation and inhibition. An example of Hull's (1943) theory of discrimination learning is indicated in Figure 13–3. Here it can be noted that the positive or reinforced stimulus has been placed at zero along the stimulus continuum whereas the negative or nonreinforced stimulus is approximately eight jnd's away from the positive stimulus. In contrast to Hull's postulation of concave generalization gradients, Spence (1936) has hypothesized that these gradients are convex in shape.

Two approaches have been taken with regard to an examination of the Spence-Hull theory of discrimination learning. One has been to make inquiry regarding the operation of some of the basic processes on which the theory rests; the second has been to examine empirically some of the specific predictions generated by this position.

A differential eyelid conditioning experiment by Gynther (1957) is an example of this second approach. His experimental procedure consisted of using two small lights, placed approximately two inches apart and directly ahead of the subject, as the

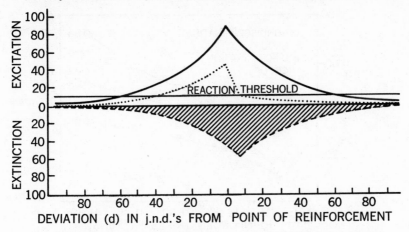

Fig. 13–3. Diagram representing the manner in which inhibitory gradients are assumed to interact with excitatory gradients. The upper curve represents excitation, the lower curve represents inhibition, while the dotted line in between represents effective reaction tendencies. *Adapted from Hull (1943)*

positive and negative stimulus conditions. The positive stimulus was followed by the UCS (puff of air), but the negative stimulus was not.

One prediction generated from the Spence-Hull analysis was that a conditioning situation which did not involve discrimination learning should result in a higher level of performance than that obtained with differential conditioning. This would follow since in the nondiscrimination learning situation there would be no generalized inhibitory tendencies arising from the negative stimulus and subtracting from the excitatory tendencies which had accrued to the positive stimulus. In an examination of this prediction, one group of subjects received fifty reinforced trials in which the positive light was always followed by the puff of air. The negative stimulus was never presented. The second group was differentially conditioned and received 50 reinforced trials with the positive stimulus and an equal number of non-reinforced trials with the negative stimulus. The results are indicated in Figure 13–4. Here, in agreement with Spence and Hull, the differentially trained group provided fewer conditioned responses than the nondifferentially trained group.

A second prediction arising from the Spence-Hull position was

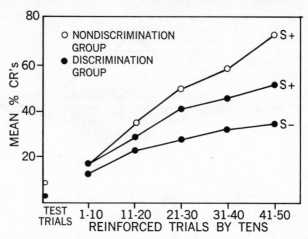

Fig. 13–4. Mean percentage of CR's in successive blocks of ten reinforced trials for the discrimination and nondiscrimination groups. *Adapted from Gynther (1957)*

that the strength of the excitatory and inhibitory tendencies might be manipulated by varying the number of reinforced and nonreinforced trials. For example, assume that the positive stimulus was provided 50 reinforcements. It would be possible to manipulate the strength of the response to that stimulus by varying the number of nonreinforced trials to the negative stimulus. As the number of nonreinforced trials increased, the strength of the response to the positive stimulus should become weaker. This would be predicted since by increasing the number of nonreinforced trials there would be increasing amounts of generalized inhibitory strength subtracted from the excitatory strength derived from the reinforced trials.

In an examination of this prediction, Gynther provided 50 reinforced trials to a positive stimulus and 50 nonreinforced trials to the negative for one differentially trained group (1:1), whereas a second group (3:1) received the same number of reinforced trials to the positive stimulus but only 17 nonreinforced trials to the negative stimulus. Figure 13–5 reveals the findings, which again support the Spence-Hull position. Not only was there a higher level of response to the positive stimulus for the group given only 17 nonreinforced trials but this group also had a higher level of response to the negative stimulus.

An important consideration in the discrimination learning

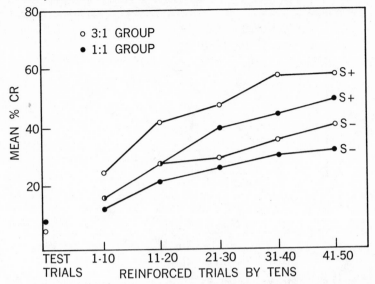

Fig. 13–5. Mean percentage of CR's in successive blocks of ten reinforced trials for the 3:1 and 1:1 discrimination groups. *Adapted from Gynther (1957)*

situation is the similarity of the stimuli that are used. The greater the dissimilarity of stimuli used as discriminanda, the more readily discrimination learning should take place. This should follow since the generalization of inhibitory strength to the positive stimulus and the generalization of excitatory strength to the negative stimulus should grow progressively weaker as the positive and negative stimulus conditions become more distant on the stimulus continuum.

Gynther, examining this prediction, increased the difference between the positive and negative stimulus by covering the negative stimulus with a piece of red plastic. Subjects trained under these conditions, it would be predicted, should respond at a higher level to the positive stimulus than a second differential training group (control) in which both the reinforced and nonreinforced stimuli were white lights. Both groups received 100 training trials in which the ratio of reinforced trials to the positive stimulus, and nonreinforced trials to the negative, was 1:1. Figure 13–6 indicates that the mean percentage of CR's to the positive stimulus for the red and white stimulus group was significantly

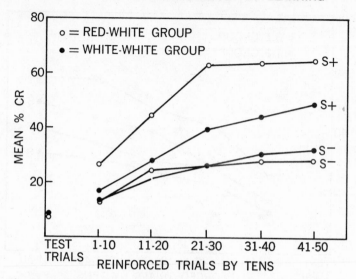

Fig. 13–6. Mean percentage of CR's in successive blocks of ten reinforced trials for the red-white discrimination group and the white-white discrimination group. *Adapted from Gynther (1957)*

greater than the number of CR's to the positive stimulus for the control group.

The Spence-Hull position also has resulted in a number of individuals' examining the nature of the basic processes upon which the theory rests. This examination has, in turn, given rise to three controversies: (1) the problem of transposition, or responding to the absolute or relational characteristics of the stimulus, (2) an incremental versus a nonincremental theory of learning, i.e., the continuity versus noncontinuity controversy, and (3) the nature of stimulus generalization. The theoretical and experimental literature related to these topics has been so extensive that only a brief outline of this material can be presented. Since the nature of stimulus generalization was discussed in the preceding chapter, only the first two topics will be discussed in this chapter.

The Problem of Transposition

In 1902, Kinnaman was interested in examining the "mental life" of monkeys, and in one part of his study he used nine painted glasses varying in brightness from a very light gray (glass 9) to black (glass 1). A discrimination experiment was then provided which consisted of presenting two of these glasses together, with the animal learning which of them contained food. More specifically, glasses 9 and 8 were presented, with food placed in the lighter of the two (glass 9). Following ten training trials, a new discrimination task was formed using glasses 8 and 7. Following additional training trials with these glasses, glasses 7 and 6 were used to form the new discriminanda, then glasses 6 and 5, and so on until all of the glasses were used. An analysis of the monkeys' responses led Kinnaman to conclude that it was possible for a monkey to have some general notion, of a low order, which might be represented by "food-always-in-the-lighter."

Kinnaman's general procedure illustrates what has been described as the transposition experiment. Two members of a stimulus dimension (light gray vs. mid-gray) are presented to the subject, and the response to one of them (mid-gray) is consistently rewarded whereas the response to the other stimulus is not. Following a number of trials in which the subject learns to choose one of them (mid-gray) consistently, this stimulus is then paired with another stimulus (dark gray) obtained from the same stimulus continuum in order to provide the subject with a second discrimination problem. The basic question is whether the subject continues to respond to the same stimulus as he had previously, in which case it is assumed that he had learned to respond to the absolute characteristics of the discriminanda in the original discrimination training, or whether he transposes his response, that is, responds relationally. Here, he would choose the dark gray stimulus. From such responding, it would be inferred that he had learned a relationship during the original training.

Following Kinnaman, a number of experimenters performed transposition studies and confirmed Kinnaman's conclusions that animals could learn to respond to relationships between stimuli [Casteel (1911), Breed (1912), Lashley (1912), Bingham (1913), Coburn (1914), and Johnson (1914)].

Other early investigators, however, obtained findings which indicated that the subject learned to respond to the absolute characteristics of the stimulus. Perkins and Wheeler (1930), employing goldfish, Warden and Winslow (1931), using the ring dove, and Taylor (1932), using chickens, found that absolute responses predominated, at least in the transposition situations

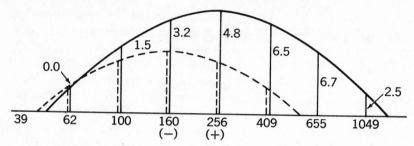

Fig. 13–7. Spence's theoretical representation of discrimination learning. *Adapted from Spence (1937)*

which they employed. Gayton (1927), using rats in a brightness discrimination study, could draw no definite conclusions for the predominance of either absolute or relative responses.

Gulliksen (1932) and Kluver (1933) were among the first investigators to indicate that the character of the transposition response was related to the distance between the training and test stimuli as measured on some stimulus dimension. In Kluver's (1933) study, Java monkeys were presented with a 300 and 150 sq. cm. rectangle, with responses to the 300 sq. cm. rectangle being reinforced. Following training, the subjects were presented with four test situations in which the rectangle sizes were as follows: (a) 1,536 and 768, (b) 600 and 300, (c) 150 and 75, and (d) 8.64 and 4.32. Kluver's findings indicated that chance responding occurred when the 1,536 vs. 768 and 8.64 vs. 4.32 test situations were presented. With the 600 vs. 300 test situation, 72 per cent of the responses were to the 600 sq. cm. rectangle, indicating a predominance of relational responding, but when the 150 vs. 75 test situation was utilized 97 per cent of the responses were relational. These results confirmed the findings obtained the previous year by Gulliksen (1932). Working with rats, he also had found that relational responding predominated when the test stimuli were quite similar to the stimuli used in the original training; as the test stimuli became more dissimilar chance responding increased.

Throughout this period, the Gestalt psychologists, notably Kohler (1918, 1929), emphasized the importance of relational responding in the transposition experiment. Spence, however, was quite dissatisfied with the Gestalt theorists' failure to provide a set of postulates from which deductions concerning transposition

TABLE 13–1

Theoretical Values and Predictions Derived from Figure 13–7

TASK	STIMULI PRESENTED		NET EXCITATORY STRENGTHS ACCRUING TO EACH STIMULUS		PREDICTIONS	
					Absolute	Relational
Original training	160(−)	256(+)	3.2	4.8		
Test situation 1	256	409	4.8	6.5	409	409
Test situation 2	409	655	6.5	6.7	Chance	655
Test situation 3	655	1049	6.7	2.5	655	1049

(Adapted from Spence, 1937)

responding could be made; as a result, in 1937 he [Spence (1937)] used his theoretical analysis which he had proposed the year before [Spence (1936)] to do just this.

Using Table 13–1 derived from Figure 13–7 as a source of reference, it can be noted that following original training, on stimuli varying in size, in which the 256 stimulus was positive and 160 negative, a transposition test consisting of stimulus 256 versus 409, or 160 versus 100, would result in responses to the larger stimulus in each instance. This would follow since the net excitatory strength of the larger stimulus in each comparison is considerably greater than that of the smaller. But such a prediction is the same as that which would be made if the organism was responding to the stimuli on a relational basis. On the other hand, if the transposition task consisted of stimulus 409 versus 655, it would be predicted that the organism should not respond to either stimulus systematically since the difference in net excitatory strength between the stimuli is quite small. Finally, if the transposition task consisted of stimulus 655 versus 1,049, it would be predicted that the subject should respond to stimulus 655. Both of these latter predictions are contrary to predictions based upon the position that the subject had learned to respond to relationships.

In a subsequent paper, Spence (1942) pointed out that the lack of knowledge concerning the nature of the generalization curves made it extremely difficult to make specific predictions for all the transposition tests which might be made at varying points along the stimulus continuum.[2] As a result, he proposed two

[2] It should be also noted that Spence (1942) applied his theoretical analysis to transposition studies in which the original discrimination problem consisted of

TABLE 13–2

Training Pairs and Various Test Pairs Used in Both Studies

STIMULUS PAIRS EXP. I.	STIMULUS CARDS DIFFUSE REFLECTION FACTORS		STIMULUS PAIRS EXP. II.
Training Pair	(4) .22 vs.	(1) .91	D
A	(5) .13	(2) .57	C
B	(6) .09	(3) .34	B
C	(7) .05	(4) .22	A
D	(8) .035	(4) .13	Training Pair

(Adapted from Ehrenfreund, 1952)

transposition predictions of a more general nature: (1) transposition (relational responding) will take place when the test stimuli are close to the original training stimuli and that (2) such relational responding will decrease as the differences between the original training and test stimuli increase.

A few years later, Kendler (1950) pointed out that Spence, in a private communication, had elaborated on this second prediction by positing that as the distance between the original training stimuli and the stimuli used in the transposition test increased the percentage of transposed responses should decrease until they dropped to well below the 50 per cent level but then rise and level off at 50 per cent.

Of the many contemporary transposition studies which have been done, Ehrenfreund's (1952) findings have been most congruent with Spence's predictions. Ehrenfreund's first experiment consisted of training rats to choose the brighter of two pathways in a discrimination apparatus. When the animals reached a criterion of 18 correct out of 20 trials, test trials were presented in which the discriminanda consisted of a number of pairs of stimuli; each pair was darker than the training stimuli. In a second experiment, a similar procedure was used except that the animals were originally trained to choose the darker of the two pathways and

three stimuli rather than two. The three-stimulus problem frequently has been identified as the "intermediate size problem" inasmuch as the middle or intermediate stimulus is reinforced during training. The test situation, of course, also utilizes three stimuli. Limitations of space require that primary consideration be given to the two-stimulus situation. The interested reader can refer to the studies of Gonzalez, Gentry, and Bitterman (1954); Stevenson and Bitterman (1955); Rudel (1957); Gonzalez and Ross (1958); Gentry, Overall, and Brown (1959); Brown, Overall, and Gentry (1959); and Zeiler (1963, 1963a) for a sampling of the experimental work dealing with this problem.

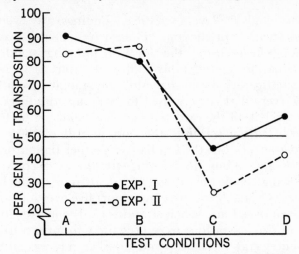

Fig. 13–8. Transposition gradients for subjects transposed down the brightness scale (Experiment I) and for subjects transposed up the brightness scale (Experiment II). *Adapted from Ehrenfreund (1952)*

then given test trials in which the pairs of stimuli were lighter than the original stimuli. Table 13–2 indicates the training stimuli and the varying test pairs which were used in each experiment. The close correspondence between the findings and Spence's predictions can be noted by examining Figure 13–8.

Other investigators, however, have not been able to obtain findings which support all of Spence's predictions. Kendler's (1950) study was similar in design and procedure to Ehrenfreund's which was cited above. Her first experiment consisted of training animals to respond to the brighter of two pathways, but in a second study animals were trained to respond to the darker of the two pathways. Transposition tests were provided with pairs of stimuli both similar to and different from those used in training. Her results are difficult to interpret. As the test stimuli departed further from those used in the original training, the results from the first experiment showed a decrease in relational responding followed by an increase; results from the second experiment, however, indicated only decreased relational responding. In neither instance did responses to test stimuli distant from the original training stimuli approach chance as Ehrenfreund's results had revealed and as would be expected from the Spence model.

Lawrence and DeRivera's (1954) findings are even more contrary to Spence's predictions. These experimenters examined transposition effects using the Lashley jumping stand and a stimulus situation considerably different from that used by previous investigators. Seven shades of gray, ranging from 1 (very light) to 7 (very dark), were used to make up stimulus cards in which the top half of the card was one shade and the bottom half was another. During training, the bottom half of the card was always mid-gray (4) but the top half was either lighter or darker than the mid-gray. Thus, the training stimulus cards could be one of the following: shade one on the top, shade four on the bottom; shade two over shade four; three over four; five over four; six over four; or seven over four. When stimulus cards one over four, two over four, or three over four were presented, forming a pattern in which a lighter gray was on top and a darker gray was on bottom, the correct response for the animal was to jump to the right window. Whenever combinations of five over four, six over four, or seven over four were used, forming a pattern in which the darker gray was on the top and lighter gray on the bottom, the animal was reinforced for jumping to the left window. Training continued until each subject was able to go through the sequence of the six different stimulus cards twice without making an error.

Lawrence and DeRivera reasoned that, in terms of a theory which emphasized responses to the absolute properties of the stimulus, grays 1, 2, and 3 should become associated with jumping to the right and grays 5, 6, and 7 should become associated with jumping to the left. In terms of relational theory, the investigators posited that specific stimulus values should be inconsequential; rather, the animals should have learned that a light-over-dark stimulus should be associated with jumping right and that a dark-over-light stimulus should be associated with jumping left.

Transposition test trials consisted of shifting the color of the bottom half of the card up or down the brightness continuum and providing 24 new patterns of light-dark or dark-light combinations. These were selected so that in six combinations both a relational theory and an absolute theory of transposition would make the same predictions, in 12 they would make opposing predictions, and in the remaining six the relational theory could make an unambiguous prediction whereas the absolute theory would not.

The findings revealed that 80 per cent of 264 test responses were in keeping with the relational hypothesis. In test situations in which the relational and the absolute theories would make directly opposing predictions, 74 per cent of the jumps were in conformity with the relational theory and only 26 per cent were in keeping with the absolute theory.

A Point of View

In view of the experimental evidence which has been brought to bear on this topic, what conclusions can be drawn? One bias would be to eschew Spence's theoretical position since predictions for transposition based upon this position are dependent upon the characteristics of the generalization gradient which, as noted in a previous chapter, appear to be reasonably specific to the experimental situation. Moreover, the fact that asymmetrical gradients are obtained when stimuli of varying intensities are used would make predictions even more difficult.[3]

There appears to be little doubt that it is possible for an organism to solve a discrimination problem in which the effective stimulus can assume either an absolute or relational role; the solution of a transposition problem usually should continue to reflect the operation of the cue which was used in the original training.[4] Such being the case, the examination of transposition learning appears to rest upon an analysis of the conditions which determine whether the effective stimulus shall consist of the absolute properties of the stimulus or a relationship between the discriminanda.[5]

One such condition would be that when the stimulus situation is so arranged that the subject has the opportunity to make a

---

[3] In this regard, it is interesting to note that most experimenters investigating transposition have assumed a symmetrical stimulus generalization gradient, even though there has been evidence [Hull (1949)] to support the position that the use of some stimulus dimension, e.g., brightness, may provide asymmetrical generalization gradients.

[4] What constitutes the absolute properties of a stimulus may be open to question. Riley (1958) has made an interesting point in that he believes, at least with regard to the brightness dimension, that the "absolute" properties of a stimulus should be defined in terms of the relationship of its brightness to its background. That is, it is the ratio of the brightness of the stimulus to the brightness of the background which makes up the "absolute" characteristics of the stimulus and to which the animal attaches a response.

[5] It seems possible, as some writers have indicated, for the subject to learn to respond to both the absolute as well as relative properties of a stimulus. When such is the case, the analysis should be related to an examination of the conditions which facilitate the utilization of one of these cues in contrast to the other.

comparison among the stimuli that are presented, the probability is increased that relational aspects of the stimulus situation will be emphasized.

One experimental procedure used to investigate comparison training in the discrimination experiment has been to employ the simultaneous and successive methods of presenting the stimuli. With the simultaneous method, the stimuli are presented together, typically side by side, so that the subject can make a direct comparison between the two discriminanda. The successive method consists of presenting only a single stimulus, with the subject learning to respond or not to respond depending upon the stimulus which is presented.

An early study by Jackson and Jerome (1940) using children and a later one by Baker and Lawrence (1951) employing rats as subjects have both indicated that relative responding is enhanced by the simultaneous presentation of the stimuli making up the discrimination task. In the Baker and Lawrence (1951) study, six and one-half cm. and nine cm. circles were used as the discriminanda. One group of rats was trained using the simultaneous presentation of stimuli, and a second group was trained with successive presentation. Following the reaching of a learning criterion of 18 correct responses out of 20 trials, a transposition problem was presented in which the six and one-half cm. circle was paired with a four cm. circle. On the first trial, all of the subjects given simultaneous discrimination training chose the four cm. circle, giving evidence of relational responding; but only six of the ten successive discrimination trained animals did so. Thus, simultaneous presentation of stimuli produced a greater amount of relational responding than the successive presentation method.

The experimental operations used by Thompson (1955) to manipulate stimulus comparison consisted of providing the subjects with two discrimination problems to learn. For the group given comparison training, a small circle versus a large circle made up one discrimination problem and a light gray stimulus versus a dark gray served as the second problem. For the group given non-comparison training, one problem consisted of a small circle versus a dark gray stimulus and the second problem consisted of a large circle versus a light gray stimulus. It can be noted for this second group that a direct comparison of the small circle with the large or the dark gray stimulus with the light was virtually

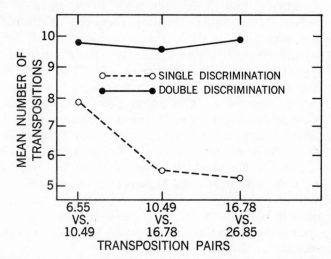

Fig. 13–9. Mean number of transposed responses for the single and double discrimination training groups. *Adapted from Johnson and Zara (1960)*

impossible because the stimuli to be compared were not presented in either spatial or temporal contiguity. Following training in which the subjects learned each discrimination to a criterion, the transposition tests were presented, with the light gray stimulus paired with a still lighter one to form one problem and the small circle paired with a still smaller one to form the second problem. Results supported Baker and Lawrence (1951) in that the group given comparison training revealed a greater amount of relational responding than the noncomparison group.

A more recent study by Riley, Ring, and Thomas (1960), using a still different procedure for examining the influence of comparison versus noncomparison training on transposition, has confirmed the findings of Baker and Lawrence (1951) and Thompson (1955).

A second condition which seems to facilitate relational responding is the utilization of more than a single discrimination task in the training session. Studies by Gonzalez and Ross (1958) and Johnson and Zara (1960) have lent support to this position. In Johnson and Zara's (1960) study, children three and one-half to five years of age were used as subjects. The stimuli were black squares measuring 1.60, 2.56, 4.09, 6.55, 10.49, 16.78, or 26.85 square inches. The original training consisted of having one group of children learn to discriminate between stimuli 4.09 and 6.55. A second group was trained on two discrimination problems: 1.60 versus 2.56 and 4.09 versus 6.55. The criterion for discrimination learning was 14 correct responses in a series of 15 trials; reward consisted of a raisin or piece of candy for each correct response. Following the reaching of the criterion in the training series, transposition tests were presented. Subjects in each group were presented with one of the following test situations: (a) 6.55 versus 10.49, (b) 10.49 versus 16.78, or (c) 16.78 versus 26.85. The results, indicated in Figure 13–9, reveal that for the single discrimination training situation transposition decreased as the transposed stimuli grew more remote from the original training, but no such decline can be noted for the group trained with two discriminations.

There is some indication, following the suggestion of Gundlach and Herington (1933), that as the discriminanda used in the original training become more different relational responding in the transposition test decreases. If two quite different stimuli were used, e.g., a circle versus a square, it would be quite difficult for the subject to conceptualize these stimuli in terms of some relationship; as a result, the absolute characteristics of the stimuli would take on cue value. Similarly, it would follow that large differences between stimuli, even though they were on the same stimulus continuum, would increase the probability that responding to the absolute characteristics of the stimuli would occur. An early study by Taylor (1932) as well as a more recent one by Rudel (1957) supported such a conjecture.

At the other end of the continuum, if the difference between the training stimuli and the test stimuli is very small, it is likely that in many instances the subject cannot detect that the test stimuli are different from those used in training; as a result, the relational responding is enhanced. Stevenson and Weiss (1955), listening to the verbal reports made by college students who served as subjects in a transposition experiment, observed that some of their subjects simply failed to notice that the training and test stimuli were different.

Some investigators have made the tacit assumption that the subject learns a discrimination using either absolute or relational cues but not both. Under certain circumstances, however, it may be that the subject learns to respond to both the absolute and relative properties of the stimulus as a number of investigators have pointed out [Nissen, Levinson, and Nichols (1953) ; Thompson (1955) ; Stevenson and Bitterman (1955) ; Riley, Goggin, and Wright (1963)]. It has been suggested, however, that the forgetting curve may decline more rapidly for absolute cues than for relational ones.[6] As a result, it would be posited that as the time interval between the training and the test situation is increased the greater forgetting of the absolute cues leads the subject to utilize relational characteristics in order to solve the problem.

Some support for this position was reported in an early study by Kohler (1929) who found that during the transposition test chicks would respond to the originally correct stimulus only about one-half of the time when the animals were tested immediately following training. If testing was delayed, relational responding increased. Thompson (1955), using rats and providing either an immediate transposition test following training or one delayed 24 hours, obtained similar findings. Finally, both Spence (1942), using chimpanzees, and Rudel (1957), employing children, also have found that absolute responding declines as a function of the length of the time interval between the training and testing period.[7]

The last condition which appears to be related to the occurrence of relational responding is verbalization. Kuenne (1946) hypothesized that the mechanism which mediated transposition in infrahumans was the same as the mechanism which mediated transposition in children in the pre-verbal stage of development. With the acquisition of verbal processes, and with much of the child's behavior dominated by this process, Kuenne believed that a child's responses in the discrimination learning situation would become cued to words related to relational responding, i.e., "bigger," "larger," "brighter," etc. A basic prediction from her position was that pre-verbal children would transpose consistently on the test stimuli which were similar to the training stimuli but reveal only chance responding on transposition tests as the stimuli

[6] One reason for this difference may be that relational learning is usually easier, and, in the typical experiment, the relational stimulus-response relationship is overlearned and thus more resistant to forgetting.

[7] Stevenson and Weiss (1955) were unable to obtain results supporting this general position. Using college students and a four-stimulus task, they reported that relational responding was maximum when ten minutes intervened between training and testing, in contrast to either immediate testing or a delay of 24 hours.

became less similar to the training stimuli—findings paralleling the results obtained with animals. With the acquisition of verbal behavior, the child would be expected to show relational responding on both of the stimulus tests.

Using preschool and kindergarten children whose mental age ranged from three years (pre-verbal) to six years (verbal), Kuenne obtained results which supported her hypothesis. Findings indicated that transposition scores for all mental age groups were quite similar when the stimuli were similar to those presented during training; when test stimuli far removed from the original training were used, however, there was a high correlation between mental age and the occurrence of relational responding. Thus, children with a mental age of three gave 50 per cent relational responses, at age four they provided 60 per cent, at age five 80 per cent, and at age six 100 per cent. Alberts and Ehrenfreund (1951) have obtained findings confirming Kuenne's results.[8]

The Continuity–Noncontinuity Controversy

In 1929, Lashley expressed the point of view that the animal in learning a discrimination problem attempts various solutions before he hits upon the right one. In addition, Lashley assumed that the actual learning took place very quickly and that both the practice preceding and the errors following were irrelevant to the formation of the association.

A few years later, Lashley's position was supported by Krechevsky who, in a series of discrimination learning experiments [Krechevsky (1932, 1932a, 1933, 1933a)], showed that the rat, prior to learning the problem, appeared to engage in a number of systematic modes of responses—alternation behavior, responding to position, etc. From this, Krechevsky was led to conclude that the animal selects out of the many possible stimuli found in the learning situation certain sets of discriminanda to which he pays attention. While paying attention to such stimuli, the animal does not learn anything about the correctness of the final discriminanda to be learned. Viewed from another vantage point, these pre-solution responses were conceptualized as hypotheses which the

---

[8] Stevenson and Bitterman (1955) and Rudel (1957), on the other hand, have been unable to find any relationship between a child's ability to verbalize and the kind of responses obtained in the transposition test.

animal first adopts and then abandons until one of them leads to the solution of the problem. Following Krechevsky, this position has become known as the noncontinuity position since it views the learning process as being of a noncontinuous nature.

In contrast, the Spence-Hull theory of discrimination learning has been called the continuity position. Briefly, and following the earlier discussion, this theory assumes that if a response is followed by reward the excitatory tendencies of the immediate stimulus components are strengthened by a certain increment but if a response is not reinforced inhibitory tendencies of the immediate stimulus components are strengthened. The algebraic summation of excitatory and inhibitory increments determine whether or not the subject will respond to a given stimulus.

A basic issue which has arisen from these diverse points of view has been whether or not the association between the stimulus components, or hypotheses, and the response is formed very quickly or whether the strength of the association increases as a function of the number of reinforcements which are received.

One experimental procedure, agreed upon by supporters on both sides of the issue, was to use the stimulus reversal situation— a procedure which represents the major contemporary approach to the problem. Briefly, this procedure consists of providing a number of trials to experimental subjects in which two stimuli, e.g., black versus white, are presented, with one, i.e., black, consistently reinforced. These trials are usually referred to as the pre-solution period inasmuch as before the subject begins to respond systematically to the positive stimulus, the cues are reversed.[9] The learning of this stimulus reversal discrimination is then carried out to some criterion. The logic of the continuity position is that the experimental group should learn the reversal more slowly than a group not given pre-solution training since the reinforced trials given to the negative stimulus during the pre-solution period should provide interference when this stimulus becomes positive. The noncontinuity position would hold that the reinforced pre-solution trials should not provide any interference since the subject was not responding to the relevant cue and

[9] It was originally assumed that the pre-solution period consisted of the trials on which the subject was not responding to the relevant cue at a level significantly higher than chance. Krechevsky (1938) subsequently took the position that a subject may be making hypotheses about a relevant stimulus feature before it begins to show a systematic tendency to respond in terms of that feature.

that practice prior to the time that the association was established was of no consequence in a later solving of the problem.

An experiment by McCulloch and Pratt (1934) was the first of many to use this design. Rats were trained to pull on one of two strings in order to obtain a tray containing food. The weight of the trays (heavy or light) was used as the relevant cue. Three experimental groups of subjects were given varying amounts of practice during the pre-solution period prior to the introduction of the reversal learning. Experimental Group I was given 28 trials, whereas Experimental Group II was given trials until it began to learn the discrimination. The criterion of "beginning to discriminate" was not more than six errors in 24 trials. Experimental Group III was given 348 trials. (This training was more than sufficient to learn the problem.) One control group did not receive training during this period, but a second control group was given 84 training trials in which the trays were equally weighted. The reversal learning situation was then presented. The results supported the continuity position in that control groups took the smallest number of trials to learn the reversal problem—there was no difference between them—whereas for the experimental groups, ease of learning was inversely related to the number of trials provided during the pre-solution period.

A subsequent study by Krechevsky (1938), however, lent some support to the noncontinuity position. In this experiment, rats were given discrimination training on a Lashley jumping stand in which difficult visual discriminanda were used. Horizontal rows of small black squares made up one stimulus card, and vertical rows of small black squares made up the second. Experimental Group I was given 20 trials, and Experimental Group II was given 40 trials. For both groups one stimulus was positive and the other negative. The cues were then reversed, and the subjects were required to reach a criterion of 18 correct responses out of 20 trials. A control group was given training only on this second task. The investigator found that Experimental Group I did not make any more errors than the control group, thus, supporting the noncontinuity position, but Experimental Group II did reveal a significant amount of negative transfer, a finding in keeping with the continuity position. Krechevsky accounted for the negative transfer behavior of Experimental Group II by suggesting that 40 trials was too long a pre-solution period, whereas Spence (1940) interpreted the findings of Experimental Group I by positing that the subjects did not "see" the rows of black squares because they were fixating upon other aspects of the stimulus complex.[10]

A few years later, Spence (1945) conducted a study which has been acknowledged to be a model of experimental procedure. Two groups of rats were first given 30 trials in learning a position habit in a discrimination apparatus painted gray. The experimental group was then given 20 trials during a pre-solution period in which the alleys of the discrimination apparatus were painted black (or white); reinforcement was always associated with the black (or white) alley. A control group was also given 20 pre-solution trials, but reinforcement was divided equally between the two alleys. It was noted that during this pre-solution period, as a result of the previous position habit training, both the experimental and control groups revealed strong position habits. Eighty-four per cent of the responses made by the control group were to the preferred side, and 78 per cent of the responses exhibited by the experimental group were to this side. Moreover, none of the animals in either group responded more than 65 per cent to either the black or the white alley. Following pre-solution training, all animals were trained to reverse the originally rewarded position habit, and again the gray apparatus was employed. The black-white discrimination task was then presented with the cues reversed and all animals run to a criterion of 18 correct out of 20 trials. The results supported the continuity position by revealing that the control group learned the discrimination task significantly more rapidly than the experimental group.

Most of the studies following Spence (1945) have also sup-

---

[10] Spence's interpretation was supported in a study conducted by Ehrenfreund (1948) who, in two experiments, had rats learn to discriminate an upright from an inverted triangle in a Lashley jumping apparatus. During the second experiment, the jumping platform of the apparatus was raised above the level of the stimulus windows, enabling the subjects to fixate upon that area of the card which provided discriminable differences between the stimuli. This was in contrast to the first experiment in which, with the lowered jumping platform, the fixation habits of the rats (a tendency to fixate upon the lower portion of the card) were likely to preclude discriminably different retinal excitations from the stimulus figures at the start of training. The results of the first experiment indicated that 40 pre-solution trials had no influence on the reversal learning situation; a similar amount of training during Experiment II did result in the experimental group's taking significantly longer to learn the reversal than the control group. Ehrenfreund, in agreement with Spence, has pointed out that it is possible for an animal not to be learning anything about the differential cues at the beginning of visual discrimination training if the specific receptor exposure fixations are such that they do not provide discriminably different excitations of the retina necessary for discrimination learning.

ported the continuity position. Ehrenfreund (1948), Gatling (1951), and Ritchie, Ebeling, and Roth (1950), using rats, and Prentice (1949) and Walk (1952), using human subjects, have all demonstrated that systematic reinforcement during the pre-solution period retards learning when the cues are reversed.

A second issue arising from the continuity–noncontinuity controversy, as Melton (1950a) has written, has been whether or not a given aspect of the stimulus, e.g., size, may become attached to a particular response through reinforcement even though it is not relevant to the solution of the current discrimination problem. The continuity theorists have posited, following Hull's (1929) early position, that ". . . all elements of a stimulus complex playing upon the sensorium of an organism at or near the time that a response is evoked tend themselves independently and indiscriminately to acquire the capacity to evoke substantially the same response." In contrast, the noncontinuity position, as posited by Lashley (1942), has held that "if the animals are given a set to react to one aspect of a stimulus situation, large amounts of training do not establish association with other aspects, so long as the original set remains effective for reaching the food."

The following study was used by Lashley (1942) to support this position. Rats (N = 4) were given discrimination training on a jumping stand in which a ten cm. circle was positive and a six cm. circle was negative, with the animals learning to respond to a criterion of 20 errorless trials. An equilateral triangle, ten cm. on each side, was then substituted for the larger circle, thus providing a new discrimination task consisting of a large triangle versus a small circle. Two hundred training trials were then given, with the subjects consistently choosing (and being reinforced for) the triangle. The subjects were then presented with both a triangle and a circle of intermediate size in a test to determine if the animals would respond to form (triangularity). The results indicated no preference for either stimulus, the animals responding only to position throughout a 20-trial period. Although form (in addition to size) had been associated with reinforcement, which according to continuity theory should have resulted in excitatory strength accruing to this stimulus dimension, test trials did not reveal it.

But a number of other experiments have been performed which have not been in keeping with the noncontinuity position. For example, in Spence's (1945) study which was cited previously, although the animals were responding on the basis of position during the pre-solution training, the reversal learning situation revealed that they had also learned something about the brightness of the alleys. Blum and Blum's (1949) replication of Lashley's study, with some minor modifications, has also supported the continuity position. Studies by Bitterman and Coate (1950), Babb (1956, 1957), and Jeeves and North (1956) are some of the more recent investigations which have also lent support to the continuity position. The experimental procedure used by these investigators has been to associate an irrelevant cue with varying percentages of reinforcement during the learning of Task I. With Task II the irrelevant cue becomes relevant for the solution of the problem and the influence of the varying percentages of reinforcement provided during Task I is assessed by examining the rate of learning this second task.

In Bitterman and Coate's (1950) study, their first experiment consisted of having rats learn a black-white discrimination task in which the white card was positive. Contrary to the usual experimental procedure, each card did not appear equally often on each side of the Lashley jumping stand. For one group, the white card appeared on the right on 80 per cent of the trials and on the left on 20 per cent of the trials. This position bias was reversed for a second group of animals so that the white card appeared on the right for 20 per cent of the trials and on the left for 80 per cent. The criterion of learning was 20 correct responses out of 20 trials. Task II consisted of having all animals learn the position habit of responding to the right. The continuity position would assume that when the problem was shifted from a brightness discrimination to a position habit the differential reinforcement for position during the brightness phase of the study should influence performance, with superior performance expected from the group which had been reinforced 80 per cent on the right side. The noncontinuity theory suggests that the differential reinforcement provided during the brightness phase of the experiment should have no effect and that both groups should learn the position habit equally well. The performance of the two groups is presented in Figure 13–10 and unequivocally supports the continuity position. A second experiment by these investigators using a somewhat similar design has confirmed these results.

In Babb's (1956) first study, four groups of rats—three experimental and one control—were trained in the first phase of the

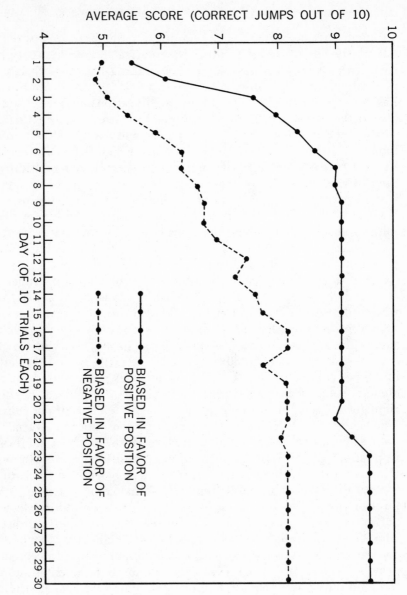

Fig. 13–10. The acquisition of the position habit. *Adapted from Bitterman and Coate (1950)*

experiment to discriminate one alley in which small pull chains hung from the top from a second alley in which chains were not present. For the control group in the experiment both alleys were painted gray. Three experimental groups also learned the chains–no chains discrimination, but one alley was painted black and the other white. For Experimental Group I, the chains (positive cue) were located in the white alley on 30 per cent of the 60 training trials; for Experimental Group II, the chains were located in the white alley on 50 per cent of the trials; for Experimental Group III, the chains were located in the white alley on 70 per cent of the trials. The second phase of the experiment consisted of having the subjects learn a white-black discrimination problem with the white alley positive; chains were not present. All subjects were run to a criterion of 18 correct responses out of 20 trials. The experimental findings, which were consistent with the findings of Bitterman and Coate (1950), revealed that the rate of learning was a function of white alley reinforcement provided during Phase I.

In summary, on both issues which have been examined, the continuity position has had more supporters. The work of Harlow (1949) and his concept of learning set, however, has provided another facet to the controversy. This topic will be discussed more fully in the chapter on transfer; but, briefly, Harlow (1949) has found that monkeys given a series of 250 to 300 discrimination problems gradually acquire the ability to solve a problem in a single trial, a finding which appears to support a noncontinuity position. Regarding this issue, Harlow (1949) indicated, however, that such apparent noncontinuity behavior has developed through a history of gradual learning, thus, emphasizing the continuous nature of the process.

14

Transfer I:

The Role of Specific and General
Factors in the Transfer Situation

TRANSFER OF TRAINING refers to the fact that the learning or training that has taken place in one task carries over, or transfers, to a second. It has been generally acknowledged that this area is one of great practical importance. Our Western culture, for example, has been responsible for organizing a large number of institutions in order to train both children and adults. The general belief has been that such training will carry over to situations in everyday living.

If the learning of one task (Task 1) aids in the learning of a second task (Task 2), it is an example of positive transfer, but if the learning of Task 1 hinders the learning of Task 2 it is negative transfer. Or, it may be that the learning of Task 1 has no influence on the learning of Task 2. Although this situation is frequently designated as one of zero transfer, it should be classified as indeterminate since to state that there is no influence of one task on the other requires the acceptance of the null hypothesis.[1,2]

[1] The reader should be aware that some writers have distinguished between transfer and transfer effects. Here, transfer means the carrying over of a behavior pattern from one performance to another, whereas transfer effect is defined as the influence of the behavior pattern upon the learning of the second task. As so defined, transfer, whenever it occurs, is always positive, although its influence on the second task may be positive, negative, or indeterminate. As Woodworth and Schlosberg (1954) have written, "A habit of speedy work carried over from a well-learned task to a new one may impede the learning of the latter—a clear case of

Transfer Design

Before examining the variables which operate in the transfer situation, transfer designs and transfer measurement should be discussed briefly.[3]

Design 1

| Group A | Learn Task 1 | Learn Task 2 |
| Group B | Learn Task 1' (or rest) | Learn Task 2 |

This design is used most frequently and often has been indicated to be the standard transfer design. Many investigators have employed a rest period for their Task 1' or, in some instances, have brought their subjects (Group B) into the experimental situation to learn only Task 2. But such a procedure does not ensure that Task 1 and Task 1' differ only in one way. If Group A learns Task 1 and then learns Task 2, but Group B learns *only* Task 2, any difference between the groups in learning Task 2 *may* arise from the specific influence of Task 1. However, the difference may also arise from general transfer variables such as warm-up, or learning to learn, brought about by the fact that Group A has engaged in some type of learning activity prior to the learning of the transfer task. Many investigators desire to differentiate transfer effects attributable to the more general transfer variables from those attributable to specific stimulus-response relationships. One solution to the problem may be to use two tasks which are basically identical for Tasks 1 and 1' but differ in that one task is relevant to Task 2 whereas the other task is not.

Design 2

| Group A | Learn Task 1 | Learn Task 2 |
| Group B | Learn Task 1 | Learn Task 2' |

Here, the investigator is interested in determining if, following the learning of Task 1, it is easier to learn Task 2 than it is to

---

positive transfer with a negative transfer effect." Most investigators, however, have not made this distinction but, rather, have written simply in terms of positive, negative, or indeterminate transfer. In so doing, they have referred to transfer effect.

    [2] The operations involved in both experimental extinction and stimulus generalization involve transfer of training situations. Contemporary usage has dictated that these areas be considered in another chapter rather than in this chapter.

    [3] For an extended discussion of this area, the reader is referred to the articles of Gagné, Foster, and Crowley (1948) and Murdock (1957).

learn Task 2'. For example, Russell and Storms (1955) had all their subjects first learn a paired-associate task (e.g., cef–flower). Task 2 consisted of a second paired-associate list which contained the same stimulus words as the first list. One group, however, had to learn responses which were part of the associative chain stemming from the response words, whereas the second group had to learn response words which were not a part of this associative chain.

With this design it is necessary to ensure that Tasks 2 and 2' are equivalent; that is, in the absence of the learning of Task 1, they should be equally difficult to learn. If this is not so, then the experimental findings are confounded since any difference between Group A and Group B may simply reflect differences in the difficulty of Task 2 and Task 2'.

Two other designs, although not frequently used, should be mentioned.

Design 3

| Group A | Learn Task 1 | Learn Task 2 |
| Group B | Learn Task 2 | Learn Task 1 |

An excellent example of this design is found in a study by Gaydos (1956) who examined the transfer of form discrimination from one sensory modality to another. Briefly, subjects learned to recognize stimulus objects (irregular-shaped pieces of masonite) through one sense-modality and then learned to identify the same shapes through a different modality. One group first learned the material using vision and was then transferred to touch, whereas the second group first learned through touch and was then transferred to vision.

Design 4

| Group A | Learn Task 1 | Learn Task 2 |
| Group B | Learn Task 1 | Learn Task 2 |

The last design is one in which the investigator is not interested in examining the influence of a task variable but, rather, is concerned with the contribution of the temporal interval interpolated between the learning of the first and second task. As indicated in Design 4, both groups learn the same tasks; the only difference is the amount of time interpolated between Tasks 1 and 2.

An example of this type of design is found in a study by Bunch (1939) who had rats first learn to go to one side of a T-maze (Task 1) and then either 0, 2, 7, 14, or 28 days later had them learn to go to the other side (Task 2).

In summary, the question which is asked by the experimenter may indicate which transfer design must be used; but, when the investigator may select among them, Design 1 is chosen most frequently. The reason for this choice is that the transfer task is identical for both the experimental and control groups; differences in learning can be readily attributed to the learning of the first task.

Transfer Measurement

In measuring transfer, most contemporary investigators use raw scores (or possibly some transformation of them) which would be obtained by using rate or probability of response measures. The direction and amount of transfer is obtained by subtracting the smaller score made by one group on Task 2 from the larger score of the other group on the same task. Sometimes this value is converted into a percentage of transfer score by dividing the control group's score into the difference and multiplying by 100. Thus, the formula:

$$\text{Percentage of transfer} = \frac{\begin{array}{c}\text{Experimental Score} - \text{Control Score} \\ \text{or} \\ \text{Control Score} - \text{Experimental Score}\end{array}}{\text{Control Score}} \times 100$$

The use of a raw score measure, or a percentage based upon raw score values, has the advantage of precision of meaning, but these measures have the obvious limitation of preventing an investigator from making comparison of the amount of transfer obtained in one task with that of another.

A second way to examine transfer measurement is to compare the amount of transfer which has taken place to the maximum amount of improvement which can take place. The latter value is determined by computing the difference between the total possible score on Task 2 and the actual performance of the control group on Task 2. If correct responses represent the response measure, the formula would be as follows:

$$\text{Percentage of transfer} = \frac{\text{Experimental Score} - \text{Control Score}}{\text{Total Possible Score} - \text{Control Score}} \times 100$$

Although Gagne, Foster, and Crowley (1948) have supported a transfer formula based upon this type of measure, Murdock (1957) has indicated that there are a number of reasons why the use of this formula may not be completely satisfactory. Two of these seem particularly cogent. The first is that the determination of the maximum amount of improvement which is possible to obtain in a given learning task may be difficult or impossible to ascertain. The second is that this formula is generally unsatisfactory for examining negative transfer. Although the upper limit for positive transfer is a value of $+100$ per cent, the lower limit is not -100 per cent but, rather, minus infinity. Moreover, a -100 per cent transfer value is not comparable to a $+100$ per cent transfer.

Murdock has suggested the following percentage of transfer formula which he believes has certain advantages over the others which have been discussed.

$$\text{Percentage of transfer} = \frac{\begin{array}{c}\text{Experimental Score} - \text{Control Score}\\ \text{or}\\ \text{Control Score} - \text{Experimental Score}\end{array}}{\text{Experimental Score} + \text{Control Score}} \times 100$$

It can be noted the denominator includes the performance of the experimental group as well as the performance of the control group, providing a formula in which positive and negative transfer are symmetrical and the upper and lower limits are 100 per cent.

Mixed versus Unmixed Lists

Before proceeding to examine the results of early studies in this area, the reader should be aware of a methodological consideration—the problem of mixed versus unmixed lists.

It will be assumed that an investigator desires to examine the amount of transfer involved in (1) learning to attach a new response to an old stimulus, i.e., A-B, A-C, and (2) learning to attach an old response to a new stimulus, i.e., A-B, C-B. A frequently used experimental design would involve the use of an unmixed list. Two paired-associate lists would be used in which all of the items in one list reflected the A-B, A-C relationship and all of the items in the second list would be of the A-B, C-B variety. It follows that if the investigator desired to study a third or fourth paradigm additional lists reflecting the relationship involved in these paradigms would have to be constructed.

With the mixed list procedure, however, only a single transfer list is used and the list is so constructed that different relationships exist among the items which make up the list. This permits the simultaneous observation of the transfer produced by the different relationships. In examining the problem which was cited previously, and assuming that the original list consisted of six paired-associates, three pairs on the transfer list would form the A-B, A-C paradigm and the remaining three would reflect the A-B, C-B relationship.

A basic question may be raised as to whether or not different experimental findings are obtained when a mixed list is used, in contrast to the use of an unmixed list. Twedt and Underwood (1959), examining four different paradigms, obtained findings which revealed no difference in transfer as a function of whether or not a mixed or unmixed list was used. As a result, they have concluded that investigators may use either type without serious concern that the transfer effects will be different.[4]

Early Work in the Area

Many of the early studies in the area of transfer had their origins in an examination of the concept of "formal discipline." It will be recalled that a number of traditional educators assumed that the individual had faculties which could be developed in much the same way that a muscle could be strengthened by exercise. Memory, reasoning power, and perception were examples of faculties which, it was assumed, could be strengthened with one type of material, which resulted in their preparation for much more general use. Thus, if an individual memorized poetry, such training resulted in the strengthening of an individual's memorial faculty so that the memorizing of any type of material was aided.

Quotations from Roark's (1895) *Psychology in Education* and

[4] A recent study by Johnson and Penney (1965), examining transfer effects of mixed and unmixed list designs in paired-associate learning by children, has not supported the Twedt and Underwood (1959) findings. Whether or not mixed and unmixed list designs can be used interchangeably in studying transfer seems open to question.

Morgan's (1906) *Psychology for Teachers* aptly describe this position. Roark stated that "faculties, like muscles, grow strong by use: therefore do nothing for the pupil that he can do for himself," whereas Morgan pointed out that "it is as a means of training the faculties of comparison and generalisation, that the study of such a language as Latin side by side with English is so valuable."

Although James (1890) was perhaps the first to attempt to test this position experimentally with his research on memory training, the early work of Thorndike and Woodworth (1901) was most noteworthy in examining as well as challenging this doctrine of formal discipline. These experimenters argued that "there is no reason to suppose that any general change occurs corresponding to the words 'improvement of the attention' or 'of the power of observation,' or 'of accuracy.' " Their experimental findings led Thorndike (1914), some years later, to conclude that (p. 268):

> . . . no careful observer would assert that the influence upon the other mental traits is comparable in amount to that upon the direct object of training. By doubling a boy's reasoning power in arithmetical problems we do not double it for formal grammar or chess or economic history or theories of evolution. By tripling the accuracy of movement in fingering exercises we do not triple it for typewriting, playing billiards or painting. The gain of courage in the game of football is never equaled by the gain in moral courage or resistance to intellectual obstacles.

In contrast to a formal discipline position, Thorndike (1914) proposed a theory of identical elements in order to account for transfer effects. As he stated, "The answer which I shall try to defend is that a change in one function alters any other only in so far as the two functions have as factors identical elements." Thorndike indicated that identical elements could be of a general nature as well as of a specific variety. Training in addition helps with multiplication since addition is typically a part of most multiplication problems. More general types of identical elements were ideas of aim and method, attitudes of confidence and care, habituation to distraction, etc. But, unfortunately, Thorndike (1914) made his identical element theory untestable when he defined it as follows: "By identical elements are meant mental processes which have the same cell action in the brain as their physical correlate. It is of course often not possible to tell just what features of two mental abilities are thus identical."

A large number of experiments followed the pioneer studies of Thorndike and Woodworth in which the main objective of the investigator was simply to examine the influence that the training on one task had on the second. What is the influence of memorizing one type of material on the memorizing of a different type [Sleight (1911), Reed (1917)]? What is the influence of canceling certain letters on canceling certain numbers [Martin (1915)] or canceling words [Kline (1914)], etc.? Unfortunately, most of these studies did not lead to a better understanding of the variables which influence transfer.

Transfer Analyzed in Terms of Stimulus and Response

As noted in previous chapters, many investigators have been interested in analyzing learning from a stimulus–response point of view. This approach also has been taken for examining transfer. Two basic paradigms, with some variations thereof, have been studied quite extensively. The verbal learning situation has been used most frequently to examine them. One of these paradigms has been to investigate the kind and amount of transfer when (1) an old response is attached to a new stimulus (A-B, C-B) and (2) when a new response is attached to an old stimulus (A-B, A-C).

Attaching Old Responses to New Stimuli (A-B, C-B)

Many of the early experimenters investigating transfer, e.g., Wylie (1919), concluded that when an old response was attached to a new stimulus (A-B, C-B) positive transfer was obtained. It was further posited that as the new stimulus (C) became more similar to the old (A) the amount of positive transfer increased. Studies by Bruce (1933), Hamilton (1943), Bugelski and Cadwallader (1956) as well as others have supported this generalization, which Osgood (1949) considered to be one of three empirical laws which govern transfer. Thus, Osgood (1946) wrote that where stimuli are varied and responses are functionally identical positive transfer and retroactive facilitation are obtained; the magnitude of both increases as the similarity among the stimulus members increases.[5]

[5] It generally has been assumed that there is a high correlation between the findings obtained in studies examining (1) transfer and (2) retroaction. Bugelski and Cadwallader (1956) have supported this assumption by reporting an r of −.85 be-

Although some question may be raised with the results obtained by Bruce (1933) and Hamilton (1943), since these studies did not control for the influence of nonspecific transfer (warm-up, learning to learn), this criticism cannot be leveled against Bugelski and Cadwallader (1956). In their experiment, thirteen nonsense forms used previously in a verbal learning study by Gibson (1941) served as stimuli and adjectives formerly employed by Osgood (1946) were used as responses.

In one part of this study, the transfer task consisted of one of four different stimulus conditions (identical, similar, less similar, or neutral when compared with the first task) paired with the responses used in the original task. The following general procedure was used: when a subject correctly anticipated a given response on two successive trials, the stimulus–response pair was dropped from the list. Learning continued until all the responses were anticipated correctly. Both original and transfer lists were learned to this criterion. Bugelski and Cadwallader found progressively easier learning of the transfer task as the stimuli comprising the transfer task grew more similar to those found on the original task. When the mean number of trials to reach the criterion for each of the experimental conditions was compared with an A-B, C-D control group (which must be used if the influence of learning to learn and warm-up is to be controlled) positive transfer was obtained for all conditions.

The more recent studies of Twedt and Underwood (1959), Postman (1962a), Jung (1962), and Dallett (1962), however, have been at variance with the general position that attaching an old response to a new stimulus provides positive transfer. In the Twedt and Underwood (1959) study, twelve paired-associates made up of two-syllable adjectives served as the material to be learned for the original and transfer tasks. Following the learning of the first list to a criterion of one perfect trial, the second list was presented for ten trials. The results of the A-B, C-B condition compared with results of the A-B, C-D control condition revealed a small amount of negative transfer; this effect was present throughout all ten transfer trials. Moreover, such an effect was present regardless of whether the experimental procedure utilized a mixed or unmixed list.

---

tween these two measures. The result has been that, although an investigator utilizes a transfer of training design, the findings are believed to have equal applicability to retroaction.

Postman (1962a) and Jung (1962) have confirmed the Twedt and Underwood (1959) findings. Postman (1962a) was interested in examining the A-B, C-B paradigm as a function of the degree of first-trial learning. Ten two-syllable adjectives were used to make up each list, and the degree of first-list learning was manipulated by having subjects learn to a criterion of (1) six correct responses on a single trial, (2) ten correct responses on a single trial, and (3) ten correct responses on a single trial plus 50 per cent overlearning. When compared to an appropriate control group (A-B, C-D), the A-B, C-B condition yielded negative transfer, with the amount of transfer not changing (at least at a statistically significant level) as a function of the degree of first-list learning. Jung's (1962) replication of Postman's (1962a) experiment yielded similar findings.

Dallett (1962) used the basic experimental material employed by Bugelski and Cadwallader (1956). In one part of this study, after the subjects had received seven trials on the first task, the transfer task was made up by pairing identical responses with stimuli which were (1) similar, (2) less similar, or (3) completely different from the stimuli used on the original list. Seven learning trials were also provided on this task. When the experimental group's findings were compared with an appropriate control group's (A-B, C-D), the different stimulus–identical response group revealed negative transfer, a finding in keeping with Twedt and Underwood (1959), Postman (1962a), and Jung (1962). The (1) similar and (2) less similar stimuli–identical response groups revealed positive transfer, although there was no significant difference between the transfer scores obtained by these groups.

Recently, Jung (1963) has reported that whether positive or negative transfer is obtained with the A-B, C-B paradigm may be a function of the meaningfulness of the material which is utilized. In this study, paired-associate lists were used in which two-syllable adjectives served as stimuli and trigrams served as responses; six pairs made up each list. Two levels (high and low) of response meaningfulness (as inferred from measures of trigram frequency) were used. Following the learning of the first list to a criterion of one perfect trial, the second list was presented for ten trials. The results, as measured by the mean number of correct responses over the ten trials, are indicated in Figure 14–1. Note that with low meaningful responses the A-B, C-B condition is superior to

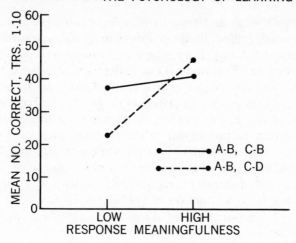

Fig. 14–1. Mean number of correct responses as a function of response meaningfulness. *Adapted from Jung (1963)*

the control group (A-B, C-D), thus, indicating positive transfer. On the other hand, with high meaningful responses, the A-B, C-B condition yields negative transfer since the performance is poorer than that obtained by the controls.[6]

In summary, it would appear that Osgood's first empirical law should be modified to include the possibility that the A-B, C-B condition does, at times, produce small amounts of negative transfer, perhaps depending upon the kind of response material that is utilized. Thus, where stimuli are varied and responses are functionally identical, small amounts of positive or negative transfer may be obtained, the magnitude of the positive transfer increasing or the negative transfer decreasing as the similarity among the stimulus members increases.

Attaching New Responses to Old Stimuli (A-B, A-C)

This paradigm has been classified as one of associative inhibition, and the results of most studies have indicated that negative transfer is obtained when the subject is required to attach a new response to an old stimulus. This area of experimental inquiry was examined initially by Müller and Schumann (1894) who formulated the Law of Associative Inhibition: "When any two

[6] It should be noted that this condition yielded a small amount of positive transfer when early trials of the transfer task were examined.

items, as A and B, have been associated, it is more difficult to form an association between either and a third item K."

Bugelski (1942), Bugelski and Cadwallader (1956) as well as Twedt and Underwood (1959), Postman (1962a), Jung (1962) and Dallett (1962), to mention only a sampling of investigators, are all in agreement—learning to attach a new response to an old stimulus leads to negative transfer. In the Twedt and Underwood (1959) experiment, for example, following the learning of one list of paired-associates, the experimenters had their subjects learn a second list in which the stimuli were identical to those in the first but the responses were different. When the results of this A-B, A-C condition were compared with those of the control group (A-B, C-D), the findings revealed negative transfer. When comparing the amount of negative transfer produced by the A-B, A-C paradigm with that of the A-B, B-C, Twedt and Underwood (1959) noted that smaller amounts of negative transfer were provided by this latter paradigm—a typical finding when this comparison is made.

It was reported earlier that Jung (1963) had found that with the A-B, C-B paradigm the meaningfulness of the responses which are used contributes to the amount of transfer which is obtained. This investigator has found a similar effect with the A-B, A-C paradigm. It will be recalled that paired-associates were used in this study, with two-syllable adjectives serving as stimuli and trigrams as responses. Two levels (high and low) of response meaningfulness were employed. Following the learning of the first list to a criterion of one perfect trial, the second list was presented for ten trials. Jung found, as Figure 14–2 indicates, that greater amounts of negative transfer were obtained when high meaningful responses were used than when the responses were of low meaningful value. Merikle and Battig (1963) have also found that negative transfer increased with increased meaningfulness of the A-B, A-C paradigm, although it must be pointed out that this increase was not statistically significant.

A number of instrumental as well as motor learning situations have also demonstrated that negative transfer is obtained when a new response is attached to an old stimulus. For example, Hunter (1922) trained rats to turn right in a T-shaped discrimination apparatus in response to light and to turn left when there was darkness. After the animals had attained a criterion of 95 per cent errorless responses on two successive days, the animals were

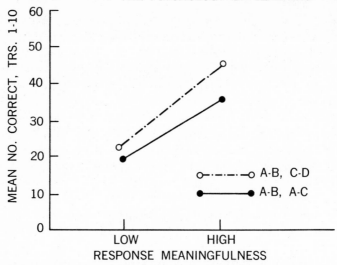

Fig. 14–2. Mean number of correct responses as a function of response meaningfulness. *Adapted from Jung (1963)*

trained to turn left for light and right for darkness. The first task was learned in an average of 286 trials, but the second task required an average of 603 trials.

Using a motor-skills task, Siipola (1941) had subjects learn to move a lever into one of ten slots when a numbered stimulus, one through ten, was presented. Following the subject's response, a buzzer sounded and the subject returned the lever to a neutral position to await presentation of the next stimulus. The transfer task was similar except that when stimulus three appeared the lever had to be placed in the slot previously associated with stimulus seven and when stimulus four appeared the lever had to be placed in the slot previously associated with stimulus eight. A considerable amount of negative transfer was obtained when the subject's performance on these two response changes was analyzed.[7]

One variation of the A-B, A-C paradigm would be to examine transfer as a function of the similarity of the responses between

[7] From time to time some investigators have reported that the A-B, A-C paradigm does not yield negative transfer. See the results obtained by Bunch (1939) using a T-maze learning situation employing rats as subjects. Porter and Duncan (1953) have also been unable to obtain negative transfer utilizing an A-B, A-C verbal learning situation.

the two tasks. In a basic study examining this relationship, Osgood (1946) used a paired-associate task in which two letters were used as stimuli (c.m., f.s., etc.) and adjectives served as responses. On the transfer task, the stimuli remained the same but the responses were varied in that they were either (1) similar, (2) neutral, or (3) opposed to the original adjectives.[8] A mixed list design was used. Subjects learned the original list to a criterion of one perfect trial and the transfer task to a criterion of two perfect trials. The results revealed negative transfer under all conditions, although it was least for the identical stimulus–similar response condition. There appeared to be no differences between the identical stimulus–neutral response condition and the identical stimulus–opposed response condition.

As an outcome of the findings from this study as well as from many others performed in this area, Osgood (1949) proposed a second empirical law stating that where stimuli were functionally identical and responses were varied negative transfer would be obtained, the magnitude of such transfer decreasing as the similarity between the responses increased.[9]

A further variation of the A-B, A-C paradigm would be to employ a transfer task in which stimuli were similar to the stimuli used in the original task and paired with different responses. Gibson (1941) has examined this type of situation. First, a number of nonsense forms were made up which resembled the standard ones in varying degrees. Figure 14–3 illustrates some of the standard forms and the forms of varying degrees of similarity. For the original task, subjects learned to attach a nonsense syllable to each of 12 standard forms. A criterion of eight out of 12 correct was employed. Following such training, a transfer task was used in which the forms, varying in similarity, were used as stimuli and nonsense syllables different from those used in the

---

[8] More specifically, similar words were not necessarily synonyms but were judged to have the same feeling-tone and were believed to be interchangeable. For example the word "low" was regarded as similar to "dejected," whereas "serious" was regarded as similar to "weighty." Words selected as being opposed in meaning were not antonyms but again were related to the feeling-tone. Thus, the opposed word for "dejected" was "high," and the opposed word for "weighty" was "humorous." Neutral words were selected on the basis of their having no recognizable similarity or opposition to the original adjectives.

[9] There is some indication that if the responses found on the transfer task are very similar to those used on the original training slight amounts of positive transfer rather than small amounts of negative transfer may be found. See Bruce's (1933) early study as well as a more recent one by Runquist and Marshall (1963).

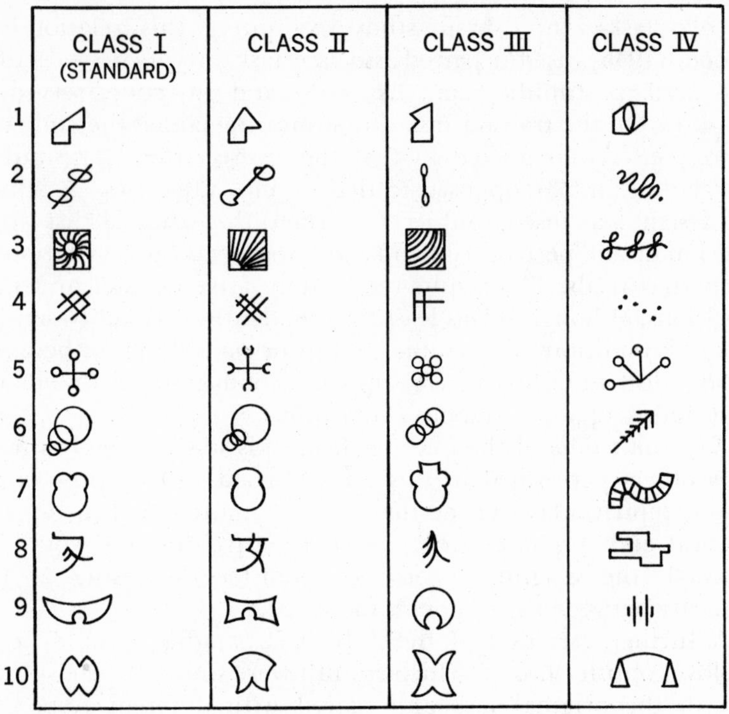

Fig. 14–3. Stimulus forms grouped in classes as a function of their similarity to the standard. *Adapted from Gibson (1941)*

original training served as responses. Maximum negative transfer was obtained when stimuli identical to those used in the original training were paired with the new responses. As the similarity of the stimuli decreased, negative transfer decreased, with zero transfer being approximated when neutral stimuli were paired with different responses. Gibson's (1941) work was largely responsible for Osgood's (1949) proposing a third transfer principle: When both stimulus and response members are simultaneously varied, negative transfer is obtained, the magnitude of such transfer increasing as stimulus similarity increases.

The Role of Mediated Responses

One variation of attaching a new response to an old stimulus has been examined under the topic of mediated association. In brief, the experimental question may be posed: If A is first associated with B, and then B with C, will the association A-C be learned more readily as a result of this previous training? Although there is the attaching of a new response to an old stimulus in this situation, and one which might normally be expected to provide negative transfer, it differs from the other studies which have been examined since it may be that Task B will mediate the connection between A and C and, thus, lead to more rapid learning and positive transfer effects.

Although Peters (1935) was one of the earliest investigators to examine the role of mediated associations, his experimental findings were not very conclusive since he was able to demonstrate mediation for only a few subjects in just two out of nine experiments. A more conclusive demonstration was provided by Bugelski and Scharlock (1952). In this study, 20 college students learned three lists of paired-associate nonsense syllables, one at each of three separate learning sessions, with subjects learning to anticipate each response to a criterion of five perfect trials. The experimental lists were A-B, B-C, and A-C; and the control lists were A-B, B-C, and A-D. Each subject learned both sets of lists.

The results showed that experimental list A-C was learned more rapidly than the A-D list, with the findings providing a clear demonstration of mediated association in the learning of verbal material. Interestingly enough, a questioning of the subjects revealed that none of the subjects reported that he was conscious of using the mediating B syllable in attempting to learn the A-C list.

A later study by Russell and Storms (1955) examined the role of the mediating verbal processes when the mediating process was implemented by pre-existing language habits and extended over more than a single implicit verbal term. Their design was similar to Bugelski and Scharlock's except that words rather than nonsense syllables were used and two implicit words rather than one linked the pairs on the test trial. List 1 consisted of a nonsense syllable which served as a stimulus; the response word was obtained from the Kent-Rosanoff association test. Russell and Storms had obtained norms for responses on this test which made it possible to infer a B-C and C-D association without establishing it experimentally. The test for the mediation effect was then made by requiring the subjects to learn a list of A-D pairings. A group which learned an A-X pairing was used as the control. The manner in which the investigators hypothesized that the associa-

TABLE 14–1

An Illustration of the Chaining and Control Paradigms

	LIST 1	ASSOCIATIONS INFERRED FROM NORMS	LIST 2 (TEST LIST)
Chaining Paradigm	$A_1 \cdots > B_1$	$(B_1 \to C_1 \to D_1)$	$A_1 \cdots\cdots\cdots > D_1$ $\searrow (B_1 \to C_1) \nearrow$
Control Paradigm	$A_2 \cdots > B_2$	$(B_2 \to C_2 \to D_2)$	$A_2 \cdots\cdots\cdots\cdots > X_2$ $\searrow (B_2 \to C_2 \to D_2)$

(Adapted from Russell and Storms, 1955)

TABLE 14–2

Nonsense Syllables, Associative Chains, and Control Words Used in Forming the Paired-Associate Lists

A NONSENSE SYLLABLE	B FIRST CHAINED WORD	C SECOND CHAINED WORD	D FINAL CHAINED WORD	X CONTROL WORD
CEF	Stem	Flower	Smell	Joy
DAX	Memory	Mind	Matter	Afraid
YOV	Soldier	Army	Navy	Cheese
VUX	Trouble	Bad	Good	Music
WUB	Wish	Want	Need	Table
GEX	Justice	Peace	War	House
JID	Thief	Steal	Take	Sleep
ZIL	Ocean	Water	Drink	Doctor
LAJ	Command	Order	Disorder	Cabbage
MYV	Fruit	Apple	Red	Hand

(Adapted from Russell and Storms, 1955)

tive chains facilitated the learning of the A-D pairs is schematically illustrated in Table 14–1. The nonsense syllables, associative chains, and control words which were used in forming the paired-associate lists are indicated in Table 14–2. Russell and Storms found that there was facilitation of learning of the A-D as contrasted with the learning of the A-X pairs.

An Attempted Integration of the Transfer Studies

A logical question which arises from a consideration of the many studies which have been reviewed in this section would be

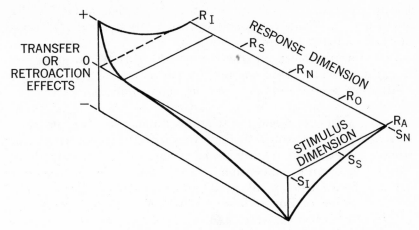

Fig. 14–4. The transfer and retroaction surface: medial plane represents transfer effects of zero magnitude; response relations distributed along length of solid and stimulus relations along its width.
Adapted from Osgood (1949)

whether or not the bulk of them can be organized into some
meaningful whole. An early attempt was made by Robinson
(1927) in his Skaggs-Robinson hypothesis. Briefly, this hypothesis
stated that facilitation, or positive transfer, was maximum when
the successively practiced material was identical; moderate degrees
of similarity between such material resulted in maximum negative transfer, with such transfer decreasing progressively as the
successively practiced material became dissimilar. Difficulties with
this hypothesis arose from conflicting experimental data [Mc-
Geoch and McDonald (1931), Johnson (1933)], but a basic problem was that there was no specification as to whether the hypothesis
applied to stimulus material, response material, or both.

Some years later, Osgood (1949) provided a three-dimensional
surface which he generated from his three empirical laws and
which in turn, as noted, had been derived from a number of
earlier experimental studies. Figure 14–4 provides this representation, and it can be observed that separate axes have been used
for the (1) stimulus, (2) response, and (3) kind and amount of
transfer. Since the stimulus and response members of the task
have been considered as representing basic dimensions, Osgood
(1949) pointed out that it has been necessary to limit this surface
to only the experimental situations in which there can be a clear
identification of the stimuli and responses which make up the

learning situation. One unusual feature of this surface is the antagonistic response category (R_A) which Osgood (1949) postulated would provide greater amounts of negative transfer than would the responses of the "opposed" variety. Most subsequent investigators have ignored this particular category since the distinction between opposed and antagonistic responses has not been clear. It should also be noted that an "opposed" stimulus category is lacking along the stimulus dimension. The probable reason for this, of course, is that Gibson's (1941) nonsense-form stimulus material frequently has been used in studies which have varied the stimulus dimension and it is impossible to obtain a stimulus figure which is "opposed" to the standard.

The studies of Bugelski and Cadwallader (1956) and Dallett (1962), parts of which were cited previously, were major attempts to examine simultaneously most of the key points on Osgood's surface. In the Bugelski and Cadwallader (1956) study, the transfer task consisted of four different stimulus conditions (identical, similar, less similar, and neutral); each of which was paired with one of four different responses (identical, similar, neutral, and opposed). Thus, 16 different experimental conditions were examined. The specific stimuli which were employed were the nonsense forms used by Gibson (1941), which have been described, and the response continuum came from the lists which Osgood (1946) had used.

The curves depicting the findings obtained by Bugelski and Cadwallader (1956) are compared with those formulated by Osgood (1949) and are presented in Figures 14–5 and 14–6. As Bugelski and Cadwallader (1956) have pointed out, specific score values actually cannot be assigned to Osgood's curves, but values can be approximated to provide some comparison. An examination of Figure 14–5 reveals that when the type of response is held constant, and the varying types of stimuli are plotted along the abscissa, there is a marked similarity between the curves generated from Bugelski and Cadwallader's data and Osgood's representation. On the other hand, as Figure 14–6 indicates, when the type of stimulus is held constant, and varying types of responses are plotted along the abscissa, there is considerable discrepancy between the two curves, with the major problem occurring in the "opposed" response category.

Dallett's (1962) paired-associate study also used Gibson's (1941) figures as stimuli and Osgood's (1946) adjectives as

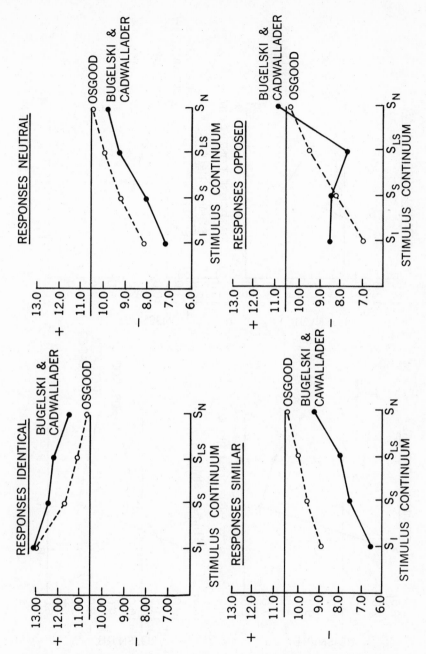

Fig. 14–5. The experimental findings of Bugelski and Cadwallader compared with Osgood's theoretical values. *Figures have been prepared from data supplied by Bugelski and Cadwallader (1956)*

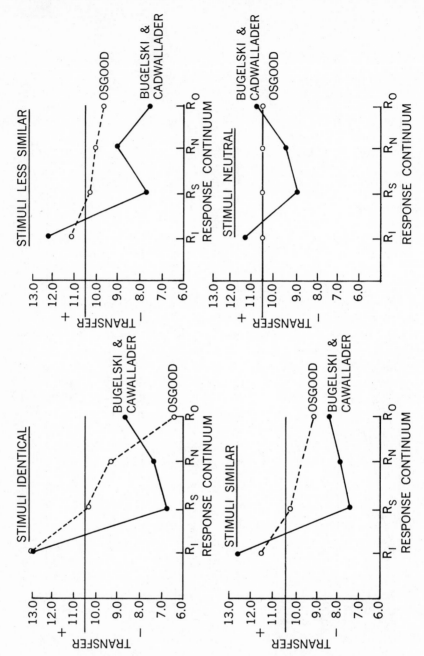

Fig. 14–6. The experimental findings of Bugelski and Cadwallader compared with Osgood's theoretical values. *Adapted from Bugelski and Cadwallader (1956)*

responses. Four degrees of stimulus similarity were combined with three degrees of response similarity to form the varying transfer tasks. For the original task, all subjects were provided only seven trials; the transfer task was also presented for seven trials. In general, the results supported Osgood's predictions and did not agree with those of Bugelski and Cadwallader (1956).

In summary, what can be concluded about Osgood's three-dimensional surface? First, his framework makes it possible to present succinctly many of the transfer findings which have been obtained when the varying stimulus and response relationships have been manipulated in the transfer situation. Many of the relationships which exist among the different paradigms have had experimental verification, although there is some question as to whether it is possible, as Osgood (1949) has done, to indicate that the kind of transfer for a number of paradigms will be positive or negative. For example, the studies of Twedt and Underwood (1959), Postman (1962a), Jung (1962) as well as others have indicated that the A-B, C-B paradigm will produce small amounts of negative transfer rather than slightly positive or zero transfer as would be predicted from Osgood's transfer surface.

It must also be recognized that the surface provides no information concerning the interaction which may exist between the similarity variable and the operation of other variables which contribute to kind and amount of transfer. Thus, Jung's (1963) finding of an interaction between the characteristic of the material used (high versus low meaningfulness) and the amount of transfer produced by a particular paradigm cannot be represented.

Similarity of Stimuli and Responses within the Task

The examination of the role of similarity of stimuli and responses existing between the original and transfer task has been limited primarily to examining the similarity between tasks. Gagne, Baker, and Foster (1950) have proposed that it is appropriate to examine the role of similarity among stimuli and responses within each task. As an example of their point of view, the following situation is outlined. The original task may be described as pressing a telegraph key on the right when a red light is presented and pressing a key on the left to the presentation of a green light. The transfer task consists of using an orange light paired with the right key and a yellow light paired with the left key. The similarity between the stimuli used in the second task is greater than that found between the stimuli used in the first task.[10]

Four general types of stimulus and response variation have been considered, and, using stimulus and response generalization concepts, the investigators have postulated varying amounts of positive and negative transfer effects. Table 14–3 provides a summary of these along with hypothesized transfer effects. Although the investigators' discussion was confined to an examination of discriminative motor tasks of a relatively simple variety, they believed that their analysis could be extended to much more complex skills.

In general, very little research has been generated as a function of this analysis, but one area deserves particular attention. An examination of the complete reversal category in Table 14–3 reveals that, although the stimuli and responses of the second task may be identical to those used in the first task, if the stimulus-response relationship is reversed, maximum negative transfer is hypothesized. (This paradigm has been depicted as A-B, A-Br.) A study by Porter and Duncan (1953) attempted to examine this prediction. Subjects, in two groups, first learned a 12-item paired-associate adjective list to one errorless trial. The transfer task was then presented; for one group the same stimuli as used in List 1 were employed but these were paired with new responses (A-B, A-C). For the second group, the same stimulus and response words as used on List 1 were employed; however, the items were re-paired so that each response was paired with a stimulus different from the stimulus with which it had been paired on List 1. The second list was learned by both groups to a criterion of one errorless trial. The results showed that the group which had the old stimulus and response re-paired, thus forming new pairs, had considerable negative transfer.

These findings were confirmed subsequently by Besch and Reynolds (1958), Twedt and Underwood (1959), Postman (1962a), and Jung (1962) but not by Mandler and Heinemann (1956) who found high positive transfer with this A-B, A-Br paradigm. Since Mandler and Heinemann (1956) used low meaningful material (consonant syllables for responses), in contrast to the high meaningful material used by the other investiga-

[10] It must be pointed out that, in the example, similarity relationships exist between tasks as well as within.

TABLE 14–3

Showing the Types of Variation Which May Be Made in a Second Learning
Task with Respect to a First Learning Task, and the Transfer Expected to
Result from Each

TYPE OF VARIATION IN SECOND TASK	STIMULI OF SECOND TASK	RESPONSES OF SECOND TASK	S-R RELATION-SHIPS OF SECOND TASK	TRANSFER
Stimulus alteration	increasingly similar	identical	identical	positive, decreasing in amount
	increasingly dissimilar	identical	identical	positive, decreasing in amount
	same degree of similarity, increasingly displaced	identical	identical	positive, decreasing in amount
Response alteration	identical	increasingly similar	identical	positive, decreasing in amount
	identical	increasingly dissimilar	identical	positive, decreasing in amount
	identical	same degree of similarity, increasingly displaced	identical	positive, decreasing in amount
Complete reversal	identical	identical	reversed	maximum negative
Partial reversal	increasingly similar, increasingly dissimilar, or increasingly displaced	identical	reversed	negative, decreasing in amount
	identical	increasingly similar, increasingly dissimilar, or increasingly displaced	reversed	negative, decreasing in amount

(Adapted from Gagne, Baker, and Foster, 1950)

tors, Merikle and Battig (1963) attempted to determine if the conflicting findings were a function of the material used. Briefly, these investigators employed three levels of meaningful material, with common CVC words representing one end of the continuum and consonant syllables the other. One group of subjects was then provided lists of high meaningful material, a second group with lists of medium meaningful material, and a third group with lists of low meaningful material. Following the learning of the first list (A-B) to a criterion of one errorless trial, a second list containing A-Br, A-C, and C-D (control) pairs was learned to a criterion of two errorless trials or a maximum of 20 trials. Note, of course, that this experiment utilized the mixed list design. The primary concern is with the A-B, A-Br paradigm, and the results indicated that when the material to be learned had high meaningfulness, negative transfer was obtained—a finding in keeping with Porter and Duncan (1953), etc. On the other hand, when low meaningful material was used, Mandler and Heinemann's findings of positive transfer were confirmed. Thus, whether or not the re-pairing of old stimuli and responses to make new pairs produces positive or negative transfer appears to be dependent upon whether or not high or low meaningful material is used.

The Role of Task Difficulty

A prediction made from Osgood's surface would be that maximum positive transfer should take place when the stimuli and responses of the second task are identical to those found on the first. Lawrence (1952) has suggested that, at least under certain circumstances, such a generalization does not hold. Rather, he has posited that a difficult discrimination may be learned more easily if the subjects are trained first on an easy discrimination of the same type than if all training is given directly on the difficult discrimination.

In an experimental test of this situation, four groups of rats were given training on a brightness discrimination problem. Group I, the hardest discrimination group, received 80 trials in learning to discriminate between stimuli which differed by approximately six foot-candles (31.8 versus 25.9). This was the test task to which all other groups would be transferred. A second group, the abrupt transition group, received 30 trials on an easy discrimination (82.9 foot-candles versus 15.2 foot-candles) and was then shifted to the test stimuli for the remaining 50 trials. A

TABLE 14–4

Mean Error Score on Last 50 Trials of the
Test Discrimination

GROUP	MEAN ERROR SCORE
Hard discrimination group	17.7
Abrupt discrimination group	12.3
Gradual discrimination group	7.9

(Adapted from Lawrence, 1952)

third group, the gradual transition group, received its first ten trials on an easy discrimination (82.9 foot-candles versus 15.2 foot-candles) and was then shifted to a more difficult problem for ten trials (53.9 versus 18.7). Ten additional problems were given on a still more difficult problem (39.9 versus 25.9). Finally, the last 50 trials were provided on the test stimuli.[11] The mean error scores for the three groups on the last 50 trials are presented in Table 14–4, and the findings indicate that the most efficient way of setting up the discrimination was to devote part of the training trials to an easier discrimination on the same continuum of stimuli. The gain in efficiency appears to be increased if the transition from the easy to the difficult discrimination involves intermediate steps of difficulty rather than being abrupt.

These findings have been confirmed by a number of investigators who used a variety of learning situations. North (1959) was interested in examining whether the phenomenon of facilitated transfer from easy to difficult problems took place under more complex stimulus conditions than were obtained in the case of a simple sensory dimension such as brightness which Lawrence employed. Results from three experiments confirmed Lawrence's (1952) findings. Baker and Osgood (1954) and Restle (1955), using adult humans as subjects, and House and Zeaman (1960), using mental defectives, have also confirmed Lawrence's findings that transfer may be facilitated by using an easy to difficult continuum.

The Role of Extraexperimental Learning

In the transfer experiments which have been reviewed, most frequently the subject first learned a specific task (Task A) to

[11] A fourth group was also employed but this served merely as a specialized control group.

enable the experimenter to determine the influence of that task on the learning of a second (Task B). This undoubtedly is the most direct, and usually easiest, way to see if a given variable has any influence on the transfer task. Recently, however, a number of investigators, using the verbal learning situation, have examined transfer by assessing the learning which has been acquired by the subject outside the experimental situation and then measuring the influence of such learning on the acquisition of material which is provided in an experimental situation. The fact that such previous learning, although not acquired in a laboratory situation, does make a basic contribution in the new learning situation dictates that this situation be considered within a transfer context.

Underwood and Postman (1960) delineated two types of verbal habits which subjects acquire and which influence the learning of the verbal material. These habits are of a unit sequence and letter sequence variety, both of which have been developed through the normal course of learning the language. By a unit sequence habit, the investigators refer to connections between verbal items which have been learned with varying degrees of strength. It has been generally accepted that one way of assessing the strength of the varying unit sequence habits is to use word association data. For example, if a subject's continuous associations to the word "hard" are "easy," "soft," "egg," "wood," and "rock," in that order, it would be assumed that the "hard-easy" relationship represents a strong unit association whereas "hard-rock" represents a weak one. Moreover, these previously learned associations should facilitate or interfere with the learning of paired-associates in the laboratory. That is, it would be expected that the paired-associate "hard-easy" would be quite easy to learn since the pre-existing association and the association to be learned in the laboratory are identical. On the other hand, if the paired-associate was "hard-rock," it would be expected that the stronger associations to "hard" would interfere with the learning of the "hard-rock" pair; in general, the subject would have to extinguish or inhibit these stronger associates before learning could take place.

By a letter sequence habit, Underwood and Postman (1960) mean that the individual has learned that certain letters (rather than words) will follow others with varying degrees of probability. For example, most individuals have learned that U almost invariably follows Q and that the probability that any other letter follows Q is quite low. Following the earlier argument, when a subject attempts to learn the bigram QJ, the previously learned habit that U follows Q will provide interference to such learning; this previously established habit will have to be inhibited or extinguished before the new bigram can be learned.

Experiments by Underwood and Postman (1960), Underwood and Schulz (1960), Postman (1962), Spence (1963), and Coleman (1963) are a few of those which have demonstrated the contribution of these previously learned habits to the learning of material provided in the laboratory. For example, in Coleman's (1963) study, subjects were first required to continuously associate adjectives to 80 nouns. As an example, the words "doughnut is" were presented and the subject was required to respond with adjectives in order to make a sensible associate to the word doughnut. Thus, a subject might first respond with "round" and then "sweet," "sugary," "powdery," and "crusty." Similarly, the words "coffee is" might elicit "brown," "bitter," "good," "black," and "sweet" in that order. Association hierarchies were then compiled for each noun on a subject-by-subject basis. It was assumed that adjectives given early in the series represented strong associations for the subject and that words given late represented weak ones. Thirteen of the pairs were then so selected that they were preceded by many stronger associates. For example, doughnut-crusty might be used since it was preceded by doughnut: round, sweet, sugary, and powdery. For thirteen other pairs, each pair was preceded by relatively few stronger associates. Thus, coffee-bitter, might be used since it would be exceeded in associative strength by only coffee-brown. Thus, for 13 pairs of words, there was strong extraexperimental interference, but for 13 other pairs, such interference was minimal. The list was presented until each subject had learned at least 20 responses. Coleman found that those paired-associates which were subject to strong extraexperimental interference (doughnut-crusty) were more difficult to learn than associates subject to minimal interference (coffee-bitter). Moreover, most of the incorrect responses made by the subjects in learning the material could be traced back to the association hierarchies provided by the subject in the association test.

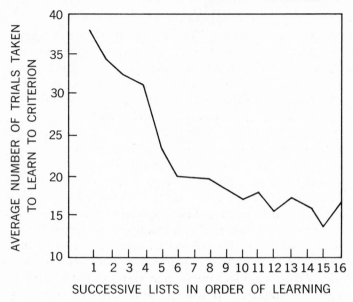

Fig. 14–7. A curve indicating the changes in rate of learning sixteen successive lists of twelve nonsense syllables. *Adapted from Ward (1937)*

GENERAL FACTORS IN TRANSFER

The experimental evidence which has been accumulated in the area reveals that all transfer effects cannot be related to an analysis of specific stimulus and response relationships. These other influences frequently have been designated as general or nonspecific factors, and some of the more important of these will be discussed in this section.

The Concept of Learning Sets

In an early study, Ward (1937) found that the number of trials required to learn a list of nonsense syllables declined as a function of the number of lists which were learned. As Figure 14–7 indicates, the average number of trials taken to learn a list after 14 lists had been learned previously was considerably fewer than those trials required to learn the first list.

Harlow (1949) has demonstrated a similar effect with monkeys learning discrimination problems in his now classic study of learning-set formation. The task was one in which the monkey was

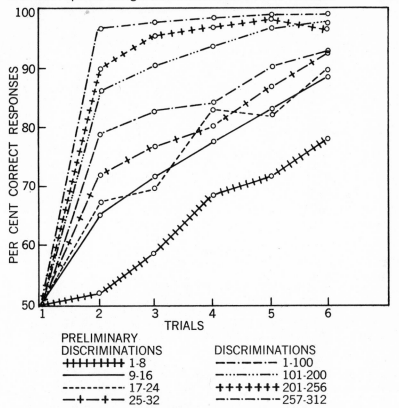

Fig. 14–8. Discrimination learning curves obtained from successive blocks of problems. *Adapted from Harlow (1949)*

required to choose the rewarded one of two objects which differed in multiple characteristics and which were shifted from left to right in a balanced, predetermined order. The apparatus (Wisconsin General Test Apparatus) is illustrated in Figure 2–8.

In an early study, a series of 344 problems, using 344 different pairs of stimuli, was run with a group of eight monkeys. Each of the first 32 problems was run for 50 trials, but only six trials were given for the next 200 problems. For the last 112 problems, an average of only nine trials was provided. Figure 14–8 presents learning curves which reveal the percentage of correct responses on the first six trials of these discriminations, and Figure 14–9 plots the percentage of correct responses on Trials 2 to 6 as a

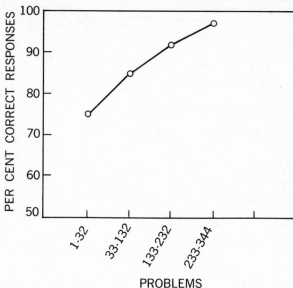

Fig. 14–9. Discrimination learning-set curve based on Trials 2–6 responses. *Adapted from Harlow (1949)*

function of the number of problems which have been presented. Both figures reveal an increase in learning efficiency as more and more problems are provided for the organism to solve, but it must be noted that this increase in efficiency does not represent positive transfer effects based upon similar stimuli used from one problem to another. Rather, another process must be involved; Harlow has called this a learning set or learning to learn.

As might be anticipated, the formation of learning sets has been investigated in a variety of species with a number of different learning situations. Warren and Baron (1956) have demonstrated the phenomenon with cats, and Koranakos and Arnold (1957) have found that rats also are able to acquire learning sets—a finding confirmed by Weaver and Michels (1961) and Wright, Kay, and Sime (1963). Kaufman and Peterson (1958) have shown that retarded children (Stanford-Binet IQ of 50 to 75) have the capacity to acquire learning sets with an object quality discrimination learning situation. Of interest also is the work of Meyer and Miles (1953) and Duncan (1960). Meyer and Miles (1953) demonstrated the formation of learning sets with college students learning 20 lists of nonsense syllables—a

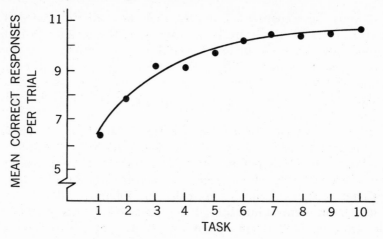

Fig. 14–10. Mean performance per trial over all twenty trials on each task. *Adapted from Duncan (1960)*

finding not unlike that obtained by Ward (1937). Finally, Duncan (1960) noted learning-set formation with human subjects using a motor-skills task. Ten paired-associate tasks with twenty trials per task were provided. In each task, the stimulus was a visual form and the response was a movement of a lever into one of 13 slots. Figure 14–10 presents the mean performance per trial for all 20 trials given on each task.

As Reese (1964) has noted, a number of experimenters have examined learning-set formation as a function of a number of variables, i.e., size and kind of stimuli, contiguity of stimulus and locus of response, and number of trials per problem. Harlow and Warren (1952) and Chow (1954), for example, demonstrated that learning-set formation is more rapid when stereometric objects are used as stimuli, in contrast to planometric objects. (Stereometric objects differ in multiple dimensions of external form, size, color, and surface properties, whereas planometric objects are similar in size and external form but differ with regard to color and surface properties.) Murphy and Miller (1955) have shown that monkeys cannot acquire a learning set if the stimulus object, which a monkey must push aside in the typical discrimination problem, does not cover the food well but, rather, is placed six inches above it. (The food wells in such instances were covered by identical pieces of wood.)

It must be recognized, however, that the contribution of the characteristics of the stimuli and the spatial contiguity of the stimulus and the response are not confined to learning-set formation but apply equally well to the learning of a single discrimination problem. The number of trials per problem, however, is a variable which is uniquely related to the formation of learning sets.

In an early study by Levine, Levinson, and Harlow (1959), two groups of rhesus monkeys were given either three trials per problem or 12 trials per problem. The three trials per problem group received 12 problems per day, each for three trials; the 12 trials per problem group received three problems per day with 12 trials per problem. Thus, all subjects received 36 trials each day. The experiment was continued for 64 days at which time all subjects appeared to have reached a performance asymptote. No differences were obtained between the two groups when performance was measured over successive blocks of trials. As a result, the investigators concluded that at least from three to twelve trials per problem yields equivalent learning-set development. A second study by Levine and Harlow (1959), in which rhesus monkeys were given either one or 12 trials per problem in solving oddity problems, and a study by Behar (1961), using an object-alternation problem, have provided similar findings; that is, learning appeared to depend only on the number of trials given, regardless of how they were organized into problems.[12]

Two hypotheses which have been presented in order to account for the learning-set phenomenon found with monkeys learning discrimination problems should be considered. The first has been derived from Harlow's (1950, 1959) conceptualization of how discrimination learning takes place. Briefly, Harlow has posited that "learning involves nothing more than the elimination of responses and response tendencies appropriate to a particular learning situation." An analysis of the data from discrimination learning-set experiments has enabled him to identify a number of

---

[12] The oddity problem is one in which the subject is presented with three objects consisting of two that are identical and one different from the other two. The task of the subject is to select the object which is different from the others.

With the object-alternation problem, the subject is required to respond alternately on successive trials to each of two dissimilar stimulus objects. It differs from the object-discrimination problem only in reward contingency. That is, the reward is obtained by the subject's responding to the object that was not rewarded on the previous trial.

distinct classes of errors—interfering tendencies which the organism must inhibit if learning is to take place. More specifically, these error factors have been designated as (1) stimulus perseveration, (2) differential cue, (3) response shift, and (4) position preferences. With the learning of a series of multiple discrimination tasks, as would be found in the learning-set situation, the subject gradually eliminates these error factors which, thus, results in his being progressively more able to solve the discrimination problems which are presented.

A second hypothesis, also derived from the analysis of discrimination learning, stems from the work of Restle (1958) and Levine (1959). As outlined by Levine, the basic feature is the adoption by the subject of a hypothesis—defined as a specified pattern of responses to selected stimuli and identified by the analysis of a subject's responses over three trials of a given problem. Although Levine has provided a list of nine different hypotheses that may be adopted by a monkey learning a discrimination problem, only three will be identified in this discussion. The first is a position preference, manifested behaviorally by a sequence of responses to one side of the test board. The second is more complex and can be identified as Win, stay with same position–Lose, shift to the other position. The third hypothesis is Win, stay with the same object; Lose, shift to the other object.

A fundamental consideration is that these hypotheses, or behavior patterns, are susceptible to the traditional effects of reinforcement operations. Thus, it is possible to reinforce some hypotheses and extinguish others. The development of a learning set involving object-discrimination problems is reflected in the gradual strengthening, via 100 per cent reinforcement, of the Win, stay with the same object–Lose, shift to the other object hypothesis and the gradual extinction, because of 50 per cent reinforcement, of other hypotheses which the subject may adopt. The results of a recent study by Schusterman (1964) are in keeping with Levine's position.

In concluding this section, it should be pointed out that recently Postman and his associates [Postman and Schwartz (1964), Postman (1964)] have undertaken a series of studies to examine learning-set formation in human subjects learning verbal materials. A basic point which Postman (1964) has made is that "while general transfer is independent of the relationship between individual items, it nevertheless reflects circumscribed

habits and skills which apply to a limited range of learning tasks."
In one experiment, Postman and Schwartz (1964) examined
interlist transfer as a function of the class of verbal material which
was used (adjectives or trigrams) as well as the type of learning
situation (paired-associate or serial). More specifically, subjects
learned List 1, which consisted of one of four different kinds of
tasks (paired-associate adjectives, serial adjectives, paired-associate
trigrams, or serial trigrams), and were then transferred to List 2,
which consisted of either paired adjectives or serial adjectives.
Intra-list and interlist similarity were minimized. The results
revealed that all conditions of training produced substantial
improvement in the performance on List 2, but, more important,
transfer effects specific to the conditions of prior learning were
demonstrated. That is, learning was superior when the method of
practice and the class of materials in the successive tasks remained
unchanged.

In a second study, Postman (1964) examined the learning of
transfer skills using four transfer situations: (1) attaching a
similar response to an identical stimulus, A-B'; (2) attaching a
new response to an identical stimulus, A-C; (3) re-pairing the
stimulus and response items of the first list to form new S-R pairs,
A-Br; and (4) a control condition which employed unrelated
stimuli and unrelated responses, C-D. In the experiment, groups
of subjects learned three sets of lists. Each set consisted of two lists
of paired-associates; eight pairs of two-syllable adjectives made
up each list. For any subject, the relationship between the
lists always conformed to the same paradigm within each of the
three sets. The first list in each set was learned to a criterion of
seven correct out of the eight presented items, but the second list
was presented for only five trials.

Of primary interest was how the amount of transfer would
vary as a function of the learning of the three sets of lists. Figure
14–11 presents this data. Note that there is a shift from an initial
small amount of negative transfer to positive transfer for the A-B'
condition and a reduction in the degree of negative transfer for
both A-C and A-Br.

Discrimination Reversal

One type of learning situation which frequently has been
subsumed under the learning-set category is the discrimination
reversal. Here, using a two-choice discrimination problem, the

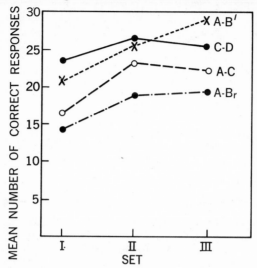

Fig. 14–11. Mean numbers of correct responses in five trials of List 2 learning as a function of set and paradigm. *Adapted from Postman (1964)*

positive stimulus in one series of trials becomes the negative stimulus for the next series. A noteworthy example of the general experimental procedure as well as a typical result is found in a study by Dufort, Guttman, and Kimble (1954), who used a two-choice discrimination apparatus. Rats were required to learn a series of ten position discriminations and were given four trials per day. A noncorrection procedure was used; that is, each time the subject made 11 of 12 correct responses, the problem was reversed. The results are indicated in Figure 14–12, and, although negative transfer was obtained for the early reversals, successive improvement can be noted over the latter reversals in the series so that by the last three problems all of the animals were reversing in a single trial.[13]

Many investigators, working under a variety of conditions and with a number of different species, have noted this same general finding. Chickens [Bacon, Warren, and Schein (1962)], racoons [Warren and Warren (1962)], horses [Warren and Warren

[13] This was the first study by an American investigator to obtain one-trial reversal learning with rats. Although Buytendijk (1930) had obtained such findings, Kreschevsky (1932b) and North (1950. 1950a) were unable to obtain findings which indicated that learning was this rapid.

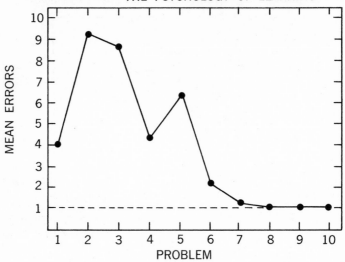

Fig. 14–12. Mean number of errors on each problem as a function of the number of problems presented. *Adapted from Dufort, Guttman, and Kimble (1954)*

(1962)], cats, [Cronholm, Warren, and Hara (1960)], chimpanzees [Schusterman (1962, 1964)], and imbecile children [House and Zeaman (1959)] have all been used as subjects in this type of study. All of the investigators cited have noted that successive improvement took place as a function of the number of reversals that were provided.[14]

What variables have been investigated within the discrimination reversal situation? In an early series of studies, North (1950, 1950a), using rats learning a position habit on a T-maze, examined (1) massed practice (one trial per minute) versus spaced practice (one trial per 12 minutes), (2) a correction versus noncorrection method of learning, and (3) the number of trials provided per reversal. Although the results of the two experiments were rather variable, it did appear that the massed versus spaced practice conditions had little influence on the differential learning of reversals, although in one case a group which was given four trials per reversal revealed a significant

[14] A few investigators have been unable to obtain this general effect. Fritz (1930) working with rats, Reid (1958) using pigeons, and Warren (1960) employing paradise fish have all reported an inability to obtain successive improvement with increasing numbers of reversals.

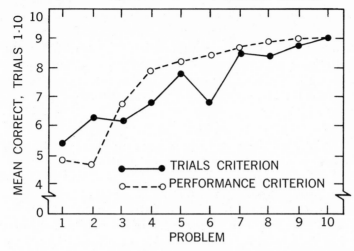

Fig. 14–13. Mean number of correct responses on the first ten trials of each problem, as a function of the ordinal position of problem. *Adapted from Pubols (1957)*

advantage in favor of massed practice, in contrast to spaced, during the last 24 of 48 reversals which were provided. Secondly, there was no convincing evidence for the superiority of the correction procedure over the noncorrection. Finally, when performance on a given reversal was examined, there appeared to be little difference in learning whether the number of trials per reversal was small (four or six) or large (eight or 30).

Some years later, in a series of studies Pubols (1957, 1962) again investigated the role of the number of trials per reversal. In his first study, Pubols (1957) was interested in examining reversal learning as a function of whether the subject was given a fixed number of trials per problem or whether each problem was learned to a criterion. In this study, successive position discrimination reversals in a Y-maze were examined as a function of whether a subject received (1) ten trials per reversal or (2) a sufficient number of trials to reach a criterion of nine correct responses on ten trials before having the problem reversed. All subjects received ten trials per day and were trained for a total of ten problems. The results, indicated in Figure 14–13, revealed that the group given ten trials per problem performed significantly better at the beginning of the problem series but after the second problem the criterion group was superior. By the end of training, however, there was little difference between the groups, a basic reason being that both groups were learning each reversal after a single trial. Note, of course, that by plotting the number of problems on the abscissa the total number of trials provided each group varied, with the ten trials per reversal group receiving significantly fewer trials throughout the course of the reversal problems.

In his second study, Pubols (1962) examined the contribution of numbers of trials per reversal. Again, the Y-maze was used, with each problem consisting of the learning of a left–right position habit. Three groups of rats were used, and 10, 20, or 40 trials per problem were provided. Each subject was given a total of 400 trials. Findings indicated that both the prior number of trials which were provided and the prior number of reversals exerted a systematic influence on performance. If the number of reversals was held constant, thus permitting trials to vary, performance was best for the 40 trials per problem group and poorest for the ten trials per problem group. On the other hand, if the number of trials was held constant, thus permitting the number of reversals to vary, performance was best for the ten trials per problem group and poorest for the 40 trials per problem group. Since efficiency of performance of reversal learning most frequently is related to the number of trials which are provided, the greatest overall efficiency of performance takes place when the trials provided for each reversal are few rather than many.

In the introduction to this topic, it was pointed out that frequently this area has been related to learning-set formation, recognizing, of course, that learning-set work with animals has generally involved multiple discrimination training. This type of training, it will be recalled, involves the introduction of new stimuli for each problem. In a recent study, Schusterman (1964), working with chimpanzees, compared the learning of a series of discrimination reversal problems with the learning of a series of multiple discrimination tasks. Furthermore, he examined the transfer value of these different learning situations on the learning of additional multiple discrimination tasks. In this study, during Phase 1 the subjects received either successive discrimination reversal training or multiple discrimination training. Each problem was presented until the subject reached a criterion of 12 consecutive correct responses; a minimum of 50 problems was provided. Training in Phase 1 ended when subjects were able to solve a problem in one trial. Following this, Phase 2 was provided

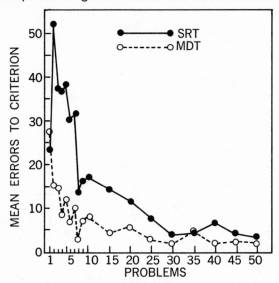

Fig. 14–14. Interproblem learning curves on a successive discrimination reversal task and on multiple discrimination tasks. *Adapted from Schusterman (1964)*

which consisted of the presentation of a series of multiple discrimination problems, with each problem presented for four trials. One control animal was used and was given only five multiple discrimination problems during Phase 1, in contrast to the minimum of 50 provided the experimental subjects prior to being shifted to Phase 2.

The results for Phase 1 are presented in Figure 14–14 and indicate that rapid learning on both tasks took place, although more efficient performance was provided by the multiple discrimination task group. Although the difference between the groups was significant early in the learning series, beyond Problems 30 to 35 there was little difference between the groups. The results for Phase 2 are indicated in Figure 14–15. Both methods of training produced a high level of correct responses on Trial 2, with the successive discrimination reversal training group being slightly superior.

The Role of Overlearning

A nonspecific transfer variable which has relevance to the discrimination reversal learning situation is overlearning; the work of Reid (1953) illustrates its operation. In this study, three

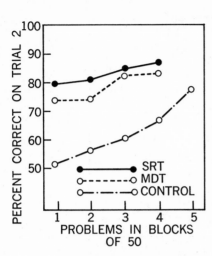

Fig. 14–15. Percentage of correct responses on Trial 2 on a learning-set series of four trial discrimination problems following differential training methods. *Adapted from Schusterman* (*1964*)

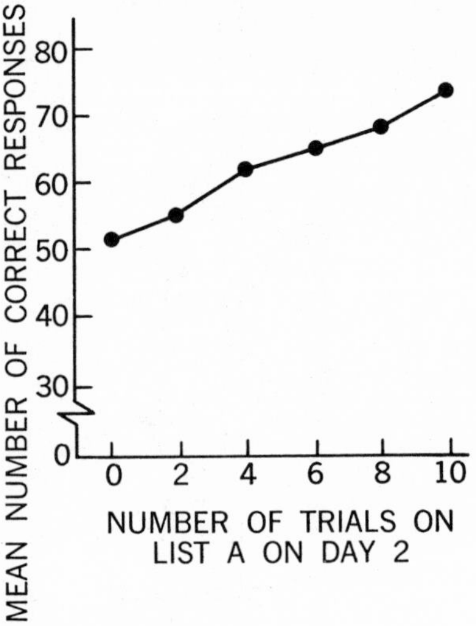

Fig. 14–16. Mean correct responses on the total of ten trials on List B. *Adapted from Thune* (*1950*)

groups of rats were trained to make a simple black–white discrimination in a Y-alley discrimination apparatus. All groups learned the problem to a criterion of nine out of ten correct responses with the black card positive. Following this, one group was reversed immediately, a second group was given 50 overlearning trials prior to being reversed, and a third group was given 150 overlearning trials before reversal. The number of trials to reach the same criterion with the white card positive was then determined for all groups. Table 14–5 presents the trials to criterion and erroneous intrusions in the discrimination reversal learning situation. It can be noted that the group which was given 150 overlearning trials learned the new task significantly more rapidly than the controls. Capaldi and Stevenson (1957), also using a black–white discrimination problem, have confirmed Reid's findings.[15]

[15] It should be recognized that overlearning trials are always relative to the learning criterion which is employed. Thus, if one investigator decides that his

TABLE 14–5

Trials to Criterion and Erroneous Intrusions
in Discrimination Reversal Learning

GROUP	TRIALS	INTRUSIONS
Immediately reversed	138.3	2.0
50 overlearning trials	129.0	8.0
150 overlearning trials	70.0	16.0

(Adapted from Reid, 1953)

Since Reid's study, a number of investigators have been interested in determining if these findings could be extended to other learning situations. Pubols (1956) demonstrated that overlearning would facilitate the learning of a position reversal. In this study, four groups of rats were trained on a position discrimination in a Y-alley maze, with two groups learning to respond to their preferred side and two to their nonpreferred side. Upon attainment of a criterion of 18 out of 20 correct responses on two consecutive days, one each of the preferred and nonpreferred groups was reversed immediately whereas the other two groups were given 150 overlearning trials and then reversed. Pubols found that the overlearning groups learned the reversal significantly faster than the immediately reversed groups. The influence of the initial position preference variable, however, was not significant. Bruner, Mandler, O'Dowd, and Wallach (1958) have also demonstrated the overlearning effect when the task consisted of a four-choice serial position task. The animals first had to learn a left-right–left-right (or right-left–right-left) problem as their original task. One group was trained to a criterion of 80 per cent correct with not more than four wrong turns on five trials which were given during a single session. A second group also learned to this criterion but was then given an additional four sessions (20 trials) of overlearning, and a third group was carried 80 trials beyond the 80 per cent correct criterion. Following reaching of the criterion, all groups were then given reversal training. Findings indicated that the group which received the maximum amount of original training learned most rapidly, followed by the

---

learning criterion shall be nine correct responses out of ten trials, trials provided after this criterion has been reached are considered overlearning trials. On the other hand, a second investigator may decide that his criterion shall be 19 correct out of 20 trials. It is obvious that some of the learning trials provided in the second experiment would be considered as overlearning trials in the first.

second overlearning group. The group given no overlearning learned the transfer task least rapidly.

A number of experimenters, however, have been unable to replicate the influence of the overlearning variable on reversal learning, and considerable question must be raised as to the generality of this effect. Some of these early studies used subjects other than rats. Boycott and Young (1958) trained octopuses to attack one figure, but not another, and then had the animals learn a reversal. They reported that the longer the original training, the greater the number of trials needed to learn the reversal.[16]

Warren (1960) and Warren, Brookshire, Ball, and Reynolds (1960) also were unable to obtain facilitating effects of overtraining with chickens or fish. Warren (1960) using a discrimination task gave paradise fish either 50 or 100 training trials beyond a criterion (18 out of 20 correct) and then had his subjects reverse the habit. Both overlearning groups required significantly more trials to learn the reversal than the group which did not have overlearning trials. Warren, Brookshire, Ball, and Reynolds (1960) had white leghorn chicks learn a spatial discrimination on a T-maze and then had the subjects reverse the habit after 0, 60, or 120 overlearning trials. In a second experiment, the arms of the maze differed in brightness, and groups of birds received either 0 or 120 overtraining trials before reversing. In both experiments 3-, 13-, 23-, 33-, 43-, and 53-day-old subjects were employed. The results in both experiments revealed that overlearning retarded reversal learning at all age levels. A subsequent study by Brookshire, Warren, and Ball (1961) also confirmed the finding that overtraining retards reversal learning in the chicken, although these investigators were able to obtain facilitation with overlearning trials when the subjects were rats.

Stevenson and Weir (1959) employing elementary school children as subjects also were unable to find a facilitating effect of overtraining. A three-choice discrimination problem was employed, with subjects learning to a criterion of six consecutive correct responses. Subjects were then divided into three groups which differed in amount of overtraining. One group was reversed upon reaching the criterion, whereas a second group was given 36 overlearning trials. A third group was given 72 overlearning

---

[16] One primary difference between this study and the others reported is that the investigators gave their subjects shock when they responded to the negative stimulus—a motivational effect not found in other studies.

trials.[17] Results showed no differences among groups in the transfer task as a function of degree of training.

Since the negative findings which have been reviewed have been obtained with subjects other than rats, it might be hypothesized that the overlearning effect is specific to the rodent. But, unfortunately, the results of a number of recent studies by D'Amato and Jagoda (1962), Hill, Spear, and Clayton (1962), Hill and Spear (1963b), Clayton (1963), and Erlebacher (1963) make it necessary to reject this hypothesis. All of these investigators used rats as their experimental subjects and were unable to obtain the overlearning effect.

To illustrate these findings, in a study by Hill, Spear, and Clayton (1962) the first experiment consisted of training rats to learn to turn right or left in a T-maze, with 36 acquisition trials being provided to all groups. One experimental group was then given 102 overtraining trials, being free to choose either side at the choice point. A second experimental group was also given 102 overtraining trials, with the subjects being forced to go to the correct side on all trials. A third experimental group was given 204 overtraining trials; for half of these trials the animals were forced to go to the correct side and for the other half forced to go to the incorrect side. The distribution of correct and incorrect forced trials was determined randomly. Finally, a control group was not given any overtraining. Following the appropriate training, the correct goal box was reversed and all subjects received 15 free trials on each of two days. The investigators reported that "reversal learning was found to be temporarily retarded by free-trial overtraining, greatly retarded by forced-trial overtraining when half the trials were to each side, and unaffected by forced-trial overtraining when all the trials were to the correct side." Two additional experiments replicated the essential procedure found in the first study. Results obtained in the latter two studies were similar to those obtained in the first, with the basic finding being a failure to obtain an overlearning effect.

In view of the difficulty that many investigators have had in obtaining the overlearning effect, there is some question of the value in reviewing the varying hypotheses which have been proposed to account for such facilitation. Nonetheless, some of them should be described briefly.

[17] A second variable—immediate or 24-hour delay between original learning and time of transfer—was also used.

Reid (1953), the first investigator to obtain the overlearning effect, proposed that the overlearning trials result in the "response of discriminating." More specifically, his observation of the animals in the learning situation suggested that the overlearning trials provided the rats with the opportunity to learn to stop at the choice point and look at both the positive and negative stimuli prior to making a response. Pubols (1956) subsequently elaborated upon the development of this kind of response within the discrimination learning experiment.[18]

In the learning of a reversal, it is generally assumed that the previously correct (reinforced) response must be extinguished prior to the new response's being learned. As a result, a number of experimenters have assumed that overlearning trials result in the strengthening or development of some process which, in turn, results in the more rapid extinction of the originally reinforced response when the discrimination is reversed.

As an example of this point of view, Capaldi and Stevenson (1957) have suggested that overtraining trials result in the subject's being better able to discriminate the change (or reversal problem). This "superior discriminability" results in a more rapid extinction of the previously correct response, and, as a result, a second response to the original stimulus can be learned more quickly.

North and Stimmel (1960) found that rats given a large (135 or 90) number of rewarded trials in a straight runway extinguished more rapidly than subjects provided an intermediate (45) number. They have suggested that the increased number of reinforcements, or overlearning, increases the strength of the fractional anticipatory goal response, which, in turn, results in greater frustration when the problem is changed and reinforcement is no longer forthcoming. This greater frustration results in

[18] Clayton (1963) suggested that the discriminating (or observing) response may be one of ignoring irrelevant stimulation and has hypothesized that if irrelevant cues were minimized or absent in the learning situation the subjects would not be expected to profit from the overlearning experience. In examining this position, two experiments were run in which the degree of learning (control versus overlearning trials) was manipulated simultaneously with irrelevant cues being (1) present and (2) absent. Using rats learning and reversing a position discrimination task, he did not obtain findings to support his hypothesis. The results revealed that overlearning, when irrelevant cues were absent, retarded learning (in contrast to the control–irrelevant cues absent group) and that learning was even more retarded by overlearning when irrelevant cues were present.

more rapid extinction of the old response which, in turn, facilitates the learning of the new problem.

The theory of overlearning that D'Amato and Jagoda (1961) have proposed is that an essential component of simple discrimination learning is the development of avoidance tendencies toward the negative stimulus. The establishment of approach tendencies toward the positive stimulus is, in their opinion, a process of secondary importance. Reversal learning requires the extinction of avoidance tendencies developed toward the former negative stimulus; it is this factor that makes reversal learning so difficult. Relating this hypothesis to the overlearning findings, the investigators maintain that during post-criterion training experience with the negative stimulus is virtually eliminated which results in a reduction or elimination of avoidance tendencies toward the negative stimulus.

D'Amato and Jagoda predicted that if their subjects were compelled during overlearning to have a reasonable number of experiences with the negative stimulus the facilitative effect of overlearning would disappear. In a test of this hypothesis, three groups of rats were trained first on a brightness discrimination problem. One group was reversed immediately upon reaching a criterion of 18 correct choices out of 20 trials. A second group was given 200 overlearning trials, 20 per cent of which were forced to the positive stimulus, and a third group had 20 per cent of its 200 overlearning trials forced to the negative stimulus. Reversal training was then instituted, with all groups reaching a criterion of 18 correct out of 20 trials. It was noted that the group given 200 overlearning trials with 20 per cent forced to the positive stimulus learned the reversal significantly more rapidly than either the control group or the experimental group which had also been given 200 overlearning trials but had 20 per cent of its trials forced to the negative stimulus. The findings were thus in keeping with the investigators' hypothesis.

The specificity of this hypothesis is indicated in a second study by D'Amato and Jagoda (1962) who conducted four experiments to examine the role of overlearning on a spatial (left–right) discrimination task. Unlike the results obtained in their previous study, utilizing a brightness discrimination, they were unable to find any overlearning effect regardless of whether some of the overlearning trials forced the animals to the negative stimulus or whether all overlearning responses were made to the positive stimulus.

The Role of Warm-up

The last nonspecific factor which will be discussed and which operates in transfer situations has been referred to as warm-up, frequently subsumed under the general rubric of set. Warm-up is not a new psychological construct since Mosso (1906), Wells (1908), and Arai (1912) all reported systematic observations of the phenomenon. Thorndike (1914) provided one of the best early definitions of the construct by defining it as "that part of an increase of efficiency during the first 20 minutes (or some other assigned early portion) of a work period, which is abolished by a moderate rest, say of 60 minutes."

The contemporary analysis of warm-up has been markedly influenced by Ammons (1947) and Irion (1948). Ammons (1947), in his examination of the variables which contribute to rotary pursuit performance, posited that the decrement in performance following a rest period after practice was due to the loss of "set," with "set" identified as those "advantageous postural adjustments" necessary for optimal performance. Irion (1948) took as his point of departure the retention of verbal material and examined the role of the subject's postural and attentive adjustments in such retention.

An examination of many of the studies in this area reveals that, in general, two experimental procedures have been used. The first and, perhaps, most frequently utilized technique has been to provide the subject with a series of trials on a single task, with rest periods provided from time to time. Thus, in a study by Adams (1952), a rotary pursuit task was used, with 36 ten-second trials given each day for five days. The sharp initial rise in performance over the first few trials of each day's session has been used from which to infer the influence of warm-up. It can be noted, however, that this is not a transfer situation but, rather, one which can be subsumed under retention.

The second experimental procedure examines the influence of warm-up within the transfer situation. One of the early experimental studies in which this procedure was used was conducted within the verbal learning situation by Heron (1928) who had his subjects learn two different lists of nonsense syllables a day on each of three different days. Heron found that the first list learned on the second day required significantly more trials to learn than did the second list on the first day. Similarly, the first list which was learned on the third day was learned less rapidly than was the second list learned on either of the two preceding days. Heron (1928) interpreted the positive transfer obtained from the first to the second list as due to a warm-up effect.

Both Thune (1950) and Hamilton (1950) also have demonstrated the influence of a warm-up effect in learning verbal material. Thune (1950) was interested in examining the effects of different amounts and types of warm-up activities upon the subsequent learning of paired-associate material. In his first study, following six trials on a practice list, List A was presented to varying groups of subjects which received either zero, two, four, six, eight, or ten trials. This list was presented again on the second day, with the varying groups receiving either ten, eight, six, four, two, or zero additional trials. The total amount of practice on the list was held constant, but the number of trials given on the second day varied depending upon the number of trials provided on Day 1. Thus, the group given ten trials on Day 1 received no trials on Day 2; the group given eight trials on Day 1 was given only two trials on Day 2, etc. Practice on the first list was considered to be warm-up, with the experimental variable being the proportion of the total practice period given on the second day. A ten-minute cartoon sorting task was given following the second day's trials on List A, with List B then being given for ten trials. The experimenter attempted to minimize proactive inhibition effects by utilizing different and unrelated words in each list. The mean number of correct anticipations on the ten trials of List B is indicated in Figure 14–16, and it can be noted that positive transfer to List B is an increasing function of the number of trials provided on List A given on Day 2, an effect which Thune attributed to warm-up.

In Thune's second study, the influence of a different warm-up task was examined by a color guessing task. The general experimental procedure for this study was similar to the previous one except that only two groups were used. For the first group, following six trials on a practice list, List A was given for ten trials immediately followed by a color guessing task for ten trials. Twenty-four hours later, List B was presented for ten trials. For the second group, following the practice list, ten trials were given on List A. Twenty-four hours later, ten color guessing trials were

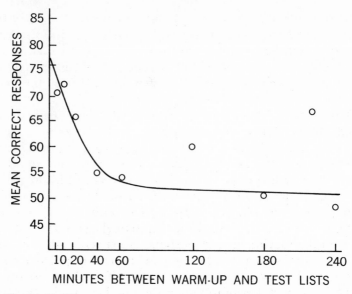

Fig. 14–17. Mean correct responses during ten trials on the test list following different intervals of rest between the test and warm-up lists. *Adapted from Hamilton (1950)*

given, immediately followed by ten trials on List B. (The color guessing task consisted of the subject's attempting to guess which one of five colors would appear in a response space of the memory drum. The same stimulus, a large X, was used for all colors on all trials.) Results were similar to those obtained in the first experiment. Ten trials of the color guessing task given just prior to the learning of List B produced a significant amount of positive transfer. The findings obtained from both studies led Thune to conclude that learning per se did not appear to be an essential element of those activities which have a facilitating warm-up effect for paired-associate learning tasks.

Hamilton (1950) was interested in demonstrating that temporal factors were important in the facilitative effect produced by warm-up. His experimental procedure closely approximated that of Thune (1950). Briefly, nine groups of subjects were given a warm-up task consisting of ten trials on a list of paired adjectives. This was followed by a rest interval of either 8 seconds, 5, 10, 20, 40, 60, 120, 180, or 240 minutes. The rest interval was followed by ten trials on a list of paired nouns which served as the test list.

The results are shown in Figure 14–17, and it can be noted that performance on the test list was an exponential decay function of the rest interval.

These studies indicate that warm-up effects in transfer are a bona fide phenomenon, but there has been a sufficient amount of negative evidence to make the careful investigator wonder what the significant variables are that contribute to its presence. For example, Heron's early positive findings were questioned by Mitchell (1933) who was unable to obtain such an effect, although it should be pointed out that Mitchell's subjects learned lists of three-digit numbers rather than nonsense syllables. Murdock (1960) also has been unsuccessful in finding such an effect when his subjects learned lists of unrelated words.

15

Transfer II:

The Role of Sensory Preconditioning,
Stimulus Predifferentiation, and Familiarity

THE SITUATIONS WHICH HAVE been selected for consideration in this chapter are different from the transfer paradigms discussed in the last chapter in that there has been a difference in the conceptualization of what constitutes the original task. More specifically, frequently it will be found that the original task does not consist of a well defined learning situation but, rather, of one in which the subject is presented some type of stimulus which is then utilized in the subsequent transfer task. The responses which the subject makes during this original training period are often irrelevant to the transfer task or of little concern to the investigator.

Three varieties of stimulus presentation have been used, and, although bearing a certain similarity one to the other, frequently each has been associated with a particular type of learning situation. As a result, they have been given specific identities; namely, (1) sensory preconditioning, (2) stimulus predifferentiation, and (3) familiarization.

SENSORY PRECONDITIONING

Presenting the subject with the stimuli to be used later in a conditioning experiment has been termed sensory preconditioning. The original study in the area was performed by Brogden (1939). In this experiment, eight dogs received 200 pairings of a light and buzzer which were presented simultaneously. A conditioning experiment was then set up in which one of these stimuli served as the CS and shock which elicited foot withdrawal served as the UCS. A criterion of 20 CR's in 20 trials was employed. Following such training, a transfer test was provided in which the other stimulus was then presented to the subjects. A control group of animals was given similar conditioning and transfer trials, but the preconditioning sessions were omitted. Animals in the experimental group produced 78 CR's during the transfer test, in contrast to only four by the control group. It is obvious that the preconditioning procedure produced an effect which somehow resulted in the transfer of the CR to the new test stimulus.

Since this early study, a number of investigators have examined sensory preconditioning under a variety of conditions. Animal studies have been run by Reid (1952), Bahrick (1953), and Silver and Meyer (1954); but only Reid (1952) was unable to obtain positive results. In Reid's study, in which pigeons were used as subjects, the experimental group was presented with a paired buzzer and light during pretraining. For the control subjects, the buzzer and light were not paired but were presented separately. The animals were then trained to peck for a food reward to the presentation of either the light or buzzer. In the test situation, the other stimulus was presented and the number of pecking responses was recorded. No significant differences were obtained between the experimental and control groups to the test stimuli.

Bahrick (1953) and Silver and Meyer (1954), on the other hand, have confirmed Brogden's early findings. In Bahrick's study, rats were divided randomly into two experimental groups and one control group. The two experimental groups differed in the deprivation conditions established during the preconditioning trials. The first group was given these trials after 14 hours of food and water deprivation, whereas a second experimental group received its trials under satiated conditions. The control group was given trials after 14 hours of deprivation. This preconditioning consisted of providing the experimental animals with 360 paired presentations of a buzzer and light whereas the control group was provided only 360 presentations of light. All animals were then satiated and taught a running response to a buzzer by pairing it with shock. Such training was administered at the rate of 30 trials per day for a maximum of two days or until a criterion of four consecutive correct avoidance responses was reached. The test procedure was then instituted and consisted of using the light as a conditioned stimulus and training the animals to make the same running response. Again, the criterion was four consecutive correct avoidance responses, with a maximum of 90 trials being provided. Bahrick found that the experimental group under high deprivation conditions learned the transfer task more rapidly than either the low deprivation group or the control group. No significant differences, however, were obtained between the latter two groups.

Silver and Meyer (1954) have likened the preconditioning trials to a conditioning procedure in which one stimulus may act as a CS whereas the other appears to have the properties of a UCS. Working within such a framework, they examined the effectiveness of simultaneous, forward, and backward presentations of a buzzer and light which were employed in the preconditioning trials. The forward and backward presentations of the stimuli employed a one and one-half-second delay between the onset of one stimulus and the onset of the second. With simultaneous presentation, both stimuli were presented together. Three control groups were also run. One group received no preconditioning trials, the second group received presentations of only the buzzer, and the third group received presentations of only the light. All groups received 3,000 presentations of the stimuli (either singly or in pairs) following which a running response was conditioned to one stimulus, with shock serving as the UCS. The criterion was seven conditioned responses. The test situation consisted of 100 transfer trials in which the stimulus, other than that employed in the preconditioning trials, was used as the CS and the animal was shocked whenever an avoidance response was not made. The results indicated that there was no difference in responding among the varying control groups during the transfer tests but that the performance of these groups was significantly poorer than any of the experimental groups. Among the latter groups, it was found that the forward preconditioning group yielded significantly more transfer than either the simultaneous or backward preconditioning groups. No difference was found between the latter groups.

A study by Hoffeld, Thompson, and Brogden (1958), also conceptualizing the preconditioning trials as a kind of conditioning procedure, examined the role of varying CS-UCS intervals.

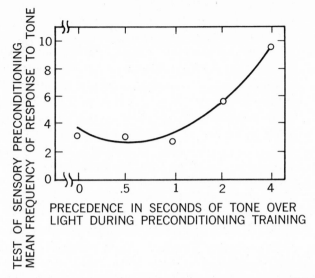

Fig. 15–1. Relation between magnitude of sensory preconditioning and precedence of tone over light during preconditioning. *Adapted from Hoffeld, Thompson, and Brogden (1958)*

Five experimental groups of cats were used, with the onset of a tone preceding the onset of a light by one of the following intervals: 0, .5, 1, 2, or 4 seconds. Both tone and light were terminated together. Twenty preconditioning trials per day for ten days were presented. The control group received neither the presentation of tone nor light although it was placed in the experimental apparatus for ten minutes per session for each of the ten preconditioning sessions. Following these sessions, instrumental avoidance training was provided. Light was used as the CS and a one-tenth-second shock was provided which elicited a cage-turning response in the subject. All groups received avoidance training until a criterion of 18 or more shock-avoiding responses to the light in one test period was reached. Tests for sensory preconditioning were then run by presenting a two-second tone until such time that the frequency of conditioned responding was 10 per cent or less (two positive responses out of 20 trials). Following the test series, extinction trials of 20 daily presentations of light were provided, also until the frequency of the conditioned response was 10 per cent or less. Findings indicated that the acquisition of the conditioned cage-turning response to light was not significantly different among any of the groups. The extinction data also re-vealed no differences among them. On the other hand, there were significant differences among the groups as a function of the time of onset and duration of the stimuli used in the preconditioning period. No responses to the tone were made by subjects in the control group, but some response to the tone was made by every one of the experimental groups. The relationship between fre-quency of responding and onset and duration time is revealed in Figure 15–1.

A number of investigators have utilized human subjects in examining sensory preconditioning. Although Brogden's (1942) early study using the conditioned GSR was unsuccessful in demonstrating sensory preconditioning, a later study by Karn (1947) was not. In this study, college students first received 50 simultaneous two-second presentations of a buzzer and light; a control group did not receive this experience. The second session consisted of utilizing a conditioned finger withdrawal situation. A buzzer was sounded one to three seconds before shock, permitting the subjects to acquire an avoidance response. Following the subject's giving a finger withdrawal to the buzzer for five succes-sive trials, the light was then presented ten times without shock. An examination of the findings indicated that the experimental group responded to the light for 75 times out of a possible maximum of 120. In contrast, the control group responded only nine times. Other studies by Brogden (1947) and Chernikoff and Brogden (1949), using reaction time as the response, have also been successful in demonstrating sensory preconditioning to be a valid phenomenon.[1]

Although Brogden (1947) concluded that "the experimental conditions of the phenomenon of sensory preconditioning are not necessarily critical for any learning theory," many investigators have not taken Brogden's position seriously and have attempted to relate the sensory preconditioning findings to some theoretical position. During the early 1950's, sensory preconditioning findings were frequently cited as embarrassing to a reinforcement position since some learning had obviously taken place between the

[1] One disturbing condition about many of the sensory preconditioning studies has been the failure on the part of most experimenters to use a control group which receives both stimuli during the sensory preconditioning phase, with such stimuli presented singly and in random order. It should be noted that Reid (1952) who was unable to obtain sensory preconditioning effects used such a control group.

Fig. 15–2. A conditioning explanation of sensory preconditioning. *Adapted from Seidel (1959)*

sensory stimuli which were used during the preconditioning period although reinforcement was not present.

Recent concern has been directed toward attempting to explain the phenomenon, with, perhaps, most interest centering around a mediation hypothesis. Numerous variations of this hypothesis have been presented and the reader can refer to Seidel (1959) for a thorough analysis of them. Briefly, the general explanation is as follows and is indicated in Figure 15–2. The preconditioning trials may be conceived of as representing the typical classical conditioning procedure except that the responses which take place are not measured. This period is illustrated by the preconditioning phase of Figure 15–2, in which the R_2 is a nonmeasured response but one which also has stimulus characteristics. In the regular conditioning, or training period, the previous UCS now serves as a CS in eliciting the overt and measured CR (R_3). In the transfer situation, it can be noted that the first preconditioning stimulus, S_1, evokes the R_2 which, in turn, has stimulus characteristics capable of eliciting R_3.

An excellent example of how a mediated response may operate in the sensory preconditioning situation is found in an experiment by Wickens and Briggs (1951). In this study, two stimuli, tone and light, were presented during preconditioning trials. Four groups of subjects were run. For Group I, the stimuli were paired for 15 trials with the subjects' being required to say "now" when the stimuli appeared. For Group II, the two stimuli were presented independently with the same response ("now") being given to each stimulus when it was presented. Fifteen presentations of each stimulus were provided. For Groups III and IV, the procedure was similar to that utilized with Group II except that the subjects were required to say "now" to one stimulus but not to the other. Following such training, a typical conditioning study was run in which the subject learned to avoid shock by lifting his finger when a tone was presented. Following 30 trials, the test period consisted of ten presentations of the light. Findings indicated that Groups I and II showed a high frequency of response transfer, or sensory preconditioning, but Groups III and IV did not. The point which is critical to this discussion is the fact that no significant difference was present between Group I and Group II. Thus, although the tone and light were presented separately for Group II, in contrast to being presented together for Group I, the fact that the subjects had to make a common response—"now"—to both stimuli resulted in this group's performing as well as the normal sensory preconditioning group. The overt verbal response served to mediate the connection between the two sensory stimuli and, in turn, was responsible for the large amount of transfer which took place during the test trials.

STIMULUS PREDIFFERENTIATION

An early series of articles by Gibson (1940, 1941, 1942) provides a background for work in the area which has become known as stimulus predifferentiation.[2] In essence, Gibson hypothesized that generalization may occur among the stimulus items that make up a list of words, so that a number of stimuli on the list become capable of eliciting the same response. One response which has been learned to a given stimulus item may be given also to other stimulus items which appear on the list. The tendency of the other responses to block the correct response is proportional to the strength of these incorrect response tendencies. Figure 15–3 illustrates a list of paired-associates in which generalization is assumed to be taking place during learning.

Gibson proposed that in order to reduce the strength of the generalization tendencies differentiation among the stimulus items should be set up through practice. When such differentiation takes place, the learning of new material which utilizes the same stimulus items should take place more rapidly. Gibson's (1940) formal hypothesis was as follows: "If differentiation has been set up within a list, less generalization will occur in learning a new list which includes the same stimulus items paired with

---

[2] A contemporary review of the area can be found in Arnoult (1957).

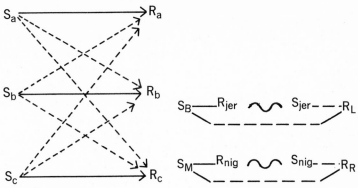

Fig. 15–3. List of paired-associates in which generalization is assumed to be taking place during learning. *Adapted from Gibson (1942)*

Fig. 15–4. An illustration of the acquired distinctiveness of cue hypothesis. *Adapted from Goss (1955)*

different responses; and the trials required to learn the new list will tend to be reduced by reduction of the internal generalization."

Gibson has stated, then, that verbal learning is not only a matter of establishing bonds or connections between a stimulus and its response. Rather, the similarity of the stimulus items is responsible for tendencies toward generalization which must be overcome. Thus, each stimulus item must become discriminable from the others in order that a correct response can be attached to it. Gibson has called attention to the von Restorff phenomenon to provide support for this hypothesis. As noted earlier, the finding that an isolated item is learned more rapidly than one placed within a homogeneous setting is in keeping with her point of view since the isolated item would enable the individual to differentiate it most rapidly from the rest of the items which, in turn, would reduce the amount of stimulus generalization.

In a test of her hypothesis, Gibson (1942) devised a paired-associate task in which the stimuli which were used were nonsense forms taken from all four classes of nonsense forms which were illustrated in Chapter 14. One list which was constructed consisted of stimulus forms which were quite different, one from the other. Presumably, such a list would generate little stimulus generalization, which, in turn, should result in the subject's being able to differentiate the items very easily and lead to rapid learning.

TABLE 15–1

A Summary of the Varying Types of Predifferentiation Training and Transfer Tasks

KIND OF PRETRAINING	PRETRAINING		TRANSFER TASK	
	Stimulus	Verbal Response	Motor Learning	Perceptual
Relevant stimulus– relevant response	Nonsense Form #1 Nonsense Form #2	Up Down	S is required to push lever up when non- sense form #1 is presented; push lever down when nonsense form #2 is presented	S is required to recognize or discriminate nonsense forms #1 and #2 from other nonsense forms which are presented
Relevant stimulus– irrelevant response	Nonsense Form #1 Nonsense Form #2	Cow Horse	As above	As above
Relevant stimulus– no response	Nonsense Form #1 Nonsense Form #2	None de- manded by experimenter	As above	As above
Irrelevant stimulus– irrelevant response	Book City	Cow Horse	As above	As above
No pretrain- ing	None	None	As above	As above

(Major portion of table adapted from Arnoult, 1957)

pair of words was presented and the subject was required to continue responding until a correct response was given. A control group was used which was provided no verbal pretraining.

Following pretraining, the subject was taken into the experimental room and shown a motor-skills apparatus for the first time. It was pointed out that the words presented during the training series represented the color and position of the lights that would appear on the stimulus panel of the apparatus and that pairs of response words which had been learned represented the position and switch number to be pushed in response to these stimulus lights. Sixty trials were given, with response time and errors recorded. Results as measured by either response measure showed that the group given 24 training trials was significantly superior to the other groups which were utilized. A subsequent study by McAllister (1953) has also demonstrated the effectiveness of the relevant stimulus–relevant response type of pretraining in producing significant amounts of positive transfer on a motor-skills task.

It has been the relevant stimulus–irrelevant response category of pretraining which has interested most investigators. In one of the early studies by Gagne and Baker (1950), groups of subjects were given either 0, 8, 16, or 32 trials in which they learned to respond with the letters J, V, S, or M to four different stimulus lights located on a panel (lower red, upper red, lower green, upper green). The presentation of these lights was in random order throughout each set of eight trials of training. Following this pretraining session, both time and error scores were obtained for each subject during 60 trials of practice on a motor-skills task in which the same four lights were presented but the subjects had to learn to attach to them four new responses (pushing one of four switches).

An examination of response times on successive sets of ten trials revealed that 8 and 16 trials of predifferentiating practice resulted in a small amount of positive transfer to the motor-skills task but that the 32 trials brought about considerably more. Error scores after 8 or 16 trials of training were only slightly (but not significantly) lower than those obtained for the control group. There was, however, a considerable and significant reduction in errors in the group given 32 trials of preliminary training, with the greatest error reduction taking place during the first 20 trials of learning. In general, these findings indicate that differentiating among the stimuli prior to the learning of a motor-skills task did aid in the learning of that task. More than a small amount of such training was apparently required, at least in this situation, in order for significant degrees of positive transfer to be obtained. A basic difficulty with the Gagne and Baker (1950) study was that there was no control for the nonspecific transfer variables of learning to learn or warm-up.

J. H. Cantor's (1955) study confirmed the influence of the relevant stimulus–irrelevant response pretraining when nonspecific transfer effects have been controlled. In this study, three groups of subjects received either 2, 4, or 12 blocks of relevant stimulus–irrelevant response pretraining. The subjects learned to associate varying letters with the presentation of each of six colors made up of red, orange, or yellow hues. These colors were later used in the transfer task. A training block consisted of the presentation of a random sequence of 36 colors in which each color was presented six times. Three irrelevant stimulus–irrelevant response pretraining groups were given corresponding amounts of practice (2, 4, or 12 blocks of trials) in associating the same letters with each of six colors consisting of a blue–green series of hues. A control group was given no pretraining. All groups were then given 40 trials on a motor-skills task which consisted of the subject's having to move a vertical wobble stick into a specific slot when a particular color (red, yellow, or orange hue) was presented.

Findings indicated that the combined relevant stimulus–irrelevant response groups' performance was reliably superior to that of the combined irrelevant stimulus–irrelevant response groups, with such facilitation being attributed to the stimulus predifferentiation which took place during the pretraining period. The amount of facilitation was not related, however, to the amount of pretraining which was provided.

Studies by Goss (1953) and Goss and Greenfeld (1958) are interesting in that these experimenters investigated the role of different types of relevant stimulus–no response (or observational) pretraining in addition, of course, to pretraining of the typical relevant stimulus–irrelevant response type. In Goss' (1953) study, three relevant stimulus–irrelevant response pretraining groups (verbal learning) learned to respond with a nonsense syllable whenever a light of a given intensity was presented. Four different intensities were used. One group learned to a criterion of nine out of twelve correct anticipations, whereas a second group learned to a criterion of eleven out of twelve correct anticipations. A third group (100 per cent over-learning) was given twice the number of trials as the 11/12 criterion group plus 12 criterion trials. Three other pretraining groups were given "seeing and discriminating" training. The subjects were told that they were participating in an experiment to determine how well they could judge stimulus differences, with the instructions emphasizing that they were to pay close attention to a series of lights that varied in intensity. These groups were then given the same number of trials as the three previous groups. Three additional pretraining groups (seeing) were employed in which these subjects were informed simply

TABLE 15-2

Summary of Type and Degree of Pretraining

GROUP	TYPE OF PREMOTOR EXPERIENCES	DEGREE OF PREMOTOR LEARNING
1a	Verbal learning	9/12 Criterion
1b	Verbal learning	11/12 Criterion
1c	Verbal learning	100% Overlearning
2a	Seeing-and-discriminating	Same as 1a
2b	Seeing-and-discriminating	Same as 1b
2c	Seeing-and-discriminating	Same as 1c
3a	Seeing	Same as 1a
3b	Seeing	Same as 1b
3c	Seeing	Same as 1c
Control	None	

(Adapted from Goss, 1953)

that the purpose of the experiment was to investigate the influence of seeing lights of varying intensity; hence, they were to pay close attention to each stimulus presentation. In effect, these instructions were designed primarily only to arouse postural adjustment and receptor exposure responses. The number of trials given to each of these groups was the same as that provided to the other two major groupings. A control group was also used which was not exposed to any light stimuli prior to the introduction to the motor-discrimination task.

A summary of the type and amount of pretraining is presented in Table 15-2. Goss found that all nine pretraining groups learned the motor discrimination task with fewer errors than the control group and that the verbal learning group which was given 100 per cent overlearning was significantly superior to all other pretraining groups. Differences among the other pretraining groups were not statistically significant.

In the Goss and Greenfeld (1958) study, the predifferentiation training for three groups consisted of having subjects associate four white lights which varied in intensity with the verbal responses of either (I) nonsense syllables, (II) words supplied by the experimenter, or (III) words supplied by the subjects. With each of these conditions, the experimenter reinforced correct responses by saying "right." The training for three other groups consisted of instructing the subject to look at the lights, discriminate among them, and either (IV) provide names which were to be said aloud, (V) provide names which were to be said covertly, or (VI) not to provide names. The experimenter did not say "right" to correct responses made by these groups. Group VII was instructed merely to see or look at the stimuli; Group VIII was a control group not given pretraining. Each of the varying experimental pretraining groups was divided into subgroups and given different amounts of pretraining. The amount of pretraining was either a fixed number of trials or determined by a criterion of performance established by the experimenter. The training task consisted of all subjects' learning to press a lever in a given direction whenever a light of a given intensity was presented. The results indicated that positive transfer was obtained for all of the experimental groups. There was no difference among the three types of verbal learning groups, but for high levels of pretraining these groups were superior to groups given pretraining which involved seeing, discriminating, and nonreinforced responses (Groups IV, V, and VI). These groups, in turn, were superior to Group VII, which was instructed only to look at the stimuli.

In summary, there is some evidence that a relevant stimulus–no response kind of pretraining may aid in the learning of a motor task. However, such training does not appear to provide as much positive transfer as the relevant stimulus–irrelevant response situation.

It should be noted that the transfer task used in all of the studies which were cited above was of a motor-skills variety. A number of investigators have been interested in examining the influence of predifferentiation training when the transfer task places greater emphasis upon perception, i.e., discrimination or recognition tasks.

In an early study by Arnoult (1953) two experiments were run in which subjects were given pretraining consisting of learning to associate a letter with a nonsense shape. For one group, the shapes which were used in pretraining were subsequently used in the transfer task; for a second group, the shapes used in the transfer task were different from those employed in pretraining. A third group was not given pretraining. In one experiment, the transfer task was a discrimination problem which consisted of having the subject report "same" or "different" when two shapes were presented. In the second experiment, the transfer task was a multiple-choice test in which a given shape was presented as a standard. It was then removed and the subject was required to choose one of five shapes which corresponded to the standard. Findings in both studies showed that pretraining with shapes which later were used in the transfer task had no influence on performance.

Subsequent studies by Campbell and Freeman (1955), Robinson (1955), and Ellis, Bessemer, Devine, and Trafton (1962), also using recognition or discrimination problems as their transfer task, have been also unable to secure positive findings.[5]

What conclusions can be drawn from the stimulus predifferentiation studies? In spite of a large number of experimental studies which have been conducted, the conclusions are surprisingly meager. It would appear that relevant stimulus–relevant response pretraining, if it is accepted as being within the stimulus predifferentiation area, is the most effective form of pretraining. Whether or not irrelevant stimulus–irrelevant response pretraining or relevant stimulus–no response (observational) pretraining is next most effective appears to be dependent upon a number of variables, only some of which have been delineated. For example, much of the experimental evidence supports the position that if the transfer task is of a motor variety then relevant stimulus–irrelevant response training is at least as effective as observational training and, in a number of instances, more effective. On the other hand, if the transfer task is of a discrimination or recognition type, it has been difficult to obtain significant differences as a function of the type of pretraining provided, although a recent study by Ellis and Muller (1964) indicated that observational training was more effective than relevant stimulus–irrelevant

---

[5] One notable exception is an experiment by G. N. Cantor (1955) in which three groups of three- to five-year-old children were given various types of stimulus pretraining. The first group (relevant stimulus–irrelevant response) learned during pretraining to associate specific female names, i.e., Jean and Peg, with each of two pictures of female faces that subsequently served as stimuli in the transfer task. A second group (irrelevant stimulus–irrelevant response) was given a comparable amount of paired-associate learning, but the training involved male faces and the names "Jack" and "Pete." A third group (relevant stimulus–no response) was merely exposed to the relevant stimuli. The transfer task involved a simple discrimination learning situation which employed two toy cars identical in appearance except that each had a female face obtained from the pretraining task mounted on its side. The subject's task consisted of learning to choose one of these and rolling it down a track. If the correct car, arbitrarily designated by the experimenter, was chosen by the subject, a marble reward was dispensed, with accumulated marbles being exchanged for toys. Cantor found that the relevant stimulus–irrelevant response group performed significantly better than did the irrelevant stimulus–irrelevant response or relevant stimulus–no response group.

response pretraining when the stimuli that were used were relatively simple.

Before it can be indicated more precisely how stimulus pretraining influences a transfer task, more attention must be given to the nature of the transfer or criterion task. The experimental evidence appears to indicate that positive transfer in a motor-skills task is much more likely to be found as a result of relevant stimulus–irrelevant response pretraining, when compared with observational training, than if the transfer task is perceptual in nature. But it is unlikely that the motor–perceptual distinction represents the critical element in this analysis. Perhaps, as Vanderplas (1963) and Ellis and Muller (1964) have indicated, the critical variable is whether the criterion task requires that new differential responses be made to the stimuli, as typically found in motor-skills learning, or that new differential responses need not be made to the stimuli, as in the case of a recognition test.

Experimenters must also give more attention to the nature of the pretraining task. Are the stimuli which are used easy or difficult to discriminate, one from the other? One study [Ellis and Muller (1964)], for example, has demonstrated that the complexity of the stimuli used in pretraining is a significant variable in determining the kind of results that are obtained. But most frequently consideration has not been given to this variable.

FAMILIARITY

The concept of familiarity was discussed briefly in an earlier chapter which dealt with the learning variables of frequency, association, and pronunciability. The concept of familiarity has an obvious relevance to frequency, and, in fact, Underwood and Schulz (1960) have considered familiarity to be a kind of manipulated frequency. Such manipulation usually involves the investigator's providing subjects with a pretraining period during which time they are familiarized with certain material which is later used as a part of the transfer task. Except for the fact that a verbal learning situation is used, in contrast to the usual perceptual or motor-skills task, the experimental methodology in this area is similar to that found with stimulus predifferentiation.

Although an early study by Waters (1939) indicated that

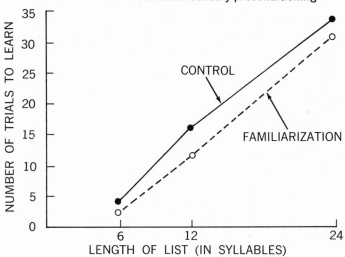

Fig. 15–5. The number of trials to learn to a criterion of one perfect recitation as a function of the length of list under familiarization and control procedures. *Adapted from Hovland and Kurtz (1952)*

familiarization training had no influence on material which subsequently was learned, Hovland and Kurtz (1952) did obtain positive findings. In this study, 12 subjects learned serial lists of 6, 12, and 24 nonsense syllables (association values ranging from 0 to 46.7 per cent) with and without familiarization training. Familiarization training consisted of presenting the syllables on three by five inch index cards to the subject one at a time, with the order changing for each presentation. After every five trials, the subject was given a test trial in which he attempted to reproduce (pronounce) each complete syllable when presented with only two of the letters. Familiarization was continued until the subject responded correctly on all syllables in a single test trial. Familiarization training was always given for 24 nonsense syllables although the subsequent list to be learned under a rote serial presentation might consist of 6, 12, or 24 syllables. The criterion of learning was one perfect recitation. The results, shown in Figure 15–5, indicated that lists learned without prior familiarization were more difficult to learn than were the same lists preceded by familiarization training. Riley and Phillips (1959) have confirmed the findings of Hovland and Kurtz (1952).

Noble (1955), using a different type of familiarization train-

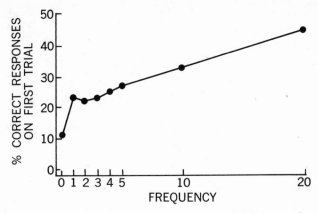

Fig. 15–6. Percentage of correct responses on Trial 1 as a function of prior frequency of experience. *Adapted from Noble* (*1955*)

ing, was also able to demonstrate that the learning of serial verbal material was a function of the amount of familiarity that was provided. Fifteen items were chosen from the low end of his meaningfulness scale (see Table 10–1). Varying groups of subjects received either 0, 1, 2, 3, 4, 5, 10, or 20 presentations of six of these items. The remaining nine items were fillers used to equalize the total number of familiarization exposures for each group. Familiarization training consisted of having each subject pronounce each item as it was presented. Two minutes following training, the six critical items were made up into a serial list and the subjects were required to learn it to a criterion of two successive trials. Noble found that the percentage of correct responses on Trial 1 was a function of the frequency with which each item had been presented during familiarization training—a finding illustrated in Figure 15–6.

The role of familiarization training in serial learning appears to be quite clear. Such learning is a function of the amount of familiarization that is provided. But the contribution of familiarization training in paired-associate learning, however, is not clear, and the experimental findings have been controversial.

The most extensive investigation in this area has been made by Underwood and Schulz (1960) who performed three studies involving the learning of paired-associates. In their first experiment, the familiarization material consisted of low association value nonsense syllables, with interlist similarity minimized.

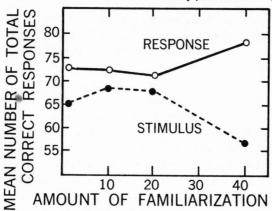

Fig. 15–7. Mean total number of correct responses on twenty trials as a joint function of locus and amount of familiarization. *Adapted from Underwood and Schulz (1960)*

Either 1, 10, 20, or 40 presentations (familiarization trials) of the appropriate syllables were provided. The training procedure was patterned after that used by Hovland and Kurtz (1952) in which subjects were presented with the syllables placed on index cards and given study trials interspersed with test trials. Irrelevant syllables were interspersed among the relevant ones to ensure that all subjects would have prior experience with the same number of presentations. The familiarized syllables then appeared as either stimuli or responses in an eight-unit paired-associate list. The varying numbers of familiarization trials and the placement of the familiarization syllables as either stimulus or response resulted in eight experimental conditions: S-1, S-10, S-20, S-40, R-1, R-10, R-20, R-40. All subjects in each group received 20 trials. The mean number of total correct responses for the learning of this list is revealed in Figure 15–7. It can be noted that the performance of the R-40 group was facilitated by familiarization training, but the learning of the S-40 group appears to have been inhibited although the interaction between locus and amount of familiarization was not statistically significant.

The investigators speculated that the method of administering familiarization training may have been responsible for the inhibitory effects noted with the S-40 group. That is, there may have been a loss of differentiation between the stimulus and response items during the learning of the paired-associate list inasmuch as subjects in the stimulus familiarization groups became accustomed to giving the stimulus units of the list as "responses" during familiarization training.

A second experiment attempted to examine this hypothesis by using, in the test list, stimulus and response material which belonged to different classes of verbal materials. This, the investigators reasoned, should reduce confusion and increase the probability that the stimuli and responses would be differentiated readily. The familiarization procedure, similar to that used in the first experiment, consisted of two groups' receiving either one or 40 presentations of nonsense syllables. For all groups, the stimuli of the paired-associate learning task continued to be nonsense syllables. However, for two subgroups, the response items were also nonsense syllables, and for two other subgroups, the response items were paralogs. An examination of the 20 learning trials revealed no difference among any of the groups; the use of paralogs as responses did not result in more rapid learning, nor did the amount of familiarization of stimuli have any influence. The puzzling finding was that the experimenters were unable to replicate the inhibition in performance on the nonsense syllable (stimulus) —nonsense syllable (response) list following 40 familiarization trials which was obtained in their first study.

In a third experiment, a different method of familiarization was used. A paired-associate task was used in which nonsense syllables were used as the response items and the stimuli were either nonsense forms or common English nouns. The nonsense syllables were then used as either the stimulus or response units in the test task which was also a paired-associate learning situation. One test list consisted of nonsense syllables which served as stimuli and paralogs as responses, whereas in the second list the paralogs became the stimuli and nonsense syllables served as responses. The results supported the findings obtained in the first study; performance was superior for subjects who were familiarized with material which later served as response units in the paired-associate list.

In general, the Underwood and Schulz findings have provided some experimental support for the position that familiarizing the subject with the to-be-learned responses in the paired-associate task facilitates the learning of that task but stimulus familiarization does not.

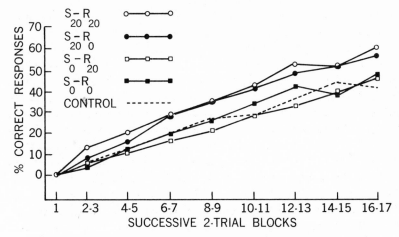

Fig. 15–8. Acquisition curves for a list of five paired-associates as a function of practice under four different combinations of low and high frequency of stimulus and response term familiarization. The control received no prior familiarization experience. *Adapted from Gannon and Noble (1961)*

This conclusion was not confirmed, however, by the experiments of either Cieutat (1960) or Gannon and Noble (1961). In the Gannon and Noble (1961) study, groups of subjects were given varying combinations of either zero or 20 presentations of paralogs during familiarization training. One group received familiarization trials on both stimulus and response units of the to-be-learned paired-associate list $(S_{20}–R_{20})$, whereas a second group received familiarization trials on the stimuli but not on the responses $(S_{20}–R_0)$. A third group received familiarization training only with the responses $(S_0–R_{20})$, and a fourth group $(S_0–R_0)$ received familiarization training with material which in the subsequent paired-associate task did not appear as either stimuli or responses. Familiarization training consisted of having each subject pronounce each paralog as it was projected on the screen. A control group given no familiarization training was also run. The test task consisted of a five-unit paired-associate list made up from the familiarization material; all groups were given 17 trials. Findings indicated, as Figure 15–8 reveals, that the group given familiarization training on both stimulus and response units was superior to all of the other groups but that the group given only stimulus familiarization was superior to the group provided with response familiarization—a finding at variance with the results of Underwood and Schulz (1960) .

Cieutat (1960) has obtained still other findings. His procedure was similar to Gannon and Noble's (1961) except that the exposure duration of the material, rather than frequency of presentation, was varied during familiarization training and the subjects were not required to pronounce each item as it appeared. Paralogs were presented for either zero or 60 seconds, with the familiarized (or nonfamiliarized) material later serving as stimuli or responses in the test task, a four-unit paired-associate list. Twenty learning trials were provided. The results showed that (1) familiarity with both stimulus and response members $(S_{60}-R_{60})$ facilitated the learning of the list, (2) familiarity with only the response member (S_0-R_{60}) inhibited such learning, (3) familiarity with only the stimulus member $(S_{60}-R_0)$ had essentially no effect.

One difficulty in attempting to reconcile the findings which have been obtained lies in the variety of familiarization procedures which have been employed. As noted, Cieutat (1960) required his subjects merely to look at the verbal material while it was being presented; Gannon and Noble (1961) , on the other hand, demanded that their subjects pronounce the material. Underwood and Schulz (1960) had their subjects either spell the nonsense syllables which were presented or learn them as paired-associate responses.

One step in examining the contribution of these varying familiarization procedures has been taken by Schulz and Tucker (1962, 1962a) who examined the role of articulation during familiarization training. These investigators proposed that the effective length of the paired-associate anticipation interval co-varies with the number of stimulus familiarization trials. Thus, it is assumed that the latency of the subject's response grows shorter as the number of familiarization trials increases, when familiarization involves articulation of each unit as it is presented. In a paired-associate learning situation which requires the subject to pronounce the stimulus term (typically this is not done) , subjects who have been familiarized with the stimulus material have a longer effective anticipation interval than unfamiliarized subjects inasmuch as the unfamiliarized subjects devote less of the anticipation interval to stimulus articulation per se. Since paired-associate learning is directly related to the length of the anticipation interval in the range from one to two and one-half seconds, the positive effect of stimulus familiarization is predictable.

The inhibitory effects of stimulus familiarization training which requires the subject to pronounce the material have been accounted for as follows. During familiarization training which requires the subject to pronounce the material, the subject develops the habit of articulating the units which subsequently will serve as stimuli in the paired-associate list. The strength of this habit is dependent upon the number of familiarization trials. However, this habit is in conflict with paired-associate instructions which require the subject not to pronounce the stimuli. Thus, under these instructions, the attempt to inhibit overt articulation of the stimuli during paired-associate performance may decrease the effective length of the anticipation interval of familiarized subjects.

Two studies [Schulz and Tucker (1962, 1962a)] have supported this hypothesis. In the first, the investigators provided three amounts of stimulus familiarization training (0, 20, or 60 trials), and all subjects were required to pronounce each stimulus unit as it appeared. The material used was identical to that employed by Gannon and Noble (1961). Following familiarization training, 17 trials on a paired-associate task were provided, with the familiarized material serving as stimuli. One-half of the subjects were required to pronounce each stimulus word during this learning period, but the other half was not. The findings supported the investigators' hypothesis. For the group required to pronounce each stimulus word during paired-associate learning, the mean number of correct responses increased as a function of the number of familiarization trials. For the group not required to pronounce the material, performance decreased as a function of the amount of familiarization. (See Figure 15–9.)

In the second study, a similar procedure was utilized in which all subjects were required to pronounce the material during stimulus familiarization training. One-half of the subjects also were required to pronounce each stimulus word during paired-associate learning, but the other half was not. In this study, the paired-associate learning situation utilized a four-second anticipation interval, in contrast to two seconds used in the previous study. According to the experimenters' hypothesis, this long anticipation interval should eliminate or substantially reduce both the facilitating and the inhibiting effects of stimulus famil-

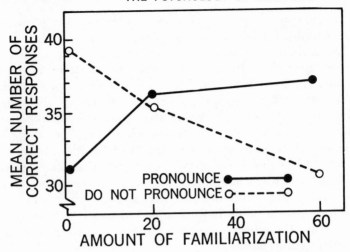

Fig. 15–9. Mean total number of correct responses during seventeen anticipation trials as a function of whether or not the subject was instructed to pronounce the stimulus word and the number of familiarization trials. *Adapted from Schulz and Tucker (1962a)*

iarization. Again the results supported Schulz and Tucker's hypothesis. Sixty stimulus familiarization trials did not influence the paired-associate performance of either articulating or non-articulating subjects.

In summary, the Schulz and Tucker studies are important in indicating that articulation is one of the important variables in determining whether or not familiarization trials will facilitate or inhibit subsequent paired-associate learning.

16

The Nature of Retention

A NUMBER OF INVESTIGATORS have not been interested in the variables which contribute to those performance changes which have been defined as learning but, rather, have centered their attention on how persistent such changes are over time. This, then, is the area of retention.

In the typical learning experiment, learning and retention are inextricably bound together. That is, any given learning trial must reflect learning which has been retained from previous trials as well as include the learning which takes place on that particular trial. But, like many other concepts which have been examined, certain operations or conventions have been used to distinguish between these two constructs. Melton (1963) has written that a change from Trial N to N + 1 is considered to be a learning change when the variable of interest is the ordinal number of Trial N and not the temporal interval between Trial N and N + 1. However, a change arising from Trial N to N + 1 is considered to be a retention change when the variable of interest is the interval itself and/or the events which fill this interval.

The concept of forgetting has not been considered yet in discussing learning. Forgetting is merely the other side of the retention coin; retention refers to the amount of previously learned material which persists or has been retained by the subject, whereas forgetting refers to the amount which has been lost or has not been retained. However, it should be acknowledged that a de facto distinction has been made between these two concepts. If the experimenter is interested in examining the lack of persistence of previously learned material, with particular reference to how certain kinds of environmental events or activities contribute to this lack, investigators frequently use the term forgetting. On the other hand, if the experimenter is interested in variables related to persistence, with the events filling the temporal interval between Trial N and N + 1 being of no particular concern, the term retention has been used to denote this interest. It is to this latter topic that major attention will be directed in this chapter.

An examination of much of the experimental work that has been done within the retention area reveals that it can be classified generally into two major sections. The first has been to relate retention to many of the variables which have already been examined as being related to learning. Thus, an experimenter may be interested in investigating the role of massed versus distributed learning trials in retention. A typical procedure would be to have two groups of subjects learn a list of words to the same criterion under either massed or distributed practice. Twenty-four hours later, a recall test is provided in order to determine the influence of this variable on the retention of the material.

The second area of interest has been to examine how or by what means the subject organizes and stores the material which has been learned. For example, if a subject is presented with 16 words in a random sequence and it is noted that these words can be grouped into four general categories, e.g., animals, trees, foods, and furniture, is there any tendency for the subject to group or cluster all of the words of a single category during the recall of this material? Before examining these areas, however, the methods for measuring retention should be presented.

Measures of Retention

1. Savings or relearning. The measurement operation used by many early investigators to measure retention was of a savings or relearning variety. Here, the subject learns the original material to a specified criterion and, following a period of time, is required to relearn the material to the same criterion. The difference between the number of trials required to learn the material and to relearn it is the savings score. This score frequently is converted to a percentage value by the following formula:

$$\frac{\text{Original Learning} - \text{New Learning}}{\text{Original Learning}} \times 100 = \text{Per cent Savings}$$

Although frequently used as a measure of retention, it must be acknowledged to be a confounded measure since it is dependent upon a second learning session, which brings into play the role of learning variables.

2. Recognition. With this technique, the subject must identify material which he has previously learned from material which has not been learned. As Murdock (1963) pointed out, different types of recognition tests may be employed. One type provides the subject with two alternatives from which to choose material which had been learned. The true-false test is essentially a recognition test of this variety. A second type of test requires the individual to select the correct item from a group of several items; this variation is exemplified by the multiple-choice test. A third type of recognition test requires the individual to select all the correct items from a larger number of them. As an example of this type, Luh (1922) provided subjects with 24 nonsense syllables from which they were to select the 12 which they had previously learned.

3. Reconstruction. The reconstruction method has been used only infrequently in experimental studies of retention, but a good example of its use is found in an experiment by Smith (1934) in which subjects were given 30 seconds to look at a pattern which was made up of varying colored squares. Figure 16–1 illustrates one such pattern. Following this presentation, the subject was provided with 16 squares of each color and given three minutes to reproduce as much of the pattern as he could remember. One point was permitted for each square which was correctly placed.

4. Recall. With this method, following the learning of the material, the subject is asked to reproduce or recall the material which had been previously learned. One recall technique has been designated as the anticipation method. As used in the paired-associate learning situation, a stimulus is first presented and the subject is required to respond with the appropriate response prior

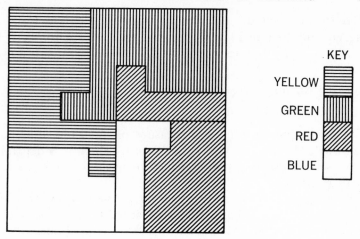

Fig. 16–1. Pattern which subjects were required to reconstruct. *Adapted from Smith (1934)*

to its exposure on the memory drum. Similarly, with serial learning, a given item will act as the stimulus, to which the subject responds with the next item on the list. With this type of situation, learning and recall trials are essentially identical, with the only difference between learning and retention measures being in the temporal interval placed between trials. Thus, a subject may learn a list of paired-associates using a ten-second intertrial interval. Such trials will be designated as learning trials. If, however, an investigator desires to examine retention, the same presentation of material will be utilized but the investigator will interpolate a period of longer than ten seconds between Trial N and N + 1.

A second recall method has been classed as free recall. In this situation, a list of material is presented to the subject (more than one presentation may be made) and he is asked to recall the items in any order in which they occur to him. In essence, then, the order is unimportant and there is no pacing of the presentation of items, although a finite period of time usually is provided for the subject to complete the task. A variation of this recall method is to use paced recall in which the subject is not permitted to distribute his recall time as he chooses but, rather, is given a limited period of time to recall each unit, although, again, the order in which he responds is not important.

Basically, many of the free-recall situations represent learning rather than retention situations. As such, they might be more accurately designated as free learning, as some investigators have suggested, since the experimenter is concerned primarily with the contribution of some variable that is related to the material itself, or its method of presentation, rather than with the temporal interval interpolated between the presentation of the material and its subsequent recall.

Retention Curves

It is obvious that the varying methods of measuring retention can be used to provide retention curves which reflect these measurement values. For a long time, the only systematic comparison of retention curves produced by different measures of retention was made in an early study by Luh (1922), who had subjects learn a list of nonsense syllables to a criterion of one perfect recitation and, then, following intervals of 20 minutes, 1, 4, 24, or 48 hours, measured the retention of this material. Relearning, recognition, and recall as measured by anticipation and written reproduction, in addition to the reconstruction method, were used to measure retention.[1] The results for all the retention intervals revealed that the recognition measures provided the highest retention score, reconstruction next, followed by written reproduction. The anticipation method provided the smallest amount of retention. The relearning measure produced variable findings and was next to the poorest value when the retention interval was 20 minutes, 1 hour, or 4 hours. At the 48-hour retention interval, however, only the recognition measure provided a higher retention score.

Recently, Postman and Rau (1957) performed a similar study, in which they examined the retention of words as well as of nonsense syllables.[2] Twelve-item lists of nonsense syllables and

[1] The written reproduction method was a type of free-recall situation. Subjects were asked to recall all of the items they could without regard to order. The reconstruction method consisted of furnishing the subjects with the original material and requiring them to arrange the items in the correct serial order.

[2] Postman and Rau pointed out that Luh's experiment suffered from two basic difficulties. First, three of the retention tests which Luh used (written reproduction, recognition, and reconstruction) were given in succession to the same subjects, and it was possible that performance on the latter two tests was influenced by previous tests which were given. Secondly, the same subjects served repeatedly under each of the experimental conditions, with some subjects serving as many as five times in each condition. Such a procedure would mean that the subjects became highly practiced learners which should result in their obtaining higher retention scores. At the same time, the learning of successive lists of nonsense syllables produced increasing amounts of interference which should reduce retention scores.

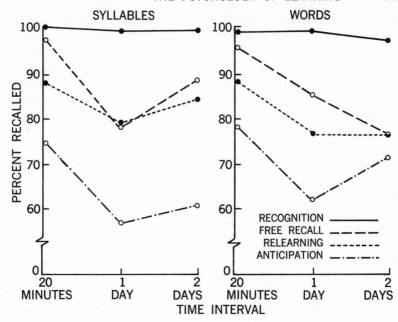

Fig. 16–2. Retention curves for nonsense syllables and words as a function of the method of measurement. *Adapted from Postman and Rau (1957)*

words were each learned to a criterion of one perfect recitation by the method of anticipation. After reaching the criterion, retention was measured after either 20 minutes, 24 hours, or 48 hours. Four measures of retention were used: (1) recognition, (2) free recall, (3) anticipation, and (4) relearning. In measuring recognition, 12-item multiple-choice tests were used in which each multiple-choice item consisted of four alternatives, one of which was correct. For the measurement of free recall, the subject, who was encouraged to guess, was instructed to write down as many of the items as he could remember, not necessarily in the order of presentation. The measure for the anticipation method was the score obtained on the first trial of the relearning series, and the relearning score was obtained by noting the number of trials the subject required to reach the same criterion as employed in original learning. The findings for the two types of material used are indicated in Figure 16–2. In general, the results confirm the findings of Luh, who also found that recognition produced best retention, and free recall and anticipation the poorest. Postman and Rau's findings indicate that relearning produces a retention score next best to recognition—a finding which Luh obtained for the 48-hour retention interval but not for the 20-minute, 1-hour, and 4-hour intervals.

It should be recognized that any comparison which is made among the varying measures of retention is relative and one which is a function of the specific operations used in the varying measurement operations. For example, in Postman and Rau's (1957) study, the recognition method of measuring retention consisted of a multiple-choice test in which each test item consisted of four alternatives, one of which was correct. Thus, the recognition score which they obtained was specific to the number of alternatives which they provided. Experimental support for this position has come from Teghtsoonian (1958) and Schwartz (1961) as well as Murdock (1963). In one experiment by Murdock, subjects were given lists of 20 words to study for 30 seconds. They then tried to identify as many of these words as possible when shown a longer list of either 40, 80, 120, or 160 words. The mean proportion of correct responses after being corrected for chance was .56, .54, .44, and .42 for lists of 40-, 80-, 120-, and 160- word alternatives. An analysis of variance indicated that the differences among the groups were significant, thus, supporting the position that any recognition test score will be a function of the number of alternatives which are provided.

A second point is that recognition score values will be related to the characteristics of the alternatives or distractors. Again using the Postman and Rau (1957) study as an example, in measuring the recognition of nonsense syllables, the distractors which the investigators used did not have more than a single letter in common with the correct item. However, by increasing (or decreasing) the similarity of the distractors to the correct response, it would have been possible to manipulate the recognition test score.[3]

Similarly, one could point out that the retention measures of anticipation, free recall, or relearning are dependent also upon

[3] The position that recognition test scores are dependent upon the particular testing conditions has been recognized by many investigators. Thus, Underwood (1949a) wrote, "If we required S to learn a list of adjectives and then placed the adjectives among a group of nonsense syllables, S would probably show very small loss in retention. Obviously the similarity of the test material to the other material is an important variable which determines the recognition score."

the operations which are used to obtain them. For example, such measures invariably will reflect the amount of time that the experimenter has provided the subject within which to respond, whether guessing has been encouraged, etc.

A final consideration in comparing retention measures concerns the type of original learning situation which is used. Most investigators have used only a single type of learning situation, e.g., anticipation, and then tested for retention by using a variety of different measures, i.e., recall, recognition, etc. A point which Bahrick (1964) recently made is that in comparing retention measures, and particularly recognition versus recall indicants, "it is necessary to train one group of subjects until all of their recall responses are correct, and another group of subjects until all of their recognition responses are correct." Furthermore, "The general conclusion that tests of recognition yield higher scores than do tests of recall has not been based upon any such comparison and is, therefore, limited to situations in which the degree of original training is not comparable." Thus, Bahrick pointed out that when an anticipation method of learning is used this type of learning situation results in a much higher level of "recognition" learning than "recall" learning and that the subsequent test for retention merely reflects this original difference.

Short Term versus Long Term Memory

Individuals working in the area of memory have often been interested in the immediate memory span. One basic question can be asked: How large a quantity of material can be recalled perfectly after a single presentation? The typical experiment involves an experimenter's presenting a number of digits or perhaps letters and then asking the subject to repeat them. The experimenter introduces relatively few items and increases the number of items presented until the total number of units cannot be perfectly recalled by the subject. The number of items which can be recalled represents the individual's immediate memory span.

Although the construct of immediate memory was introduced by Jacobs in 1887, until a short time ago it was considered separate and distinct from typical experiments on retention and forgetting in which the time interval interpolated between the last learning trial and the test for retention would be measured in terms of minutes or hours. The latter situation frequently has been referred to as long term memory. It was Brown (1958) and Peterson and Peterson (1959) who introduced an experimental procedure which bridges the gap between the memory span and long term memory. In the Peterson and Peterson (1959) study, trigrams consisting of three consonants were auditorily presented and immediately following such presentation a three-digit number was presented. The subject counted backward by three's or four's from that number until, after an appropriate interval, he received a cue to recall the syllables. Intervals of three, six, nine, twelve, fifteen, or eighteen seconds were interpolated between the presentation of the material and a cue for recall. The results revealed that the amount of material recalled was a decreasing function of the length of the retention interval.

Murdock (1961a) and Peterson and Peterson (1962) examined paired-associate learning within the short term retention situation. Murdock's technique consisted of presenting a list of paired-associates and then testing for recall for only one of the pairs in the list. Subjects were given no information prior to the recall test as to which pair would be selected. Peterson and Peterson (1962), on the other hand, presented a stimulus word followed by the presentation of a response word. Following the response word, a randomly selected three-digit number appeared on the memory drum, with the subjects counting backward by three's or four's until the stimulus word was again presented. The subject then was required to make the appropriate response.

Short term memory has been examined also in a continuous or sequential task situation. In one experimental procedure, a long series of items is presented and the experimenter interrupts the presentation from time to time to request that the subject recall a particular item which has been presented previously. In the Lloyd, Reid, and Feallock (1960) study, the subjects might hear the words: pine, tin, polo, METAL, copper, TREE. . . . With the presentation of the word METAL, the subject would be expected to recall the word denoted by METAL, i.e., "tin," and when TREE was presented, he would be expected to recall "pine." In a second procedure, introduced by Shepard and Teghtsoonian (1961), different three-digit numbers were placed on index cards, on each of which was a single number. The subject was given a pack of cards and instructed to examine the number on each card and to indicate whether that number was "old" or "new," depending upon whether he remembered having seen that number on a card presented earlier. Subjects were permitted to proceed through the deck at their own rate but were not permitted to look back to an earlier card. Feedback to indicate the correctness of a response was not provided.

Although some experimenters believe that short term memory represents a category of retention qualitatively different from that of long term, other investigators believe that this is not, at least at this time, a meaningful distinction. As a result, and wherever possible, both types will be considered as members of a single class.

THE INFLUENCE OF LEARNING VARIABLES ON RETENTION

In some of the earlier chapters it was noted that a number of variables made significant contributions to the ease of learning. In this section, the contribution of some of these variables to retention will be examined.

The Role of Overlearning

A finding that would be expected most frequently is that when the amount or degree of original learning varies such differences will be reflected on the retention test. In Underwood's study (1954b), one group of subjects learned a serial list of 12 nonsense syllables which was presented until the subject achieved seven correct responses on a single trial. A second group of subjects was given trials until one perfect recitation was obtained. Paired-associate lists also were utilized, with one group learning a ten-pair list until five correct responses were made on a single trial and a second group learning the list to a criterion of one perfect trial. The data showed that recall scores obtained 24 hours later for both serial and paired-associate lists reflected the differences which were present at the end of the training period.

One question which follows from this general finding relates to the effect of providing learning trials beyond a criterion of one perfect recitation: Once perfect recitation is achieved, what is the influence of providing additional learning trials? Such a procedure means that performance measures cannot reflect the contribution of these added learning trials since asymptote has been reached.

TABLE 16–1

Recall Scores as a Function of Degree of Learning

INTERVAL	DEGREE OF LEARNING		
(DAYS)	100	150	200
	MEAN WORDS RECALLED		
1	3.10	4.60	5.83
2	1.80	3.60	4.65
4	.50	2.05	3.30
7	.20	1.30	1.65
14	.15	.65	.90
28	.00	.25	.40

(Adapted from Krueger, 1929)

Although the classical study of the influence of overlearning was performed by Krueger (1929), the Underwood study should be mentioned again. In addition to the two degrees of learning which were employed in the learning of the serial and paired-associate lists, a third degree of learning was also utilized. Here, paired-associate and serial lists were learned to a criterion of one perfect trial plus seven additional trials. The results indicated that the groups receiving the overlearning trials recalled more items 24 hours later than the groups which had learned to a criterion of only one perfect trial.

In Krueger's (1929) classic study, lists of monosyllabic nouns were used as the material to be learned. Groups of subjects learned either to one perfect recitation or were provided additional trials amounting to 50 per cent or 100 per cent of those taken to reach the criterion. These degrees of learning have been designated as 100 per cent, 150 per cent, and 200 per cent. Following such learning, 1, 2, 4, 7, 14, or 28 days later relearning trials were provided in which the first trial provided a recall score. Table 16–1 reveals the scores obtained as a function of the degree of learning and the interval between the last learning trial and the test for retention. It can be noted that overlearning trials significantly aided retention, with the increased retention scores being smaller from 150 per cent to 200 per cent than from 100 per cent to 150 per cent. In a subsequent study examining the subjects' retention of a path on a finger maze, with the same degrees of learning being employed and utilizing retention intervals of 1, 2,

3, 4, 7, and 14 days, Krueger obtained similar findings. Postman (1962b) recently replicated Krueger's first study and confirmed Krueger's findings.

Most investigators, however, have not been interested in examining retention when different degrees of learning are present at the end of the learning trials since, as noted, any difference in retention merely reflects the difference which was present at the end of the original training. Rather, experimenters have been interested in determining if different materials or procedures result in varying amounts of retention when the amount of the original learning has been held constant.

With this experimental objective, the most frequently used procedure has been to present the material until all experimental groups achieve the same criterion. If the experimental variable does influence the rate of learning, such a procedure means that the different experimental groups receive varying numbers of trials prior to reaching the criterion. However, most investigators have assumed that once the criterion has been reached the degree of learning for the different groups is equivalent. Following such learning, retention tests are provided at some later time and differences among groups are noted.

Underwood (1964a) recently pointed to a major difficulty with this assumption. But, prior to the specific examination of the use of a criterion measure from which to infer the equivalence of learning, it is first necessary to examine the general problem of determining the "true" amount of material which has been learned at the conclusion of a given learning trial. When the anticipation method of measuring learning is used, for example, the number of items which are correct on the last anticipation trial, although often used from which to infer the amount of learning that has taken place, is not a true measure since it does not include the learning which has occurred on the last trial. For example, if the subject fails to respond to a given stimulus on this trial, the correct response member is exposed and the subject has the opportunity to learn the response at that time. Thus, performance on the last trial does not reflect this additional learning.[4]

---

[4] Underwood (1964a) did not limit his position to the anticipation method but indicated that it had greater generality. He wrote, "The use of alternate study and test trials [rather than anticipation] does not avoid this problem, for most assuredly some change in performance must occur as a consequence of a test trial even without knowledge of the correctness of performance."

Underwood indicated that the number of correct responses which would have been given had there been another trial should be determined. He suggested a number of solutions to this problem. An obvious one is to use a control group which is given the extra trial; the mean score for this group then is used as an estimate of the immediate recall for the experimental group. Other procedures which he suggested are those which he designated as single- and multiple-entry projection. Although these methods cannot be discussed in detail at this time, the procedures involve an estimation or a projection of the expected performance (projected score) on a hypothetical trial which would follow the last learning trial. It is these projected scores which are used as a base learning score from which to measure the amount of retention (or forgetting) that has taken place.

As indicated earlier, investigators examining retention as a function of the operation of some learning variable have assumed that when material has been learned to the same criterion equivalent degrees of learning are present. But, according to Underwood's position, it follows that the trial on which the criterion has been reached does not reflect the true amount of learning that has taken place. Thus, if an experimenter is examining the learning of easy and difficult verbal items, with the learning of such items taking place at different rates, although the performance measure on the criterion trial is the same for both the true amount of learning is different. Figure 16–3 illustrates the hypothetical growth of learning easy and difficult items as a function of the number of trials which are provided. Although a criterion of 100 per cent has been achieved in each case, it is assumed that the associative strength of the easy and difficult items continues to grow, with the strength of the easy items increasing at a faster rate.

Underwood's projection techniques may provide true measures of learning if the criterion which is used is less than one perfect trial or if a constant number of learning trials is provided. But, if the criterion is one perfect trial appropriate projections cannot be made and differences in associative strength cannot be assessed.

Since many investigators have used a criterion of one perfect trial for learning material in attempting to assess retention differences, many of these studies undoubtedly have been confounded by differences in associative strength being present at the end of the learning trials.

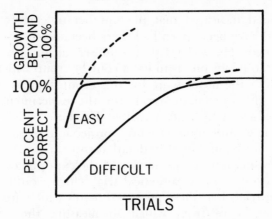

Fig. 16–3. Hypothetical growth of degree of learning beyond 100 per cent as a function of continued trials after reaching asymptote for easy and difficult items. *Adapted from Underwood (1964a)*

Retention as a Function of Speed of Learning

An examination of retention related to the speed of learning provides a good example of Underwood's multiple-entry projection technique. In an early study, in which an adjusted learning procedure was used, Gillette (1936) concluded that "the slow learner when given sufficient time to learn the *same amount* as the fast learner, but not allowed to *overlearn* the material, is not able to retain as much as the fast learner." [5] A basic assumption which this investigator made was that the associative strength for all items at the end of the learning trials was the same for fast and for slow subjects.

Using the results of a series of prior studies, Underwood (1954), using an adjusted learning technique, confirmed Gillette's conclusions. That is, when items were equated for number of "reinforcements" during learning, retention was consistently superior for the fast learner. But Underwood pointed out that this conclusion was based on the assumption that reinforcement

[5] The adjusted learning technique as used by Gillette is one in which the items in a list are "dropped out" after being learned to some specified criterion. Thus, if one correct anticipation is used as the criterion in a paired-associate learning situation, the first time that the subject correctly anticipates the response that stimulus–response pair is dropped from the list. The subject continues to be given trials on those items which he has not correctly anticipated. In this way, all items of a list are given the same number of "reinforcements."

(making a correct response) for a slow learner results in the same associative strength as a reinforcement for the fast learner. However, it may be that one reinforcement adds more strength to an association which is acquired by a fast learner than it does to an association for a slow learner, with the result that the degree of learning of the material is not equal prior to the introduction of the retention interval.

In order to make an appropriate comparison of the retention of the fast and slow learners, Underwood indicated that it is essential that the response strength of the items for fast and slow learners be equated at the end of the learning trials. The adjusted learning technique does not assure this to be the case, and the solution which Underwood provided was a successive probability analysis of learning which he later termed multiple-entry projection.

Using experimental data obtained from earlier studies, Underwood (1954) obtained a population of 90 fast and 90 slow learners, each having learned and recalled three lists of paired-associates. Two hundred and seventy lists were thus available for each group. Since each list consisted of ten S-R pairs, 2,700 responses per group were available for examination. The analysis consisted of determining the growth of the associative strength for each item. This was accomplished by observing when a response was first correctly anticipated. It was then noted whether that response was anticipated correctly or incorrectly on the next trial, the trial following that, and so on until the last learning trial.

When such an analysis is made for each item for a large number of subjects, one is in a position to make a prediction about the probability of the subject's making a correct response on a succeeding trial when this response has been correctly anticipated on previous trials once, twice, three times, etc. Successive probability curves for fast and slow subjects, using this method of analysis, are plotted in Figure 16–4. Thus, for the slow learner the probability of making a correct response on the trial which followed one reinforcement was .50. After nine previous reinforcements, the probability of obtaining a correct response on the next trial increased to approximately .85. An examination of the fast learners reveals that their probability of securing a correct response on the next trial after one reinforcement was approximately .62 and after nine reinforcements it increased to approximately .91. It is clear, then, that reinforcement does not

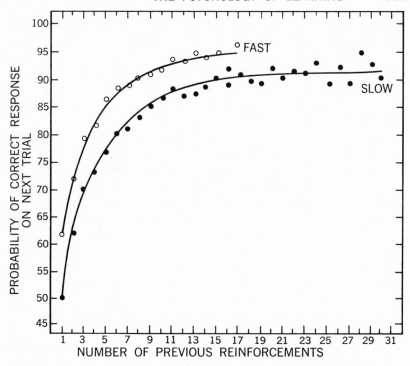

Fig. 16–4. The relationship between number of reinforcements during learning and the probability of correct response on next trial for
fast and slow learners. *Adapted from Underwood (1954)*

result in equal probability that a response will be correct on the
next trial for fast and slow learners. It is equally clear that the
studies which have equated fast and slow learners by equating the
number of reinforcements have not equated these learners for
associative strength. In order to provide such equality, more
reinforcements have to be provided for slow learners than for fast
learners. Thus, as Figure 16–4 indicates, six reinforcements for
slow learners provide about the same associative strength during
learning as three reinforcements for fast learners. When the
proportion of items recalled after 24 hours for fast and slow
learners for each level of associative strength was plotted, as has
been done in Figure 16–5, no consistent differences existed
between the two groups. Underwood (1954) concluded that
when associative strength at the end of learning is equivalent for
fast and slow learners no difference in retention can be expected.

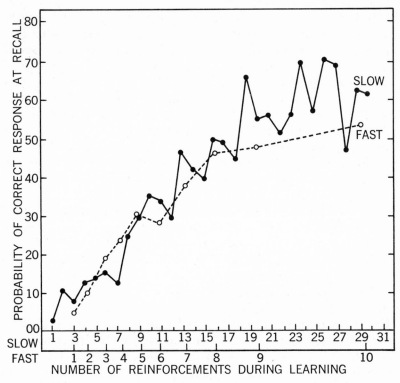

Fig. 16–5. Retention of fast and slow learners after twenty-four hours when associations are equated for strength at the end of learning. *Adapted from Underwood (1954)*

Retention as a Function of Serial Position

Although Hovland (1940a) did not obtain differential retention values for items in a serial list which were recalled 24 hours following learning, Underwood and Richardson (1956) and Postman and Rau (1957) obtained findings which revealed that recall of items was a function of the position of the item in the list. More specifically, the typical bow-shaped curve as found in learning was obtained.[6]

---

[6] Underwood and Richardson (1956) stated that Hovland's (1940a) findings might be related to differences in interlist interference existing between the two studies. Hovland's subjects, in contrast to those used by Underwood and Richardson, had learned many serial lists which undoubtedly interfered with recall. As Underwood and Richardson stated (p. 125):

Not only would there be interference among specific items but also among lists as wholes, since the same anticipatory cue for the first syllable was the

THE PSYCHOLOGY OF LEARNING   564

In keeping with the previous analysis of retention, the associative strength for the varying items was not equivalent. That is, a successive probability analysis made during learning trials would undoubtedly reveal that the probability of a subject's making a correct response for the first and last items would be much greater than for the items appearing in the middle of the list. Underwood and Richardson (1956), who examined the recall of nonsense syllables that made up a serial list and adjusted values so that the expected probabilities of immediate recall were the same for all positions, concluded that there was no evidence that the first and last sections of the list were recalled better than the middle section.

An interesting examination of serial position within the short term retention context was made by Peterson and Peterson (1962). In one study, two paired-associates were presented. Thus, a stimulus word was followed by the presentation of a response word; this procedure was repeated for the second pair. Following the presentation of the second response, a retention interval of either 4, 8, or 16 seconds was utilized. This period of time was filled by having the subjects count backward by two's, three's, or four's. In one condition, following an appropriate time interval, the subject was asked to recall the response associated with the first stimulus word, whereas in a second condition the subject was asked to recall the response associated with the second stimulus word. Recall scores revealed that performance was superior when the response of the first pair was asked for rather than the response of the second pair. This is somewhat unusual since the presentation of the second response was closer in time to the recall period than the first. The investigators called this a primacy effect and its influence was examined in another experiment which utilized three paired-associates. In this study, three pairs of items were presented, and, following a retention interval of 12 seconds, one of

---

same for all lists. The interference should be greatest during the attempted recall of the first several items as S would have difficulty in establishing "which list this was." Thus, recall of the first items should be severely depressed. By the time the middle items appeared, however, S should have established what list was involved so that these items could be as well recalled as the first items even though they are weaker. Yet by this reasoning the items in the last portion of the list should be better recalled than any; this is not the case, and at the present time we have no resolution of this difficulty. Nevertheless, the fact that in Hovland's study the bowed curve was very apparent on the second relearning trial is quite in line with previous findings of the transitoriness of interference among serial lists.

the three stimuli appeared to cue the subject's response. The results revealed no bowing of the position curve; instead, the primacy effect continued to be present. In general, the response to the first stimulus was recalled most frequently, followed by the response to the second stimulus. The response to the third stimulus was recalled least frequently.

Retention as a Function of Meaningfulness

Davis (1935) examined 18 studies which used meaningless material and 24 studies using meaningful material and derived retention curves from these investigations. Although he indicated that satisfactory comparisons could not always be made because the data were not always comparable, he did conclude that meaningful material was retained better than meaningless material. McGeoch and Irion (1952) have also written that "there is good ground for concluding that meaningful materials . . . are usually much better retained than are nonsense materials and others learned by rote."

However, the recent studies of Underwood and Richardson (1956) and Postman and Rau (1957) have not supported this position. In the Underwood and Richardson study, ten-item nonsense syllable lists were used. Two lists were made up of high association values (e.g., sar, bil, gab) and two were made up of low association values (e.g., gyk, zyw, neq). The lists were learned to one perfect trial and then relearned after 24 hours. The first relearning trial provided recall scores. An analysis of the raw data revealed that association value or meaningfulness was not a significant variable in recall. The investigators pointed out that since wide differences in the rate of learning the lists were evident the analysis of the raw recall scores was inappropriate as a means of securing the best possible estimate of the influence of the meaningfulness variable. As a result, their major analysis was based on a probability analysis of acquisition curves as a means of adjusting for different response strengths at the end of learning. This analysis also revealed that meaningfulness did not significantly influence recall, although, as Figure 16–6 indicates, if any trend is discernible it is that the low meaningfulness list was better recalled than the high.

Postman and Rau's (1957) study was cited previously in examining the retention of nonsense syllables and words. It will be recalled that these experimenters had their subjects learn

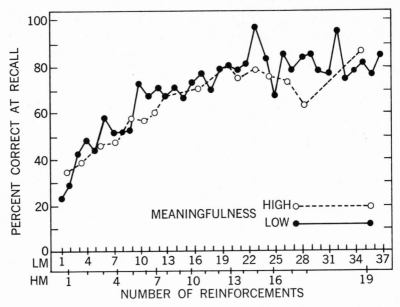

Fig. 16–6. Recall as a function of meaningfulness when strength of associations have been equalized at the end of learning. *Adapted from Underwood and Richardson (1956)*

serial lists of this material to a criterion of one perfect trial and obtained retention scores either 20 minutes, 24, or 48 hours later. Statistical analysis of the findings indicated no difference between the two types of material when retention was measured by using recognition, free recall, or anticipation values. Like Underwood and Richardson (1956), Postman and Rau found that when the relearning measure was used meaningful material was relearned more quickly than the nonmeaningful.[7]

The meaningfulness of material as related to short term retention has been examined by a number of investigators. Lindley (1963a) examined the short term retention of trigrams which differed in meaningfulness. High meaningful trigrams were words, medium meaningful trigrams were syllables, and low

[7] Postman and Rau (1957) did not apply the successive probability analysis to their anticipation scores. They did, however, use the findings of the Underwood and Richardson study to estimate the relative rates of associative growth and, from this estimate, inferred that the associative strengths of nonsense syllables and words were approximately equal at the end of the original learning.

meaningful trigrams were nonsyllables. Following one presentation of a single item, retention intervals of either 3, 13, or 39 seconds were provided, after which the subject was asked to recall the material which had been presented. Lindley found that the proportion of items recalled correctly increased as a function of increasing meaningfulness. As Underwood (1964a) pointed out, however, it is assumed that the degree of learning or amount of associative strength for the three kinds of material is equivalent since presentation time was equivalent—an assumption which probably is erroneous.

Retention as a Function of Distribution of Practice

Although this has been an area of considerable experimental interest, the findings obtained have been sufficiently controversial that no general conclusions can be made. In an early study [Hovland (1940)], subjects learned serial lists of nonsense syllables under massed (six seconds) or distributed (two minutes) practice. Following the reaching of one perfect trial, a retention interval of six seconds, two minutes, or 24 hours was utilized. The findings indicated that the distributed practice groups provided better recall at all retention intervals. But a series of studies by Underwood (1952, 1952a, 1953c) did not support Hovland's findings. In these studies, Underwood found that the retention of serial nonsense syllables was better following massed than following distributed practice.

The complexity of the area is indicated in a study by Underwood and Richardson (1955). Seven serial lists of consonant syllables with high interlist similarity were used. For the first list, one half of the subjects were given massed practice (two-second intertrial interval) and the other half were given distributed practice (30-second intertrial interval). Twenty-four hours later, a retention test was given. Five additional lists were then learned by all subjects under massed practice conditions. For the seventh list, half of the subjects were given massed practice and the other half distributed, with the latter group being subdivided into three groups with either one-, two-, or three-minute intertrial intervals. Retention of list seven was also measured after 24 hours. The total experiment covered a five-day period. The first list was learned on Day 1 and its retention was measured on Day 2, after which the subjects learned two additional lists. On Day 3, the subjects learned three additional lists, and on Day 4 the seventh list was learned. The retention of this list was measured on Day 5.

The results revealed that the retention of list one was better following massed than following distributed practice whereas the reverse was true for list seven. In general, the findings suggest that massed practice of serial lists results in better retention than does distributed practice when interlist interference is low; when interlist interference is high, distributed practice results in superior retention.

When massed versus distributed practice effects were examined to determine the retention of paired-associate lists, Underwood (1951, 1953, 1953a) found that retention following distributed practice was better than retention following massed. Such a conclusion must be tempered by the fact, however, that differences have not always approached statistical significance.

A major difficulty with the studies that have been cited is that the experimenters have had their subjects learn the material to a criterion of one perfect trial. Typically, the distributed practice groups learn the material with fewer trials, and it is quite likely that the associative strengths for the materials learned under different distributions of practice are not equivalent at the end of the original learning, thus making it difficult to draw any firm conclusions concerning the relative effectiveness of massed versus distributed practice.

Retention as a Function of the Similarity of the Material Learned

An examination of a large number of verbal learning studies revealed that such learning was a function of the similarity of the material which was used. As the material making up a list of words, for example, increases in similarity, the learning of such material becomes more difficult. In many of the studies which have been performed in this area, retention of such material also has been examined. In one study of serial learning, Underwood (1952a) constructed lists of nonsense syllables which varied in similarity (low, medium, and high). Each list was learned (serial anticipation) to a criterion of one perfect trial, and 24 hours later the list was recalled. The investigator found that recall did not vary as a function of intra-list similarity.

In a study using paired-associates, similar findings were obtained. In this study [Underwood (1953a)], six experiments were run in which the intra-list similarity of the stimuli and responses was varied. All lists were learned to a criterion of one perfect trial, and the retention of the material was measured 24 hours following learning. The findings indicated that neither response similarity nor stimulus similarity had any influence on retention.

In an examination of much of the experimental work, Underwood (1954a) concluded that "data from these experiments have shown that, over a wide range of response strengths, recall and intralist similarity are not systematically related. Items in a list with high similarity among these items are as well recalled as are items from a list in which the similarity is low."

Examination of the role of meaningfulness, distribution of practice, and similarity of retention has resulted in findings which are similar in each case. When the associative strengths of the varying types of experimental material are held constant, the amount of material retained is also constant. Although some investigators have obtained results which are not in keeping with this position, when such findings have been reported it is likely that the associative strengths of the varying experimental materials have varied.

Retention as a Function of Delay of Reinforcement

In examining the role of reward in learning, it was pointed out that learning was a function of the amount of time interpolated between the making of the correct response and the securing of reward. Brackbill and her associates examined the influence of the delay of reinforcement variable on retention. In the first study [Brackbill and Kappy (1962)], third-grade boys learned a series of two-choice discrimination problems, with delay of reinforcement intervals of either zero, five, or ten seconds. The general procedure was to expose two pictures; the child pushed a lever to designate the correct one. Reinforcement, in the form of marbles which could later be exchanged for a toy, was provided either zero, five, or ten seconds following each correct response. Following the reaching of a learning criterion, one or eight days later the children were required to relearn the task. In the relearning situation, zero delay of reinforcement was provided for all subjects. The results revealed that the mean numbers of trials to reach the original learning criterion for the zero-, five-, and ten-second delay groups were 17.67, 17.91, and 19.83—a finding in keeping with the general position that delay of reinforcement retards learning, although the differences among the groups were not statistically significant. Of primary interest, however, was retention performance, which the investigators expressed in terms of saving scores.

Results for the one-day retention test revealed that the group provided ten seconds of delay during acquisition had the best retention scores, the zero group the poorest. Thus, the zero-second delay group had a savings score of 65.27 per cent; the five-second delay group, 71.94 per cent; the ten-second delay group, 83.38 per cent. The superiority for the ten-second group tended to disappear when retention was tested after eight days.

In an effort to account for their findings, Brackbill and Kappy hypothesized that, in delay of reinforcement studies, if the subjects are capable of using distinctive response-produced cues and if the experimental task is one which permits the subject to make use of the cues, then, (1) the potentially deleterious effects of delay on learning efficiency will be reduced by virtue of a mediation effect operating from the learned response to reinforcement and (2) retention will be enhanced in proportion to the extent that distinctive response-produced cues have been utilized during acquisition. Thus, in the Brackbill and Kappy (1962) study, the distinctive response-produced cues were verbal. That is, the subjects were required to call out the name of the correct stimulus on each trial. Moreover, the investigators hypothesized that the naming tended to continue covertly after the overt response had been made. Such covert responding became a much stronger habit for the five- and ten-second delay groups than it did for the zero-delay group since for the five-second and ten-second delay groups it was *followed* by reinforcement but any covert responses by the zero-second delay group came after reinforcement.

In a second study [Brackbill, Bravos, and Starr (1962)], the difficulty of the task was increased by (1) using the same discrimination task and using kindergarten children as subjects or (2) requiring third-grade children to learn the material in a single session rather than in two sessions as had been done in the earlier study. In the first study, response-reinforcement delays of zero, five, and ten seconds were used; but in the second study, only two levels of response-reinforcement delay (zero and ten seconds) were employed. The results confirmed the findings of the original study [Brackbill and Kappy (1962)]. The delay-retention effect was obtained which, as a result of the large number of acquisition trials needed to reach the criterion, presumably increasing covert responding, was both initially stronger and longer lasting than that obtained previously.

The delay-retention effect was confirmed further in studies by Brackbill, Boblitt, Davlin, and Wagner (1963) and Brackbill, Isaacs, and Smelkinson (1962). In the latter study, the generality of the effect was extended to the use of material of low familiarity. Bigrams were used as the material to be learned, in contrast to the highly familiar material (names and pictures of common objects) which had been used in previous studies.

The Role of Warm-up in Retention

In the first chapter in which transfer was discussed, the construct of warm-up was introduced and some of the studies which investigated its influence within the transfer situation were examined. As indicated at that time, another area of inquiry has been the examination of the contribution of warm-up to retention.

One of the early studies examining warm-up effects on the recall of verbal material was performed by Irion (1949). In this study (Exp. II), subjects were required to learn a 15-unit list of paired, two-syllable adjectives. All groups were given ten trials of original learning. Group A was then given 24 hours of rest followed by one trial of color naming. The latter task was the warm-up task, in which the colors were arranged in paired-associate fashion and presented on the memory drum at the same rate of presentation as the adjectives. Subjects were instructed not to attempt to learn the colors but merely to name the second color of each pair as it appeared in the window of the drum. Thus, the task which was provided was similar to the learning task but one, it was believed, which would not increase the degree of learning on the originally learned activity. Ten relearning trials were then provided. Group B was also given a 24-hour rest period, but the color naming task was not provided prior to the ten relearning trials. Finally, Group C was given the ten relearning trials immediately following the first ten.

Using the total number of correct anticipations during the first ten learning trials as the initial measure, three analyses of covariance were conducted on the scores obtained on the first relearning trial. The first of these compared Group C (no-rest condition) with Group B (24-hour rest without warm-up). This analysis revealed that the no-rest condition was significantly

TABLE 16–2

Plan of Experiment

CONDI-TION	NO. TRIALS ORIGINAL LEARNING	LENGTH OF REST	NO. TRIALS WARMING UP	NO. TRIALS RELEARN-ING
I	20	no rest	0	10
II	20	35'0''	0	10
III	20	34'50''	0.5	10
IV	20	34'36''	1	10
V	20	34'12''	2	10
VI	20	33'24''	4	10

(Adapted from Irion and Wham, 1951)

superior on this trial. The second analysis compared Group C with Group A (24-hour rest and one warm-up trial) and revealed a nonsignificant difference. A comparison of Group B (24-hour rest without warm-up) with Group A (24-hour rest with warm-up) revealed a significantly superior retention score for Group A. From these findings, Irion concluded that a significant amount of forgetting took place over the 24-hour rest period when the subject was not warmed-up before recall and that the warming-up technique produced a significant reduction in the amount of this forgetting.

In a second study, Irion and Wham (1951) examined the influence of the amount of warming-up activity on recall and predicted that the greater the amount of such warm-up, the higher the level of recall performance. Six groups of subjects were first given 20 trials to learn a list of nine nonsense syllables in rote serial fashion. One group was then given ten additional relearning trials. The remaining groups were provided rest intervals of varying lengths and varying numbers of warm-up trials just prior to being given ten relearning trials. The specific length of the rest periods along with the number of warm-up trials is presented in Table 16–2. The warm-up task consisted of the recitation of a list of nine three-digit numbers, with the presentation of the digits being similar to the presentation of the original learning material. In order to minimize the possibility that learning would take place during this period, the digits were arranged in order: 1–2–3, 4–5–6, 7–8–9, 1–2–3, etc. Since the subjects were informed of this arrangement, it was possible for all subjects to anticipate correctly each number beginning with the

TABLE 16–3

Mean Correct Anticipations on Trials
Twenty and Twenty-one

CONDI-TION	WARMING-UP TRIALS	MEAN CORRECT ANTICIPATIONS		DIFFERENCE
		Trial 20	Trial 21	
I	—	6.00	6.00	0.00
II	0	6.07	4.40	−1.62
III	0.5	6.00	5.67	−0.33
IV	1	6.20	5.46	−0.74
V	2	5.87	5.53	−0.34
VI	4	4.53	5.87	+1.34

(Adapted from Irion and Wham, 1951)

first warm-up trial. The general findings are indicated in Table 16–3. Again, warm-up had a facilitating effect, with all three warm-up conditions producing recall scores on the first relearning trial which were superior to those obtained in the condition in which the subjects did not receive warm-up.[8]

[8] Some investigators have had difficulty confirming Irion's and Irion and Wham's findings. Rockway and Duncan (1952) gave ten groups of subjects ten trials learning a list of 15 paired adjectives. Twenty-four hours later an additional ten trials were given to all groups. The total number of correct responses on the first relearning trial was used as the recall score. Immediately prior to the first relearning trial, nine of the groups were given a color naming task which consisted of naming the second member of either 5, 15, or 30 pairs of colors presented at either a 1-, 2-, or 4-second anticipation rate. The tenth group (control) did not name colors prior to the relearning trials. A second experiment was also run in which Irion's (1949) materials and procedures were replicated but one group was told the purpose of the color naming whereas the second group was not. In neither experiment was any influence of this type of warm-up activity on recall demonstrated.

In a second study, Dinner and Duncan (1959) believed that warm-up might facilitate recall after a given degree of original learning, although not after the medium degree as used in the Rockway and Duncan (1952) experiment. The learning task and general procedure was the same as that used in the Rockway and Duncan study. The experimental variable was the amount of original learning provided—either 3, 8, or 15 (one errorless trial) correct anticipations. Experimental (warm-up) and control (no warm-up) groups learned lists of paired adjectives to each degree on Day 1 and returned 24 hours later for either warm-up trials (color naming) and relearning or for only relearning trials. The results revealed that warm-up significantly facilitated recall only after the highest degree of original learning; it had no influence on recall after the medium or low degrees of original learning. The complexity of the problem, however, is indicated by the fact that over the ten relearning trials, warm-up significantly facilitated performance for the group provided the low degree of learning but not after the medium or high degree of original learning.

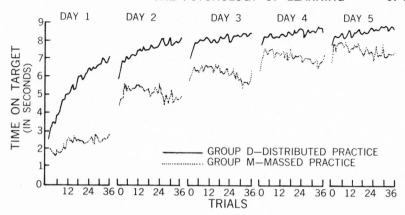

Fig. 16–7. Illustrations of warm-up decrement under conditions of massed and distributed practice on a Rotary Pursuit Test. *Adapted from Adams (1952)*

Motor learning represents a second situation which investigators have used to examine the influence of warm-up on retention. There is no doubt that decrements similar to warm-up are found in some, although certainly not all, motor learning tasks.[9] For example, Adams (1952), employing the rotary pursuit task, administered 36 ten-second trials each day for five days. For the massed practice group, these trials consisted of six minutes of continuous practice; for the distributed practice group, 40 seconds of rest were interpolated between each trial. Figure 16–7 reveals time on target for both groups over the five-day practice period. It can be noted that for both groups warm-up effects were obtained. Such effects are reflected in the sharp initial rise in the early trials of each day's session; this rise was independent of the influence of an overall gain or loss from the preceding day's trials.

Adams (1961) acknowledged that although performance decrements may be characterized as being due to a lack of warm-up, it may be postulated that such effects might arise from forgetting factors as well. More specifically, the learning of a specific task is assumed to involve the extinction of conflicting responses which have arisen from prior tasks which the individual has learned.

[9] Printing the alphabet upside-down which frequently has been used in the study of inhibition appears to be immune to warm-up effects [Archer (1954), Kimble (1949), Wasserman (1951)]; Bilodeau (1952, 1952a) was unable to find warm-up effects in a manual crank turning task.

When a rest period is introduced, these extinguished responses spontaneously recover some of their strength and compete with the responses demanded in the laboratory task. Such competition may be expected to produce a behavior decrement just as the lack of attentive and postural adjustments which define warm-up would also be expected to produce a decrement.[10]

The technique for differentiating a warm-up effect from a forgetting effect in the recall of verbal material, as Adams (1961) has written, has been ". . . to show positive effects of goal behavior from performance on neutral tasks that could not reasonably be thought as strengthening goal responses and therefore must be enhancing something else. . . ." This "something else" generally has been acknowledged to be related to set or warm-up. Thus, a color naming task introduced just prior to the recall of verbal material could not be considered to strengthen the specific verbal responses demanded by the test for recall. But when such activity aids recall, it can be attributed only to the enhancement of those attentive and postural adjustments demanded by the verbal learning task.

Adams (1961) indicated that the difficulty in examining warm-up effects in motor learning is that neutral tasks—tasks which can be demonstrated not to strengthen the original motor learning task but nonetheless do strengthen attentive and postural adjustments—have not been discovered. As a result, warm-up effects can just as well be explained by the forgetting factor. One study which attempted to provide a neutral task within the motor learning situation was performed by Ammons (1951). In this study, subjects were given continuous practice on a rotary pursuit task for 12 minutes, allowed to rest for 17 minutes, and then continuous practice for 12 more minutes. The experimental conditions relevant for this discussion consisted of providing, just prior to the second 12-minute period, the following types of warm-up activities: (1) ocular practice, in which the subjects merely followed the target for two minutes with their eyes, (2) blindfolded manual practice in which a blindfolded subject followed a small rivet head set into the rotor plate for two minutes with the

---

[10] Although warm-up effects have not been formally investigated in animal studies, a number of investigators in their examination of other problem areas [Schlosberg (1934, 1936), Ellson (1938), Finger (1942a), and Verplanck (1942)] observed performance decrements which they attributed to lack of warm-up. But, as with motor learning situations, such decrements could have arisen from forgetting factors as well.

index finger, (3) imaginary practice which consisted of the subject's standing before the rotary pursuit with eyes blindfolded and imagining for two minutes that she was practicing, although overt movements were not permitted. An examination of the difference between the first and second minutes of the second 12-minute practice period revealed no difference between any of the experimental groups and a control group, which was not given any type of warm-up activity prior to the second 12-minute practice period.

The conclusions on the influence of warm-up on retention are similar to those which were reached following an examination of warm-up within the transfer situation. The experimental evidence points to warm-up effects, particularly in the area of verbal learning and recall, as being a bona fide phenomenon; but as Adams (1961) noted, in reviewing much of the work that has been done in this area, "there is a disconcerting number of negative findings." More research is needed in order to be able to specify which variables are contributing to the discrepant results.

RETENTION AS RELATED TO ORGANIZATION AND STORAGE VARIABLES

Thus far, the primary concern has been how task variables influence retention, but any complete examination of this area should include organization and storage variables as well.

The experimental procedure used in almost all the studies which will be reviewed in this section employed free learning trials, although they frequently have been classed as recall trials. In keeping with this recall classification, most investigators have assumed that the variables which have been investigated provide information about how the individual *retains* material rather than how such material is *learned*. Because of the prevalence of this practice, the material will be considered within this framework, although the reader should recognize that these variables could be related to the learning process just as readily.

Transformation or the Process of Encoding

When an individual recalls a response, for example, the trigram RIV, it is possible that the unit which is placed in his memory is isomorphic to the material which was objectively presented. In this case, the trace or memory unit would simply consist of some direct representation of RIV. But a more realistic position would be that the subject frequently transforms the unit for memory storage into something different from that which has been presented. For example, mnemonic devices, or associational aids, often are utilized in the memory process. In the example cited, the subject may code or transform RIV into "river" and store this word along with the additional memory unit—"the first three letters." The retrieval of the trigram takes place by the individual first remembering "river" but then modifying the response by the additional instructions "first three letters." Inasmuch as in most learning experiments the subject is not instructed how the material which is presented should be transformed or coded, this process is frequently idiosyncratic, i.e., the individual provides a transformation or code of his own which is determined by his previous experiences.

A good example of this is found in an experiment by Allan (1961) in which servicemen had to learn a randomized order of the letters of the alphabet. The sequence of the letters was as follows: N A J S T W H I D Q V F Z C E P G O K B X R Y L M U, each of which was placed on an index card. The general procedure was for the subject to turn over each card and say the letter aloud until all 26 letters were repeated. A recall trial followed this presentation. Learning and recall trials continued until each subject was able to recall all of the letters. It was noted that all the subjects attempted to organize the material into manageable units with frequent meaningful translations. Thus, O K was recalled by some as a slang expression, and H I D was remembered as a word. Q V was remembered by one subject as Queen Victoria, and Q V F was recalled by another as a code used in the Navy. Allan noted that the coding of letters was highly individualistic and a noticeable feature was the diversity of the categorical groupings.

Coding operations may inhibit recall as well as facilitate it. Studies by Lindley (1963a) and Underwood and Keppel (1963) provide interesting illustrations. In the latter study, the investigators presented ten trigrams to subjects for five alternate study and recall trials. Each trigram could be coded into either of two words by rearranging the letters. Thus, UTB could be arranged to spell either TUB or BUT. Parallel groups were either given or not given instructions indicating that these trigrams could be coded into words. Within each of these major groups, four subgroups were differentiated on the basis of the nature of the correct response which was demanded by the experimenter. The first subgroup was instructed, prior to the first learning trial, that the letters could be written in any order. The second subgroup was instructed that the order of the letters must be recalled in the order presented to be counted correct. Following the first recall trial, they were reinstructed that on subsequent trials the letters could be written in any order. For the third subgroup, the instructions to write the letters as presented held until after the third recall trial at which time they were reinstructed that on subsequent trials the letters could be written in any order. Subjects in the fourth subgroup were required to write the letters as they were presented on all recall trials. The data showed that if the subjects were permitted to recall the letters of each trigram in any order performance was facilitated if the trigrams were encoded into words, with the instructed group being superior to the noninstructed. On the other hand, if the subject was required to recall the trigrams as they were presented, the noninstructed group revealed superior performance. The reason for the inhibitory effect of coding was that, although coding was simple, a specific decoding rule had to be learned for each coded trigram. Thus, if TFA was encoded to "fat," the decoding rule had to be something like "put last letter first." But for the trigram BSU, which had been coded to "bus," a different decoding rule was necessary. Since no single decoding rule could apply to all trigrams, there were numerous possibilities for interference among the decoding rules, which undoubtedly contributed to poorer performance.

Lindley (1963a) demonstrated that coding can facilitate as well as inhibit performance in the short term retention situation. Trigrams which differed in level of meaningfulness were used as the material to be recalled. High meaningful trigrams were words (WAS, CUT, etc.) ; medium meaningful trigrams were syllables (JUM, VER, FRO, etc.) ; and the low meaningful trigrams were nonsyllables (XPO, NPA, RCH, etc.). Three retention intervals were utilized: 3, 13, or 39 seconds; one half of the subjects were given coding cues, but the other half were not. The recoding cues consisted of having the trigram which was to be recalled typed in capital letters and then providing additional lower case letters in the appropriate positions to make a complete English word. Thus, the trigram CQU was coded by presenting the additional lower case letters to make the word aCQUire, and the trigram WAS, although a word in itself, was coded into a different word by the addition of the letter h, i.e., WASh. Subjects who were not given coding cues were not presented with these additional lower case letters but with only the trigram itself. As with typical short term retention studies, only a single item was presented, followed by a retention interval, with recall following this interval. The retention interval (3, 13, or 39 seconds) was filled by the subject's reading a row of random digits, with instructions to perform this task as rapidly as possible and not to rehearse the items which had been presented. The results revealed that the proportion of items correctly recalled decreased as a function of the retention interval and as a function of decreasing meaningfulness. A basic concern, however, is the coding function, and an interaction was found between recoding cues and meaningfulness. In brief, the presence of coding cues facilitated the recall of low meaningful items but interfered with the retention of the high meaningful items. No effect was noted for items of medium meaningfulness.

An excellent example of how coding can distort the recall of visual forms is illustrated in an early study by Carmichael, Hogan, and Walter (1932), although it should be pointed out that this study was not conducted with this objective in mind. In this experiment, a set of 12 relatively ambiguous figures was prepared, some of which are indicated in Figure 16–8. Two names were assigned to each figure. All subjects were presented with the same figures, but for one group one list of names was provided and for the other group a second list of names was given. Prior to each figure's being presented, the experimenter stated: "The next figure resembles. . . ." Following this presentation, subjects were instructed to draw the figures as accurately as possible. Two judges rated the subjects' drawings, with the results being that 74 per cent of the figures that had been named by the words in the first list were found to be similar to the visual representation of the figure named in the first list. Seventy-three per cent of the figures named by the second word list were like visual representations of the figure named in that list. In essence, what appeared to happen was that the subjects used the word provided by the experimenter to encode in the memory a visual figure. When they were then asked to reproduce this figure, the coding operation resulted in its distortion.

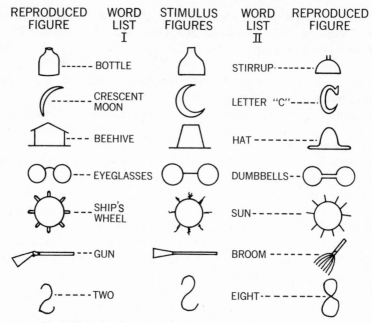

Fig. 16–8. A sampling of the stimulus figures which were used appears in the middle column. *Adapted from Carmichael, Hogan, and Walter (1932)*

Recoding and the Immediate Memory Span

Another example of the coding process can be found in the examination of the individual's immediate memory span. This span, of course, refers to the number of items which can be recalled immediately after a single presentation. The memory span may be conceptualized as representing one point on the memory continuum with immediate, or short term, memory being placed at one end and long term memory at the other. It has been demonstrated that if digits or letters are used as the basic unit the average adult is able to recall about seven of them accurately 50 per cent of the time. But the number of letters that can be recalled increases substantially if they are arranged into words. In essence, there has been a kind of encoding operation which plays an important role in the determination of how much is recalled.

Miller (1956) primarily has been responsible for calling

attention to the fact that within the immediate memory span the individual codes material into familiar units. These units he has called "chunks." The basic point which Miller has made is that, although the span for immediate memory appears to be relatively fixed at about seven chunks, the amount of material that is recalled can be increased effectively by building larger and larger chunks. That is, by appropriate coding operations, the individual can combine a number of small chunks into a larger one and, thus, increase the amount of material that can be recalled. An excellent example which he uses to illustrate this phenomenon is the man just beginning to learn telegraphic code. At first he hears each dit and dah as a separate chunk, but soon he is able to organize these sounds into letters so that he deals with letters as chunks. After some practice, the letters organize themselves into words which become larger chunks. Following this, he begins to hear whole phrases as chunks. As Miller points out, as larger and larger chunks emerge in the learning of the code, the amount of the message that the operator can remember increases accordingly.

Support for Miller's chunk hypothesis is found in a short term retention study by Murdock (1961a). In one session, the Peterson and Peterson (1959) experimental procedure was replicated in which the subject had to recall three letters which made up a trigram. In a second session, the items that were presented were single monosyllabic words selected from the Thorndike-Lorge (1944) list of 1,000 most common words, and in the third session, three monosyllabic words were presented. In selecting these word triads, the only stipulation was that the three words could be spoken clearly in the same length of time required to say the three-consonant syllables presented in the first session. The duration of the retention interval was either 0, 3, 6, 9, 12, or 18 seconds. The chunk hypothesis would predict that no differences should be found between the recall of the three letters and the recall of the three words since three chunks are involved in each case. On the other hand, where only a single chunk was presented (one word), retention of this material should be superior. Murdock's experimental findings confirmed Miller's position.

Cohen (1963) reasoned that, if the chunk hypothesis is correct, groups of words that go together, or are related in some manner, should be recoded and given a new name or label. A group of related words may function as a single unit in memory.

Applied to the free-recall situation, a list made up of more than 20 words but comprising only 20 categories and a list of 20 unrelated words should be equivalent in the sense that each contains 20 units or chunks of information. In the 20-category word list, each unit or chunk comprised a set of related words belonging to a given category, but in the unrelated word list, the unit or chunk was the set of letters making up a given word. Cohen attempted to examine this position in his study. Twenty unrelated words were presented to a group of subjects, with each word presented for ten and one-half seconds. Another group of subjects was presented 70 words which were arranged in 20 categories, each of which was made up of three or four sets of words. In order to equate total presentation time, each word from the 70-word list was presented for three seconds. The results supported the chunk hypothesis. That is, the number of words recalled from the list of 20 unrelated words did not differ from the number of categories recalled in the 70-word list.

Organization as Revealed by Clustering

If a list of unrelated words is presented only once to a subject, with the instructions that he recall them immediately following their presentation, most experimental results reveal that the last items which were presented are recalled most frequently, the items appearing at the beginning of the list next most frequently, and the middle items least frequently. Recall in this situation appears to be determined by the serial position of the material—a task variable.

But at times, there may be some relationship among the words in the list. When such a situation prevails, recall scores reveal that the findings obtained with the single presentation of unrelated words do not hold; rather, the recall of the material appears to indicate that the subject has introduced some type of organization into the situation. One of the early studies in which this phenomenon was noted was conducted by Bousfield (1953). In this study, subjects were presented with a randomized list of 60 items made up of four 15-item categories: animals, names, professions, and vegetables. Immediately following the presentation, the subjects were given ten minutes to list all of the words they could recall. The experimenter found that the subjects showed a greater than chance tendency to place items in clusters or groups which contained members of the same general category. From such recall data, Bousfield inferred an organizing tendency on the part of the subject which he termed "clustering."

It is reasonable to assume that clustering may be found whenever the list of material which is presented is made up of words which can be categorized in some way or another. Support for this assumption can be found in a study by Cofer (1959). One list of 40 words was composed of eight groups of synonyms, and a second list was composed of unrelated words. The general procedure used by Bousfield (1953) was employed. Although results revealed no difference in number of words recalled between the lists, there was evidence for clustering appearing in the list containing the synonyms. These findings support the position that synonymity can serve as a basis for clustering.

A question which follows from the research which has been reported is how recall is influenced by the number of clusters or categories which make up the list. An early study by Mathews (1954) indicated that, when the total number of items which made up a list was held constant, recall was an increasing function of the number of categories, or clusters, which were used. In this study, 24 items (individual's names) were divided into either two, three, or six categories—a category being defined as a profession or occupation, i.e., artist, athlete, scientist, etc. The names comprising each category were presumably equated on the basis of controlled-association data. The general procedure was for the subject to first identify each of 24 individuals as belonging to one of either two, three, or six categories. Following this, a retention test was provided in which subjects had to recall the names which they had previously identified. It was found that subjects who previously had to identify individuals belonging to six categories recalled significantly more names than those who had to identify individuals belonging to only three. This group, in turn, recalled significantly more names than the group using only two categories to classify the items.

Bousfield and Cohen (1956), using a word list comprised of 40 items and divided into two, four, or eight categories, were able to confirm Mathew's findings—the number of words recalled was a function of the number of categories which were used. However, a second experiment by these investigators which replicated the experimental procedure of the first revealed opposite findings.

The mean number of words recalled for the eight-category list in this second experiment was 19.71, in contrast to 23.54 for the four-category list and 25.50 for the two-category list.[11]

A recent and extensive study by Dallett (1964) indicated that the area is a rather complex one and that the length of the list appears to make an important contribution to the findings which are obtained. Of five experiments which were conducted, four of them have primary relevance to this discussion. The general procedure utilized in all experiments was to present, on a tape recorder, the items to be recalled by the groups of five subjects. Following the presentation of the last item, the subjects were given one minute to recall as many of the items as they could. Control lists were constructed by taking one of the experimental lists and matching it, word for word, with words of the same frequency, number of syllables, and initial letters. A control list, an experimental list, and a control list, in that order, were presented to each group of subjects during a given experimental session.

The specific experimental conditions utilized in Experiment I consisted of a list of 12 words in which the number of categories used was either 1, 2, 3, 4, or 6 and in which all words within a given category were presented contiguously. Experiment II replicated Experiment I except that the words within a given category were distributed randomly throughout the list. Experiments IV and V were similar to Experiments I and II except that the lists were 24 words in length, rather than 12, and the number of categories was changed to 2, 4, 6, 8, and 12. The results for Experiments I and II are indicated in Figure 16–9, and Figure 16–10 presents the findings for Experiments IV and V. The findings suggested that the relationship between recall and the number of categories which comprised the list differed for different lengths of list. With a list of 12 words, recall was a curvilinear function of the number of categories, but with a list consisting of 24 words recall increased as the number of categories decreased—

[11] The investigators have taken the position that the results of the first study reveal the more general relationship between free recall and number of categories which make up a list. They have pointed out that the subjects used in Experiment II had served previously in a word-category study and hypothesized that this previous experience produced a particular set in these subjects to look for word categories, a set which was not present in subjects serving in Experiment I. Thus, they attributed the different findings in the two experiments to differences in the set of the subjects employed.

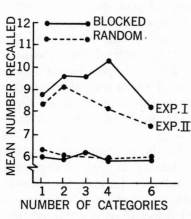

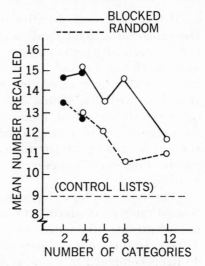

Fig. 16–9. Mean number of items recalled as a function of the number of categories. The upper curves represent performance on the category lists while the lower curves are control-list scores and are keyed to correspond to the category-list curves above. *Adapted from Dallett (1964)*

Fig. 16–10. Mean number of items recalled as a function of the number of categories. Experiment IV (open circles) examined 2 and 4; Experiment V (filled circles) examined 4, 6, 8 and 12. *Adapted from Dallett (1964)*

a finding also obtained by Bousfield and Cohen (1956) in their second experiment.

It seems reasonable to assume that the categories which are used may vary. For example, Cohen (1963a) called attention to the fact that the words making up a category may be exhaustive whereas at other times the words may form a nonexhaustive category. Thus, an exhaustive category may be defined as one where the number of words contained in the group represent all or nearly all of the words in the category. For example, the words north, south, east, and west exhaust the members of the category which might be termed cardinal points of the compass. On the other hand, the words dog, lion, horse, and bear represent members of a nonexhaustive category since they represent only a small sample from a large pool of animal names. Cohen (1963a) attempted to determine whether the exhaustive–nonexhaustive dimension was an important one in the free recall of categorized word lists. A second objective was to determine if this variable also contributed to the recall of categories. Four experiments were run, in each of which the same general procedure and material were employed. Lists of 70 words comprising ten exhaustive and ten nonexhaustive categories of words were presented. The results showed that significantly more words of the exhaustive categories were recalled, indicating that an important variable in the presentation of a categorized word list is related to whether the words exhaust the varying categories which are used. There was no difference, however, in the number of categories which were recalled.

The type of clustering which has been illustrated has been termed category clustering [Cofer (1964)], in contrast to associative clustering illustrated in a study by Jenkins and Russell (1952). In this study, subjects recalled a list of words consisting of 48 items composed of stimulus and response pairs obtained from the Kent-Rosanoff association test. Although the words were presented in random order, subjects showed a highly significant tendency to recall words in their stimulus-response sequence. For example, although words intervened between the presentation of "table" and "chair," recall scores revealed that "table" and "chair" were recalled together. Reversed associations, "chair"–"table," occurred significantly more than chance pairings but significantly less than the forward sequence.

In a second study, Jenkins, Mink, and Russell (1958) demonstrated that such clustering was a function of the associative strength of the stimulus and response pairs which were used. In this experiment, groups of subjects were asked to recall four different word lists; each list was made up of 12 stimulus and response pairs (24 words) also obtained from the Kent-Rosanoff association test. The average associative strength of the stimulus and response pairs, as measured by frequency of occurrence in word association norms, varied systematically from list to list. Thus, the first list had the highest associative strength, being comprised of such pairs as man-woman, table-chair, black-white, etc., whereas the fourth list had the lowest associative strength, with such pairs as cheese-crackers, child-baby, earth-round, etc. The words were not used in their paired order, of course, but were randomly distributed throughout the list. A significant tendency to recall the words in their stimulus-response sequence appeared —a finding which confirmed the earlier Jenkins and Russell

(1952) study. More important was the fact that the average amount of such forward associative clustering was closely related to the average free associative strength of the pairs in each list. Thus, List 1, which had the highest associative strength, provided the largest number of associative pairs recalled. List 2 revealed the next largest, followed by Lists 3 and 4.

The large and consistent clustering effects obtained in the studies of Jenkins and Russell (1952) and Jenkins, Mink, and Russell (1958) suggested to Deese (1959) that it would be fruitful to examine the more general case of associative relationship between all items that make up the list of words and not between just particular items. As a result, the principal independent variable which he examined has been described as inter-item associative strength, defined as the average relative frequency with which all items in a list tend to elicit, as free associates, all other items in the same list. This measure is obtained from single response free association data, and an example of how it is computed can be found in Table 16–4.

In Deese's (1959) study, 18 lists of 15 words per list were used for the free-recall tests. Each of the first six lists consisted of high frequency response items to a single word obtained from the Kent-Rosanoff word list. Six other lists consisted of low frequency associations to the same six stimulus words, and the last six lists consisted entirely of response words which had never been given as associations to these words. For example, using the stimulus word "butterfly," the following words were used to make up one of the high frequency lists: moth, insect, wing, bird, fly, yellow, net, pretty, flower, bug, cocoon, color, stomach, blue, and bees. The inter-item associative strength for this list was calculated to be 28.3. Words used to make up the low frequency list (also using butterfly as a stimulus word) were as follows: garden, sky, flutter, sunshine, nature, chase, spring, collection, beautiful, caterpillar, summer, flight, wasp, colorful, and grace. The inter-item associative strength for this list was 4.3. Finally, the zero frequency list consisted of the following: book, tutor, government, study, early, velvet, winter, payroll, line, zebra, spray, arrow, help, arithmetic, and typical.

Six groups of subjects were used, and each group of subjects was given two high frequency lists, two low frequency lists, and two zero frequency lists. For one-half of the subjects, the Kent-Rosanoff stimulus word was given to the subjects as a means

TABLE 16–4

An Index of Inter-Item Associative Strength

	PIG	HORSE	DEER	DONKEY
Pig	—	0	0	0
Horse	1	—	0	2
Deer	0	0	—	0
Donkey	0	0	0	—
Totals	1	0	0	2

Computation of the index is accomplished by summing the column totals and dividing by the number of columns:

$$\frac{1\% + 0 + 0 + 2\%}{4} = .75\%$$

Data: Assume the words PIG, HORSE, DEER, and DONKEY are used in a free association test and presented to 100 subjects. The object of the inter-item associative strength index is to measure the extent to which each of these words will elicit the other in the free association test.

In order to obtain such a measure, a matrix is set up with the words used in the test listed across the top row. The same words also are listed down the left column. The percentage of frequency with which a word in the column is a response to the word at the head of the column is entered in the appropriate cell. The percentage of frequency with which a word elicits itself is not used. An examination of the matrix presented reveals that one subject out of 100 responded with the word "horse" when PIG was presented and that two subjects out of 100 responded with the word "horse" when DONKEY was presented.

(Adapted from Marshall and Cofer, 1963)

whereby the list was identified, but for the other half of the subjects, the word which was given did not bear any relationship to the response words. The general procedure was to read the list of words to the subjects, and, immediately following such reading, they were to write down all of the words that they could remember.

Deese found that the identification of the lists by appropriate or inappropriate stimulus words did not contribute to the number of items recalled. However, the inter-item associative strength did significantly determine the number of words which were recalled. Lists with high inter-item associative strength were recalled significantly better than lists with low inter-item associative strength which, in turn, were recalled better than lists with zero inter-item associative strength.

Must there be some associative connection or relationship among the material in order for the subject to exhibit organizational tendencies during recall? It may be recalled that when a series of unrelated words is presented for a single trial such organizational tendencies are not observed. But perhaps this failure merely reflects the lack of opportunity for the subject to demonstrate such a tendency. There appears to be some evidence that such is the case.

Tulving (1962) presented a list of 16 disyllabic nouns to subjects for 16 trials, using a different serial order of presentation on each trial. At the end of each trial, the subject was asked to recall as many words from the list as he could. As would be expected, Tulving found that the number of words recalled increased as a function of the number of trials. But of greater importance was the fact that he found a tendency on the part of the subjects to recall words in the same order on different trials. Moreover, this type of subjective organization increased systematically with repeated exposures to the material. Thus, although the experimenter may presume that the words which are to be recalled are unrelated one to the other, the subject, if given the opportunity, will provide his own organization.

17

The Nature of Forgetting

In the preceding chapter, in discussing the use of the terms retention and forgetting, it was pointed out that the concept of forgetting has been reserved primarily for experimental situations in which the investigator was interested in examining the characteristics and nature of the events which fill the temporal interval between Trial N and N + 1 and which, of course, produce a performance decrement.

No one retains all the material which he has learned. Over a period of time an individual forgets, often regardless of the conditions under which the learning took place. For many individuals, it has been this time period which provides the fundamental reason as to why we forget. Poems, speeches, definitions, and formulas which once have been learned, following the passage of time, can no longer be recalled. Since time appears to be the common denominator in all such instances, it is not surprising that time has been looked upon as the basic contributor to forgetting.

Other investigators have emphasized time-related variables, with perhaps the most important of these being disuse. During the period of time between learning and the attempted recall, the material which has been learned has not been used; hence, it is forgotten. Physiologically oriented theorists have conceptualized forgetting in terms of a fading or decay of the memory trace

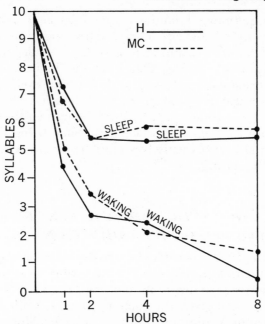

Fig. 17–1. Average number of syllables recalled after intervals of
sleeping and waking. *Adapted from Jenkins and Dallenbach (1924)*

taking place with the passage of time or disuse of the material.
Thus, as time passes, normal bodily processes produce a disinte-
gration of the memory trace which is mirrored in the behavioral
changes which we term forgetting.

Although many early investigators supported a disuse position
as a primary explanation of forgetting, the experimental work of
Jenkins and Dallenbach (1924) and a replication of this study by
Van Ormer (1932) were the initial attacks against such a
position. In the Jenkins and Dallenbach study, subjects first
learned a list of ten nonsense syllables to a criterion of one perfect
trial. After one, two, four, or eight hours of (1) ordinary waking
activity or (2) sleeping, they were asked to recall the material.
The results, revealed in Figure 17–1, indicated that nonsense
syllables were retained better after intervals of sleeping than after
corresponding intervals of waking. Since the same amount of time,
or lack of using the material, took place between the original
learning and the test for recall, it is difficult to account for the
differential forgetting using time or disuse as an explanation.

These experimental findings were used as a basic point in McGeoch's (1932) now classic paper attacking disuse as a fundamental variable in explaining forgetting. A second point which this investigator made was that time should be thought of as merely a conceptual framework within which events take place. The iron bar that is tossed in the field does not rust because of time; rather, it is time which permits the oxygen from the air to combine with the iron to produce rust. Such being the case, the environmental events themselves must be considered in order to account for forgetting.[1]

THE ROLE OF ENVIRONMENTAL EVENTS: RETROACTIVE AND PROACTIVE INHIBITION

McGeoch (1932) considered the basic condition which contributed to forgetting to be the activity which was interpolated between the original learning and the test for retention. This condition has been given the name retroactive inhibition, following the usage of Müller and Pilzecker (1900). More specifically, the term refers to a retention decrement resulting from activity which has been interpolated between the original learning and the test for retention. The experimental design that typically has been utilized is as follows:

Retroactive Inhibition

Exp. Group	Learn A	Learn B	Recall A
Control Group	Learn A	Rest	Recall A

It has been also acknowledged that learning which has taken place prior to the learning and recall of material may inhibit recall. The interference that such activity provides has been classed as proactive inhibition and the experimental design that has been utilized in such experiments is as follows:

Proactive Inhibition

Exp. Group	Learn B	Learn A	Recall A
Control Group	Rest	Learn A	Recall A

[1] It is interesting to note that McGeoch (1932) believed that if the interval of time interpolated between the learning and recall was entirely devoid of activity retention would be perfect. Thus, he stated, "Recall after sleep is sufficiently high to support the inference that, could an interval be rendered absolutely empty of events, a vacuum mentally, and the conditions of learning and of recall equated, there would be no forgetting."

It should be noted that these designs may provide facilitation, as well as inhibition, of retention. Most investigators, however, have been concerned primarily with inhibition (and forgetting) and have, accordingly, attempted to manipulate the conditions in order to achieve this result.

An Examination of the Variables Which Contribute to Proactive and Retroactive Inhibition

The experimental work that has been done in this area is so extensive that only some of the more fundamental investigations can be cited.[2]

SIMILARITY OF MATERIAL. It has been generally accepted that the experimental findings which are obtained using a transfer design parallel those which would be obtained if a proaction or retroaction experimental design was used. Thus, the Skaggs-Robinson hypothesis which was presented in Chapter 14 to account for the role of similarity in transfer also has application to proaction and retroaction situations. It will be recalled that this hypothesis stated that facilitation is maximum when successively practiced material is identical. Moderate degrees of similarity between such material result in maximum inhibition, with such inhibition decreasing progressively as the successively practiced materials become dissimilar. Studies by Robinson (1927), Harden (1929), and Kennelly (1941), investigating retroactive inhibition as a function of the similarity of the materials used, confirmed this hypothesis. Thus, it was agreed that for relatively high degrees of similarity the *greater* the similarity between the original and interpolated materials, the *less* the retroactive inhibition.

However, the retroactive inhibition studies of McGeoch and McDonald (1931), Johnson (1933), and McGeoch and McGeoch (1937) did not confirm the findings of the previous investigators. In the McGeoch and McDonald (1931) study, for example, subjects learned a list of two-syllable adjectives to a criterion of one perfect trial. Following such learning, one of the following types of interpolated material was presented: synonyms, antonyms, unrelated adjectives, nonsense syllables, three-digit numbers, and rest. The materials had been ranked previously by

---

[2] For example, three reviews of the literature [Britt (1935), Swenson (1941), and Slamecka and Ceraso (1960)] contain more than 300 experimental studies devoted to this topic.

judges on the basis of their similarity to the original list of adjectives. Following the learning of the interpolated materials, relearning trials on the original list were provided. The score on the first relearning trial was used as a recall score. The results revealed that the rest condition provided the largest number of words recalled (4.50), followed by three-digit numbers (3.68), nonsense syllables (2.58), unrelated adjectives (2.17), antonyms (1.83), and synonyms (1.25).

In a second experiment by these investigators, a similar experimental design and procedure were utilized except that three different groups of synonyms, varying in degree of similarity to the original material, served as the interpolated material. Original list retention scores showed that the learning of the synonyms which were most closely related to the original list adjectives produced the largest amount of retroactive inhibition. In short, this study, as well as the others which have been cited, indicated that the greater the similarity between the original and interpolated material, the greater the amount of retroactive inhibition—a position contrary to the Skaggs-Robinson hypothesis.

A basic difficulty with the Skaggs-Robinson formulation is that the similarity dimension is not related to either stimuli or responses. Osgood (1949), recognizing this difficulty, proposed his three-dimensional surface, which was presented in Chapter 14, in which the similarity dimension of the stimulus is separated from the response.

A survey of the retroactive and proactive inhibition experimental literature in which Osgood's three-dimensional surface was examined reveals that primarily two paradigms have been investigated. The first is one in which the response dimension of the interfering material has been varied, i.e., A-B, A-C; and the second is one in which the stimulus aspect of the interfering material has been varied, i.e., A-B, C-B.

Examining the A-B, A-C situation, Osgood's surface predicts that retroactive (or proactive) facilitation should be obtained when response members are highly similar but increasing amounts of retroactive (or proactive) inhibition should be obtained as the responses go from similar to antagonistic. As noted in Chapter 14, Bugelski and Cadwallader (1956) obtained inhibitory effects when either similar, neutral, or opposed responses were attached to identical stimuli and used as the interpolated material in a retroactive inhibition situation. But, as Figure

14–5 shows, the specific curve form which these investigators obtained is somewhat different from that formulated by Osgood. In contrast, Young (1955), Gladis and Braun (1958), and Dallett (1962) confirmed that portion of Osgood's surface which posits that inhibitory effects should increase as the interfering responses go from similarity through neutrality.

In the Gladis and Braun (1958) study, for example, subjects learned to associate two-syllable adjectives with two-letter stimuli, i.e., TL–insane, HX–winding. Eight such paired-associates comprised the original learning material. Interpolated materials consisted of identical stimuli to which were attached responses which varied in similarity to the original responses; high, moderate, and low degrees of response similarity as well as those classed as neutral were used. The original list was learned to a criterion of one perfect trial plus one additional trial, following which the interpolated list was learned to the same criterion. After the subjects learned the interpolated list, they were asked to recall the original list. The investigators found that retroactive inhibition increased (reflected by decreased recall scores) as the degree of similarity between the response members of the original and interpolated list decreased. Thus, the recall scores for the varying groups, as measured by the number of items recalled, were as follows: [3]

High similarity	5.4
Moderate similarity	4.3
Low similarity	3.1
Neutral	2.6

It will be recalled that one part of Osgood's surface would predict retroactive facilitation when the interpolated material consisted of identical stimuli, with responses highly similar to the original material. Parducci and Knopf's (1958) experiment is one of the few in which such a finding was obtained. In their study, geometric figures served as the stimuli and four-digit numbers were used as responses. Identical stimuli with one of three degrees of response similarity were used as the interpolated materials. A control group copied a complex abstract design during the

[3] Gladis and Braun's (1958) failure to use a learn-rest-recall control group makes it difficult to determine whether retroactive facilitation or retroactive inhibition was obtained.

interpolated learning period. The findings indicated that retroactive facilitation increased with increased similarity of response. The differentiating feature of the Parducci and Knopf study, in contrast to the others which have been presented, was their use of a recognition test for the original learning and retention situation, whereas the interpolated task involved a recall measure. They proposed that the relationship between retroactive facilitation and response similarity postulated by Osgood may hold only for those situations in which the subject can easily discriminate among the successive stages of the experiment.

In the studies which have been presented a retroaction design was used, although Osgood's surface has application to proaction as well. Studies by Morgan and Underwood (1950) and Dallett (1962) demonstrated proactive inhibition effects as a function of the similarity of first and second list responses—a finding in keeping with the retroactive inhibition studies. In the Morgan and Underwood study, subjects learned lists of 12 paired two-syllable adjectives; the stimuli on the two lists were identical, and the degree of synonymity among the response items was varied through five conditions. The first condition utilized dissimilar responses, the second slightly similar, and so on to the fifth condition in which the responses were highly similar. The two lists were learned to a criterion of seven correct anticipations on a single trial, with the second list being relearned to a criterion of one perfect trial after a 20-minute rest interval. The findings showed that proactive inhibition tended to increase as response similarity decreased. Dallett (1962), using stimuli selected from Gibson's figures and responses obtained from those previously used by Osgood (1946), was able to demonstrate a similar finding.[4]

The second paradigm is one in which the interfering responses remain identical to original list responses but the stimuli are varied from identity through dissimilarity (A-B, C-B). Bugelski and Cadwallader (1956) obtained findings which indicated that retroactive facilitation increased with increasing similarity of stimuli, thus supporting the Osgood surface. A description of this

---

[4] It must be noted that Young (1955), using lists of eight two-syllable paired adjectives, with the stimuli for the interfering list being identical to those used in the original list but with the responses varying from a high degree of similarity through medium to low, found that proactive inhibition was not related to response similarity—a finding in contrast to Morgan and Underwood (1950) and Dallett (1962).

experiment along with the experimental findings is presented in Chapter 14 where this effect was examined within a transfer context. Dallett (1962) obtained similar facilitating effects using a proactive type design.

It may be noted that this examination of the role of similarity has been confined to the specific learning material. There is no reason, however, why the study of this variable cannot be extended to the learner's set or the stimuli which comprise the learning environment. Studies by Postman and Jenkins (1948), Postman and Postman (1948), Jenkins and Postman (1949) and Postman and Stark (1962) are but a few of the many experiments designed to investigate the role of similarity of set within the retroactive inhibition situation.

In the Postman and Postman (1948) study, set was defined as the subject's expectation to form associations which embody a given type of logical relationship. Pairs of meaningful words were used as the experimental material, and they were so chosen that members of the pair were either compatible or incompatible with each other with regard to meaning and connotation. An example of a compatible pair would be doctor-heal or war-bloodshed; an incompatible pair would be doctor-harm or war-peaceful. Four groups of subjects were used with the original and interpolated learning situations as follows:

GROUP	ORIGINAL LEARNING	INTERPOLATED LEARNING	
I	Compatible pairs	Compatible pairs	⎤ Similar
II	Incompatible pairs	Incompatible pairs	⎦ Set
III	Compatible pairs	Incompatible pairs	⎤ Different
IV	Incompatible pairs	Compatible pairs	⎦ Set

The learning of both the original and interpolated task was by the method of anticipation. Each pair of words was printed on a card and presented for one second. After one presentation of the list, the first word was presented and the subject was required to anticipate its associate. The interpolated learning took place immediately after original learning. Fifteen minutes later, all subjects were retested on the original list. In analyzing the results, Groups I and II were combined since the same set was present during the original and interpolated learning, and Groups III and IV were combined since the set present during the interpolated learning was different from that in the original learning and test for retention. The results revealed that if the

TABLE 17–1

Experimental Design Examining Retroactive Inhibition as a
Function of Set

GROUP	TEST FOR ORIGINAL LEARNING	TEST FOR INTERPOLATED LEARNING	RETEST	
I	Anticipation	Anticipation	Anticipation	Same Set
II	Recognition	Recognition	Recognition	Same Set
III	Anticipation	Recognition	Anticipation	Different Set
IV	Recognition	Anticipation	Recognition	Different Set

(Adapted from Jenkins and Postman, 1949)

same set was present the percentage of materials retained was
significantly lower than if different sets were used.

In another experiment, Jenkins and Postman (1949) demonstrated a similar finding when the subject's set was manipulated
by varying the testing procedures employed during the original
and interpolated learning. The original learning task consisted of
presenting a list of 25 two-syllable adjectives for five presentations. More specifically, the words were read to subjects at a rate
of one every two seconds, with the list being read through five
times. Following the fifth presentation, either an anticipation
method of testing was used (subjects were permitted four seconds
for recalling each successive item) or a recognition test was
employed. In the latter test, subjects were instructed to select the
25 items from a list containing 100 alphabetized adjectives.
Interpolated learning took place immediately after the original
learning. Twenty-five two-syllable adjectives made up the second
list. This list was also presented five times followed by either the
recognition or anticipation test. Recall of the original material
immediately followed the interpolated learning; again, either
anticipation or recognition was employed. The varying experimental conditions are presented in Table 17–1. The results were
in keeping with the Postman and Postman (1948) findings. When
original, interpolated, and relearning activities were carried out
under the same set, a greater amount of retroactive inhibition
resulted than was found when the original learning and interpolated learning took place under different sets.

The role of the similarity of the environmental stimuli within
a retroactive inhibition design was investigated by Bilodeau and

Schlosberg (1951) and Greenspoon and Ranyard (1957). In the Bilodeau and Schlosberg study, the original learning consisted of eight repetitions of ten paired-associates. In the first experiment, all original learning took place in what the investigators described as a "drum room"—a dingy storeroom filled with old apparatus. The subject stood as he attempted to learn the material presented on a memory drum. The learning of the interpolated material for the first group was done in a room identified as the "card room"— a room made as different as possible from the room in which the original learning took place. The card room was a large basement classroom in which the material was presented on a card-flipping device similar to a desk calendar. The subject sat in front of the apparatus, and the experimenter flipped the cards every two seconds. A second group learned the interpolated material in the same room where the original learning took place. A third group's interpolated activity consisted of doing long-division problems for eight minutes, also in the original learning room. Following the interpolated activity, all groups relearned the original material in the drum room. In a second experiment the original learning took place in the card room and the drum room was used for the interpolated learning of one of the experimental groups.

The findings revealed that the control group showed the best recall. A primary concern, however, is with the findings of the experimental groups. The experimental group which learned the interpolated material in the environmental setting different from that in which the original material was learned recalled the original material significantly better than the second experimental group, which learned the original and interpolated material in the same room. More recently, Greenspoon and Ranyard (1957) confirmed the Bilodeau and Schlosberg (1951) findings.

These findings, in which the subject's set, as well as the experimental environment, has been manipulated, demonstrate that interfering effects can be reduced by reducing the similarity of conditions existing between the original and interpolated learning situations.

DEGREE OF LEARNING. A second area of interest has been to examine retroactive and proactive inhibition effects when the degree of original learning as well as the degree of learning the interfering material has been manipulated. For ease of presentation, the experimental evidence which has been obtained within the retroactive inhibition experimental design will be examined first and then the influence of this variable on proactive inhibition will be examined.

Before proceeding, it should be pointed out that retroactive (as well as proactive) inhibition values may be expressed in relative as well as absolute terms. An absolute difference refers to the numerical difference obtained by subtracting the experimental group's retention score from that of the control group. Relative retroactive inhibition values, however, represent the percentage difference between them and are expressed by the following formula:

$$\frac{\text{Control Group Retention Score} - \text{Exp. Group Retention Score}}{\text{Control Group Retention Score}} \times 100$$

In most experimental situations, the findings obtained by using an absolute measure of retroactive (or proactive) inhibition will parallel those obtained by a relative measure. But this parallelism does not necessarily hold when such inhibition effects are examined as a function of the degree of original learning. As Slamecka and Ceraso (1960) pointed out, using the retroactive inhibition situation as an example, when the degree of original learning is small, the control group's retention score is also small, and slight departures from this base line on the part of the experimental group will represent a substantial percentage difference. On the other hand, when a large number of original training trials has been provided, thus producing large retention values in the control group, the same absolute difference between the control and experimental group will reflect a much smaller percentage change. Thus, although relative retroactive inhibition values will have decreased, the absolute amount of retroactive inhibition will have remained the same. It appears that when the degree of original learning is manipulated relative retroactive inhibition scores provide the most appropriate type of analysis.

Retroactive Inhibition   One of the early studies in which the degree of original learning was varied was performed by McGeoch (1929) who used lists of nine nonsense syllables as the material to be learned. Either 6, 11, 16, 21, or 26 presentations of the original list were provided. The number of interpolated list presentations was held constant at 11. The original list was then relearned to a criterion of one perfect recitation, with the first relearning trial providing a measure of recall. The investigator found that relative retroactive inhibition values decreased with increases in the degree of original learning.

A few years later, McGeoch (1932) performed a similar experiment in which the degree of the interpolated learning was varied but the degree of original learning was held constant. The materials and conditions were the same as in the previous study except that the original material was presented for only 11 trials and the interpolated material was presented for either 6, 11, 16, 21, or 26 trials. Recall scores obtained on the first relearning trial of the original materials provided the basic data. Both absolute and relative amounts of retroactive inhibition increased as the interpolated learning trials were increased from 6 to 11 trials, but further increases in the degree of interpolated learning had no additional effect. One interesting finding was that if relearning scores were used as the basic data there was some indication that the highest degree of interpolated learning produced some decrease in the amount of retroactive inhibition. Thus, the percentage of retroactive inhibition dropped from 74.3 per cent after 21 trials of interpolated learning to 59.4 per cent after 26 trials.

Melton and Irwin (1940), also varying the amount of interpolated learning, obtained findings supporting those of McGeoch (1932). In their study, serial lists of nonsense syllables were used as the learning material. Five trials of original learning were provided followed by either 5, 10, 20, or 40 trials of the interpolated material. The original list was then relearned to a criterion of two perfect recitations. Retroactive inhibition, as measured by recall scores on the first relearning trial, increased from 5 to 20 trials of interpolated learning and then showed a slight decline at 40 trials. Similar findings were obtained when relearning scores were used, except that with 40 trials of interpolated learning there was a pronounced decline in the amount of retroactive inhibition obtained, a finding which supported the inversion reported by McGeoch.

Thune and Underwood (1943) extended Melton and Irwin's findings to the paired-associate learning situation. The original and interpolated lists consisted of ten paired-associates which were learned by the anticipation method, comprising an A-B, A-C relationship. Five original learning trials were provided followed by either 2, 5, 10, or 20 trials of interpolated learning. The original list was then relearned to a criterion of two perfect trials. The results closely paralleled the findings of previous investigators in that increasing the amount of interpolated learning up to a point (10 trials) resulted in increased retroactive inhibition as measured by recall scores. After ten trials, additional interpolated learning (20 trials) did not produce increased retroactive inhibition.

Contemporary investigators [Richardson (1956), Briggs (1957), and Postman and Riley (1959)] have examined retroactive inhibition as a function of the degree of original and interpolated learning and obtained findings which confirmed those obtained by earlier investigators.

Underwood (1945) demonstrated that increases in retroactive inhibition take place as a function of the number of interpolated lists which are learned, in contrast to the numbers of trials which previous experimenters have employed. In this study, paired two-syllable adjectives comprised the learning material, with the original lists being learned to a criterion of six or more correct responses. Following this, subjects learned either zero, two, four, or six interpolated lists; each list was presented for only four trials. Each interpolated list had the same stimulus words as the original list although they were paired with different responses. Following the presentation of the appropriate number of interpolated lists, the subjects relearned the original list to a criterion of two successive errorless trials. The results, as Figure 17–2 reveals, indicated that retroactive inhibition, as measured by the mean number of correct responses on the first relearning trial, increased as a function of the number of interpolated lists which were presented.

An experiment by Lewis, Smith, and McAllister (1952) is one of the few motor skills learning studies in which retroactive inhibition as a function of the degree of interpolated learning was investigated. Their apparatus provided a small target which revolved once per minute through the same irregular pathway; the subject's task was to turn two lathe-like handles in such a way as to keep a button on top of the moving target. Subjects were first given original learning so that they reached a performance criterion of 40 seconds on target during two consecutive trial periods of 30 seconds in length. Following this, varying experimental groups were given sufficient interpolated training so that they could reach a criterion consisting of two trials of either 24, 32, 40, 48, or 56 seconds on target. During this training the subjects had to turn the lathe handles in the opposite direction from which they had to be turned during the original task. The amount of retroactive inhibition, as reflected by losses in proficiency during relearning, was a function of the level of proficiency (or amount of learning) attained on the reverse task during interpolated learning. The group which was given the most difficult criterion for interpolated learning had the poorest relearning score; the group provided the next most difficult interpolated learning criterion had the next poorest relearning score, etc.

In summary, over a rather wide range of situations, the experimental work investigating the degree of original and interpolated learning on retroactive inhibition has given rise to two general conclusions: (1) As original learning increases, holding the degree of interpolated learning constant, the relative amount of retroactive inhibition decreases; (2) As the degree of interpolated learning increases, holding the degree of original learning constant, the amount of retroactive inhibition increases. Both functions appear to level off at some particular point beyond which increasing the degree of either original or interpolated learning does not lead to decreasing or increasing amounts of retroactive inhibition.

Proactive Inhibition   In one of the early studies examining proactive inhibition as a function of degree of first list learning [Underwood (1949)], subjects learned lists of ten paired two-syllable adjectives in the traditional A-B, A-C paradigm. For one group, the first list was presented until three or more responses were anticipated correctly on a single trial, whereas for the second group, the first list was presented until eight or more responses were correctly anticipated. The third condition consisted of presenting the first list until all ten items had been anticipated correctly on a single trial, after which five additional trials were given. A control group was employed which was not given any trials on the first list. Following presentation of the first list, the second list was presented until six or more responses were anticipated on a single trial. Either 20 minutes (Experiment I) or 75 minutes (Experiment II) following such learning, the second list was recalled. Underwood found that proactive inhibition increased as the degree of first list learning increased. Thus, significant amounts of proactive inhibition were produced by the two highest degrees of first list learning when retention was measured 20 minutes after the learning of the second list. When proactive

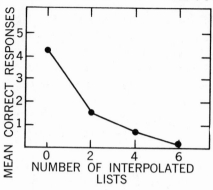

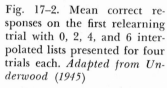

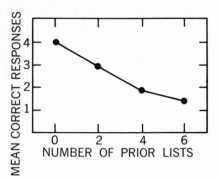

Fig. 17–2. Mean correct responses on the first relearning trial with 0, 2, 4, and 6 interpolated lists presented for four trials each. *Adapted from Underwood (1945)*

Fig. 17–3. Mean correct responses on the first relearning trial with 0, 2, 4, and 6 prior lists presented for four trials each. *Adapted from Underwood (1945)*

inhibition was measured after 75 minutes, the results revealed that only the highest degree of first list learning produced a significant amount of proactive inhibition.

Atwater (1953), also examining proactive inhibition as a function of the degree or amount of first list learning, obtained similar findings. He also used the traditional A-B, A-C paired-associate learning situation; each list contained ten pairs of three-letter words. Four degrees of first list learning were used, and the degree of learning was defined by a performance criterion. Under Condition I (control) the first list was not presented, but under Condition II, the first list was learned to a criterion of six correct responses on one trial. For Condition III, the criterion was one perfect trial plus five additional trials, and for Condition IV, the criterion was one perfect trial plus fifteen additional trials. Second list learning was carried to a criterion of one perfect trial plus five additional trials. A ten-minute rest period was then provided, followed by the relearning of the second list to a criterion of one perfect trial. The findings, supporting those obtained by Underwood (1949), indicated that proactive inhibition increased, as the degree of first list or prior learning increased, until a relatively high degree of first list learning was reached after which no further proactive inhibition increases were obtained.

Underwood (1945) examined proactive inhibition when the

TABLE 17–2

Relative Amounts of Proactive Inhibition
(In Per Cent)

FIRST LIST LEARNING TRIALS	SECOND LIST LEARNING TRIALS			
	5	10	20	40
5	32.4	−11.9	−7.9	16.5
10	38.2	−7.1	−3.2	26.8
20	50.0	−4.5	25.4	30.9
40	32.4	2.4	17.5	33.0

− Values reflect facilitation

(Adapted from Postman and Riley, 1959)

first material to be learned consisted of a number of different lists rather than when the number of trials on a single list was manipulated. In this study, similar to one which was examined in the retroactive inhibition section, either zero, two, four, or six lists of paired adjectives were presented; four trials were provided on each list. Following this, a second list was presented and learned to a criterion of six correct responses. Following 25 minutes of rest, the second list was relearned to a criterion of two successive errorless trials. The results are presented in Figure 17–3 and show that proactive inhibition increased as a function of the number of prior lists which were learned—a finding in keeping with the results of other investigators who manipulated learning trials.

One of the most extensive factorial studies examining the degree of both first and second list learning on proactive inhibition was performed by Postman and Riley (1959). Serial lists of nonsense syllables served as the material to be learned. Subjects were given either 5, 10, 20, or 40 trials on the first list followed by 5, 10, 20, or 40 trials on the second list. Thirty minutes after the last trial on the second list, the second list was relearned to a criterion of two perfect recitations; the first relearning trial provided the recall scores. Appropriate control groups were used.

The results are found in Table 17–2. Using relative proactive inhibition scores, the findings parallel those obtained by previous investigators. It can be noted that by increasing the number of first list learning trials, keeping the number of second list learning trials constant, increasing amounts of proactive inhibition are obtained. There is some indication, however, that when the number of second list learning trials are minimal increasing the number of first list learning trials results in increases of proactive inhibition only up to a point. Beyond this, further increases in first list learning trials produce a decrement in proactive inhibition. When first list learning trials are held constant, and second list learning trials varied, a curvilinear relationship is obtained, with small and large amounts of second list learning providing maximum amounts of proactive inhibition within each first list learning trial condition.

In summary, the experimental evidence supports the position that (1) increasing the degree of first list learning, and holding the degree of second list learning constant, increases the relative amount of proactive inhibition and (2) as the degree of second list learning increases, holding the amount of first list learning constant, the relative amount of proactive inhibition first increases but then decreases as greater degrees of learning are provided.

The first conclusion is in keeping with the retroactive inhibition studies and can be stated in the more general case that as the interfering responses, whether arising from prior or interpolated learning, increase in strength, retention decreases. With regard to the second conclusion, there appears to be some disparity between the conclusions drawn from the retroactive and proactive inhibition studies. Thus, holding the strength of the interfering responses constant, and increasing the strength of original list responses, appears to result in decreasing the amount of retroactive inhibition, but increasing and then decreasing the amount of proactive inhibition. Inasmuch as the proactive inhibition findings have been based upon only a single study [Postman and Riley (1959)], the verification of this unusual finding must await further experimental test.

The Generality of Retroactive and Proactive Inhibition

An examination of the experimental literature has revealed that retroactive and proactive inhibition play an important role in forgetting. It must be acknowledged, however, that the experimental work which has been cited has typically used serial or paired-associate learning situations in which nonsense syllables or adjectives served as the material to be learned. Moreover, situations which were previously described as long term memory situations have been examined primarily. If these inhibitory effects are to be firmly established as primary contributors to forgetting, the generality of their contribution must be extended to other kinds of material with other types of learning and retention situations, and it must be demonstrated that they are applicable to organisms other than human beings. It is these areas which will be examined now.

SHORT TERM RETENTION. In the short term retention study of Peterson and Peterson (1959), it will be remembered that the procedure was one in which a consonant syllable was presented and 3, 6, 9, 12, 15, or 18 seconds later the subject was asked to recall it. The interval of time between the presentation of the syllable and its recall was filled by the subject's counting backwards by three's or four's from some random number that was presented following the presentation of the syllable. The experimental design was a counterbalanced one in which each subject was tested eight times at each of the varying recall intervals so that at the end of the experimental session each subject had been exposed to 48 syllables.

Presumably, syllables which were learned late in the experimental session should be subject to a greater number of potentially interfering associations than would the syllables which were presented early. However, this finding was not obtained. When the number of correct responses within each successive block of 12 presentations was analyzed, with short recall intervals (3 and 6 seconds) analyzed separately from long recall intervals (15 and 18 seconds), the findings revealed that the proportions of correct responses for the short recall interval were .57, .66, .70, and .74, with the difference between the first and last blocks significant at the .02 level. The proportions of correct responses for the long recall interval were .08, .15, .09, and .12, with the gain from the first to the last blocks not being significant. Since there was no decline in the number of syllables recalled over blocks of presentations, Peterson and Peterson interpreted these results as providing no evidence for proactive inhibition. The logical question raised by this study, then, is whether such inhibitory effects can be demonstrated within the short term memory situation.

Melton (1963) pointed out the difficulty of assessing the role

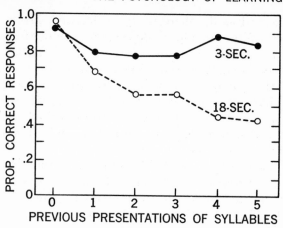

Fig. 17–4. Retention as a function of number of prior syllables and length of retention interval. *Adapted from Keppel and Underwood (1962)*

of proactive inhibition with this type of study since as the subject proceeds through the experiment there is a learning-to-learn effect which may serve to counteract any decrement in retention which takes place as a function of the increasing number of potentially interfering associations.

Keppel and Underwood (1962) also acknowledged the role of learning-to-learn in this situation and posited that with short retention intervals the learning-to-learn, or practice, effect more than compensates for the increased interference provided by the increasing number of consonants which are presented. With long retention intervals, however, the interference is of sufficient magnitude to mask the practice effect. In one experiment demonstrating such an effect, the short-term retention procedure was used in which single consonant syllables of low association value were employed as the material to be learned. Retention intervals of either three or 18 seconds were utilized. One subgroup received such intervals in the order of 3–18–3–18–3–18, whereas the other subgroup had them presented in the reverse order. This procedure permitted an examination of retention of the syllables after three and 18 seconds following zero, one, two, three, four, and five presentations. The proportions of correct responses for both intervals are presented in Figure 17–4. As can be noted, with 18-second intervals, retention declined with successive tests, but this did not

TABLE 17–3

Mean Proportion of Correct Recalls at
Each Retention Interval

RETENTION INTERVAL	NUMBER OF PRIOR WORDS					MEAN
	0	3	6	9	12	
0 sec.	.995	1.000	.985	.985	.974	.988
3 sec.	1.000	.959	.927	.948	.969	.960
6 sec.	.953	.834	.896	.901	.865	.890
9 sec.	.938	.844	.860	.849	.875	.873
12 sec.	.938	.771	.834	.818	.860	.844
18 sec.	.907	.823	.802	.828	.823	.836
Mean	.955	.872	.884	.888	.894	

(Adapted from Murdock, 1961)

take place with the three-second interval. The findings indicate that short term memory is subject to proactive inhibition and support the investigators' hypothesis of an interaction between the amount of interference and the length of retention interval.

Murdock (1961) also examined proactive inhibition effects within the short term memory situation but utilized an experimental situation somewhat different from that employed by Keppel and Underwood (1962). The first task was the reading of either 0, 3, 6, 9, or 12 words obtained from the Thorndike-Lorge word list of the 1,000 most common English words. A single monosyllabic word was then presented as the stimulus word, and, following this, the subject was required to count backward for either 0, 3, 6, 9, 12, or 18 seconds. The subject was then asked to recall the stimulus word. The mean proportion of correct words recalled at each retention interval as a function of the number of prior words presented is indicated in Table 17–3. With the exception of the zero-second retention interval, where there was a slight inversion of values, the presentation of three words prior to the presentation and recall of the experimental word resulted in poorer retention than if no prior words were presented. The presentation of more than three prior words appeared to have little additional influence on retention values, although there is the suggestion that such additional words provided the paradoxical result of lesser rather than greater amounts of proactive inhibition.

Wickens, Born, and Allen (1963) also obtained proactive inhibition effects in the short term retention situation; in this instance it was noted that such inhibition varied as a function of the similarity of the materials used.

RETROACTIVE INHIBITION OF CONNECTED DISCOURSE. One of the early studies examining the susceptibility of connected discourse to retroactive inhibition was performed by McGeoch and McKinney (1934). The original material consisted of prose obtained from an elementary psychology text; the subjects were permitted five minutes to study it. The amount learned was measured by answers to 20 questions covering the facts presented in the original material. Three groups of subjects were then asked to either (1) study a second section of prose on the same topic as the original material, (2) learn 20 nonsense syllables, or (3) take a pitch discrimination test. The findings indicated that the differences in the amount recalled among the varying groups were not satisfactorily reliable. In subsequent experimental studies Deese and Hardman (1954), Hall (1955b), and Ausubel, Robbins, and Blake (1957) also were unable to demonstrate retroactive inhibition effects when prose or connected discourse was used as the material to be learned and recalled.

The more recent studies of Slamecka (1959, 1960, 1960a, 1961, 1962) have shown, however, that the retention of passages of connected discourse is subject to retroactive as well as proactive inhibition effects. In one study (1960), a single sentence 20 words in length served as the original material. An example of such a sentence was as follows: "We must postulate that from strictly semantic points of vantage, most confusions in communication revolve about inadequate stipulation of meaning." Sentences of either high, intermediate, or low similarity to the original material were utilized as the interpolated material. The high similarity passage also dealt with the topic of semantics, the intermediate similarity passage was concerned with mathematics, and the low similarity passage dealt with government. All learning was by the method of serial anticipation, with each word presented at a three-second rate and with a six-second intertrial interval. Both the original and interpolated passages were learned to a criterion of one perfect trial. The time between the end of the original learning and the start of the relearning of the original passage was held constant at 12 minutes and 6 seconds. Absolute retroactive inhibition effects were obtained for all work groups, with the group provided the high similarity interpolated material showing the poorest recall scores, followed by the intermediate group, and then the low. In a second study, Slamecka (1961) demonstrated that this type of material was also susceptible to proactive inhibition effects. In a third study, Slamecka (1960a) investigated retroactive inhibition as related to the degree of interpolated and original learning. The results supported the findings obtained when more traditional verbal learning methods and materials were used.

As Slamecka pointed out, the phenomenon of retroactive and proactive inhibition based upon unconnected materials can now be generalized to connected discourse. King and Tanenbaum (1963) confirmed the findings of Slamecka (1960), extending them to group learning situations in which there was unlimited time available for written recall.

PROACTIVE AND RETROACTIVE INHIBITION IN ANIMALS. In contrast to the large amount of work utilizing human subjects, in relatively few studies have retroactive and proactive inhibition effects been examined with animals. It will be recalled that McGeoch (1932) in his paper on disuse suggested that if the retention interval was entirely devoid of activity there should be no forgetting. Some experimenters have employed animals in an effort to test this hypothesis. In an early study, Hunter (1932) investigated the retention of cockroaches which had previously learned an avoidance response to darkness. After they had reached a learning criterion, the experimental animals were made inactive by placing them in temperatures of three to six degrees Centigrade for either two or four hours. The general influence of lowered temperature is to make the cockroach completely inactive. Following such interpolated activity, the animals were required to relearn the original response. The results, contrary to what might be expected, revealed that the performance of the experimental subjects was poorer than that obtained with control animals, which had been kept at normal temperatures and permitted normal activity during the interpolated period. Moreover, Hunter found that such retardation was greater after an exposure to four hours of cold than after two hours. Presumably, the extreme environmental temperature which was used to produce inactivity had an effect of its own which decreased retention.

The subsequent studies of Russell and Hunter (1937), using sodium amytal to produce inactivity in rats, and French (1942), using lowered temperatures to inhibit the activity of goldfish, were not successful in demonstrating increased retention as a function of the amount of inactivity produced by these procedures. A basic difficulty with this type of experimental situation is that the technique used to produce the inactivity appears to produce effects of its own which interfere with the subject's making the previously learned response.

One of the successful experiments demonstrating the role of inactivity as well as activity in the retention of a learned response, in species other than man, was performed by Minami and Dallenbach (1946). Like Hunter, some years before, the experimenters used cockroaches as their experimental animals. In their first experiment, they sought to determine the effect of forced activity upon the retention and relearning of an avoidance response to darkness. The criterion for the original learning task was nine correct responses in ten successive trials. The interval between the original learning and the relearning was either 10, 20, or 30 minutes or 1, 2, 3, 8, or 24 hours. Experimental animals were provided a period of either 10, 20, or 30 minutes of forced activity. Here, they were placed on a small treadmill and forced to run for a fixed period of time. Control animals were returned to their cages immediately following the original learning. After an appropriate interval, the subjects were then required to relearn the original task. Findings revealed that relearning scores at all time intervals were poorer after forced activity than after rest. In fact, the relearning scores were even poorer than those made during the original learning. As the investigators pointed out, the forced running appeared to produce a general irritability on the part of the subjects which was hypothesized to account for the learning decrement.

In a second experiment, there was an attempt to assess the role of inactivity. The well known fact that cockroaches, when in bodily contact with external objects, tend to become inactive was utilized to produce a quiescent state. Again, the avoidance response to darkness was used as the learning task. Following such learning, an inactivity period of one, two, or three hours was provided prior to relearning. Inactivity in the experimental animals was produced by using a small box lined with tissue paper so that the farther the insect crawled into it, the greater would be the bodily contact and resultant inactivity. Control animals were permitted normal activity within the confines of a

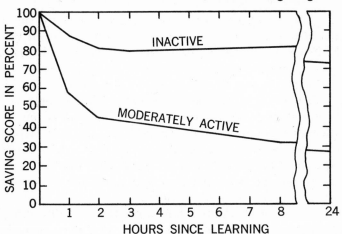

Fig. 17–5. Retention as a function of interpolated periods of activity or inactivity. *Adapted from Minami and Dallenbach (1946)*

small cage. Relearning after one, two, or three hours of inactivity was markedly superior to that obtained after corresponding intervals of normal activity. A further study extended these findings to 8- and 24-hour periods. Figure 17–5 reveals these findings. The similarity between these findings and those obtained by Jenkins and Dallenbach (1924) is noteworthy.

A second field of interest for a number of experimenters using animals has been to examine retroactive inhibition as a function of the similarity or degree of learning of the interpolated material. The early studies of Webb (1917) and Wiltbank (1919) as well as a later one by Marx (1944) demonstrated that interpolated learning of one or more maze problems interfered with the retention of one learned earlier.[5] In Marx's (1944) study, rats first learned to swim a 14-unit multiple T-maze to a criterion of one perfect trial. These animals were then divided into four experimental groups and one control group. The experimental groups were given an interpolated learning task consisting of either 0, 1, 4, 8 or 12 short mazes which were constructed from parts of the original maze. The interpolated training consisted of ten trials per day for five days. Fifteen days following the original learning, relearning trials on the original maze were provided. The findings

[5] Hunter and Yarbrough (1917) and Waters and Vitale (1945) were unable to obtain retroactive inhibition effects using animals in maze situations.

showed that retroactive inhibition increased with increasing amounts of interpolated learning up to eight mazes but then declined when four additional mazes were added to the interpolated task.

Marx hypothesized that his findings showed that considering retroactive inhibition as a major factor in explaining forgetting was of limited value since such inhibition did not become greater with increased amounts of interpolated training. It is possible, however, that the animals gradually acquired a learning set during the experimental period which eventually reached sufficient strength to counteract further decrements in retention occasioned by the learning of the four additional mazes.

The studies of Wickens, Hall, and Reid (1949) and, more recently, Kehoe (1963) are interesting in that these investigators attempted to examine retroactive and proactive inhibition effects as a function of the specific stimulus-response relationships which made up the tasks to be learned. In the Wickens, Hall, and Reid (1949) study, retroactive inhibition as influenced by the similarity of the drive stimulus was examined. One group of rats was first placed under 22 hours of water deprivation, and a second group was placed under 22 hours of food deprivation. Both groups were then given 27 trials in learning to turn right in a T-maze. The interpolated task was then presented; here, the animals had to learn to turn left in order to receive the appropriate goal object. For this task, the motivation was changed for half of the animals in each group. Thus, one-half of the original water deprived group was placed on food deprivation, but the other half remained under water deprivation. Similarly, one-half of the food deprivation group was placed under water deprivation and the other half continued to be food deprived. Learning continued until the animals reached a criterion of ten correct responses in 12 trials. Following this, the goal object was shifted back to the right arm, and the animals which had been shifted to a different drive state during the interpolated learning were returned to the original drive. Relearning trials were continued until the animals reached a criterion of ten correct responses out of 12 trials. An examination of the relearning scores on the first task revealed that the groups which did not have their drive changed took significantly longer to relearn the original task than the groups which had their drive shifted during the interpolated task. If the drive stimulus is conceptualized as making up an important part of the

TABLE 17–4

Mean Correct Responses at Recall

MEASURE	CONDI-TION	RETENTION INTERVAL (DAYS)		
		1	10	30
No. correct Rs at recall	Control	48.6	46.9	42.3
	PI	47.5	48.7	39.6
	RI	4.5	5.8	15.8

(Adapted from Kehoe, 1963)

total stimulus complex, then these findings are in keeping with the results of the verbal learning studies which indicate that the similarity of the original and interpolated stimulus conditions is important in determining the amount of retroactive inhibition.

Kehoe (1963) examined retroactive and proactive inhibition with pigeons in a discrimination situation. The animals were placed in a compartment, and five illuminated keys which varied in color were presented. The task consisted of the subjects' learning to peck at a key illuminated with a green (or red) light. The position of the correct key was varied from trial to trial. In contrast to the typical Skinner-box situation, trials were discrete in that the box was blacked out after each response, which thus defined a trial. The learning of the first task consisted of the animals' reaching a criterion of 45 or more correct responses in the 50 trials which were provided each day. Following the learning of the first task, the experimental animals were given a second task, which consisted of learning to peck at a different colored key. The criterion for the second task was also 45 or more correct responses out of the 50-trial period. After the second task had been learned, a 1-, 10-, or 30-day retention interval was given after which the subjects were required to relearn either the first or second task depending upon whether proactive or retroactive inhibition was to be measured. The findings are indicated in Table 17–4.

When the number of correct responses on the first relearning day of the subjects in the retroactive inhibition group was compared with the control group at each of the retention intervals, there was little doubt that the learning of the interpolated task had a detrimental effect on the retention of the original task. What is surprising, however, is that there was a performance increment for the retroactive inhibition group as a function of the time interval between the original learning and the test for retention.

A comparison of the proactive inhibition group with the control group revealed no difference between them at any of the retention intervals. This finding that the learning of the first task had no influence on the recall of the second was at variance with a number of verbal learning studies which have demonstrated proactive inhibition effects.

One possible explanation for this discrepancy, Kehoe pointed out, is that, with the verbal learning situation, in the learning of the second task the presentation of the stimulus is always followed in a few seconds by the presentation of the correct response, independent of the subject's behavior. Consequently, if the subject makes the proper response, he is reinforced by its presentation; if he makes an error, he is corrected. In the animal discrimination situation, there is no indication following an error as to which response should have been made. As a result, it is quite possible that the old response extinguishes differently in the two situations. That is, in the verbal learning task, the new response is learned more rapidly and gains strength over the old response prior to the complete extinction of the old response. On the other hand, in the animal discrimination task the old response must be quite well extinguished before the new response even occurs. Moreover, the discrimination situation differs from the verbal learning task in the number of extinction sessions that the to-be-recalled response undergoes prior to the recall test. In Kehoe's study, there were many sessions during which the first learned response underwent extinction. Since these sessions were separated by a 24-hour interval it is possible that spontaneous recovery of the extinguished response occurred during this time. The response then underwent repeated extinction during the following session. The investigator pointed out that such repeated extinction sessions undoubtedly reduced the amount of recovery that took place during the retention interval, much in the same manner that repeated extinctions of a conditioned response have been shown to reduce greatly the amount of spontaneous recovery that takes place following the last extinction session. In the verbal learning situation, where typically the learning criterion is met in a single session, this repeated recovery-extinction process would appear not to be as prominent; thus, greater first task recovery would be likely to take place during the retention interval. Whether Kehoe's explanation for her failure to find proactive inhibition is correct will have to be determined by further experimental testing.

AN ANALYSIS OF RETROACTIVE AND PROACTIVE INHIBITION

Most contemporary investigators account for retention decrement in terms of proactive and retroactive inhibition which, in turn, make up what has been called an interference theory of forgetting. An early formulation of this position was provided by McGeoch (1942) who, primarily concerned with retroactive inhibition, believed that the forgetting produced by interpolated material could be reduced to competition between responses. More specifically, the two responses acquired during the original and interpolated learning situations, and attached to identical or similar stimuli, remained available and competed with each other during the recall of the original material. As already noted, the similarity variable is a significant factor in obtaining proactive and retroactive inhibition effects—a finding in keeping with the response competition position.

It must be acknowledged that any competition of response position must include generalized as well as specific responses which make up the learning situation. The studies of Postman and Postman (1948), Postman and Jenkins (1948), Jenkins and Postman (1949), Postman and Stark (1962), Bilodeau and Schlosberg (1951), and Greenspoon and Ranyard (1957), many of which were discussed earlier, demonstrated that decreasing the similarity of the subject's set or learning environment found in the original list–interpolated list learning situation may tend to increase retention. These changes reduce the strength of the subject's tendency to continue responding with items from the interfering list at the time of recall.

Studies by Newton and Wickens (1956) and Postman and Riley (1959) called attention to other evidences of the competition among generalized responses. Within this experimental context, generalized response competition takes on the characteristics of a set to give responses to the most recent list learned. In the Postman and Riley study (1959), serial lists of nonsense syllables

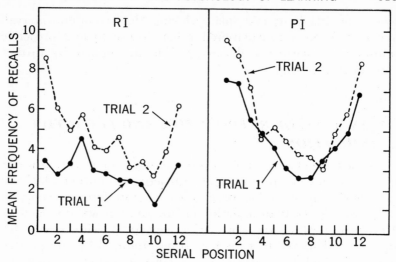

Fig. 17–6. Average serial-position curves of retroactive-inhibition and proactive-inhibition work groups at recall. *Adapted from Postman and Riley (1959)*

were used to measure both retroactive and proactive inhibition as a function of the degree of original and interfering learning. Figure 17–6 presents the serial position curves for both the retroactive inhibition and proactive inhibition groups at recall. As Postman (1961) pointed out, there was a flattening of the curve at the beginning of the list for the retroactive inhibition group, and the primacy effect which is usually observed in this kind of situation was absent. On the second trial, the curve of the retroactive inhibition group recovered its typical bow-shaped appearance and was comparable to the proactive inhibition groups. The retention decrement found in the initial portion of the list for the retroactive inhibition group Postman attributed to "generalized competition, which is reduced or eliminated once the context of the original list is reestablished."

In 1940, Melton and Irwin postulated a second factor which they believed also made an important contribution to a better understanding of retroactive inhibition. The primary purpose of this study was to examine retroactive inhibition as a function of the amount of interpolated activity. This study was cited previously, and it will be recalled that the original learning material

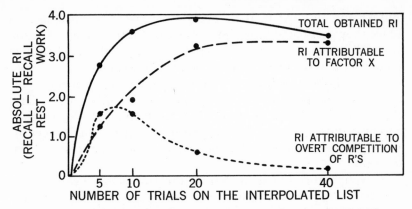

Fig. 17–7. Relationship between the amount of retroactive inhibition and the degree of learning of the interpolated material. *Adapted from Melton and Irwin (1940)*

consisted of a list of 18 nonsense syllables presented in serial order for five trials. An interpolated 18-item list of nonsense syllables was then presented for either 5, 10, 20, or 40 trials, followed by the relearning of the original list. In addition to examining the total amount of retroactive inhibition, the investigators looked at the number of responses which could be identified as belonging to the interpolated list–overt interpolated list intrusions. This measure, the investigators believed, provided an index of the amount of competition between the original and the interpolated responses at recall. The findings have been plotted in Figure 17–7.

It can be noted that there was no consistent relationship between the number of such interlist intrusions and the total amount of retroactive inhibition. The amount of retroactive inhibition attributable to competition increased to a maximum at a point between five and ten trials of interpolated training and then declined. Since the total amount of retroactive inhibition increased to an asymptote at approximately 20 trials of interpolated learning and then remained relatively constant, Melton and Irwin reasoned that some factor other than competition was contributing to the recall decrement. This factor was labeled Factor X and was tentatively identified as the unlearning of the original responses. More specifically, Melton and Irwin suggested that when the original responses intruded during the learning of the interpolated list they were not reinforced since they were incorrect in that context and this led to their being unlearned, or extinguished. Thus, they postulated a two-factor theory of retroactive inhibition in which a competition between responses at recall was identified as one factor and an unlearning factor as the second.

It should be noted that the unlearning factor is not contradictory to the competition of response position. Rather, the unlearning factor is posited to produce a weakening of the original responses during the interpolated learning which then changes the relative response strengths of the original and interpolated items at recall.

One hypothesis generated from the two-factor theory is that retroactive inhibition, which presumably arises from both unlearning and competition of responses, should be greater than proactive inhibition, which is presumed to arise as a result of response competition alone. Melton and Von Lackum (1941) examined this hypothesis. In their study, lists consisting of ten three-consonant syllables were used as the material to be learned. In addition, the syllables comprising two of the lists, which made up one experimental condition, had considerable inter-item similarity, but the two other lists, which made up a second experimental condition, consisted of syllables which were quite dissimilar. List 1 was presented for five trials followed by List 2 which was also presented for five trials. Retroactive inhibition was examined by having the first list relearned to a criterion of two successive errorless trials, and proactive inhibition was measured by having the subjects relearn the second list to the same criterion. The findings revealed that the control groups exhibited highly significant amounts of both retroactive and proactive inhibition when compared with their appropriate control groups. Furthermore, in keeping with the two-factor theory, the amount of retroactive inhibition was significantly greater than that found for proactive inhibition. These findings held regardless of whether similar or dissimilar lists made up the experimental material. A number of subsequent studies, e.g., Underwood (1945, 1948), confirmed these findings.

Thune and Underwood (1943) attempted to examine the role of Factor X in the paired-associate learning situation. Subjects were given five trials of original learning on a ten-item paired adjective list. This was followed by either 0, 5, 10, or 20 interpolated trials on a list containing the same stimulus words but unrelated responses. The original material was then relearned

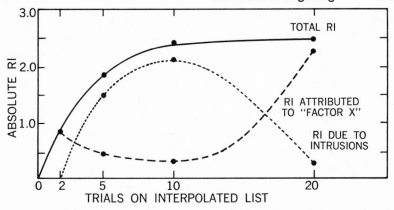

Fig. 17–8. Relationship between the absolute retroactive inhibition and the degree of learning of the interpolated list. *Adapted from Thune and Underwood (1943)*

to a criterion of two perfect trials. Their findings paralleled those obtained by Melton and Irwin (1940) on serial lists of nonsense syllables in that a negatively accelerated function was obtained between the amount of retroactive inhibition and the number of trials on the interpolated list. When overt intrusions were plotted, however, and the Factor X curve drawn, findings different from those obtained by Melton and Irwin (1940) were observed. As revealed in Figure 17–8, the number of overt intrusions increased and then declined precipitously, and inhibition attributed to Factor X first decreased and then increased as increasing numbers of trials on the interpolated list were provided. Thune and Underwood (1943) argued that if Factor X represented the functioning of a single mechanism it was not in keeping with any known psychological function with which it might be legitimately compared. A second consideration that the investigators pointed out was that in order for the original responses to be unlearned such responses would have to occur with sufficient frequency to be subject to extinction; and, yet, the number of related original list intrusions which were noted during the interpolated learning was quite small.

The investigators did acknowledge, however, that the unlearning factor was a fruitful concept, and two subsequent studies by Underwood (1948, 1948a) were helpful in delineating some of its characteristics. In the first study [Underwood (1948)], subjects learned each of two lists of paired adjectives to a criterion of one perfect trial. Both lists employed the same stimulus words; unrelated responses were employed. The two lists were learned in each of four conditions with the recall and relearning situation for the varying conditions as follows: (1) List 1 recalled after five hours (RI) ; (2) List 2 recalled after five hours (PI) ; (3) List 1 recalled after 48 hours (RI) ; (4) List 2 recalled after 48 hours (PI).

Underwood found that after a five-hour retention interval the recall of the first list (RI paradigm) was significantly less than the recall of the second list (PI paradigm), confirming the findings of earlier studies which indicated that the amount of retroactive inhibition was greater than proactive inhibition. After 48 hours, however, there was no difference in the recall of the two lists. In addition, the recall and relearning scores of the first list were as high after 48 hours as after five.

As previously noted, one hypothesis derived from the positing of an unlearning factor is that if two tasks are learned to an equal degree the retention of the first task will be less than the retention of the second. Underwood's study confirmed this position when the retention interval was five hours but not when 48. The findings also provided a problem in that they demonstrated equally good retention for the first list after 48 hours as after five. Underwood suggested that if the basic unlearning postulate is extended to include the spontaneous recovery by the associations which were unlearned during presentation of the second list these findings could be adequately handled. More specifically, it was proposed that the unlearning factor was analogous to experimental extinction of a conditioned response. Like extinguished responses, the unlearned verbal associations spontaneously recover strength with the passage of time.

In Underwood's (1948a) second study, this spontaneous recovery by verbal associations was further investigated, with an interesting feature being the use of a modified free-recall (MFR) procedure. The experiment consisted of subjects' learning two lists of ten paired two-syllable adjectives to a criterion of one perfect recitation. These lists were of the A-B, A-C relationship in which the second list had the same stimulus words as the first list but unrelated responses. Following the learning of the second list and after the time interval of either one minute, 5, 24, or 48 hours, the modified free-recall situation was employed. This consisted of presenting the subject with the common stimulus

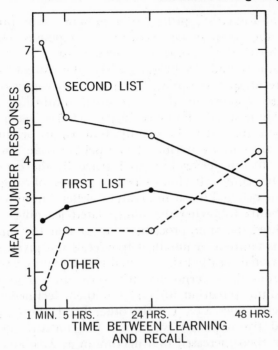

Fig. 17–9. Mean frequency of response on the free-recall trial for the four different time intervals. *Adapted from Underwood (1948a)*

words and asking him to say the first of the two response words which might come to him. If no response was given by the end of ten seconds, the subject was asked "What response does the stimulus word make you think of?" If no response was given by the end of 30 seconds, the experimenter instructed the subject to "Give any word which occurs to you." The mean frequency of responses on the modified free-recall trial over the four time intervals is indicated in Figure 17–9. As the time interval increased between the learning of the second list and the modified free-recall test, there was a consistent decrease in the frequency of responses from the list which was learned second. In contrast, no decrease in frequency of responses from the first list can be observed. Underwood believed that these findings further confirmed the usefulness of the unlearning construct. That is, since no decrease in effective strength of first list responses took place over 48 hours, the results suggested that a process running counter to the usual forgetting process was present. This process was likened to the spontaneous recovery by responses which were unlearned during the learning of the second list.

A subsequent study by Briggs (1954), also using the modified free-recall technique to examine the relative strengths of competing response systems in the retroactive inhibition situation, confirmed Underwood's findings. Briggs' (1954) general experimental procedure was to have subjects learn an original list of paired adjectives to a criterion of one perfect trial. Twenty-four hours later, an interfering list was learned by the experimental group to the same criterion. Varying groups of subjects then relearned the original list at intervals of either 4 minutes or 6, 24, 48, or 72 hours following the interpolated learning. A control group followed the same procedure except that the interpolated learning was omitted. A modified free-recall test given just prior to the traditional recall of the original list responses revealed that responses from the interpolated list were quite high following the four-minute retention interval but then declined as the retention interval increased. On the other hand, the frequency of the original list responses was quite low for the four-minute interval but then increased to a maximum at 24 hours and continued at approximately this level for both the 48- and the 72-hour period.

The "fate" of the first list associations during the learning of a second list was further explicated in a study by Barnes and Underwood (1959). The experimental procedure was one in which subjects first learned a paired-associate list in which nonsense syllables served as stimuli and two-syllable adjectives served as responses. Following the learning of the first list, a second list was presented for either 1, 5, 10, or 20 trials. The second list consisted of either identical stimuli and unrelated responses (A-B, A-C) or identical stimuli and highly similar responses (A-B, A-B′)—the latter condition being one which typically produces positive transfer. Following the appropriate number of interpolated trials, the memory drum was stopped and the subject was provided with a piece of paper on which each stimulus word was printed. The subject was then asked to write down the two responses which had been associated with each stimulus. In addition, the subject was asked whether the responses were written as they had come to mind or if there was first a deliberate attempt to recall the adjectives from a given list. The subjects also

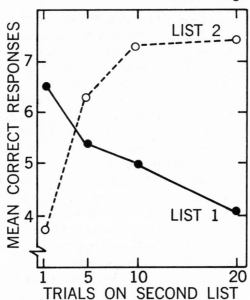

Fig. 17–10. Mean number of responses correctly recalled and identified with stimulus and list in the A-B, A-C paradigm. *Adapted from
Barnes and Underwood (1959)*

were asked whether or not they had used first list responses to
mediate the learning of those found on the second list. The results
for the A-B, A-C situation are presented in Figure 17–10. Here it
can be noted that as the number of trials on the second list
increased the number of correct responses from this list also
increased but the responses from the first list showed a gradual
decline. Since the subjects were instructed to recall these adjectives if possible, it is as if the A-B associations were extinguished
during the learning of the A-C pairs.

The results from the A-B, A-B′ paradigm revealed an entirely
different picture. Findings indicated that the recall of second list
responses was nearly perfect after only a single trial on the second
list and remained high over the 20-trial period. Moreover, first list
associations showed no appreciable decline.

The present findings, then, provide additional support for the
conception of unlearning, or of extinction, in the A-B, A-C
paradigm. With regard to the A-B, A-B′ situation, the experimenters supported a mediation hypothesis in which A leads to B

and B leads to B′ at recall. The data reveal that B was more often recalled first, although after 20 trials, B and B′ were recalled about equally often. Nearly all of the subjects reported using B as a mediator to learn A-B′, although the use of B as a mediator tended to drop out as learning of A-B′ proceeded.

A recent study by McGovern (1964) represents an attempt to examine the characteristics of the extinction, or unlearning, factors as they apply to four of the basic transfer paradigms (i.e., A-B, C-D; A-B, C-B; A-B, A-C; A-B, A-Br). McGovern assumed that three types of unlearning, or extinction, factors were operating during the transfer situation: (1) the extinction of first list S-R (forward) associations, (2) the extinction of first list R-S (backward) associations, and (3) the extinction of associations between environmental stimuli and first list responses. The investigator further posited that these different unlearning, or extinction, factors combined in different ways during the learning of the varying experimental paradigms. More specifically, she hypothesized that:

(1) the A-B, C-D paradigm involves the extinction of context associations.

(2) the A-B, C-B paradigm involves the extinction of backward associations.

(3) the A-B, A-C paradigm involves the extinction of forward and context associations.

(4) the A-B, A-Br paradigm involves the extinction of forward and backward associations.

Inasmuch as the last two paradigms have two sources of unlearning operating to reduce recall, in contrast to only one source for the first two, it was predicted that retroactive inhibition should be greatest for the A-C and A-Br conditions.

The experimental procedure consisted of having four groups of subjects learn the varying transfer paradigms which previously were described. The first list was learned to a criterion of one perfect trial, and 15 trials were provided on the second list. Following the fifteenth trial, all subjects were given a list of the stimuli used on List 1. One-half of the subjects in each transfer group were given a free-recall test in which they had to recall the first list responses and pair them with their appropriate stimuli, whereas the other half of the subjects in each group were given the List 1 responses and instructed to pair them with List 1 stimuli.

When the mean number of correct responses in the transfer

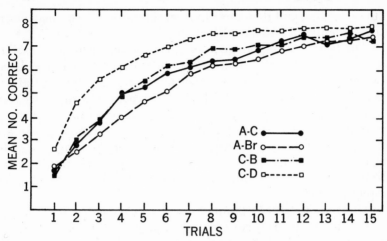

Fig. 17–11. Mean number of correct responses in second-list learn-ing plotted over fifteen trials as a function of transfer conditions. Free and list recall subgroups of each paradigm have been com-bined. *Adapted from McGovern (1964)*

task was plotted over the fifteen trials as a function of the different transfer conditions, the results, as indicated in Figure 17–11, revealed that retention scores for original list learning, as measured by either free recall or list recall, paralleled the findings obtained with second list learning. The fact that the A-C and A-Br conditions provided poorest recall of A-B supported one aspect of McGovern's hypothesis. It will be recalled that since these two paradigms had two sources of extinction operating during the second list learning, in contrast to only one source hypothesized for the C-B and C-D conditions, the investigator had hypothesized that the recall of A-B should be best for the C-B and C-D situations.

McGovern's analysis of the source and locus of the varying unlearning factors which she hypothesized to operate during second list learning is too complex to discuss in detail since it in-volved comparisons not only among the varying transfer paradigms but also between the retention values obtained with free recall and list recall. But in brief, her hypotheses, which were outlined earlier, were confirmed. In addition, the comparison between retention, as measured by free recall, and list recall confirmed Underwood's position that paired-associate recall may be divided into two phases and that a loss in retention in one phase may occur independently of a loss in the other.

The factors of response competition and unlearning, or extinction, do not, however, exhaust all of the variables which have been postulated in accounting for forgetting. A third is differentiation, proposed by Underwood (1945). Phenomenologically, this concept is related to the verbally reported experiences of "knowing" on the part of the subject that the responses from one list are inappropriate during the attempted recall of the other list. The degree of differentiation in this sense is thus an indication of the degree to which the subject identified the list to which each response belonged.

Underwood (1945) pointed out that two conditions appear to be the major determinants of the degree of differentiation that exists between two response systems. The first is the relative strengths of the two lists. Assuming that a constant number of trials have been provided on the original list, Underwood posited that differentiation increases very slowly with each successive trial of interpolated list training and that the function is a slowly rising positively accelerated one, in contrast to the rapidly rising negatively accelerated function assumed to define the development of associative strength of the interpolated list. Thus, with a small number of trials provided on the interpolated list, differentiation between this list and the original list would be quite low, and the subject, in recalling the original list, would tend to respond with some responses from the interpolated list. Up to a point, the greater the number of interpolated trials, the greater would be the occurrence of these overt interpolated list intrusions during the recall of the original list. This would take place since the associative strengths of the interpolated responses would be increasing relatively to those of the original learning. A still greater number of interpolated trials, however, would result in a rapid increase in differentiation. Here the subject would begin to recognize that the interpolated responses were inappropriate and would begin to inhibit them. As a consequence, the number of overt intrusions would decrease, although the total amount of retroactive inhibition would not. Both the Melton and Irwin (1940) and Thune and Underwood (1943) studies revealed this increase and then decrease in overt intrusions as interpolated learning increased.

The second differentiation variable is related to the time

interval existing between the end of the interpolated learning and the recall of the original learning. Differentiation should increase as the amount of time between the interpolated learning and the recall of the original material decreases. Some support for this position was provided by Underwood (1949) in a study which was cited previously. In a proactive inhibition situation, Underwood examined the retention of second list material after either a 20- or 75-minute retention interval. An analysis of the number of intrusions during the recall period revealed that the greatest number of these took place when the longer interval between learning and recall was provided.

An Analysis of Error Characteristics in Retroactive Inhibition

Most experimenters examining retroactive (or proactive) inhibition effects have been content to use numerical indices, and an examination of the characteristics of the actual errors that have been made during recall has been limited to an examination of intrusions from interpolated lists. Studies by Deese and Hardman (1954) and Deese and Marder (1957) are noteworthy in their attempt to examine the characteristics of the varying types of errors which have been made during recall.

In the Deese and Hardman (1954) study, the analysis of errors was examined with three types of learning tasks. The first was serial anticipation learning. The experiment consisted of providing two groups of subjects with four learning trials on a list of two-syllable adjectives, following which the experimental group received four trials on an interpolated list composed of adjectives highly similar to the original material. The control group practiced an irrelevant task. The second task was paired-associate learning consisting of a stimulus item, i.e., *Arsenic is,* with the subject having to learn a response item, i.e., *deadly.* Following four trials on 12 items, the experimental group was given interpolated learning consisting of identical stimulus items with different responses, e.g., (S) Arsenic is . . . (R) poisonous. The control group was also given identical stimulus items but neutral responses, e.g., (S) Arsenic is . . . (R) tasteless. The third task involved the learning of connected discourse as the original learning material. Interpolated material similar to the original was learned by one group, whereas the control group was given a sorting task. In order to facilitate the obtaining of responses, in all the experiments the subjects were given unlimited response time. Thus, with the anticipation learning task, for example, the subject was given ample opportunity to anticipate the next adjective. If he was unable to make a response he so informed the experimenter, who then presented the next item.

The findings revealed that retroactive inhibition was obtained with the anticipation and paired-associate learning tasks but not with connected discourse. The major concern of the investigators, however, was the nature of the errors made during the recall sessions. Four classes of errors were denoted: (1) within-list, (2) extra-list, (3) between-list, (4) failure of response. The data clearly indicated differences in the patterns of errors as a function of the type of task. With the serial anticipation task, most of the increase in errors, which arose from the learning of the interpolated list, between the experimental and control groups was the result of either within-list errors or failures of response. Only a very small portion of errors was actually due to intrusions from the interpolated list.

With the paired-associate task, most of the difference in errors between the experimental and control group was the result of between-list errors. Finally, with connected discourse learning, although there was a lack of retroactive inhibition effects, the pattern of errors produced by interpolation was similar to that found with the paired-associate task. Between-list errors were increased by interpolation, but within-list errors were reduced.

The findings indicated that interference from interpolated learning at the time of recalling a serial list of material does not appear to be the most important cause of inhibition—a finding which contrasts with the results obtained when a paired-associate or connected discourse learning situation is used.

The Deese and Marder (1957) study was designed to study further the pattern of errors in the recall of a serial learning task. The investigators hypothesized that between-list errors, which contributed so little to retroactive inhibition in the Deese and Hardman study, should increase as the delay interval between interpolated learning and the recall test increased. In the experiment, the subjects learned a list of adjectives for seven trials. Immediately following, an interpolated list of similar adjectives was practiced for six trials. Following delay intervals of either four minutes, 2, 24, or 48 hours, an additional anticipation trial was provided. As with the previous study, in order to obtain as many responses as possible all subjects were given unlimited time for responding. The results supported the investigators' hypothesis in that between-list errors increased as a function of the time between interpolated learning and recall but within-list errors decreased.

The Relative Contribution of Retroactive and Proactive Inhibition to Forgetting

Most of the early investigators who acknowledged the contribution of an interference theory of forgetting considered retroactive inhibition as the prime contributor. However, in 1957, in an extremely important paper, Underwood (1957a) attempted to demonstrate that proactive inhibition made a much greater contribution to forgetting than had been believed previously.

The problem, briefly, was as follows: A subject learned a list of adjectives, and after a period of 24 hours, his retention of this list was measured. Most investigators assumed that the forgetting which took place was due largely to the interference of other tasks learned during the 24-hour retention interval. An examination of many of the earlier rote learning studies indicated that approximately 75 per cent of the material was forgotten during this 24-hour period. That is, if a 12-item list was learned to a criterion of one perfect trial, 24 hours later only three of the items would be recalled. The usual interference explanation for such forgetting was that during the 24-hour interval subjects learned interpolated material which interfered with the recall of the list. But, as Underwood reasoned, it appears to be an incredible stretch of an interference hypothesis to hold that the 75 per cent forgetting was caused by material which the subjects had learned outside the laboratory during this 24-hour period. Moreover, if nonsense syllables represented the material learned, what kind of material could have been learned during the retention interval to provide interfering responses?

A basic point which Underwood made is that the classical studies which examined retention over a 24-hour period and which indicated 75 per cent forgetting used subjects who had learned many previous lists in the experimental situation. When the percentage of recall was plotted as a function of the number of previous lists learned, the curve shown in Figure 17–12 was found. Underwood's examination of contemporary studies in which the subjects learned no previous lists prior to the learning of the first led him to estimate that the amount of forgetting over a 24-hour period would be only 25 per cent. This means, then, that the

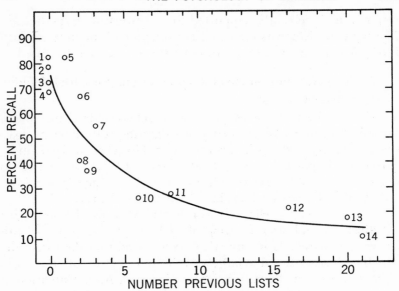

Fig. 17–12. Recall as a function of number of previous lists learned as determined from a number of studies. (1) Weiss and Margolius (1954), (2) Gibson (1942), (3) Belmont and Birch (1951), (4) Underwood and Richardson (1955), (5) Williams (1950), (6) Williams (1950), (7) Johnson (1939), (8) Underwood (1952a, 1953, 1953a, 1953b), (9) Lester (1932), (10) Krueger (1929), (11) Cheng (1929), (12) Hovland (1940), (13) Luh (1922), and (14) Youtz (1941). *Adapted from Underwood (1957a)*

major factor in forgetting in many of the earlier studies arose from proactive inhibition rather than retroactive inhibition.[6]

A study by Greenberg and Underwood (1950) supported such an interpretation. These investigators examined the learning and recall of paired adjectives as a function of the number of previous lists learned. More specifically, subjects learned a list of ten paired adjectives to a criterion of eight out of ten correct on a

[6] Underwood (1957a) indicated that this amount of forgetting could be reduced further by recognizing that these studies make the assumption that if a recall trial had been provided immediately following the subject's reaching the criterion, the material would have been recalled perfectly. Such an assumption, Underwood avers, is not true; rather, there would be a retention score of something less than this. Therefore, forgetting scores should be obtained using this base value rather than the criterion score.

This assumption, however, is in contrast to another hypothesis that Underwood (1964a) has made: In the anticipation type of learning situation, there is an underestimation of the amount of learning that takes place on any trial.

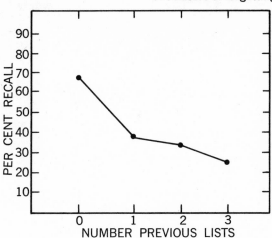

Fig. 17–13. Recall of paired adjectives as a function of number of previous lists learned. *Adapted from Greenberg and Underwood (1950)*

single trial. Forty-eight hours later, the list was recalled. The following day a new list was learned to the same criterion. This list was also recalled after 48 hours. The same procedure continued for the learning and recalling of two additional lists so that the subjects recalled four lists in all. The findings, indicated in Figure 17–13, revealed that the amount of recall diminishes as a function of the number of previous lists which were learned.

Underwood and Postman (1960) suggested that the forgetting which takes place in many of the laboratory learning tasks, which is not attributable to formal interfering tasks, is a product of what they termed extraexperimental sources of interference. That is, the major source of inhibition for forgetting may arise not from the learning of interpolated lists, but from letter sequence and unit sequence habits which have been learned outside the laboratory. In an earlier chapter, the character and contribution of these habits in the transfer situation was discussed; their contribution to forgetting follows a parallel course.

<h1 align="right">References</h1>

Abbott, D. W., and Price, L. E. (1964) Stimulus generalization of the conditioned eyelid response to structurally similar nonsense syllables. *J. exp. Psychol.*, 68, 368–371.

Aborn, M., and Rubenstein, H. (1952) Information theory and immediate recall. *J. exp. Psychol.*, 44, 260–266.

Adams, J. A. (1952) Warm-up decrement in performance on the pursuit-rotor. *Amer. J. Psychol.*, 65, 404–414.

Adams, J. A. (1954) Psychomotor performance as a function of intertrial rest interval. *J. exp. Psychol.*, 48, 131–133.

Adams, J. A. (1961) The second facet of forgetting: A review of warm-up decrement. *Psychol. Bull.*, 58, 257–273.

Adams, J. A., and Reynolds, B. (1954) Effect of shift in distribution of practice conditions following interpolated rest. *J. exp. Psychol.*, 47, 32–36.

Adelman, H. M., and Maatsch, J. L. (1955) Resistance to extinction as a function of the type of response elicited by frustration. *J. exp. Psychol.*, 50, 61–65.

Adelman, H. M., and Maatsch, J. L. (1956) Learning and extinction based upon frustration, food reward, and exploratory tendency. *J. exp. Psychol.*, 52, 311–315.

Alberts, E., and Ehrenfreund, D. (1951) Transposition in children as a function of age. *J. exp. Psychol.*, 41, 30–38.

Allan, M. D. (1961) Memorizing, recoding and perceptual organization. *Brit. J. Psychol.*, 52, 25–30.

Ammons, R. B. (1947) Acquisition of motor skill: I. Quantitative analysis and theoretical formulation. *Psychol. Rev.,* 54, 263–281.

Ammons, R. B. (1950) Acquisition of motor skill: III. Effects of initially distributed practice on rotary pursuit performance. *J. exp. Psychol.,* 40, 777–787.

Ammons, R. B. (1951) Effects of pre-practice activities on rotary pursuit performance. *J. exp. Psychol.,* 41, 187–191.

Amsel, A. (1950) The combination of a primary appetitional need with primary and secondary emotionally derived needs. *J. exp. Psychol.,* 40, 1–14.

Amsel, A. (1951) A three-factor theory of inhibition: An addition to Hull's two-factor theory. *Amer. Psychologist,* 6, 487.

Amsel, A. (1958) The role of frustrative nonreward in noncontinuous reward situations. *Psychol. Bull.,* 55, 102–119.

Amsel, A. (1962) Frustrative nonreward in partial reinforcement and discrimination learning: Some recent history and a theoretical extension. *Psychol. Rev.,* 69, 306–328.

Amsel, A., and Penick, E. C. (1962) The influence of early experience on the frustration effect. *J. exp. Psychol.,* 63, 167–176.

Amsel, A., and Roussel, J. (1952) Motivational properties of frustration: I. Effect on a running response of the addition of frustration to the motivational complex. *J. exp. Psychol.,* 43, 363–368.

Amsel, A., and Work, M. S. (1961) The role of learned factors in "spontaneous" activity. *J. comp. physiol. Psychol.,* 54, 527–532.

Anderson, E. E. (1941) The externalization of drive: I. Theoretical considerations. *Psychol. Rev.,* 48, 204–224.

Anderson, E. E. (1941a) The externalization of drive: II. The effect of satiation and removal of reward at different stages in the learning process of the rat. *J. genet. Psychol.,* 59, 359–376.

Anderson, E. E. (1941b) The externalization of drive: III. Maze learning by non-rewarded and by satiated rats. *J. genet. Psychol.,* 59, 397–426.

Anderson, N. H. (1963) Comparison of different populations: Resistance to extinction and transfer. *Psychol. Rev.,* 70, 162–179.

Andersson, B., and Larsson, S. (1956) An attempt to condition hypothalamic polydipsia. *Acta physiol. Scandinav.,* 36, 377–382.

Angermeier, W. F. (1960) Some basic aspects of social reinforcements in albino rats. *J. comp. physiol. Psychol.,* 53, 364–367.

Annau, Z., and Kamin, L. J. (1961) The conditioned emotional response as a function of intensity of the US. *J. comp. physiol. Psychol.,* 54, 428–432.

Appel, J. B. (1963) Punishment and shock intensity. *Science,* 141, 528–529.

Applezweig, M. H. (1951) Response potential as a function of effort. *J. comp. physiol. Psychol.,* 44, 225–235.

Arai, T. (1912) Mental fatigue. *Teach. Coll. Contr. Educ.,* No. 54.

Archer, E. J. (1954) Postrest performance in motor learning as a function of prerest degree of distribution of practice. *J. exp. Psychol.,* 47, 47–51.

Archer, E. J. (1960) A re-evaluation of the meaningfulness of all possible CVC trigrams. *Psychol. Monogr.*, 74, No. 10.

Archer, E. J. (1961) Some comments on Noble's "Measurement of association value (a) , etc. . . ." *Psychol. Repts.*, 9, 679–680.

Armus, H. L. (1958) Drive level and habit reversal. *Psychol. Repts.*, 4, 31–34.

Armus, H. L. (1959) Effect of magnitude of reinforcement on acquisition and extinction of a running response. *J. exp. Psychol.*, 58, 61–63.

Armus, H. L., and Garlich, M. M. (1961) Secondary reinforcement strength as a function of schedule of primary reinforcement. *J. comp. physiol. Psychol.*, 54, 56–58.

Arnold, W. J. (1945) An exploratory investigation of primary response generalization. *J. comp. Psychol.*, 38, 87–102.

Arnoult, M. D. (1953) Transfer of predifferentiation training in simple and multiple shape discrimination. *J. exp. Psychol.*, 45, 401–409.

Arnoult, M. D. (1957) Stimulus predifferentiation: Some generalizations and hypotheses. *Psychol. Bull.*, 54, 339–350.

Atwater, S. K. (1953) Proactive inhibition and associative facilitation as affected by degree of prior learning. *J. exp. Psychol.*, 46, 400–404.

Ausubel, D., Robbins, L., and Blake, E., Jr. (1957) Retroactive inhibition and facilitation in the learning of school materials. *J. educ. Psychol.*, 48, 334–343.

Axelrod, H. S., Cowen, E. L., and Heilizer, F. (1956) The correlates of manifest anxiety in stylus maze learning. *J. exp. Psychol.*, 51, 131–138.

Babb, H. (1956) Proportional reinforcement of irrelevant stimuli and transfer value. *J. comp. physiol. Psychol.*, 49, 586–589.

Babb, H. (1957) Transfer from a stimulus complex to differentially discriminable components. *J. comp. physiol. Psychol.*, 50, 288–292.

Bacon, H. R., Warren, J. M., and Schein, M. W. (1962) Non-spatial reversal learning in chickens. *Anim. Behav.*, 10, 239–243.

Bahrick, H. P. (1953) Sensory preconditioning under two degrees of deprivation. *J. comp. physiol. Psychol.*, 46, 39–42.

Bahrick, H. P. (1964) Retention curves: Facts or artifacts? *Psychol. Bull.*, 61, 188–194.

Bahrick, H. P., Fitts, P. M., and Briggs, G. E. (1957) Learning curves—Facts or artifacts? *Psychol. Bull.*, 54, 256–268.

Bakan, D. (1954) A generalization of Sidman's results on group and individual functions and criterion. *Psychol. Bull.*, 51, 63–64.

Baker, K. E., and Wylie, R. C. (1950) Transfer of verbal training to a motor task. *J. exp. Psychol.*, 40, 632–638.

Baker, R. A., and Lawrence, D. H. (1951) The differential effects of simultaneous and successive stimuli presentation on transposition. *J. comp. physiol. Psychol.*, 44, 378–382.

Baker, R. A., and Osgood, C. W. (1954) Discrimination transfer along a pitch continuum. *J. exp. Psychol.*, 48, 241–246.

Barnes, G. W. (1956) Conditioned stimulus intensity and temporal factors in spaced-trial classical conditioning. *J. exp. Psychol.*, 51, 192–198.

Barnes, G. W., and Kish, G. B. (1961) Reinforcing properties of the onset of auditory stimulation. *J. exp. Psychol.*, 62, 164–170.

Barnes, J. M., and Underwood, B. J. (1959) "Fate" of first-list associations in transfer theory. *J. exp. Psychol.*, 58, 97–105.

Baron, A., and Kish, G. B. (1962) Low-intensity auditory and visual stimuli as reinforcers for the mouse. *J. comp. physiol. Psychol.*, 55, 1011–1013.

Baron, M. R. (1952) The effect of long intertrial intervals on the limit of eyelid conditioning. *J. exp. Psychol.*, 44, 438–441.

Baron, M. R., and Connor, J. P. (1960) Eyelid conditioned responses with various levels of anxiety. *J. exp. Psychol.*, 60, 310–313.

Barry, H., III. (1958) Effects of strength of drive on learning and on extinction. *J. exp. Psychol.*, 55, 473–481.

Bass, M. J., and Hull, C. L. (1934) The irradiation of a tactile conditioned reflex in man. *J. comp. Psychol.*, 17, 47–65.

Batten, D. E., and Shoemaker, H. A. (1961) The effect of incentive palatability on a conditioned operant response. *J. comp. physiol. Psychol.*, 54, 577–579.

Battig, W. F. (1964) Procedural problems in paired-associate learning research. Unpublished manuscript.

Battig, W. F., and Spera, A. J. (1962) Rated association values of numbers from 0–100. *J. verb. Learn. and verb. Behav.*, 1, 200–202.

Beach, F. A. (1942) Analysis of the stimuli adequate to elicit mating behavior in the sexually inexperienced male rat. *J. comp. Psychol.*, 33, 163–207.

Bechterev, V. M. (1932) *General principles of human reflexology*. New York: International.

Beck, R. C. (1961) On secondary reinforcement and shock termination. *Psychol. Bull.*, 58, 28–45.

Beck, S. B. (1963) Eyelid conditioning as a function of CS intensity, UCS intensity, and manifest anxiety scale score. *J. exp. Psychol.*, 66, 429–438.

Behan, R. A. (1953) Expectancies and Hullian theory. *Psychol. Rev.*, 60, 252–256.

Behar, I. (1961) Analysis of object-alternation learning in rhesus monkeys. *J. comp. physiol. Psychol.*, 54, 539–542.

Belmont, L., and Birch, H. G. (1951) Re-individualizing and the repression hypothesis. *J. abnorm. soc. Psychol.*, 46, 226–235.

Bendig, A. W. (1952) Latent learning in a water maze. *J. exp. Psychol.*, 43, 134–137.

Berkson, G. (1962) Food motivation and delayed response in gibbons. *J. comp. physiol. Psychol.*, 55, 1040–1043.

Berkun, M. M., Kessen, M. L., and Miller, N. E. (1952) Hunger-reducing effects of food by stomach fistula versus food by mouth measured by a consummatory response. *J. comp. physiol. Psychol.*, 45, 550–554.

Berlyne, D. E. (1950) Novelty and curiosity as determinants of exploratory behavior. *Brit. J. Psychol.*, 41, 68–80.

Berlyne, D. E. (1960) *Conflict, arousal, and curiosity.* New York: McGraw-Hill.

Bernstein, A. L. (1934) Temporal factors in the formation of conditioned eyelid reactions in human subjects. *J. gen. Psychol.*, 10, 173–197.

Bersh, P. J. (1951) The influence of two variables upon the establishment of a secondary reinforcer for operant responses. *J. exp. Psychol.*, 41, 62–73.

Besch, N. F., Morris, H., and Levine, S. (1963) A comparison between correction and noncorrection method in drive discrimination. *J. exp. Psychol.*, 65, 414–419.

Besch, N. F., and Reynolds, W. F. (1958) Associative interference in verbal paired-associate learning. *J. exp. Psychol.*, 55, 554–558.

Bevan, W., and Adamson, R. (1960) Reinforcers and reinforcement: Their relation to maze performance. *J. exp. Psychol.*, 59, 226–232.

Bevan, W., and Dukes, W. F. (1955) Effectiveness of delayed punishment on learning performance when preceded by premonitory cues. *Psychol. Repts.*, 1, 441–448.

Bexton, W. H., Heron, W., and Scott, T. H. (1954) Effects of decreased variation in the sensory environment. *Canad. J. Psychol.*, 8, 70–76.

Bilodeau, E. A. (1952) Decrements and recovery from decrements in a simple work task with variation in force requirements at different stages of practice. *J. exp. Psychol.*, 44, 96–100.

Bilodeau, E. A. (1952a) Massing and spacing phenomena as a function of prolonged and extended practice. *J. exp. Psychol.*, 44, 108–113.

Bilodeau, E. A., and Bilodeau, I. McD. (1958) Variable frequency of knowledge of results and the learning of a simple skill. *J. exp. Psychol.*, 55, 379–383.

Bilodeau, E. A., and Bilodeau, I. McD. (1958a) Variation of temporal intervals among critical events in five studies of knowledge of results. *J. exp. Psychol.*, 55, 603–612.

Bilodeau, E. A., and Bilodeau, I. McD. (1961) Motor-skills learning. *Annual Rev. Psychol.*, 12, 243–280.

Bilodeau, E. A., Brown, J. S., and Merryman, J. J. (1956) The summation of generalized reactive tendencies. *J. exp. Psychol.*, 51, 293–298.

Bilodeau, I. McD., and Schlosberg, H. (1951) Similarity in stimulating conditions as a variable in retroactive inhibition. *J. exp. Psychol.*, 41, 199–204.

Bindra, D. (1959) *Motivation.* New York: Ronald.

Bindra, D. (1961) Components of general activity and the analysis of behavior. *Psychol. Rev.*, 68, 205–215.

Bingham, H. C. (1913) Size and form perception in Gallus domesticus. *J. anim. Behav.*, 3, 65–113.

Birch, D. (1955) Discrimination learning as a function of the ratio of nonreinforced to reinforced trials. *J. comp. physiol. Psychol.*, 48, 371–374.

Birch, D., Burnstein, E., and Clark, R. A. (1958) Response strength as a function of hours of food deprivation under a controlled maintenance schedule. *J. comp. physiol. Psychol.*, 51, 350–354.

Birch, H. G. (1945) The relation of previous experience to insightful problem solving. *J. comp. Psychol.*, 38, 367–383.

Birch, H. G., and Bitterman, M. E. (1949) Reinforcement and learning: The process of sensory integration. *Psychol. Rev.*, 56, 292–307.

Bitterman, M. E. (1962) Techniques for the study of learning in animals: Analysis and classification. *Psychol. Bull.*, 59, 81–92.

Bitterman, M. E., and Coate, W. B. (1950) Some new experiments on the nature of discrimination learning in the rat. *J. comp. physiol. Psychol.*, 43, 198–210.

Bitterman, M. E., and Holtzman, W. H. (1952) Conditioning and extinction of the galvanic skin response as a function of anxiety. *J. abnorm. soc. Psychol.*, 47, 615–623.

Black, R., Adamson, R., and Bevan, W. (1961) Runway behavior as a function of apparent intensity of shock. *J. comp. physiol. Psychol.*, 54, 270–274.

Blackwell, H. R., and Schlosberg, H. (1943) Octave generalization, pitch discrimination, and loudness thresholds in the white rat. *J. exp. Psychol.*, 33, 407–419.

Blodgett, H. C. (1929) The effect of the introduction of reward upon the maze performance of rats. *Univ. Calif. Pub. in Psychol.*, 4, 113–134.

Blodgett, H. C., and McCutchan, K. (1947) Place vs. response learning in the simple T-maze. *J. exp. Psychol.*, 37, 412–422.

Blodgett, H. C., McCutchan, K., and Mathews, R. (1949) Spatial learning in the T-maze: The influence of direction, turn, and food location. *J. exp. Psychol.*, 39, 800–809.

Blum, R. A., and Blum, J. S. (1949) Factual issues in the "continuity" controversy. *Psychol. Rev.*, 56, 33–50.

Bolles, R. C. (1963) Effect of food deprivation upon the rat's behavior in its home cage. *J. comp. physiol. Psychol.*, 56, 456–460.

Bolles, R. C., and deLorge, J. (1962) Exploration in a Dashiell maze as a function of prior deprivation, current deprivation, and sex. *Canad. J. Psychol.*, 16, 221–227.

Boneau, C. A. (1958) The interstimulus interval and the latency of the conditioned eyelid response. *J. exp. Psychol.*, 56, 464–472.

Book, W. F. (1908) The psychology of skill. *Univ. Montana Pub. in Psychol.* 1, p. 12.

Boren, J. J., Sidman, M., and Herrnstein, R. J. (1959) Avoidance, escape, and extinction as functions of shock intensity. *J. comp. physiol. Psychol.*, 52, 420–425.

Boring, E. G., Langfeld, H. S., and Weld, H. P. (1948) *Foundations of psychology*. New York: Wiley.

Bourne, L. E., Jr. (1957) Effects of delay of information feedback and task complexity on the identification of concepts. *J. exp. Psychol.*, 54, 201–207.

Bousfield, W. A. (1953) The occurrence of clustering in the recall of randomly arranged associates. *J. gen. Psychol.*, 49, 229–240.

Bousfield, W. A., and Cohen, B. H. (1955) The occurrence of clustering in the recall of randomly arranged words of different frequencies of usage. *J. gen. Psychol.*, 52, 83–95.

Bousfield, W. A., and Cohen, B. H. (1956) Clustering as a function of the number of word-categories in stimulus-word lists. *J. gen. Psychol.*, 54, 95–106.

Bousfield, W. A., Cohen, B. H., and Whitmarsh, G. A. (1958) Associative clustering in the recall of words of different taxonomic frequencies of occurrence. *Psychol. Repts.*, 4, 39–44.

Bousfield, W. A., Whitmarsh, G. A., and Esterson, J. (1958) Serial position effects and the "Marbe effect" in the free recall of meaningful words. *J. gen. Psychol.*, 59, 255–262.

Bower, G. H. (1961) A contrast effect in differential conditioning. *J. exp. Psychol.*, 62, 196–199.

Bower, G. H. (1962) The influence of graded reductions in reward and prior frustrating events upon the magnitude of the frustration effect. *J. comp. physiol. Psychol.*, 55, 582–587.

Bower, G. H., and Miller, N. E. (1958) Rewarding and punishing effects from stimulating the same place in the rat's brain. *J. comp. physiol. Psychol.*, 51, 669–674.

Bower, G. H., and Miller, N. E. (1960) Effects of amount of reward on strength of approach in an approach-avoidance conflict. *J. comp. physiol. Psychol.*, 53, 59–62.

Boycott, B. B., and Young, J. Z. (1958) Reversal of learned responses in Octopus vulgaris Lamarck. *Anim. Behav.*, 6, 45–52.

Brackbill, Y. (1964) The impairment of learning under immediate reinforcement. *J. exp. child Psychol.*, 1, 199–207.

Brackbill, Y., Boblitt, W. E., Davlin, D., and Wagner, J. E. (1963) Amplitude of response and the delay-retention effect. *J. exp. Psychol.*, 66, 57–64.

Brackbill, Y., Bravos, A., and Starr, R. H. (1962) Delay-improved retention of a difficult task. *J. comp. physiol. Psychol.*, 55, 947–952.

Brackbill, Y., Isaacs, R. B., and Smelkinson, N. (1962) Delay of reinforcement and the retention of unfamiliar, meaningless material. *Psychol. Repts.*, 11, 553–554.

Brackbill, Y., and Kappy, M. S. (1962) Delay of reinforcement and retention. *J. comp. physiol. Psychol.*, 55, 14–18.

Bragiel, R. M., and Perkins, C. C., Jr. (1954) Conditioned stimulus intensity and response speed. *J. exp. Psychol.*, 47, 437–441.

Brandauer, C. M. (1953) A confirmation of Webb's data concerning the action of irrelevant drives. *J. exp. Psychol.*, 45, 150–152.

Braun, H. W., and Heymann, S. P. (1958) Meaningfulness of material, distribution of practice, and serial-position curves. *J. exp. Psychol.,* 56, 146–150.

Braun, H. W., Wedekind, C. E., and Smudski, J. F. (1957) The effect of an irrelevant drive on maze learning in the rat. *J. exp. Psychol.,* 54, 148–152.

Breed, F. S. (1912) Reactions of chicks to optical stimuli. *J. anim. Behav.,* 2, 280–295.

Briggs, G. E. (1954) Acquisition, extinction, and recovery functions in retroactive inhibition. *J. exp. Psychol.,* 47, 285–293.

Briggs, G. E. (1957) Retroactive inhibition as a function of degree of original and interpolated activity. *J. exp. Psychol.,* 53, 60–67.

Britt, S. H. (1935) Retroactive inhibition: A review of the literature. *Psychol. Bull.,* 32, 381–440.

Broadhurst, P. L. (1957) Emotionality and the Yerkes-Dodson law. *J. exp. Psychol.,* 54, 345–352.

Brogden, W. J. (1939) Sensory pre-conditioning. *J. exp. Psychol.,* 25, 323–332.

Brogden, W. J. (1942) Tests of sensory pre-conditioning with human subjects. *J. exp. Psychol.,* 31, 505–517.

Brogden, W. J. (1947) Sensory pre-conditioning of human subjects. *J. exp. Psychol.,* 37, 527–539.

Brogden, W. J. (1949) Acquisition and extinction of a conditioned avoidance response in dogs. *J. comp. physiol. Psychol.,* 42, 296–302.

Brogden, W. J. (1951) Animal studies of learning. In Stevens, S. S., Ed., *Handbook of experimental psychology.* New York: Wiley.

Brogden, W. J., Lipman, E. A., and Culler, E. (1938) The role of incentive in conditioning and extinction. *Amer. J. Psychol.,* 51, 109–117.

Brookshire, K. H., Warren, J. M., and Ball, G. G. (1961) Reversal and transfer learning following overtraining in rat and chicken. *J. comp. physiol. Psychol.,* 54, 98–102.

Brown, G. W., and Cohen, B. D. (1959) Avoidance and approach learning motivated by stimulation of identical hypothalamic loci. *Amer. J. Physiol.,* 197, 153–157.

Brown, J. (1958) Some tests of the decay theory of immediate memory. *Quart. J. exp. Psychol.,* 10, 12–21.

Brown, J. L. (1956) The effect of drive on learning with secondary reinforcement. *J. comp. physiol. Psychol.,* 49, 254–260.

Brown, J. S. (1942) The generalization of approach responses as a function of stimulus intensity and strength of motivation. *J. comp. Psychol.,* 33, 209–226.

Brown, J. S. (1953) Problems presented by the concept of acquired drives. In *Current theory and research in motivation: A symposium.* Lincoln, Nebraska: Univ. Nebraska Press.

Brown, J. S. (1961) *The motivation of behavior.* New York: McGraw-Hill.

Brown, J. S., and Bass, B. (1958) The acquisition and extinction of an instrumental response under constant and variable conditions. *J. comp. physiol. Psychol.,* 51, 499–504.

Brown, J. S., Bilodeau, E. A., and Baron, M. R. (1951) Bidirectional gradients in the strength of a generalized voluntary response to stimuli on a visual-spatial dimension. *J. exp. Psychol.,* 41, 52–61.

Brown, J. S., and Farber, I. E. (1951) Emotions conceptualized as intervening variables—with suggestions toward a theory of frustration. *Psychol. Bull.,* 48, 465–480.

Brown, J. S., Kalish, H. I., and Farber, I. E. (1951) Conditioned fear as revealed by magnitude of startle response to an auditory stimulus. *J. exp. Psychol.,* 41, 317–328.

Brown, W. L., Overall, J. E., and Gentry, G. V. (1959) "Absolute" versus "relational" discrimination of intermediate size in the rhesus monkey. *Amer. J. Psychol.,* 72, 593–596.

Bruce, R. H. (1937) An experimental investigation of the thirst drive in rats with especial reference to the goal-gradient hypothesis. *J. genet. Psychol.,* 17, 49–60.

Bruce, R. W. (1933) Conditions of transfer of training. *J. exp. Psychol.,* 16, 343–361.

Bruner, J. S., Mandler, J. M., O'Dowd, D., and Wallach, M. A. (1958) The role of overlearning and drive level in reversal learning. *J. comp. physiol. Psychol.,* 51, 607–613.

Brush, F. R. (1957) The effects of shock intensity on the acquisition and extinction of an avoidance response in dogs. *J. comp. physiol. Psychol.,* 50, 547–552.

Brush, F. R., Brush, E. S., and Solomon, R. L. (1955) Traumatic avoidance learning: The effects of the CS-UCS interval with a delayed-conditioning procedure. *J. comp. physiol. Psychol.,* 48, 285–293.

Bryan, J. H., and Carlson, P. V. (1962) Spontaneous activity and food deprivation in human subjects. *Percept. mot. Skills,* 15, 123–126.

Bryan, W. L., and Harter, N. (1897) Studies in the physiology and psychology of a telegraphic language. *Psychol. Rev.,* 4, 27–53.

Buchwald, A. M., and Yamaguchi, H. G. (1955) The effect of change in drive level on habit reversal. *J. exp. Psychol.,* 50, 265–268.

Bugelski, B. R. (1938) Extinction with and without sub-goal reinforcement. *J. comp. Psychol.,* 26, 121–134.

Bugelski, B. R. (1942) Interference with recall of original responses after learning new responses to old stimuli. *J. exp. Psychol.,* 30, 368–379.

Bugelski, B. R. (1956) *The psychology of learning.* New York: Holt.

Bugelski, B. R., and Cadwallader, T. C. (1956) A reappraisal of the transfer and retroaction surface. *J. exp. Psychol.,* 52, 360–365.

Bugelski, B. R., Coyer, R. A., and Rogers, W. A. (1952) A criticism of pre-acquisition and pre-extinction of expectancies. *J. exp. Psychol.,* 44, 27–30.

Bugelski, B. R., and Scharlock, D. P. (1952) An experimental demonstration of unconscious mediated association. *J. exp. Psychol.,* 44, 334–338.

Bunch, M. E. (1939) Transfer of training in the mastery of an antagonistic habit after varying intervals of time. *J. comp. Psychol.,* 28, 189–200.

Buss, A. H. (1961) Stimulus generalization and aggressive verbal stimuli. *J. exp. Psychol.*, 61, 469–473.

Butler, R. A. (1953) Discrimination learning by rhesus monkeys to visual-exploration motivation. *J. comp. physiol. Psychol.*, 46, 95–98.

Butler, R. A. (1954) Incentive conditions which influence visual exploration. *J. exp. Psychol.*, 48, 19–23.

Butler, R. A. (1957) The effect of deprivation of visual incentives on visual exploration motivation in monkeys. *J. comp. physiol. Phychol.*, 50, 177–179.

Butler, R. A. (1957a) Discrimination learning by rhesus monkeys to auditory incentives. *J. comp. physiol. Psychol.*, 50, 239–241.

Butler, R. A. (1960) Acquired drives and the curiosity-investigative motives. In Waters, R. H., Rethlingshafer, D. A., and Caldwell, W. E., Eds., *Principles of comparative psychology*. New York: McGraw-Hill.

Butler, R. A., and Harlow, H. F. (1954) Persistence of visual exploration in monkeys. *J. comp. physiol. Psychol.*, 47, 258–263.

Butter, C. M., and Thomas, D. R. (1958) Secondary reinforcement as a function of the amount of primary reinforcement. *J. comp. physiol. Psychol.*, 51, 346–348.

Buxton, C. E. (1940) Latent learning and the goal-gradient hypothesis. *Contr. psychol. Theor.*, 2, No. 2.

Buytendijk, F. J. J. (1930) Über das Umlernen. *Arch. nëerl Physiol.*, 15, 283–310.

Caldwell, D. F., and Cromwell, R. L. (1959) Replication report: The relation of manifest anxiety and electric shock to eyelid conditioning. *J. exp. Psychol.*, 57, 348–349.

Calvin, J. S., Bicknell, E. A., and Sperling, D. S. (1953) Establishment of a conditioned drive based on the hunger drive. *J. comp. physiol. Psychol.*, 46, 173–175.

Calvin, J. S., Bicknell, E. A., and Sperling, D. S. (1953a) Effect of a secondary reinforcer on consummatory behavior. *J. comp. physiol. Psychol.*, 46, 176–179.

Campbell, A. A. (1938) The interrelations of two measures of conditioning in man. *J. exp. Psychol.*, 22, 225–243.

Campbell, A. A., and Hilgard, E. R. (1936) Individual differences in ease of conditioning. *J. exp. Psychol.*, 19, 561–571.

Campbell, B. A., and Kraeling, D. (1953) Response strength as a function of drive level and amount of drive reduction. *J. exp. Psychol.*, 45, 97–101.

Campbell, B. A., and Pickleman, J. R. (1961) The imprinting object as a reinforcing stimulus. *J. comp. physiol. Psychol.*, 54, 592–596.

Campbell, B. A., and Sheffield, F. D. (1953) Relation of random activity to food deprivation. *J. comp. physiol. Psychol.*, 46, 320–322.

Campbell, V., and Freeman, J. T. (1955) Some functions of experimentally induced language in perceptual learning. *Percept. mot. Skills*, 1, 71–79.

Cantor, G. N. (1955) Effects of three types of pretraining on discrimination learning in preschool children. *J. exp. Psychol.*, 49, 339–342.

Cantor, G. N., and Spiker, C. C. (1954) Effects of nonreinforced trials on discrimination learning in preschool children. *J. exp. Psychol.*, 47, 256–258.

Cantor, J. H. (1955) Amount of pretraining as a factor in stimulus predifferentiation and performance set. *J. exp. Psychol.*, 50, 180–184.

Capaldi, E. J., Hart, D., and Stanley, L. R. (1963) Influence of intertrial reinforcement on the aftereffect of nonreinforcement and resistance to extinction. *J. exp. Psychol.*, 65, 70–74.

Capaldi, E. J., and Spivey, J. E. (1963) Effect of goal-box similarity on the aftereffect of nonreinforcement and resistance to extinction. *J. exp. Psychol.*, 66, 461–465.

Capaldi, E. J., and Stevenson, H. W. (1957) Response reversal following different amounts of training. *J. comp. physiol. Psychol.*, 50, 195–198.

Capehart, J., Viney, W., and Hulicka, I. M. (1958) The effect of effort upon extinction. *J. comp. physiol. Psychol.*, 51, 505–507.

Carmichael, L., Hogan, H. P., and Walter, A. A. (1932) An experimental study of the effect of language on the reproduction of visually perceived form. *J. exp. Psychol.*, 15, 73–86.

Carper, J. W. (1953) A comparison of the reinforcing value of a nutritive and non-nutritive substance under conditions of specific and general hunger. *Amer. J. Psychol.*, 66, 270–277.

Carr, H. A. (1917) The distribution and elimination of errors in the maze. *J. anim. Behav.*, 7, 145–159.

Carr, H. A. (1925) *Psychology, a study of mental activity.* New York: Longmans, Green.

Carter, L. F. (1941) Intensity of conditioned stimulus and rate of conditioning. *J. exp. Psychol.*, 28, 481–490.

Cason, H. (1935) Backward conditioned eyelid reactions. *J. exp. Psychol.*, 18, 599–611.

Castaneda, A. (1956) Effects of stress on complex learning and performance. *J. exp. Psychol.*, 52, 9–12.

Castaneda, A., and Palermo, D. S. (1955) Psychomotor performance as a function of amount of training and stress. *J. exp. Psychol.*, 50, 175–179.

Casteel, D. B. (1911) The discriminative ability of the painted turtle. *J. anim. Behav.*, 1, 1–28.

Cautela, J. R. (1956) Experimental extinction and drive during extinction in a discrimination habit. *J. exp. Psychol.*, 51, 299–302.

Chambers, R. M. (1956) Effects of intravenous glucose injections on learning, general activity, and hunger drive. *J. comp. physiol. Psychol.*, 49, 558–564.

Champion, R. A. (1962) Stimulus-response contiguity in classical aversive conditioning. *J. exp. Psychol.*, 64, 34–39.

Champion, R. A. (1962a) Stimulus intensity effects in response evocation. *Psychol. Rev.*, 69, 428–449.

Champion, R. A., and McBride, D. A. (1962) Activity during delay of reinforcement in human learning. *J. exp. Psychol.*, 63, 589–592.

Chatterjee, B. B., and Eriksen, C. W. (1962) Cognitive factors in heart rate conditioning. *J. exp. Psychol.*, 64, 272–279.

Cheng, N. Y. (1929) Retroactive effect and degree of similarity. *J. exp. Psychol.*, 12, 444–449.

Chernikoff, R., and Brogden, W. J. (1949) The effect of different instructions upon the occurrence of sensory preconditioning. *J. exp. Psychol.*, 39, 200–207.

Chow, K. L. (1954) Effects of temporal neocortical ablation on visual discrimination learning sets in monkeys. *J. comp. physiol. Psychol.*, 47, 194–198.

Christie, R. (1951) The role of drive discrimination in learning under irrelevant motivation. *J. exp. Psychol.*, 42, 13–19.

Christie, R. (1952) The effect of some early experiences in the latent learning of adult rats. *J. exp. Psychol.*, 43, 281–288.

Church, R. M. (1963) The varied effects of punishment on behavior. *Psychol. Rev.*, 70, 369–402.

Church, R. M., Brush, F. R., and Solomon, R. L. (1956) Traumatic avoidance learning: The effects of CS-UCS interval with a delayed conditioning procedure in a free-responding situation. *J. comp. physiol. Psychol.*, 49, 301–308.

Cicala, G. S. (1961) Running speed in rats as a function of drive level and presence or absence of competing response trials. *J. exp. Psychol.*, 62, 329–334.

Cieutat, V. J. (1960) Differential familiarity with stimulus and response in paired-associate learning. *Percept. mot. Skills*, 11, 269–275.

Cieutat, V. J., Stockwell, F. E., and Noble, C. E. (1958) The interaction of ability and amount of practice with stimulus and response meaningfulness (m, m') in paired-associate learning. *J. exp. Psychol.*, 56, 193–202.

Clayton, F. L. (1958) Light reinforcement as a function of water deprivation. *Psychol. Repts.*, 4, 63–66.

Clayton, K. N. (1963) Reversal performance by rats following overlearning with and without irrelevant stimuli. *J. exp. Psychol.*, 66, 255–259.

Coate, W. B. (1956) Weakening of conditioned bar-pressing by prior extinction of its subsequent discriminated operant. *J. comp. physiol. Psychol.*, 49, 135–138.

Coburn, C. A. (1914) The behavior of the crow, Corvus Americanus. *J. anim. Behav.*, 4, 185–201.

Cochran, S. W., and Wickens, D. D. (1963) Supplementary Report: Rated association values of numbers from 0–100. *J. verb. Learn. and verb. Behav.*, 2, 373–374.

Cofer, C. N. (1959) A study of clustering in free recall based on synonyms. *J. gen. Psychol.*, 60, 3–10.

Cofer, C. N. (1964) On some factors in the organizational characteristics of free recall. *O.N.R. Tech. Rept. No. 1.*

Cofer, C. N., and Appley, M. H. (1964) *Motivation: theory and research.* New York: Wiley.

Cohen, B. D., Brown, G. W., and Brown, M. L. (1957) Avoidance learning motivated by hypothalamic stimulation. *J. exp. Psychol.*, 53, 228–233.

Cohen, B. H. (1963) An investigation of recoding in free recall. *J. exp. Psychol.*, 65, 368–376.

Cohen, B. H. (1963a) Recall of categorized word lists. *J. exp. Psychol.*, 66, 227–234.

Cole, L. W. (1911) The relation of strength of stimulus to rate of learning in the chick. *J. anim. Behav.*, 1, 111–124.

Coleman, E. B. (1963) The association hierarchy as an indicator of extraexperimental interference. *J. verb. Learn. and verb. Behav.*, 2, 417–421.

Coleman, E. B. (1963a) Approximations to English. *Amer. J. Psychol.*, 76, 239–247.

Collier, G., Knarr, F. A., and Marx, M. H. (1961) Some relations between the intensive properties of the consummatory response and reinforcement. *J. exp. Psychol.*, 62, 484–495.

Collier, G., and Willis, F. N. (1961) Deprivation and reinforcement. *J. exp. Psychol.*, 62, 377–384.

Conrad, D. G., and Sidman, M. (1956) Sucrose concentration as reinforcement for lever pressing by monkeys. *Psychol. Repts.*, 2, 381–384.

Cook, S. W., and Harris, R. E. (1937) The verbal conditioning of the galvanic skin reflex. *J. exp. Psychol.*, 21, 202–210.

Coppock, H. W., and Chambers, R. M. (1954) Reinforcement of position preference by automatic intravenous injections of glucose. *J. comp. physiol. Psychol.*, 47, 355–357.

Cotton, J. W. (1953) Running time as a function of amount of food deprivation. *J. exp. Psychol.*, 46, 188–198.

Cotton, J. W. (1955) On making predictions from Hull's theory. *Psychol. Rev.*, 62, 303–314.

Cotton, J. W., and Lewis, D. J. (1957) Effect of intertrial interval on acquisition and extinction of a running response. *J. exp. Psychol.*, 54, 15–20.

Cowles, J. T. (1937) Food tokens as incentives for learning by chimpanzees. *Comp. Psychol. Monogr.*, 14, No. 5.

Cowles, J. T., and Nissen, H. W. (1937) Reward expectancy in delayed responses of chimpanzees. *J. comp. Psychol.*, 24, 345–358.

Crespi, L. P. (1942) Quantitative variation of incentive and performance in the white rat. *Amer. J. Psychol.*, 55, 467–517.

Crespi, L. P. (1944) Amount of reinforcement and level of performance. *Psychol. Rev.*, 51, 341–357.

Cronholm, J. N., Warren, J. M., and Hara, K. (1960) Distribution of training and reversal learning by cats. *J. genet. Psychol.*, 96, 105–113.

Crowder, W. F. (1958) Secondary reinforcement and shock termination. Unpublished doctoral dissertation, Univ. Illinois.

Crowder, W. F., and Crowder, T. H. (1961) Duration of weak light reinforcement. *Psychol. Repts.*, 8, 130.

Crowder, W. F., Gay, B. R., Bright, M. G., and Lee, M. F. (1959) Secondary reinforcement or response facilitation?: III. Reconditioning. *J. Psychol.*, 48, 307–310.

Crowder, W. F., Gay, B. R., Fleming, W. C., and Hurst, R. W. (1959) Secondary reinforcement or response facilitation?: IV. The retention method. *J. Psychol.*, 48, 311–314.

Crowder, W. F., Gill, K., Jr., Hodge, C. C., and Nash, F. A., Jr. (1959) Secondary reinforcement or response acquisition?: II. Response acquisition. *J. Psychol.*, 48, 303–306.

Crowder, W. F., Morris, J. B., and McDaniel, M. H. (1959) Secondary reinforcement or response facilitation?: I. Resistance to extinction. *J. Psychol.*, 48, 299–302.

Crum, J., Brown, W. L., and Bitterman, M. E. (1951) The effect of partial and delayed reinforcement on resistance to extinction. *Amer. J. Psychol.*, 64, 228–237.

Dallett, K. M. (1962) The transfer surface re-examined. *J. verb. Learn. and verb. Behav.*, 1, 91–94.

Dallett, K. M. (1962a) The role of response similarity in proactive inhibition. *J. exp. Psychol.*, 64, 364–372.

Dallett, K. M. (1964) Number of categories and category information in free recall. *J. exp. Psychol.*, 68, 1–12.

D'Amato, M. R. (1955) Secondary reinforcement and magnitude of primary reinforcement. *J. comp. physiol. Psychol.*, 48, 378–380.

D'Amato, M. R., and Jagoda, H. (1961) Analysis of the role of overlearning in discrimination learning. *J. exp. Psychol.*, 61, 45–50.

D'Amato, M. R., and Jagoda, H. (1962) Overlearning and position reversal. *J. exp. Psychol.*, 64, 117–122.

D'Amato, M. R., Lachman, R., and Kivy, P. (1958) Secondary reinforcement as affected by reward schedule and the testing situation. *J. comp. physiol. Psychol.*, 51, 737–741.

Dashiell, J. F. (1925) A quantitative demonstration of animal drive. *J. comp. Psychol.*, 5, 205–208.

Dashiell, J. F. (1928) *Fundamentals of objective psychology.* Boston: Houghton-Mifflin.

Dashiell, J. F. (1937) *Fundamentals of objective psychology.* (2d ed.) Boston: Houghton-Mifflin.

Dashiell, J. F., and Bayroff, A. G. (1931) A forward-going tendency in maze running. *J. comp. Psychol.*, 12, 77–94.

Daub, C. T. (1933) The effect of doors on latent learning. *J. comp. Psychol.*, 15, 49–58.

Davenport, J. W. (1963) Spatial discrimination and reversal learning based upon differential percentage of reinforcement. *J. comp. physiol. Psychol.*, 56, 1038–1043.

Davis, J. D. (1958) The reinforcing effect of weak-light onset as a function of amount of food deprivation. *J. comp. physiol. Psychol.*, 51, 496–498.

Davis, R. A. (1935) *Psychology of learning.* New York: McGraw-Hill.

Davitz, J. R., Mason, D. J., Mowrer, O. H., and Viek, P. (1957) Conditioning of fear: A function of the delay of reinforcement. *Amer. J. Psychol.*, 70, 69–74.

Deese, J. (1951) The extinction of a discrimination without performance of the choice response. *J. comp. physiol. Psychol.*, 44, 362–366.

Deese, J. (1958) *The psychology of learning.* (2d ed.) New York: McGraw-Hill.

Deese, J. (1959) Influence of inter-item associative strength upon immediate free recall. *Psychol. Repts.*, 5, 305–312.

Deese, J. (1960) Frequency of usage and number of words in free recall: The role of associations. *Psychol. Repts.*, 7, 337–344.

Deese, J. (1961) From the isolated verbal unit to connected discourse. In Cofer, C. N., Ed., *Verbal learning and verbal behavior.* New York: McGraw-Hill.

Deese, J., and Hardman, G. W., Jr. (1954) An analysis of errors in retroactive inhibition of rote verbal learning. *Amer. J. Psychol.*, 67, 299–307.

Deese, J., and Kaufman, R. A. (1957) Serial effects in recall of unorganized and sequentially organized verbal material. *J. exp. Psychol.*, 54, 180–187.

Deese, J., and Marder, V. J. (1957) The pattern of errors in delayed recall of serial learning after interpolation. *Amer. J. Psychol.*, 70, 594–599.

Delgado, J. M. R., Roberts, W. W., and Miller, N. E. (1954) Learning motivated by electrical stimulation of the brain. *Amer. J. Physiol.*, 179, 587–593.

Denenberg, V. H., and Karas, G. C. (1960) Supplementary report: The Yerkes-Dodson law and shift in task difficulty. *J. exp. Psychol.*, 59, 429–430.

Denny, M. R. (1946) The role of secondary reinforcement in a partial reinforcement learning situation. *J. exp. Psychol.*, 36, 373–389.

Denny, M. R., and Behan, R. A. (1956) Conditioned hunger drive or conditioned approach? *Psychol. Repts.*, 2, 192–193.

Denny, M. R., and Davis, R. H. (1951) A test of latent learning for a non-goal significate. *J. comp. physiol. Psychol.*, 44, 590–595.

Denny, M. R., and Dunham, M. D. (1951) The effect of differential non-reinforcement of the incorrect response on the learning of the correct response in the simple T-maze. *J. exp. Psychol.*, 41, 382–389.

Denny, M. R., Frisbey, N., and Weaver, J. W., Jr. (1955) Rotary pursuit performance under alternate conditions of distributed and massed practice. *J. exp. Psychol.,* 49, 48–54.

Denny, M. R., and King, G. F. (1955) Differential response learning on the basis of differential size of reward. *J. genet. Psychol.,* 87, 317–320.

Denny, M. R., and Ratner, S. C. (1959) Distal cues and latent extinction. *Psychol. Rec.,* 9, 33–35.

Desiderato, O. (1964) Generalization of acquired fear as a function of CS intensity and number of acquisition trials. *J. exp. Psychol.,* 67, 41–47.

DeVito, J. L, and Smith, O. A., Jr. (1959) Effects of temperature and food deprivation on the random activity of macaca mulatta. *J. comp. physiol. Psychol.,* 52, 29–32.

Dews, P. (1960) Free-operant behavior under conditions of delayed reinforcement: I. CRF-type schedules. *J. exp. anal. Behav.,* 3, 221–234.

Diesenroth, C. F., and Spence, K. W. (1941) An investigation of latent learning in the white rat. *Psychol. Bull.,* 38, 706.

Dinner, J., and Duncan, C. P. (1959) Warm-up in retention as a function of degree of verbal learning. *J. exp. Psychol.,* 57, 257–261.

Dinsmoor, J. A. (1950) A quantitative comparison of the discriminative and reinforcing functions of a stimulus. *J. exp. Psychol.,* 40, 458–472.

Dinsmoor, J. A. (1954) Punishment: I. The avoidance hypothesis. *Psychol. Rev.,* 61, 34–46.

Dinsmoor, J. A. (1955) Punishment: II. An interpretation of empirical findings. *Psychol. Rev.,* 62, 96–105.

Diven, K. (1936) Certain determinants in the conditioning of anxiety reactions. *J. Psychol.,* 3, 291–308.

Dmitriev, A. S., and Kochigina, A. M. (1959) The importance of time as stimulus of conditioned reflex activity. *Psychol. Bull.,* 56, 106–132.

Dodson, J. D. (1915) The relation of strength of stimulus to rapidity of habit-formation in the kitten. *J. anim. Behav.,* 5, 330–336.

Dodson, J. D. (1917) Relative values of reward and punishment in habit formation. *Psychobiol.,* 1, 231–276.

Dollard, J., Doob, L. W., Miller, N. E., Mowrer, O. H., and Sears, R. R. (1939) *Frustration and aggression.* New Haven: Yale Univ. Press.

Dollard, J., and Miller, N. E. (1950) *Personality and psychotherapy.* New York: McGraw-Hill.

Dowling, R. M., and Braun, H. W. (1957) Retention and meaningfulness of material. *J. exp. Psychol.,* 54, 213–217.

Drew, G. C. (1939) The speed of locomotion gradient and its relation to the goal gradient. *J. comp. Psychol.,* 27, 333–372.

Duda, J. J., and Bolles, R. C. (1963) Effects of prior deprivation, current deprivation, and weight loss on the activity of the hungry rat. *J. comp. physiol. Psychol.,* 56, 569–571.

Dufort, R. H., Guttman, N., and Kimble, G. A. (1954) One-trial discrimination reversal in the white rat. *J. comp. physiol. Psychol.,* 47, 248–249.

Duncan, C. P. (1953) Transfer in motor learning as a function of degree of first-task learning and inter-task similarity. *J. exp. Psychol.*, 45, 1–11.

Duncan, C. P. (1955) Development of response generalization gradients. *J. exp. Psychol.*, 50, 26–30.

Duncan, C. P. (1960) Description of learning to learn in human subjects. *Amer. J. Psychol.*, 73, 108–114.

Dyal, J. A. (1962) Latent extinction as a function of number and duration of pre-extinction exposures. *J. exp. Psychol.*, 63, 98–104.

Dyal, J. A., and Holland, T. A. (1963) Resistance to extinction as a function of number of reinforcements. *Amer. J. Psychol.*, 76, 332–333.

Earl, R. W. (1957) Motivation, performance, and extinction. *J. comp. physiol. Psychol.*, 50, 248–251.

Ebbinghaus, H. (1885) *Memory: A contribution to experimental psychology.* (Translated by Ruger, H. A., and Bussenius, C. E., 1913) New York: Teachers College, Columbia Univ.

Ebel, H. C., and Prokasy, W. F. (1963) Classical eyelid conditioning as a function of sustained and shifted interstimulus intervals. *J. exp. Psychol.*, 65, 52–58.

Edgington, E. S. (1960) Contradictory conclusions from two speed of performance measures. *Psychol. Bull.*, 57, 315–317.

Edmonson, B. W., and Amsel, A. (1954) The effects of massing and distribution of extinction trials on the persistence of a fear-motivated instrumental response. *J. comp. physiol. Psychol.*, 47, 117–123.

Egger, M. D., and Miller, N. E. (1962) Secondary reinforcement in rats as a function of information value and reliability of the stimulus. *J. exp. Psychol.*, 64, 97–104.

Egger, M. D., and Miller, N. E. (1963) When is a reward reinforcing?: An experimental study of the information hypothesis. *J. comp. physiol. Psychol.*, 56, 132–137.

Ehrenfreund, D. (1948) An experimental test of the contiguity theory of discrimination learning with pattern vision. *J. comp. physiol. Psychol.*, 41, 408–422.

Ehrenfreund, D. (1952) A study of the transposition gradient. *J. exp. Psychol.*, 43, 81–87.

Ehrenfreund, D., and Badia, P. (1962) Response strength as a function of drive level and pre- and postshift incentive magnitude. *J. exp. Psychol.*, 63, 468–471.

Eisman, E., Asimow, A., and Maltzman, I. (1956) Habit strength as a function of drive in a brightness discrimination problem. *J. exp. Psychol.*, 52, 58–64.

Ekstrand, B., and Underwood, B. J. (1963) Paced versus unpaced recall in free learning. *J. verb. Learn. and verb. Behav.*, 2, 288–290.

Elliott, M. H. (1929) The effect of appropriateness of rewards and of complex incentives on maze performance. *Univ. Calif. Pub. in Psychol.*, 4, 91–98.

Elliott, M. H. (1929a) The effect of change in drive on maze performance. *Univ. Calif. Pub. in Psychol.,* 4, 185–188.

Ellis, H. C., Bessemer, D. W., Devine, J. V., and Trafton, C. L. (1962) Recognition of random tactual shapes following predifferentiation training. *Percept. mot. Skills,* 10, 99–102.

Ellis, H. C., and Muller, D. G. (1964) Transfer in perceptual learning following stimulus predifferentiation. *J. exp. Psychol.,* 68, 388–395.

Ellis, N. R. (1957) The immediate effects of emotionality upon behavior strength. *J. exp. Psychol.,* 54, 339–344.

Ellis, W. D. (1938) *A source book of Gestalt psychology.* New York: Harcourt Brace.

Ellson, D. G. (1938) Quantitative studies of the interaction of simple habits. I. Recovery from specific and generalized effects of extinction. *J. exp. Psychol.,* 23, 339–358.

Eninger, M. U. (1952) Habit summation in a selective learning problem. *J. comp. physiol. Psychol.,* 45, 604–608.

Epstein, W. (1961) The influence of syntactical structure on learning. *Amer. J. Psychol.,* 74, 80–85.

Epstein, W. (1962) A further study of the influence of syntactical structure on learning. *Amer. J. Psychol.,* 75, 121–126.

Epstein, W., Rock, I., and Zuckerman, C. B. (1960) Meaning and familiarity in verbal learning. *Psychol. Monogr.,* 74, No. 491.

Erickson, R. L. (1963) Relational isolation as a means of producing the von Restorff effect in paired-associate learning. *J. exp. Psychol.,* 66, 111–119.

Erlebacher, A. (1963) Reversal learning in rats as a function of percentage of reinforcement and degree of learning. *J. exp. Psychol.,* 66, 84–90.

Estes, B. W., Miller, L. B., and Curtin, M. E. (1962) Supplementary report: Monetary incentive and motivation in discrimination learning—sex differences. *J. exp. Psychol.,* 63, 320.

Estes, W. K. (1944) An experimental study of punishment. *Psychol. Monogr.,* 57, No. 3.

Estes, W. K. (1950) Toward a statistical theory of learning. *Psychol. Rev.,* 57, 94–107.

Estes, W. K. (1956) The problem of inference from curves based on group data. *Psychol. Bull.,* 53, 134–140.

Estes, W. K. (1956a) Learning. In *Annual Rev. Psychol.,* 7, 1–38.

Estes, W. K. (1958) Comments on Dr. Bolles' paper. In Jones, M. R., Ed., *Nebraska symposium on motivation.* Lincoln, Nebraska: Univ. Nebraska Press.

Estes, W. K. (1960) Learning theory and the new "mental chemistry." *Psychol. Rev.,* 67, 207–223.

Estes, W. K., Koch, S., MacCorquodale, K., Meehl, P., Mueller, C. G., Jr., Schoenfeld, W. N., and Verplanck, W. S. (1954) *Modern learning theory.* New York: Appleton-Century-Crofts.

Farber, I. E., and Spence, K. W. (1953) Conditioning and extinction as a function of anxiety. *J. exp. Psychol.*, 45, 116–125.

Fehrer, E. (1951) Latent learning in the sophisticated rat. *J. exp. Psychol.*, 42, 409–416.

Fehrer, E. (1956) The effects of hunger and familiarity of locale on exploration. *J. comp. physiol. Psychol.*, 49, 549–552.

Fehrer, E. (1956a) Effects of amount of reinforcement and of pre- and postreinforcement delays on learning and extinction. *J. exp. Psychol.*, 52, 167–176.

Felsinger, J. M., Gladstone, A. I., Yamaguchi, H. G., and Hull, C. L. (1947) Reaction latency (s'r) as a function of the number of reinforcements (N). *J. exp. Psychol.*, 37, 214–228.

Ferster, C. B. (1953) Sustained behavior under delayed reinforcement. *J. exp. Psychol.*, 45, 218–224.

Ferster, C. B. (1953a) The use of the free operant in the analysis of behavior. *Psychol. Bull.*, 50, 263–274.

Ferster, C. B., and Skinner, B. F. (1957) *Schedules of reinforcement.* New York: Appleton-Century-Crofts.

Fields, P. E. (1928) Form discrimination in the white rat. *J. comp. Psychol.*, 8, 143–158.

Finan, J. L. (1940) Quantitative studies in motivation: I. Strength of conditioning in rats under varying degrees of hunger. *J. comp. Psychol.*, 29, 119–134.

Finger, F. W. (1942) The effect of varying conditions of reinforcement upon a simple running response. *J. exp. Psychol.*, 30, 53–68.

Finger, F. W. (1942a) Retention and subsequent extinction of a simple running response following varying conditions of reinforcement. *J. exp. Psychol.*, 31, 120–133.

Finger, F. W. (1951) The effect of food deprivation and subsequent satiation upon general activity in the rat. *J. comp. physiol. Psychol.*, 44, 557–564.

Finger, F. W., and Reid, L. S. (1952) The effect of water deprivation and subsequent satiation upon general activity in the rat. *J. comp. physiol. Psychol.*, 45, 368–372.

Finger, F. W., Reid, L. S., and Weasner, M. H. (1957) The effect of reinforcement upon activity during cyclic food deprivation. *J. comp. physiol. Psychol.*, 50, 495–498.

Fiske, D. W., and Maddi, S. R. (1961) *Functions of varied experience.* Homewood, Illinois: Dorsey Press.

Fitts, P. M. (1964) Perceptual-motor skill learning. In Melton, A. W., Ed., *Categories of human learning.* New York: Academic Press.

Fitzwater, M. E. (1952) The relative effect of reinforcement and nonreinforcement in establishing a form discrimination. *J. comp. physiol. Psychol.*, 45, 476–481.

Fitzwater, M. E., and Reisman, M. N. (1952) Comparison of forward, simultaneous, backward, and pseudo-conditioning. *J. exp. Psychol.*, 44, 211–214.

Fitzwater, M. E., and Thrush, R. S. (1956) Acquisition of a conditioned response as a function of forward temporal contiguity. *J. exp. Psychol.*, 51, 59–61.

Forgays, D. G., and Levin, H. (1958) Learning as a function of change of sensory stimulation in food-deprived and food-satiated animals. *J. comp. physiol. Psychol.*, 51, 50–54.

Fowler, H., and Trapold, M. A. (1962) Escape performance as a function of delay of reinforcement. *J. exp. Psychol.*, 63, 464–467.

Fox, R. E., and King, R. A. (1961) The effects of reinforcement scheduling on the strength of a secondary reinforcer. *J. comp. physiol. Psychol.*, 54, 266–269.

Franks, C. M. (1957) Effect of food, drink, and tobacco deprivation on the conditioning of the eyeblink response. *J. exp. Psychol.*, 53, 117–120.

French, J. W. (1942) The effect of temperature on the retention of a maze habit in fish. *J. exp. Psychol.*, 31, 79–87.

Fritz, M. F. (1930) Long time training of white rats on antagonistic visual habits. *J. comp. Psychol.*, 11, 171–184.

Fromer, R. (1962) The effect of several shock patterns on the acquisition of the secondary drive of fear. *J. comp. physiol. Psychol.*, 55, 142–144.

Furchtgott, E., and Rubin, R. D. (1953) The effect of magnitude of reward on maze learning in the white rat. *J. comp. physiol. Psychol.*, 46, 9–12.

Gagne, R. M. (1941) The effect of spacing of trials on the acquisition and extinction of an operant response. *J. exp. Psychol.*, 29, 201–216.

Gagne, R. M. (1950) The effect of sequence of presentation of similar items on the learning of paired associates. *J. exp. Psychol.*, 40, 61–73.

Gagne, R. M., and Baker, K. E. (1950) Stimulus pre-differentiation as a factor in transfer of training. *J. exp. Psychol.*, 40, 439–451.

Gagne, R. M., Baker, K. E., and Foster, H. (1950) On the relation between similarity and transfer of training in the learning of discriminative motor tasks. *Psychol. Rev.*, 57, 67–79.

Gagne, R. M., Foster, H., and Crowley, M. E. (1948) The measurement of transfer of training. *Psychol. Bull.*, 45, 97–130.

Galanter, E. H., and Shaw, W. A. (1954) "Cue" vs. "reactive inhibition" in place and response learning. *J. comp. physiol. Psychol.*, 47, 395–398.

Gannon, D. R., and Noble, C. E. (1961) Familiarization (*n*) as a stimulus factor in paired-associate verbal learning. *J. exp. Psychol.*, 62, 14–23.

Ganz, L. (1962) Hue generalization and hue discriminability in macaca mulatta. *J. exp. Psychol.*, 64, 142–150.

Ganz, L., and Riesen, A. H. (1962) Stimulus generalization to hue in the dark-reared Macaque. *J. comp. physiol. Psychol.*, 55, 92–99.

Gates, A. I. (1917) Recitation as a factor in memorizing. *Arch. Psychol.*, 6, No. 40.

Gatling, F. P. (1951) A study of the continuity of the learning process as measured by habit reversal in the rat. *J. comp. physiol. Psychol.*, 44, 78–83.

Gatling, F. P. (1952) The effect of repeated stimulus reversals on learning in the rat. *J. comp. physiol. Psychol.*, 45, 347–351.

Gaydos, H. F. (1956) Intersensory transfer in the discrimination of form. *Amer. J. Psychol.*, 69, 107–110.

Gayton, A. H. (1927) The discrimination of relative and absolute stimuli by albino rats. *J. comp. Psychol.*, 7, 93–105.

Geer, J. H., and Buss, A. H. (1962) Supplementary report: Generalization of a nonverbal response to aggressive verbal stimuli. *J. exp. Psychol.*, 63, 413–414.

Gentry, G. V., Overall, J. E., and Brown, W. L. (1959) Transpositional responses of rhesus monkeys to stimulus-objects of intermediate size. *Amer. J. Psychol.*, 72, 453–455.

Gerall, A. A., and Woodward, J. K. (1958) Conditioning of the human pupillary dilation response as a function of the CS-UCS interval. *J. exp. Psychol.*, 55, 501–507.

Gewirtz, J. L., Jones, L. V., and Waerneryd, K. (1956) Stimulus units and range of experienced stimuli as determinants of generalization-discrimination gradients. *J. exp. Psychol.*, 52, 51–57.

Gibson, E. J. (1939) Sensory generalization with voluntary reactions. *J. exp. Psychol.*, 24, 237–253.

Gibson, E. J. (1940) A systematic application of the concepts of generalization and differentiation of verbal learning. *Psychol. Rev.*, 47, 196–229.

Gibson, E. J. (1941) Retroactive inhibition as a function of degree of generalization between tasks. *J. exp. Psychol.*, 28, 93–115.

Gibson, E. J. (1942) Intra-list generalization as a factor in verbal learning. *J. exp. Psychol.*, 30, 185–200.

Gibson, E. J., Bishop, C. H., Schiff, W., and Smith, J. (1964) Comparison of meaningfulness and pronunciability as grouping principles in the perception and retention of verbal material. *J. exp. Psychol.*, 67, 173–182.

Gibson, J. J. (1960) The concept of the stimulus in psychology. *Amer. Psychologist*, 15, 694–703.

Gilchrist, J. C. (1952) Characteristics of latent and reinforcement learning as a function of time. *J. comp. physiol. Psychol.*, 45, 198–203.

Gillette, A. L. (1936) Learning and retention: A comparison of three experimental procedures. *Arch. Psychol.*, 28.

Gladis, M., and Braun, H. W. (1958) Age differences in transfer and retroaction as a function of intertask response similarity. *J. exp. Psychol.*, 55, 25–30.

Glanzer, M. (1953) The role of stimulus satiation in response alternation. *J. exp. Psychol.*, 45, 387–393.

Glaze, J. A. (1928) The association value of non-sense syllables. *J. genet. Psychol.*, 35, 255–269.

Gleitman, H. (1950) Studies in motivation and learning: II. Thirsty rats trained in a maze with food but no water, then run hungry. *J. exp. Psychol.,* 40, 169–174.

Gleitman, H., Nachmias, J., and Neisser, U. (1954) The S-R reinforcement theory of extinction. *Psychol. Rev.,* 61, 23–33.

Glickman, S. E., and Hartz, K. E. (1964) Exploratory behavior in several species of rodents. *J. comp. physiol. Psychol.,* 58, 101–104.

Glickman, S. E., and Jensen, G. D. (1961) The effects of hunger and thirst on Y-maze exploration. *J. comp. physiol. Psychol.,* 54, 83–85.

Goldstein, M. L. (1960) Acquired drive strength as a joint function of shock intensity and number of acquisition trials. *J. exp. Psychol.,* 60, 349–358.

Gonzalez, R. C., Eskin, R. M., and Bitterman, M. E. (1962) Extinction in the fish after partial and consistent reinforcement with number of reinforcements equated. *J. comp. physiol. Psychol.,* 55, 381–386.

Gonzalez, R. C., Eskin, R. M., and Bitterman, M. E. (1963) Further experiments on partial reinforcement in the fish. *Amer. J. Psychol.,* 76, 366–375.

Gonzalez, R. C., Gentry, G. V., and Bitterman, M. E. (1954) Relational discrimination of intermediate size in the chimpanzee. *J. comp. physiol. Psychol.,* 47, 385–388.

Gonzalez, R. C., Gleitman, H., and Bitterman, M. E. (1962) Some observations on the depression effect. *J. comp. physiol. Psychol.,* 55, 578–581.

Gonzalez, R. C., and Ross, S. (1958) The basis of solution by preverbal children of the intermediate size problem. *Amer. J. Psychol.,* 71, 742–746.

Goodrich, K. P. (1959) Performance in different segments of an instrumental response chain as a function of reinforcement schedule. *J. exp. Psychol.,* 57, 57–63.

Goodrich, K. P. (1960) Running speed and drinking rate as functions of sucrose concentration and amount of consummatory activity. *J. comp. physiol. Psychol.,* 53, 245–250.

Gormezano, I., and Moore, J. W. (1962) Effects of instructional set and UCS intensity on the latency, percentage, and form of the eyelid response. *J. exp. Psychol.,* 63, 487–494.

Goss, A. E. (1953) Transfer as a function of type and amount of preliminary experience with the task stimuli. *J. exp. Psychol.,* 46, 419–428.

Goss, A. E. (1955) A stimulus-response analysis of the interaction of cue-producing and instrumental responses. *Psychol. Rev.,* 62, 20–31.

Goss, A. E., and Greenfeld, N. (1958) Transfer to a motor task as influenced by conditions and degree of prior discrimination training. *J. exp. Psychol.,* 55, 258–269.

Goss, A. E., Morgan, C. H., and Golin, S. J. (1959) Paired-associates learning as a function of percentage occurrence of response members (reinforcement). *J. exp. Psychol.,* 57, 96–104.

Grant, D. A. (1943) The pseudo-conditioned eyelid response. *J. exp. Psychol.,* 32, 139–149.

Grant, D. A. (1943a) Sensitization and association in eyelid conditioning. *J. exp. Psychol.,* 32, 201–212.

Grant, D. A. (1945) A sensitized eyelid reaction to the conditioned eyelid response. *J. exp. Psychol.,* 35, 393–402.

Grant, D. A. (1964) Classical and operant conditioning. In Melton, A. W., Ed., *Categories of human learning.* New York: Academic Press.

Grant, D. A., Hake, H. W., and Hornseth, J. P. (1951) Acquisition and extinction of a verbal conditioned response with differing percentages of reinforcement. *J. exp. Psychol.,* 42, 1–5.

Grant, D. A., and Hilgard, E. R. (1940) Sensitization as a supplement to association in eyelid conditioning. *Psychol. Bull.,* 37, 478–479.

Grant, D. A., and Meyer, H. I. (1941) The formation of generalized response sets during repeated electric shock stimulation. *J. gen. Psychol.,* 24, 21–38.

Grant, D. A., and Norris, E. B. (1947) Eyelid conditioning as influenced by the presence of sensitized Beta-responses. *J. exp. Psychol.,* 37, 423–433.

Grant, D. A., Norris, E. B., and Boissard, S. (1947) Dark adaptation and the pseudo-conditioned eyelid response. *J. exp. Psychol.,* 37, 434–439.

Grant, D. A., Riopelle, A. J., and Hake, H. W. (1950) Resistance to extinction and the pattern of reinforcement. I. Alternation of reinforcement and the conditioned eyelid response. *J. exp. Psychol.,* 40, 53–60.

Grant, D. A., and Schiller, J. J. (1953) Generalization of the conditioned galvanic skin response to visual stimuli. *J. exp. Psychol.,* 46, 309–313.

Grant, D. A., and Schipper, L. M. (1952) The acquisition and extinction of conditioned eyelid responses as a function of the percentage of fixed-ratio random reinforcement. *J. exp. Psychol.,* 43, 313–320.

Grant, D. A., Schipper, L. M., and Ross, B. M. (1952) Effect of inter-trial interval during acquisition on extinction of the conditioned eyelid response following partial reinforcement. *J. exp. Psychol.,* 44, 203–210.

Grant, D. A., and Schneider, D. E. (1948) Intensity of the conditioned stimulus and strength of conditioning: I. The conditioned eyelid response to light. *J. exp. Psychol.,* 38, 690–696.

Grant, D. A., and Schneider, D. E. (1949) Intensity of the conditioned stimulus and strength of conditioning: II. The conditioned galvanic skin response to an auditory stimulus. *J. exp. Psychol.,* 39, 35–40.

Green, R. T. (1956) Surprise as a factor in the von Restorff effect. *J. exp. Psychol.,* 52, 340–344.

Greenberg, I. (1954) The acquisition of a thirst drive. Unpublished doctoral dissertation, University of Pennsylvania.

Greenberg, R., and Underwood, B. J. (1950) Retention as a function of stage of practice. *J. exp. Psychol.,* 40, 452–457.

Greene, J. E. (1953) Magnitude of reward and acquisition of a black-white discrimination habit. *J. exp. Psychol.,* 46, 113–119.

Greenspoon, J. (1955) The reinforcing effect of two spoken sounds on the frequency of two responses. *Amer. J. Psychol.*, 68, 409–416.

Greenspoon, J., and Foreman, S. (1956) Effect of delay of knowledge of results on learning a motor task. *J. exp. Psychol.*, 51, 226–228.

Greenspoon, J., and Ranyard, R. (1957) Stimulus conditions and retroactive inhibition. *J. exp. Psychol.*, 53, 55–59.

Grether, W. F. (1938) Pseudo-conditioning without paired stimulation encountered in attempted backward conditioning. *J. comp. Psychol.*, 25, 91–96.

Grice, G. R. (1942) An experimental study of the gradient of reinforcement in maze learning. *J. exp. Psychol.*, 30, 475–489.

Grice, G. R. (1948) The relation of secondary reinforcement to delayed reward in visual discrimination learning. *J. exp. Psychol.*, 38, 1–16.

Grice, G. R. (1949) Visual discrimination learning with simultaneous and successive presentation of stimuli. *J. comp. physiol. Psychol.*, 42, 365–373.

Grice, G. R., and Goldman, H. M. (1955) Generalized extinction and secondary reinforcement in visual discrimination learning with delayed reward. *J. exp. Psychol.*, 50, 197–200.

Grice, G. R., and Hunter, J. J. (1964) Stimulus intensity effects depend upon the type of experimental design. *Psychol. Rev.*, 71, 247–256.

Grice, G. R., and Saltz, E. (1950) The generalization of an instrumental response to stimuli varying in the size dimension. *J. exp. Psychol.*, 40, 702–708.

Grindley, G. C. (1929) Experiments on the influence of the amount of reward on learning in young chickens. *Brit. J. Psychol.*, 20, 173–180.

Grings, W. W., and Lockhart, R. A. (1963) Effects of "anxiety-lessening" instructions and differential set development on the extinction of GSR. *J. exp. Psychol.*, 66, 292–299.

Grings, W. W., and O'Donnell, D. E. (1956) Magnitude of response to compounds of discriminated stimuli. *J. exp. Psychol.*, 52, 354–359.

Gross, C. G. (1963) Effect of deprivation on delayed response and delayed alternation performance by normal and brain operated monkeys. *J. comp. physiol. Psychol.*, 56, 48–51.

Grosslight, J. H., Hall, J. F., and Murnin, J. (1953) Patterning effect in partial reinforcement. *J. exp. Psychol.*, 46, 103–106.

Grosslight, J. H., and Radlow, R. (1956) Patterning effect of the non-reinforcement–reinforcement sequence in a discrimination situation. *J. comp. physiol. Psychol.*, 49, 542–546.

Grosslight, J. H., and Radlow, R. (1957) Patterning effect of the non-reinforcement–reinforcement sequence involving a single non-reinforced trial. *J. comp. physiol. Psychol.*, 50, 23–25.

Gulliksen, H. (1932) Studies of transfer of response. I. Relative versus absolute factors in the discrimination of size by the white rat. *J. genet. Psychol.*, 40, 37–51.

Gundlach, R. H., and Herington, G. B., Jr. (1933) The problem of relative and absolute transfer of discrimination. *J. comp. Psychol.*, 16, 199–206.

Guthrie, E. R. (1935) *The psychology of learning*. New York: Harper.

Guttman, N. (1953) Operant conditioning, extinction, and periodic reinforcement in relation to concentration of sucrose used as reinforcing agent. *J. exp. Psychol.*, 46, 213–224.

Guttman, N., and Kalish, H. I. (1956) Discriminability and stimulus generalization. *J. exp. Psychol.*, 51, 79–88.

Gynther, M. D. (1957) Differential eyelid conditioning as a function of stimulus similarity and strength of response to the CS. *J. exp. Psychol.*, 53, 408–416.

Hall, J. F. (1951) Studies in secondary reinforcement: I. Secondary reinforcement as a function of the frequency of primary reinforcement. *J. comp. physiol. Psychol.*, 44, 246–251.

Hall, J. F. (1951a) Studies in secondary reinforcement: II. Secondary reinforcement as a function of the strength of drive during primary reinforcement. *J. comp. physiol. Psychol.*, 44, 462–466.

Hall, J. F. (1954) Learning as a function of word-frequency. *Amer. J. Psychol.*, 67, 138–140.

Hall, J. F. (1955) Activity as a function of a restricted drinking schedule. *J. comp. physiol. Psychol.*, 48, 265–266.

Hall, J. F. (1955a) Extinction as a function of altered stimulating conditions. *J. genet. Psychol.*, 87, 155–158.

Hall, J. F. (1955b) Retroactive inhibition in meaningful material. *J. educ. Psychol.*, 46, 47–52.

Hall, J. F. (1956) The relation between external stimulation, food deprivation, and activity. *J. comp. physiol. Psychol.*, 49, 339–341.

Hall, J. F. (1958) The influence of learning in activity wheel behavior. *J. genet. Psychol.*, 92, 121–125.

Hall, J. F. (1961) *Psychology of motivation*. Philadelphia: Lippincott.

Hall, J. F., and Kobrick, J. L. (1952) The relationships among three measures of response strength. *J. comp. physiol. Psychol.*, 45, 280–282.

Hall, J. F., Low, L., and Hanford, P. (1960) The activity of hungry, thirsty, and satiated rats in the Dashiell checkerboard maze. *J. comp. physiol. Psychol.*, 53, 155–158.

Hall, J. F., and Prokasy, W. F. (1961) Stimulus generalization to absolutely discriminable tones. *Percept. mot. Skills*, 12, 175–178.

Hamilton, C. E. (1950) The relationship between length of interval separating two learning tasks and performance on the second task. *J. exp. Psychol.*, 40, 613–621.

Hamilton, E. L. (1929) The effect of delayed incentive on the hunger drive in the white rat. *Genet. Psychol. Monogr.*, 5, 131–207.

Hamilton, R. J. (1943) Retroactive facilitation as a function of degree of similarity between tasks. *J. exp. Psychol.*, 32, 363–376.

Hamilton, W. F., and Coleman, T. B. (1933) Trichromatic vision in the pigeon as illustrated by the spectral hue discrimination curve. *J. comp. Psychol.*, 15, 183–191.

Hammes, J. A. (1956) Visual discrimination learning as a function of shock-fear and task difficulty. *J. comp. physiol. Psychol.*, 49, 481–484.

Haney, G. W. (1931) The effect of familiarity on maze performance of albino rats. *Univ. Calif. Pub. in Psychol.*, 4, 319–333.

Hanson, H. M. (1959) Effects of discrimination training on stimulus generalization. *J. exp. Psychol.*, 58, 321–334.

Hanson, H. M. (1961) Stimulus generalization following three-stimulus discrimination training. *J. comp. physiol. Psychol.*, 54, 181–185.

Hara, K., and Warren, J. M. (1961) Stimulus additivity and dominance in discrimination performance by cats. *J. comp. physiol. Psychol.*, 54, 86–90.

Harden, L. M. (1929) A quantitative study of the similarity factor in retroactive inhibition. *J. gen. Psychol.*, 2, 421–430.

Harlow, H. F. (1939) Forward conditioning, backward conditioning and pseudo-conditioning in the goldfish. *J. genet. Psychol.*, 55, 49–58.

Harlow, H. F. (1948) Studying animal behavior. In Andrews, T. G., Ed., *Methods of psychology*. New York: Wiley.

Harlow, H. F. (1949) The formation of learning sets. *Psychol. Rev.*, 56, 51–65.

Harlow, H. F. (1950) Analysis of discrimination learning by monkeys. *J. exp. Psychol.*, 40, 26–39.

Harlow, H. F. (1952) Learning. *Annual Rev. Psychol.*, 3, 29–54.

Harlow, H. F. (1953) Motivation as a factor in the acquisition of new responses. In *Current theory and research in motivation: A symposium*. Lincoln, Nebraska: Univ. Nebraska Press.

Harlow, H. F. (1959) Learning set and error factor theory. In Koch, S., Ed., *Psychology: A study of a science*, Vol. II. New York: McGraw-Hill.

Harlow, H. F., Harlow, M. K., and Meyer, D. R. (1950) Learning motivated by a manipulation drive. *J. exp. Psychol.*, 40, 228–234.

Harlow, H. F., and Hicks, L. H. (1957) Discrimination learning theory: Uniprocess vs. duoprocess. *Psychol. Rev.*, 64, 104–109.

Harlow, H. F., and Toltzien, F. (1940) Formation of pseudo-conditioned responses in the cat. *J. gen. Psychol.*, 23, 367–375.

Harlow, H. F., and Warren, J. M. (1952) Formation and transfer of discrimination learning sets. *J. comp. physiol. Psychol.*, 45, 482–489.

Harris, J. D. (1941) Forward conditioning, backward conditioning, and pseudo-conditioning, and adaptation to the conditioned stimulus. *J. exp. Psychol.*, 28, 491–502.

Harris, J. D. (1943) Studies in non-association factors inherent in conditioning. *Comp. Psychol. Monogr.*, 18, No. 1.

Harris, P., and Nygaard, J. E. (1961) Resistance to extinction and number of reinforcements. *Psychol. Repts.*, 8, 233–234.

Hartman, T. F., and Grant, D. A. (1962) Differential eyelid conditioning as a function of the CS-UCS interval. *J. exp. Psychol.*, 64, 131–136.

Hartman, T. F., Grant, D. A., and Ross, L. E. (1960) An investigation of the latency of "instructed voluntary" eyelid responses. *Psychol. Repts.*, 7, 305–311.

Hartman, T. F., and Ross, L. E. (1961) An alternative criterion for the elimination of "voluntary" responses in eyelid conditioning. *J. exp. Psychol.*, 61, 334–338.

Hayes, K. J. (1953) The backward curve: A method for the study of learning. *Psychol. Rev.*, 60, 269–275.

Hebb, D. O. (1961) Introduction to cognitive and physiological effects of perceptual isolation. In Solomon, P., Kubzansky, P. E., Leiderman, P. H., Mendelson, J. H., Trumbull, R., and Wexler, D., Eds., *Sensory deprivation*. Cambridge, Mass.: Harvard Univ. Press.

Helson, H. (1959) Adaptation-level theory. In Koch, S., Ed., *Psychology: A study of a science*, Vol. I. New York: McGraw-Hill.

Hendry, D. P., and Rasche, R. H. (1961) Analysis of a new nonnutritive positive reinforcer based on thirst. *J. comp. physiol. Psychol.*, 54, 477–483.

Herb, F. H. (1940) Latent learning–non-reward followed by food in blinds. *J. comp. Psychol.*, 29, 247–255.

Heron, W. T. (1928) The warming-up effect in learning nonsense syllables. *J. genet. Psychol.*, 35, 219–228.

Hicks, V. C., and Carr, H. (1912) Human reactions in a maze. *J. anim. Behav.*, 2, 98–125.

Hilgard, E. R. (1938) A summary and evaluation of alternative procedures for the construction of Vincent curves. *Psychol. Bull.*, 35, 282–297.

Hilgard, E. R. (1951) Methods and procedures in the study of learning. In Stevens, S. S., Ed., *Handbook of experimental psychology*. New York: Wiley.

Hilgard, E. R. (1956) *Theories of learning*. (2d ed.) New York: Appleton-Century-Crofts.

Hilgard, E. R., Jones, L. V., and Kaplan, S. J. (1951) Conditioned discrimination as related to anxiety. *J. exp. Psychol.*, 42, 94–99.

Hilgard, E. R., and Marquis, D. G. (1935) Acquisition, extinction, and retention of conditioned eyelid responses to light in dogs. *J. comp. Psychol.*, 19, 29–58.

Hilgard, E. R., and Marquis, D. G. (1936) Conditioned eyelid responses in monkeys, with a comparison of dog, monkey, and man. *Psychol. Monogr.*, 47, No. 212.

Hilgard, E. R., and Marquis, D. G. (1940) *Conditioning and learning*. New York: Appleton-Century-Crofts.

Hill, F. A., and Wickens, D. D. (1962) The effect of stimulus compounding in paired-associate learning. *J. verb. Learn. and verb. Behav.*, 1, 144–151.

Hill, W. F. (1956) Activity as an autonomous drive. *J. comp. physiol. Psychol.*, 49, 15–19.

Hill, W. F. (1958) The effect of varying periods of confinement on activity in tilt cages. *J. comp. physiol. Psychol.*, 51, 570–574.

Hill, W. F. (1958a) The effect of long confinement on voluntary wheel-running by rats. *J. comp. physiol. Psychol.*, 51, 770–773.

Hill, W. F., and Spear, N. E. (1963) Choice between magnitudes of reward in a T-maze. *J. comp. physiol. Psychol.*, 56, 723–726.

Hill, W. F., and Spear, N. E. (1963a) Extinction in a runway as a function of acquisition level and reinforcement percentage. *J. exp. Psychol.*, 65, 495–500.

Hill, W. F., and Spear, N. E. (1963b) A replication of overlearning and reversal in a T maze. *J. exp. Psychol.*, 65, 317.

Hill, W. F., Spear, N. E., and Clayton, K. N. (1962) T-maze reversal learning after several different overtraining procedures. *J. exp. Psychol.*, 64, 533–540.

Hillman, B., Hunter, W. S., and Kimble, G. A. (1953) The effect of drive level on the maze performance of the white rat. *J. comp. physiol. Psychol.*, 46, 87–89.

Hiss, R. H., and Thomas, D. R. (1963) Stimulus generalization as a function of testing procedure and response measure. *J. exp. Psychol.*, 65, 587–592.

Hitchcock, F. A. (1927) The total energy requirement of the albino rat for growth and activity. *Amer. J. Physiol.*, 83, 28–36.

Hoffeld, D. R., Thompson, R. F., and Brogden, W. J. (1958) Effect of stimuli time relations during preconditioning training upon the magnitude of sensory preconditioning. *J. exp. Psychol.*, 56, 437–442.

Homme, L. E., DeBaca, P. C., Devine, J. V., Steinhorst, R., and Rickert, E. J. (1963) Use of the Premack principle in controlling the behavior of nursery school children. *J. exp. anal. Behav.*, 6, 544.

Homzie, M. J., and Ross, L. E. (1962) Runway performance following a reduction the concentration of a liquid reward. *J. comp. physiol. Psychol.*, 55, 1029–1033.

Honig, W. K. (1961) Generalization of extinction on the spectral continuum. *Psychol. Rec.*, 11, 269–278.

Honzik, C. H. (1936) The sensory basis of maze learning in rats. *Comp. Psychol. Monogr.*, 13.

Hopkins, C. O. (1955) Effectiveness of secondary reinforcing stimuli as a function of the quantity and quality of food reinforcement. *J. exp. Psychol.*, 50, 339–342.

Horenstein, B. R. (1951) Performance of conditioned responses as a function of strength of hunger drive. *J. comp. physiol. Psychol.*, 44, 210–224.

Horowitz, L. M. (1961) Free recall and ordering of trigrams. *J. exp. Psychol.*, 62, 51–57.

House, B. J., and Zeaman, D. (1959) Position discrimination and reversals in low-grade retardates. *J. comp. physiol. Psychol.*, 52, 564–565.

House, B. J., and Zeaman, D. (1960) Transfer of a discrimination from objects to patterns. *J. exp. Psychol.*, 59, 298–302.

Hovland, C. I. (1937) The generalization of conditioned responses. I. The sensory generalization of conditioned responses with varying frequencies of tone. *J. gen. Psychol.*, 17, 125–148.

Hovland, C. I. (1937a) The generalization of conditioned responses. II. The sensory generalization of conditioned responses with varying intensities of tone. *J. genet. Psychol.*, 51, 279–291.

Hovland, C. I. (1937b) The generalization of conditioned responses. III. Extinction, spontaneous recovery, and disinhibition of conditioned and of generalized responses. *J. exp. Psychol.*, 21, 47–62.

Hovland, C. I. (1937c) The generalization of conditioned responses. IV. The effects of varying amounts of reinforcement upon the degree of generalization of conditioned responses. *J. exp. Psychol.*, 21, 261–276.

Hovland, C. I. (1938) Experimental studies in rote-learning theory. III. Distribution of practice with varying speeds of syllable presentation. *J. exp. Psychol.*, 23, 172–190.

Hovland, C. I. (1939) Experimental studies in rote-learning theory: V. Comparison of distribution of practice in serial and paired-associate learning. *J. exp. Psychol.*, 25, 622–633.

Hovland, C. I. (1940) Experimental studies in rote-learning theory. VI. Comparison of retention following learning to same criterion by massed and distributed practice. *J. exp. Psychol.*, 26, 568–587.

Hovland, C. I. (1940a) Experimental studies in rote-learning theory: VII. Distribution of practice with varying lengths of list. *J. exp. Psychol.*, 27, 271–284.

Hovland, C. I. (1949) Experimental studies in rote-learning theory: VIII. Distributed practice of paired-associates with varying rates of presentation. *J. exp. Psychol.*, 39, 714–718.

Hovland, C. I. (1951) Human learning and retention. In Stevens, S. S., Ed., *Handbook of experimental psychology*. New York: Wiley.

Hovland, C. I., and Kurtz, K. H. (1952) Experimental studies in rote learning: X. Pre-syllable familiarization and the length-difficulty relationship. *J. exp. Psychol.*, 44, 31–39.

Howard, T. C., and Young, F. A. (1962) Conditioned hunger and secondary rewards in monkeys. *J. comp. physiol. Psychol.*, 55, 392–397.

Howat, M. G., and Grant, D. A. (1958) Influence of intertrial interval during extinction on spontaneous recovery of conditioned eyelid responses. *J. exp. Psychol.*, 56, 11–15.

Hubbert, H. B. (1915) Elimination of errors in the maze. *J. anim. Behav.*, 5, 66–72.

Hubbert, H. B., and Lashley, K. S. (1917) Retroactive association and the elimination of errors in the maze. *J. anim. Behav.*, 7, 130–142.

Hughes, D., Davis, J. D., and Grice, G. R. (1960) Goal box and alley similarity as a factor in latent extinction. *J. comp. physiol. Psychol.*, 53, 612–614.

Hulicka, I. M. (1960) Additive versus multiplicative combination of drive and incentive. *Psychol. Repts.*, 6, 403–409.

Hull, C. L. (1929) A functional interpretation of the conditioned reflex. *Psychol. Rev.*, 36, 498–511.

Hull, C. L. (1932) The goal-gradient hypothesis and maze learning. *Psychol. Rev.*, 39, 25–43.

Hull, C. L. (1933) The meaningfulness of 320 selected nonsense syllables. *Amer. J. Psychol.*, 45, 730–734.

Hull, C. L. (1934) The rat's speed of locomotion gradient in the approach to food. *J. comp. Psychol.*, 17, 393–422.

Hull, C. L. (1935) The conflicting psychologies of learning—A way out. *Psychol. Rev.*, 42, 491–516.

Hull, C. L. (1937) Mind, mechanism, and adaptive behavior. *Psychol. Rev.*, 44, 1–32.

Hull, C. L. (1939) The problem of stimulus equivalence in behavior theory. *Psychol. Rev.*, 46, 9–30.

Hull, C. L. (1940) Explorations in the patterning of stimuli conditioned to the GSR. *J. exp. Psychol.*, 27, 95–110.

Hull, C. L. (1943) *Principles of behavior.* New York: Appleton-Century-Crofts.

Hull, C. L. (1949) Stimulus intensity dynamism (V) and stimulus generalization. *Psychol. Rev.*, 56, 67–76.

Hull, C. L. (1950) Behavior postulates and corollaries—1949. *Psychol. Rev.*, 57, 173–180.

Hull, C. L. (1951) *Essentials of behavior.* New Haven: Yale Univ. Press.

Hull, C. L. (1952) *A behavior system.* New Haven: Yale Univ. Press.

Hull, C. L., Livingston, J. R., Rouse, R. O., and Barker, A. N. (1951) True, sham, and esophageal feeding as reinforcements. *J. comp. physiol. Psychol.*, 44, 236–245.

Hull, C. L., and Spence, K. W. (1938) Correction vs. noncorrection method of trial-and-error learning in rats. *J. comp. Psychol.*, 25, 127–145.

Hulse, S. H., Jr. (1958) Amount and percentage of reinforcement and duration of goal confinement in conditioning and extinction. *J. exp. Psychol.*, 56, 48–57.

Hulse, S. H., Jr., and Stanley, W. C. (1956) Extinction by omission of food as related to partial and secondary reinforcement. *J. exp. Psychol.*, 52, 221–227.

Hume, D. (1939) An enquiry concerning human understanding. In Burtt, E. A., Ed., *The English Philosophers from Bacon to Mill.* New York: Modern Library.

Humphreys, L. G. (1939) The effect of random alternation of reinforcement on the acquisition and extinction of conditioned eyelid reactions. *J. exp. Psychol.*, 25, 141–158.

Humphreys, L. G. (1939a) Generalization as a function of method of reinforcement. *J. exp. Psychol.*, 25, 361–372.

Humphreys, L. G. (1940) Distributed practice in the development of the conditioned eyelid reaction. *J. gen. Psychol.*, 22, 379–385.

Humphreys, L. G. (1943) Measures of strength of conditioned eyelid responses. *J. gen. Psychol.*, 29, 101–111.

Hunt, D. P. (1962) The effect of stimulus similarity on the acquisition and extinction of a conditioned response. *J. exp. Psychol.*, 63, 278–283.

Hunt, J. McV., and Quay, H. C. (1961) Early vibratory experience and the question of innate reinforcement value of vibration and other stimuli. *Psychol. Rev.*, 68, 149–156.

Hunter, W. S. (1922) Habit interference in the white rat and in human subjects. *J. comp. Psychol.*, 2, 29–59.

Hunter, W. S. (1929) Experimental studies in learning. In Murchison, C., Ed., *Foundations of experimental psychology*. Worcester: Clark Univ. Press.

Hunter, W. S. (1930) A further consideration of the sensory control of the maze habit in the white rat. *J. genet. Psychol.*, 38, 3–19.

Hunter, W. S. (1932) The effect of inactivity produced by cold upon learning and retention in the cockroach, blattella germanica. *J. genet. Psychol.*, 41, 253–265.

Hunter, W. S. (1934) Learning. IV. Experimental studies of learning. In Murchison, C., Ed., *Handbook of general experimental psychology*. Worcester: Clark Univ. Press.

Hunter, W. S. (1935) Conditioning and extinction in the rat. *Brit. J. Psychol.*, 26, 135–148.

Hunter, W. S., and Yarbrough, J. U. (1917) The interference of auditory habits in the white rat. *J. anim. Behav.*, 7, 49–65.

Hurwitz, H. M. B., and De, S. C. (1958) Studies in light reinforced behavior: II. Effect of food deprivation and stress. *Psychol. Repts.*, 4, 71–77.

Hutt, P. J. (1954) Rate of bar pressing as a function of quality and quantity of food reward. *J. comp. physiol. Psychol.*, 47, 235–239.

Ingebritsen, O. C. (1932) Maze learning after lesion in the cervical cord. *J. comp. Psychol.*, 14, 279–294.

Irion, A. L. (1948) The relation of "set" to retention. *Psychol. Rev.*, 55, 336–341.

Irion, A. L. (1949) Retention and warming-up effects in paired-associate learning. *J. exp. Psychol.*, 39, 669–675.

Irion, A. L., and Wham, D. S. (1951) Recovery from retention loss as a function of amount of pre-recall warm-up. *J. exp. Psychol.*, 41, 242–247.

Ishihara, S. (1954) An experimental investigation of partial reinforcement. *Jap. J. Psychol.*, 25, 9–100.

Ison, J. R. (1962) Experimental extinction as a function of number of reinforcements. *J. exp. Psychol.,* 64, 314–317.

Iwahara, S., and Marx, M. (1950) Cognitive transfer in discrimination learning. *Amer. Psychologist,* 5, 479.

Jackson, T. A., and Jerome, E. (1940) Studies in the transposition of learning by children: IV. A preliminary study of patternedness in discrimination learning. *J. exp. Psychol.,* 26, 432–439.

Jacobs, A. (1955) Formation of new associations to words selected on the basis of reaction-time-GSR combinations. *J. abnorm. soc. Psychol.,* 51, 371–377.

Jacobs, J. (1887) Experiments on "prehension." *Mind,* 12, 75–79.

Jacobson, A. L. (1963) Learning in flatworms and annelids. *Psychol. Bull.,* 60, 74–94.

Jahnke, J. C. (1963) Serial position effects in immediate serial recall. *J. verb. Learn. and verb. Behav.,* 2, 284–287.

James, W. (1890) *Principles of psychology,* Vol. I. New York: Holt.

Jeeves, M. A., and North, A. J. (1956) Irrelevant or partially correlated stimuli in discrimination learning. *J. exper. Psychol.,* 52, 90–94.

Jenkins, H. M., and Harrison, R. H. (1960) Effect of discrimination training on auditory generalization. *J. exp. Psychol.,* 59, 246–253.

Jenkins, J. G., and Dallenbach, K. M. (1924) Obliviscence during sleep and waking. *Amer. J. Psychol.,* 35, 605–612.

Jenkins, J. J., Mink, W. D., and Russell, W. A. (1958) Associative clustering as a function of verbal association strength. *Psychol. Repts.,* 4, 127–136.

Jenkins, J. J., and Russell, W. A. (1952) Associative clustering during recall. *J. abnorm. soc. Psychol.,* 47, 818–821.

Jenkins, W. O. (1950) A temporal gradient of derived reinforcement. *Amer. J. Psychol.,* 63, 237–243.

Jenkins, W. O., and Clayton, F. L. (1949) Rate of responding and amount of reinforcement. *J. comp. physiol. Psychol.,* 42, 174–181.

Jenkins, W. O., and Postman, L. (1949) An experimental analysis of set in rote learning: Retroactive inhibition as a function of changing set. *J. exp. Psychol.,* 39, 69–72.

Jenkins, W. O., and Stanley, J. C., Jr. (1950) Partial reinforcement: A review and critique. *Psychol. Bull.,* 47, 193–234.

Jensen, A. R. (1961) On the reformulation of inhibition in Hull's system. *Psychol. Bull.,* 58, 274–298.

Jensen, A. R. (1962) Is the serial-position curve invariant? *Brit. J. Psychol.,* 53, 159–166.

Jensen, G. D. (1960) Learning and performance as functions of ration size, hours of privation, and effort requirement. *J. exp. Psychol.,* 59, 261–268.

Jensen, G. D. (1963) Preference for bar pressing over "freeloading" as a function of number of rewarded presses. *J. exp. Psychol.,* 65, 451–454.

Jensen, G. D., and Cotton, J. W. (1961) Running speed as a function of stimulus similarity and number of trials. *J. comp. physiol. Psychol.*, 54, 474–476.

Johnsgard, K. W. (1957) The role of contrast in stimulus intensity dynamism (V). *J. exp. Psychol.*, 53, 173–179.

Johnson, E. E. (1952) The role of motivational strength in latent learning. *J. comp. physiol. Psychol.*, 45, 526–530.

Johnson, G. J., and Penney, R. K. (1965) Transfer effects of mixed and unmixed list designs in paired associate learning of children. *Psychonomic Sci.*, 2, 171–172.

Johnson, H. M. (1914) Visual pattern discrimination in the vertebrate. *J. anim. Behav.*, 4, 319–361.

Johnson, L. M. (1933) Similarity of meaning as a factor in retroactive inhibition. *J. gen. Psychol.*, 9, 377–388.

Johnson, L. M. (1939) The relative effect of a time interval upon learning and retention. *J. exp. Psychol.*, 24, 169–179.

Johnson, R. C. (1962) Reanalysis of "meaningfulness and verbal learning." *Psychol. Rev.*, 69, 233–238.

Johnson, R. C., and Zara, R. C. (1960) Relational learning in young children. *J. comp. physiol. Psychol.*, 53, 594–597.

Jones, A., Wilkinson, H. J., and Braden, I. (1961) Information deprivation as a motivational variable. *J. exp. Psychol.*, 62, 126–137.

Jones, F. M., and Jones, M. H. (1942) Vividness as a factor in learning lists of nonsense syllables. *Amer. J. Psychol.*, 55, 96–101.

Jones, J. E. (1961) The CS–UCS interval in conditioning short- and long-latency responses. *J. exp. Psychol.*, 62, 612–617.

Jones, J. E. (1962) Contiguity and reinforcement in relation to CS-UCS intervals in classical aversive conditioning. *Psychol. Rev.*, 69, 176–186.

Judd, C. H. (1905) Practice without knowledge of results. *Psychol. Rev. Monogr. Suppl.*, 7, No. 29.

Jung, J. (1962) Transfer of training as a function of degree of first-list learning. *J. verb. Learn. and verb. Behav.*, 1, 197–199.

Jung, J. (1963) Effects of response meaningfulness (m) on transfer of training under two different paradigms. *J. exp. Psychol.*, 65, 377–384.

Kagan, J., and Berkun, M. (1954) The reward value of running activity. *J. comp. physiol. Psychol.*, 47, 108.

Kalish, D. (1946) The non-correction method and the delayed response problem of Blodgett and McCutchan. *J. comp. Psychol.*, 39, 91–108.

Kalish, H. I. (1954) Strength of fear as a function of the number of acquisition and extinction trials. *J. exp. Psychol.*, 47, 1–9.

Kalish, H. I. (1958) The relationship between discriminability and generalization: A re-evaluation. *J. exp. Psychol.*, 55, 637–644.

Kalish, H. I., and Guttman, N. (1957) Stimulus generalization after equal training on two stimuli. *J. exp. Psychol.*, 53, 139–144.

Kalish, H. I., and Haber, A. (1963) Generalization: I. Generalization gradients from single and multiple stimulus points. II. Generalization of inhibition. *J. exp. Psychol.*, 65, 176–181.

Kamin, L. J. (1954) Traumatic avoidance learning: The effects of CS-US interval with a trace-conditioning procedure. *J. comp. physiol. Psychol.,* 47, 65–72.

Kamin, L. J. (1959) The delay-of-punishment gradient. *J. comp. physiol. Psychol.,* 52, 434–437.

Kamin, L. J. (1963) Backward conditioning and the conditioned emotional response. *J. exp. Psychol.,* 56, 517–519.

Karn, H. W. (1947) Sensory preconditioning and incidental learning in human subjects. *J. exp. Psychol.,* 37, 540–544.

Karn, H. W., and Porter, J. M., Jr. (1946) The effect of certain pretraining procedures upon maze performance and their significance for the concept of latent learning. *J. exp. Psychol.,* 36, 461–469.

Katz, I., and Greenbaum, C. (1963) Effects of anxiety, threat, and racial environment on task performance of negro college students. *J. abnorm. soc. Psychol.,* 66, 562–567.

Kaufman, M. E., and Peterson, W. M. (1958) Acquisition of a learning set by normal and mentally retarded children. *J. comp. physiol. Psychol.,* 51, 619–621.

Keesey, R. (1964) Intracranial reward delay and the acquisition rate of a brightness discrimination. *Science,* 143, 702.

Kehoe, J. (1963) Effects of prior and interpolated learning on retention in pigeons. *J. exp. Psychol.,* 65, 537–545.

Kelleher, R. T., and Gollub, L. R. (1962) A review of positive conditioned reinforcement. *J. exp. anal. Behav.,* Supplement to Vol. 5, 543–597.

Kellogg, W. N., and Walker, E. L. (1938) An analysis of the bilateral transfer of conditioning in dogs, in terms of the frequency, amplitude, and latency of the responses. *J. gen. Psychol.,* 18, 253–265.

Kendler, H. H. (1945) Drive interaction: Learning as a function of the simultaneous presence of the hunger and thirst drives. *J. exp. Psychol.,* 35, 96–109.

Kendler, H. H. (1947) A comparison of learning under motivated and satiated conditions in the white rat. *J. exp. Psychol.,* 37, 545–549.

Kendler, H. H. (1947a) An investigation of latent learning in a T-maze. *J. comp. physiol. Psychol.,* 40, 265–270.

Kendler, H. H. (1952) "What is learned?"—A theoretical blind alley. *Psychol. Rev.,* 59, 269–277.

Kendler, H. H., and Kanner, J. H. (1950) A further test of the ability of rats to learn the location of food when motivated by thirst. *J. exp. Psychol.,* 40, 726–765.

Kendler, H. H., and Levine, S. (1953) A more sensitive test of irrelevant-incentive learning under conditions of satiation. *J. comp. physiol. Psychol.,* 46, 271–273.

Kendler, H. H., Pliskoff, S. S., D'Amato, M. R., and Katz, S. (1957) Nonreinforcements versus reinforcements as variables in the partial-reinforcement effect. *J. exp. Psychol.,* 53, 269–276.

Kendler, T. S. (1950) An experimental investigation of transposition as a function of the difference between training and test stimuli. *J. exp. Psychol.,* 40, 552–562.

Kennelly, T. W. (1941) The role of similarity in retroactive inhibition. *Arch. Psychol.,* 37, No. 260.

Keppel, G., and Underwood, B. J. (1962) Proactive inhibition in short-term retention of single items. *J. verb. Learn. and verb. Behav.,* 1, 153–161.

Kessen, W. (1953) Response strength and conditioned stimulus intensity. *J. exp. Psychol.,* 45, 82–86.

Kientzle, M. J. (1946) Properties of learning curves under varied distribution of practice. *J. exp. Psychol.,* 36, 187–211.

Kimble, G. A. (1947) Conditioning as a function of the time between conditioned and unconditioned stimuli. *J. exp. Psychol.,* 37, 1–15.

Kimble, G. A. (1949) An experimental test of a two factor theory of inhibition. *J. exp. Psychol.,* 39, 15–23.

Kimble, G. A. (1949a) Performance and reminiscence in motor learning as a function of the degree of distribution of practice. *J. exp. Psychol.,* 39, 500–510.

Kimble, G. A. (1951) Behavior strength as a function of the intensity of the hunger drive. *J. exp. Psychol.,* 41, 341–348.

Kimble, G. A. (1955) Shock intensity and avoidance learning. *J. comp. physiol. Psychol.,* 48, 341–348.

Kimble, G. A. (1961) *Hilgard and Marquis' conditioning and learning.* New York: Appleton-Century-Crofts.

Kimble, G. A., and Bilodeau, E. A. (1949) Work and rest variables in cyclical motor learning. *J. exp. Psychol.,* 39, 150–157.

Kimble, G. A., and Dufort, R. H. (1955) Meaningfulness and isolation as factors in verbal learning. *J. exp. Psychol.,* 50, 361–368.

Kimble, G. A., Mann, L. I., and Dufort, R. H. (1955) Classical and instrumental eyelid conditioning. *J. exp. Psychol.,* 49, 407–417.

Kimmel, H. D. (1959) Amount of conditioning and intensity of conditioned stimulus. *J. exp. Psychol.,* 58, 283–288.

Kimmel, H. D., Hill, F. A., and Morrow, M. C. (1962) Strength of GSR and avoidance conditioning as a function of CS intensity. *Psychol. Repts.,* 11, 103–109.

Kimmel, H. D., and Pennypacker, H. S. (1963) Differential GSR conditioning as a function of the CS-UCS interval. *J. exp. Psychol.,* 65, 559–563.

King, D. J., and Tanenbaum, S. (1963) Comparison of two procedures in the study of retroactive interference in connected meaningful material. *J. exp. Psychol.,* 65, 420–421.

King, M. S., Kimble, G. A., Gorman, J., and King, R. A. (1961) Replication report: Two failures to reproduce effects of anxiety on eyelid conditioning. *J. exp. Psychol.,* 62, 532–533.

Kinnaman, A. J. (1902) Mental life of two macacus rhesus monkeys in captivity: II. *Amer. J. Psychol.,* 13, 173–218.

Kintsch, W. (1962) Runway performance as a function of drive strength and magnitude of reinforcement. *J. comp. physiol. Psychol.*, 55, 882–887.

Kish, G. B. (1955) Learning when the onset of illumination is used as reinforcing stimulus. *J. comp. physiol. Psychol.*, 48, 261–264.

Kjerstad, C. L. (1919) The form of the learning curves for memory. *Psychol. Monogr.*, 26, No. 116.

Klee, J. B. (1944) The relation of frustration and motivation to the production of abnormal fixations in the rat. *Psychol. Monogr.*, 56, No. 257.

Klein, R. M. (1959) Intermittent primary reinforcement as a parameter of secondary reinforcement. *J. exp. Psychol.*, 58, 423–427.

Kline, L. W. (1914) Some experimental evidence in regard to formal discipline. *J. educ. Psychol.*, 5, 259–266.

Kling, J. W. (1952) Generalization of extinction of an instrumental response to stimuli varying in the size dimension. *J. exp. Psychol.*, 44, 339–346.

Kling, J. W. (1956) Speed of running as a function of goal-box behavior. *J. comp. physiol. Psychol.*, 49, 474–476.

Kling, J. W., Horowitz, L., and Delhagen, J. E. (1956) Light as a positive reinforcer for rat responding. *Psychol. Repts.*, 2, 337–340.

Klinman, C., and Bitterman, M. E. (1963) Classical conditioning in fish: The CS-US interval. *J. comp. physiol. Psychol.*, 56, 578–583.

Kluver, J. (1933) *Behavior mechanisms in monkeys.* Chicago: Univ. Chicago Press.

Kobrick, J. L. (1956) The relationships among three measures of response strength as a function of the numbers of reinforcements. *J. comp. physiol. Psychol.*, 49, 582–585.

Koch, S. (1954) Clark L. Hull. In Estes, W. K., Koch, S., MacCorquodale, K., Meehl, P., Mueller, C. G., Jr., Schoenfeld, W. N., and Verplanck, W. S. *Modern learning theory.* New York: Appleton-Century-Crofts.

Koch, S., and Daniel, W. J. (1945) The effect of satiation on the behavior mediated by a habit of maximum strength. *J. exp. Psychol.*, 35, 167–187.

Kohler, W. (1918) Nachweis einfacher Strukturfunktionen beim Schimpansen und beim Haushuhn. *Abh. d. konig. Preuss. Ak. d. Wissen, Phys. Math. Klasse,* Nr. 2, 1–101. (Translated and condensed as "Simple structural functions in the chimpanzee and in the chicken.") In Ellis, W. D. (1938) 217–227.

Kohler, W. (1929) *Gestalt psychology.* New York: Horace Liveright.

Kohn, M. (1951) Satiation of hunger from food injected directly into the stomach versus food ingested by mouth. *J. comp. physiol. Psychol.*, 44, 412–422.

Koppman, J. W., and Grice, G. R. (1963) Goal-box and alley similarity in latent extinction. *J. exp. Psychol.*, 66, 611–612.

Koronakos, C., and Arnold, W. J. (1957) The formation of learning sets in rats. *J. comp. physiol. Psychol.*, 50, 11–14.

Kothurkar, V. K. (1963) Effect of stimulus-response meaningfulness on paired associate learning and retention. *J. exp. Psychol.,* 65, 305–308.

Krechevsky, I. (1932) "Hypothesis" in rats. *Psychol. Rev.,* 39, 516–532.

Krechevsky, I. (1932a) "Hypotheses" versus "chance" in the pre-solution period in sensory discrimination-learning. *Univ. Calif. Pub. in Psychol.,* 6, 27–44.

Krechevsky, I. (1932b) Antagonistic visual discrimination habits in the white rat. *J. comp. physiol. Psychol.,* 14, 263–277.

Krechevsky, I. (1933) Hereditary nature of "hypotheses." *J. comp. Psychol.,* 16, 99–116.

Krechevsky, I. (1933a) The docile nature of "hypotheses." *J. comp. Psychol.,* 15, 429–443.

Krechevsky, I. (1938) A study of the continuity of the problem-solving process. *Psychol. Rev.,* 45, 107–133.

Krueger, W. C. F. (1929) The effect of overlearning on retention. *J. exp. Psychol.,* 12, 71–78.

Krueger, W. C. F. (1930) Further studies in overlearning. *J. exp. Psychol.,* 13, 152–163.

Krueger, W. C. F. (1932) Learning during directed attention. *J. exp. Psychol.,* 15, 517–527.

Krueger, W. C. F. (1934) The relative difficulty of nonsense syllables. *J. exp. Psychol.,* 17, 145–153.

Kuenne, M. R. (1946) Experimental investigation of the relation of language to transposition behavior in young children. *J. exp. Psychol.,* 36, 471–490.

L'Abate, L. (1959) Manifest anxiety and the learning of syllables with different associative values. *Amer. J. Psychol.,* 72, 107–110.

Lacey, J. I., and Smith, R. L. (1954) Conditioning and generalization of unconscious anxiety. *Science,* 120, 1045–1052.

Lacey, J. I., Smith, R. L., and Green, A. (1955) Use of conditioned autonomic responses in the study of anxiety. *Psychosom. Med.,* 17, 208–217.

Lachman, R. (1961) The influence of thirst and schedules of reinforcement-nonreinforcement ratios upon brightness discrimination. *J. exp. Psychol.,* 62, 80–87.

Lang, P. J., Geer, J., and Hnatiow, M. (1963) Semantic generalization of conditioned autonomic responses. *J. exp. Psychol.,* 65, 552–558.

Lashley, K. S. (1912) Visual discrimination of size and form in the albino rat. *J. anim. Behav.,* 2, 310–331.

Lashley, K. S. (1915) The acquisition of skill in archery, as cited in Ruch, T. C. (1928).

Lashley, K. S. (1918) A simple maze: with data on the relation of the distribution of practice to rate of learning. *Psychobiol.,* 1, 353–367.

Lashley, K. S. (1929) Learning: I. Nervous-mechanisms of learning. In

Murchison, C., Ed., *The foundations of experimental psychology*. Worcester: Clark Univ. Press.

Lashley, K. S. (1929a) *Brain mechanisms and intelligence*. Chicago: Univ. Chicago Press.

Lashley, K. S. (1930) The mechanism of vision. I. A method for rapid analysis of pattern-vision in the rat. *J. genet. Psychol.*, 37, 453–460.

Lashley, K. S. (1938) Experimental analysis of instinctive behavior. *Psychol. Rev.*, 45, 445–471.

Lashley, K. S. (1942) An examination of the "continuity theory" as applied to discriminative learning. *J. gen. Psychol.*, 26, 241–265.

Lashley, K. S., and Ball, J. (1929) Spinal conduction and kinaesthetic sensitivity in the maze habit. *J. comp. Psychol.*, 9, 71–106.

Lashley, K. S., and Wade, M. (1946) The Pavlovian theory of generalization. *Psychol. Rev.*, 53, 72–87.

Lawrence, D., and Hommel, L. (1961) The influence of differential goal boxes on discrimination learning involving delay of reinforcement. *J. comp. physiol. Psychol.*, 54, 552–555.

Lawrence, D. H. (1949) Acquired distinctiveness of cues: I. Transfer between discriminations on the basis of familiarity with the stimulus. *J. exp. Psychol.*, 39, 770–784.

Lawrence, D. H. (1950) Acquired distinctiveness of cues: II. Selective association in a constant stimulus situation. *J. exp. Psychol.*, 40, 175–188.

Lawrence, D. H. (1952) The transfer of a discrimination along a continuum. *J. comp. physiol. Psychol.*, 45, 511–516.

Lawrence, D. H., and DeRivera, J. (1954) Evidence for relational transposition. *J. comp. physiol. Psychol.*, 47, 465–471.

Lawson, R. (1953) Amount of primary reward and strength of secondary reward. *J. exp. Psychol.*, 46, 183–187.

Lawson, R. (1957) Brightness discrimination performance and secondary reward strength as a function of primary reward amount. *J. comp. physiol. Psychol.*, 50, 35–39.

Leary, R. W. (1958) Homogeneous and heterogeneous reward of monkeys. *J. comp. physiol. Psychol.*, 51, 706–710.

Lee, C. L. (1961) The effects of anxiety level and shock on a paired-associate verbal task. *J. exp. Psychol.*, 61, 213–217.

Leeper, R. (1935) The role of motivation in learning; a study of the phenomenon of differential motivational control of the utilization of habits. *J. genet. Psychol.*, 46, 3–40.

Lester, O. F. (1932) Mental set in relation to retroactive inhibition. *J. exp. Psychol.*, 15, 681–699.

Levine, M. (1959) A model of hypothesis behavior in discrimination learning set. *Psychol. Rev.*, 66, 353–366.

Levine, M., and Harlow, H. F. (1959) Learning-sets with one-and twelve-trial oddity-problems. *Amer. J. Psychol.*, 72, 253–257.

Levine, M., Levinson, B., and Harlow, H. F. (1959) Trials per problem as a variable in the acquisition of discrimination learning set. *J. comp. physiol. Psychol.,* 52, 396–398.

Levine, S., and England, S. J. (1960) Temporal factors in avoidance learning. *J. comp. physiol. Psychol.,* 53, 282–283.

Levine, S., Staats, S. R., and Frommer, G. (1959) Drive summation in a water maze. *Psychol. Repts.,* 5, 301–304.

Lewis, D., Smith, P. N., and McAllister, D. E. (1952) Retroactive facilitation and interference in performance on the modified two-hand coordinator. *J. exp. Psychol.,* 44, 44–50.

Lewis, D. J. (1952) Partial reinforcement in the gambling situation. *J. exp. Psychol.,* 43, 447–450.

Lewis, D. J. (1956) Acquisition, extinction, and spontaneous recovery as a function of percentage of reinforcement and intertrial intervals. *J. exp. Psychol.,* 51, 45–53.

Lewis, D. J. (1960) Partial reinforcement: A selective review of the literature since 1950. *Psychol. Bull.,* 57, 1–28.

Lewis, D. J., and Cotton, J. W. (1957) Learning and performance as a function of drive strength during acquisition and extinction. *J. comp. physiol. Psychol.,* 50, 189–194.

Lewis, D. J., and Cotton, J. W. (1960) Effect of runway size and drive strength on acquisition and extinction. *J. exp. Psychol.,* 59, 402–408.

Lewis, D. J., and Duncan, C. P. (1956) Effect of different percentages of money reward on extinction of a lever pulling response. *J. exp. Psychol.,* 52, 23–27.

Lewis, D. J., and Duncan, C. P. (1957) Expectation and resistance to extinction of a lever-pulling response as functions of percentage of reinforcement and amount of reward. *J. exp. Psychol.,* 54, 115–120.

Lewis, D. J., and Duncan, C. P. (1958) Expectation and resistance to extinction of a lever-pulling response as a function of percentage of reinforcement and number of acquisition trials. *J. exp. Psychol.,* 55, 121–128.

Lewis, D. J., and Duncan, C. P. (1961) Effects of variable magnitude of reward on a lever-pulling response. *J. exp. Psychol.,* 62, 203–205.

Lichtenstein, P. E. (1950) Studies of anxiety: I. The production of a feeding inhibition in dogs. *J. comp. physiol. Psychol.,* 43, 16–29.

Lindley, R. H. (1960) Association value and familiarity in serial verbal learning. *J. exp. Psychol.,* 59, 366–370.

Lindley, R. H. (1963) Association value, familiarity, and pronunciability ratings as predictors of serial verbal learning. *J. exp. Psychol.,* 65, 347–351.

Lindley, R. H. (1963a) Effects of controlled coding cues in short-term memory. *J. exp. Psychol.,* 66, 180–187.

Lindley, R. H., and Moyer, K. E. (1961) Effects of instructions on the extinction of a conditioned finger-withdrawal response. *J. exp. Psychol.,* 61, 82–88.

Littman, R. A. (1950) Latent learning in a T-maze after two degrees of training. *J. comp. physiol. Psychol.,* 43, 135–147.

Littman, R. A., and Wade, E. (1955) A negative test of the drive-reduction hypothesis. *Quart. J. exp. Psychol.,* 7, 56–66.

Lloyd, K. E., Reid, L. S., and Feallock, J. B. (1960) Short-term retention as a function of the average number of items presented. *J. exp. Psychol.,* 60, 201–207.

Logan, F. A. (1954) A note on stimulus intensity dynamism (V). *Psychol. Rev.,* 61, 77–80.

Logan, F. A. (1956) A micromolar approach to behavior theory. *Psychol. Rev.,* 63, 63–73.

Logan, F. A. (1960) *Incentive.* New Haven: Yale Univ. Press.

Logan, F. A., Beier, E., and Ellis, R. A. (1955) Effect of varied reinforcement on speed of locomotion. *J. exp. Psychol.,* 49, 260–266.

Logan, F. A., Beier, E. M., and Kincaid, W. D. (1956) Extinction following partial and varied reinforcement. *J. exp. Psychol.,* 52, 65–70.

Longenecker, E. G., Krauskopf, J., and Bitterman, M. E. (1952) Extinction following alternating and random reinforcement. *Amer. J. Psychol.,* 65, 580–587.

Longo, N., and Bitterman, M. E. (1960) The effect of partial reinforcement with spaced practice on resistance to extinction in the fish. *J. comp. physiol. Psychol.,* 53, 169–172.

Longstreth, L. E. (1962) Incentive stimuli as determinants of instrumental response strength in children. *J. comp. physiol. Psychol.,* 55, 398–401.

Lorge, I., and Thorndike, E. L. (1935) The influence of delay in the after-effect of a connection. *J. exp. Psychol.,* 18, 186–194.

Lovaas, O. I. (1960) The relationship of induced muscular tension, tension level, and manifest anxiety in learning. *J. exp. Psychol.,* 59, 145–152.

Low, L. A., and Low, H. I. (1962) Effects of CS-US interval length upon avoidance responding. *J. comp. physiol. Psychol.,* 55, 1059–1061.

Luh, C. W. (1922) The conditions of retention. *Psychol. Monogr.,* 31, No. 142.

Lyon, D. O. (1914) The relation of length of material to time taken for learning and the optimum distribution of time. *J. educ. Psychol.,* 5, 1–9, 85–91, 155–163.

Maatsch, S. L., Adelman, H. M., and Denny, M. R. (1954) Effort and resistance to extinction of the bar-pressing response. *J. comp. physiol. Psychol.,* 47, 47–50.

MacCorquodale, K., and Meehl, P. E. (1951) On the elimination of cul entries without obvious reinforcement. *J. comp. physiol. Psychol.,* 44, 367–371.

MacCorquodale, K., and Meehl, P. E. (1954) Edward C. Tolman. In Estes, W. K., Koch, S., MacCorquodale, K., Meehl, P., Mueller, C. G., Jr.,

Schoenfeld, W. N., and Verplanck, W. S. *Modern learning theory.* New York: Appleton-Century-Crofts.

MacDuff, M. M. (1946) The effect on retention of varying degrees of motivation during learning in rats. *J. comp. Psychol.,* 39, 207–240.

MacKinnon, J. R., and Amsel, A. (1964) Magnitude of the frustration effect as a function of confinement and detention in the frustrating situation. *J. exp. Psychol.,* 67, 468–474.

Maher, W. B., and Wickens, D. D. (1954) Effect of differential quantity of reward on acquisition and performance of a maze habit. *J. comp. physiol. Psychol.,* 47, 44–46.

Maltzman, I. (1950) An experimental study of learning under an irrelevant need. *J. exp. Psychol.,* 40, 788–793.

Mandler, G. (1955) Associative frequency and associative prepotency as measures of response to nonsense syllables. *Amer. J. Psychol.,* 68, 662–665.

Mandler, G., and Campbell, E. H. (1957) Effect of variation in associative frequency of stimulus and response members on paired-associate learning. *J. exp. Psychol.,* 54, 269–273.

Mandler, G., and Heinemann, S. H. (1956) Effect of overlearning of a verbal response on transfer of training. *J. exp. Psychol.,* 52, 39–46.

Mandler, G., and Huttenlocher, J. (1956) The relation between associative frequency, associative ability, and paired-associate learning. *Amer. J. Psychol.,* 69, 424–428.

Margolius, G. (1955) Stimulus generalization of an instrumental response as a function of the number of reinforced trials. *J. exp. Psychol.,* 49, 105–111.

Marks, M. R., and Jack, O. (1952) Verbal context and memory span for meaningful material. *Amer. J. Psychol.,* 65, 298–300.

Marshall, G. R., and Cofer, C. N. (1963) Associative indices as measures of word relatedness: A summary and comparison of ten methods. *J. verb. Learn. and verb. Behav.,* 1, 408–421.

Martin, M. A. (1915) The transfer effects of practice in cancellation tests. *Arch. Psychol.,* 4, No. 32.

Marx, M. H. (1944) The effects of cumulative training upon retroactive inhibition and transfer. *Comp. Psychol. Monogr.,* 18, No. 2.

Marx, M. H. (1956) Some relations between frustration and drive. In Jones, M. R., Ed., *Nebraska symposium on motivation.* Lincoln, Nebraska: Univ. Nebraska Press.

Marx, M. H. (1958) Resistance to extinction as a function of continuous or intermittent presentation of a training cue. *J. exp. Psychol.,* 56, 251–255.

Marx, M. H. (1960) Resistance to extinction as a function of degree of reproduction of training conditions. *J. exp. Psychol.,* 59, 337–342.

Marx, M. H., and Brownstein, A. J. (1963) Effects of incentive magnitude on running speeds without competing responses in acquisition and extinction. *J. exp. Psychol.,* 65, 182–189.

Marx, M. H., Henderson, R. L., and Roberts, C. L. (1955) Positive reinforcement of the bar-pressing response by a light stimulus following dark operant pretests with no aftereffect. *J. comp. physiol. Psychol.,* 48, 73–76.

Marx, M. H., and Murphy, W. W. (1961) Resistance to extinction as a function of the presentation of a motivating cue in the start-box. *J. comp. physiol. Psychol.,* 54, 207–210.

Marx, M. H., Tombaugh, J. W., Cole, C., and Dougherty, D. (1963) Persistence of nonreinforced responding as a function of the direction of a prior-ordered incentive shift. *J. exp. Psychol.,* 66, 542–546.

Mason, D. J. (1957) The relation of secondary reinforcement to partial reinforcement. *J. comp. physiol. Psychol.,* 50, 264–268.

Masserman, J. H. (1943) *Behavior and neurosis.* Chicago: Univ. Chicago Press.

Mathers, B. L. (1957) The effect of certain parameters on the acquisition of fear. *J. comp. physiol. Psychol.,* 50, 329–333.

Mathews, R. (1954) Recall as a function of the number of classificatory categories. *J. exp. Psychol.,* 47, 241–247.

May, M. A. (1948) Experimentally acquired drives. *J. exp. Psychol.,* 38, 66–77.

May, M. A. (1949) An interpretation of pseudo-conditioning. *Psychol. Rev.,* 56, 177–183.

McAllister, D. E. (1953) The effects of various kinds of relevant verbal pretraining on subsequent motor performance. *J. exp. Psychol.,* 46, 329–336.

McAllister, W. R. (1953) Eyelid conditioning as a function of the CS-US interval. *J. exp. Psychol.,* 45, 417–422.

McAllister, W. R. (1953a) The effect on eyelid conditioning of shifting the CS-US interval. *J. exp. Psychol.,* 45, 423–428.

McAllister, W. R., and McAllister, D. E. (1958) Effect of knowledge of conditioning upon eyelid conditioning. *J. exp. Psychol.,* 55, 579–583.

McAllister, W. R., and McAllister, D. E. (1963) Increase over time in the stimulus generalization of acquired fear. *J. exp. Psychol.,* 65, 576–582.

McClelland, D. C. (1942) Studies in serial verbal discrimination learning. I. Reminiscence with two speeds of pair presentation. *J. exp. Psychol.,* 31, 44–56.

McClelland, D. C. (1951) *Personality.* New York: Dryden.

McCrary, J. W., and Hunter, W. S. (1953) Serial position curves in verbal learning. *Science,* 117, 131–134.

McCulloch, T L., and Pratt, J. G. (1934) A study of the pre-solution period in weight discrimination by white rats. *J. comp. Psychol.,* 18, 271–290.

McGeoch, J. A. (1929) The influence of degree of learning upon retroactive inhibition. *Amer. J. Psychol.,* 41, 252–262.

McGeoch, J. A. (1930) The influence of associative value upon the difficulty of non-sense syllable lists. *J. genet. Psychol.*, 37, 421–426.

McGeoch, J. A. (1932) Forgetting and the law of disuse. *Psychol. Rev.*, 39, 352–370.

McGeoch, J. A. (1942) *The psychology of human learning.* New York: David McKay Company.

McGeoch, J. A., and Irion, A. L. (1952) *The psychology of human learning.* (2d ed.) New York: David McKay Company.

McGeoch, J. A., and McDonald, W. T. (1931) Meaningful relation and retroactive inhibition. *Amer. J. Psychol.*, 43, 579–588.

McGeoch, J. A., and McGeoch, G. O. (1937) Studies in retroactive inhibition: X. The influence of similarity of meaning between lists of paired associates. *J. exp. Psychol.*, 21, 320–329.

McGeoch, J. A., and McKinney, F. (1934) The susceptibility of prose to retroactive inhibition. *Amer. J. Psychol.*, 46, 429–436.

McGovern, J. B. (1964) Extinction of associations in four transfer paradigms. *Psychol. Monogr.*, 78, No. 16.

McGuigan, F. J., and Crockett, F. (1958) Evidence that the secondary reinforcing stimulus must be discriminated. *J. exp. Psychol.*, 55, 184–187.

McHose, J. H. (1963) Effects of continued nonreinforcement on the frustration effect. *J. exp. Psychol.*, 65, 444–450.

Mednick, S., and Freedman, J. L. (1960) Stimulus generalization. *Psychol. Bull.*, 57, 169–200.

Meehl, P. E. (1950) On the circularity of the law of effect. *Psychol. Bull.*, 47, 52–75.

Meehl, P. E., and MacCorquodale, K. (1948) A further study of latent learning in the T-maze. *J. comp. physiol. Psychol.*, 41, 372–396.

Meehl, P. E., and MacCorquodale, K. (1951) A failure to find the Blodgett effect and some secondary observations on drive conditioning. *J. comp. physiol. Psychol.*, 44, 178–183.

Meehl, P. E., and MacCorquodale, K. (1953) Drive conditioning as a factor in latent learning. *J. exp. Psychol.*, 45, 20–24.

Melton, A. W. (1936) The end-spurt in memorization curves as an artifact of the averaging of individual curves. *Psychol. Monogr.*, 47, No. 212.

Melton, A. W. (1950) Learning. In Monroe, W. S., Ed., *Encycl. of educational research.* New York: Macmillan.

Melton, A. W. (1950a) Learning. *Annual Rev. Psychol.*, 1, 9–30.

Melton, A. W. (1963) Implications of short-term memory for a general theory of memory. *J. verb. Learn. and verb. Behav.*, 2, 1–21.

Melton, A. W., and Irwin, J. M. (1940) The influence of degree of interpolated learning on retroactive inhibition and the overt transfer of specific responses. *Amer. J. Psychol.*, 53, 173–203.

Melton, A. W., and Von Lackum, W. J. (1941) Retroactive and proactive inhibition in retention: evidence for a two-factor theory of retroactive inhibition. *Amer. J. Psychol.*, 54, 157–173.

Menzel, E. W., Jr., Davenport, R. K., Jr., and Rogers, C. M. (1961) Some aspects of behavior toward novelty in young chimpanzees. *J. comp. physiol. Psychol.*, 54, 16–19.

Merikle, P. M., and Battig, W. F. (1963) Transfer of training as a function of experimental paradigm and meaningfulness. *J. verb. Learn. and verb. Behav.*, 2, 485–488.

Merrill, M. (1931) The relationship of individual growth to average growth. *Human Biol.*, 3, 37–70.

Metzger, R., Cotton, J. W., and Lewis, D. J. (1957) Effect of reinforcement magnitude and of order of presentation of different magnitudes on runway behavior. *J. comp. physiol. Psychol.*, 50, 184–188.

Meyer, D. R. (1951) Food deprivation and discrimination reversal learning by monkeys. *J. exp. Psychol.*, 41, 10–16.

Meyer, D. R. (1951a) The effects of differential rewards on discrimination reversal learning by monkeys. *J. exp. Psychol.*, 41, 268–274.

Meyer, D. R. (1953) On the interaction of simultaneous responses. *Psychol. Bull.*, 50, 204–220.

Meyer, D. R., and Miles, R. C. (1953) Intralist-interlist relations in verbal learning. *J. exp. Psychol.*, 45, 109–115.

Miles, R. C. (1956) The relative effectiveness of secondary reinforcers throughout deprivation and habit-strength parameters. *J. comp. physiol. Psychol.*, 49, 126–130.

Miles, R. C. (1958) The effect of an irrelevant motive on learning. *J. comp. physiol. Psychol.*, 51, 258–261.

Miles, R. C. (1959) Discrimination in the squirrel monkey as a function of deprivation and problem difficulty. *J. exp. Psychol.*, 57, 15–19.

Miles, R. C. (1962) Effect of food deprivation on manipulatory reactions in cat. *J. comp. physiol. Psychol.*, 55, 358–362.

Miller, G. A. (1956) Magical number 7, plus or minus two. *Psychol. Rev.*, 63, 81–97.

Miller, G. A., and Selfridge, J. A. (1950) Verbal context and the recall of meaningful material. *Amer. J. Psychol.*, 63, 176–185.

Miller, J. (1939) The effect of facilitatory and inhibitory attitudes on eyelid conditioning. Ph. D. dissertation, Yale Univ.

Miller, J. (1939a) The rate of conditioning of human subjects to single and multiple conditioned stimuli. *J. gen. Psychol.*, 20, 399–408.

Miller, L. B., and Estes, B. W. (1961) Monetary reward and motivation in discrimination learning. *J. exp. Psychol.*, 61, 501–504.

Miller, N. E. (1948) Studies of fear as an acquirable drive: I. Fear as motivation and fear-reduction as reinforcement in learning of new responses. *J. exp. Psychol.*, 38, 89–101.

Miller, N. E. (1948a) Theory and experiment relating psychoanalytic displacement to stimulus-response generalization. *J. abnorm. soc. Psychol.*, 43, 155–178.

Miller, N. E. (1951) Learnable drives and rewards. In Stevens, S. S., Ed., *Handbook of experimental psychology.* New York: Wiley.

Miller, N. E. (1957) Experiments on motivation: Studies combining psychology, physiology and pharmacological techniques. *Science,* 126, 1271–1278.

Miller, N. E. (1959) Liberalization of basic S-R concepts: extensions to conflict behavior, motivation and social learning. In Koch, S., Ed., *Psychology: A study of a science,* Vol 2. New York: McGraw-Hill.

Miller, N. E. (1963) Some reflections on the law of effect produce a new alternative to drive reduction. In Jones, M. R., Ed., *Nebraska symposium on motivation.* Lincoln, Nebraska: Univ. Nebraska Press.

Miller, N. E., Coons, E. E., Lewis, M., and Jensen, D. D. (1961) A simple technique for use with the rat. In Sheer, D. E., Ed., *Electrical stimulation of the brain.* Austin: Univ. Texas Press.

Miller, N. E., and Dollard, J. C. (1941) *Social learning and imitation.* New Haven: Yale Univ. Press.

Miller, N. E., and Kessen, M. L. (1952) Reward effects of food via stomach fistula compared with those of food via mouth. *J. comp. physiol. Psychol.,* 45, 555–564.

Miller, W. C., and Greene, J. E. (1954) Generalization of an avoidance response to various intensities of tone. *J. comp. physiol. Psychol.,* 47, 136–139.

Minami, H., and Dallenbach, K. M. (1946) The effect of activity upon learning and retention in the cockroach. *Amer. J. Psychol.,* 59, 1–58.

Minturn, L. (1954) A test for sign-gestalt expectancies under conditions of negative motivation. *J. exp. Psychol.,* 48, 98–100.

Mitchell, M. B. (1933) The effect of serial position in the continuous memorization of numbers. *Amer. J. Psychol.,* 45, 493–494.

Moeller, G. (1954) The CS-UCS interval in GSR conditioning. *J. exp. Psychol.,* 48, 162–166.

Moltz, H. (1957) Latent extinction and the fractional anticipatory response mechanism. *Psychol. Rev.,* 64, 229–241.

Moltz, H., and Maddi, S. R. (1956) Reduction of secondary reward value as a function of drive strength during latent extinction. *J. exp. Psychol.,* 52, 71–76.

Montague, E. K. (1953) The role of anxiety in serial rote learning. *J. exp. Psychol.,* 45, 91–96.

Montgomery, K. C. (1951) Spontaneous alternation as a function of time between trials and amount of work. *J. exp. Psychol.,* 42, 82–93.

Montgomery, K. C. (1953) The effect of hunger and thirst drives upon exploratory behavior. *J. comp. physiol. Psychol.,* 46, 315–319.

Montgomery, K. C. (1953a) The effect of activity deprivation upon exploratory behavior. *J. comp. physiol. Psychol.,* 46, 438–441.

Montgomery, K. C. (1954) The role of exploratory drive in learning. *J. comp. physiol. Psychol.,* 47, 60–64.

Montgomery, K. C., and Segall, M. (1955) Discrimination learning based upon exploratory drive. *J. comp. physiol. Psychol.*, 48, 225–228.

Moon, L. E., and Lodahl, T. M. (1956) The reinforcing effect of changes in illumination on lever-pressing in the monkey. *Amer. J. Psychol.*, 69, 288–290.

Morgan, C. L. (1906) *Psychology for teachers.* New York: Scribner.

Morgan, C. T., and Fields, P. E. (1938) The effect of variable preliminary feeding upon the rat's speed of locomotion. *J. comp. Psychol.*, 26, 331–348.

Morgan, R. L., and Underwood, B. J. (1950) Proactive inhibition as a function of response similarity. *J. exp. Psychol.*, 40, 592–603.

Moskowitz, M. J. (1959) Running-wheel activity in the white rat as a function of combined food and water deprivation. *J. comp. physiol. Psychol.*, 52, 621–625.

Moss, E., and Harlow, H. F. (1947) The role of reward in discrimination learning in monkeys. *J. comp. physiol. Psychol.*, 40, 333–342.

Mosso, A. (1906) *Fatigue* (Translated by Drummond, M.) New York: Putnam.

Mowrer, O. H. (1947) On the dual nature of learning—A reinterpretation of "conditioning" and "problem solving." *Harv. educ. Rev.*, 17, 102–148.

Mowrer, O. H. (1960) *Learning theory and behavior.* New York: Wiley.

Mowrer, O. H., and Jones, H. M. (1943) Extinction and behavior variability as functions of effortfulness of task. *J. exp. Psychol.*, 33, 369–386.

Mowrer, O. H., and Jones, H. M. (1945) Habit strength as a function of the pattern of reinforcement. *J. exp. Psychol.*, 35, 293–311.

Moyer, K. E., and Korn, J. H. (1964) Effect of UCS intensity on the acquisition and extinction of an avoidance response. *J. exp. Psychol.*, 67, 352–359.

Muenzinger, K. F., Brown, W. C., Crow, W. J., and Powloski, R. F. (1952) Motivation in learning: XI. An analysis of electric shock for correct responses into the avoidance and accelerating components. *J. exp. Psychol.*, 43, 115–119.

Muenzinger, K. F., and Conrad, D. G. (1953) Latent learning observed through negative transfer. *J. comp. physiol. Psychol.*, 46, 1–8.

Muenzinger, K. F., and Powloski, R. F. (1951) Motivation in learning: X. Comparison of electric shock for correct turns in a corrective and a noncorrective situation. *J. exp. Psychol.*, 42, 118–124.

Müller, G. E., and Pilzecker, A. (1900) Experimentelle Beiträge zur Lehre vom Gedächtnis. *Z. Psychol.*, Ergbd. 1, 1–300.

Müller, G. E., and Schumann, F. (1894) Experimentelle Beiträge zur Untersuchung des Gedächtnisses. *Z. Psychol.*, 6, 81–90.

Munn, N. L. (1946) *Psychology.* New York: Houghton Mifflin.

Munn, N. L. (1950) *Handbook of psychological research on the rat.* New York: Houghton Mifflin.

Murdock, B. B., Jr. (1957) Transfer designs and formulas. *Psychol. Bull.,* 54, 313–326.

Murdock, B. B., Jr. (1960) The distinctiveness of stimuli. *Psychol. Rev.,* 67, 16–31.

Murdock, B. B., Jr. (1960a) The immediate retention of unrelated words. *J. exp. Psychol.,* 60, 222–234.

Murdock, B. B., Jr. (1961) The retention of individual items. *J. exp. Psychol.,* 62, 618–625.

Murdock, B. B., Jr. (1961a) Short-term retention of single paired associates. *Psychol. Repts.,* 8, 280.

Murdock, B. B., Jr. (1962) The serial position effect of free recall. *J. exp. Psychol.,* 64, 482–488.

Murdock, B. B., Jr. (1963) An analysis of the recognition process. In Cofer, C. N., and Musgrave, B. S., Eds., *Verbal behavior and learning.* New York: McGraw-Hill.

Murphy, J. V., and Miller, R. E. (1955) The effect of spatial contiguity of cue and reward in the object-quality learning of rhesus monkeys. *J. comp. physiol. Psychol.,* 48, 221–224.

Murphy, J. V., and Miller, R. E. (1956) Spaced and massed practice with a methodological consideration of avoidance conditioning. *J. exp. Psychol.,* 52, 77–81.

Myers, A. K., and Miller, N. E. (1954) Failure to find a learned drive based on hunger; evidence for learning motivated by "exploration." *J. comp. physiol. Psychol.,* 47, 428–436.

Myers, J. L. (1958) Secondary reinforcement: A review of recent experimentation. *Psychol. Bull.,* 55, 284–301.

Myers, J. L., and Myers, N. A. (1963) Secondary reinforcement in children as a function of conditioning associations, extinction percentages, and stimulus types. *J. exp. Psychol.,* 65, 455–459.

Myers, N. A. (1960) Extinction following partial and continuous primary and secondary reinforcement. *J. exp. Psychol.,* 60, 172–179.

Nachmias, J., Gleitman, H., and McKenna, V. V. (1961) The effect of isolation of stimuli and responses in paired associates. *Amer. J. Psychol.,* 74, 452–456.

Nefzger, M. D. (1957) The properties of stimuli associated with shock reduction. *J. exp. Psychol.,* 53, 184–188.

Newman, S. E., and Buckhout, R. (1962) S-R and R-S learning as functions of intralist similarity. *Amer. J. Psychol.,* 75, 429–436.

Newton, J. M., and Wickens, D. D. (1956) Retroactive inhibition as a function of the temporal position of the interpolated learning. *J. exp. Psychol.,* 51, 149–154.

Nicholls, M. F., and Kimble, G. A. (1964) Effect of instructions upon eyelid conditioning. *J. exp. Psychol.,* 67, 400–402.

Nissen, H. W. (1930) A study of exploratory behavior in the white rat by means of the obstruction method. *J. genet. Psychol.,* 37, 361–376.

Nissen, H. W., and Elder, J. H. (1935) The influence of amount of incentive on delayed response performances of chimpanzees. *J. genet. Psychol.,* 47, 49–72.

Nissen, H. W., Levinson, B., and Nichols, J. W. (1953) Reinforcement and "hypothesis" in the discrimination behavior of chimpanzees. *J. exp. Psychol.,* 45, 334–340.

Noble, C. E. (1952) An analysis of meaning. *Psychol. Rev.,* 59, 421–430.

Noble, C. E. (1952a) The role of stimulus meaning (*m*) in serial verbal learning. *J. exp. Psychol.,* 43, 437–446.

Noble, C. E. (1953) The meaning-familiarity relationship. *Psychol. Rev.,* 60, 89–98.

Noble, C. E. (1955) The effect of familiarization upon serial verbal learning. *J. exp. Psychol.,* 49, 333–338.

Noble, C. E. (1961) Measurements of association value (a), rated associations (a'), and scaled meaningfulness (m') for the 2100 CVC combinations of the English alphabet. *Psychol. Repts.,* 8, 487–521.

Noble, C. E. (1963) Meaningfulness and familiarity. In Cofer, C. N., and Musgrave, B. S., Eds., *Verbal behavior and learning.* New York: McGraw-Hill.

Noble, C. E., and Alcock, W. T. (1958) Human delayed-reward learning with different lengths of task. *J. exp. Psychol.,* 56, 407–412.

Noble, C. E., Stockwell, F. E., and Pryer, M. W. (1957) Meaningfulness (m') and association value (a) in paired-associate syllable learning. *Psychol. Repts.,* 3, 441–452.

Noble, M., and Adams, C. K. (1963) The effect of length of CS-US interval as a function of body temperature in a cold-blooded animal. *J. gen. Psychol.,* 69, 197–201.

Noble, M., and Adams, C. K. (1963a) Conditioning in pigs as a function of the interval between CS and US. *J. comp. physiol. Psychol.,* 56, 215–219.

Noble, M., Gruender, A., and Meyer, D. R. (1959) Conditioning in fish (Molienisia Sp.) as a function of the interval between CS and US. *J. comp. physiol. Psychol.,* 52, 236–239.

Noble, M., and Harding, G. E. (1963) Conditioning in rhesus monkeys as a function of the interval between CS and US. *J. comp. physiol. Psychol.,* 56, 220–224.

Norris, E. B., and Grant, D. A. (1948) Eyelid conditioning as affected by verbally induced inhibitory set and counter reinforcement. *Amer. J. Psychol.,* 61, 37–49.

North, A. J. (1950) Improvement in successive discrimination reversals. *J. comp. physiol. Psychol.,* 43, 442–460.

North, A. J. (1950a) Performance during an extended series of discrimination reversals. *J. comp. physiol. Psychol.,* 43, 461–470.

North, A. J. (1959) Acquired distinctiveness of form stimuli. *J. comp. physiol. Psychol.,* 52, 339–341.

North, A. J., and Stimmel. D. T. (1960) Extinction of an instrumental response following a large number of reinforcements. *Psychol. Repts.,* 6, 227–234.

Notterman, J. M., Schoenfeld, W. N., and Bersch, P. J. (1952) Partial reinforcement and conditioned heart rate response in human subjects. *Science,* 115, 77–79.

Novin, D., and Miller, N. E. (1962) Failure to condition thirst induced by feeding dry food to hungry rats. *J. comp. physiol. Psychol.,* 55, 373–374.

Nygaard, J. E. (1958) Cue and contextual stimulus intensity in discrimination learning. *J. exp. Psychol.,* 55, 195–199.

O'Kelley, L. I., and Heyer, A. W., Jr. (1951) Studies in motivation and retention. V. The influence of need duration in retention of a maze habit. *Comp. Psychol. Monogr.,* 20, 287–301.

Olds, J., and Milner, P. (1954) Positive reinforcement produced by electrical stimulation of septal area and other regions of rat brain. *J. comp. physiol. Psychol.,* 47, 419–427.

Osgood, C. E. (1946) Meaningful similarity and interference in learning. *J. exp. Psychol.,* 36, 277–301.

Osgood, C. E. (1949) The similarity paradox in human learning: a resolution. *Psychol. Rev.,* 56, 132–143.

Osgood, C. E. (1953) *Method and theory in experimental psychology.* New York: Oxford Univ. Press.

Palermo, D. S. (1957) Proactive interference and facilitation as a function of amount of training and stress. *J. exp. Psychol.,* 53, 293–296.

Parducci, A., and Knopf, N. B. (1958) Retroactive facilitation when new responses have been learned to old stimuli. *Amer. J. Psychol.,* 71, 426–428.

Passey, G. E. (1948) The influence of intensity of unconditioned stimulus upon acquisition of a conditioned response. *J. exp. Psychol.,* 38, 420–428.

Patten, E. F. (1938) The influence of distribution of repetitions on certain rote learning phenomena. *J. Psychol.,* 5, 359–374.

Pavlik, W. B., and Reynolds, W. F. (1963) Effects of deprivation schedule and reward magnitude on acquisition and extinction performance. *J. comp. physiol. Psychol.,* 56, 452–455.

Pavlov, I. P. (1927) *Conditioned reflexes.* (Translated by Anrep, G. V.). London: Oxford Univ. Press.

Pavlov, I. P. (1928) *Lectures on conditioned reflexes.* (Translated by Gantt, W. H.). New York: International.

Pearl, J. (1963) Intertrial interval and acquisition of a lever press avoidance response. *J. comp. physiol. Psychol.,* 56, 710–712.

Penney, R. K. (1960) The effects of non-reinforcement on response strength as a function of number of previous reinforcements. *Canad. J. Psychol.,* 14, 206–215.

Pennypacker, H. S. (1964) Measurement of the conditioned eyelid reflex. *Science,* 144, 1248–1249.

Pereboom, A. C., and Crawford, B. M. (1958) Instrumental and competing behavior as a function of trials and reward magnitude. *J. exp. Psychol.,* 56, 82–85.

Perin, C. T. (1942) Behavior potentiality as a joint function of the amount of training and the degree of hunger at the time of extinction. *J. exp. Psychol.,* 30, 93–113.

Perin, C. T. (1943) A quantitative investigation of the delay-of-reinforcement gradient. *J. exp. Psychol.,* 32, 37–51.

Perkins, C. C., Jr. (1947) The relation of secondary reward to gradients of reinforcement. *J. exp. Psychol.,* 37, 377–392.

Perkins, C. C., Jr. (1953) The relation between conditioned stimulus intensity and response strength. *J. exp. Psychol.,* 46, 225–231.

Perkins, C. C., Jr., and Weyant, R. G. (1958) The interval between training and test trials as a determiner of the slope of generalization gradients. *J. comp. physiol. Psychol.,* 51, 596–600.

Perkins, F. T., and Wheeler, R. H. (1930) Configuration learning in the goldfish. *Comp. Psychol. Monogr.,* 7, No. 1.

Perrin, F. A. C. (1914) An experimental and introspective study of the human learning process in the maze. *Psychol. Monogr.,* No. 70.

Peters, H. N. (1935) Mediate association. *J. exp. Psychol.,* 18, 20–48.

Peters, H. N. (1936) The relationship between familiarity of words and their memory value. *Amer. J. Psychol.,* 48, 572–585.

Peterson, L. R. (1956) Variable delayed reinforcement. *J. comp. physiol. Psychol.,* 49, 232–234.

Peterson, L. R., and Peterson, M. J. (1959) Short term retention of individual verbal items. *J. exp. Psychol.,* 58, 193–198.

Peterson, L. R., and Peterson, M. J. (1962) Minimal paired-associate learning. *J. exp. Psychol.,* 63, 521–527.

Peterson, N. (1962) Effect of monochromatic rearing on the control of responding by wavelength. *Science,* 136, 774–775.

Pieper, W., and Marx, M. H. (1963) Conditioning of a previously neutral cue to the onset of a metabolic drive: two instances of negative results. *Psychol. Rec.,* 13, 191–195.

Porter, J. M. (1938) Extinction of an acquired response as a function of the interval between successive non-rewarded trials. *J. comp. Psychol.,* 26, 261–270.

Porter, J. M. (1939) Experimental extinction as a function of the interval between successive nonreinforced elicitations. *J. gen. Psychol.,* 20, 109–134.

Porter, L. W., and Duncan, C. P. (1953) Negative transfer in verbal learning. *J. exp. Psychol.,* 46, 61–64.

Postman, L. (1947) The history and present status of the law of effect. *Psychol. Bull.,* 44, 489–563.

Postman, L. (1961) The present status of interference theory. In Cofer, C. N., Ed., *Verbal learning and verbal behavior.* New York: McGraw-Hill.

Postman, L. (1962) The effects of language habits on the acquisition and retention of verbal associations. *J. exp. Psychol.*, 64, 7–19.

Postman, L. (1962a) Transfer of training as a function of experimental paradigm and degree of first-list learning. *J. verb. Learn. and verb. Behav.*, 1, 109–118.

Postman, L. (1962b) Retention as a function of degree of overlearning. *Science*, 135, 666–667.

Postman, L. (1963) One-trial learning. In Cofer, C. N., and Musgrave, B. S., Eds., *Verbal behavior and learning*. New York: McGraw-Hill.

Postman, L. (1964) Studies of learning to learn. II. Changes in transfer as a function of practice. *J. verb. Learn. and verb. Behav.*, 3, 437–447.

Postman, L., and Adams, P. A. (1960) Studies in incidental learning: VIII. The effects of contextual determination. *J. exp. Psychol.*, 59, 153–164.

Postman, L., and Jenkins, W. O. (1948) An experimental analysis of set in rote learning: the interaction of learning instruction and retention performance. *J. exp. Psychol.*, 38, 683–689.

Postman, L., and Postman, D. L. (1948) Change in set as a determinant of retroactive inhibition. *Amer. J. Psychol.*, 61, 236–242.

Postman, L., and Rau, L. (1957) Retention as a function of the method of measurement. *Univ. Calif. Pub. in Psychol.*, 8, 217–270.

Postman, L., and Riley, D. A. (1959) Degree of learning and interserial interference in retention. *Univ. Calif. Pub. in Psychol.*, 8, 271–396.

Postman, L., and Schwartz, M. (1964) Studies of learning to learn. I. Transfer as a function of method of practice and class of verbal material. *J. verb. Learn. and verb. Behav.*, 3, 37–49.

Postman, L. and Stark, K. (1962) Retroactive inhibition as a function of set during the interpolated task. *J. verb. learn. and verb. behav.*, 1, 304–311.

Powell, D. R., Jr., and Perkins, C. C., Jr. (1957) Strength of secondary reinforcement as a determiner of the effects of duration of goal response on learning. *J. exp. Psychol.*, 53, 106–112.

Premack, D. (1959) Toward empirical behavior laws: I. Positive reinforcement. *Psychol. Rev.*, 66, 219–233.

Premack, D. (1961) Predicting instrumental performance from the independent rate of the contingent response. *J. exp. Psychol.*, 61, 163–171.

Prentice, W. C. H. (1949) Continuity in human learning. *J. exp. Psychol.*, 39, 187–194.

Prokasy, W. F., Ebel, H. C., and Thompson, D. D. (1963) Response shaping at long interstimulus intervals in classical eyelid conditioning. *J. exp. Psychol.*, 66, 138–141.

Prokasy, W. F., Fawcett, J. T., and Hall, J. F. (1962) Recruitment, latency, magnitude, and amplitude of the GSR as a function of interstimulus interval. *J. exp. Psychol.*, 64, 513–518.

Prokasy, W. F. Jr., Grant, D. A., and Myers, N. A. (1958) Eyelid conditioning as a function of unconditioned stimulus intensity and intertrial interval. *J. exp. Psychol.*, 55 242–246

Prokasy, W. F., and Hall, J. F. (1963) Primary stimulus generalization. *Psychol. Rev.,* 70, 310–322.

Prokasy, W. F., Hall, J. F., and Fawcett, J. T. (1962) Adaptation, sensitization, forward and backward conditioning, and pseudo-conditioning of the GSR. *Psychol. Repts.,* 10, 103–106.

Prokasy, W. F., and Truax, C. B. (1959) Reflex and conditioned responses as a function of manifest anxiety. *Amer. J. Psychol.,* 72, 262–264.

Prokasy, W. F., and Whaley, F. L. (1961) The intertrial interval in classical conditioning. *J. exp. Psychol.,* 62, 560–564.

Prokasy, W. F., and Whaley, F. L. (1962) Manifest anxiety scale score and the ready signal in classical conditioning. *J. exp. Psychol.,* 63, 119–124.

Pubols, B. H., Jr. (1956) The facilitation of visual and spatial discrimination reversal by overlearning. *J. comp. physiol. Psychol.,* 49, 243–248.

Pubols, B. H., Jr. (1957) Successive discrimination reversal learning in the white rat: A comparison of two procedures. *J. comp. physiol. Psychol.,* 50, 319–322.

Pubols, B. H., Jr. (1958) Delay of reinforcement, response perseveration, and discrimination reversal. *J. exp. Psychol.,* 56, 32–40.

Pubols, B. H., Jr. (1960) Incentive magnitude, learning, and performance in animals. *Psychol. Bull.,* 57, 89–115.

Pubols, B. H., Jr. (1962) Constant versus variable delay of reinforcement. *J. comp. physiol. Psychol.,* 55, 52–56.

Pubols, B. H. (1962a) Serial reversal learning as a function of the number of trials per reversal. *J. comp. physiol. Psychol.,* 55, 66–68.

Ramond, C. K. (1953) Anxiety and tasks as determiners of verbal performance. *J. exp. Psychol.,* 46, 120–124.

Ramond, C. K. (1954) Performance in instrumental learning as a joint function of delay of reinforcement and time of deprivation. *J. exp. Psychol.,* 47, 248–250.

Ratner, C. S. (1956) Effect of extinction of dipper approaching on subsequent extinction of bar pressing and dipper approaching. *J. comp. physiol. Psychol.,* 49, 576–581.

Razran, G. H. S. (1935) Conditioned responses: An experimental study and a theoretical analysis. *Arch. Psychol.,* 28, No. 191.

Razran, G. H. S. (1939) A quantitative study of meaning by a conditioned salivary technique (semantic conditioning). *Science,* 90, 89–90.

Razran, G. H. S. (1949) Stimulus generalization of conditioned responses. *Psychol. Bull.,* 46, 337–365.

Razran, G. H. S. (1956) Backward conditioning. *Psychol. Bull.,* 53, 55–69.

Razran, G. H. S. (1957) The dominance-contiguity theory of the acquisition of classical conditioning. *Psychol. Bull.,* 54, 1–46.

Razran, G. H. S. (1961) The observable unconscious and the inferable conscious in current Soviet psychophysiology. *Psychol. Rev.,* 68, 81–147.

Razran, G. H. S. (1963) Nature and varieties and level-varieties of conditioned stimulus generalization (CSG). *Stimulus Generalization Conference,* Boston Univ.

Reed, H. B. (1917) A repetition of Ebert and Meumann's practice experiment on memory. *J. exp. Psychol.,* 2, 315–346.

Reese, H. W. (1964) Discrimination learning set in rhesus monkeys. *Psychol. Bull.,* 61, 321–340.

Reid, L. S. (1953) The development of noncontinuity behavior through continuity learning. *J. exp. Psychol.,* 46, 107–112.

Reid, R. L. (1952) A test of sensory preconditioning in pigeons. *Quart. J. exp. Psychol.,* 4, 49–56.

Reid, R. L. (1958) Discrimination-reversal learning in pigeons. *J. comp. physiol. Psychol.,* 51, 716–720.

Renner, K. E. (1963) Influence of deprivation and availability of goal box cues on the temporal gradient of reinforcement. *J. comp. physiol. Psychol.,* 56, 101–104.

Renner, K. E. (1964) Delay of reinforcement: A historical review. *Psychol. Bull.,* 61, 341–361.

Restle, F. (1955) A theory of discrimination learning. *Psychol. Rev.,* 62, 11–19.

Restle, F. (1957) Discrimination of cues in mazes: A resolution of the "place-vs.-response" question. *Psychol. Rev.,* 64, 217–228.

Restle, F. (1958) Toward a quantitative description of learning set data. *Psychol. Rev.,* 65, 77–91.

Restorff, H. von (1933) Uber die Wirkung von Bereichsbildungen im Spurenfeld. (Analyse von Vorgangen im Spurenfeld) *Psychol. Forsch.,* 18, 299–342.

Reynolds, B. (1945) The acquisition of a trace conditioned response as a function of the magnitude of the stimulus trace. *J. exp. Psychol.,* 35, 15–30.

Reynolds, B. (1945a) A repetition of the Blodgett experiment on latent learning. *J. exp. Psychol.,* 35, 504–516.

Reynolds, B. (1949) The acquisition of black-white discrimination habit under two levels of reinforcement. *J. exp. Psychol.,* 39, 760–769.

Reynolds, B. (1950) Resistance to extinction as a function of the amount of reinforcement present during acquisition. *J. exp. Psychol.,* 40, 46–52.

Reynolds, B. (1950a) Acquisition of a simple spatial discrimination as a function of the amount of reinforcement. *J. exp. Psychol.,* 40, 152–160.

Reynolds, G. S. (1961) Behavioral contrast. *J. exp. anal. Behav.,* 4, 57–71.

Reynolds, G. S. (1961a) Contrast, generalization and the process of discrimination. *J. exp. anal. Behav.,* 4, 289–297.

Reynolds, W. F., Blau, B. I., and Hurlbut, B. (1961) Speed in simple tasks as a function of MAS score. *Psychol. Repts.,* 8, 341–344.

Reynolds, W. F., and Pavlik, W. B. (1960) Running speed as a function of deprivation period and reward magnitude. *J. comp. physiol. Psychol.,* 53, 615–618.

Richards, W. J., and Leslie, G. R. (1962) Food and water deprivation as influences on exploration. *J. comp. physiol. Psychol.*, 55, 834–837.

Richardson, J. (1956) Retention of concepts as a function of degree of original and interpolated learning. *J. exp. Psychol.*, 51, 358–364.

Richardson, P., and Voss, J. F. (1960) Replication report: Verbal context and the recall of meaningful material. *J. exp. Psychol.*, 60, 417–418.

Richter, C. P. (1922) A behavioristic study of the activity of the rat. *Comp. Psychol. Monogr.*, 1, No. 2.

Riess, B. F. (1946) Genetic changes in semantic conditioning. *J. exp. Psychol.*, 36, 143–152.

Riley, D. A. (1958) The nature of the effective stimulus in animal discrimination learning: transposition reconsidered. *Psychol. Rev.*, 65, 1–7.

Riley, D. A., Goggin, J. P., and Wright, D. C. (1963) Training level and cue separation as determiners of transposition and retention in rats. *J. comp. physiol. Psychol.*, 56, 1044–1049.

Riley, D. A., and Phillips, L. W. (1959) The effects of syllable familiarization on rote learning, association value, and reminiscence. *J. exp. Psychol.*, 57, 372–379.

Riley, D. A., Ring, K., and Thomas, J. (1960) The effect of stimulus comparison on discrimination learning and transposition. *J. comp. physiol. Psychol.*, 53, 415–421.

Ritchie, B. V., Ebeling, E., and Roth, W. (1950) Evidence for continuity in the discrimination of vertical and horizontal patterns. *J. comp. physiol. Psychol.*, 43, 168–180.

Roark, R. N. (1895) *Psychology in education.* New York: American.

Roberts, C. L., Lebow, K. E., and Yoder, R. M. (1961) Secondary reinforcement based on stimulus-change primary reinforcement. *J. exp. Psychol.*, 61, 339–344.

Roberts, C. L., Marx, M. H., and Collier, G. (1958) Light onset and light offset as reinforcers for the albino rat. *J. comp. physiol. Psychol.*, 51, 575–579.

Roberts, W. W. (1958) Both rewarding and punishing effects from stimulation of posterior hypothalamus of cat with same electrode at same intensity. *J. comp. physiol. Psychol.*, 51, 400–407.

Robinson, E. S. (1927) The "similarity" factor in retroaction. *Amer. J. Psychol.*, 39, 297–312.

Robinson, E. S. (1932) *Association theory today.* New York: Century.

Robinson, E. W., and Wever, E. G. (1930) Visual distance discrimination in the rat. *Univ. Calif. Pub. in Psychol.*, 4, 233–239.

Robinson, H. B. (1961) Persistence of a response in the apparent absence of motivation. *J. exp. Psychol.*, 61, 480–488.

Robinson, J. S. (1955) The effect of learning verbal labels for stimuli on their later discrimination. *J. exp. Psychol.*, 49, 112–115.

Robinson, J. S. (1959) Light onset and termination as reinforcers for rats living under normal light conditions. *Psychol. Repts.*, 5, 793–796.

Rockway, M. R., and Duncan, C. P. (1952) Pre-recall warming-up in verbal retention. *J. exp. Psychol.*, 43, 305–312.

Rohrer, J. H. (1947) Experimental extinction as a function of the distribution of extinction trials and response strength. *J. exp. Psychol.*, 37, 473–493.

Rohrer, J. H. (1949) A motivational state resulting from nonreward. *J. comp. physiol. Psychol.*, 42, 476–485.

Rosenbaum, G. (1951) Temporal gradients of response strength with two levels of motivation. *J. exp. Psychol.*, 41, 261–267.

Ross, L. W., and Spence, K. W. (1960) Eyelid conditioning performance under partial reinforcement as a function of UCS intensity. *J. exp. Psychol.*, 59, 379–382.

Rotberg, I. C., and Woolman, M. (1963) Verbal paired-associate learning as a function of grouping similar stimuli or responses. *J. exp. Psychol.*, 65, 47–51.

Rozeboom, W. W. (1957) Secondary extinction of lever-pressing behavior in the albino rat. *J. exp. Psychol.*, 54, 280–287.

Rubenstein, H., and Aborn, M. (1954) Immediate recall as a function of degree of organization and length of study period. *J. exp. Psychol.*, 48, 146–152.

Rubin, L. S. (1953) A demonstration of superior resistance to extinction following continuous reinforcement as compared with partial reinforcement. *J. comp. physiol. Psychol.*, 46, 28–32.

Ruch, T. C. (1928) Factors influencing the relative economy of massed and distributed practice in learning. *Psychol. Rev.*, 35, 19–45.

Rudel, R. G. (1957) Transposition of response by children trained in intermediate-size problems. *J. comp. physiol. Psychol.*, 50, 292–295.

Runquist, W. N., and Marshall, M. A. (1963) Transfer, synonymity, and anticipatory interval in paired-associate verbal learning. *Amer. J. Psychol.*, 76, 281–286.

Runquist, W. N., and Ross, L. E. (1959) The relation between physiological measures of emotionality and performance in eyelid conditioning. *J. exp. Psychol.*, 57, 329–332.

Runquist, W. N., Spence, K. W., and Stubbs, D. W. (1958) Differential conditioning and intensity of the UCS. *J. exp. Psychol.*, 55, 51–55.

Russell, R. W., and Hunter, W. S. (1937) The effects of inactivity produced by sodium amytal on the retention of the maze habit in albino rats. *J. exp. Psychol.*, 20, 426–436.

Russell, W. A., and Storms, L. H. (1955) Implicit verbal chaining in paired-associate learning. *J. exp. Psychol.*, 49, 287–293.

Saltz, E., and Ager, J. W. (1962) Issues in scaling meaningfulness: Noble's revised CVC norms. *Psychol. Repts.*, 10, 25–26.

Saltzman, I. J. (1949) Maze learning in the absence of primary reinforcement: a study of secondary reinforcement. *J. comp. physiol. Psychol.*, 42, 161–173.

Saltzman, I. J. (1951) Delay of reward and human verbal learning. *J. exp. Psychol.*, 41, 437–439.

Saltzman, I. J., Kanfer, F. H., and Greenspoon, J. (1955) Delay of reward and human motor learning. *Psychol. Repts.*, 1, 139–142.

Saltzman, I. J., and Koch, S. (1948) The effect of low intensities of hunger on the behavior mediated by a habit of maximum strength. *J. exp. Psychol.*, 38, 347–370.

Sarason, I. G. (1958) Effects on verbal learning of anxiety, reassurance, and meaningfulness of material. *J. exp. Psychol.*, 56, 472–477.

Scharlock, D. P. (1954) The effects of a pre-extinction procedure on the extinction of place and response performance in a T maze. *J. exp. Psychol.*, 48, 31–36.

Scharlock, D. P. (1955) The role of extramaze cues in place and response learning. *J. exp. Psychol.*, 50, 249–254.

Schlosberg, H. (1934) Conditioned responses in the white rat. *J. genet. Psychol.*, 45, 303–335.

Schlosberg, H. (1936) Conditioned responses in the white rat. II. Conditioned responses based upon shock to the foreleg. *J. genet. Psychol.*, 49, 107–138.

Schneirla, T. C. (1933) Some comparative psychology. *J. comp. Psychol.*, 16, 307–315.

Schoenfeld, W. N., Antonitis, J. J., and Bersh, P. J. (1950) A preliminary study of training conditions necessary for secondary reinforcement. *J. exp. Psychol.*, 40, 40–45.

Schrier, A. M. (1958) Comparison of two methods of investigating the effect of amount of reward on performance. *J. comp. physiol. Psychol.*, 51, 725–731.

Schrier, A. M., and Harlow, H. F. (1956) Effect of amount of incentive on discrimination learning by monkeys. *J. comp. physiol. Psychol.*, 49, 117–125.

Schulz, R. W., and Runquist, W. N. (1960) Learning and retention of paired adjectives as a function of percentage occurrence of response members. *J. exp. Psychol.*, 59, 409–413.

Schulz, R. W., and Tucker, I. F. (1962) Stimulus familiarization and length of the anticipation interval in paired-associate learning. *Psychol. Rec.*, 12, 341–344.

Schulz, R. W., and Tucker, I. F. (1962a) Supplementary report: Stimulus familiarization in paired-associate learning. *J. exp. Psychol.*, 64, 549–550.

Schusterman, R. J. (1962) Transfer effects of successive discrimination-reversal training in chimpanzees. *Science*, 137, 422–423.

Schusterman, R. J. (1964) Successive discrimination-reversal training and multiple discrimination training in one-trial learning by chimpanzees. *J. comp. physiol. Psychol.*, 58, 153–156.

Schwartz, F. (1961) Immediate memory and amount of information. Paper presented at Eastern Psychol. Assoc. meeting, Philadelphia.

Scott, E. D., and Wike, E. L. (1956) The effect of partially delayed reinforcement and trial-distribution on the extinction of an instrumental response. *Amer. J. Psychol.*, 69, 264–268.

Seidel, R. J. (1959) A review of sensory preconditioning. *Psychol. Bull.*, 56, 58–73.

Seward, J. P. (1943) An experimental analysis of maze discrimination. *J. comp. Psychol.*, 35, 17–27.

Seward, J. P. (1949) An experimental analysis of latent learning. *J. exp. Psychol.*, 39, 177–186.

Seward, J. P. (1950) Secondary reinforcement as tertiary motivation: A revision of Hull's revision. *Psychol. Rev.*, 57, 362–374.

Seward, J. P. (1951) Experimental evidence for the motivating function of reward. *Psychol. Bull.*, 48, 130–149.

Seward, J. P. (1952) Introduction to a theory of motivation in learning. *Psychol. Rev.*, 59, 405–413.

Seward, J. P. (1956) Reinforcement and expectancy: two theories in search of a controversy. *Psychol. Rev.*, 63, 105–113.

Seward, J. P., Datel, W. E., and Levy, N. (1952) Test of two hypotheses of latent learning. *J. exp. Psychol.*, 43, 274–280.

Seward, J. P., and Levy, N. (1949) Sign learning as a factor in extinction. *J. comp. physiol. Psychol.*, 39, 660–668.

Seward, J. P., Levy, N., and Handlon, J. H., Jr. (1950) Incidental learning in the rat. *J. comp. physiol. Psychol.*, 43, 240–251.

Seward, J. P., and Procter, D. M. (1960) Performance as a function of drive, reward, and habit strength. *Amer. J. Psychol.*, 73, 448–453.

Seward, J. P., Shea, R. A., and Davenport, R. H. (1960) Further evidence for the interaction of drive and reward. *Amer. J. Psychol.*, 73, 370–379.

Seward, J. P., Shea, R. A. and Elkind, D. (1958) Evidence for the interaction of drive and reward. *Amer. J. Psychol.*, 71, 404–407.

Sharp. H. C. (1958) Effect of contextual constraint upon recall of verbal passages. *Amer. J. Psychol.*, 71, 568–572.

Shaw, M. E., and Waters, R. H. (1950) An experimental test of latent learning in a relatively free-choice situation. *J. genet. Psychol.*, 77, 283–292.

Shearn, R. W. (1961) Operant conditioning of heart rate. Unpublished doctoral dissertation, Indiana University.

Sheer, D. E., Ed. (1961) *Electrical stimulation of the brain.* Austin: Univ. Texas Press.

Sheffield, F. D. (1949) Hilgard's critique of Guthrie. *Psychol. Rev.*, 56, 284–291.

Sheffield, F. D., and Campbell, B. A. (1954) The role of experience in the "spontaneous" activity of hungry rats. *J. comp. physiol. Psychol.*, 47, 97–100.

Sheffield, F. D., and Roby, T. B. (1950) Reward value of a non-nutritive sweet taste. *J. comp. physiol. Psychol.,* 43, 471–481.

Sheffield, F. D., Roby, T. B., and Campbell, B. A. (1954) Drive reduction versus consummatory behavior as determinants of reinforcement. *J. comp. physiol. Psychol.,* 47, 349–354.

Sheffield, F. D., Wulff, J. J., and Backer, R. (1951) Reward value of copulation without sex drive reduction. *J. comp. physiol. Psychol.,* 44, 3–8.

Sheffield, V. F. (1949) Extinction as a function of partial reinforcement and distribution of practice. *J. exp. Psychol.,* 39, 511–526.

Sheffield, V. F. (1950) Resistance to extinction as a function of the distribution of extinction trials. *J. exp. Psychol.,* 40, 305–313.

Shepard, R. N., and Teghtsoonian, M. (1961) Retention of information under conditions approaching a steady state. *J. exp. Psychol.,* 62, 302–309.

Sherrington, C. S. (1906) *The integrative action of the nervous system.* New Haven: Yale Univ. Press.

Shirley, M. (1928) Studies in activity: II. Activity rhythms; age and activity; activity after rest. *J. comp. Psychol.,* 8, 159–186.

Sidman, M. (1952) A note on functional relations obtained from group data. *Psychol. Bull.,* 49, 263–269.

Siegel, P. S. (1946) Activity level as a function of physically enforced inaction. *J. Psychol.,* 21, 285–291.

Siegel, P. S. (1946a) Alien drive, habit strength and resistance to extinction. *J. comp. physiol. Psychol.,* 39, 307–317.

Siegel, P. S., and Alexander, I. E. (1948) A further observation on the effect of physically enforced inaction on the activity level of the rat. *J. genet. Psychol.,* 72, 57–62.

Siegel, P. S., and MacDonnell, M. F. (1954) A repetition of the Calvin-Bicknell-Sperling study of conditioned drive. *J. comp. physiol. Psychol.,* 47, 250–252.

Siegel, P. S., and Steinberg, M. (1949) Activity level as a function of hunger. *J. comp. physiol. Psychol.,* 42, 413–416.

Siegel, S., and Andrews, J. M. (1962) Magnitude of reinforcement and choice behavior in children. *J. exp. Psychol.,* 63, 337–341.

Siegel, S., and Wagner, A. R. (1963) Extended acquisition training and resistance to extinction. *J. exp. Psychol.,* 66, 308–310.

Siipola, E. M. (1941) The relation of transfer to similarity in habit-structure. *J. exp. Psychol.,* 28, 233–261.

Silver, C. A., and Meyer, D. R. (1954) Temporal factors in sensory preconditioning. *J. comp. physiol. Psychol.,* 47, 57–59.

Silverman, R. E. (1960) Eliminating a conditioned GSR by the reduction of experimental anxiety. *J. exp. Psychol.,* 59, 122–125.

Simmons, R. (1924) The relative effectiveness of certain incentives in animal learning. *Comp. Psychol. Monogr.,* 2, 1–79.

Simon, C. W., Wickens, D. D., Brown, U., and Pennock, L. (1951) Effect of the secondary reinforcing agents on the primary thirst drive. *J. comp. physiol. Psychol.*, 44, 67–70.

Skinner, B. F. (1938) *The behavior of organisms; an experimental analysis.* New York: Appleton-Century-Crofts.

Skinner, B. F. (1959) A case history in scientific method. In Koch, S., Ed., *Psychology: A study of a science,* Vol. 2. New York: McGraw-Hill.

Slamecka, N. J. (1959) Studies of retention of connected discourse. *Amer. J. Psychol.*, 72, 409–416.

Slamecka, N. J. (1960) Retroactive inhibition of connected discourse as a function of similarity of topic. *J. exp. Psychol.*, 60, 245–249.

Slamecka, N. J. (1960a) Retroactive inhibition of connected discourse as a function of practice level. *J. exp. Psychol.*, 59, 104–108.

Slamecka, N. J. (1961) Proactive inhibition of connected discourse. *J. exp. Psychol.*, 62, 295–301.

Slamecka, N. J. (1962) Retention of connected discourse as a function of duration of interpolated learning. *J. exp. Psychol.*, 63, 480–486.

Slamecka, N. J., and Ceraso, J. (1960) Retroactive and proactive inhibition of verbal learning. *Psychol. Bull.*, 57, 449–475.

Sleight, W. G. (1911) Memory and formal training. *Brit. J. Psychol.*, 4, 386–457.

Slivinske, A. J., and Hall, J. F. (1960) The discriminability of tones used to test stimulus generalization. *Amer. J. Psychol.*, 73, 581–586.

Small, W. S. (1899) Notes on the psychic development of the young white rat. *Amer. J. Psychol.*, 11, 80–100.

Small, W. S. (1900) An experimental study of the mental processes of the rat. *Amer. J. Psychol.*, 11, 133–165.

Small, W. S. (1901) Experimental study of the mental processes of the rat. II. *Amer. J. Psychol.*, 12, 206–239.

Smith, F. O. (1933) Repetition without knowledge of results as a factor in learning. *Psychol. Bull.*, 30, 673–674.

Smith, J. G. (1954) Influence of failure, expressed hostility, and stimulus characteristics on verbal learning and perception. *J. Pers.*, 22, 475–493.

Smith, K. (1954) Conditioning as an artifact. *Psychol. Rev.*, 61, 217–225.

Smith, M. D. (1934) The reproduction of colour patterns. *Brit. J. Psychol.*, 25, 63–76.

Smith, M. H., Jr. (1949) The influence of isolation on immediate memory. *Amer. J. Psychol.*, 62, 405–411.

Smith, M. H., Jr., and Stearns, E. G. (1949) The influence of isolation on the learning of surrounding materials. *Amer. J. Psychol.*, 62, 369–381.

Smith, M. P. (1951) The stimulus trace gradient in visual discrimination learning. *J. comp. physiol. Psychol.*, 44, 154–161.

Smith, M. P., and Buchanan, G. (1954) Acquisition of secondary reward by cues associated with shock reduction. *J. exp. Psychol.*, 48, 123–126.

Smith, W. G. (1896) The place of repetition in memory. *Psychol. Rev., 3,* 21–31.

Snyder, H. L. (1962) Saccharine concentration and deprivation as determinants of instrumental and consummatory response strengths. *J. exp. Psychol., 63,* 610–615.

Snyder, H. L., and Hulse, S. H. (1961) Effects of volume of reinforcement and number of consummatory responses on licking and running behavior. *J. exp. Psychol., 61,* 474–479.

Snygg, D. (1935) The relative difficulty of mechanically equivalent tasks. II. Animal learning. *J. genet. Psychol., 47,* 321–336.

Solomon, P., Kubzansky, P. E., Leiderman, P. H., Mendelson, J. H., Trumbull, R., and Wexler, D. (1961) *Sensory deprivation.* Cambridge: Harvard Univ. Press.

Solomon, R. L. (1948) Effort and extinction rate: A confirmation. *J. comp. physiol. Psychol., 41,* 93–101.

Solomon, R. L. (1964) Punishment. *Amer. Psychologist, 19,* 239–253.

Solomon, R. L. and Wynne, L. C. (1954) Traumatic avoidance learning: the principles of anxiety conservation and partial irreversibility. *Psychol. Rev., 61,* 353–385.

Spelt, D. K. (1948) The conditioning of the human fetus in utero. *J. exp. Psychol., 38,* 338–346.

Spence, J. T. (1963) Associative interference on paired-associate lists from extraexperimental learning. *J. verb. Learn. and verb. Behav., 2,* 329–338.

Spence, K. W. (1932) The order of eliminating blinds in maze learning by the rat. *J. comp. Psychol., 14,* 9–27.

Spence, K. W. (1936) The nature of discrimination learning in animals. *Psychol. Rev., 43,* 427–449.

Spence, K. W. (1937) The differential response in animals to stimuli varying within a single dimension. *Psychol. Rev., 44,* 430–444.

Spence. K. W. (1937a) Analysis of the formation of visual discrimination habits in chimpanzee. *J. comp. Psychol., 23,* 77–100.

Spence, K. W. (1940) Continuous versus non-continuous interpretations of discrimination learning. *Psychol. Rev., 47,* 271–288.

Spence, K. W. (1942) The basis of solution by chimpanzees of the intermediate size problem. *J. exp. Psychol., 31,* 257–271.

Spence, K. W. (1945) An experimental test of the continuity and non-continuity theories of discrimination learning. *J. exp. Psychol., 35,* 253–266.

Spence, K. W. (1947) The role of secondary reinforcement in delayed reward learning. *Psychol. Rev., 54,* 1–8.

Spence, K. W. (1953) Learning and performance in eyelid conditioning as a function of the intensity of the UCS. *J. exp. Psychol., 45,* 57–63.

Spence, K. W. (1956) *Behavior theory and conditioning.* New Haven: Yale Univ. Press.

Spence, K. W. (1958) A theory of emotionally based drive (D) and its relation to performance in simple learning situations. *Amer. Psychologist,* 13, 131–141.

Spence, K. W. (1960) *Behavior theory and learning.* Englewood Cliffs, New Jersey: Prentice-Hall.

Spence, K. W. (1964) Anxiety (drive) level and performance in eyelid conditioning. *Psychol. Bull.,* 61, 129–139.

Spence, K. W., and Beecroft, R. S. (1954) Differential conditioning and level of anxiety. *J. exp. Psychol.,* 48, 399–403.

Spence, K. W., Bergmann, G., and Lippitt, R. A. (1950) A study of simple learning under irrelevant motivational-reward conditions. *J. exp. Psychol.,* 40, 539–551.

Spence, K. W., Buxton, C. E., and Melton, A. W. (1950) The effect of massing and distribution of practice on rotary pursuit test scores. *Civil Aeronautics Admini., Div. of Research, Report No. 44,* Washington, D. C.

Spence, K. W., and Farber, I. E. (1953) Conditioning and extinction as a function of anxiety. *J. exp. Psychol.,* 45, 116–119.

Spence, K. W., and Farber, I. E. (1954) The relation of anxiety to differential eyelid conditioning. *J. exp. Psychol.,* 47. 127–134.

Spence, K. W., Farber, I. E., and McFann, H. H. (1956) The relation of anxiety (drive) level to performance in competitional and noncompetitional paired-associates learning. *J. exp. Psychol.,* 52, 296–305.

Spence, K. W., Farber, I. E., and Taylor, E. (1954) The relation of electric shock and anxiety to level of performance in eyelid conditioning. *J. exp. Psychol.,* 48, 404–408.

Spence, K. W., and Goldstein, H. (1961) Eyelid conditioning performance as a function of emotion-producing instructions. *J. exp. Psychol.,* 62, 291–294.

Spence, K. W., Haggard, D. F., and Ross, L. E. (1958) UCS intensity and the associative (habit) strength of the eyelid CR. *J. exp. Psychol.,* 55, 404–411.

Spence, K. W., Homzie, M. J., and Rutledge, E. F. (1964) Extinction of the human eyelid CR as a function of the discriminability of the change from acquisition to extinction. *J. exp. Psychol.,* 67, 545–552.

Spence, K. W., and Lippitt, R. (1940) "Latent" learning of a simple maze problem with relevant needs satiated. *Psychol. Bull.,* 37, 429.

Spence, K. W., and Lippitt, R. (1946) An experimental test of the sign-gestalt theory of trial-and-error learning. *J. exp. Psychol.,* 36, 491–502.

Spence, K. W., and Norris, E. B. (1950) Eyelid conditioning as a function of the inter-trial interval. *J. exp. Psychol.,* 40, 716–720.

Spence, K. W., and Ross, L. E. (1959) A methodological study of the form and latency of eyelid responses in conditioning. *J. exp. Psychol.,* 58, 376–381.

Spence, K. W., and Taylor, J. (1951) Anxiety and strength of the UCS as determiners of the amount of eyelid conditioning. *J. exp. Psychol.*, 42, 183–188.

Spence, K. W., Taylor, J., and Ketchel, R. (1956) Anxiety (drive) level, and degree of competition in paired-associates learning. *J. exp. Psychol.*, 52, 306–310.

Spence, K. W., and Weyant, G. F. (1960) Conditioning performance of high- and low-anxious Ss in the absence of a warning signal. *J. exp. Psychol.*, 60, 146–149.

Spencer, L. T. (1923) Effects of practice without knowledge of results. *Amer. J. Psychol.*, 34, 107–111.

Spiker, C. C. (1956) Effects of stimulus similarity on discrimination learning. *J. exp. Psychol.*, 51, 393–395.

Spooner, A., and Kellogg, W. N. (1947) The backward conditioning curve. *Amer. J. Psychol.*, 60, 321–334.

Stabler, J. R. (1962) Performance in instrumental conditioning as a joint function of time of deprivation and sucrose concentration. *J. exp. Psychol.*, 63, 248–253.

Stanley, W. C. (1952) Extinction as a function of the spacing of extinction trials. *J. exp. Psychol.*, 43, 249–260.

Stanley, W. C., and Aamodt, M. A. (1954) Force of responding during extinction as a function of force requirement during conditioning. *J. comp. physiol. Psychol.*, 47, 462–464.

Starkweather, J. A., and Duncan, C. P. (1954) A test for conditioned inhibition in motor learning. *J. exp. Psychol.*, 47, 351–356.

Stein, L. (1958) Secondary reinforcement established with subcortical stimulation. *Science,* 127, 466–467.

Stevens, S. S. (1951) Mathematics, measurement, and psychophysics. In Stevens, S. S., Ed., *Handbook of experimental psychology.* New York: Wiley.

Stevenson, H. W., and Bitterman, M. E. (1955) The distance effect in the transposition of intermediate size by children. *Amer. J. Psychol.*, 68, 274–279.

Stevenson, H. W., and Weir, M. W. (1959) Response shift as a function of overtraining and delay. *J. comp. physiol. Psychol.*, 52, 327–329.

Stevenson, H. W., and Weiss, E. S. (1955) Time as a variable in transposition. *Amer. J. Psychol.*, 68, 285–288.

Stevenson, J. A. F., and Rixon, R. H. (1957) Environmental temperature and deprivation of food and water on the spontaneous activity of rats. *Yale J. Biol. Med.*, 29, 575–584.

Stone, C. P. (1922) The congenital sexual behavior of the young male albino rat. *J. comp. Psychol.*, 2, 95–153.

Stone, C. P., and Nyswander, D. B. (1927) The reliability of rat learning scores from the multiple-T maze as determined by four different methods. *J. genet. Psychol.*, 34, 497–524.

Storms, L. H., Boroczi, G., and Broen, W. E., Jr. (1962) Punishment inhibits an instrumental response in hooded rats. *Science,* 135, 1133–1134.

Strain, E. R. (1953) Establishment of an avoidance gradient under latent learning conditions. *J. exp. Psychol.,* 46, 391–399.

Strange, J. R. (1950) Latent learning under conditions of high motivation. *J. comp. physiol. Psychol.,* 43, 194–197.

Strassburger, R. C. (1950) Resistance to extinction of a conditioned operant as related to drive level at reinforcement. *J. exp. Psychol.,* 40, 473–487.

Strong, P. N., Jr. (1957) Activity in the white rat as a function of apparatus and hunger. *J. comp. physiol. Psychol.,* 50, 596–600.

Sundland, D. M., and Wickens, D. D. (1962) Context factors in paired-associate learning and recall. *J. exp. Psychol.,* 63, 302–306.

Swenson, E. J. (1941) Retroactive inhibition: A review of the literature. *Minn. Stud. Educ.,* 1941, No. 1.

Swift, E. J. (1903) Studies in the psychology and physiology of learning. *Amer. J. Psychol.,* 14, 201–251.

Switzer, S. A. (1930) Backward conditioning of the lid reflex. *J. exp. Psychol.,* 13, 76–97.

Symmes, D., and Leaton, R. N. (1962) Failure to observe reinforcing properties of sound onset in rats. *Psychol. Repts.,* 10, 458.

Szymanski, J. S. (1918) Versuche uber die wirkung der Factoren, die als Antrieb zum Erlernen einer Handlung dienen, Können. *Pflüger's Arch. ges. Physiol.,* 171, 374–385.

Taylor, H. (1932) A study of configuration learning. *J. comp. Psychol.,* 13, 19–26.

Taylor, J. A. (1951) The relationship of anxiety to the conditioned eyelid response. *J. exp. Psychol.,* 41, 81–92.

Taylor, J. A., and Chapman, J. P. (1955) Paired-associate learning as related to anxiety. *Amer. J. Psychol.,* 68, 671.

Taylor, J. A., and Spence, K. W. (1952) The relationship of anxiety to performance in serial learning. *J. exp. Psychol.,* 44, 61–64.

Teel, K. S. (1952) Habit strength as a function of motivation during learning. *J. comp. physiol. Psychol.,* 45, 188–191.

Teghtsoonian, R. (1958) The influence of amount of information on performance in a recognition test of verbal learning. Unpublished doctoral dissertation, Harvard Univ.

Teichner, W. H. (1952) Experimental extinction as a function of the intertrial intervals during conditioning and extinction. *J. exp. Psychol.,* 44, 170–178.

Terwilliger, R. F. (1962) Note on familiarity and verbal learning. *Psychol. Repts.,* 10, 409–410.

Theios, J. (1962) The partial reinforcement effect sustained through blocks of continuous reinforcement. *J. exp. Psychol.,* 64, 1–6.

Thistlethwaite, D. (1951) A critical review of latent learning and related experiments. *Psychol. Bull.,* 48, 97–129.

Thistlethwaite, D. (1951a) An experimental test of a reinforcement interpretation of latent learning. *J. comp. physiol. Psychol.,* 44, 431–441.

Thistlethwaite, D. (1952) Conditions of irrelevant-incentive learning. *J. comp. physiol. Psychol.,* 45, 517–525.

Thomas, A. R. (1958) Some variables affecting latent extinction. *J. exp. Psychol.,* 56, 203–212.

Thomas, D. R. (1962) The effects of drive and discrimination training on stimulus generalization. *J. exp. Psychol.,* 64, 24–28.

Thomas, D. R., and Hiss, R. H. (1963) A test of the "units hypothesis" employing wave-length generalization in human subjects. *J. exp. Psychol.,* 65, 59–62.

Thomas, D. R., and Lopez, L. J. (1962) The effects of delayed testing on generalization slope. *J. comp. physiol. Psychol.,* 55, 541–544.

Thomas, D. R., and Mitchell, K. (1962) Instructions and stimulus categorizing in a measure of stimulus generalization. *J. exp. anal. Behav.,* 5, 375–381.

Thomas, D. R., Ost, J., and Thomas, D. H. (1960) Stimulus generalization as a function of the time between training and testing procedures. *J. exp. anal. Behav.,* 3, 9–14.

Thomas, D. R., and Williams, J. L. (1963) A further study of stimulus generalization following three-stimulus discrimination training. *J. exp. anal. Behav.,* 6, 171–176.

Thompson, M. E. (1944) An experimental investigation of the gradient of reinforcement in maze learning. *J. exp. Psychol.,* 34, 390–403.

Thompson, M. E., and Thompson, J. P. (1949) Reactive inhibition as a factor in maze learning: II. The role of reactive inhibition in studies of place learning versus response learning. *J. exp. Psychol.,* 39, 883–891.

Thompson, R. (1955) Transposition in the white rat as a function of stimulus comparison. *J. exp. Psychol.,* 50, 185–190.

Thompson, R., and McConnell, J. (1955) Classical conditioning in the planarian, dugesia dorotocephala. *J. comp. physiol. Psychol.,* 48, 65–68.

Thorndike, E. L. (1898) Animal intelligence: an experimental study of the associative process in animals. *Psychol. Rev. Monogr.,* 2, No. 8.

Thorndike, E. L. (1913) *Educational psychology,* Vol. II. *The psychology of learning.* New York: Teachers College, Columbia Univ.

Thorndike, E. L. (1914) *Educational psychology: briefer course.* New York: Columbia Univ. Press.

Thorndike, E. L. (1932) *The fundamentals of learning.* New York: Teachers College, Columbia Univ.

Thorndike, E. L. (1932a) Reward and punishment in animal learning. *Comp. Psychol. Monogr.,* 8, 1–65.

Thorndike, E. L. (1933) An experimental study of rewards. *Teach. Coll. Contr. Educ.,* No. 580.

Thorndike, E. L., and Lorge, I. (1944) *The teacher's word book of 30,000 words.* New York: Columbia Univ. Press.

Thorndike, E. L., and Woodworth, R. S. (1901) The influence of improvement in one mental function upon the efficiency of other functions. I. *Psychol. Rev.*, 8, 247–261.

Thorndike, E. L., and Woodworth, R. S. (1901a) The influence of improvement in one mental function upon the efficiency of other functions. II. The estimation of magnitudes. *Psychol. Rev.*, 8, 384–395.

Thorndike, E. L., and Woodworth, R. S. (1901b) The influence of improvement in one mental function upon the efficiency of other functions. III. Functions involving attention, observation, and discrimination. *Psychol. Rev.*, 8, 553–564.

Thorpe, W. H. (1956) *Learning and instinct in animals.* London: Methuen.

Thune, L. E. (1950) The effect of different types of preliminary activities on subsequent learning of paired-associate material. *J. exp. Psychol.*, 40, 423–438.

Thune, L. E., and Underwood, B. J. (1943) Retroactive inhibition as a function of degree of interpolated learning. *J. exp. Psychol.*, 32, 185–200.

Tinklepaugh, O. L. (1928) An experimental study of representative factors in monkeys. *J. comp. Psychol.*, 8, 197–236.

Titchener, E. B. (1919) *A text-book of psychology.* New York: Macmillan.

Tolman, E. C. (1932) *Purposive behavior in animals and men.* New York: Appleton-Century-Crofts.

Tolman, E. C. (1938) The determiners of behavior at a choice point. *Psychol. Rev.*, 45, 1–41.

Tolman, E. C. (1949) There is more than one kind of learning. *Psychol. Rev.*, 56, 144–155.

Tolman, E. C. (1955) Principles of performance. *Psychol. Rev.*, 62, 315–326.

Tolman, E. C., and Gleitman, H. (1949) Studies in learning and motivation: I. Equal reinforcements in both end-boxes, followed by shock in one end-box. *J. exp. Psychol.*, 39, 810–819.

Tolman, E. C., and Honzik, C. H. (1930) Introduction and removal of reward and maze performance in rats. *Univ. Calif. Pub. in Psychol.*, 4, 257–275.

Tolman, E. C., Ritchie, B. F., and Kalish, D. (1946) Studies in spatial learning. II. Place learning versus response learning. *J. exp. Psychol.*, 36, 221–229.

Tolman, E. C., Ritchie, B. F., and Kalish, D. (1947) Studies in spatial learning. V. Response learning vs. place learning by the non-correction method. *J. exp. Psychol.*, 37, 285–292.

Trabasso, T. R. (1960) Additivity of cues in discrimination learning of letter patterns. *J. exp. Psychol.*, 60, 83–88.

Trapold, M. A., and Fowler, H. (1960) Instrumental escape performance as a function of the intensity of noxious stimulation. *J. exp. Psychol.*, 60, 323–326.

Trapold, M. A., Homzie, M., and Rutledge, E. (1964) Backward conditioning and UCR latency. *J. exp. Psychol.*, 67, 387–391.

Treichler, F. R., and Hall, J. F. (1962) The relationship between deprivation weight loss and several measures of activity. *J. comp. physiol. Psychol.*, 55, 346–349.

Tulving, E. (1962) Subjective organization in free recall of "unrelated" words. *Psychol. Rev.*, 344–354.

Turner, L. H., and Solomon, R. L. (1962) Human traumatic avoidance learning: Theory and experiments on the operant-respondent distinction and failures to learn. *Psychol. Monogr.*, 76, No. 559.

Twedt, H. M., and Underwood, B. J. (1959) Mixed vs. unmixed lists in transfer studies. *J. exp. Psychol.*, 58, 111–116.

Tyler, D. W., Wortz, E. C., and Bitterman, M. E. (1953) The effect of random and alternating partial reinforcement on resistance to extinction in the rat. *Amer. J. Psychol.*, 66, 57–65.

Ulrich, J. L. (1915) The distribution of effort in learning in the white rat. *Behav. Monogr.*, 2, No. 5.

Umemoto, T. and Hilgard, E. R. (1961) Paired-associate learning as a function of similarity: common stimulus and response items within the list. *J. exp. Psychol.*, 62, 97–104.

Underwood, B. J. (1945) The effect of successive interpolations on retroactive and proactive inhibition. *Psychol. Monogr.*, 59, No. 3.

Underwood, B. J. (1948) Retroactive and proactive inhibition after five and forty-eight hours. *J. exp. Psychol.*, 38, 29–38.

Underwood, B. J. (1948a) "Spontaneous recovery" of verbal associations. *J. exp. Psychol.*, 38, 429–439.

Underwood, B. J. (1949) Proactive inhibition as a function of time and degree of prior learning. *J. exp. Psychol.*, 39, 24–34.

Underwood, B. J. (1949a) *Experimental psychology*. New York: Appleton-Century-Crofts.

Underwood, B. J. (1951) Studies of distributed practice: II. Learning and retention of paired-adjective lists with two levels of intralist similarity. *J. exp. Psychol.*, 42, 153–161.

Underwood, B. J. (1951a) Studies of distributed practice: III. The influence of stage of practice in serial learning. *J. exp. Psychol.*, 42, 291–295.

Underwood, B. J. (1952) Studies of distributed practice: VI. The influence of rest-interval activity in serial learning. *J. exp. Psychol.*, 43, 329–340.

Underwood, B. J. (1952a) Studies of distributed practice: VII. Learning and retention of serial nonsense lists as a function of intralist similarity. *J. exp. Psychol.*, 44, 80–87.

Underwood, B. J. (1953) Studies of distributed practice: VIII. Learning and retention of paired nonsense syllables as a function of intralist similarity. *J. exp. Psychol.*, 45, 133–142.

Underwood, B. J. (1953a) Studies of distributed practice: IX. Learning and retention of paired adjectives as a function of intralist similarity. *J. exp. Psychol.*, 45, 143–149.

Underwood, B. J. (1953b) Studies of distributed practice: X. The influence of intralist similarity on learning and retention of serial adjective lists. *J. exp. Psychol.*, 45, 253–259.

Underwood, B. J. (1953c) Studies in distributed practice: XI. An attempt to resolve conflicting facts on retention of serial nonsense lists. *J. exp. Psychol.*, 45, 355–359.

Underwood, B. J. (1954) Speed of learning and amount retained: A consideration of methodology. *Psychol. Bull.*, 51, 276–282.

Underwood, B. J. (1954a) Intralist similarity in verbal learning and retention. *Psychol. Rev.*, 61, 160–166.

Underwood, B. J. (1954b) Studies of distributed practice: XII. Retention following varying degrees of original learning. *J. exp. Psychol.*, 47, 294–300.

Underwood, B. J. (1957) A graphical description of rote learning. *Psychol. Rev.*, 64, 119–122.

Underwood, B. J. (1957a) Interference and forgetting. *Psychol. Rev.*, 64, 49–60.

Underwood, B. J. (1963) Stimulus selection in verbal learning. In Cofer, C. N., and Musgrave, B. S., Eds., *Verbal behavior and learning.* New York: McGraw-Hill.

Underwood, B. J. (1964) The representativeness of rote verbal learning. In Melton, A. W., Ed., *Categories of human learning.* New York: Academic Press.

Underwood, B. J. (1964a) Degree of learning and the measurement of forgetting. *J. verb. Learn. and verb. Behav.*, 3, 112–129.

Underwood, B. J., and Archer, E. J. (1955) Studies of distributed practice: XIV. Intralist similarity and presentation rate in verbal discrimination learning of consonant syllables. *J. exp. Psychol.*, 50, 120–124.

Underwood, B. J., and Goad, D. (1951) Studies of distributed practice: I. The influence of intralist similarity in serial learning. *J. exp. Psychol.*, 42, 125–134.

Underwood, B. J., Ham, M., and Ekstrand, B. (1962) Cue selection in paired-associate learning. *J. exp. Psychol.*, 64, 405–409.

Underwood, B. J., and Hughes, R. H. (1950) Gradients of generalized verbal responses. *Amer. J. Psychol.*, 63, 422–430.

Underwood, B. J., and Keppel, G. (1963) Coding processes in verbal learning. *J. verb. Learn. and verb. Behav.*, 1, 250–257.

Underwood, B. J., and Postman, L. (1960) Extraexperimental sources of interference in forgetting. *Psychol. Rev.*, 67, 73–95.

Underwood, B. J., and Richardson, J. (1955) Studies of distributed practice: XIII. Interlist interference and the retention of serial nonsense lists. *J. exp. Psychol.*, 50, 39–46.

Underwood, B. J., and Richardson, J. (1956) The influence of meaningfulness, intralist similarity, and serial position on retention. *J. exp. Psychol.*, 52, 119–126.

Underwood, B. J., and Schulz, R. W. (1959) Studies of distributed practice:

XIX. The influence of intralist similarity with lists of low meaningfulness. *J. exp. Psychol.,* 58, 106–110.

Underwood, B. J., and Schulz, R. W. (1960) *Meaningfulness and verbal learning.* Philadelphia: Lippincott.

Underwood, B. J., and Schulz, R. W. (1961) Studies of distributed practice: XX. Sources of interference associated with differences in learning and retention. *J. exp. Psychol.,* 61, 228–235.

Underwood, B. J., and Schulz, R. W. (1961a) Studies of distributed practice: XXI. Effect of interference from language habits. *J. exp. Psychol.,* 62, 571–575.

Underwood, B. J., and Viterna, R. O. (1951) Studies of distributed practice: IV. The effect of similarity and rate of presentation in verbal-discrimination learning. *J. exp. Psychol.,* 42, 296–299.

Van Buskirk, W. L. (1932) An experimental study of vividness in learning and retention. *J. exp. Psychol.,* 15, 563–573.

Vandament, W. E., and Price, L. E. (1964) Primary stimulus generalization under different percentages of reinforcement in eyelid conditioning. *J. exp. Psychol.,* 67, 162–167.

Vandermeer, S., and Amsel, A. (1952) Work and rest factors in eyelid conditioning. *J. exp. Psychol.,* 43, 261–266.

Vanderplas, J. M. (1963) Associative processes and task relations in perceptual learning. *Percept. mot. Skills,* 16, 501–509.

Van Ormer, E. B. (1932) Sleep and retention. *Psychol. Bull.,* 30, 415–439.

Verplanck, W. S. (1942) The development of discrimination in a simple locomotor habit. *J. exp. Psychol.,* 31, 441–464.

Verplanck, W. S., and Hayes, J. R. (1953) Eating and drinking as a function of maintenance schedule. *J. comp. physiol. Psychol.,* 46, 327–333.

Vincent, S. B. (1912) The function of the vibrissae in the behavior of the white rat. *Behav. Monogr.,* 1, No. 5.

Vincent, S. B. (1915) The white rat and the maze problem. I. Introduction of a visual control. *J. anim. Behav.,* 5, 1–24.

Vincent, S. B. (1915a) The white rat and the maze problem. IV. The number and distribution of errors. *J. anim. Behav.,* 5, 367–374.

Waddel, D., Gans, S., Kempner, P., and Williams, A. (1955) A comparison of place and response learning in very young rats. *J. comp. physiol. Psychol.,* 48, 375–377.

Wagner, A. R. (1961) Effects of amount and percentage of reinforcement and number of acquisition trials on conditioning and extinction. *J. exp. Psychol.,* 62, 234–242.

Wagner, A. R. (1963) Conditioned frustration as a learned drive. *J. exp. Psychol.,* 64, 142–148.

Wald, G., and Jackson, B. (1944) Activity and nutritional deprivation. *Proc. Nat. Acad. Sci.,* Washington, 30, 255–263.

Walk, R. D. (1952) Effect of discrimination reversal on human discrimination learning. *J. exp. Psychol.,* 44, 410–419.

Walker, E. (1960) Eyelid conditioning as a function of intensity of conditioned and unconditioned stimuli. *J. exp. Psychol.*, 59, 303–311.

Walker, E. L. (1948) Drive specificity and learning. *J. exp. Psychol.*, 38, 39–49.

Walker, E. L. (1951) Drive specificity and learning: demonstration of a response tendency acquired under a strong irrelevant drive. *J. comp. physiol. Psychol.*, 44, 596–603.

Walker, E. L., Knotter, M. C., and DeValois, R. L. (1950) Drive specificity and learning: the acquisition of a spatial response to food under conditions of water deprivation and food satiation. *J. exp. Psychol.*, 40, 161–168.

Wallace, S. R., Jr., Blackwell, M. G., Jr., and Jenkins, G. (1941) Pre-reward and post-reward performance in the "latent learning" of an elevated maze. *Psychol. Bull.*, 38, 694.

Wallach, M. A. (1958) On psychological similarity. *Psychol. Rev.*, 65, 103–116.

Walters, G. C., and Rogers, J. V. (1963) Aversive stimulation of the rat: Long term effects on subsequent behavior. *Science,* 142, 70–71.

Walton, A. (1930) Visual cues in maze running by the albino rat. *J. genet. Psychol.*, 38, 50–77.

Ward, L. B. (1937) Reminiscence and rote learning. *Psychol. Monogr.*, 49, No. 220.

Warden, C. J. (1923) Some factors determining the order of elimination of culs-de-sac in the maze. *J. exp. Psychol.*, 6, 192–210.

Warden, C. J., and Cummings, S. B. (1929) Primacy and recency factors in animal motor learning. *J. genet. Psychol.*, 36, 240–254.

Warden, C. J., and Dymond, S. (1931) A preliminary study of the effect of delayed punishment on learning in the white rat. *J. genet. Psychol.*, 39, 455–461.

Warden, C. J., and Winslow, C. N. (1931) The discrimination of absolute versus relative size in the ring dove, Turtus Risorius. *J. genet. Psychol.*, 39, 328–341.

Warren, J. M. (1953) Additivity of cues in visual pattern discrimination by monkeys. *J. comp. physiol. Psychol.*, 46, 484–486.

Warren, J. M. (1954) Perceptual dominance in discrimination learning by monkeys. *J. comp. physiol. Psychol.*, 47, 290–292.

Warren, J. M. (1960) Reversal learning by paradise fish (Macropodus opercularis) . *J. comp. physiol. Psychol.*, 53, 376–378.

Warren, J. M. (1964) Additivity of cues in conditional discrimination learning by rhesus monkeys. *J. comp. physiol. Psychol.*, 58, 124–126.

Warren, J. M. (1965) Learning in paramecia and planaria. *Annual Rev. Psychol.*, 17, 95–118.

Warren, J. M., and Baron, A. (1956) The formation of learning sets by cats. *J. comp. physiol. Psychol.*, 49, 227–231.

Warren, J. M., Brookshire, K. H., Ball, G. G., and Reynolds, D. V. (1960)

Reversal learning by white leghorn chicks. *J. comp. physiol. Psychol.*, 53, 371–375.

Warren, J. M., and Hall, J. F. (1956) Discrimination of visual patterns as a function of motivation and frequency of reinforcement. *J. genet. Psychol.*, 88, 245–250.

Warren, J. M., and Warren, H. B. (1962) Reversal learning by horse and racoon. *J. genet. Psychol.*, 100, 215–220.

Warren, R. P., and Pfaffmann, C. (1959) Early experience and taste aversion. *J. comp. physiol. Psychol.*, 52, 263–266.

Wasserman, H. N. (1951) The effect of motivation and amount of pre-rest practice upon inhibitory potential in motor learning. *J. exp. Psychol.*, 42, 162–172.

Waters, R. H. (1939) The law of acquaintance. *J. exp. Psychol.*, 24, 180–191.

Waters, R. H., and Vitale, A. G. (1945) Degree of interpolated learning and retroactive inhibition in maze learning. I. Animal subjects. *J. comp. Psychol.*, 38, 119–126.

Watson, J. B. (1907) Kinaesthetic and organic sensations: their role in the reactions of the white rat. *Psychol. Rev. Monogr.*, 8, No. 2.

Watson, J. B. (1914) *Behavior, an introduction to comparative psychology.* New York: Holt.

Watson, J. B. (1917) The effect of delayed feeding upon learning. *Psychobiol.*, 1, 51–59.

Weasner, M. H., Finger, F. W., and Reid, L. S. (1960) Activity changes under food deprivation as a function of recording device. *J. comp. physiol. Psychol.*, 53, 470–474.

Weaver, L. A., Jr., and Michels, K. M. (1961) Methodological factors affecting the formation of learning sets by rats. *Anim. Behav.*, 9, 4–7.

Webb, L. W. (1917) Transfer of training and retroaction. *Psychol. Monogr.*, 24, No. 3.

Webb, W. B. (1949) The motivational aspect of an irrelevant drive in the behavior of the white rat. *J. exp. Psychol.*, 39, 1–14.

Webb, W. B. (1955) Drive stimuli as cues. *Psychol. Repts.*, 1, 287–298.

Webb, W. B., and Goodman, I. J. (1958) Activating role of an irrelevant drive in absence of the relevant drive. *Psychol. Repts.*, 4, 235–238.

Webb, W. B., and Nolan, C. Y. (1953) Cues for discrimination as secondary reinforcing agents: A confirmation. *J. comp. physiol. Psychol.*, 46, 180–181.

Weinstock, S. (1954) Resistance to extinction of a running response following partial reinforcement under widely spaced trials. *J. comp. physiol. Psychol.*, 47, 318–322.

Weinstock, S. (1958) Acquisition and extinction of a partially reinforced running response at a 24-hour intertrial interval. *J. exp. Psychol.*, 56, 151–158.

Weiss, R. F. (1960) Deprivation and reward magnitude effects on speed throughout the goal gradient. *J. exp. Psychol.,* 60, 384–390.

Weiss, W., and Margolius, G. (1954) The effect of context stimuli on learning and retention. *J. exp. Psychol.,* 48, 318–322.

Wells, F. L. (1908) Normal performance on the tapping test before and during practice with special reference to fatigue phenomenon. *Amer. J. Psychol.,* 19, 437–483.

Wendt, G. R. (1936) An interpretation of inhibition of conditioned reflexes as competition between reaction systems. *Psychol. Rev.,* 43, 258–281.

White, C. T., and Schlosberg, H. (1952) Degree of conditioning of the GSR as a function of the period of delay. *J. exp. Psychol.,* 43, 357–362.

Wickens, D. D. (1938) The transference of conditioned excitation and conditioned inhibition from one muscle group to the antagonistic muscle group. *J. exp. Psychol.,* 22, 101–123.

Wickens, D. D. (1939) A study of voluntary and involuntary finger conditioning. *J. exp. Psychol.,* 25, 127–140.

Wickens, D. D. (1939a) The simultaneous transfer of conditioned excitation and conditioned inhibition. *J. exp. Psychol.,* 24, 332–338.

Wickens, D. D. (1943) Studies in response generalization in conditioning. I. Stimulus generalization during response generalization. *J. exp. Psychol.,* 33, 221–227.

Wickens, D. D. (1954) Stimulus-response theory as applied to perception. In *Learning theory, personality theory, and clinical research: The Kentucky symposium.* New York: Wiley.

Wickens, D. D. (1959) Conditioning to complex stimuli. *Amer. Psychologist,* 7, 180–188.

Wickens, D. D., Allen, C. K., and Hill, F. A. (1963) Effect of instructions and UCS strength on extinction of the conditioned GSR. *J. exp. Psychol.,* 66, 235–240.

Wickens, D. D., Born, D. G., and Allen, C. K. (1963) Proactive inhibition and item similarity in short-term memory. *J. verb. Learn. and verb. Behav.,* 2, 440–445.

Wickens, D. D., Born, D. G., and Wickens, C. D. (1963) Response strength to a compound conditioned stimulus and its elements as a function of the element interstimulus interval. *J. comp. physiol. Psychol.,* 56, 727–731.

Wickens, D. D., and Briggs, G. E. (1951) Mediated stimulus generalization as a factor in sensory preconditioning. *J. exp. Psychol.,* 42, 197–200.

Wickens, D. D., Gehman, R. S., and Sullivan, S. N. (1959) The effect of differential onset time on the conditioned response strength to elements of a stimulus complex. *J. exp. Psychol.,* 58, 85–93.

Wickens, D. D., Hall, J. F., and Reid, L. S. (1949) Associative and retroactive inhibition as a function of the drive stimulus. *J. comp. physiol. Psychol.,* 42, 398–403.

Wickens, D. D., Schroder, H. M., and Snide, J. D. (1954) Primary stimulus generalization of the GSR under two conditions. *J. exp. Psychol.,* 47, 52–56.

Wickens, D. D., and Wickens, C. D. (1940) A study of conditioning in the neonate. *J. exp. Psychol.,* 26, 94–102.

Wickens, D. D., and Wickens, C. D. (1942) Some factors related to pseudo-conditioning. *J. exp. Psychol.,* 31, 518–526.

Wike, E. L., and Barrientos, G. (1957) Selective learning as a function of differential consummatory activity. *Psychol. Repts.,* 3, 225–258.

Wike, E. L., and Kintsch, W. (1959) Delayed reinforcement and runway performance. *Psychol. Rec.,* 9, 19–28.

Wike, E. L., and Platt, J. R. (1962) Reinforcement schedules and bar pressing: Some extensions of Zimmerman's work. *Psychol. Rec.,* 12, 273–278.

Wike, E. L., Platt, J. R., and Knowles, J. M. (1962) The reward value of getting out of a starting box: Further extensions of Zimmerman's work. *Psychol. Rec.,* 12, 397–400.

Wike, E. L., Platt, J. R., and Scott, D. (1963) Drive and secondary reinforcement: Further extensions of Zimmerman's work. *Psychol. Rec.,* 13, 45–49.

Wike, E. L., and Remple, R. (1959) Delayed reinforcement, selective learning and habit reversal. *Psychol. Rec.,* 9, 179–187.

Willett, R. A., and Eysenck, H. J. (1962) Experimentally induced drive and difficulty level in serial rote learning. *Brit. J. Psychol.,* 53, 35–39.

Williams, K. A. (1929) The reward value of a conditioned stimulus. *Univ. Calif. Pub. in Psychol.,* 4, 31–55.

Williams, M. (1950) The effects of experimentally induced needs upon retention. *J. exp. Psychol.,* 40, 139–151.

Williams, S. B. (1938) Resistance to extinction as a function of the number of reinforcements. *J. exp. Psychol.,* 23, 506–522.

Wilson, W., Weiss, E. J., and Amsel, A. (1955) Two tests of the Sheffield hypothesis concerning resistance to extinction, partial reinforcement and distribution of practice. *J. exp. Psychol.,* 50, 51–60.

Wiltbank, R. T. (1919) Transfer of training in white rats upon various series of mazes. *Behav. Monogr.,* 4, No. 1.

Wischner, G. J. (1947) The effect of punishment on discrimination learning in a non-correction situation. *J. exp. Psychol.,* 37, 271–284.

Wischner, G. J., Fowler, H., and Kushnick, S. A. (1963) Effect of strength of punishment for "correct" or "incorrect" responses on visual discrimination performance. *J. exp. Psychol.,* 65, 131–138.

Witmer, L. R. (1935) The association value of three-place consonant syllables. *J. genet. Psychol.,* 47, 337–360.

Wodinsky, J., and Bitterman, M. E. (1959) Partial reinforcement in the fish. *Amer. J. Psychol.,* 72, 184–199.

Wodinsky, J., and Bitterman, M. E. (1960) Resistance to extinction in the fish after extensive training with partial reinforcement. *Amer. J. Psychol.,* 73, 429–434.

Wolfe, J. B. (1934) The effect of delayed reward upon learning in the white rat. *J. comp. Psychol.,* 17, 1–21.

Wolfe, J. B., and Kaplon, M. D. (1941) Effect of amount of reward and consummative activity on learning in chickens. *J. comp. Psychol.,* 31, 353–361.

Wolfle, H. M. (1930) Time factors in conditioning finger-withdrawal. *J. gen. Psychol.,* 4, 372–378.

Wolfle, H. M. (1932) Conditioning as a function of the interval between the conditioned and the original stimulus. *J. gen. Psychol.,* 7, 80–103.

Woodworth, R. S. (1958) *Dynamics of behavior.* New York: Holt.

Woodworth, R. S., and Schlosberg, H. (1954) *Experimental psychology.* New York: Holt.

Wright, P. L., Kay, H., and Sime, M. E. (1963) The establishment of learning sets in rats. *J. comp. physiol. Psychol.,* 56, 200–203.

Wyckoff, L. B., Sidowski, J., and Chambliss, D. (1958) An experimental study of the relationship between secondary reinforcing and cue effects of a stimulus. *J. comp. physiol. Psychol.,* 51, 103–109.

Wylie, H. H. (1919) An experimental study of transfer of response in the white rat. *Behav. Monogr.,* 3, No. 16.

Yamaguchi, H. G. (1951) Drive (D) as a function of hours of hunger (h). *J. exp. Psychol.,* 42, 108–117.

Yamaguchi, H. G. (1952) Gradients of drive stimulus (S_D) intensity generalization, *J. exp. Psychol.,* 43, 298–304.

Yamaguchi, H. G. (1961) The effect of continuous, partial, and varied magnitude reinforcement on acquisition and extinction. *J. exp. Psychol.,* 61, 319–321.

Yerkes, R. M. (1916) The mental life of monkeys and apes: a study of ideational behavior. *Behav. Monogr.,* 3, No. 1.

Yerkes, R. M., and Dodson, J. D. (1908) The relation of strength of stimulus to rapidity of habit-formation. *J. comp. Neurol. and Psychol.,* 18, 459–482.

Yerkes, R. M., and Watson, J. B. (1911) Methods of studying vision in animals. *Behav. Monogr.,* 1, No. 2.

Young, P. T., and Shuford, E. H., Jr., (1955) Quantitative control of motivation through sucrose solutions of different concentrations. *J. comp. physiol. Psychol.,* 48, 114–118.

Young, R. K. (1955) Retroactive and proactive effects under varying conditions of response similarity. *J. exp. Psychol.,* 50, 113–119.

Young, R. K. (1961) Paired-associate learning when the same items occur as stimuli and responses. *J. exp. Psychol.,* 61, 315–318.

Young, R. K., Mangum, W. P., Jr., and Capaldi, E. J. (1960) Temporal factors associated with nonresponse extinction. *J. comp. physiol. Psychol.,* 53, 435–438.

Youtz, A. C. (1941) An experimental evaluation of Jost's laws. *Psychol. Monogr.*, 53, No. 1.

Youtz, R. E. P. (1939) The weakening of one Thorndikean response following the extinction of another. *J. exp. Psychol.*, 24, 294–304.

Zeaman, D. (1949) Response latency as a function of the amount of reinforcement. *J. exp. Psychol.*, 39, 466–483.

Zeiler, M. D. (1963) The ratio theory of intermediate size discrimination. *Psychol. Rev.*, 70, 516–533.

Zeiler, M. D. (1963a) New dimensions of the intermediate size problem: Neither absolute nor relational response. *J. exp. Psychol.*, 66, 588–595.

Zener, K. (1937) The significance of behavior accompanying conditioned salivary secretion for theories of the conditioned response. *Amer. J. Psychol.*, 50, 384–403.

Zimbardo, P. G., and Miller, N. E. (1958) Facilitation of exploration by hunger in rats. *J. comp. physiol. Psychol.*, 51, 43–46.

Zimbardo, P. G., and Montgomery, K. C. (1957) The relative strengths of consummatory responses in hunger, thirst, and exploratory drive. *J. comp. physiol. Psychol.*, 50, 504–508.

Zimmerman, D. W. (1957) Durable secondary reinforcement. Method and theory. *Psychol. Rev.*, 64, 373–383.

Zimmerman, D. W. (1959) Sustained performance in rats based on secondary reinforcement. *J. comp. physiol. Psychol.*, 52, 353–358.

Name Index

725